THE LETTERS OF SAMUEL WESLEY

Samuel Wesley, aged around 60, from the portrait by John Jackson, RA.
By courtesy of the National Portrait Gallery, London.

THE LETTERS OF
SAMUEL WESLEY

Professional and Social Correspondence,
1797–1837

Edited by
PHILIP OLLESON

OXFORD
UNIVERSITY PRESS

OXFORD

UNIVERSITY PRESS

Great Clarendon Street, Oxford OX2 6DP
Oxford University Press is a department of the University of Oxford.
It furthers the University's objective of excellence in research, scholarship,
and education by publishing worldwide in

Oxford   New York

Athens Auckland Bangkok Bogotá Buenos Aires Cape Town
Chennai Dar es Salaam Delhi Florence Hong Kong Istanbul Karachi
Kolkata Kuala Lumpur Madrid Melbourne Mexico City Mumbai
Nairobi Paris São Paulo Singapore Taipei Tokyo Toronto Warsaw

and associated companies in Berlin Ibadan

Oxford is a registered trade mark of Oxford University Press
in the UK and certain other countries

Published in the United States
by Oxford University Press Inc., New York

British Library Cataloguing in Publication Data
Data available

Library of Congress Cataloging in Publication Data
Data available

ISBN 0–19–816423–8

1 3 5 7 9 10 8 6 4 2

Typeset by Graphicraft Limited, Hong Kong
Printed in Great Britain
on acid-free paper by
Biddles Ltd
Guildford & Kings Lynn

To Hilary

PREFACE

The life of the composer and organist Samuel Wesley (1766–1837) encompassed momentous changes in British society. Born in the early years of the reign of George III, Wesley died in the first months of the reign of Victoria. He saw equally momentous changes in music. As a child he was taught by musicians who remembered and in some cases had played for Handel; in adult life, he witnessed the introduction of the music of Haydn, Mozart, and Beethoven into England, and late in his career saw the visits to London of Liszt, Weber, and Mendelssohn.

Wesley's life on both a personal and professional level was highly unconventional. Born into the first family of Methodism—his father was the hymn-writer Charles Wesley (1708–88), his uncle was John Wesley (1703–91)—he converted in his teens to Roman Catholicism and spent most of his life alienated from his family and from his Methodist upbringing. His marriage to Charlotte Louisa Martin in 1793 followed years of family opposition and a period when the couple lived together unmarried. In 1810 he left her for his teenage housekeeper, with whom he lived until his death. His professional career was brilliant but uneven, bedevilled by periods of mental illness which left him incapacitated for long periods.

Wesley was a prolific correspondent: over 600 letters out of a far larger number that he is known to have written are extant. This output would have been enough to fill two large volumes. Fortunately, the letters fall into two fairly distinct categories: those to members of his family, and those to correspondents outside the family. This division is paralleled to a large degree in the subject matter of the letters. In general, Wesley kept his family and his professional and social life well apart. He discusses family matters only rarely in his professional and social letters; conversely, although there are many mentions of his professional and social life in the family correspondence, they do not form a very large proportion of it as a whole. The two sequences of letters are thus largely (though obviously not entirely) self-contained.

The present volume reflects this division, and brings together all of Wesley's known professional and social correspondence from 1797 until his death. It also includes a few family letters where the subject matter is wholly or largely music: further details are given in the Textual Introduction. It can therefore be seen as the first part of a complete edition of Wesley's letters. The second part, containing the family letters, will, I hope, follow in due course.

ACKNOWLEDGEMENTS

I gratefully acknowledge the assistance of the University of Nottingham, which provided funds for the initial purchase of microfilms and photocopies under the Humanities Rolling Small Grants Scheme and have given generous support subsequently, including a period of study leave in 1997–8.

A number of individuals have been particularly closely involved with this volume. Robert Pascall first suggested that I might look at Wesley's letters. Michael Kassler has shared with me his extensive knowledge of Wesley's life and has made a large contribution to establishing the chronology and dating of the letters, and to innumerable other points of detail. Fr. Alvaro Ribeiro, SJ, editor of the correspondence of Charles Burney, has answered numerous queries about Burney, provided advice and wisdom on editorial procedures, and given much support and encouragement. Ian Wells has provided information on matters of Roman Catholic liturgy. Andrew Drummond has identified and translated Wesley's quotations from Greek and Latin. To all of these I am grateful. I must also express my particular thanks and gratitude to Cyril Ehrlich, who has been involved in this project since its beginning and has been characteristically generous in his advice, support, and encouragement. At OUP, I would like to thank Helen Peres da Costa, Dorothy McLean, Janet Moth, and Mary Worthington.

I acknowledge with thanks permission granted by the following libraries and private individuals to publish letters in their collections: Bath Public Libraries; Beinecke Rare Book and Manuscript Library, Yale University; Boston Public Library; The British Library, London; Michael Burney-Cumming; Cambridge University Library; Cheshire Record Office; Christ Church, Oxford; the late John R. G. Comyn; Raymond C. Currier; Drew University, Madison, New Jersey; Duke University, Durham, North Carolina; Edinburgh University Library; Emory University, Atlanta, Georgia; Fitzwilliam Museum, Cambridge; Gloucestershire County Library; Hampshire Record Office; Houghton Library, Harvard University; John Wesley's Chapel, Bristol; Library of Congress, Washington; Michael and Jamie Kassler; London University Library; Methodist Archives and Research Centre, John Rylands University of Manchester; London Metropolitan Archives; National Library of Scotland; The National Trust; New

Acknowledgements

York Public Library; Norfolk Record Office; Princeton University; The Royal College of Music; The Royal Institution of Great Britain; Royal Ontario Museum, Toronto; Southern Methodist University, Dallas, Texas; University of California at Santa Barbara; The Upper Room, Nashville, Tennessee.

Investigating Wesley's letters has involved me in correspondence with, and visits to, a large number of libraries and record offices. In addition to the institutions listed above, I would like to thank the following: Birmingham Archives; Bodleian Library, Oxford; British Library Newspaper Library; Bristol Public Library; The Brotherton Library, University of Leeds; Dorset Record Office; Guildhall Library; Hertfordshire Record Office; the National Maritime Museum; the Pendlebury Library, Cambridge; The Royal Literary Fund; The Royal Society of Musicians; St Albans Public Library; Suffolk Record Office; Watford Public Library; Wesley College, Bristol; The United Grand Lodge of England.

I am also grateful to the following, who have answered queries or provided assistance in other ways: Mark Argent, Chris Banks, Christina Bashford, the Revd Mark Beach, Heather Blackburn, Barra Boydell, the late Revd Frank Baker, Donald Burrows, David Byers, Rachel Cowgill, Donald Cullington, Oliver Davies, Nigel Day, Fr. Ian Dickie, Gabriella Dideriksen, Sally Drage, Pippa Drummond, Michelle Elverson, Kathy Flewitt, Peter Forsaith, Maggie Gibb, Jane Girdham, Leo Gooch, Bette Gray-Fow, Celia Hall, Sam Hammond, Jane Hatcher, John Henderson, Peter Holman, Peter Horton, Bronwen Jenkins, H. Diack Johnstone, Jamie Kassler, Christopher Kent, S T Kimbrough, Jr., Leanne Langley, Gareth Lloyd, Simon McGuire, Simon McVeigh, The Ven. John Marsh, Sander Meredeen, Anne Micallef, John Morehen, Kenneth Newport, Peter Nockles, John Ogasapian, Michael Ogden, Guy Oldham, Edward Olleson, Robert Parker, Stephen Parks, Stanley Pelkey, Bruce Phillips, Lynda Prescott, Peter Preston, Rebecca Preston, Kenneth E. Rowe, Brian Robins, Graça Almeida Rodrigues, Stephen Roe, Alan E. Rose, Francis Routh, Gillian Ward Russell, Wendy Sharpe, Hilary Silvester, the Revd William Simpson, Christopher Smith, Meg Smith, Alan Sommerstein, Nicholas Temperley, Richard Turbet, John Vickers, Arthur Wainwright, John Wardroper, Paul Weaver, William Weber, John Whittle, David Wickens, Rosemary Williamson, Peter Wright, Carlton Young, Bennett Zon.

My greatest thanks, however, are due to my wife Hilary, who has shared with good humour and tolerance the ups and downs of a project which at times must have seemed never-ending. This volume is dedicated to her.

Contents

LIST OF ILLUSTRATIONS

Abbreviations and Cue Titles

Manuscript collections

Argory	The Argory, near Moy, Co. Armagh
Austin	Harry Ransom Humanities Research Centre, The University of Texas at Austin
BL	British Library, London
Bristol	John Wesley's Chapel, Bristol
Cambridge	Cambridge, University Library
Christ Church	Christ Church, Oxford
Drew	Methodist Collection, Drew University Library, Madison, NJ
Duke	Special Collections Library, Duke University, Durham, NC
Edinburgh	Edinburgh University Library
Emory	John Wesley Collection, Special Collections Department, Robert W. Woodruff Library, Emory University, Atlanta, Ga.
Fitzwilliam	Fitzwilliam Museum, Cambridge
Foundling Hospital	Foundling Hospital Archives, London Metropolitan Archives
Gloucester	Local Studies Library, Gloucestershire County Library, Gloucester
Harvard	Shaw Theatre Collection, Houghton Library, Harvard University, Cambridge, Mass.
Kassler	Private collection of Jamie and Michael Kassler, Northbridge, NSW, Australia
LC	Library of Congress, Washington
London	Senate House Library, University of London
NRO	Norfolk Record Office, Norwich, Norfolk
NYPL (Berg)	The Henry W. and Albert A. Berg Collection, New York Public Library
NYPL (Music)	Music Division, New York Public Library
Osborn	The James Marshall and Marie-Louise Osborn Collection, Yale University Library, New Haven, Conn.

RCM	Royal College of Music, London
RSCM	Royal School of Church Music, Dorking
Rylands	Methodist Archives and Research Centre, John Rylands University Library of Manchester
SMU	Southern Methodist University, Dallas, Texas
UCSB	University of California at Santa Barbara, California

OTHER MANUSCRIPT SOURCES

Loan 48	Royal Philharmonic Papers, BL Loan 48
MADSOC	BL, Madrigal Society papers
Reminiscences	Wesley's manuscript Reminiscences (1836) (BL, Add. MS 27593)
RSM	Royal Society of Musicians Records

FREQUENTLY CITED WORKS

The place of publication is London unless otherwise indicated.

Altick	Richard Altick, *The Cowden Clarkes* (1948)
Anstruther	Godfrey Anstruther, OP, *The Seminary Priests: A Dictionary of the Secular Clergy of England and Wales, 1558–1830*, 4 vols. (Great Wakering, 1969–77)
Argent	*Recollections of R. J. S. Stevens: An Organist in Georgian London*, ed. Mark Argent (1992)
Bach Letters	Samuel Wesley, *Letters of Samuel Wesley to Mr Jacobs, Organist of Surrey Chapel, Relating to the Introduction into this Country of the Works of John Sebastian Bach*, ed. Eliza Wesley (1875). Facsimile edn. with Introduction by Peter Williams as *The Wesley Bach Letters* (1988)
BCP	Book of Common Prayer (1662)
BD	*A Biographical Dictionary of Actors, Actresses, Musicians, Dancers, Managers & Other Stage Personnel in London, 1660–1800*, ed. Philip H. Highfill, Jr., Kalman A. Burnim, and Edward A. Langhans, 16 vols. (Carbondale and Edwardsville, Ill., 1973–93)
Bicknell	Stephen Bicknell, *The History of the English Organ* (Cambridge, 1996)
Boeringer	James Boeringer, *Organica Britannica: Organs in Great Britain 1660–1860*, 3 vols. (London and Toronto, 1989)
Brown and Stratton	James D. Brown and Stephen S. Stratton, *British Musical Biography* (1897; repr. New York, 1971)

Burney, *History*	Charles Burney, *A General History of Music, from the Earliest Ages to the Present Period*, 4 vols. (1776–89)
Burney, *Letters I*	*The Letters of Dr Charles Burney*, Vol i: *1751–1784*, ed. Alvaro Ribeiro, SJ (Oxford, 1991)
Burrows	*George Frideric Handel: The Complete Hymns and Chorales*, facscimile edn. with introduction by Donald Burrows (1987)
Busby	[Thomas Busby], 'Dr Busby', *Public Characters* 5 (1803), 388–411
Clarke, *Life and Labours*	Mary Cowden Clarke, *Life and Labours of Vincent Novello* (1864)
Clarke, *My Long Life*	Mary Cowden Clarke, *My Long Life: An Autobiographic Sketch* (1896)
Colvin	Howard Colvin, *A Biographical Dictionary of British Architects 1600–1840* (London, 1978)
Court Guide	*Boyle's New Fashionable Court and Country Guide and Town Visiting Directory*, published annually
CPM	*The Catalogue of Printed Music in the British Museum until 1980*, 62 vols. (1987)
Dawe	Donovan Dawe, *Organists of the City of London 1666–1850* (Padstow, 1983)
DEB	*A Dictionary of Evangelical Biography*, ed. Donald M. Lewis, 2 vols. (Oxford, 1995)
DNB	*Dictionary of National Biography*
Doane	John Doane, *A Musical Directory for the Year 1794* (1794)
Edwards	F. G. E[dwards], 'Bach's Music in England', *MT* 37 (1896), 585–7, 652–7, 722–6, 797–800
Ehrlich, *Music Profession*	Cyril Ehrlich, *The Music Profession in Britain since the Eighteenth Century: A Social History* (Oxford, 1985)
Ehrlich, *First Philharmonic*	Cyril Ehrlich, *First Philharmonic: A History of the Royal Philharmonic Society* (Oxford, 1995)
Elkin	R. Elkin, *Royal Philharmonic: The Annals of the Royal Philharmonic Society* [1946]
Elvin	Laurence Elvin, *Bishop and Son, Organ Builders: The Story of J. C. Bishop and his Successors* (Lincoln, 1984)
Emery, 'Jack Pudding'	Walter Emery, 'Jack Pudding', *MT* 107 (1966), 301–6
EM	*The European Magazine and London Review* (1782–1826)
Encyclopaedia of London	*An Encyclopaedia of London*, ed. William Kent (1937)
Farmer	D. H. Farmer, *The Oxford Dictionary of Saints*, 3rd edn. (Oxford, 1992)

Fenner	Theodore Fenner, *Opera in London: Views of the Press, 1785–1830* (Carbondale and Edwardsville, Ill., 1994)
Foster	*Alumni Oxonienses*, ed. Joseph Foster, 1st ser., *1500–1714*, 4 vols. (Oxford, 1891–2); 2nd. ser., *1715–1886*, 4 vols. (Oxford, 1887–8)
Foster, *Philharmonic*	Myles Birkett Foster, *The History of the Philharmonic Society of London, 1813–1912* (1912)
Fulford	Roger Fulford, *Royal Dukes: The Father and Uncle of Queen Victoria* (1933)
Gill	Frederich C. Gill, *Charles Wesley: The First Methodist* (New York, and London, 1964)
GM	*The Gentleman's Magazine*, 1731–1880. References are to the year and part
Grove	*Grove's Dictionary of Music and Musicians*, followed by edition number (Grove[6]: *The New Grove Dictionary of Music and Musicians*, ed. Stanley Sadie, 20 vols., 1980)
Harmonicon	*The Harmonicon: A Journal of Music* (1823–33)
Humphries and Smith	Charles Humphries and William C. Smith, *Music Publishing in the British Isles from the Beginning until the Middle of the Nineteenth Century* (Oxford, 1970)
Jackson	Thomas Jackson, *The Life of the Rev. Charles Wesley, MA*, 2 vols. (1841)
JBIOS	*Journal of the British Institute of Organ Studies*, 1977–
Kassler, 'Lectures'	Jamie Croy Kassler, 'The Royal Institution Lectures 1800–1831: A Preliminary Study', *Royal Musical Association Research Chronicle* 19 (1983–5), 1–30
Kassler, *Science of Music*	Jamie Croy Kassler, *The Science of Music in Britain, 1714–1830: A Catalogue of Writings, Lectures and Inventions*, 2 vols. (New York, 1979)
King	Alec Hyatt King, *Some British Collectors of Music* (Cambridge, 1963)
Langley	Leanne Langley, 'The English Musical Journal in the Early Nineteenth Century', Ph.D. diss., University of North Carolina at Chapel Hill, 1983
Law Lists	*Clarke's New Law List*, published annually
Lightwood	James T. Lightwood, *Samuel Wesley, Musician: The Story of his Life* (1937)
London Encyclopaedia	*The London Encyclopaedia*, ed. Ben Weinreb and Christopher Hibbert (1983)
London Stage	*The London Stage 1660–1800*, 5 pts. in 11 vols. (Carbondale, Ill., 1960–8)

Lonsdale	Roger Lonsdale, *Dr Charles Burney: A Literary Biography* (Oxford, 1965)
Matthews	Betty Matthews, *The Royal Society of Musicians of Great Britain: List of Members 1738–1984* (1985)
Mercer	Charles Burney, *A General History of Music*, ed. Frank Mercer, 2 vols. (1935; repr. New York, 1957)
ML	*Music and Letters*, 1920–
MM	*The Monthly Magazine and British Register* (1790–1826)
MQ	*Musical Quarterly*, 1915–
MR	*Music Review*, 1940–84
MT	*Musical Times*, 1844–
Munby	A. N. L. Munby, *The Cult of the Autograph Letter in England* (1962)
MW	*The Musical World. A Weekly Record of Musical Science, Literature and Intelligence*, 1836–91
MW Obituary	'Professional Memoranda of the Late Mr. Samuel Wesley's Life', *MW* 7 (1837), 81–93, 113–18
Neighbour and Tyson	Oliver Neighbour and Alan Tyson, *English Music Publishers' Plate Numbers in the First Half of the Nineteenth Century* (1965)
New Bach Reader	*The New Bach Reader: A Life of Johann Sebastian Bach in Letters and Documents*, ed. Hans T. David and Arthur Mendel, rev. and enlarged by Christoph Wolff (New York and London, 1998)
Nichols and Wray	R. H. Nichols and F. A. Wray, *The History of the Foundling Hospital* (1935)
NMMR	*The New Musical Magazine, Review, and Register of Valuable Musical Publications, Ancient and Modern*, 1809–10
OCEL	*The Oxford Companion to English Literature*, ed. Margaret Drabble, rev. 5th edn. (Oxford, 1998)
OED	*Oxford English Dictionary*
Olleson	Philip Olleson, 'Samuel Wesley and the *European Magazine*', *Notes* 52 (1996), 1097–111
Oxford	Arnold Whitaker Oxford, *No 4: An Introduction to the History of the Royal Somerset House and Inverness Lodge* (1928)
Plantinga	Leon Plantinga, *Muzio Clementi: His Life and Music* (1977)
Plumley	Nicholas M. Plumley, *The Organs of the City of London* (Oxford, 1996)
QMMR	*Quarterly Musical Magazine and Review*, 1818–29

Rees	*The Cyclopaedia; or, Universal Dictionary of Arts, Sciences and Literature*, ed. Abraham Rees, 45 vols. (1802–20)
Sainsbury	John H. Sainsbury, *A Dictionary of Musicians* (1824)
Shaw	Watkins Shaw, *The Succession of Organists of the Chapel Royal and the Cathedrals of England and Wales from c.1538* (Oxford, 1991)
Stevenson, *City Road*	George J. Stevenson, *City Road Chapel London and its Associations, Historical, Biographical, and Memorial* [1872]
Stevenson, *Memorials*	George J. Stevenson, *Memorials of the Wesley Family* (1876)
Sullivan, *AAAJ*	Alvin Sullivan, *British Literary Magazines: The Augustine Age and the Age of Johnson, 1698–1788* (Westport, Conn., and London, 1983)
Sullivan, *TRA*	Alvin Sullivan, *British Literary Magazines: The Romantic Age, 1789–1896* (Westport, Conn., and London, 1983)
Survey of London	*Survey of London*, 46 vols. (1900–)
Thistlethwaite	Nicholas Thistlethwaite, *The Organs of Cambridge: An Introduction to the Organs of the University and City of Cambridge* (Oxford, 1983)
Venn	*Alumni Cantabrigienses*. Part II: *1752–1900*, ed. J. A. Venn, 6 vols. (Cambridge, 1940–54)
Wainwright	*Wesley/Langshaw Correspondence: Charles Wesley, his Sons, and the Lancaster Organists*, ed. Arthur Wainwright and Don E. Saliers ([Atlanta, Ga.], 1993)
Warrack	John Warrack, *Carl Maria von Weber* (Cambridge, 1968; 2nd edn., 1976)
WBRR	*Wesley Banner and Revival Record*, 1849–52
WMM	*The Wesleyan Methodist Magazine*, 1822–1913
Wroth	Warwick Wroth, *The London Pleasure Gardens in the Eighteenth Century* (1896)
Young	Percy M. Young, *Beethoven: A Victorian Tribute based on the Papers of Sir George Smart* (1976)

References to Shakespeare are to the *Complete Works*, ed. Stanley Wells and Gary Taylor (Oxford, 1988).

References to the Bible are to the Authorized Version.

Chronology

1766	Samuel Wesley (SW) born in Bristol, 24 Feb., the son of Charles and Sarah Gwynne Wesley.
1769	First musical activities: a child prodigy.
1771	Charles Wesley takes lease on house in Marylebone. Composes an oratorio, *Ruth*, to words by the Revd Thomas Haweis.
1772–3	First keyboard lessons from David Williams, a Bristol organist.
1774	Family visited by Boyce, who proclaims SW 'a second Mozart'.
1776	SW moves permanently to Marylebone. Visits Russell family in Guildford, summer. Portrait painted by John Russell, RA.
1778	Beginning of involvement with Roman Catholicism.
1779–87	Family concerts, involving SW and his brother Charles. Many compositions.
1780	First Latin church music compositions, Nov.
1780–4	Many further Latin church music compositions.
1782	Beginning of relationship with Charlotte Louisa Martin, Oct.
1783	Death of SW's friend James Price, who leaves him £1,000 and a house at Guildford, Aug.
1784	Converts to Roman Catholicism. Composes *Missa de Spiritu Sancto*, May; sends a revised version to Pope Pius VI, Sept.
1784	Starts to teach at Mrs Barnes's girls' school, Marylebone.
1788	Death of Charles Wesley, 29 Mar.
1788	Becomes a Freemason: admitted to the Lodge of Antiquity, 17 Dec.
1792	Moves to Ridge, Hertfordshire, and sets up house with Charlotte, Oct.
1793	Marries Charlotte, 5 Apr. Son Charles born, 25 Sept.
1794	Completes *Ode to St Cecilia*, 21 Oct.
1798	Applies unsuccessfully for the post of organist at the Foundling Hospital, May.
1799	Renews his acquaintance with Burney, Jan. *Ode to St Cecilia* performed at Covent Garden, 22 Feb. Son John William born, probably June. Completes *Confitebor tibi, Domine*, 14 Aug.
1800	Performs an organ concerto at a performance of Haydn's *Creation*, 21 Apr.
1802	Unsuccessful concert series at Tottenham Street Rooms, Feb.–May.

1802–5	Period of depression and inactivity.
1805	Rapprochement with Charlotte, spring.
1806	Daughter Emma Frances born, Jan. or Feb. Completes manuscript copy of '48', by 21 May.
1808	Starts to promote Bach. Gives recital at Surrey Chapel, 15 Mar. Benefit concert at Hanover Square Rooms, 11 June. Visits Cambridge and performs Bach there, June–July. Beginning of correspondence with Jacob, Aug. Te Deum and Jubilate performed at St Paul's Cathedral, 30 Oct.
1809	Visits Bath, Jan.–Feb. Lectures on music at the Royal Institution of Great Britain, Mar.–May. Benefit concert at Hanover Square Rooms, 3 June. Created a Master Mason at Somerset House Lodge, 27 June. Directs music festival at Tamworth, 21–2 Sept. Performs in a concert in Birmingham, 23 Sept. With C. F. Horn, publishes an edition of Bach organ trio sonatas. Lectures at Surrey Institution, Nov.–Dec. Gives recital of Bach's music at Surrey Chapel with Jacob and Salomon, 29 Nov.
1810	Marriage breakdown, probably Jan. Sets up house with Sarah Suter. Benefit concert at Hanover Square Rooms, 19 May. Son Samuel Sebastian born, 14 Aug.
1810–13	With C. F. Horn, publishes an edition of Bach's '48' in four parts.
1811	Visits Christopher Jeaffreson in Tunstall, Suffolk, Jan. Lectures at Surrey Institution, Feb.–Mar. Benefit concert at Hanover Square Rooms, 27 Apr. First extant letter to Novello, May. Directs Birmingham Music Festival, 2–4 Oct.
1812	Appointed masonic Grand Organist, May. Benefit concert at Hanover Square Rooms, 5 June. Visits Ramsgate and Margate and gives concerts with Samuel Webbe II, Sept.–Oct.
1813	Becomes organist at Covent Garden Lenten oratorio concerts, Mar. Benefit concert at Argyll Rooms, 4 May. Visits Ipswich and performs at the festival, June–July. Becomes an associate member of the Philharmonic Society, autumn. Applies unsuccessfully for Foundling Hospital organist's appointment, Nov. Plays at union of the two masonic Grand Lodges of England, 27 Dec.
1814	Begins to write reviews of music for the *European Magazine*, Feb. Daughter Rosalind born? Visits and performs in Norwich, Oct.
1815	Benefit concert at Covent Garden, 13 May (with C. J. Ashley). Visits and performs in Great Yarmouth and Norwich, July. Becomes a full member of the Philharmonic Society, 1 June, and a Director, 22 Nov.
1816	Motet 'Father of Light' performed at Philharmonic Society concert, 29 Apr. Benefit concert at Covent Garden, 1 June (with Ashley). Collapses while travelling to Norwich following the death of a child, early Aug. Recovers temporarily, but health declines.

1817	Continuing decline in health culminating in serious breakdown, early May. Benefit concert at Covent Garden held in his absence, 24 May. Confined in Blacklands House, Chelsea, a private lunatic asylum, July.
1818	Discharged from Blacklands House, late June.
1818–23	Period of depression and slow recuperation.
1819	Resumes position as organist at Covent Garden oratorio concerts, Feb. Daughter Eliza born, 6 May.
1821	Applies unsuccessfully for organist's position at St Pancras New Church, Feb. Son Matthias Erasmus born, 19 Apr.
1822	Accepts invitation to become an honorary member of the Royal Academy of Music, Sept. Arranges music for the barrels of the organ being built for Walter McGeough by James Bishop, Oct.–Nov. Composes Anglican Magnificat and Nunc Dimittis, thus completing his Service, Nov. Mother dies, 28 Dec.
1823	Applies unsuccessfully for organist's position at St Lawrence, Jewry, Jan. Magnificat and Nunc Dimittis from Service performed at St Paul's Cathedral, 25 Dec.
1824	Applies unsuccessfully for organist's position at St George's, Hanover Square, Feb. Proposals for publication of Service issued, Feb. Service performed in full at St Paul's, 3 and 25 Apr. Appointed organist at Camden Chapel, May. Publication of Sainsbury's *Dictionary of Music*, containing article stating that SW had died 'around 1815', Oct. Service published, late Oct.
1825	Service reviewed in *Harmonicon*, Jan., and in *QMMR*, Apr. Arrested and imprisoned for debt following financial crisis, 4 May. Released, 8 May. Son John born, late June or early July. Visits Cambridge for a week in June and two weeks in July and Aug. Performs *Confitebor* with Vincent Novello on the organ of Trinity College chapel to an invited audience.
1826	Granted permission by University of Cambridge to transcribe and publish music in the Fitzwilliam collection, 1 Mar. Visits Cambridge, Mar.–Apr., and issues proposals for an edition of Byrd antiphons from a Fitzwilliam Museum manuscript. Lectures at Royal Institution, Apr.–May. *Confitebor* performed at the Argyll Rooms, 4 May. Visits Cambridge again and discovers a manuscript of hymn tunes by Handel to words by his father, Sept. Publishes an edition of the hymns, Nov.
1827	Publishes a second edition of the Handel hymns, Mar. Lectures at Royal Institution, Mar.–May. Attends Breakfast for the Children of the Methodist Preachers at City Road Chapel, 3 May. Daughter Thomasine born, Oct.–Nov.
1828	Lectures at London Institution, Jan., and Royal Institution, Mar.–Apr. Publishes *Original Hymn Tunes Adapted to Every Metre in the Collection by the Rev. John Wesley*, Aug. Gives the inaugural organ recital at Brunswick Methodist Chapel, Leeds, 12 Sept. Sister Sarah dies, 19 Sept.

1829	Visits Bristol and gives organ recitals at St Mary Redcliffe and other Bristol churches, Sept.–Oct.
1830	Lectures at Bristol Institution, Jan. Further breakdown in health, followed by virtual retirement from public life, summer. Son Robert Glenn born, 21 Nov.
1834	Brother Charles dies, 23 May. Composes funeral anthem 'All go unto one place', which he directs at a Sacred Harmonic Society concert, 7 Aug.
1835	Composes hymn tunes for Novello's *The Psalmist*.
1836	Contributes historical article to the first issue of *The Musical World*, 18 March. Writes his manuscript Reminiscences, Apr.
1837	Copies out score of *Ode to St Cecilia* from memory, July. Meets and plays to Mendelssohn at Christ Church, Newgate Street, 12 Sept. Composes eight further hymns for *The Psalmist*, Oct. Dies, 11 Oct.

Biographical Introduction

Samuel Wesley was born in Bristol on 24 February 1766 into a family of extraordinary achievements and high-mindedness. Charles Wesley, his father, was the principal poet and hymn-writer of Methodism; his uncle John was the movement's founder. Samuel was to be the youngest child, joining Charles, eight years his senior, and Sarah, almost seven years older. The family was a musical one: Samuel's father had played the flute in his youth, his mother sang, and his brother Charles was a child prodigy whose musical abilities had brought a steady stream of visitors to the family home since his earliest childhood.

It was not long before Samuel was showing unmistakable signs of musicality himself. His father later recorded Samuel's delight at a very early age at hearing music, and his insistence on attending Charles's harpsichord lessons and accompanying him 'on the chair'.[1] According to the same account, he played his first tune at just under 3, taught himself to read from a copy of Handel's *Samson* at 4, and at 5 'had all the recitatives, and choruses of *Samson* and the *Messiah*: both words and notes by heart'. At the age of 6 he had some keyboard lessons from David Williams, a Bristol organist, although according to his father 'it was hard to say which was the master and which the scholar'. He also had violin and organ lessons, and at 7 played a psalm at a service at St James's church. His first compositions apparently pre-dated his learning to write music: according to his father he frequently improvised scenes from oratorio texts at the keyboard, and the family noticed that when he came to repeat them, the music was always the same. Before he was 6 he had composed the airs for an entire oratorio, *Ruth*, which he then held in his memory until he was able to write them down, over two years later.

These exploits predictably attracted attention. In 1774, shortly after Samuel had written down the music of *Ruth*, William Boyce visited the family, announcing that he had heard that there was 'an English Mozart' in the house. The comparison

---

[1] Charles Wesley senior's account of the musical talents of his two sons, as given to Daines Barrington, was included in Barrington's *Miscellanies* (1781), 291–310, and forms the basis of much of the following paragraphs.

would readily have come to mind: the young Mozart, ten years Samuel's senior, had spent fifteen months in London in 1764–5, exhibiting much the same near-miraculous precocity. Boyce's comment after looking over the score of *Ruth* was: 'these airs are some of the prettiest I have seen; this boy writes by nature as true a bass as I can by rule and study.' His remark went to the heart of the matter: like Mozart, his brother, and other musical child prodigies before and since, Samuel possessed from his earliest years musical accomplishments that normally took years of concentrated work to acquire.

The education of children as talented as Charles and Samuel caused obvious problems. It would have been unthinkable for one in Charles Wesley senior's position to have exhibited them in public for financial gain; in fact he appears to have kept them as much as possible out of the public gaze, and to have strictly rationed their appearances at public concerts. At the same time, he would have realized that if they were to develop their full potential they would need to learn from the best teachers and to be exposed to as many musical experiences as possible. Such considerations were no doubt uppermost in his mind when he decided to move the family from Bristol to London. In 1771 he was given the use of a house in Marylebone—at the time a village on the outskirts of London—by a wealthy well-wisher. For some time the family kept on their Bristol house and divided their time between Bristol and London, but in 1776 Samuel moved permanently to Marylebone, and two years later the family moved entirely from Bristol.

Perhaps inevitably, Samuel spent much of his childhood in the company of adults. For some of the time he was entrusted to the care of his godfather, the evangelical clergyman and amateur musician Martin Madan. Madan would later achieve notoriety for his controversial *Thelyphthora; or a Treatise on Female Ruin* (1780). At this time, however, he was chiefly known as a charismatic preacher and as the chaplain of the Lock Hospital, an asylum for men and women with venereal diseases, where the chapel had achieved renown because of the excellence of its music. Madan took Samuel on visits to his friends and acquaintances, where his musical abilities inevitably made him the object of much attention. Another child might have enjoyed the experience, but Samuel stated later that he had felt humiliated by it, and had resented his father's behaviour in allowing Madan to carry him around 'like a raree show': 'This soured my temper toward him at an early age. I contracted a dislike of my father's conduct, which grew with my growth, and strengthened with my strength.'[2]

But Samuel's visits to Madan's friends were not entirely taken up with music: family letters from the summer of 1776 include descriptions of an extended stay with the Russell family in Guildford, which included games of cricket,

---

[2] Rylands, DDCW 6/93Q.

experiments with home-made explosives, and firework displays. John Russell senior (1711–1804), the head of the family, was a printer and several times mayor of Guildford; John Russell, RA (1745–1806), his elder son, was a portrait painter who during this visit painted the well-known portrait of Samuel as a boy which now hangs at the Royal Academy of Music. Also among the Guildford circle was the experimental scientist James Price, sometimes described as the last of the alchemists, who in 1783 committed suicide after being unable to substantiate claims that he was able to transmute mercury into silver and gold, and who left Samuel a house at Guildford and £1,000 in his will.

Some of the problems faced by Charles Wesley senior in deciding how best to manage the upbringing of Charles and Samuel were those which have always confronted the parents of exceptionally gifted children.[3] But these were compounded by Charles's prominent position within Methodism and by other, class-related, factors. As a music-lover himself, and as a Christian father mindful of the parable of the talents, he would have considered it his duty to ensure that Charles and Samuel were given every opportunity to develop their abilities to their fullest extent. On the other hand, many Methodists, including Charles's brother John, looked with considerable suspicion on the sensual appeal of music and its use in any other context than that of worship. Public concerts, with their close associations with the theatre, were a cause of particular disapproval, and even religious music was suspect if it was at all elaborate. Charles was already criticized in some Methodist circles for the worldliness of his social circle. John Fletcher voiced what was presumably a widely felt concern when he wrote to Charles in 1771: 'You have your *enemies*, as well as your brother, they complain of your *love for musick, company, fine people, great folks*, and of the *want of your former zeal and frugality*. I need not put you in mind to cut off *sinful appearances*.'[4] Charles Wesley tended to react robustly to criticisms of his children's musical activities, replying on one occasion to a correspondent who had criticized him for allowing Charles to play in public that he had intended him for the Church, but that nature had intended otherwise, and that the only way he could have prevented him from being a musician would have been by cutting off his fingers.

It is apparent, however, that for all his love of music and his desire to see his children receive the best possible musical education, Charles Wesley senior had considerable misgivings about music as a suitable profession for them. His unease, although it may have been magnified by the particular circumstances of his position, did not arise specifically from his Methodist background, but would have been shared by most parents of his time and class. Irrespective of the value

---

[3] See Philip Olleson, 'The Wesleys at Home: Charles Wesley and his Children', *Methodist History*, 36 (1998), 139–52.   [4] Fletcher to Charles Wesley, 13 Oct. 1771, quoted in Gill, 190.

one might individually place on music, one would not welcome the prospect of one's children entering a profession with such a low status and high degree of insecurity.[5]

For the moment, however, Charles Wesley's first priority was to advance his sons' musical education, and allowing them to organize concerts at the family home must have appeared to him as an ideal way of achieving this aim. He set out his motives in a document headed 'reasons for letting my sons have a concert at home' dated 14 January 1779, which reveals much of the ambivalence of his attitudes:

(1) To keep them out of harm's way: the way (I mean) of bad music and bad musicians who by a free communication with them might corrupt both their taste and their morals.

(2) That my sons may have a safe and honourable opportunity of availing themselves of their musical abilities, which have cost me several hundred pounds.

(3) That they may enjoy their full right of private judgment, and likewise their independency; both of which must be given up if they swim with the stream and follow the multitude.

(4) To improve their play and their skill in composing: as they must themselves furnish the principal music of every concert, although they do not call their musical entertainment a concert. It is too great a word. They do not presume to rival the *present great masters* who excel in the variety of their accompaniments. All they aim at in their concert music is *exactness*.[6]

The family concerts, which ran for nine seasons from 1779 to 1787, included examples of music in both the 'ancient' and modern styles, performed by a small professional ensemble which included both Charles and Samuel, to audiences which on occasion numbered over fifty. In addition to giving both boys experience of performing, the concerts were also ideal opportunities for them to try out their compositions, and all of Samuel's instrumental music of the period—including five symphonies and a number of organ and violin concertos—can be assumed to have been written for them. Recent recordings and performances have shown them to be highly competent and attractive works, if sometimes understandably derivative in style.

Although the family concerts did much to fulfil Charles Wesley senior's aim of furthering his sons' musical education while keeping them 'out of harm's way', it is not clear how they fitted into any longer-term plans he may have had for their

---

[5] See Simon McVeigh, *Concert Life in London from Mozart to Haydn* (Cambridge, 1993), 199–201; Deborah Rohr, 'A Profession of Artisans: The Careers and Social Status of British Musicians, 1750–1850', Ph.D. diss., University of Pennsylvania, 1983.

[6] Rylands, DDWES 14/65, quoted in Lightwood, 51–2.

future. If, on the one hand, the concerts reflected his reluctant acceptance that they would probably eventually become professional musicians despite all his misgivings, he may have looked on them as a sheltered apprenticeship, in which they could gain necessary experience without being exposed too early to the potentially corrupting professional music world. But both sons would sooner or later need to make the transition, and the family concerts only delayed the moment when this would need to happen. In fact, by the time of the final series of concerts in 1787, they were both of an age when their less privileged contemporaries would long have been earning a living in music. If, on the other hand, he envisaged that his sons would eventually earn their living in other fields, he would have seen the concerts as a way of allowing them for the moment to practise music at the highest level with professionals, while still remaining gentlemen amateurs. But if this was what he had in mind, it too was unsatisfactory, in that the concerts effectively provided a full professional training that led nowhere.

Sheltered though he was from the world of professional music-making during the late 1770s and early 1780s, Samuel was nonetheless searching out new musical experiences wherever he could find them. He would no doubt have attended services at St Paul's Cathedral, Westminster Abbey, and other Anglican establishments. Rather more surprising, however, was his discovery of Roman Catholic worship, and a very different set of religious and musical traditions. From remarks in two letters from Charles Wesley to his wife, the date can be established as the late summer of 1778. Samuel's involvement must have been with one or more of the embassy chapels, which were at this time the main centres of worship for London Roman Catholics. The three largest chapels were those of the Bavarian, Sardinian, and Portuguese embassies, where the Mass and the Offices were celebrated with considerable splendour of liturgy and ritual. At an early stage Samuel would have met Samuel Webbe I (1740–1816), the organist of the Sardinian and Portuguese chapels, and the most important figure in Roman Catholic church music in London at this time. Webbe would have welcomed Samuel and would have given him the opportunity to sing in the choir, play the organ, and in time to compose for the services.

Charles Wesley's reaction to Samuel's continuing involvement with Roman Catholicism is not recorded, but can readily be imagined: intense disapproval, coupled with anxiety for Samuel's spiritual welfare, and above all a fear that he might convert. At the same time, it would have been inconsistent with his views on freedom of conscience for him to have considered forbidding Samuel's continued attendance. He was also no doubt sufficiently realistic to realize that any attempt to do so would be counter-productive, as by this time Samuel was exhibiting a rebellious streak and becoming increasingly resistant to any form of parental discipline. His worries may have been to some extent assuaged by the thought of the musical benefits that Samuel was deriving from his attendance, and the assurances that Samuel may well have given that his reasons for continuing to attend were exclusively musical.

In fact, Samuel did convert in early 1784: a course of action which dismayed and sorrowed Charles Wesley and further contributed to the already deteriorating relationship between father and son. To mark the event, in May Samuel composed a large-scale setting of the Mass which he later fair-copied and had bound and sent off to Pope Pius VI. The *Missa de Spiritu Sancto*, scored for soloists, chorus, and orchestra and lasting for around ninety minutes in performance, was Wesley's longest and most ambitious work to date, written on a scale matched by few other Mass settings of the period either in England or on the continent, and suitable for liturgical use on only the grandest of occasions. It seems unlikely that Samuel expected that it would be performed in Rome, and there were certainly no opportunities for it to be used in the London embassy chapels. He probably regarded it as a presentation piece, written to demonstrate at the same time his seriousness of commitment and his technical prowess.

Samuel's period of whole-hearted commitment to Roman Catholicism appears to have lasted for some years, although as time went on there were increasing tensions between his own convictions and the teachings of the Church. Some correspondence of early 1792 shows him unprepared to accept the Church's authority on certain points of doctrine. Uncertain whether or not his views were to be regarded as heretical, he stated that until the matter was resolved he no longer intended to attend services at 'public chapels'. This disagreement may in fact have marked the end of his active spiritual involvement with Roman Catholicism, and when he returned to the Church some years later, it was for purely musical reasons. In later life he regarded the episode of his conversion with embarrassment and tried to pretend that it had never happened, claiming that 'although the Gregorian music had seduced him to their chapels, the tenets of the Romanists never obtained any influence over his mind'.[7] His subsequent attitude to the Roman Catholic Church was highly ambivalent, consisting of a fascination with its liturgy and music combined with a deep distaste for its teaching and doctrines, summed up in his remark that 'if the Roman Doctrines were like the Roman *Music* we should have Heaven upon Earth'.[8]

Samuel's conversion to Roman Catholicism was only one of a number of factors adversely affecting his relations with his family at this time. Another was his passionate relationship with Charlotte Louisa Martin, whom he first met in October 1782 and was to marry in April 1793. The daughter of George Martin, variously described as a demonstrator of anatomy and a surgeon at St Thomas's

[7] Obituary in *The Times*, 12 Oct. 1837.   [8] SW to Jacob, 5 Nov. [1809].

hospital, she was four or five years older than Samuel, and may have been a teacher at one of the schools at which Samuel gave music lessons. The family disapproved of her and her background from the start, claiming that she was vain and extravagant, and pointing to a history of financial imprudence in her family. At some stage Charles Wesley appears to have attempted to insist that Samuel should break off the relationship and have nothing more to do with her. The result was predictable: Samuel refused, the relationship between him and his father—already under strain because of Samuel's involvement with Roman Catholicism—further deteriorated, and the bond between him and Charlotte was further strengthened.

Inextricably entangled with Samuel's family problems during his adolescence were the beginnings of the mental illness which so markedly affected his later career. His tendency to depression, leading on occasion to periods of prolonged incapacity, has always been recognized by his biographers. It is clear, however, that this was only one aspect of his illness, and that a more accurate diagnosis is of manic depression, in which periods of depression alternate with periods of hypomania. Hypomanic periods are typically characterized by a wide range of uninhibited behaviour, and in the case of creative artists often by great creativity. The irregular pattern of Samuel's compositional output in the 1780s, varying between great productivity and almost complete inactivity, is consistent with such a diagnosis. So is his behaviour at the same time, as reported in family letters: it included incidents of drunkenness, staying out all night, and the physical abuse of servants, all of which suggest something more than the normal mood-swings of adolescence. A low point must have been reached in the summer of 1785, when his father felt it necessary to take the extraordinary and humiliating step of begging Bishop Talbot, the Roman Catholic Vicar Apostolic of the London district, to assert his spiritual authority to keep Samuel under control, as he was no longer able to do so himself.

Wesley attained his majority in February 1787. Now that he was no longer either a child prodigy or a precocious adolescent, he needed to find a role in the adult world. He seems to have regarded a future as a musician with scant enthusiasm. As subsequent remarks scattered through the correspondence reveal, he deeply resented the quirk of fate which had given him such outstanding musical abilities, and which he considered had at the same time disqualified him from following any other profession. Much of this resentment was directed at his father, for encouraging his musical education and 'suffering' him to be a musician. By the time he entered adult life, the unglamorous reality of much of the musician's life must have become ever more apparent to him: the low status of the professional musician, the large amount of teaching that all but the most eminent performers needed to undertake in order to earn a basic living, the frequent physical discomforts of concert life, and the lack of any career progression.

In fact, Wesley appears for the moment to have turned away from music: there are no records of him performing in public and he seems to have stopped composing. His sole musical activity was his teaching, both in schools and privately. This was undemanding work for one of his abilities, and had little to recommend it beyond the money it brought in. Otherwise, little is known about his activities at this period, and his life appears to have been one of aimlessness and lack of direction, very probably punctuated by shorter or longer periods of depression.

In 1787, according to his obituary notice in *The Times*, Wesley suffered a serious head injury which he subsequently blamed for his mental health problems. But there is no mention of such an incident in family letters or papers, and the first signs of Wesley's condition had manifested themselves at least three years earlier. As the account of the head injury apparently came from Wesley himself, it should not be dismissed as a fiction, but there must be doubt about the precise date at which it occurred, to say nothing of its effects.

In December 1788 Wesley became a Freemason. Little is known about this event; it should be stressed, however, that it is not (as has sometimes been supposed) of any relevance to the question of his continued commitment to Roman Catholicism, as there was no ideological incompatibility at this time in England between Roman Catholicism and Freemasonry, and many English Catholics were also Freemasons.

Throughout the 1780s, Wesley and Charlotte remained as committed to each other as ever, their relationship no doubt gaining in strength with each additional instance of family opposition. After the death of Charles Wesley in March 1788, it might have been expected that they would consider marriage: by this time they had known each other for over five years, and their commitment had been tested by constant family opposition, at least on Wesley's side. In addition, Wesley had on his majority come into money left to him in various bequests, including the substantial one from James Price. As he and Charlotte intended to spend the rest of their lives together and were openly conducting a passionately physical relationship, there were no compelling reasons, apart from family disapproval, why they should not marry, and several reasons why they should.

In fact, the question of marriage does not seem for the moment to have been considered, and when the subject came up again some time later, the grounds of the family's concern had shifted. By now, they recognized the strength and apparent permanence of Wesley's commitment to Charlotte, and had abandoned their former attempts to persuade him to give her up. Instead, they now tried to persuade him to regularize the situation by marrying her. Part of their concern undoubtedly stemmed from worries about Charlotte becoming pregnant, and the stigma of illegitimacy which would attend any resulting children. Indeed, it appears from a reference in a family letter of 1791 that Charlotte had by this time already had a child by Samuel;[9] nothing further is known of this child and its fate, however, and it seems most likely that it was either stillborn or died in early infancy, or possibly that it was given away for adoption.

It is at this point that the story takes a totally unexpected turn. Wesley's response to family suggestions that he and Charlotte should marry was a flat refusal, on the surprising grounds that he considered them to be married already by virtue of their sexual intimacy, and that going through a religious ceremony would do nothing to alter matters. This stance, which he set out in detail in a remarkable series of letters to his sister Sarah in the summer of 1791, derived from arguments which his godfather Martin Madan had elaborated, but for very different purposes, in *Thelyphthora*. In an attempt to force men to take responsibility for their sexual behaviour, Madan had argued that the essence of marriage lay not in a legal ceremony but in sexual intercourse. If this could be established and enshrined into law, a man who had sexual intercourse with a woman could be held responsible for her maintenance and that of any resulting child or children. Madan claimed that this well-intentioned but eccentric position was supported by scriptural authority, arguing that there was nothing in the Bible to suggest that a religious ceremony was an essential component of marriage. One very obvious problem with this position was posed by men who had sexual intercourse with more than one woman. To cope with this, Madan was obliged to argue for polygamy, once more citing the Bible. Not surprisingly, it was this aspect of his argument that attracted the most attention and opposition—often from those who had not troubled to familiarize themselves with the entirety of his argument—and which led first to his public notoriety and ultimately to his disgrace.

In Wesley's hands, Madan's arguments were given a new and personal application. If the essence of marriage was indeed in sexual intercourse, then he and Charlotte were already married, and there could be no reason for them also to go through a church ceremony. It is difficult to think of a position which could have caused more offence and hurt to his family. In his refusal to marry, Samuel was claiming to be adopting not a libertarian stance, but a position of principle, backed by the full weight of biblical authority. At the same time he paraded his physical intimacy with Charlotte in front of his family, expressed his contempt for the marriage ceremony, and impugned the integrity of all those who celebrated it. It was an extraordinary position to take, and one which—Madan and *Thelyphthora* apart—finds no resonance in any thinking of the time.

Although Madan's arguments gave Samuel's position intellectual backing of a sort, he had more down-to-earth reasons for his refusal to marry, which on occasion he was prepared to acknowledge. One was financial; the other purely a

---

[9] Sarah Wesley to SW, 27 May 1791 (Emory).

matter of his refusal to conform to expected norms of behaviour. As he explained to Sarah in June 1791:

I have but two objections to marrying. The first is I am not rich enough: the second that to tie my person wd be to lose my heart: and she who valued it would hardly consent to that. It is impossible for me to explain to another the reason of some irresistible anti-pathies, and I can only declare this truth, that my aversion to constraint is invincible.[10]

For all the vehemence of Wesley's arguments and his repeated protestations of his commitment to Charlotte, it was not until the autumn of 1792 that they decided to set up house together and live together as man and wife. Samuel described this move in an important letter to his mother which more than any other document conveys his own feelings for Charlotte, his family's opposition, and his views on marriage:

I think I need not be told that every grand Step in Life ought to be well weighed, & thoroughly considered before it be taken:—It is certain that I have taken one of these grand Steps within this Month past, & I hope, not without having previously & seriously reflected on the Consequences of it.

An Acquaintance of ten Years duration has confirmed me in the Resolution of passing 'Life's Sea' with that 'Mate', whose every Action has given the Lye to her Accusers.—It is true that her Enemies have been found only among the Base & Unworthy, yet as their cruel & unfounded Aspersions have unfortunately sunk too deep in the Minds of those who deserve to be undeceived, I shall not believe it Time lost, to animadvert upon a few of their Charges. Charlotte Louisa Martin has been represented as a fickle & unsteady Character. Whether this be true or false, let the following Fact decide.—It was in October 1782 that I first became acquainted with her; soon after which time, she acknowledged that she loved me: since then she has to my Knowledge had repeated & eligible Offers not of a dishonourable Connexion but of an honourable Alliance; *not of Concubinage* but of *Marriage*, from Men qualified to support her in a Style similar to that in which she was originally educated: but to these she has preferred Me in my wooden Cottage, with my splendid Fortune of 150 Pounds a Year!

Again, she has been held forth as of a careless, prodigal Disposition, & as closely resembling an extravagant Father & a vain Mother, whose Iniquities she has (indeed most unjustly) borne.—But how does this Charge agree with another Fact? (which let him deny who can): Mr King, (a Bristol Merchant who has the Management of the desperate Affairs of the Family) has allowed her, for several Years past, 30 Pounds per Annum, on which she has hitherto lived, decently, & out of debt. That she was ever assisted by me in pecuniary Matters, I can safely & solemnly declare to be untrue.—From me she never received or would accept aught but mere Trifles, although amongst the other diabolical Slanders it was affirmed (by him who is gone to his own Place) that I had engaged to liquidate her Debts & administer to her Luxuries, as soon as I should become of Age.

[10] SW to Sarah Wesley, 5 June [1791] (Fitzwilliam).

She has been called a Coquette, nay more; a wanton.—On these Accusations, as false as God is true, I can reflect with no Patience: they were engendered in the Heart of Envy, & vomited from the Mouth of Malice.—Suffice it to say that I have had personal Proofs that till she was mine, she was pure & untouched: proofs which it would not be delicate to adduce.—If she was seduced, I alone was her Seducer.

It may easily be believed that the Woman whom I so well love I would ever wish to render respected by all those whose good Opinion may be valuable: & if I were to con-sider Her as anything else than my Wife, I should confess that I was adding Insult to Injury. But she is truly & properly my Wife by all the Laws of God & Nature. She never can be made more so, by the mercenary Tricks of divine Jugglers; but yet, if a Million of Ceremonies, repeated Myriads of Times, by as many Successors & Imitators of Simon Magus, can serve to make her more happy, or more honourable, I am ready to *pay* them for their Hocus Pocus, for I am told that in this Evangelical Age, 'the Gift of God is' *not* 'to be purchased' *without* Money.[11]

The house described here as a 'wooden Cottage' was in Ridge, a small village in Hertfordshire near St Albans, some thirteen miles outside London, and Wesley and Charlotte were to live there for the next four years. The decision to move there was on the face of it a bizarre one. It was probably prompted in the first place by Wesley's disenchantment with London, coupled with a desire to live out a rural idyll with Charlotte, far from the intrusive and censorious attentions of family and acquaintances. Another factor was no doubt his 'splendid Fortune of 150 Pounds a Year', which was—notwithstanding his dismissive comment—in fact quite sufficient to free him from the necessity of full-time work and hence the obligation to live in London.

If worries about the prospect of illegitimate children were the main factor in the family's attempts to persuade Wesley and Charlotte to marry, these must have increased after the move to Ridge. The issue soon became pressing, for early in 1793 Charlotte became pregnant. The impending birth of a child was evidently successful in inducing a change of attitude where repeated arguments and pleas from the family had failed: Wesley and Charlotte rapidly abandoned their previously cherished principles and married in early April. Not surpris-ingly, given the circumstances and the vehemence with which they had held their former position, the ceremony was quiet, not to say secretive: it was by special licence, thus obviating the need to call the banns, and not at Ridge but at Hammersmith, where presumably neither Wesley nor Charlotte was known. None of Wesley's family was present, and they were not informed that the marriage had taken place until much later. Incredibly, in letters to Sarah of late August Wesley was still arguing his old position on the redundancy of the marriage ceremony and making no mention of the fact that he and Charlotte were now

---

[11] SW to his mother, 7 Nov. 1792 (Rylands, DDWF 15/5).

married.[12] It was not until the following January that Sarah could record that she had had their marriage 'confirmed' and had met Charlotte for the first time as SW's wife.[13]

In this way Wesley and Charlotte embarked on married life. Their first child, Charles, was born on 25 September 1793. But the relationship which had thrived on ten concentrated years of family opposition before the marriage rapidly deteriorated after it. As early as October 1794, as Charlotte's confinement with a second child approached, Wesley was confessing to Sarah: 'I love her, as you know, but the event has proved that she was never designed for my second self. I dwell on her virtues even now, and as little on her faults as she will let me. But where can esteem be for her or him who knows not to bridle the tongue?'[14]

From this point, Wesley made no attempt to conceal his marital unhappiness from his family, and his letters to his mother and sister describe frequent quarrels, on occasion escalating into physical violence. Perhaps not surprisingly, his complaints about Charlotte's character and behaviour bore a great similarity to those expressed by his family before the marriage. By July 1795, he was considering separation as his only way of escaping a situation that he was finding increasingly intolerable, and predicting that Charlotte's 'open violence' would drive him 'more speedily to comfort' than he had previously expected.[15] Eighteen months later, he was confiding to his old friend James Kenton that life with Charlotte had adversely affected his health: his memory was weakened, he was seldom calm, and he had aged a dozen years since the marriage. There was no arguing with Charlotte's 'diabolical, ungovernable, ferocious, ungrateful disposition', and he and Kenton were agreed that she was 'incurable among lunaticks'.[16]

Despite repeated crises, resulting from time to time in periods of temporary separation, Wesley and Charlotte remained together until 1810. There may, of course, have been peaks of happiness to match the troughs of misery, and more settled and uneventful times which went unrecorded in the family correspondence. For a while, at least, some of the strong attraction that had sustained their commitment through their ten-year courtship appears to have survived: in an undated letter from around this time, Charlotte confided to Sarah that Wesley had been 'the love of her youth', that she had loved him 'better than mortal', and that he had 'taken too strong root' for her ever to stop loving him, even though she considered that some aspects of his behaviour disgraced him.[17]

---

[12] SW to [Sarah Wesley], [22 Aug. 1793] (Rylands, DDWF 15/6), selectively quoted in Lightwood, 84.   [13] Sarah Wesley, 'Mercies of the Year 1794', entry for 18 Jan. 1794 (Emory).

[14] SW to Sarah Wesley, 26 Oct. 1794 (Emory).

[15] SW to Sarah Wesley, [8] July 1795 (Fitzwilliam).   [16] SW to Kenton, 18 Jan. 1797 (Duke).

[17] Charlotte Wesley to Sarah Wesley, undated [?1795–7] (Drew).

Musically, Wesley's time at Ridge seems to have been almost entirely fallow. He continued with his teaching, but there is no evidence of him performing in public during the period, and apart from one major work (the *Ode to St Cecilia*) there were no compositions of any significance.

By 1797, any attractions which Ridge may have once have possessed had evidently long since disappeared, and the Wesleys moved to Finchley: now a suburb of London, but at the time still an outlying village. They were to be there until some time after May of the following year, when they moved to Hornsey Lane, near Highgate. The move appears to have had a dramatic effect on Wesley's life. Participation in London musical life immediately became feasible, even if Wesley still needed on occasion to use the Marylebone house for overnight stays after evening engagements, as he had when he lived at Ridge. The change in Wesley's circumstances is apparent in a fresh crop of compositions. A number of glees, catches, and other small-scale vocal compositions points to his involvement with the world of the glee clubs and other more informal private gatherings where professionals joined with amateurs for relaxed and convivial music-making.

After a long silence, Wesley was also once more composing Latin church music. His compositions of this period include such pieces as the ambitious eight-part settings of 'Deus Majestatis intonuit' and 'Dixit Dominus' and a five-part setting of 'Exultate Deo', all of them reflecting his by now considerable knowledge of English and continental Renaissance polyphonic styles. As with his earlier Latin church music, there is no evidence to link these works with any one location, but it is probable that they were written for the Portuguese embassy chapel, where the 16-year-old Vincent Novello had recently taken up the post of organist.

The rise in spirits that can be inferred from Wesley's sudden resumption of composition can also be seen in the earliest letters in this volume. Many are to Joseph Payne Street, a City businessman and a prominent member of the Madrigal Society, whom Wesley may have got to know through one or other of the glee clubs, or as a pupil. It was also at around this time that Wesley renewed his acquaintance with the music historian Charles Burney, and laid the foundations of a friendship that would continue until Burney's death in 1814.

Wesley's one large-scale work of the period was his *Confitebor tibi, Domine*, an hour-long setting for soloists, chorus, and orchestra of Psalm 111, which he completed in August 1799. The *Confitebor* is the most successful of Wesley's large-scale choral works, combining choruses in the 'ancient' Handelian manner with florid solo sections in a more modern idiom in a manner which demonstrates Wesley's easy mastery of both styles. As with the earlier *Ode to St Cecilia*, we know nothing about the circumstances of its composition, and can only speculate on the plans that Wesley may have had for its performance. It seems most likely that he wrote it with performance at one of the Lenten oratorio concerts in mind. If so, he may have intended it for the 1800 Covent Garden season, following the belated first performance of his *Ode to St Cecilia* there in February 1799. What is less certain, however, is how acceptable a setting of a Latin sacred text would have been at an oratorio concert at this time, and it may have been for this reason that plans for its performance eventually foundered.

The abortive *Confitebor* project notwithstanding, it is clear that by 1799 Wesley was beginning to establish himself in London professional musical life. In the spring of 1798 he had applied unsuccessfully for the post of organist at the chapel of the Foundling Hospital, where the musical traditions inaugurated during the lifetime of Handel still continued. His failure to be elected on this occasion was one of many similar disappointments throughout his life, and appears to have had nothing to do with his abilities or his fitness for the post: his reputation as an organist, and particularly as an extempore player, was by this time well established. In April 1800 he appeared at the King's Theatre in one of the earliest performances in England of Haydn's *Creation*, playing continuo and performing his own recently composed D major organ concerto between the acts. In addition, his most recent music was beginning to appear in print: a set of twelve sonatinas for piano was published in late 1798 or early 1799, followed around two years later by a further set of piano sonatas and duets.

A more determined effort to break into London musical life was the ill-starred series of subscription concerts at the Tottenham Street rooms that Wesley and his brother Charles arranged in early 1802. It was for performance at one of these that Wesley composed his Symphony in B flat, his only mature work in the genre, and a piece which, like the *Confitebor*, amply demonstrates Wesley's familiarity with the late music of Haydn. Contemporary information on the concert series is sparse, consisting only of a single press advertisement and a letter to Burney which gives details of the programme of one of the concerts and expresses Wesley's regret that they had not been able to engage the services of the soprano Elizabeth Billington.[18] Nonetheless, it is clear from remarks in subsequent letters that the series was an expensive and embarrassing failure which cost Wesley and Charles around £100 each.

Notwithstanding the performance of the *Ode to St Cecilia*, a few concert appearances, and the promotion of the Tottenham Street series, it cannot be said that Wesley was a major figure in London's music at this time: the picture is one of isolated events rather than of sustained activity. A large part of the reason no doubt lay in his continuing mental health problems, the cyclical nature of which

[18] SW to Burney, [Feb.–May 1802].

must have made any long-term career development difficult, if not impossible. At the same time, his relationship with Charlotte continued to be stormy. Family letters, not always precisely datable, reveal a long catalogue of quarrels and unhappiness, culminating in Wesley's love affair in or around 1799 with Anne Deane, a close friend of his sister Sarah. The result, in the autumn of 1801, was a separation from Charlotte and a serious rift with Sarah, followed by an extended period of depression which appears to have been at its most severe in the summer of 1802 and to have rendered Wesley for a time incapable of any but the most routine activities. The house at Five Mile Stone, Highgate, where he and Charlotte had been living since the summer of 1799, was sold, and for a while nothing is known of Wesley's activities, either private or public.

Wesley and Charlotte appear to have had some sort of rapprochement in the spring of 1805, and it was probably at around this time that they moved into the house in Arlington Street, Camden Town that they were to occupy until the final breakdown of their marriage in 1810. Another child, Emma Frances, was born in January or February 1806, joining Charles, now 12, and John William, born in the summer of 1799 and now 6. But although differences had been patched up and accommodations reached for the moment, the relationship was evidently as highly charged as before, and as likely to turn to acrimony and violence. The Roman Catholic bluestocking Mary Freeman Shepherd, who had known Wesley since his boyhood and had been his confidante at the time of his conversion in 1784, took a jaundiced view of the relationship. Learning in January 1806 of Charlotte's impending confinement, she remarked contemptuously in a letter to Wesley's sister Sarah: 'his wife I find is ready to lay in. By and by they will be quarrelling again, like cats that fight when they cease caterwauling.'[19]

With the move to Camden Town and the birth of Emma, some degree of domestic normality appears to have returned, although Wesley's depression continued. He was dissatisfied with his lot as a musician, in particular the school teaching by which he was obliged to make his main living. He was also plagued with money worries—some of them no doubt the result of the domestic problems of the previous few years—and could no longer afford to maintain Charles at St Paul's School, where he had placed him only the previous year. For the moment he felt himself trapped by debt and a heavy load of family responsibilities, and his mood was one of grim resignation. In a letter of April 1806 to his mother he set out the grounds for his discontent:

It is absolutely impossible for me to maintain myself & four other People (not reckoning the infant) upon my present Income, especially when it is considered that the Person

---

[19] Mary Freeman Shepherd to Sarah Wesley, 15 Jan. 1806 (Rylands).

whose sole Care & Business ought to be to make the most of every Thing, is & ever will be, a thoughtless, not to say a determined Spendthrift. If another School, equal in Emolument to Mrs Barnes's were to offer (which is not very likely) even then the Matter would not be mended, because the simple Fact is that my Head & Nerves will not bear the Drudgery of more Dunces assaulting my Ears for six Hours together. It is not that I am averse from Employment; no, not of the closest Kind, for those who know me best know that Application has been my Delight; but this contemptible, frivolous Work of hammering Sounds into blockheads, which at last they never rightly comprehend, is an Avocation, which I cannot increase, without driving myself either into Madness or Ideotism.[20]

This shows Wesley at his most despairing. Other letters of the period show him in a happier and more active frame of mind. By mid-January 1807, he was able to profess himself in a letter to his mother 'much more recovered' in bodily health than he ever expected to be.[21] Although elsewhere in the letter he expresses more gloomy thoughts, the tenor of the whole is cheerful enough, and his letter of the same date to his brother Charles (included in this volume) extends to eleven pages of lively news and gossip. The contrast with the despairing letters of the previous year could not be stronger.

At around the same time as Wesley's reconciliation with Charlotte and the resumption of a more settled domestic life was an event which was both to transform his professional fortunes and to give him a cause into which to concentrate his considerable energies: his discovery of the music of J. S. Bach.

Although Wesley may have come across a few isolated examples of Bach's music earlier in publications by A. F. C. Kollmann, William Shield, and Clementi, which appeared between 1796 and 1800, they do not seem to have made very much of an impression on him. Nor does he appear to have encountered the three continental editions of the '48' published around 1801, copies of which presumably arrived in England shortly afterwards. In fact, according to his account in his *Reminiscences*, written in 1836, Wesley's first encounter with the '48' was through the violinist and composer George Frederick Pinto. This fixes the date with some precision: it cannot have been later than early 1806, as Pinto died at the early age of 20 on 23 March of that year. Wesley subsequently made his own manuscript copy from a copy lent to him by the flautist John George Graeff.[22] Thereafter, for the moment, his interest appears to have lain dormant.

The explosive awakening of Wesley's interest in Bach's music can probably be dated to early 1808. In April, Wesley wrote to Burney to tell him about his enthu-

---

[20] SW to his mother, 21 Apr. [1806] (BL, Add. MS 35012, fo. 11).

[21] SW to his mother, 15 Jan. 1807 (BL, Add. MS 35012, fo. 15).

[22] SW to Graeff, 21 May [?1806].

siasm for Bach, subsequently visiting him at Chelsea College to play examples from the '48' to him. As a result of Wesley's advocacy, Burney became an enthusiastic convert to the Bach cause, and Wesley came to rely on him for advice on how Bach's music could best be promoted. By this time Wesley was also asking Burney for his opinion on the likely demand for an English edition of the '48', to be published by subscription. As a result of Burney's advice that Bach's music might be 'played into fashion',[23] Wesley arranged an evidently successful concert of Bach's music at the Hanover Square Rooms on 11 June. At the same time, Wesley consulted Burney on the advisability of lecturing on Bach, and in another letter recounted his success in playing Bach while on a visit to Cambridge.[24]

From August 1808 to the following December the main source of information on Wesley's activities in promoting Bach is his letters to Benjamin Jacob, organist of the Surrey Chapel. First published in 1875 in an edition by Wesley's daughter Eliza as *Letters of Samuel Wesley to Mr Jacobs, relating to the Introduction into this Country of the works of John Sebastian Bach*, the *Bach Letters* are the most widely known of Wesley's letters. With their excitable tone, extravagant language, and all-pervading use of religious imagery, they convey Wesley's enthusiasm for Bach at its height. In addition, they are an invaluable source of information on the day-to-day progress of the English Bach movement at a crucial early stage.

In the earliest letter of the collection Wesley proposes the formation of a 'junto' of Bach enthusiasts and a programme of concerted action to counter the resistance to Bach's music that he was evidently encountering among more conservative musicians, including his brother Charles.[25] A month later he gives Jacob his celebrated account of the conversion of Burney to the Bach cause.[26] Subsequent letters contain a wealth of information on a number of Bach-related activities: the projected publication by Wesley and C. F. Horn of an English translation of Forkel's biography of Bach,[27] their edition of the organ trio sonatas,[28] and Wesley's insertion of an arrangement of a Bach fugue in a performance of one of his own organ concertos at a music festival at Tamworth.[29] Letters of late 1809 contain details of encouraging sales of the organ trios, which Wesley and Horn had been issuing in individual numbers since the spring of that year, and in a letter which is probably addressed to Horn, a report of strong public demand for their proposed new edition of the '48'.[30] There is also discussion of plans for a large-scale recital of Bach's music at the Surrey Chapel, to include one or more of the violin sonatas in addition to Preludes and Fugues from the '48', and

---

[23] Quoted in SW to Burney, 23 June [1808].   [24] SW to Burney, 7 July 1808.
[25] SW to [Jacob], 13 Aug. [1808].   [26] SW to Jacob, 17 Sept. 1808.
[27] SW to Jacob, 17 Oct. 1808.   [28] SW to Jacob, 3 Mar. 1809.
[29] SW to Jacob, 25 Sept. 1809.   [30] SW to [?C. F. Horn], *c*.30 Sept. 1809.

evidence of a strong pro-Bach lobby among the London banking community.[31] Other letters show Wesley taking care to keep Burney fully informed of the progress of his activities, and on occasion arranging private performances of Bach's music for him at his apartments in Chelsea. One such was in September 1809, when Wesley on the violin and Jacob on the piano performed one or more of the violin sonatas;[32] another was in July 1810, when Wesley and Novello performed the *Goldberg Variations* on two pianos, one of which had to be specially moved into Burney's apartments for the purpose.[33]

It was during this exceptionally busy period that the final breakdown of the Wesleys' marriage occurred. Although details are sparse, it is clear that the immediate cause was Wesley's liaison with his domestic servant or housekeeper Sarah Suter, at the time 15 or at most 16 years old. The final separation, no doubt precipitated by the discovery of Sarah's pregnancy, was in early 1810, whereupon Wesley and Sarah set up house together. They were to live together unmarried until Wesley's death. Samuel Sebastian, their first child, was born on 14 August 1810, followed by eight further children over the next twenty years.

Wesley's abandonment of his wife and family for his teenage servant was naturally a great scandal. Divorce was not a practical possibility at this time for any but the wealthy, and Wesley and Charlotte thus had no option but to remain married. As Charlotte outlived him, Wesley's relationship with Sarah Suter remained irregular until the end, and all their children were illegitimate. In 1812 a Deed of Separation was drawn up which put the separation on a formal basis and awarded Charlotte annual maintenance of £130, an amount which probably represented around a third of Wesley's income at the time.[34]

Little is known about Sarah Suter, and she remains a peculiarly shadowy figure. In accordance with Wesley's compartmentalization of his life, she is mentioned only rarely in the letters in this volume. Wesley's early biographers, anxious to maintain propriety, make no mention of her and the twenty-seven years that she and Wesley lived together, even though their relationship must have been common knowledge. Almost the only documentary evidence of her existence is a series of forty-two letters that Wesley wrote to her between 1810 and 1830[35] and which now forms part of the collection of family manuscripts, letters, and papers bequeathed to the British Museum by Eliza in 1895. From these, it is apparent that Wesley enjoyed a measure of domestic stability and contentment with Sarah and their many children that had been lacking in his marriage to Charlotte.

---

[31] SW to Jacob, [24 Nov. 1809].   [32] SW to Jacob, 4 Sept. [1809] and [?30 Sept. 1809].

[33] SW to Burney, 17 July 1810.

[34] Rylands, DDCW 6/88. For private separation at this time, see Lawrence Stone, *Road to Divorce* (Oxford, 1990), 149–82.   [35] BL, Add. MS 35012.

The incident of the *Goldberg Variations* performance marks the entry of Vincent Novello into the correspondence and provides the first evidence of his friendship with Wesley. Wesley may in fact have known Novello since a good deal earlier, but his absence from the letters until 1810 suggests that Wesley's closer association with him did not begin until around this time.

From May 1811, Wesley's letters to Novello dominate the correspondence. By this time, Wesley was acting as Novello's assistant at the Portuguese Embassy Chapel, and in this capacity needed to be in frequent contact with him to discuss arrangements for the chapel's music, particularly on those occasions when Novello was absent and Wesley deputized for him. This appears to have been how the correspondence began, and many of the early letters are largely if not entirely concerned with one aspect or another of the music of the chapel.

But Portuguese Embassy Chapel matters account for only part of the contents of the letters to Novello, which over the next five years contain a host of details of Wesley's increasingly crowded life as a performer, composer, concert organizer, reviewer for the *European Magazine*, and teacher. In addition, they chronicle the continuing story of Wesley's promotion of Bach, often now with Novello as his partner in duet performances of the organ music. Finally, they show Wesley's promotion of his own music, both at his annual benefit concerts and at the Covent Garden Lenten oratorio concerts, where he was the regular organist from the beginning of the 1813 season.

This appointment immediately put Wesley at the heart of London's concert world and gave him a markedly higher public profile. The period from 1813 to 1816 marked the peak of Wesley's career, when for the first time, and in his late forties, he at last achieved a central position in London's musical life. In addition he was busy making the social contacts, both within and outside the profession, which were vital if his career was to prosper. In May 1812 he had been appointed masonic Grand Organist, a position which involved him in regular contact with many in the highest reaches of London society. In June 1815 he was appointed to full membership of the recently founded Philharmonic Society and in November of the same year became a Director, subsequently playing a significant role in the affairs of the Society.

The letters of this period also show Wesley's involvement in music-making outside London. For Wesley, as for most of his fellow musicians in the capital, London offered concert engagements for only part of the year. After the main winter season and the series of self-promoted or benefit concerts that followed it, the season petered out in June. But part of the off-season period could be filled by concert engagements out of London, principally on the provincial music festival circuit. Such festivals, in towns and cities such as Norwich, Birmingham, Manchester, and Liverpool, provided provincial audiences with their only opportunities to hear large-scale choral and orchestral music performed by professional forces, mostly drawn from London.

Wesley's first involvement with this world had been in 1809 in Tamworth, and he had subsequently been invited to direct the 1811 Birmingham festival. On both of these occasions he would have been engaged by a local committee for a set fee and possibly a share of box-office takings. But he also on occasion promoted his own concerts. A speculative visit in September 1812 with Samuel Webbe II to Ramsgate and Margate on this basis narrowly escaped failure, largely because of a lack of local knowledge and poor forward planning.[36] Wesley had happier experiences in East Anglia, however, where a visit to the Ipswich festival in July 1813 at the invitation of his old friend Charles Hague was followed by successful visits to Norwich in 1814 and to Norwich and Great Yarmouth in 1815.

Wesley's long run of success came to an end in August 1816. Early in the month an infant child had died, just as he was preparing to go to Norwich for a third concert visit. This event appears to have set in train a rapid deterioration in his mental and physical health which eventually culminated in a serious breakdown the following May.

Although Wesley managed to set off for Norwich, he collapsed on the way and never arrived. The loss of the £100 that he was expecting from the trip plunged him into a financial crisis which no doubt compounded his mental problems. By early October, in an attempt to regain his health in the purer air of what was still a country area, he had moved out of the family home into lodgings in Hampstead. A few isolated letters from this time chart his decline and his increasing reliance on Novello to deputize for him in his teaching.

In spite of everything, however, Wesley was for the moment still continuing to work: he was able to fulfil his teaching commitments for most of the time, and was at his usual place at the organ for the Covent Garden Lenten oratorio concerts in February and March 1817. But his health was evidently continuing its downward spiral. The crisis came on 6 May, when, imagining himself to be pursued by creditors set on him by Charlotte, he flung himself from an upper-storey window. According to his sister Sarah's account, written a few days later, the fall was '25 feet, upon stones', and his injuries were so severe that he was given only hours to live.[37]

Wesley's fall and subsequent incapacity turned what was already a serious financial situation into a desperate one. He was now completely out of action for the foreseeable future, and he and his family—by this time consisting of Sarah Suter, Samuel Sebastian, and Rosalind, aged 2 or 3—faced the prospect of immediate and total financial ruin.

[36] SW to Novello, 1 Oct. [1812].
[37] Sarah Wesley to William Wilberforce, [c.12 May 1817] (Emory); see also Sarah's diary entry for 6 May 1817, quoted in Lightwood, 183.

It was at this point that William Linley and some of SW's other musical and masonic friends stepped in. Their immediate priority was to cope with the aftermath of the fall, but they soon also needed to consider how best to manage what was evidently going to be a protracted period of illness and convalescence. Eventually the decision was taken to place Wesley in Blacklands House, Chelsea, a private lunatic asylum. He remained there until late June 1818, when he was pronounced cured and discharged.[38]

Wesley wrote few letters during his illness, and the period from his breakdown until his recovery around 1823 is particularly poorly documented. Nonetheless, it is clear that by late 1818 he was attempting to pick up the threads of his career. In a letter to Novello he enquired about the appropriate level of payment for a copying job which William Hawes had asked him to undertake, no doubt out of kindness.[39] By the beginning of the 1819 season he was back in action at the Covent Garden oratorio concerts, his place during the previous season having been taken by Jacob. But he was for the moment only partly recovered, and for some time to come his spirits were low.

Wesley's breakdown had had a disastrous effect on his finances. Arrangements painstakingly built up over a period of years were disrupted, some never to return. In his absence, other musicians no doubt gladly stepped into his shoes, and many of his pupils would have found other teachers. For the next few years, Wesley would need to take work wherever he could find it, however menial. Two affecting letters to Novello show him begging for copying work of any sort, literary or musical,[40] one of them eliciting the comment from Novello that he was placing it on record as

an eternal disgrace to the pretended Patrons of good music in England, who could have the contemptible bad taste to undervalue & neglect the masterly productions of such an extraordinary Musician as Sam Wesley, and who had the paltry meanness of spirit, to allow such a real Genius . . . to sink into such poverty, decay and undeserved neglect, as to be under the necessity of seeking employment as a mere drudging *Copyist* to prevent himself from starvation!

Notwithstanding letters such as these, the picture was not entirely negative, and Wesley was gradually able to resume some of his former activities and to take on some new ones. In June 1819 he applied to R. M. Bacon, proprietor of the recently launched *Quarterly Musical Magazine and Review*, with an enquiry about work on Bacon's projected dictionary of music,[41] and in October 1821, amidst protestations of his lack of ability as a composer, he composed a Latin

---

[38] Charles Wesley's pocket book, 25 June 1818 (Dorset Record Office): see Betty Matthews, 'Charles Wesley on Organs: 2', *MT* 112 (1971), 1111–12.   [39] SW to Novello, 17 Nov. [?1818].

[40] SW to Novello, 20 Nov. [1820], 27 Nov. 1821.   [41] SW to Bacon, 5 June 1819.

Magnificat setting for a projected publication of Novello's.[42] A different side to his activities is shown in letters of late 1822 to the wealthy Irish landowner Walter McGeough concerning the arrangements of music that he was making for the barrel organ that McGeough had commissioned for The Argory, his new house in Co. Armagh.[43]

Perhaps the clearest sign of Wesley's return to health was his composition of his Anglican Magnificat and Nunc Dimittis in late 1822. These two settings were companion-pieces to the Te Deum and Jubilate that he had written as long ago as 1808, and completed a full Anglican morning and evening service. They were first performed at St Paul's on Christmas Day 1823, just as the Te Deum and Jubilate had been on the same day fifteen years earlier. No doubt as a result of favourable comments received on this occasion, Wesley decided early in 1824 to publish the full Service by subscription. Proposals were issued in February, the Service received two complete performances at St Paul's in April, and was published in October.

By the time of the publication of the Service, Wesley's recovery was complete and he was once more playing an active part in London's musical life. As before, he was making a living from a number of different activities, of which performing and teaching were the most important. Some of his former activities had disappeared, however, and the pattern of his employment was now rather different from before his illness.

One activity which did not survive Wesley's illness was his musical journalism. It is one of the greatest ironies of Wesley's career that his illness in 1817 had exactly coincided with the preparations for the launch, and the launch itself, of *QMMR*, London's first long-run music journal. Had Wesley been in good health during this crucial period, his strong opinions, trenchant prose style, and experience in musical journalism would no doubt have ensured him a role of some sort in the new journal. In the event, by the time Wesley had sufficiently recovered his health to be thinking about writing for *QMMR*, its organization was well established and a team of contributors headed by William Horsley was in place.

Another casualty of Wesley's illness was his involvement with the Philharmonic Society. As we have seen, for a short time in 1815 and 1816 Wesley had played a prominent part in the Society's affairs in a way which suggests that he had become firmly established as a member of the most influential group of musicians in London. His motet 'Father of Life' had been performed at one of the Society's concerts in April 1816, and he was no doubt looking forward both to further performances of his music and to his own continuing participation as a performer

---

[42] SW to Novello, 2 Oct. [1821], 9 Oct. 1821.
[43] SW to McGeough, 12 Oct. 1822, 11 Nov. 1822.

and, on occasion, as director. He could also have been confident that the contacts with his fellow directors would be fruitful in other ways not directly connected with the Society. All of this ceased with his breakdown. His membership appears to have lapsed at the time of his illness, and he never subsequently rejoined. He performed at no more of the Society's concerts, and no more of his music was included in its programmes.

In the absence of further information it is impossible to do more than speculate on the reasons for the severing of relations with the Philharmonic Society. In the years following his breakdown Wesley must have cut a sorry figure, and it is possible that his former fellow directors, always concerned with respectability and the reputation of their fledgeling organization, would have been unenthusiastic about reinstating his lapsed membership, let alone restoring him to his former position on the board. It is also possible that there was a quarrel or a more general cooling of relations with the Society or with some of its leading members.

Whatever the truth of the matter, Wesley's absence from the Philharmonic Society and its concerts is indicative of a more general change in his position in London's concert life. Before his illness he had been fully involved in all the activities of a busy freelance musician: a hectic schedule of oratorio and other concerts in London during the season, supplemented with appearances at provincial music festivals and other out-of-town concerts during the off-season. After his recovery, much of that involvement is missing. Although he continued to play at the Covent Garden oratorio concerts, he was now appearing increasingly as a solo recitalist rather than as a soloist in choral and orchestral concerts. Perhaps in consequence of a reluctance to undertake the necessary travelling, he was also undertaking fewer engagements out of London, and he seems entirely to have given up his involvement with the provincial music festival scene. Later in the decade he would once more venture out of London for concert engagements: to Birmingham in May 1828, to Leeds in September of the same year, and finally to his native Bristol in September 1829, but for the moment he appears to have been content to remain close to home.

This change in direction may have been the result of a deliberate choice. Wesley was always ambivalent about the music profession and his own role in it, and frequently scathing about his fellow professionals. He may now have felt wearied with large-scale concerts and have decided to concentrate as much as possible on solo recitals and lectures, where contact with other musicians could be kept to a minimum. But other factors may also have contributed. Wesley, always conservative by temperament, must have felt increasingly out of place in the transformed London concert world of the 1820s, which featured music by a new generation of composers and the extended visits of Rossini and Liszt in 1824 and of Weber in 1826. One looks in vain in the letters for anything but brief and derogatory comments on these composers and their music. It is clear that by the mid-1820s Wesley was no longer making any attempt to keep up with modern developments.

One area in which a conservative outlook was no disadvantage was Anglican church music, and it is not surprising to find Wesley turning his attention once again to church appointments. As early as 1821 he had been an unsuccessful candidate for the new parish church of St Pancras, and further unsuccessful applications to St Lawrence, Jewry in January 1823 and to St George's, Hanover Square in February 1824 followed. In May 1824, he was appointed organist at Camden Chapel, a new church in the St Pancras parish. This was by no means a prestigious appointment for one of Wesley's abilities, and the salary of £63 per annum was not princely, but it was no doubt a welcome addition to the family finances.

For the 1820s, as for earlier periods, Wesley's output of letters is a good indicator of his general health and level of activity. The trickle of letters of 1822 and 1823 increased dramatically in 1824, and by 1825 had reached a spate comparable to the high points of the period immediately before his illness. As before, most were to Novello, and although the subject matter is varied, two topics occur again and again: Wesley's reactions to reviews of his Service, and the protracted negotiations with the University of Cambridge over the granting of permission to publish music from the Fitzwilliam collection. As Wesley's discussion of these matters occurs in a fragmentary fashion over a number of letters and a considerable period of time, it may be helpful to summarize the sequence of events here.

Wesley's Service was first reviewed in the January 1825 number of the *Harmonicon*, following its publication the previous October. The anonymous reviewer was on the whole respectful and deferential, acknowledging Wesley's learning and distinction as a church musician, and commending the overall high quality of the music. At the same time he permitted himself some criticisms of infelicities in the harmony, commenting on one progression that it included 'the chord of the 7th and 2nd in an extremely bare, crude, state, and to our ears very cacophonous, though Dr. Blow might have enjoyed it much'. Wesley was outraged by these criticisms and immediately planned a reply, to be published if possible in a future number of the *Harmonicon*, or, failing that, elsewhere. Perhaps surprisingly, he had no idea who had written the review, although he quickly discovered that William Ayrton, Thomas Attwood, and William Crotch were considered to be the most likely authors.[44] By 27 January he had finished his reply and was ready to submit it to the *Harmonicon*, although with no great confidence that it would be printed. When in time the *Harmonicon* declined to

---

[44] SW to Novello, 27 Jan. [1825].

publish it, Wesley discussed with Novello the possibility of placing his reply in a number of other journals, including the *Examiner*, the *Gentleman's Magazine*, and, eventually, the *News of Literature and Fashion*. None of these negotiations came to anything.

Even as Wesley was still attempting to secure a reply to the *Harmonicon* review, the Service received its second review, in *QMMR*.[45] The new review was three times the length of the earlier one, and far more detailed in its comments. It was also, after its initial courtesies, decidedly more hostile, containing many detailed criticisms of specific points of harmony in a manner very close to that practised by Wesley himself in his *European Magazine* reviews. Although Wesley seems not to have known who had written it, his enquiries soon revealed that it was generally thought to be by Horsley, and Wesley accordingly wrote an 'inquisitorial Line' to him on the subject in late April.[46] Unsurprisingly, Horsley denied any involvement, but Wesley by now had few doubts that he was the author, and Horsley's reply did nothing to persuade him otherwise.[47] In fact, given Horsley's position as Bacon's leading associate on *QMMR* and its chief reviewer of church music, his authorship of the review cannot ever have been seriously in doubt to anyone familiar with the journal's organization.

Even after the appearance of the *QMMR* review, Wesley still tried to find a publication which would be prepared to print his reply to the original *Harmonicon* review. Despite the growing staleness of the topic, he was eventually successful, and his article eventually appeared in the *Literary Chronicle* in June. It was presumably its polemical tone and panache rather than the precise details of its content that secured its appearance, for the *Literary Chronicle* did not generally include articles on music, and five months on from the original review the matter must have lost any topical interest it ever have had for the journal's readership.

Meanwhile, Wesley was seeking to gain separate redress for the injustices done to his reputation in *QMMR*. As with the *Harmonicon*, his first attempt was to try to have a reply published in *QMMR* itself, and to this end he wrote to Bacon in August 1825.[48] Following Bacon's refusal to comply with his demands, Wesley turned to Novello's friend (and future son-in-law) Charles Cowden Clarke, claiming that Clarke was 'the only man to give my paper to the world' and hoping that Clarke's contacts in the world of periodical journalism would help to find it a home.[49] Clarke seems to have used his good offices on Wesley's behalf with Henry Southern, the editor of the *London Magazine*, and for a while Wesley was confident that his article would appear in the November number. All, however,

---

[45] *QMMR* 7 (1825), 95–101.   [46] SW to Novello, [27 Apr. 1825].   [47] Ibid.
[48] Not preserved, but see SW to Novello, [12 Aug. 1825] and [19 Aug. 1825].
[49] SW to Novello, 31 Aug. 1825.

came to nothing,[50] and it was at this point, almost eleven months after the appearance of the *Harmonicon* review, that Wesley tacitly admitted defeat and allowed the matter to drop.

Wesley was also involved in smaller and less complicated publishing ventures throughout the 1820s, much as he had been before his illness. Most of these publications, which included a number of organ voluntaries, involved the outright sale of the copyright to the publisher, thus avoiding the capital investment and risk involved with self-publication.

Perhaps emboldened by his experiences with the Service—or, at any rate, aware of the healthy profits that could be made from such ventures—Wesley was soon considering plans for future publications. A further possible opportunity almost immediately presented itself. In December 1824 the University of Cambridge had set up a syndicate to consider how parts of the important collection of music manuscripts bequeathed to the University in 1816 by Lord Fitzwilliam might be published. Following an invitation from the University to catalogue and examine the collection and recommend possible schemes of publication, Novello visited Cambridge in late December 1824 and early January 1825 and duly submitted his catalogue and report.[51] The Senate considered these on 18 March and immediately granted a Grace which gave Novello permission to publish any parts of the collection that he should think fit, but at his own expense and at his own risk. Novello made at least one further visit to Cambridge in the course of the year to work on the publication, and the first part of his five-volume selection, consisting entirely of sacred choral music by Italian composers of the sixteenth to eighteenth centuries, was published as *The Fitzwilliam Music* in December 1825 or January 1826.[52]

It must have quickly become apparent to Novello as he examined and catalogued the Fitzwilliam collection that it contained material for more than one selection, and it was not long before Wesley was enquiring whether the University would consider granting him permission to publish his own. Wesley's initial enquiries appear to have been made in late April or early May 1825 through the Hebrew scholar Daniel Guilford Wait, at this time in Cambridge cataloguing the oriental manuscripts in the University Library; how he and Wesley had come to know each other is not known. The matter needed careful handling in the light of Novello's continuing work on his own selection, and Wesley was anxious to avoid any appearance of underhandedness. As can be seen in the letters of 1825, he consulted with Novello at every stage of the negotiations and kept him fully in

---

[50] SW to Novello, 23 Nov. 1825.

[51] Novello to Thomas Le Blanc, 27 Jan. 1825 (Cambridge, CUR 30.1). The catalogue is not preserved.

[52] Preface dated Dec. 1825. Subsequent parts appeared at intervals in 1826 and early 1827.

touch with their progress. An early stage in the negotiations is marked by a letter of 11 May from Wait, in which Wait reported that he had discussed the matter with Thomas Le Blanc, the Vice Chancellor. Le Blanc had given his opinion that the Senate would be likely to grant Wesley the necessary permission, but not until Novello had completed his own selection;[53] he had also advised that Novello should provide Wesley with a letter of recommendation, making it clear that he was aware of and had no objections to Wesley's plans.

This was the background to Wesley's visit to Cambridge in June 1825. Although he had not as yet been granted formal permission to publish by the University, Wesley was confident that it would eventually be forthcoming, and was evidently already making a start on his transcriptions. It was important that his work did not duplicate that of Novello, and accordingly he wrote to Novello to ask for a list of all the pieces that Novello was intending to publish, and a confirmation that he was not proposing to include any music by Paradies or Scarlatti.[54] As is clear from a letter to Samuel Sebastian, Wesley was similarly occupied on a second visit to Cambridge in late July and early August, and was already anticipating a healthy financial return from his activities.[55]

Although Wesley's preoccupation with the critical reception of the Service and his negotiations with the Cambridge authorities over the publication of the Fitzwilliam music loom largest in the letters of 1825, these were far from being the only matters concerning him. In terms of organ playing, he was as busy as he had ever been. In February and March he was involved once more as organist in the Covent Garden oratorio concerts, and he now also had a regular Sunday commitment at Camden Chapel. At the same time, as we know from a letter to Mary Ann Russell, he was making piano reductions for music published by the Royal Harmonic Institution, and thus too busy to have any part in performing the same task for her proposed edition of her late husband's oratorio *Job*.[56] Less than a month later, however, presumably after her failure to find others prepared to carry it out, he agreed to take on the arrangement single-handed.[57] Meanwhile, Wesley's financial and personal problems continued. On 7 May Charlotte had him arrested and briefly imprisoned in a debtors' prison, doubtless for nonpayment of maintenance. It is a mark of Wesley's recovered health that he seems to have viewed this evidently distressing experience as no more than a temporary nuisance.[58]

The Fitzwilliam project was not the only large-scale publishing venture that Wesley was pursuing during the summer of 1825: he was also thinking about

[53] Wait to SW, 11 May 1825 (BL, Add. MS 11729, fo. 258): see SW to Novello, 15 May [1825], n. 2.
[54] SW to Novello, 21 June 1825. [55] SW to Samuel Sebastian Wesley, 1 Aug. 1825.
[56] SW to Mary Ann Russell, 16 Apr. 1825. [57] SW to Novello, 10 May [1825]. [58] Ibid.

the possibility of publishing the still unperformed *Confitebor*. He had already remarked to Novello that it was the 'least imperfect' of his compositions, and the one which might have a chance of success if published;[59] he was now proposing to take the matter further.

The lack of performance of the *Confitebor* was a major obstacle to its successful publication, as few people would be prepared to subscribe for a piece they had not heard, no matter how glowingly it was presented in the prospectus. Accordingly, during his Cambridge visit Wesley arranged a performance with Novello in a four-hands arrangement on the organ of Trinity College chapel before an invited audience. This was an experiment, designed to allow him to gauge public response without financial risk, and to help him make up his mind about the likely success of a subsequent full-scale performance in London, to be followed in due course by publication if there were sufficient demand. As Wesley was able to report to Samuel Sebastian, the response was encouraging, and several subscriptions appeared to be assured from among the audience.[60] On his return to London, he arranged to have a paragraph written by himself inserted in the *Examiner* describing the Cambridge performance and its enthusiastic reception, and announcing that the *Confitebor* would be performed in the following year's Lenten oratorio season.

Wesley's more immediate thoughts, however, were on his projected publication of selections from the Fitzwilliam collection. During the summer, as we have seen, he had been sufficiently confident that permission to publish would be forthcoming to make a start on his own transcriptions. In September, however, he received news from Wait of complications which threatened the granting of permission. In the absence of the relevant letter from Wait and other crucial parts of the correspondence it is impossible to establish the full details of what was evidently a complex situation. It appears, however, that some members of the Senate were concerned about the apparent clash of interest between Wesley and Novello, and were unhappy about granting Wesley permission to publish a selection which might appear to be in competition with Novello's own. Faced with the threat of such a major upset to his plans and the prospect of the transcriptions he had already made going to waste, Wesley contemplated writing directly to the Vice Chancellor to put his case. It is not known if he did in fact do so, and if he did, what effect his letter had. In a later attempt to resolve the situation, Wesley wrote to ask Novello if he would be prepared to state that his intention was to publish music only from Italian composers, and that he was happy for others to publish selections from composers of other schools. Such a declaration would make it clear that Wesley's publication was not in any way in competition with

---

[59] SW to Novello, 9 Oct. 1821.   [60] SW to Samuel Sebastian, 1 Aug. 1825.

l

Novello's. Whether this suggestion came from Wesley himself or from the University authorities, Novello acceded to it, and included a statement along the lines suggested by Wesley in his Preface to the *Fitzwilliam Music*.

Novello's declaration appears to have had the desired effect, and Wesley was duly granted his Grace by the Senate on 1 March 1826. But the agreement may not have represented what either Novello or Wesley had originally intended. Novello may originally have had long-term plans to publish music by English or German composers which he was now not able to carry out; in particular, he may have hoped to explore some of the riches of the collection's Handel manuscripts. For his part, Wesley may have originally intended to publish music by Italian composers. In the summer of 1825, as we have seen, he had music by Paradies and Scarlatti in his sights, and he may have spent time in the summer transcribing music by these and other Italian composers. If this was the case, all this work was now rendered useless.

It is apparent that the Fitzwilliam affair was the cause of a serious quarrel between Wesley and Novello. It certainly marked the end of the main sequence of Wesley's letters to Novello, which ceased abruptly at the end of 1825.[61] One looks in vain for further information of this rift in Wesley's other letters of the period, which shed no further light on the matter and contain no mention of Novello. Evidence of the quarrel is, however, contained in the June 1826 number of the *Harmonicon*, in the form of a letter from a correspondent signing himself 'Jubal'.[62] By this time, Wesley had issued proposals for his own *Fitzwilliam Music*, and 'Jubal' felt it incumbent on him to draw some aspects of the situation to the attention of the readers of the *Harmonicon*. He found it strange that Wesley should be intending to publish a selection of music from the Fitzwilliam collection so soon after Novello's own, and insinuated that this behaviour was a betrayal of Novello's friendship and generosity in introducing him to the Fitzwilliam collection in the first place. The identity of 'Jubal' is not known. As can be seen from Wesley's letters to Novello of 1825, his grasp of the situation was imperfect, and his accusations of bad faith were ill-founded and malicious. Nonetheless, his letter clearly indicates the existence of a disagreement between the two men in early 1826, and gives some of the reasons for it.

No copies of Wesley's proposals have survived, but it is clear that the intended first volume was to have been an edition of antiphons from Byrd's *Gradualia*, which Wesley had transcribed from an eighteenth-century score in the Fitzwilliam collection. The Byrd publication never appeared, for reasons explained by Wesley over four years later in a long and revealing letter to Street:

---

[61] Novello and SW in time resolved their differences and resumed contact: see SW to Novello, 10 June 1830, which appears to date from the time of their reconciliation.   [62] *Harmonicon* 4 (1826), 113.

despite a lively interest in the publication, a healthy subscription list of over two hundred names which would have guaranteed a profit on the venture, and the completion of nine of the plates, Wesley was unable to find sufficient money to pay his engraver for the remainder of the work.[63]

Wesley did not go into details in his letter to Street about the nature and cause of his financial problems. It is apparent from family letters, however, that in the summer of 1826 he was being particularly hard pressed by his creditors, while at the same time himself being owed money from a number of quarters. His first priority was to cast around for short-term loans to avert the threat of immediate imprisonment for debt. Under these circumstances, finding additional money to pay his engraver would have been out of the question, and the project was accordingly shelved.

Part of the reason for Wesley's financial problems may have been the expenses incurred in his *Confitebor* performance, which had finally taken place on 4 May, the projected performance as part of the Covent Garden Lenten oratorio season having failed to materialize. Despite the involvement of singers of the calibre of Mary Ann Paton and Henry Phillips, at presumably heavy expense, the *Confitebor* appears to have aroused little interest or subsequent comment in the press beyond a brief paragraph in the *Harmonicon*, and Wesley seems for the moment to have abandoned his plans to publish it.

In September 1826, with financial crises held for the moment at bay, Wesley was able to make a further visit to Cambridge to continue his examination of the Fitzwilliam manuscripts. He had now turned his attention to the extensive collection of Handel autographs, and was confident that everything he was transcribing was unpublished and would 'therefore prove an entire novelty'.[64] His most profitable find on this visit was completely unexpected: a single sheet of Handel's autograph containing three tunes by Handel to well-known hymns by his father. This link between Charles Wesley and Handel was hitherto unknown, and Wesley correctly saw that the hymns would be of great interest, especially to Methodists. Moreover, as the hymns were already familiar to Methodist congregations, the newly discovered Handel tunes could be put to immediate use in Methodist chapels. Publication of the hymns could be done cheaply, quickly, and easily, and there was every likelihood of large sales.

Wesley was sufficiently confident of the commercial possibilities of the hymns to have the hymns engraved even before sounding out his few contacts in the Methodist community. His first approach on 31 October was to Eliza Tooth, a close friend of his brother and sister and a member of a prominent Methodist

---

[63] SW to Street, 25 May 1830.
[64] SW to Sarah Suter, [13 Sept. 1826] (BL, Add. MS 35012, fo. 61).

family whose links with the Wesleys went back to his parents' generation. A week later, at Tooth's suggestion, he wrote to the Revd Thomas Jackson, the Methodist Connexional Editor and editor of the *Wesleyan Methodist Magazine*. This letter, although apparently not intended by Wesley for publication, conveniently set out the background to the hymns and was included by Jackson in the December number of the *Magazine*. It must have done much to publicize Wesley's edition, which had appeared by the end of November.

This was in fact the first of two editions by Wesley of the hymns. Containing only a title page and three pages of music, it would have cost little to produce, and the high price of 1s. 6d. would have ensured good profits. But the format, consisting only of the melody and bass and the words of the first verse of each hymn, was not as useful as it might have been. At the suggestion of friends Wesley prepared a second edition, this time containing a four-part harmonization of the tunes and the words of all the verses. This appeared in March 1827.

One consequence of Wesley's contact with Jackson over the Handel hymns was an opening up of relations with the Methodist congregation at the City Road Chapel. For most of his adult life, Wesley had had no dealings with Methodism, and his links with Roman Catholicism and his irregular private life had for long made him an embarrassment in Methodist circles. With the publication of the Handel hymns, however, came friendly overtures from the Methodists, leading to an invitation to attend the annual Breakfast for the Children of the Methodist Preachers at the City Road Chapel on 3 May.[65] It was probably through the same process that Wesley was invited to open the organ at Brunswick Chapel, Leeds, in September 1828.[66]

The success of the Handel hymns and the establishment of friendly relations with Jackson also prompted Wesley to turn his attention to other ways in which he could make the most of his name and family background. One obvious option was to compose tunes of his own for the hymns currently in use in Methodist congregations. As with the Handel Hymns, Wesley moved quickly: less than a month after a first exploratory letter to Jackson in late April 1828, he was writing again to announce that he had composed the tunes and to offer the copyright to the Book Room Committee.[67] As the Book Room minutes reveal, this proposal was turned down, and Wesley proceeded to publish at his own expense: a more risky, but a potentially more profitable course of action. The *Original Hymn Tunes, adapted to every Metre in the collection by the Rev. John Wesley* were published by late

---

[65] SW to Sarah Wesley, 29 Apr. 1827 (Fitzwilliam); SW to Charles Wesley jun., [4 May 1827] (Fitzwilliam).

[66] SW to Sarah Suter, [10 Sept. 1828] and 13 Sept. [1828] (BL, Add. MS 35012, fos. 50 and 73).

[67] SW to Jackson, 21 Apr. 1828 and 17 May 1828.

August,[68] and received a glowing review in the *Wesleyan Methodist Magazine* in October, where the writer hoped that the publication would obtain a large share of the public attention, 'a distinction to which it is justly entitled'.[69]

After the cessation of the letters to Novello at the end of 1825, it becomes more difficult to chart Wesley's activities in any detail. As we have seen, some letters of 1825 and 1826 document his publishing ventures; others concern arrangements for various lecture courses in early 1828. At the same time, family letters reveal a partial rapprochement with his brother and sister, occasioned perhaps by Sarah's declining health. After Sarah's death in September 1828, however, information from family letters largely disappears too. As his surviving letters show, Charles Wesley junior had little taste or aptitude for correspondence. Wesley's contacts with him had never been extensive, and after Sarah's death appear to have been almost non-existent.

The final events in Wesley's public career took him back to his native Bristol. In September and October 1829 he gave a number of organ recitals there, including three at St Mary Redcliffe, the parish church, when he was joined by Samuel Sebastian, now aged 19 and at the beginning of his own career. Wesley's powers were evidently still undiminished. The local organist Edward Hodges ecstatically described his playing as

the most wonderful I ever heard, more even than I had before been capable of conceiving; the flow of melody, the stream of harmony, was so complete, so unbroken, so easy, and yet so highly wrought and so superbly scientific, that I was altogether knocked off my stilts . . . I walked home afterwards, but my head was full of naught but Samuel Wesley and his seraphic genius . . . He is the Prince of Musicians and Emperor of organists.[70]

In the following January Wesley returned to give a course of lectures at the Bristol Institution. Both this and the earlier visit were probably arranged through Wait, who in addition to his Cambridge connections was curate of Blagdon, near Bristol. The second also involved Hodges, at whose house Wesley stayed during part of his visit.

In the summer of 1830 Wesley was incapacitated by another severe attack of depression. A subscription was arranged by a group of his musical and masonic friends led by John Capel, MP, Linley, and Novello,[71] which no doubt helped to alleviate the inevitable financial hardship for Wesley and his family. By now, Samuel Sebastian was approaching 20 and had probably left home, but there were still five children to be supported: Rosalind, aged around 16, Eliza (11),

---

[68] See SW to Upcott, 20 Aug. [1828].   [69] Quoted in Lightwood, 211.

[70] Quoted in Lightwood, 215.

[71] Copy at BL, Add. MS 56411, fo. 34, printed in Lightwood, 219–20.

Matthias Erasmus (9), John (5), and Thomasine (2); in addition, Sarah Suter was pregnant with another child.[72]

Although depression seems to have affected Wesley for some of the time during his final years, he appears to have continued to teach, to compose, and publish. Among his compositions were a large number of hymn tunes for Novello's mammoth four-volume collection *The Psalmist* (1835–42): of its 400 tunes, no fewer than fifty-five are by Wesley, most of them specially written for the volume, and there are a further twenty-five arrangements by him of Gregorian melodies and tunes by other composers.

There are even a few signs of him attempting to return to public performance. In March 1834 he wrote to suggest himself as a director of one of the concerts of the Handel Commemoration, to be held at Westminster Abbey in the June of that year. Whether or not this was a proposal that he expected to be taken seriously, he was not appointed. His last public appearance was on 7 August 1834 at a Sacred Harmonic Society concert, when he accompanied a performance of his anthem 'All go unto one Place', written for the memorial service for Charles, who had died earlier in the year.

Little is known of how Wesley and his family managed financially during his final years: with extreme difficulty, on the evidence of the letters to Thomas Jackson which are among the last in this volume. Wesley had renewed his contacts with Jackson following the death of his brother, when the annuity granted to his mother by the Methodist Book Room in respect of the copyright of his father's hymns descended to him as the last surviving member of the family. As the Secretary of the Book Room, it was Jackson's responsibility to make the small weekly payments.

By 1836, perhaps at the suggestion or with the encouragement of Sarah Suter and their children, Wesley wrote his manuscript Reminiscences, in which he recorded on scraps of paper all he could remember of his life in music. Although containing much of interest, the Reminiscences are anodyne in style and completely lack the outspokenness and sardonic wit of the letters, while the laboriousness of the handwriting and the frequent repetitions show all too clearly how much Wesley's physical and mental powers had declined. The same manuscript also contains passages of historical writing, clearly written with publication in mind and relating to Wesley's last piece of published work, an article entitled 'A Sketch of the State of Music in England, from the year 1778 up to the Present Time', which appeared in the first number of the *Musical World* on 18 March 1836. In fact the article only covered the period up to around 1800, and was intended to be continued in a subsequent number. The second instalment never

---

[72] Robert Glenn Wesley, born 21 Nov. 1830.

appeared, however, possibly because of factual errors and other inadequacies in the first, or because of Wesley's inability to provide a satisfactory sequel.[73]

Wesley appears to have had a remarkable recovery of health shortly before his death. In July 1837 he wrote out from memory the full score of his *Ode to St Cecilia* of 1794, which he believed that he had lost, and in October wrote a further eight tunes for *The Psalmist*, which were his last compositions.

On 12 September he was taken by Eliza and Rosalind to Mendelssohn's recital at Christ Church, Newgate Street. Afterwards, as Mendelssohn recorded:

Old Wesley, trembling and bent, shook hands with me and at my request sat down at the organ bench to play, a thing he had not done for many years. The frail old man improvised with great artistry and splendid facility, so that I could not but admire. His daughter [Eliza] was so moved by the sight of it all that she fainted and could not stop crying and sobbing. She believed she would certainly never hear him play like that again; and alas, shortly after my return to Germany I learned of his death.[74]

This was the last time that Wesley left his house. He died on 11 October after a short illness and was buried on 17 October at Marylebone parish church, where his father, mother, and brother were also interred. The service was attended by many of the leading figures in the London church music and organ world, including a large body of singers who sang the music of the burial service to settings by Purcell and Croft, concluding with 'His body is buried in peace, but his name liveth for evermore' the words adapted from Handel's *Funeral Anthem for Queen Caroline*. Directing the proceedings was James Turle, organist of Westminster Abbey and a former chorister at the Portuguese Embassy Chapel under Wesley and Novello.[75]

---

[73] Olleson, 1111.

[74] Diary entry for 11–12 Sept. 1837: see Peter Ward Jones (trans. and ed.), *The Mendelssohns on Honeymoon: The 1837 Diary of Felix and Cécile Mendelssohn Bartholdy together with Letters to their Families* (Oxford, 1997), 103.   [75] *The Times*, 18 Oct. 1837.

Textual Introduction

The Manuscripts and their Provenance

The survival of any corpus of letters depends on a combination of factors, amongst which are the fame of the writer, the presence of family members or others with strong preserving habits, and pure chance. In the case of Wesley's letters, an unusually large number of which has survived, we have principally to thank four individuals—Wesley's elder sister Sarah, his daughter Eliza, his friend and colleague Vincent Novello, and Eliza Tooth, an active Methodist and a close friend of Sarah and Charles Wesley junior.[1] Also involved were the family connection with Methodism, the highly distinctive character of Wesley's handwriting, and his attractive literary style, all of which made his letters eminently collectable.

Sarah was responsible for the amassing and preservation of an extremely large collection of letters of her father, mother, and other members of the family, including many family letters to and from Wesley himself. After her death the collection first passed to her brother Charles; on his death, much of it was sold to the Book Room attached to the Methodist chapel in City Road, London, where it was over the years augmented by similar materials from other members of the family and from others. It is now in the Methodist Archives and Research Centre at the John Rylands University Library of Manchester, where the collections moved in 1977.

Eliza, Wesley's second daughter by Sarah Suter, did much after her father's death to keep his memory alive and promote his music. Like her aunt, but for rather different reasons, she was assiduous in preserving family letters and other memorabilia, and was responsible for the collection of letters to her mother and to other members of Wesley's second family which she bequeathed to the British Library along with large quantities of autograph manuscripts of her father's music.

As Wesley's closest professional colleague and friend over a long period, Vincent Novello was the recipient of a large number of letters from Wesley between 1811

---

[1] For biographical details, see SW to Tooth, 31 Oct. 1826.

and 1825. Many, particularly the most ephemeral, must have been discarded, but in 1840 he donated over 170 letters to the British Museum, describing them in his covering letter as being all he could at that time find, and continuing:

As these curious specimens of Mr Samuel Wesley's singular talent for the more familiar and quaintly humorous style of letter-writing may probably be considered very acceptable and interesting to some future musical historian, Mr Novello is desirous of confiding them to the safe custody of the Museum to preserve them in such manner as to render them easily accessible to those of his brother Professors who may wish to consult them for the purpose of ascertaining what were the exact opinions of so superior a musical Genius, upon various subjects connected with English Composers, Performers and Musicians in general, during the latter part of Mr S. Wesley's career. The only stipulation which Novello makes in presenting these original Mss to the British Museum is that nothing shall be *published* from them of a *personal* nature, during the *Lifetime* of any of the individuals relative to whom Mr S. Wesley has expressed any opinion in the course of the correspondence.[2]

The role of Eliza Tooth as collector is clear in outline, although difficult to document in detail. As a friend of Wesley's brother and sister, she was much involved in the sorting of the family papers after the death of Charles, and many of them bear datings and annotations in her distinctively spiky hand. In the process, she acquired a substantial number of family papers herself. This collection, known to and consulted by Wesley's early biographers,[3] was in time dispersed; items from it, identifiable from their inclusion in early biographical accounts and in some cases from the datings and annotations that they bear, can now be found in a variety of repositories, including Emory University and the Fitzwilliam Museum, Cambridge.

Among smaller collections of letters are those to Benjamin Jacob, largely on the subject of the introduction of J. S. Bach's music into England (the *Bach Letters*). Published in an edition by Eliza in 1875, they have long been familiar to students of the English Bach Movement; the originals are now at the RCM, having previously been owned by William Sterndale Bennett, Novello's, and the Sacred Harmonic Society.

Very few letters to Wesley have survived, and it is clear that he made no attempt to preserve his routine professional and social correspondence. On the other hand, a considerable number of letters to him from his father, mother, brother, and sister are contained in the collection amassed by Sarah, and it is apparent that Wesley not only preserved this correspondence but later returned it to Sarah at her request.

---

[2] Copy at BL, Add. MS 11729, fo. 1.   [3] See Jackson, vol. i, p. iv; Stevenson, *Memorials*, 473.

PUBLICATION HISTORY

Only a small proportion of Wesley's surviving letters has been published. A few were included in the first extended biographical account of Wesley, which appeared anonymously in four numbers of *Wesley Banner and Revival Record* for 1851.[4] Many of these subsequently appeared in the chapter on Wesley in Stevenson's *Memorials of the Wesley Family* (1876), its exceptionally close similarity with the *Wesley Banner* account suggesting that Stevenson had written this too. In April 1875 the letters to Jacob had appeared at Sterndale Bennett's auction sale, and had been acquired by Novello's. Little more than a month later, some individual letters began to appear in *Concordia*, a weekly Novello publication. Meanwhile Eliza had been preparing her edition, based on transcripts she had made some time earlier, probably when the letters were owned by Sterndale Bennett. It was published later in 1875, probably at some time in the summer.[5]

The publication of the *Bach Letters* was part of a renewal of interest in Wesley and his music, much of it instigated and promoted by Eliza; other later advocates were F. G. Edwards (1853-1909), editor of the *Musical Times*, and W. Barclay Squire (1855-1927), librarian of the printed music collections of the British Museum. A further landmark came in 1894 with James Higgs's paper to the Musical Association.[6] Written with the assistance of Eliza, who was present at the meeting, it drew its material not only from previously published accounts and the letters to Novello, but also from Wesley's manuscript lectures and from his letters and Reminiscences, which Eliza had made available to him.

Another important stage in Wesley biography, if not in the actual publication of the letters, was marked by the appearance in 1899 of Edwards's article on Wesley in *DNB*. By this time, Eliza had died and had bequeathed all the manuscripts in her possession relating to her father to the British Museum. Included were the family letters to her mother and other members of Wesley's second family. For wholly understandable reasons of tact and propriety, Sarah Suter's role as Wesley's partner over a period of twenty-seven years and the mother of seven children who had survived to adulthood had been omitted from all previous biographical accounts, apart from a very oblique mention in *Memorials of the Wesley Family*.[7] By now, however, Wesley's letters to Sarah were publicly available, and Edwards

---

[4] 'Memoir of Samuel Wesley, the Musician', *WBRR* 3 (1851), 321-8, 361-70, 401-11, 441-53.

[5] Eliza's Preface is dated 11 May 1875.

[6] J. Higgs, 'Samuel Wesley: His Life, Times and Influence on Music', *Proceedings of the Musical Association* 20 (1893-4), 125-47.

[7] Stevenson makes no mention of Sarah Suter in the text of his chapter on SW, but she is included in the fold-out genealogy of the Wesley family at the front of the volume.

felt able to include the bare statement that Wesley had formed a relationship with her 'around 1809', and that he had several children by her, including Samuel Sebastian and Eliza.

Subsequent interest in Wesley's letters has been small. In 1917 Squire published a small selection of Wesley's letters to Novello and others in a *Musical Quarterly* article,[8] but no attempt was made to publish a larger selection of these or any other of Wesley's letters, lying readily available and in great abundance in the British Museum and at the Methodist archives in City Road. James T. Lightwood drew upon some hitherto unpublished letters, including some to Sarah Suter, in his *Samuel Wesley, Musician* (1937), thus providing for the first time in print a full acknowledgement of her position in Wesley's life. Since then, there has been a facsimile reprint of Eliza's edition of the *Bach Letters*, and a few further letters have appeared in studies of Wesley's music, in Methodist periodicals, and elsewhere.[9]

EDITORIAL METHOD

The Basis of Selection

Within its terms of reference, this edition aims at completeness: that is, it includes all known letters by Wesley to correspondents outside his immediate family, from 1799 to 1837, irrespective of their subject matter. A letter is understood as a communication written to a private recipient or recipients; accordingly, letters written for publication, whether as letters to the press and journals, or as epistles dedicatory, are not included.

Wherever possible, the original text or a photocopy or microfilm has been consulted. Printed sources have been used where the present location of the original is not known or where it was not available for consultation. Letters known only from their descriptions in sale catalogues are also included, with a summary of their contents.

A few letters to family members are also included where the subject matter is entirely or predominantly music. One such is Wesley's long letter to his brother Charles of 15 January 1807, in which Wesley addresses Charles as much as a fellow professional as a brother. To omit this letter (the longest in this volume)

---

[8] W. B. Squire, 'Some Novello Correspondence', *MQ* 3 (1917), 206–42.

[9] Two letters to Alfred Pettet and one to Charles Wesley jun., now at Drew but at the time in private ownership, appeared in *Methodist History* 11 (1972), 54–5. For Wesley's letters to Burney, see Samuel J. Rogal, 'For the Love of Bach: The Charles Burney–Samuel Wesley Correspondence', *Bach* 23 (1992), 31–7; for his letters to McGeough, see Elvin, 97–9 and pl. xii.

on the grounds that it is to a family member would be perverse. Other letters not included in this edition but containing important references to music are cited, and, where appropriate, selectively quoted, in the annotations.

The concentration on the non-family letters, and thus broadly speaking on Wesley's professional and social life, has inevitably led to the exclusion of most of Wesley's most intimate and revealing correspondence. The letters in this volume offer comparatively few insights into his relationships and dealings with his mother, brother, and sister, his wife Charlotte, with Sarah Suter, and his children by both Charlotte and Sarah. This side of Wesley's life will, I hope, be revealed in time by a second, complementary volume of family letters, forming the second part of his complete correspondence. In the meantime, I have attempted in the Biographical Introduction to set the letters of the present volume in the total context of Wesley's life.

Samuel Wesley: A Source Book

In its latter stages the edition has proceeded side by side with the preparation of *Samuel Wesley: A Source Book* (Ashgate, forthcoming, 2001), which I have compiled with Michael Kassler of Northbridge, NSW, Australia. The *Source Book* aims to document Wesley's life by means of a chronology, a calendar of correspondence, and a musical worklist; it also includes sections on Wesley's family, his places of residence, the history and provenance of the manuscripts, a bibliography, an iconography, and a discography.

By far the longest section of the *Source Book* is the calendar. This comprises detailed summaries of all Wesley's correspondence, and also of letters written to him and relating to him written in his lifetime: over 1,100 items. The preparation of these summaries has involved us in the scrutiny of each relevant document, followed by subsequent discussion, often prolonged and on occasion heated, in order to reach agreement on datings and interpretations.

Work on the *Source Book* has thus provided the infrastructure for this edition. It goes without saying that our collaborative work is reflected in countless ways in the edition in the dating of letters, the identification of recipients, and in the detail of the annotations. I here pay tribute to Michael Kassler, and thank him most warmly for his many contributions, for his tenacity and determination, and for the warmth of his friendship.

The *Source Book* goes to press at the same time as this edition, and for this reason it has not been possible to provide cross-references to it here. From the description of its contents above, however, readers will be aware that they will find there summaries and manuscript locations of all Wesley's letters not included here.

Editorial Conventions

Each letter is headed by the name of the recipient, the place of writing, and the date. Names of recipients, dates, and places supplied by the editor are enclosed in square brackets. This is followed by a description of the letter: ALS (autograph letter, signed); AL (autograph letter, not signed); ANS (autograph note, signed); AN (autograph note, not signed); L (letter, neither autograph nor signed); followed by its number of pages and its location. Where appropriate, a note gives the condition of the letter: whether incomplete, damaged, or mounted. There then follows a transcription of the address panel (if any), together with any post-marks, docketings, and endorsements. Where the identity of the recipient is not specifically stated in the letter or its address portion, a note gives the reason for the identification. For undated or incompletely dated letters, a note gives the dating reason, as derived from the addresses of Wesley and/or the recipient, any postmarks or watermarks, and the content of the letter. Letters which have proved impossible to date with confidence have been placed in an Appendix in approximately chronological order, with the range of their possible dates noted, and numbered consecutively.

Wesley's spelling, use of capital letters, and punctuation have been retained. No attempt has been made to reproduce either the varying lengths of long dash with which Wesley frequently ends a sentence, or the placing on the page of his complimentary closes, and these have been standardized. Wesley's double quota-tion marks have been replaced by single quotation marks. Editorially supplied material is placed in square brackets. Editorial conjectures of passages missing in the text are placed within angle brackets (< >); missing passages are indicated by an ellipsis within angle brackets.

Dates of birth and death in annotations sometimes take the form '1758/9'. This indicates a date derived from sources which give the age at (e.g.) matriculation or death.

The Annotation

Because of the circumstances in which they were written—in many cases to col-leagues with whom Wesley was in regular, often daily, contact, and fulfilling the function of a present-day telephone conversation or e-mail message—the letters are often highly allusive and compressed, and on occasion pose considerable problems of interpretation. My aim has been to explain as many of Wesley's refer-ences and allusions as possible, in sufficient detail to allow comprehensibility. I have cited sources for information given in the annotations. For books, it should be noted that the place of publication is London unless otherwise stated. For

Wesley's letters, full location details are given only for letters not contained in this volume. Inevitably, some annotations are extensive. In Wesley's letter to Novello of 27 January 1825, for instance, his throwaway comment that the theatre manager Robert Elliston 'would have extorted £2000 from poor Kean if he had not risked his, & 5000 more Peoples' Lives on Monday Night' required a particularly long note to explain the background, and why it was feared that Edmund Kean's appearance at Drury Lane on this occasion might have caused a riot.

In the case of individuals, two factors have guided the amount of annotation: their importance in the letters, and the extent of their fame. Those who have only walk-on parts in the letters receive less annotation than those who play an important role, and those well known from other contexts receive less attention than the more obscure. More generally, the principle that I have adopted is a familiar one: in the words of Alvaro Ribeiro, 'to explain obscurities adequately and to hold a decent silence with regard to the obvious'.[10] But—and as Ribeiro goes on to say— it is often difficult to know what the obvious is: this is dependent on the presumed interests and knowledge of the reader, so that a level of annotation appropriate for one reader may be too little for a second, and too much for a third. As Samuel Johnson put it in the Preface to his edition of Shakespeare:

It is impossible for an expositor not to write too little for some, and too much for others. He can only judge what is necessary by his own experience; and how long soever he may deliberate, will at last explain many lines which the learned will think impossible to be mistaken, and omit many for which the ignorant will want his help. These are censures merely relative, and must be quietly endured.[11]

---

[10] Burney, *Letters I*, p. xxxiv.   [11] Quoted in Burney, *Letters I*, p. xxxiv.

The Letters

1797–1837

To Joseph Payne Street[1]   [Ridge],[2] 21 February 1797

ALS, 1 p. (BL, Add. MS 56228)
Addressed To | Mʳ Street | N. 17 | Mark Lane | Tuesday. paid.
Pmk 21 FE 97
Endorsed by Street: S. Wesley | Febry 21 1797

Dear Sir

I have received a Letter from our Friend Vincent,[3] stating that he is at present sustaining an Attack of the Rheumatism, nevertheless he hopes to be able to join our Party on Friday,[4] if there be possibility of venturing so far as Paddington.— I hear that young Danby[5] will be among us, so that we shall not be left quite desolate, in case of a Disappointment in the first Instance.

The principal Motive of this Letter is to acquaint you that I am desirous of singing over a Miserere which I have composed several Years ago, for two Voices,[6] and I think you and I could manage it very well.—Perhaps you would like to con it a little previously; therefore if you will favour me with a Line, by Thursday next, informing me where it may be left for your Perusal *on Friday Morning*, you may depend upon my conveying it to you for that purpose.

---

[1] Joseph Payne Street (*c.*1770–*post* 1848), an amateur musician friend of SW. On the evidence of remarks in this and later letters, he was a businessman in the City: probably the J. Street who appears as a stockbroker in London directories of this time. He and his family were prominent members of the Madrigal Society: he was elected to membership on 13 Oct. 1795 and was until 1848 the society's librarian; his son Joseph Edward and grandson Oscar were also secretary in their turn. He was a member of the social circle of R. J. S. Stevens, and is frequently mentioned in Stevens's *Recollections* (Argent). This letter is the first of eleven to him from SW, donated to the BL by Mrs Hilda L. Whittaker, his great-granddaughter, in 1971. Some manuscripts in his hand containing music by SW and others are also at the BL (*Grove*[1], under 'Madrigal Society'; Argent).

[2] SW had been living at Ridge, a small village near St Albans, Hertfordshire, some thirteen miles from London, since Oct. 1792.

[3] Either J. Vincent or Zelophead Wyeth Vincent, both of whom are listed as male altos in Doane.

[4] 24 Feb. 1797; the party was to be held at the home of Mrs Deane at the Manor House, Paddington (see next letter).

[5] Probably Eustace Danby (1781–1824), nephew of the Roman Catholic composer and organist John Danby (*c.*1757–1798).

[6] 'Miserere mei, Deus', for alto, bass, and organ. SW's autograph, dated 7 Apr. 1792, is at BL, Add. MS 14342; an undated copy in the hand of Street is at BL, Egerton MS 2571.

We expect to assemble in the Evening by 7 at the latest, when I hope we shall all meet, free from Coughs, Hoarseness, or any other vocal Obstacles to Perfection.

> Believe me
> truly yours
> S Wesley

Tuesday 21. Feby 1797

To George Polgreen Bridgetower[1]   Chesterfield Street,[2]
23 February 1797

AL, third person, 1 p. (BL, Add. MS 56411, fo. 7)
Addressed To | Mr Bridgetower | N. 20 | Eaton Street | Pimlico

Mr Samuel Wesley presents his best Compliments to Mr Bridgetower, requesting the Favour of his Company, if he should not be better engaged, to a little musical Party among a few Friends To-morrow Evening, which will meet at Mrs Deane's,[3] near the Church, Paddington. Mr Wesley is conscious of presuming upon Mr Bridgetower's Indulgence, in consequence of so slight an Acquaintance, and can only say in excuse of the Liberty he takes, that Mr B. may freely command S.W's Services upon a similar Occasion.

If Mr Bridgetower should oblige S. W. and his Friend so far as to acquiesce in their Request, and will have the Goodness to return a Line by the Bearer, informing at what hour M^r B could suffer his violin to be brought, a proper & careful Porter shall attend for that purpose.

---

[1] The violinist George Polgreen Bridgetower (?1779–1860), the son of an African father and a European mother, was first heard in England in 1790, when he came under the patronage of the Prince of Wales (later the Prince Regent and George IV), who arranged for him to be taught the violin by Barthélemon and Jarnovick, and composition by Attwood. He is best remembered as the violinist for whom Beethoven wrote his Sonata in A, Op. 47 (later dedicated to the French violinist Rodolphe Kreutzer and known as the 'Kreutzer Sonata'), which he and Beethoven first performed in Vienna in May 1803 (F. G. Edwards, 'George P. Bridgetower and the Kreutzer Sonata', *MT* 49 (1908), 302–8; Betty Matthews, 'George Polgreen Bridgetower', *MR* 29 (1968), 22–6).

[2] During his time at Ridge, and later when he was living at Finchley and Highgate, SW used the family home at 1 Chesterfield Street (now Wesley Street), Marylebone, as a convenient London base, staying overnight there as necessary.

[3] A family friend. SW's love affair with her daughter Anne, a particular friend of his sister Sarah, around 1799 gave rise to much family ill will and an estrangement with Sarah.

Chesterfield Street Marybone. Thursday Feb. 23^d 1797

Mrs Deane | Manor House | Paddington | near the Church[4]

To Thomas Merryweather[1] [Chesterfield Street],[2]
6 March 1798

ALS, 1 p. (Foundling Hospital, A/FH/A06/001/051/21/1)
Addressed To | Mr Merryweather | Secretary's Office | Foundling Hospital
Pmk 6 MR 98 Penny Post Pd 1d Marybone

Sir

It being my Intention to offer myself as a Candidate for the Vacancy of Organist at the Foundling Chapel,[3] I shall esteem myself much obliged by a Line of Information concerning the Nature of the Duty & c directed either to N. 1 Great Chesterfield Street, Marybone, or to Church End, Finchley;[4]

remaining, with Respect
Sir
your very obed^t humble Servant
    S Wesley

P.S. Had I not been under the Necessity of going out of Town early To-morrow, I would have waited upon you in Person.

Tuesday. March 6. 1798

[4] The Manor House, north of the churchyard, was purchased by the parish in 1810 and demolished in 1824 to allow the enlargement of the churchyard (J. S. Cockburn, H. P. F. King, and K. G. T. McDonnell (eds.), *A History of the County of Middlesex*, 9 vols. (Oxford, 1911–95), ix. 187).

[1] Thomas Merryweather (d. 1799), Secretary to the Foundling Hospital from 1790 to his death (Nichols and Wray, 412).

[2] It is evident from the postmark, which bears the Marylebone stamp, that SW wrote this letter from his mother's house.

[3] The Foundling Hospital (now the Thomas Coram Foundation for Children) was founded in 1742 by Thomas Coram, a retired sea-captain, for the benefit of children abandoned by their parents. Its chapel had a long and distinguished musical history. In its early days Handel was a generous benefactor: he gave annual performances of his music in the chapel from 1749, donated an organ in 1750, and left the autograph score of *Messiah* to the hospital in his will (Nichols and Wray; Ruth K. McClure, *Coram's Children: The London Foundling Hospital in the Eighteenth Century* (New Haven, 1981)). The vacancy had been created by the resignation of the blind organist Tom Grenville.

[4] SW had moved from Ridge to Church End, Finchley, in or around July 1797. He lived there until some time after May 1798, when he moved to Hornsey Lane, near Highgate.

To [William Seward]¹

[Finchley or Hornsey Lane,
16 June 1798]

ALS, 3 pp. (Sotheby's, 6 July 1977, Lot 389; present whereabouts unknown)

SW is sorry if he disappointed Seward by not sending him the advertisement he published to thank those who voted for him in the recent Foundling Hospital election. He 'doubts not that their kind & liberal Exertions would have been attended with good Success had the Election been fairly conducted'.² He fears no vote of censure that the Governors might choose to put on the advertisement. He regrets that he expended so much time and trouble in applying for the post, and trusts that Seward will think him 'no Coxcomb for thinking that my Rejection has been rather the Charity's Loss than mine'. He guesses that the Hospital's Governor to whom Seward alluded is 'a certain great Commissioner of Customs'.³ He encloses the text of a ballad satirising Bates,⁴ which 'has lately appeared printed by Wornum, at the Music Shop in Wigmore Street, Cavendish Square'. He looks forward to visiting Seward at Richmond, and will send him the Overture in Ptolemy⁵ soon.

¹ The name of the addressee of this letter is given as 'Sewart' in Sotheby's sale catalogue, but it is evident from its contents that it is in fact to William Seward (1747–99). In his Reminiscences, SW commented: 'many years ago, when I was a candidate for the place of organist to the Foundling Chapel, William Seward, Esq., the biographer and intimate friend of the great Dr Johnson, interested himself very warmly in my favour, invited me to his apartments at Richmond, and there gave me the kindest reception possible. He also introduced me there to all his numerous and brilliant acquaintances, to the late Duke of Queensbury, and a large circle of the most eminent and celebrated characters then in being.' A poem entitled 'Lines addressed to Mr Samuel Wesley on his visiting Mr S—at Richmond, a second time, in the Summer of 1798', unsigned but evidently by Seward, appeared in the 'Helicon Bag' section of the *Whitehall Evening Post*, 21–2 Aug. 1798; it was reprinted the following month in the 'Drossiana' section of *EM* together with a short paragraph describing SW's prowess as an extempore player (*EM* 34 (1798), 161–2).

² After a long appointment process, during which the eight candidates were required to play the services on successive Sundays, there was an election and John Immyns was appointed on 9 May. SW suspected, probably correctly, that Immyns's appointment came about largely through the patronage of Joah Bates, one of the Governors (Nichols and Wray; Foundling Hospital Minute Books (Foundling Hospital).

³ i.e. Joah Bates (1740–99). After education at Eton and King's College, Cambridge, where he became a fellow and tutor, Bates had a successful career as a civil servant, culminating in the post mentioned here. He was also extensively involved in music, where he was 'a fierce champion of Baroque music and particularly of Handel's work in the face of strong competition in the form of the *galant* music of J. C. Bach's generation' (*Grove*⁶). He was one of the founders of the Concert of Ancient Music in 1776 and its director until succeeded in 1793 by Greatorex. In 1784 he was one of the organizers of the Handel Commemoration festival and directed its concerts from the harpsichord (*Grove*⁶).

⁴ '*The Organ laid open, or, The True Stop Discovered, a New Song*', beginning 'Come all my brave boys who want organists' places'. The text, which comments scurrilously on the part in the affair played by 'Jo Bates', is given in Lightwood; the autograph is at the Fitzwilliam Museum, Cambridge. SW and Immyns were friends, and SW did not bear Immyns any personal ill will for having been appointed instead of him. According to Lightwood, Immyns composed an equally scurrilous rejoinder to SW's ballad, which Lightwood declines to quote as being 'not suitable for reproduction'; he does not give its location, and it has not been traced (Lightwood, 92–3).   ⁵ By Handel.

To [Christian Ignatius Latrobe]¹   [Hornsey Lane, *post*
                                              22 February 1799]²

ALS, 3 pp. (Rylands)

Dear Sir

I have known enough of Printers to be but little surprised at the Delay of your Work:³ but a Pleasure delayed is not therefore lost: nay, rather often enhanced thereby, when we obtain it.

Good comes out of Evil. Though 40 Names are fewer by some *Fifties* than I wish added to your List of Subscribers, yet perhaps, had not this typographic Disappointment happened, your Desire of ending a troublesome Job might have induced you to bring the Publication forward with so much less of Advantage to yourself.⁴

---

¹ The identity of the addressee of this letter as the prominent Moravian minister, composer, and editor of music Christian Ignatius Latrobe (1758–1836) is established by the reference to Burney's 'handsome note' (see n. 8). After initial education and a subsequent period of teaching at the Moravian college at Niesky, Upper Lusatia, Latrobe returned to England in 1784 and was ordained. He was appointed secretary to the Society for the Furtherance of the Gospel in 1787, and in 1795 succeeded James Hutton as Secretary to the Unity of the Brethren in England. Although never a professional musician and apparently self-taught, his significance as a composer and editor was considerable. In addition to composing and editing several volumes of church music for Moravian use, he was the editor of the six-volume *Selection of Sacred Music* (1806–20), which introduced church music by such composers as Graun, Hasse, Pergolesi, Haydn, and Mozart for the first time to British audiences, and anticipated the publications of Vincent Novello (*DNB*; *Grove*⁶). Latrobe's letter to SW to which this is a reply has not been traced.

² The date is established by the reference to the trial of Joseph Bazley (see n. 5). SW had moved from Finchley to Hornsey Lane, near Highgate, some time after the end of May and before the end of August 1798. A letter of 23 May of this year to his sister Sarah (Rylands, DDWF 15/7) discusses arrangements for a music party at Finchley later in the month, while the Hornsey Lane address appears on the autograph of his part-song 'Roses, their sharp spines being gone', dated 29 Aug. 1798, at BL, Add. MS 14343.

³ Latrobe's *Dies Irae & c, an Ancient Hymn on the Last Judgment, translated . . . by . . . the Earl of Roscommon . . . Adapted for the Piano Forte, and Four Voices* (R. Birchall, for the author, 1799).

⁴ Latrobe had earlier requested SW to solicit subscriptions for the *Dies Irae*. He had also approached Burney, with whom he was in frequent correspondence, with the same request (see Burney to Latrobe, *c*.5 Feb. 1799 (Osborn); Latrobe to Burney, 7 Feb. 1799 (Osborn)). Latrobe had complained to Burney: 'to have to do with engravers & printers is fit to make a parson swear—such lying & deceiving & promise-breaking wretches cannot surely exist in any other profession. My work is not yet printed off, tho' promised before the 1ˢᵗ of January. When I went to Cambridge about 3 weeks ago I was promised by the Printer, that all the Copies bespoke should be sent home before my return, but on my return, not a stroke had been done.' Latrobe's letter to SW had presumably contained a similar complaint. There were in the end 185 subscribers, who between them purchased 212 copies. One of the two copies bought by Burney is now at the RCM.

I am grieved more than Words can declare in being obliged to beg you to withdraw one Name from those I gave You; a Name which, till very lately, I thought I had every Cause to respect, & whose Person & various good Qualities I still do & always shall love. Poor Mr Bazley[5] is the unfortunate Man whom you have seen announced in the Papers as having committed a Fraud upon Hamet & Esdaile in Lombard Street, in whose House he had been for upwards of 16 Years. If there be a Man for whose Integrity & strict Principle of Justice I would have answered sooner than for most others, it was Bazley.—The little we *can* know of our Neighbour's Perseverance in Right, should make us tremble at the Danger of Error to which we are hourly exposed.—Thomas à Kempis[6] well says, 'He rideth easily enough, whom the Grace of God carrieth.' Without the kind, restraining Hand of an almighty Parent, what poor Wretches we all are!

I thank you for Dr Burney's[7] very handsome Note,[8] which shall be safely returned, & *most* willingly if you could make up your Mind to come hither & fetch it. I know your Pressure of Engagements, and therefore do not add my Pressure of Invitation; but nevertheless, as I sometimes *make* Time to see a Friend, I am not without Hopes that you will resolve upon some such Feat before long.—I am a very accessible *Personage* on most Wednesdays & Saturdays, & on the first of these that may happen to suit you, I shall be very ready to grant you an Audience, even without a Fee to the Porter.

I was introduced to Dr Jowett[9] many Years ago, at Cambridge, where I remained a Week;[10] but probably he may have forgotten me long ere now. I remember also

[5] *The Times*, 23 Feb. 1799, reported the trial at the Old Bailey of Joseph Bazley, who was found guilty of stealing a £100 banknote from his employers, the bankers Sir James Esdaile, Esdaile, Hammett, Esdaile, & Hammett.

[6] Thomas à Kempis (1380–1471), Augustinian monk and author of Christian mystical works. The quotation is from *De imitatione Christi*, his best-known work and a favourite devotional text of SW's father and uncle.

[7] Dr Charles Burney (1726–1814), historian of music, author of *The Present State of Music in France and Italy*, 2 vols. (1771 and 1773), *The Present State of Music in Germany, the Netherlands, and the United Provinces*, 2 vols. (1773 and 1775), and *A General History of Music*, 4 vols. (1776–89) (*DNB*; *Grove*[6]; Lonsdale).

[8] Burney to Latrobe, *c*.5 Feb. 1799 (Osborn), in which he had written: 'I had the pleasure to meet Sam Westley, of whom I had lost sight almost since his childhood, if ever he was a *child*. In Music now, he is somewhat more than *Man*. He pleased me very much, both by his performance & compositions; & I think him a credit to our country, wch certainly does not abound in native composers of the first class.' This encounter was the beginning of a friendship between the two men which was to last until Burney's death.

[9] Dr Joseph Jowett (1752–1813), matric. Trinity College, Cambridge (1769), migrated to Trinity Hall (1773), LL B (1775), LL D (1780), Fellow of Trinity Hall (1773–95), Regius Professor of Civil Law (1782–1813). He was a keen amateur musician and a long-standing friend of Latrobe, who frequently visited him in Cambridge (Venn; *DNB*).

[10] SW had first visited Cambridge in or around 1788 (see SW to Burney, 7 July [1808]).

Mr Jowett (his Brother, I think),[11] a very musical Man, with whom I sang Glees & Catches: they were both great Lovers of Harmony.[12]

I have no present Appetite for a Doctorship,[13] & altho' Cambridge, as an antient Seat of Learning & true Worth must be ever an interesting & beloved place of one, whose Ancestors were distinguished by both,[14] yet I doubt whether the Station of musical Professor would not prove nearly as laborious as that at which I am now posted.—How much Fatigue may be *lightened by a Weight of Honour*, may perhaps be a Question worthy to be proposed at the next public Disputation. I have an old fashioned Prejudice about Honour, namely that I cannot help thinking it consists not in what a Man is *called*, but what he *is*.

I have another odd Whim about Professorships, & *Successorships*. I hate the thought of waiting for dead Men's Shoes.—I had almost as soon *die in my own*.—

Believe me,

yours, dear Sir, with great Esteem & Regard,

S Wesley

P.S. When you next pass Birchall's Shop,[15] pray tell him to hand you over a copy of my newly published Sonatinas;[16] they are very trifles, sed Datorem non Datum considerabis.[17]

---

[11] Henry Jowett (b. 1756/7), matric. Magdalene College, Cambridge (1774), BA (1778), MA (1781) (Venn).

[12] For a description of the musical talents of the Jowett family and Latrobe's friendship with them, see Latrobe's *Letters to my Children* (1851), 5–12. Latrobe describes how he first met Henry Jowett and a third brother, John, in 1790 at the house of the Revd James Edward Gambier, Rector of Langley, Kent. He later visited John Jowett on a number of occasions at his house in Newington Butts and there met the remainder of the family, including Joseph. Following one of these visits Joseph Jowett invited the whole party to stay with him for several days at Trinity Hall, where, as Latrobe records, they 'spent several days in the enjoyment of every thing that could afford rational and intellectual delight, under the direction of the most cheerful, sweet-tempered, hospitable man existing; whose chief pleasure it was, to please his friends, and to do good to all mankind'. Latrobe's friendship with Joseph Jowett continued until Jowett's death. See also the Preface to vol. 3 of Latrobe's *Selection of Sacred Music*, published shortly after the death of Joseph Jowett, which contains a further tribute to the family.

[13] Latrobe had presumably enquired if SW was interested in taking a Cambridge music degree and in pursuing an academic career. His enquiry may have been prompted by the illness of the Professor of Music, John Randall (1717–99), who died shortly afterwards and was succeeded by SW's friend Charles Hague.

[14] i.e. by both Cambridge and Oxford: SW's grandfather Samuel Wesley (1662–1735) matric. Exeter College, Oxford (1684), BA (1688), MA Corpus Christi College, Cambridge (1694); SW's uncle Samuel Wesley (1691–1739) entered Christ Church, Oxford (1711), BA (1715), MA (1718); SW's uncle John Wesley (1703–91) matric. Christ Church (1720), BA (1724), MA (1727), Fellow of Lincoln College, Oxford (1725); SW's father Charles Wesley (1707–88) matric. Christ Church, Oxford (1726), BA (1730), MA (1733) (Foster).

[15] The premises of Robert Birchall (c.1760–1819), music seller, instrument dealer, and publisher, at 133 New Bond Street. Birchall also published many of SW's later works (Humphries and Smith).

[16] SW's *Twelve Sonatinas for the Piano-Forte or Harpsichord*, Op. 4, published by Birchall for SW.

[17] 'You will consider the giver, not the gift'.

To [Joseph Payne Street]   [Hornsey Lane], 1 May 1799

ALS, 1 p. (BL, Add. MS 56228)

Dear Sir

As I happened to pick up the most correct perfect Edition of Mr Chillingworth's Works which is extant, I hope you will favour me by accepting it.[1]—A Folio I own is a frightful Thing, but yet such a Folio as Mr Locke[2] declares to be capable of making Men reason *always* justly, is not to be met with from every Pen.[3]—

The other ugly old Book (which I believe is in some Places scarcely legible) you can leave out for the Carrier when he shall call next on you in Mark Lane.— It belongs to my Brother,[4] who whenever he is disposed to study Chillingworth (an Event rather to be *wished* than *expected*) I shall advise to read him from a better Print.

Yours sincerely

S Wesley

Wednesday May 1. 1799

---

[1] William Chillingworth (1602–44), Scholar and Fellow of Trinity College, Oxford, and one of the literary circle that gathered round Lucius Cary Falkland (1610–43) at Great Tew, Oxfordshire. He converted to Roman Catholicism in 1630, but rejected it in 1634; the controversial *The Religion of the Protestants a safe Way to Salvation* (1637) was his most celebrated work. There were many editions of his works; the one referred to here was possibly the one including his life by Birch, published in 1742 (*DNB*; *OCEL*).   [2] John Locke (1632–1704), English philosopher.

[3] Locke had commented in *Some Thoughts concerning Reading and Study for a Gentleman*, first published in *A Collection of Several Pieces of Mr. John Locke, Never before Printed, or Not Extant in his Works* (1720): 'Besides perspicuity, there must be also right reasoning; without which perspicuity serves but to expose the speaker. And for the attaining of this I should propose the constant reading of Chillingworth, who by his example will teach both perspicuity and the way of right reasoning, better than any book that I know; and therefore will deserve to be read on that account over and over again; not to say anything of his argument.'

[4] Charles Wesley jun. (1757-1834), SW's elder brother. Like SW, he had been a musical child prodigy, and his precocity as a performer and composer had astounded all who heard him. He did not fulfil his youthful promise, however, and his later musical career was one of relative obscurity. He was a noted harpsichordist and organist, held various church appointments, and was organist to the Prince of Wales (later the Prince Regent and George IV), but took no major part in London's professional musical life. His few later compositions are conservative in style. As SW's subsequent comment suggests, he was not a great reader.

10

To Joseph Payne Street

ALS, 2 pp. (BL, Add. MS 56228)
Addressed To | Mr Street | N. 17 | Mark Lane | Paid
Pmk 7 OC 99

Dear Sir

I have appointed to be at Mr Ball's[2] Piano Forte Manufactory on Friday next[3] exactly at one o'Clock, p.m. whither I shall bring the Confitebor[4] in order to run it over upon an Organ which he has there at present.—I know that the Middle of the Day is somewhat inconvenient for you to leave the City, but as this is the first Opportunity which has yet presented upon the Subject, & as you seemed desirous that Mr Carter[5] should get an early Sight of the Work, I resolved to lose no Time in fixing a Place for that Purpose.—In case you may be able to favour us with your Company, I will thank you to signify to Mr C. that the above Arrangement is made, when if he can manage to join us, & *will part with his Coals for a Song* on that Day, it will be a great Acquisition, especially if he can prevail on that *Busby-wigged Parson*[6] whom we saw at his House, to come & assist in the Bass.

As the Psalm is one of those sung in the Roman Vespers on a Sunday, perhaps his filial Piety towards holy Mother Church may influence him to sacrifice Lucre to Devotion.—

All this, of course, *entre nous*.

Yours sincerely

S Wesley

Sunday 6 Oct. 1799

---

[1] In June or July 1799 SW had moved from Hornsey Lane to an address variously described as '5th Mile Stone' or '5 Mile Stone', Highgate. He lived there until late spring 1803.

[2] James Ball (*fl. c.*1780–1832), piano maker, music seller, publisher, and printer. His premises were at 27 Duke Street, Grosvenor Square, Mayfair (Humphries and Smith; Brown and Stratton).

[3] 11 Oct.

[4] SW's recently completed large-scale setting for soloists, choir, and orchestra of the Vesper psalm 'Confitebor tibi, Domine' (Ps. 111), the autograph of which (BL, Add. MS 35002) is dated 14 Aug. 1799.

[5] Probably the Irish composer and alto singer Thomas Carter (ii) (1769–1800). As SW's remark later in this letter implies, he was also a coal merchant (*Grove*[6] under Carter, Thomas (ii); Doane; *Holden's Triennial Directory*, 1799). The autograph of SW's setting of 'Near Thame's Fam'd Banks' (BL, Add. MS 56411) is annotated as having been 'composed expressly for the performance of Mr Carter and for the use of the ad Libitum Society, Decr 22 1799.' He was also a friend of R. J. S. Stevens (Argent, *passim*).

[6] Not certainly identified, but possibly one of the two brothers mentioned in the following letter: in his letter to his brother of 15 Jan. 1807, SW refers to a 'Parson Barry of Dulwich' who was the host of a music party that SW attended there. A busby was a large bushy wig (*OED*). The party also included Wright (see next letter).

Please to direct to Marybone.

Turn over if you please.

I will thank you to look into the Answer to the 4th Chapter in Chillingworth.[7]—Sect. 4. as I think there must be a false Print in mine Edition—it occurs, about 16 Lines from the Beginning; thus:

'The Necessity of believing them being inforced upon us by a Necessity of believing this essential & Fundamental Article of Faith, *That all Divine Revelations are true*, which to disbelieve, or not to *disbelieve*, is, for any Christians, not only impious, but impossible'—

Surely the latter *disbelieve*, ought to be printed, *believe*; the other plainly enforcing a Contradiction.[8]—I trust that your Edition has no such Blunder.—I took up the Book the other Night, by Way of *Relaxation* after hard Work, & imagined the Difficulty to arise out of my Stupidity, & so kept stirring my Brains about till they boiled over like Cream in a Saucepan & I knew not whether 2 & 2 made 4, or a 100, but was yet certain, that Chillingworth must be right, (& true enough:) but little suspecting the *Fallibility* of the Compositor; otherwise I might have spared myself much absurd Labour.

To Joseph Payne Street   Highgate, 18 October 1799

ALS, 2 pp. (BL, Add. MS 56228)
Addressed To | Mr Street | N. 17 | Mark Lane | London
Pmk OC 19 99

Dear Sir

We were much disappointed in not having the Pleasure of your Company on Wednesday last,[1] although your Words to me were not sufficiently strong to make me rely on seeing you with as much Confidence as I could have wished. —Our little Party was a remarkably pleasant one, consisting only of Mr Barry & his Brother[2] (besides M^{rs} W,[3] & myself) who were extremely agreeable, &

---

[7] i.e. *The Religion of the Protestants a safe Way to Salvation* (1637).

[8] SW was correct in his conjecture. The corrupt edition has not been identified.

---

[1] 16 Oct.

[2] Neither brother has been certainly identified; one was a pupil of SW who lived at 37 Queen's Square, Bloomsbury; the other may have been 'Mr Parson Barry of Dulwich', mentioned in SW to Charles Wesley jun., 15 Jan. 1807.   [3] SW's wife Charlotte Louisa, née Martin (1761–1845).

seemed mightily to enjoy themselves.—I happened to draw two or three Corks, *the Liquid belonging to which* met most extraordinary Approbation, & really we had nothing to regret but your Absence: the Gents talked of returning to Town about 9 in the Evening (altho' I offered them Lodging here which they said an early matutinal Engagement w^d prevent their accepting) but behold! it became past the Hour of *One* on the Thursday Morning before they resolved to depart, & it was absolutely *then*, with Reluctance.—I discover that Barry (my Scholar) is a Man of much quick Sentiment, & Kindness of Heart: a thorough Lover, (& no indifferent Judge) of real good Musick: a perfect Gentleman in his Manners, & an exceedingly good Companion.—All these Qualifications engage me not to slight his Society, & I am therefore determined to shew him any obliging Attentions in my Power.

He much wishes to make up a little Glee Concert among ourselves, to which he means to invite Mr Wright^4 (who stood on the left of the Book at Ball's on Friday 11th)^5 whom he represents to me as a very profound Connoisseur in Harmony, & a good Sight's Man, of which *Propositions* we shall be able to form a good Opinion, when we come to the Test of singing *with him*: Barry is anxious to form a Party for some Evening when I can remain in Town, & desired me to say that he will be particularly glad of your Company with that of any other Friend to re-inforce our musical Corps.

If you can prevail on Mr Drummer^6 to accompany us, I know nothing to prevent my going to Barry's *on Friday next**^7 in the Evening:—I shall thank you for an immediate Answer to this, directed hither, which I shall obtain by Sunday, or at latest, on Monday Morning.—His Address is 37 Queen Square Bloomsbury.

> I am
> Dear Sir
> sincerely yours
> S Wesley

5 Mile Stone. | Highgate. | Friday 18 Octr. 1799

* I had written *Tuesday* at first, but upon Recollection, I cannot go on that Evening.

---

^4 Not certainly identified; possibly the banker of this name mentioned in SW to Jacob, [24 Nov. 1809].   ^5 The play-through of the *Confitebor* mentioned in the previous letter.

^6 Either John or William Drummer, two brothers who were amateur musician friends of SW and Street, and who feature in SW's letters over a period of thirty years. John Drummer was probably the coal merchant of this name listed in *Holden's Triennial Directory* for 1799.   ^7 25 Oct.

To [Charles Burney]¹   Highgate, 5 November [?1799]²

ALS, 1 p. (Osborn, MSS 3, Box 16, Folder 1192)

5ᵗʰ Mile Stone
Highgate
Nov. 5.

My dear Sir

I address you *at a Venture* of speedy Success; but whenever you shall have returned from the Country,³ I trust that you will favour me by your wonted Permission to attend you on some Morning which may happen to suit your Convenience, for allowing me the Instruction & Comfort of your Conversation, & the Happiness of re-assuring you that I remain always most respectfully & most cordially.

Your obliged & devoted Friend
S Wesley

To Joseph Payne Street   Highgate, 9 November [1799]¹

ALS, 2 pp. (BL, Add. MS 56228)
Addressed To | Mʳ Street. | N. 17 | Mark Lane
Pmk NO 9 99

5 Mile Stone
Highgate
Saturday Nov 9.
'Combe for ever'!²

¹ Although lacking an address portion, the deferential tone, content, and present location of this letter in the Osborn Collection leave little doubt that it is to Burney.

² The year of this letter is conjectural, but can only be between 1799 and 1802, as SW moved to this address in Highgate in the summer of 1799 and left in late spring 1803. SW's reference to Burney's forthcoming return from the country (see n. 3) may be to the visit mentioned in SW to Burney, 28 Nov. 1799, and suggests that 1799 is the most probable year.   ³ No details are known of this visit.

¹ The year is given by 9 Nov. falling on a Saturday and SW's Highgate address.

² The significance of this remark is not known.

Dear Sir

M^r and Mrs Kingston[3] hope for the Pleasure of your Company together with Mr Drummer's on Tuesday next,[4] as near *6* in the Evening as you can manage to meet us.—I mean to bring with me a new Chorus for a double Choir,[5] (as well as the Confitebor) of which I played you the Subject when we met last at Mr Drummer's, & which I was unable to finish in fair Copy till within this last Week.

Your Intelligence concerning the Discovery in the News-Paper surprized me a little. I called to Day upon Ball, (from whom I had obtained Mr Howard's Invitation) to have an explanation of the Business.—I know not whether I remarked to you that he wished me to oblige him *on Sunday next*, (the 10th Inst) which was impossible, on Account of an Engagement at Watford;[6] I therefore informed him that if he could defer the Charity Sermon until the 17th, I would then attend him: but it appears that the Preacher (whoever he is) is determined upon *mounting Timber* on the very *next immediate, consecutive, & proximate* Lord's Day, so that Mr Howard must thumb the *Musicks* himself, all alone, & no-body with him.[7]

By the Way, it would have been full as civil in the aforesaid Organist to have signified to me the State of the Circumstances, *before* he had inserted his Advertisement, stating the *Reasons* that made it necessary to decline mine Assistance.—However we know that **Politesse** is no **sine quâ non** in the Composition of a Crotchet-Monger, & by this same Omission of his, I am fully liberated from the Necessity of attending him in future.

I have been reading, in the Monthly Magazine for Decr 1799. a very pretty Account of Mozart, written by Mr Busby:[8] If you have not seen it (the contrary to which is most likely) I would advise you to give it a Perusal: You will find the Style very respectable, & the whole, interesting.

If the Biographer write *ex Corde*, he is superior to that mean Jealousy which pervades, (I may say 9 tenths) of us professional Vagabonds.

---

[3] Clearly amateur musician friends of SW and his wife. Kingston can probably be identified as William B. Kingston, who appears intermittently in the letters. For his involvement with the care of SW during his serious illness of 1817–18, see SW to Glenn, 23 Mar. 1818, n. 3.   [4] 12 Nov.

[5] Probably the setting of 'Deus majestatis intonuit' for double SATB chorus with orchestra and organ, the two autographs of which (LC, ML 96.W49; BL, Add. MS 71107) are dated 26 Sept. 1799.

[6] Not traced.

[7] It appears from this paragraph that SW had been approached by Howard with an invitation to play at a charity sermon at Howard's church. SW was unable to play on 10 Sept., the date originally suggested, as he already had an engagement in Watford on that day; accordingly, he had suggested the following Sunday, 17 Sept. The 'discovery in the newspaper' (untraced) was presumably an advertisement announcing SW's appearance on the date originally suggested. Howard was probably Thomas Howard, who in 1802 entered into an agreement to erect an organ and supply organists at St Mary le Bow (Dawe, 111–12).

[8] The 'Life of Mozart' by Thomas Busby had in fact appeared in *MM* for Dec. 1798, pp. 445–50. For Busby, see SW to Busby, 21 Mar. 1800, n. 1.

I hope Carter will come on Tuesday: I said nothing of him to the Kingstons, that it may be an agreeable Surprize.

Y^rs dear Sir
Very sincerely
S Wesley

To Charles Burney   Highgate, 28 November 1799

ALS, 4 pp. (Rylands, DDWF 15/8; address portion Osborn, MSS 3, Box 5, Folder 319).[1]
Addressed To | Dr Burney | Chelsea College.
Endorsed by Burney: Mr S. Wesley 1799
Docketed by Mme d'Arblay: ※[2]
Pmk 28 NO 99

Dear Sir,

Your last obliging Letter[3] having exprest the Probability of your Return from the Country about this Time, it is with much Satisfaction that I embrace the first Opportunity of assuring you of the Happiness I promise myself in attending you at Chelsea[4] one morning, e'er long.

My present professional Engagements occupy so much time (& consequently deprive me of those Hours which I long to devote to Study) that I am convinced of the Truth of the Proverb—'We may buy Gold too dear.' Nevertheless I have lately stolen an Hour in every Day, for the worthy Purpose of perusing attentively your invaluable History of Musick,[5] which, although I had seen several Years ago, yet I was then unable to study with much Profit, being 'A man of but little Latin, & less Greek':[6] however, having since acquired a slight Smattering of these two Languages, I am better qualified for applying to your excellent Work with Advantage, sincerely regretting the Neglect of *earlier Cultivation*, which would

---

[1] The address portion contains Burney's draft reply to this letter.

[2] This editorial symbol was added by Burney's daughter Frances (Mme d'Arblay) as part of her classification of her father's letters into various categories of interest for inclusion in her projected edition of the correspondence. For her activities as editor, see Joyce Hemlow with Curtis D. Cecil and Althea Douglas (eds.), *The Journals and Letters of Fanny Burney (Madame d'Arblay)* (Oxford, 1972), vol. i, pp. xxxvi–xliv; Burney, *Letters I*, p. xxxii. This symbol is interpreted by Hemlow and Ribeiro as denoting a letter 'in a second category of interest'.   [3] Not preserved.

[4] Burney had been appointed organist at Chelsea College in Dec. 1783. The post included rent-free accommodation at the college (Lonsdale, 295–6).

[5] *A General History of Music, from the Earliest Ages to the Present Period*, 4 vols. (1776–89).

[6] Cf. Ben Jonson, *To the Memory of Shakespeare* (1623): 'Thou hadst small Latin, and less Greek'.

have discovered to me hidden Treasures:—I might then have *borrowed* some of them, but now I can only *peep* at them.

I presume on your indulgent Permission to ask you Questions for Information upon musical Matters, especially since you have so kindly assisted me by your Advice in several Points concerning the Composition you condescended to revise.[7]

In the course of reading To-day, I studied the Table of the Greek Modes in your 1st Vol p. 48.[8]

In p. 49[9] you observe:—'There is a passage in Aristides Quintilianus,[10] which seems to point out something like *Connection* & *Relation* between the five original Modes, & those above & below them.' He says, after having enumerated the 15 Modes, 'By this means, each Mode has βαρύτητα και μεσοτητα και ὀξυτητα—its *Bottom*, its *Middle*, & its *Top*, or its grave, mean, & acute.'

'This seems to imply that the three Modes of DORIAN, Hypodorian, & Hyperdorian, for instance, were considered, in a Manner, as one: & as if the two Modes belonging to each of the five middle ones, *a fourth above*, & *a fourth below*, were regarded as necessary Adjuncts, without which they were not complete.'

A Doubt has occurred to me, respecting the Manner in which the **Ionian**, Hypoiastian, & Hyperiastian Modes have been printed in the 48th Page, which is the Subject of my present Enquiry.

Hypoiastian

Ionian

Hyperiastian

---

[7] SW's *Confitebor*. In his Reminiscences, SW wrote: 'In the Year 1799 I composed a Confitebor . . . I sent the score of this work to the late worthy Doctor Charles Burney for his Revision and opinion. He examined each movement critically with the nicest observations on them. He concluded by saying "Upon the whole it is an admirable composition in florid Counterpoint and in the best style of Church Music".'   [8] Mercer, i. 53.

[9] Ibid. i. 54.

[10] Aristides Quintilianus (*fl. c.*200 AD), a Greek music theorist, author of an influential treatise *Peri mousikes* ('On music'), described in *Grove*[6] as 'heavily derivative, with nothing by way of content or organization that can safely be attributed to Aristides himself'. It was included in Marcus Meibomius's *Antiquae musicae auctores septem, Graece et Latine*, 2 vols. (Amsterdam, 1652), a copy of which Burney owned (Burney, *History*, i. 11, 441; Mercer, i. 30–1, 349; Burney, *Letters I*, 55 n. 8).

It appeared to me that the lower Note ought to have been placed upon the 5th Line, with *five* Flats, thus: for otherwise, as there is a Diesis between G$\sharp$ & A$\flat$, the Ratio seems to be broken between the ὑπο & the ὑπερ Modes. And *this Conjecture of mine you support* in page 50, where in enumerating the 5 principal Modes with their *Collaterals*, you observe that they answer to the following Keys in present Use,

Hypo:	Dorian	Hyperdo:
A	D	G
B$\flat$	E$\flat$	A$\flat$
Hypoiast:	Iastian	Hyperiastian

I searched the Table of Errata, in which I found no Notice taken of any Mistake relative to the *Sharps*; I therefore wish to know whether you might have marked 5$\sharp\sharp$ instead of 5$\flat\flat$ for a better Reason than I am able to give; & yet this seems to be not perfectly consistent with the Account given of the *Relation* of the Modes to each other in the 50th Page, where the A$\flat$ is marked instead of G$\sharp$, & according to my *present* Notion of the Truth.

Whether I am *more nice than wise* upon this Occasion, or not, (the former of which is very probable) an illuminating Line from your Pen, at any future Moment of your Leisure, will be received as one more among the many kind Attentions already shewn to

Dear Sir
Your most obliged Friend
& devoted Servant
    S Wesley

5 Mile Stone | Highgate | Thursday. Nov. 28. 1799

To Charles Burney   [Highgate, 30 Nov 1799][1]

ALS, 2 pp. (UCSB)
Endorsed by Burney: 30 Novr 1799

My Dear Sir
    This is really pestering you with my Letters, but it were more than 'a venial sin' to delay for a moment offering you my Thanks for your signal Attention &

---

[1] The date is given by Burney's endorsement.

satisfactory Answer to the Question I took the Liberty of proposing,[2] which I hope & trust you will believe was asked *merely* for the Sake of Information without the least Affectation of Sagacity.

You have clearly shewn that I understood *myself* only by Halves, & that by placing the Hyperionian mode in A♭ Major I had forgotten 'the Beam in mine own Eye.'[3]

If I at last understand the matter, the Table ought to be arranged thus:

I have just finished the 8th section of the Dissertation,[4] in which appears to me, that the 'Question concerning *Counterpoint* among the Antients', is so demonstratively decided, no man in his Wits, or whose Prejudices did not suffocate them (which perhaps may be—could offer a Word in arrest of Judgement.

Mr. Locke's *mixed Modes*[5] are by far more intelligible than those which M. Burette[6] contends to have been used in Greek Musick: surely it is impossible that

---

[2] In his draft reply to SW's previous letter, Burney had stated: 'with respect to your remark on the mistake in the Notation of the Hypoiastian Mode, without look[ing] into my Hist[y] I am certain prima facie that your suggestion is right; the Tetrachord to E♭ minor must be A♭. As every one knows that has dipt into harmonics that G♯ & A♭, though produced on keyed Instrum[ts] is wth the voice, & violin a different sound; nor can any of the sounds of the 2 scales be the same . . . How this blunder escaped me I cannot imagine: for the moment I saw your transcript of the passage from my Dissertation, I was struck with its inaccuracy.'   [3] Matt. 7: 3; Luke 6: 41.

[4] 'Whether the Ancients had Counterpoint or Music in Parts', Part 8 of the lengthy *Dissertation on the Music of the Ancients* which opens Burney's *History*.

[5] A reference to the classification of abstract concepts in Locke's *An Essay concerning Human Understanding*, bk. II. ch. xxii. Locke states: '*mixed modes* [are] the complex *ideas* we mark by the names *obligation*, *drunkenness*, a *lie*, etc.; which consisting of several combinations of simple *ideas* of different kinds, I have called *mixed modes*, to distinguish them from the more simple modes, which consist only of simple *ideas* of the same kind. These mixed modes, being also such combinations of simple *ideas* as are not looked upon to be characteristical marks of any real beings that have a steady existence, but scattered and independent *ideas* put together by the mind, are thereby distinguished from the complex *ideas* of substances.'

[6] Pierre-Jean Burette (1665–1747), a French musician and scholar who wrote extensively on aspects of ancient Greek music (*Grove*[6]). His works were published as *Mémoires de littérature . . . de l'Académie des inscriptions et belles lettres*, 17 vols. (Paris, 1717–48), and his views remained standard for many years. He is frequently cited by Burney in his *History of Music*.

any Ears could have borne an Air even in the Lydian & Dorian mode either sung or played together.—Your confirmation of the Argument by the experiment of the Diapason, Principal, 12th, 15th & Tierce in an Organ[7] is an invincible Proof that no Euphony could possibly be produced 'were not the small harmonic Pipes governed by the greater.'

Indeed every fresh Page of this Dissertation carries with it such irresistible Evidence, that no musical enquiries need say δός που στῶ[8] respecting the Subject of Greek Counterpoint: & among the many who must acknowledge their obligations for your illuminating Researches, believe me there is no one who feels them more forcibly nor more gratefully than

> Dear Sir
> Your much indebted
> & obedient Servant
>> S Wesley

To unidentified lawyers[1]   Highgate, 5 January 1800

ALS, 3 pp. (Rylands, DDWF 15/10)

Gentlemen

Having been in Town almost all last Week, I did not obtain your Letter till Yesterday Evening.—I should otherwise have given you an immediate answer. —It seems plain that Mr Sibthorpe[2] is determined upon being as litigious, & proving as troublesome & irrational as he can: I have no other vouchers for my legal Claim to the Estate at Guildford, than what Dr Price's Will, & the Title Deeds have given;[3]—Why these are considered insufficient I am at a Loss to

---

[7] i.e. the playing together of various organ stops sounding at the unison and at the intervals of an octave, twelfth, two octaves, and two octaves and a major third higher. The intervals specified are those of successive overtones in the harmonic series. Burney's discussion of this point is not included in his draft reply.   [8] 'Give me somewhere to stand'.

[1] This letter, evidently addressed to a firm of lawyers, concerns SW's right of title to a house and land in Guildford left to him in the will of James Price (see n. 3).

[2] Thomas Sibthorpe of Guildford, the attorney acting for Dr Broxham, who was attempting to purchase the property from SW (*Law Lists*).

[3] Dr James Price (1752–83), English experimental scientist, sometimes described as 'the last of the alchemists'. He was one of the circle of friends at Guildford visited by SW and other members of his family during SW's boyhood. He committed suicide on 3 or 8 Aug. 1783, having failed to replicate in

account, nor is it possible for me to bring forward a State of Facts which happened long before I had an Acquaintance with the Testator.—Nothing can be more evident to me than that all these Delays have been contrived by M^r S on purpose to revenge the Pique he felt in my not entrusting the Papers unreservedly into his Possession.—You must be better Judges than I, whether herein I did wisely or not.—I acted upon the Advice of Mr Foster,[4] who thought it highly imprudent to trust them entirely to the Mercy of the Purchaser's Attorney, therefore if I have done wrong in this Respect, Mr Foster is the Author, who I think would not have intentionally given me improper Counsel.

It is very vexatious to find this Business so shamefully (& I believe) *wantonly* procrastinated.—Mr Sibthorpe had as well go about to deny *my Right* to the Estate at once, as to confound & perplex Matters concerning my Power of disposing of it; & in that Case, Dr Broxham[5] will be found to have made no *legal* Purchase, and the Property will be *Nobody's*.—

This must be clear to you, & therefore I have only to add, that if the Vouchers & Instruments already produced, be not available to enable me to receive the Purchase Money, Dr Broxham must adopt some other Plan than any I know of for the Purpose of making his claim legal & indisputable.

If I had had any other explanatory Papers upon the Subject, you may be assured that I should have readily produced them, in order to expedite & conclude an Affair which has caused me so much Trouble, & which will bring me (after all) an Advantage by far inadequate to the real Value of the Premises.

I remain
Gentlemen
Y^r obedient Servant
    S Wesley

P.S. If an Answer to *me* be necessary, please to direct to Chesterfield Street Marybone—Mr S. Wesley.

Highgate. 5 Jany 1800

---

public the experiments carried out at his house at Stoke, near Guildford, in 1782, in which he claimed to have turned mercury into silver and gold. In his will he left SW £1,000 and the house at Guildford discussed in this letter. A letter from him to SW of 28 July 1783 is printed in Lightwood; in it he relates his latest experiments with heating alloys in a wind furnace (*DNB*; Lightwood, 57–9).

4 The attorney acting for SW: probably John Foster of 32 Southampton Buildings (*Law Lists*).

5 The purchaser: not otherwise identified.

To Joseph Reid[1] Chesterfield Street, 7 January 1800

ALS, 1 p. (Duke) (photocopy; location of original unknown)
Addressed To | Joseph Reid Esqre | Staples Inn[2] | Holborn

Sir

I am really at a Loss how to apologize for a Neglect which no Apology can sufficiently excuse, by which I mean my shameful Delay in not having rendered you very long ago my best Thanks for the Volume which you were so good as to bestow upon me, viz; the life of Chillingworth,[3] which I obtained from our late & good Friend, Mr Seward.[4]

So valuable a Present will ever be remembered with Gratitude towards the Donor, but I fear that the Acknowledgement of it will scarcely convince you that I am, with much Respect,

Sir
Your truly obliged,
& grateful Servant
S Wesley

Chesterfield Street. Marybone | Tuesday. Jan. 7. 1800

---

[1] Not positively identified. From his address (see n. 2) he was evidently a lawyer. He may have been the Proctor and Notary Joseph Read of Doctor's Commons included in contemporary Law Lists.

[2] In fact, Staple Inn, one of the Inns of Chancery, affiliated to Gray's Inn and occupied by firms of attorneys and solicitors. The building still stands, and is occupied by the Institute of Actuaries (*London Encyclopaedia*, under 'Inns of Chancery').

[3] Pierre des Maizeaux, *An Historical and Critical Account of the Life and Writings of Wm Chillingworth* (1725).   [4] Seward had died on 24 Apr. 1799.

To Thomas Busby[1]   Charterhouse,[2] 21 March 1800

ALS, 2 pp. (Christ Church, MS 347/24)
Addressed To | M[r] Busby: | N. 9 | China Terrace | near | the Asylum[3]

Charter House.
Friday. 21st of March. 1800

Dear Sir

I received your Letter[4] last Night, & presume that before then you had received mine.—I am glad to find so promising an account of the Business in Hand,[5] &

---

[1] Thomas Busby (1755–1838), composer and writer on music. After early study in music with Jonathan Battishill (see n. 11), Samuel Champness, and Charles Knyvett, he was articled to Battishill for five years from around 1769, when he was also able to take full advantage of Battishill's extensive library, said by Busby to have contained between 6,000 and 7,000 volumes. He was probably the 'Mr Busby' who sang at the Handel Commemoration in 1784, and in 1786 is known to have been teaching singing; in the same year he also became organist of St Mary, Stoke Newington. From early in his career he combined musical with literary pursuits. For a time he was a parliamentary reporter for the *London Courant*; later, he collaborated with Samuel Arnold on *A Universal Dictionary of Musical Dictionary* (*c*.1783–6), which was never completed but ran to 197 numbers. His other early publications included *The Divine Harmonist* (1788) and *Melodia Britannica, or the Beauties of British Song* (*c*.1794). Around 1796 he met the publisher Richard Phillips, and contributed extensively to his various publishing ventures, including the *Monthly Magazine* (for which he wrote regular music reviews) and the annual *Public Characters*, for which he is assumed to have written his own (extremely laudatory) article. His oratorio *The Prophecy* (*c*.1784), based on Pope's *Messiah*, was first performed in 1799, and his oratorio *Britannia* (discussed in this letter) in June 1800. He was awarded a Cambridge Mus.D. in 1801 for his *Thanksgiving Ode on the Naval Victories*, which continued the patriotic theme of *Britannia*. His work for the theatre included the music for *A Tale of Mystery* (Covent Garden, 1802), and *The Fair Fugitives* (Covent Garden, 1803). In later life, he turned increasingly away from composition and to literary works. Among his publications were *A Complete Dictionary of Music* (*c*.1801), *A Grammar of Music* (1818), *A General History of Music, from the Earliest Times to the Present* (1819), *Concert Room and Orchestra Anecdotes* (1825), and *A Musical Manual* (1828) (*DNB*; Grove[6]; *BD*; Kassler, *Science of Music*, 141–3; Busby).

[2] A charitable institution in the City of London consisting of a school and accommodation for pensioners. SW was probably writing from the address of James Kenton, an old family friend, who is known to have been living there at this time.

[3] Off the present Kennington Road, close to its junction with Lambeth Road. 'The Asylum' was Bethlem Hospital, on the site now occupied by the Imperial War Museum.   [4] Not preserved.

[5] Preparations for the first performance of Busby's 'New, Grand, Commemorative Oratorio' *Britannia* at the King's Theatre on 28 May, in aid of the Fund for Raising a National Monument of National Gratitude to the Brave Defenders of our King and Country. According to the account in *Public Characters*, Busby had offered to compose *Britannia* for the fund, for performance 'at the opera house, as a national concert, upon a scale adequate to the great occasion'. The committee initially accepted Busby's offer but later, hoping that George III might attend the concert, and in view of his love of Handel, they decided not to have the oratorio performed in its entirety on this occasion. Instead, there was a 'Grand Concert of Miscellaneous Music', consisting of Handel's music together with extracts from *Britannia*. The first complete performance was at Covent Garden on 16 June, for the benefit of the Humane Society. The

that Matters are likely to be carried so triumphantly.—Gray[6] has sent to inform me that he has been unable to explore any organ likely to merit a Place upon such an Occasion as the present.—Surely (as I before observed) no Instrument could be so singularly appropriate to the purpose, (not only on account of its intrinsick Excellence but also by reason of the loyal Tendency of the Exhibition) as that in the King's Concert Room.[7]—At all events, it must be a Machine of similar *Power* to deserve a Situation in such a Band, & in such a House.—Verbum sat *sapienti*.[8]

You will of course acquaint me with the Result of your Enquiries concerning the Possibility of obtaining the King's Organ, as soon as you possibly can, because I must take my Measures, in consequence.[9]—I am fully resolved (& so you know I ought to be) to perform upon no other than a capital Instrument: neither shall I lose any Time in seeking for some Substitute[10] in case of *a Disappointment*, which in *some* Part or other of any long-planned Scheme, I always expect.—You will oblige me by a Line directed to Marybone on some Day in next Week.

It will give me much Pleasure (as it always has given) to meet my Friend Battishill,[11] & particular Satisfaction in so doing at your own House, where I promise myself abundant Gratification in the Opportunity of examining some of your masterly Productions, & of improving an Acquaintance & Intercourse which I trust may be mutually agreeable and advantageous.—If musical Englishmen were laudably unanimous, a Phalanx might easily be formed against the Invasion of *continental Locusts.—this, by the bye.—*

---

setting up of the fund, described as for the erection of a 'Naval Monument to Perpetuate the Glorious Victories of the British Navy' was announced in *The Times* on 27 Jan. 1800. Various designs for the monument, otherwise known as the 'naval pillar' were submitted: one, by John Flaxman, was for a 200-foot statue of Britannia, to be sited on Greenwich Hill. The monument was never erected (Rodney Mace, *Trafalgar Square: Emblem of Empire* (1976), 48–50; John Physick, *Design for English Sculpture 1680–1860* (1969), 165, 167–9; *The Times*, 27 Jan. 1800, 28 May 1800; Busby, 388–90).

    [6] Presumably the organ builder William Gray (*c*.1757–1820) (*Grove[6]*).

    [7] i.e. the Concert Room at the King's Theatre. The organ there was a two-manual 1794 instrument by Samuel Green (Boeringer, iii. 206).   [8] 'A word is sufficient to the wise'.

    [9] Busby had presumably asked SW to perform at the concert.

    [10] It is not clear whether SW is referring to a substitute organ or a substitute organist. In the event, he did not perform in the concert.

    [11] The organist and composer Jonathan Battishill (1738–1801). He was a chorister at St Paul's Cathedral, where he studied with William Savage, and later the deputy of William Boyce at the Chapel Royal. His main musical career was during the period 1760–75, when he was active both as a theatre and a church musician and as a keyboard player. His later years were marred by the frequently 'violent and erratic behaviour' (R. J. S. Stevens) which was a concomitant of his increasing dependence on alcohol, about which many anecdotes were told (*DNB*; *Grove[6]*; *BD*; Thomas Busby, 'Original Memoirs of the late Mr Jonathan Battishill', in John Page, ed., *Six Anthems and Ten Chants Composed by the Late Mr Jonathan Battishill* (1804); J. B. Trend, 'Jonathan Battishill, from the Unpublished Recollections of R. J. S. Stevens', *ML* 13 (1932), 264–71).

I fear that I cannot name any earlier Period than the Week after next for attending you at China Row, neither can I at this moment fix a Day in that same Week: however, be assured that I will endeavour as soon as possible to *secure* a Day for the Purpose of accepting your friendly Invitation, & to give you the earliest Intelligence of my Success in that Particular.

With Compliments to Mrs Busby,[12] believe me to remain, with Esteem,

Dear Sir
Your sincere
& obliged humble Servant

S Wesley

P.S. You know that Ld Chesterfield[13] says to his Son, 'Whatever is worth doing at all, is worth doing *well*.'[14]—It is upon the Strength & good Sense of this Observation, that I mean to manage to attend *two* of your Rehearsals, instead of one, if I possible can.

To Joseph Payne Street   [Highgate, 3 May 1800][1]

AL, 3 pp. (BL, Add. MS 56228); damaged and incomplete
Addressed To | Mr Street. | N.17. | Mark Lane
Pmk 3 MY 1800

Dear Sir

Mr Drummer has made a Promise of coming over hither in about a Fortnight or three Weeks hence, & I shall reckon upon the Pleasure of your accompanying him: I also think of requesting his Brother's Company together; if the Day appointed should happen to suit him.—I dined with M^r T Attwood[2] on Friday last,[3] who has also given his Word to give me a Day at Highgate before long.—If we can but

---

[12] Priscilla, née Angier, whom Busby had married in 1786 (*DNB*).

[13] Philip Dormer Stanhope, 4th Earl of Chesterfield (1694–1773), statesman, diplomat, writer, whose letters to his natural son were published by his widow in 1774.

[14] Philip Dormer Stanhope, *Letters written by the ... Earl of Chesterfield to his Son Philip Stanhope*, 2 vols. (1774), Letter 71.

[1] The date is given by the postmark.

[2] Thomas Attwood (1765–1838) had begun his musical career as a chorister in the Chapel Royal, where he came to the attention of the Prince of Wales, who paid for him to continue his musical education abroad. He was in Italy from 1783 to 1785 and was a pupil of Mozart in Vienna from 1785 to 1787. He was music teacher to the Duke of York (from 1791), to the Princess of Wales (from 1795), and composer to the Chapel Royal (from 1796). He was appointed organist of St Paul's Cathedral in 1796, a position he held until his death.   [3] 25 Apr.

manage to match all Parties on the same Day, I shall be very much gratified, & intend to contrive in my best Manner to bring it about.—You know that the Diminutiveness of my Palace admits not the round Sort of Party which I should be more happy to make, but which, for the sake of *their* Comfort, I must be at present compelled to forego: especially as I have not more than *one* spare Bed.— However, let me inform you, that I can secure *two* Beds in the Neighbourhood, so that your Distance from Town here must not be an Obstacle to your indulging us, as we will take Care you shall not be at a Loss for a safe & comfortable Lodging.—

You will oblige me by referring [to] Chillingworth's V^th Chapter. Sect.59— Title,—'Separation of Protestants from the Church of Rome, not guilty of Schism.'[4]—I am inclined to think that there must be some considerable Error in the Print of the following Passage—'Or would you have him believe those Things true, which together with him you have supposed to be Errors? This is such an one, as is assured or persuaded of that, which your here suppose, that your Church doth err, (& such only, we say, are obliged to forsake your Communion) **is**, as Schoolmen speak, Implicatio in Terminis, a Contradiction so plain, that one Word destroyeth another; as if one should say, living dead Man.

The verb **is**, immediately after the Parenthesis, I cannot connect grammatic-ally with any one Word which preceded; I have tried several Ways, but none suc-cessfully, & therefore would gladly know how the Sentence runs in your Edition, which as I am informed, is in all Respects the most correct that has hitherto appeared.[5]

It little matters what Blunders Compositors may make in a Novel, or any other modern Nonsense called *sentimental*; but in Works of moral & metaphysical Truth, Carelessness is the most inexcusable Dishonesty.—Although Chillingworth's is never a *tangled Chain*,[6] yet as it is wrought exquisitely fine, great Danger there is of Confusion, unless every Word & Point be rendered with the utmost Accuracy; & it is with profound Reasoners on abstract moral Truth, as with Mathematicians upon Lines & Quantities: one Link of their Series being either lost or impaired, the whole Symmetry is destroyed, & the whole Order of the Reasoning is disturbed & disjointed; all of which may easily happen by one typographical Mistake.

---

[4] In *The Religion of the Protestants a safe Way to Salvation* (1637).

[5] SW was right in his suspicion of a misprint. As he correctly conjectured in his postscript, the text should read 'this *in* such a one' (editor's italics).

[6] Theseus's description of the Prologue's speech in the mechanicals' play in *A Midsummer Night's Dream*, v. i. 124.

I find that Salomon[7] intends to repeat the Oratorio of Haydn[8] on Thursday 15th inst.—He has of course made it necessary for me to lend a helping Hand.— Barthelemon[9] has pleaded hard, (but in vain) for a Copy of the 'Dixit Dominus',[10] & (as some People will never lose for Want of asking) he requested me to play at his *Jerusalem Chamber*[11] (to boot) on Thursday 22^{d} of this Month.—But this too has been answered in the Negative.—My real Friends have a just Claim on my musical Services, which I think you know I am always ready to render them, but with the *Trade*, I will deal sharply, well knowing that it is merely from *Necessity*, & never from *Good Will* that they apply to me for Assistance.

Mrs W. joins < . . . > hoping that y<ou . . . >[12]

P.S. Since I wrote the under Part[13] I think I have guessed how the Blunder is in Chillingworth's Text.—Instead of 'This *is* such an one,' if we read 'this *in* such an one as is assured &c—& if this be right (as I suspect it is, the sense being then logical & compleat) the **IS** after the Parenthesis is right, as you will find upon a Moment's Examination.—

---

[7] Johann Peter Salomon (1745–1815), German violinist, impresario, and composer. His first position was at the age of 13 as a violinist at the Bonn court. By 1764 he was music director to Prince Heinrich of Prussia at Rheinsberg. Through him he met Carl Philipp Emanuel Bach (1714–88) and became familiar with the music of J. S. Bach. He later moved via Paris to London, where he made his first public appearance in 1781. He soon turned his attention to directing and promoting concerts, and arranged subscription concerts in London from 1783. He was responsible for arranging the visits of Haydn to London in 1791–2 and 1794–5.

[8] Salomon had promoted one of the first performances in England of Haydn's *Creation* at the King's Theatre on 21 Apr., at which SW had played the organ and piano and performed one of his own organ concertos between the acts. The performance under discussion here did not take place. For the first London performances of *The Creation*, see H. C. Robbins Landon, *Haydn: Chronicle and Works. The Years of 'The Creation' 1796–1800* (1977), 572–7.

[9] François-Hippolyte Barthélemon (1741–1808), French violinist and composer. He moved to London in about 1761, where he enjoyed a long career as a performer on the violin and a composer, mostly of theatre music. He was one of the leading violinists of his age, much admired by Burney, who commented on his 'powerful hand and truly vocal adagio'. He was a friend of Haydn's during his two visits to London, and is said to have suggested the subject of *The Creation* to him.

[10] The 'Dixit Dominus' a 8, the two autographs of which (RCM, MS 639; BL, Add. MS 71107, fo. 35) are dated 13 Jan. 1800.

[11] i.e. the Swedenborgian New Jerusalemite Chapel in Friar St, Blackfriars, where Barthélemon worshipped and directed the music. SW's allusion is to the chapter room at Westminster Abbey, so called because of the tapestries depicting scenes of Jerusalem on its walls. For Barthélemon's involvement with Swedenborgianism, see Charles Higham, 'Francis Barthélemon', *New-Church Magazine* 15 (1896), 1–13.

[12] The bottom of the leaf, consisting of the right-hand part of two lines and SW's close and signature, is missing.   [13] SW's postscript is at the top of the final page.

To [Charles Burney][1]   [Highgate], 12 May 1800

ALS, 2 pp. (UCSB)
Docketed by Mme d'Arblay: ※

Marybone.
Monday 12th of May.
1800.

I trust, my dear Sir, that no bad Omen threatens me for Friday next,[2] when I fully purpose attending you at Ten o'Clock.—I know not any probable Obstacle, excepting Mr Salomon's Repetition of the Oratorio,[3] which if it should happen, will render it necessary for me to transfer my usual Business on Thursday to Friday instead, & in that Case, I should be again disappointed: but, by what I have just now heard, I conjecture that we shall not be able to ensure a second Performance, Mr Salomon being baulked of his Singers, who indeed gave him Abundance of Trouble in the *former* Instance; & I am sorry to add that a most malevolent Party Spirit appears to have raged against the whole Undertaking, so that little Probability remains of any handsome Encouragement during the Remainder of this Season.

The musical Publick seem at present to be oddly divided into three Classes: they who allow nothing good but Handel, Corelli, and what are absurdly called the *old* Masters—(for how lately was it when even *these* were Moderns!)—others, who will hear no other Musick than of Mozart, Haydn, and the few excellent of our own Day: and the third august Society of ἐπιστάμενοι[4] consists chiefly of those Admirers of *Simplicity* who relish no other Strains than what proceeds from Messrs Kelly[5] & R<auzzini>,[6] together with such *Waltzes* as can assist τοῦ <u>ταμβουρινίζειν</u>:[7]

At least I guess you will thus far agree with me, that a very very few constitute that little flock who 'prove all things, and hold fast that which is good.'[8]

> I am always,
> my dear Sir
> your obliged Friend
> & faithful Servant
>
> S Wesley

---

[1] Burney is identified as the addressee of this letter by his daughter's characteristic docketing (see SW to Burney, 28 Nov. 1799, n. 2).   [2] 16 May.

[3] Salomon made a number of unsuccessful attempts to mount this performance: it was also announced for 5 May and 9 June.   [4] 'Experts'.

[5] All except the first letter has been heavily scored through, but 'Kelly' is just decipherable. For Michael Kelly (1762–1826), see SW to Charles Wesley jun., 15 Jan. 1807, n. 29.

[6] All except the first letter has been heavily scored through; 'Rauzzini' is conjectural. For Venanzio Rauzzini (1746–1810), see SW to Charles Wesley jun., 15 Jan. 1807, n. 30.

[7] 'Dancing': not in Classical Greek, and apparently a coinage of SW's own.   [8] 1 Thess. 5: 21.

To [Thomas Busby][1]   Charterhouse, [3] June 1800[2]

ALS, 4 pp. (Christ Church, MS 347/25)

Dear Sir

I this Morning received yours,[3] the Contents of which require some Consideration, previous to a final Answer upon the Subject of your intended Performance
on the 16th.[4]—I am apprehensive that you will experience more Difficulties in
the Execution of your Plan than you at present seem to anticipate.—In the first
Place, it appears to me that the *Season* is too far advanced to afford you any
clear Prospect of a full House; & a thin Audience would be another mortifying
Event added to those which Have already occurred.[5]—To-morrow you know
is the King's Birth Day,[6] after which, all the fine Folk hurry out of Town, & the
rest who remain it are likely to be deterred from attending by the Heat of the
Weather, which in a Fortnight hence will in all Probability be very considerably
encreast.

You will perhaps answer, that the Summer Theatres[7] are as full as the
Winter, & therefore you may expect a crowded House also; but on this, I must
observe, that all manner of Rabble will go to a *Play* in any Weather, as you well
know, whereas the number of those who have either Curiosity to hear an Oratorio,
or Knowledge enough to relish it when they *do* hear it is comparatively small,
even in the Winter Season, when they need not dread Fevers or Fainting.

Another Obstacle, (& which seems at last the most material) is the Difficulty
I fear you will find in securing a Band competent to the Task of doing the Justice
to your Work, *without which it had better not be undertaken.*—You remember
what Horace[8] says concerning Poetry—

—*Mediocribus* esse *Poetis*

Non Dii, non Homines, non concessere <co>lumnae[9]—and the like I think
may be applied to both the *Composition*, & the *Execution* of an Oratorio—To

---

[1] Although this letter lacks an address panel, there can be no doubt from its content that it is to Busby.

[2] This corrects SW's misdating of 4 June (see n. 22).   [3] Busby's letter is not preserved.

[4] The first performance of *Britannia* (*London Stage*; *The Times*, 16 June 1800).

[5] No doubt the events which resulted in the non-performance of *Britannia* in its entirety at the
concert on 28 May.   [6] George III's birthday was on 4 June.

[7] The London theatres were divided into 'winter' and 'summer' houses. The 'winter theatres' were
the two patent houses (Covent Garden and Drury Lane), which confined their activities to the main
winter season; the 'summer theatres' were smaller houses which were licensed to perform in the summer
months.   [8] Quintus Horatius Flaccus (65–8 BC), Roman poet and satirist.

[9] 'Neither gods, nor men, nor bookshops will allow poets to be second-rate' (*Ars Poetica*, 372–3).

witness Chorusses *indifferently* performed, is to me (& must be to you) the most exasperating of musical Miseries:—There is indeed scarcely any *Mean* between the *Extremes* of excellent & execrable, in these Matters.—

However, do not imagine that I can believe you likely to trust your Music into lame Hands, or Mouths not *responsible*; but I really question the Possibility of your raising a sufficient Force to assert your Dignity of Style, at this late Period of the Season.—and even then,—*can you safely depend on those who promise?*—Are they '*all honourable Men*'?[10]—Are even all the *Principal* Assistants so?—Do they never break their Word? (as well as their *Time?*)—You remember how Salomon was mis-used. Mr Denman[11] had engaged to sing a principal Bass in the Creation; & permitted his Name to be repeatedly advertized.—He attended not *one* of the Rehearsals, & on the Evening of the Performance, at *5 o'Clock*, sent to say, that he could not sing at all, unless he would risk forfeiting this Engagement at the Theatre![12]

You may call me 'Doctor all the Worse',[13] & perhaps not without Reason.—To say the Truth, I have experienced so often how little Dependence a rational Man ought to place upon the Generality of Professions, & *Professors*, that whenever the Execution of any Plan consists in the Co-incidence of *many*, I am ever agreeably disappointed when it succeeds.

I am fully sensible of the Compliment which the Literary Fund have passed upon me,[14] as well as yourself, & am not likely (I hope) to be wanting in a due Acknowledgement of their Distinction. Doubtless any Assistance at any Performance for the Benefit of the Institution would be as *plenary* a Testimony of Respect as could be in my Power to shew, & indeed nothing would be less according to my Wish than to neglect an Opportunity of proving that a handsome Attention is never lost upon me. You must inform me what you have already done, in this Business, & what you are *about* to do, & to be able to get *done by others*; for this last, after all, is the knotty Rub.—N.B. No Concerto *can* be played upon

---

[10] *Julius Caesar*, III. ii. 84.

[11] Henry Denman (1744–1816), actor, instrumentalist, and singer. He sang in the chorus at Drury Lane in the 1791–2 and 1794–5 seasons and also took small acting parts there in the 1790s. As SW states, his name had appeared among the vocal soloists in advertisements for Salomon's performance of *The Creation* on 21 April; he was also advertised as a soloist for *Britannia*. (*BD*; *London Stage*).

[12] Covent Garden, where Denman was employed in the 1799/1800 season as an actor and as a singer in the oratorio concerts. On the evening of the *Creation* performance he was due to appear there in Dibdin's farce *St David's Day* (*London Stage*).   [13] i.e. a pessimist.

[14] The Literary Fund had the previous month elected Busby as one of their governors. SW had presumably also been honoured in the same way (Busby, 382).

Ashley's[15] Organ at Covent Garden:[16] at least, not by *me*.—It is the most uncertain & intractable of all the Instruments I ever touched, & I have sworn, by the *Diapason of Heaven*, that I will have no more to do with it.[17]

I shall be at Leisure for half an Hour on Friday next, either at *10*, or at $\frac{1}{2}$ past 12, in Chesterfield Street, where if it may suit you to call, you may more fully explain your Plan of Operations.—Or if 'the Affair cries Haste, & Speed must answer it',[18] perhaps it may be well for you to send me an immediate Line upon Receipt of this, which will come to Hand on Thursday, when I expect to be at Marybone for a few Minutes only, till late at Night.

I know not that my Letter to Davison[19] has any Claim to our Friend Battishill's hyperbolical Commendation.—We know his Enthusiastic Prepossession in Favour of his Friends, which, *to those Friends themselves*, is highly satisfactory & delightful; but a partial Friend has but little Influence in *making Enemies think with him* on the same Subjects, or Person.

'Get your Enemies (says Swift)[20] to criticize your Works;—for your Friend is so much your Self, that he will judge too like you.'[21]

I am, in Haste (tho' you will scarce believe it, by the Length of all this)

Dear Sir
Very sincerely Yours
  S Wesley

Charter House

Tuesday. June 4.[22] 1800

---

[15] The bassoonist John Ashley (1734–1805), director of the Lenten Oratorios at Covent Garden from 1795 until his death (*Grove*[6]; *BD*). For his four sons, also musicians and involved with the management of the Lenten Oratorios, see SW to Novello, 6 May [1812], n. 4.

[16] A one-manual instrument (*c.*1733) by Abraham Jordan (Boeringer, iii. 207).

[17] Busby had doubtless asked SW to play an organ concerto at the concert.

[18] *Othello*, I. iii. 276: one of SW's favourite quotations.

[19] Alexander Davison (1750–1829), government contractor, and prize-agent and confidential friend of Lord Nelson. He was the treasurer of the fund for the erection of the naval pillar. According to Busby, after the concert on 28 May SW and other musicians, including Battishill, Burney, and Charles Wesley jun., had written to the fund to attest to the merits of *Britannia* (*DNB*; Busby, 390).

[20] Jonathan Swift (1667–1745), satirist. [21] The source of this quotation has not been traced.

[22] 4 June was a Wednesday, not a Tuesday, in 1800. It is evident from SW's reference to George III's birthday 'tomorrow' that he was writing on Tuesday, 3 June.

To Joseph Payne Street   Chesterfield Street, 18 August 1801

ALS, 3 pp. (BL, Add. MS 56228)
Addressed To | Mr Street | N. 17. | Mark Lane. | Tuesday Morning
Pmk 18 AU 1801

Marybone.
Tuesday 18 Augt 1801

My dear Sir

I believe that Saturday Week[1] will be the first Day in my Power to appoint for meeting Mr Bell's Party at Palmer's Green,[2] & at present I know of nothing very likely to prevent my Acceptance of his Invitation: I conclude by your Letter that he wishes the Appointment to be made without Loss of Time, therefore perhaps you will now speedily communicate to him this Intelligence.

With respect to your late 'Delirium' (for I am to suppose it now *over*, for which I am sorry, as it appears to have been so agreeable to you) I can only say that I fully understand the Situation you describe, & although I have not experienced it in consequence of our last Sunday's Recreation, yet I know it to be a most pleasant occasional Effect of the *Fillip* to Nature[3] which Dr Cadogan[4] talks about, but which (by the Way) will become less elastic & forcible, & consequently less effective, if too frequently repeated.—However, it did not seem to me as if you had secured to yourself any Right to become so enlightened, enlivened, & *metaphysicized* by my Wine, for really we took but a very moderate Dose of it, &, (if I am any Judge of my *own* State on Sunday) I thought that we were all perfectly steady at the Hour of Parting. I am truly vexed that W. D.[5] should have excoriated any one of his precious Limbs in returning from my Roof; but this you know being la Fortune de la Guerre, it is in vain to fret about it.

I will be with you on Saturday next[6] by half past 2, as I suspect that Business is to be done before Dinner—I wish you to take me rightly about the Sponsorship— I could have no possible Objection to the Favour you design me from any other Consideration than that of answering for Impossibilities.—I really look upon the Duty of a Godfather (admitting that it *could* be performed) as one of the most solemn & obligatory in the whole theological System, but when I reflect on what I believe is (after all) the Truth, that no one can be justly accountable for all the Sins & Imperfections of another, (he having generally enow to answer for on his own

---

[1] 29 Aug.   [2] Then, a village on the outskirts of London. Bell has not been identified.

[3] i.e. alcohol.

[4] William Cadogan, MD (1711–97), in his influential and frequently reprinted *A Dissertation on the Gout and on all Chronic Diseases* (1771).   [5] Presumably William Drummer.

[6] 22 Aug.

Score) the Affair of Sponsor becomes rather a Thing of complimentary Ceremony than of probable Damnation: so having endeavoured to quiet my Conscience (which is seldom difficult to do when Gratification follows its Repose) 'I promise & vow to renounce' my Fear of Hell & to suffer my future Godson to take his own Path, either thither or to the *other* Place, which however, I confess I should rather wish him to *prefer*, in which I suspect that you will second my Inclination.[7]

The Ladies are all sound, Wind & Limb, Miss R.[8] & my Mother arrived here yesterday about half an Hour before me, & I went through my Monday's Drudgery with great Christian Forbearance & Resignation.

With best Wishes to your whole House, I am

Dear Sir
Ever yours truly
　S Wesley

To Charles Burney　　　　　　　　　Highgate, 11 November [1801][1]

ANS, 1 p. (Private collection of Cynthia Comyn)
Addressed　To | Dr Burney, | Chelsea College. | Thursday Morning
Pmk　7 o'Clock NO 12 1801

　　　　　　　　　　　　　　　　　Highgate. Wednesday.
　　　　　　　　　　　　　　　　　　11th of Nov^r

I trust, my dear Sir, to be with you on Tuesday next[2] at 10, & will arrange Matters so as to steal half a Holiday; for I have to ask your Opinion & Advice upon a Business of more Moment & Magnitude than Organ Voluntaries,[3] although it be intimately concerned with them—sat verbum sapienti—en attendant,

Yours faithfully
　SW

---

[7] Street's child, to whom SW was to be godfather, may have been Joseph Edward, subsequently mentioned in SW to Street, 30 May 1806.

[8] Not certainly identified: perhaps the Miss Richardson who attended SW's music party on 10 Oct. 1801 (SW to his mother, 16 Oct. 1801 (Rylands, DDWes 6/49)), and sang in the concert series in 1802 discussed in SW to Burney, [Feb.–May 1802].

[1] The year is given by the postmark.　　[2] 17 Nov.

[3] Probably the series of subscription concerts which SW was promoting with his brother Charles in the coming season (see next letter).

To [Charles Burney]¹   [February–May 1802]²

ALS, 3 pp. (Osborn MSS 3, Box 12, Folder 867).
Docketed by Mme d'Arblay: ✕³

My dear Friend

Your kind Note⁴ I would sooner have acknowledged had an earlier Moment from excessive Pressure of harassing Business been allowed me.—'Nunc animo Opus, nunc Pectore firmo',⁵ is peculiarly applicable to my present Affairs: of Difficulties & Dangers there is not now *Time* to discourse; we shall have more Leisure in future perhaps than we wish, for proving how much better Things *might* have been.⁶

Billington⁷ would have laid us the golden Eggs; & would have been a *cheap* Bargain at any Price:—but this won't *argufy* now.⁸

---

¹ Burney is identified as the addressee of this letter by his daughter's characteristic docketing (see SW to Burney, 28 Nov. 1799, n. 2, and n. 3 below).

² The discussion of the concert series (see n. 6) establishes that this letter was written between February and May 1802; it is not clear, however, whether it was written before the series started or during its course. The address portion of a letter to Burney in SW's hand, dated 9 Mar. 1802 and postmarked 10 Mar. 1802 (NYPL (Berg)), may belong to this letter; if so, it establishes the date. If the symphony by SW mentioned here is the Symphony in B flat, on the other hand (see n. 12), the programme can only be of the final concert of the series, and the letter can be dated to late Apr. or early May.

³ This symbol is interpreted by Ribeiro as denoting a letter 'of tertiary interest'.

⁴ Not preserved.

⁵ 'Now courage is required, now a stout heart is needed': an adaptation of the sybil's exhortation to Aeneas just before they enter the underworld in Virgil, *Aeneid*, 6. 621.

⁶ A series of six subscription concerts promoted by SW and his brother Charles at Hyde's Concert Rooms, Tottenham Street was advertised in *The Times* on 29 Jan. 1802; it was to begin on 4 Feb., with subsequent concerts on 25 Feb., 11 and 25 Mar., 22 Apr., and 6 May. No other contemporary evidence of this series has been found, but it is clear from references in subsequent correspondence that it was not a success and resulted in substantial financial loss for both SW and his brother. In a letter of 31 May 1811 to Charles (BL, Add. MS 35012, fo. 117), SW remembered 'those concerts which failed at the Tottenham Street Rooms', and the refusal of many of the performers to 'relax in any part of their demands'.

⁷ The leading English soprano Elizabeth Billington, née Weichsell (?1765–8–1818) had initially established her reputation in London during the 1780s and early 1790s. In 1794 she went to Italy, where she had many successes in Naples and Milan. She returned to London in the summer of 1801 to great acclaim and resumed her career.

⁸ Mrs Billington, in her first full season in London since her return from Italy, would have been a star attraction, but SW and his brother Charles had either been unable or had decided not to secure her services. Long afterwards, SW's brother Charles remembered that 'the last and only Public Concert we had at the old Antient Music Room did not answer, because we neglected to engage the Late Mrs Billington, who was just arrived in England' (Charles Wesley jun. to John Langshaw jun., 11 Jan. 1827 (Emory); Wainwright, 86).

I wrote a Duet for the Organs,[9] lately, which upon Trial, I find too complicated for any Chance of *general* Approbation:—We therefore think to play one on Thursday next, adapted from the last Chorus in Esther,[10] (which you know is as easily understood as the Coronation Anthem,)[11] & which will be but little deserving of your particular Attention, having been so long remembered:—It will *happen* near the Finale of the *Job*, of which accept the following Order,

1. Symphony. S.W.[12]
2. Glee. 3 Voices. C.W.[13]
3. Song. Miss Richardson.[14] (Cimarosa)[15]
4. Trio. Tenor,[16] Bassoon & Violoncello. Shield.[17] Holmes[18] & Lindley.[19]
5. Song. M[rs] Dussek[20] (with the Harp). Sarti.[21]
6. Organ Concerto. C.W.[22]

2[d] Part

1. Symphony. Mozart.[23]
2. Song. Morelli.[24]
3. Concerto. Piano Forte.
   Master Peile.[25] (Dussek)[26]

[9] Not preserved: doubtless the duet included in the worklist appended to SW's obituary in *MW*, where it is described as 'unpublished; the composer preferred this to the other, and considered it his best composition for the organ'.

[10] 'The Lord our Enemy has slain', from Handel's oratorio *Esther* (?1718, rev. 1732).

[11] Handel's anthem 'Zadok the Priest', written for the coronation of George II in 1727.

[12] Either one of the symphonies of 1784 written for the family concerts, or the Symphony in B flat, SW's only mature work in the genre, the autograph of which (BL, Add. MS 35011) is dated 27 Apr. 1802, and which was probably written for and performed at the final concert in this series.

[13] i.e. Charles Wesley jun.: not identified.

[14] Not identified; presumably the Miss Richardson who attended SW's music party on 10 Oct. 1801 (SW to his mother, 16 Oct. 1801 (Rylands, DDWes 6/49)); conceivably one of the four daughters of the playwright and poet Joseph Richardson (1755–1803), one of the proprietors of Drury Lane Theatre, and MP for Newport, Cornwall.   [15] Domenico Cimarosa (1749–1801), Italian opera composer.

[16] i.e. viola.

[17] Presumably by William Shield (1748–1829), who also played the viola ('tenor'): not identified. For Shield, see SW to Shield, [13] Sept. 1815.

[18] The bassoonist James Holmes (1755/6–1820) (Doane; Matthews; Sainsbury).

[19] The cellist Robert Lindley (1776–1855), the leading player of his generation (*Grove*[6]).

[20] Sophia Dussek, née Corri (1775–1847), daughter of the composer, music publisher, and teacher Domenico Corri (1746–1825), who had married Jan Ladislav Dussek (see n. 26) in 1792. She was also well known as a harpist and pianist.   [21] Giuseppe Sarti (1729–1802), Italian opera composer.

[22] Charles Wesley jun.: perhaps one of his six Concertos, Op. 2 (*c*.1781).

[23] Wolfgang Amadeus Mozart (1756–91): the symphony has not been identified.

[24] The operatic bass Giovanni Morelli (*fl*.1787–1815) (*BD*).

[25] The pianist Joseph Stageldoir Peile (1787–1840) (*BD*).

[26] Jan Ladislav Dussek (1760–1812), pianist and composer. He had fled France at the time of the French Revolution, and had first appeared as a pianist in London in 1789.

4. Duetto. Mrs Dussek & Mrs Cimador.²⁷ ('Ah perdona,') Mozart.²⁸

5. Duet. 2 Organs.²⁹

6. Full Piece. Handel. (from the Ov. to Atalanta).³⁰

Yours, my kind Friend,
Most faithfully

S Wesley

To Charles Stokes¹   [?London]², 2 October 1804

ALS, 2 pp. (BL, Add. MS 31764, fo. 18)
Addressed Mr Stokes.

Dear Charles³

I am unable to account for the Reason of y^r never having either called, or written to me so long.—*You* of Course know the Cause yrself—I must own that I believe if you *had wished* to have been in my Society (tho' it is none of the best in my State of Health & Circumstances) you w^d surely have contrived Ways & Means *long ere now* of our meeting.—You see I write as one hurt at the Slight of a Person for whom he has a Regard.—had I *not*, I assure you I should not

---

²⁷ Presumably the wife of the composer, singer, violinist, and music publisher Giambattista Cimador (1761–1805), who had settled in London in 1791. He had gone into partnership with Tebaldo Monzani around 1800 (*Grove*⁶).

²⁸ A duet from Act I of Mozart's *La clemenza di Tito* (1791). Sophia Dussek was closely involved with the introduction of Mozart's music to London audiences: she included 'Ah perdona' in her benefit concert on 23 Apr. 1800, and sang in the first London performance of the *Requiem* in 1801. *La clemenza di Tito* was the first of Mozart's operas to be performed in full in London, on 27 Mar. 1806.

²⁹ The arrangement of the final chorus from Handel's *Esther*, discussed above.

³⁰ The Overture to Handel's opera *Atalanta* (1736).

---

¹ Charles Stokes (1784–1839), pianist, organist, and composer of anthems, glees, songs, and organ music. According to his own biographical sketch (BL, Add. MS 11730, fos. 204–6), he was admitted as a chorister at St Paul's Cathedral in 1792 through his godfather Samuel Webbe I, leaving the choir in 1798. He was a pupil successively of Webbe, Charles Wesley jun., and SW. With SW and Vincent Novello he gave the first performance of SW's Trio for Three Pianofortes in 1811. He owned several manuscripts of SW's music.

² SW moved from his Highgate house in late spring 1803, probably as a result of financial crises following his separation from Charlotte in (probably) late 1801. There are few letters for the next two years or so. During some of this time SW appears to have suffered from severe depression, and his address or addresses during this period are not known.

³ SW's use of the Christian name in the salutation of a letter to a recipient outside his immediate family is unparalleled, and suggests a particularly close relationship with Stokes at this time.

have thus remonstrated—I am conscious of not having done the civil Thing by the Coopers,[4] who wrote me the kindest Invitation in the World.—Illness & Distraction of Mind must, & I trust will excuse—let them know I am truly sensible for their Goodness.—

You will I think give me some Answer upon this:—had you been disengaged to-day I would have gone out with you on a ramble somewhere after 12 o'Clock.—

Should you return home by 1 o'Clock To-day & will leave a Note for me, stating when or whether we are soon to meet, I will call at a Venture, about 2.

Yrs truly

SW

Tuesday. Octr 2. 1804

To John George Graeff[1]   Camden Town,[2] 21 May [?1806][3]

ALS, 2 pp. (BL, Add. MS 60753, fo. 120)
Addressed To John George Graeff

Camden Town. 21 May.

---

[4] Not certainly identified: one of the Coopers may have been George Cooper (?1783–1843), organist of St Sepulchre and assistant organist of St Paul's Cathedral (see SW to Novello, 25 Sept. [1824], n. 2).

[1] John George Graeff (*c*.1762–*post* 1824) came to London around 1784, where he became one of the most prominent flautists of his day and appeared frequently as a concerto soloist. He was evidently a long-standing friend of SW, although on the evidence of his infrequent appearances in the letters he and SW may have met only occasionally. SW mentions him in a letter to his mother of 16 Oct. 1801 (Rylands, DDWes 6/49) as having been a member of a music party at SW's house in Highgate on 10 Oct. 1801 which also included Miss Richardson, Francis Cramer, Pinto, and Moralt, 'who formed the sweetest Harmony consisting principally of Mozart & Haydn's Musick, which of course they performed with the most exquisite Precision & Effect'.

[2] SW had moved to Arlington Street (now Arlington Road), Camden Town, some time before 1 Apr. 1806, when this address appears on a letter to his mother (Fitzwilliam). Because of the paucity of correspondence from the immediately preceding period, the date of the move is impossible to establish. SW and Charlotte appear to have been reconciled some time in the early part of 1805, and their daughter Emma Frances was born in Feb. 1806. The move to Arlington Street can be presumed to have coincided with or to have shortly followed their reconciliation. This was to be their address until the final breakdown of their marriage in early 1810.

[3] The year of this letter is suggested by SW's Camden Town address and his discussion of making his own copy of the '48'. If this copy is the one mentioned in SW to Burney, 12 Apr. [1808], the year can only be 1806 or 1807. SW's discussion of his financial problems and money owed by a 'great man' (see n. 5), strongly points to 1806, although 1807 must still be regarded as a possibility.

My dear Friend,

At length I am enabled to announce to you the good News of my having compleated the Transcript of Seb. Bach's inimitable & immortal Preludes & Fugues,[4] for which Privilege I shall always consider myself inexpressibly obliged, & particularly for the great Patience with which you have excused my unavoidable Delay in returning your valuable Book.—Had I been Master of my own Time, you would have received your Volume with many Thanks some Months ago, for if I could have devoted 4 Hours per Day to copying, I calculated that I could easily have transcribed from 6 to 8 Pages without Inconvenience; but as my Attention is by Necessity principally devoted to others, & *their* Improvement, instead of my own, I have been compelled to snatch whatever moments could be stolen out of the 24 Hours, & these were consequently irregular & uncertain.— I was however so determinedly bent upon finishing the Job, in consequence of your very kind Indulgence of so long a Loan, that it would have extremely vexed me to have quitted it without Accomplishment, & I have now one Proof among many which we daily meet, of the Advantages resulting from steady Perseverance in a rational Cause.—

As I wish that not a single Error may remain in my Manuscript, I shall request the additional Favour that you will permit me to keep the Book to the latter End of the next Week, during which Time I shall have sufficient Opportunities to revise & compare the Copy with the Original, Note by Note.—You may depend on obtaining the latter before Saturday next.

I have likewise to trust that you will pardon my Deficiency in Punctuality respecting the Kindness you did me in the pecuniary Accommodation.—The Sum would have been returned precisely at the Termination of the Month (as stated & fully intended) if a great Man,[5] who is now in Arrears £60 to me, & who gave me to expect it in the Month of *February* last, had not chosen to delay his Payment.—The Money however is as safe as if it were in my Pocket at this Moment, but still there is nothing that teazes me more than the Necessity of

[4] The two books of *Das wohltemperiertes Clavier*, BWV 846–93 (the '48') by J. S. Bach (1685–1750). Each book consists of twenty-four preludes and fugues, one for each of the major and minor keys. In his Reminiscences, SW stated that he was first introduced to the '48' by George Frederick Pinto (1785–1806); this must have been some time before 23 Mar. 1806, the date of Pinto's early death. It is apparent from SW's remarks in later letters that Graeff's copy was of the edition of around 1801 by Nägeli of Zurich. SW's manuscript copy is at BL, Add. MS 14330.

[5] Probably Justinian Casamajor (1746–1820), a wealthy businessman with property near Ridge, who is also mentioned in a number of family letters. In a letter to his mother of 1 Apr. 1806 (Fitzwilliam), SW discussed problems which had arisen from the non-payment of various amounts due to him, including £60 from Casamajor, which he had at this stage decided to write off.

the least Breach or *Delay* of an Engagement, especially with a Friend for whom I have so high & so just an Esteem as yourself.

With best Respects to Mrs Graeff & our young Friends,

believe me,
My dear Sir,
Most cordially & faithfully yours
    S Wesley

To Joseph Payne Street   Camden Town, 30 May 1806

ALS, 2 pp. (BL, Add. MS 56228)
Addressed To | Mr Street. | N. 17 | Mark Lane | Friday Morn^g | p.p. 2.^d
Pmk 30 MY 1 <80> 6

My dear Sir,

I have a little Scheme to propose, to which if you have any material Objection, I will give it up without further Argument.

My son Charles[1] has lately been so diligent & assiduous in endeavouring to improve himself in such Exercises as have appeared to me for his future Benefit, that I judge him very meritorious of what is called a Holiday or of any innocent Recreation for a few Hours on a leisure Day.—Now I think I can manage to command Wednesday, June 4.[2] & as Charles has a great Desire to hear the Tower Guns fired,[3] he has asked me to permit him to go thither that Day, to which I have consented; & my subsequent Notion was, that if you were unengaged, we might contrive to pass the Remainder of the Day entre nous trois, & what I thought of proposing was to go down to *Billingsgate*,[4] & dine upon some fresh Fish, if so be there should be any left by that Time: to stay there just as long or as short as we might find it pleasant, & then stroll towards Chalk Farm[5] (which is the best Prospect I know among the Tea-Gardens), & finally, if we were not quite sick of

---

[1] SW's son, born 25 Sept. 1793. Following a recent financial crisis, SW had been obliged to remove him from St Paul's School, and was now taking care of his education himself.

[2] The birthday of George III.

[3] It was (and is still) the custom to fire the guns at the Tower of London at noon on the sovereign's birthday.

[4] London's principal fish market, where most of the trade was done in the early hours of the morning.

[5] East of Primrose Hill, at the lower end of Haverstock Hill, not far from SW's house in Camden Town. The tea gardens may have been those attached to Chalk House Farm, an inn on the site of the present Chalk Farm Tavern on England's Lane (*Encyclopaedia of London*, under 'Chalk Farm').

one another's Company, repair to N. 9 Arlington Street, & take an unceremonious Crust of Bread & Cheese.—Here is the grand Plan of Operation, which if it meet your Suffrage, shall certainly be put into Execution.—If there were a Possibility of changing his Majesty's Birth Day from June 4. 'at 22 Minutes past 2 in the Morn',[6] I should have been glad, because Wednesday is *now* one of the Days on which I have the most oppressive Work but as I think I can engage my Assistant[7] to mount Guard for me throughout the whole of the Afternoon Business, I trust, that in Case of your Coincidence I shall be able to make all smooth on the Occasion.

Your early Opinion & Decision upon this momentous Stratagem, will oblige

My dear Sir,
Yours ever truly

S Wesley

P.S. I hope to be informed that your Son Joseph[8] is better than when we last met.

9. Arlington Street. Camden Town | Friday 30. May. 1806

To Charles Wesley Junior   Camden Town, 15 January 1807

ALS, 11 pp. (Rylands, DDWF 15/12)

Dear Charles,

I should certainly have sent you a Line long before now,[1] but have been waiting an Opportunity of accompanying it with a Copy of the Glee,[2] which you desired, as also an *Epitome*[3] (for I have not had Time to transcribe the Score) of the Responses in the Litany,[4] & I thought you would also be pleased in my adding a Copy of a new 'Dixit Dominus' for three Voices, which was performed lately at

---

[6] A quotation from 'Hurly burly, blood and thunder', a 'Burlesque Ode for the Birthday of George III' by Edward Thurlow (1731–1806), Lord Chancellor 1778–92, which SW later set for three voices. It concludes: 'This is a day for Fun and drinking | This is a day for dancing and sinking | For on this day Big George was born | At twenty three minutes past two in the morn'. Thurlow, a keen amateur musician, was the patron of R. J. S. Stevens, and is frequently mentioned in his *Recollections*. (*DNB*; Argent, *passim*).

[7] Possibly Matthew Cooke (1760/1–1829), who was SW's assistant in 1809: see SW to Smith, 23 Apr. [1809].   [8] Joseph Edward; he may have been the son mentioned in SW to Street, 18 Aug. 1801.

[1] Charles Wesley jun. was in Bath with his mother: see SW to his mother of this date (BL, Add. MS 35012, fo. 15).

[2] No doubt 'When Bacchus, Jove's Immortal Boy', a setting of a translation by Thomas Moore of an Ode by Anacreon, performed at the Society of Harmonists on 18 Dec. 1806 and subsequently published (see n. 22).   [3] i.e. a short score; not preserved.

[4] The autograph of SW's setting of the Litany Responses, dated 29 Nov. 1806, is at BL, Add. MS 71107. For plans for the first performance, see n. 41.

what is called the *Concentores Society*,[5] of which you may have heard, and which consists solely of 12 select musical Professors, each of whom is expected to produce a new Canon, and a new Glee, on whatever Day he happens to be chosen President.—My Invitation thither was as a Visitor only, from *Elliott*[6] (Master Elliott in Days of yore) who is a very amiable sensible Man, & I need not say much to you of his Skill and Taste in singing.—What will I think amuse you in the present Instance is, that at the *broaching* of this Dixit D̅n̅s̅ were aiding and assisting Mess.rs *Harrison*[7] & Greatorex,[8] together with Stevens,[9] Callcott,[10] *little Master*

---

[5] The Concentores Society was active *c.*1798–1812 and *c.*1818–1847. The autograph of SW's three-part setting of 'Dixit Dominus' discussed here (BL, Add. MS 71107, fo. 111), notes that it was 'presented & performed' at the meeting of the Concentores on 27 Dec. 1806. In his journal, R. J. S. Stevens records SW's presence on this date, but states that only the compositions of Samuel Webbe were performed: 'the rule of this Society, when any member is President for the day'. Stevens also records SW's presence at the previous meeting on 18 Dec. (Argent, 150, 291).

[6] James Elliott (1783–1856), singer and composer, chiefly of glees. He had appeared (as 'Master Elliott') as a boy treble soloist at the 1799 Birmingham festival, and had a successful later career as a bass. He was later to appear with SW as one of the soloists at the Tamworth Festival (Brown and Stratton).

[7] Samuel Harrison (1760–1812), a leading tenor of the day, well known from his appearances over the years at the Handel Commemoration, the Concert of Ancient Music, and the oratorio concerts. In 1791 he founded the Vocal Concerts with Charles Knyvett. He was also active in the world of glee singing: he was elected to membership of the Catch Club in the same year as Stevens, and was a founder member of the Glee Club (*Grove*[6]; Argent, 292–3).

[8] Thomas Greatorex (1758–1831), conductor, teacher, organist, and composer. He became a pupil of Benjamin Cooke in 1772 and in 1774 attracted the patronage of Joah Bates and of the Earl of Sandwich. He was organist of Carlisle Cathedral from 1781 to about 1784, after which he went to live at Newcastle upon Tyne. After studying singing in Italy between 1786 and 1788 he returned to London, where he established himself as a teacher of music. He succeeded Bates as conductor of the Ancient Concerts in 1793 (a post he held until his death), and was prominent as a conductor both in London and at music festivals at Birmingham, York, Derby, and elsewhere. He became organist of Westminster Abbey in 1819 and professor of organ and piano at the Royal Academy of Music on its foundation in 1822 (*Grove*[6]; Anon, 'Mr Greatorex', *QMMR* 1 (1818), 466–9).

[9] Richard John Samuel Stevens (1757–1837), English glee composer, teacher, and lecturer. He was organist at St Michael's, Cornhill (1781), the Temple Church (1786), and the Charterhouse (1796), Gresham Professor of Music (1801), and music master at Christ's Hospital (1808), where he was succeeded in 1810 by SW's friend and future son-in-law Robert Glenn. His somewhat plodding *Recollections*, a condensation of five volumes of diaries kept between 1802 and 1837, are nonetheless a valuable and detailed source of information on his activities and the various musical circles in which he moved (*Grove*[6]; Argent). For an astringent assessment of his position in the musical society of his day, see Ehrlich, *Music Profession*, 32–5.

[10] John Wall Callcott (1766–1821), organist, teacher, composer, music historian, and theorist. A noted composer of glees, he had in his youth been notorious for the single-mindedness of his approach to the annual Glee Club competitions, for which in one year he had submitted no fewer than 120 entries. In later life, his interests turned increasingly to music theory. His projected history and dictionary of music were abandoned following his mental collapse in Apr. 1808, after which he was confined to a lunatic asylum near Bristol. His daughter Elizabeth married SW's near-contemporary William Horsley in 1813 (*Grove*[6]).

Tommy,[11] cum *septem* aliis quæ nunc præscribere longum est.[12] In fine, the Verse made a great *Splash*, or as the English *French* Phrase is, a great Sensation. Old Horsefall[13] was Bawler Maximus, as usual, & he was so transported that I feared he would be seized with some mortal Spasm or other, which (as I want no more Deaths laid at my Door) I was glad to find averted.

I know not the Rules of your Harmonic Club,[14] therefore cannot determine whether they perform such a Thing as I have been writing about,[15] but if they admit Latin & Scripture among festive & Cytherean Lays,[16] & you think it would suit any of their Voices, you are quite welcome to make what Use you will of it, *only* that I should by no means like any Copies to get abroad, until it be published, (in Case I should so resolve) for various Reasons, among which the Danger (or rather the Certainty) of its being mangled & mutilated in Transcription is not the least.—You remember what a perfect Scaramouch[17] the *learned* Miss Abrams[18] made of Goosy Gander![19]

And now to the Contents of your Letter.[20] I have no Objection to my Music appearing at any of the *first-rate Shops* in Bath, (for *there*, as well as elsewhere, I presume are Orders of Dignity), but I should not like them to be set in an inferior Window, as if *soliciting* Purchase.—If the Person you mention is inclined to order a Number of Copies, either of the Voluntaries,[21] the new Glee,[22] or whatever else I may *vomit* out next, (I would have said sh—te, but the Word is already engaged

[11] Attwood.

[12] 'With seven others, whom it would take too long to describe'. In addition to those mentioned by SW, Stevens records the presence of the glee composer Reginald Spofforth (1768/70–1827) and Robert Cooke (1768–1814), organist of Westminster Abbey.

[13] James Horsfall: not otherwise identified (Argent).

[14] The Bath Harmonic Society, founded by Henry Harington (see n. 31). Charles Wesley jun. is known to have directed a concert of glees at its Ladies' Night at the Lower Assembly Rooms on 19 Dec. 1806 (programme and texts at Drew (shelfmark BY 321 A5 G555g)), and it was no doubt for a subsequent meeting of this society that SW was offering his new 'Dixit Dominus' setting.

[15] i.e. SW's setting of 'Dixit Dominus'.

[16] Cytherea was Venus, the goddess of love; SW's 'Cytherean Lays' are therefore glees on the subject of love.

[17] This use of 'scaramouch', evidently meaning a poor performance or a botched job, is not recorded in *OED*.

[18] Probably Harriett Abrams (*c*.1758–*c*.1822), the best known and most popular of three Abrams sisters who all sang professionally at this time; the others were Theodosia (*c*.1765–*post* 1834) and Eliza (*c*.1772–*c*.1830) (*Grove*⁶).

[19] Presumably SW's three-voice setting of this popular song, composed *c*.1781 and published *c*.1800.

[20] Not preserved.

[21] SW's Op. 6 organ voluntaries, the first six of which had been published individually by this time.

[22] 'When Bacchus, Jove's Immortal Boy', published as *A New Glee, for three voices . . . performed at the Society of Harmonists, on Thursday Decr 18th, 1806*, reviewed in *MM* Feb. 1807.

by Mr Geminiani)[23] & will signify his Wish either by you or otherwise, it shall be speedily complied with.

Apropos of Geminiani.—Master Jacky Owen, Arch-Deacon of York,[24] & own Brother in Law to John Beardmore Esqre[25] Crewel Manufacturer (not cruel Malefactor) Milk Street Cheapside hath lately fallen deeply in Love with Geminiani's Solos, & his Niece[26] having recommended her musical *Studies* with me, was desirous of knowing whether they were practicable in the Form they appear for the Violin? to which I ventured to answer in the Negative; but added, that I knew they were to be obtained, (altho' scarce) as adapted for a keyed Instrument by the Author himself.[27]—I also promised to get them for her if possible.—Now I really am rather at a Loss to say how, for modern Music Shops disdain such Trash, & those who love such obsolete Stuff are so bigotted to their fond Prejudices that you might as easily wrest a Bone from Cerberus,[28] or a good harmony from K-ll-y,[29]

---

[23] Francesco Geminiani (1687–1762), Italian composer, virtuoso violinist, and theorist, who after an early career in Italy settled in London in 1714 and established a considerable reputation as a violin virtuoso, composer, and teacher. In the 1730s he made two lengthy visits to Dublin and moved there permanently in 1759 (*Grove*^{6}).

[24] John Owen (1773–1824), matric. Hertford College, Oxford (1793), BA (1797), MA, Christ's College, Cambridge (1801), Archdeacon of Richmond, Yorkshire (1801), Rector of East Horsley and of St Bennet's, Paul's Wharf (1802), later Chaplain General to the Armed Forces (Venn; *GM*, 1824^2, 18).

[25] SW's reference appears to be to *Joseph* Beardmore (1745/6–1829), listed in commercial directories of the period as a wholesale hosier with premises at 38 Milk Street, Cheapside. He was a prominent Methodist who had been a personal friend of John Wesley and was one of the trustees of the City Road Chapel. He had married Mary Owen (1750–1809), presumably John Owen's sister, in 1776. Their daughters Mary (1778/9–1838) and Frances (1789/90–1868) were pupils of SW. Other Beardmores who appear in directories and membership lists at this time were probably members of the same family: Thomas Beardmore of 4 Castle Alley, Cornhill, was a contributor to the library of the Royal Institution, and George Beardmore of Crown Office Row, Temple, was elected to membership of the Madrigal Society on 13 Mar. 1810. Frances Mary Beardmore (1840–1921), a member of a later generation of the family, was married to the poet and man of letters Austin Dobson (1840–1921), and SW's two letters to Mary Beardmore are preserved with other family papers in the Austin Dobson collection at London University. Also included in this collection are some letters to John Owen (Stevenson, *City Road*, 384–5; commercial directories). [26] i.e. John Owen's niece, either Mary or Frances Beardmore.

[27] *Pièces de Clavecin, tirée des différens Ouvrages de Mr. F. Geminiani, adaptées par luy même à cet Instrument* (London, 1743, reissued c.1780), or *The Second Collection of Pieces for the Harpsichord. Taken from different Works of G. Geminiani, and adapted by Himself to that Instrument* (London, 1762) (*CPM*).

[28] In Greek mythology, the dog with three heads which guarded the entrance to Hades; here, evidently the nickname of one of SW's acquaintances. For another reference, see SW to Jacob, [?29 May 1809].

[29] The Irish tenor, composer, theatre manager, and music publisher Michael Kelly (1762–1826), best known for his Reminiscences (1826) and for having in his youth created the roles of Don Curzio and Don Basilio in Mozart's *Le nozze di Figaro*. Following his return to London in 1787 he pursued a successful career as a singer and composer of theatre music. As a composer, 'he commanded a limited but prolific vein of melodic invention and seems to have relied on others for harmony and orchestrations' (*Grove*^{6}). Thomas Moore commented in 1801 that 'Poor Mick is rather an imposer than a composer. He cannot mark the time in writing three bars of music: his understrappers, however, do all that for him'.

as persuade them to part with a Copy on any Terms.—therefore I desire your Advice & Assistance upon this Point.

I dare say that your Selection by Rauzzini[30] was a good one.—You have already discovered (I presume) that he is thoroughly versed in every Species of good Music, & that he knows & values appropriately the *everlasting Bulwarks* of Canto Fermo, as well as the Refinements of those who have since (by Degrees) almost entirely anatomized the chromatic (& even the *enharmonic*) Scale.

I am glad to hear so favourable an Account of D[r] H.'s[31] Health.—I wish we could say the same of his worthy & learned Contemporary D[r] B.[32]

With regard to a *real* Judge of Music disliking Haydn & Mozart, it is a Thing so strange to me, that I have been frequently endeavouring how to account for it.—Thus far is certain, that the Sounds which we have been *earliest* delighted with, will claim a Preference, from the very Circumstance you instance, to wit, *the Ideas annexed to those Things of which they remind us*, & for the same Reason, there are certain Strains, (even in modern Authors) which altho' not eminently beautiful, yet as they immediately bring me into the Situation where I first heard them, they exceedingly distress and torment me.

How far *Taste* in Music is inherent, I will not attempt here to enquire, but sure it is, that Taste (however acquired) may be wonderfully improved by Cultivation, & Acquaintance with the best Authors; & I have remarked, that even those who have in Words reprobated all modern Innovations in musical Style, yet when they came to *write*, imperceptibly slipped into several of the very Phrases with which they professed to wage War.

Haydn & Mozart must be heard often before they are thoroughly understood, (as it strikes me) even by those who have heard *much* Music of more *gradual* Modulation; but I do think, that when the Ear & Mind become perfectly habituated to their rapid Successions of Harmony, the Feast is rich indeed, & the *Surprize* is still maintained, notwithstanding *Familiarity*, which to me is a very extraordinary Circumstance.

---

[30] Venanzio Rauzzini (1746–1810), Italian soprano castrato, composer, and harpsichordist. He moved to London from Italy in 1774 and sang regularly at the King's Theatre from 1774 to 1777. He then moved to Bath, where he managed concerts at the New Assembly Rooms (*Grove*[6]; M. Sands, 'Venanzio Rauzzini—Singer, Composer, Traveller', *MT* 94 (1953), 15–19, 108–11).

[31] Henry Harington, MD (1727–1816), doctor, musician, and author, matric. Queen's College Oxford (1745); BA (1749), MA (1752), MD (1772). While at Oxford he joined an amateur musical society founded by William Hayes, the Professor of Music, membership of which was restricted to those who could read music at sight. He set up in medical practice at Wells in 1753 and moved to Bath in 1771, where in addition to continuing to practise medicine he became in turn an alderman, magistrate, and mayor, and founded the Bath Harmonic Society. Although an amateur, he was a noted composer of glees, many of which appear in the anthologies of the period, and one of which is still known as a hymn tune under the alternative titles 'Retirement' and 'Harington' (*DNB*; *Grove*[6]). [32] Burney.

You speak of a Movement in Handel's original MS.[33] I have lately seen a very curious Original of Marcello's Psalms,[34] which become of Course more valuable from their being almost impossible to read.—They were placed upon a Desk before a young Friend of ours, who was wholly puzzled, & *no Marvel* (as J. W.[35] would say) for really they might have made *Argus*[36] stare to no Purpose.

By the Way I think very moderately of Marcello, as far as Spirit & Effect are concerned.—His Writing is chaste; his Style generally solemn, & his Harmonies occasionally rich—but he wants the Sweetness of Steffani,[37] the Strength of Purcell,[38] & certainly the Fire of Handel.—If I am not mistaken, Boyce[39] thought that Marcello has been over-rated.—Whoever thinks so, I am quite of his Mind.

Now to the Business of the Litany.—Little Master Tommy, altho' he has been a Year or *two* (at least) the doughty Organist of Paul's Church,[40] yet, it seems, has never studied those Parts of the Church Service called Rubricks, one of which directs that the Litany is to be read or sung on all Sundays, Wednesdays, & Fridays throughout the Year.—Christmas-Day, you may remember, happened on a Thursday: therefore the Consequence was that no Litany was to be had for Love or Money, the latter of which I could not offer, & the former, among Musicians & Church Dignitaries I was not Fool enough to expect.[41]

However, to do Justice to the Sub-Dean, & Honour to myself *all under one*, I must observe, that he wrote me a very handsome Excuse for the Disappointment,

---

[33] Possibly one of the collection of Handel autographs owned by Richard, Viscount Fitzwilliam (1745–1816), to which Charles had access.

[34] Benedetto Marcello (1686–1739), Italian composer, writer, and theorist. The *Psalms* referred to here were his settings of the first fifty psalms in paraphrases by his friend G. A. Giustianini, published in Venice in eight volumes between 1724 and 1726, which became widely known and went into several subsequent editions, including an English one of 1757. SW's 'very curious original', whether an autograph or a first edition, has not been identified.   [35] John Wesley.

[36] In Greek mythology, a monster with a hundred eyes.

[37] Agostino Steffani (1654–1728), Italian composer.

[38] Henry Purcell (1659–1695), English composer.

[39] The English composer William Boyce (1711–79), who had known both SW and Charles as boys, and whose views would have been well known to them.

[40] Attwood had been organist of St Paul's Cathedral since 1796.

[41] As is clear from a letter from SW to his mother of Dec. 1806 (Rylands, DDWes 6/50), the original plan had been to perform SW's setting of the Litany Responses on Christmas Day 1806, along with the Sanctus setting of his brother Charles: 'I wanted to have found the Sanctus of my Brother, which he wrote, & wished to have performed at St Paul's—this I think may be easily done, on Christmas Day, if I can but get at it in Time, & that must be soon, because Attwood has been very urgent for my *Litany*, which I have now sent him, & which he is so desirous of having well-performed, that he chuses to have it well studied previously.—This is kind, & handsome; & I wish the same by the *Sanctus* in Question.' SW here explains why the projected Christmas Day performance failed to take place. The Litany Responses were first performed on Easter Day (29 Mar.): see SW to Charles, 21 Mar. 1807. Charles's Sanctus has not been traced.

& a Panegyric upon the Composition (which it seems he had heard in private) & added his Testimony of *Approbation* concerning the Manner in which it was produced.

Attwood has since been anxious to have it sung, on *any* Sunday I may appoint. —I shew him my Indifference upon this Head, by leaving it from Time to Time without fixing any Day—But he means very well, tho' occasionally a Marplot, & one never can be thoroughly angry with an honest Blunderer.

All I regretted was, the Disappointment of some People, who I know went to Church on Purpose.—It only remains now with me to perform the said Article, together with your Sanctus, whenever most convenient to myself.

I hope that D[r] Shepherd[42] is recovered of his Gout.—You remember my Father's speech to Petit Andrews[43]—'M[r] Andrews, pray where did you pick up your Greek? I thought that a Man of Fashion had nothing to do with Greek.' So I say, 'Where did D[r] Shepherd pick up his Gout? I thought that a Man of Temperance had nothing to do with Gout.'

He is a very sensible (& evidently a learned) Man, with a Degree of Energy & Originality which to me were excessively interesting: he is just the Man whom I could hear talk for four Hours together, & be sorry that he would not talk *six*.

I send herewith a few Lines to M[r] Bowen,[44] which you will forward at your first convenient Opportunity.

Pray give my old Love & good Will in return to M[r] Millgrove,[45] & ask him whether he remembers my pestering him about a Solo of Giardini, beginning[46]

You are very sarcastic (tho' very just) about a certain English-German-Musician-Divine.[47]—You describe him *between Bath & Bristol*: is this to express his halting between the Love of this World & the next?—I do not wonder that

---

[42] Dr Edward Sheppard (1731–1813) of Chatham Row, Bath, an old friend of the Wesleys, and a well-known and somewhat eccentric figure in Bath. A number of letters from him to SW's sister Sarah are preserved at Rylands; in one, dated 16 Nov. 1804 (DDWF 26/66), he proposed marriage to her.

[43] James Pettit Andrews (*c*.1737–1797), magistrate, historian, and antiquarian, author of *History of Great Britain connected with the Chronology of Europe from Caesar's Invasion to the Accession of Edward VI* (1794–5) and *History of Great Britain from the death of Henry VIII to the Accession of James VI of Scotland* (1796); he also contributed many papers on topographical subjects to *Archaeologia* and *GM* (*DNB*).   [44] Not identified: evidently a family friend in Bath.

[45] Not identified: evidently a family friend in Bath.

[46] The Sonata no. 4 in A of his *Sei Sonate*, Op. 1.

[47] Not certainly identified, but probably Latrobe.

not only musical Professors, but *all* Professors 'stare at him, & know not what to make of his odd way of Humour.'—

I do not think if we had seen St Paul personating *Punch*, we should have extremely respected his Apostleship.—I would have a Tom T—dman remain a Tom T—dman, & not carry on the Perfumery Trade at the same Time.

I called on Gray the Organ Builder,[48] who has been closely confined by reason of an Accident he met in coming out of his Carriage by which he has hurt his Leg so as to have been laid up for this Month past.—The organ of Mr Hoare[49] cannot be finished (in Consequence of this Mischance) for some Weeks to come, therefore, of Course, the Remuneration due to you[50] will be deferred till this Event shall take Place.

John Cramer[51] has lately sent me some charming Scraps of his for the Piano Forte, among which is a *Toccata*, which if you can get at Bath, I think I can answer that you will be much delighted with it.—[52] The Subject is quite in an Organ Style, & conducted throughout in the most Cantabile Way, altho' very difficult in various Passages, from the great Number of double Semiquavers in the Bass: but it is a Nut worth the cracking.

If Fame & Flattery would make a Man fat, Sir John Falstaff would be a Shrimp to me, as far as musical *Flummery* is concerned.—My Nerves having been (thank

---

[48] William Gray.

[49] Very probably Henry Hoare of Mitcham (1750–1828), senior partner in the banking firm of Henry Hoare and Co. If so, the organ mentioned is almost certainly the one built by Gray in 1807 for Hoare's daughter Lydia Elizabeth in advance of her marriage the following year to Sir Thomas Dyke Acland (1787–1871), and installed at their home at Killerton House, near Exeter. Thirty years later, during his time as organist of Exeter Cathedral, SW's son Samuel Sebastian taught Lady Acland; his two sets of *Three Pieces for a Chamber Organ* (1838, published 1842) are dedicated to her ([Henry Peregrine Rennie Hoare], *Hoare's Bank: A Record 1672–1955: The Story of a Private Bank* (London, 1955), 41–2; Paul Chappell, *Dr S. S. Wesley, 1810–1876: Portrait of a Victorian Musician* (Great Wakering, 1977), 39–40; *DNB*, under 'Acland, Thomas Dyke').   [50] CW's commission for recommending Gray to Hoare.

[51] Johann Baptist Cramer (1771–1858), composer, pianist, and publisher, the son of Wilhelm Cramer (1746–99). He studied with J. S. Schroeter from 1780 to 1783 and then for one year with Clementi, who exerted a decisive influence on his musical character. He made his London début in 1781, and quickly established himself as an outstanding performer. He made extensive foreign tours in 1788–91 and 1799–1800. After 1800 his career was almost entirely in England, although he made another tour in 1816–18. His playing was highly influential on several generations of pianists, and Beethoven regarded him as the finest pianist of his day. As a prolific composer, mostly of piano music, he liked to regard himself as a latter-day Mozartian: *Grove*[6] describes his music as combining 'a conservative bias with the most advanced, idiomatically pianistic passage-work' and as 'nearly always skilful, pleasant and sophisticated'. He entered the music publishing business in 1805 (*Grove*[6]).

[52] *A Collection of Rondos, Airs with Variations and Toccata*, published in separate numbers between 1805 and 1807 (*Grove*[6]). The Toccata in G (No. 7 in the collection) had been advertised in *The Times* for 13 Nov. 1806 (Thomas B. Milligan and Jerald Graue, *Johann Baptist Cramer (1771–1850): A Thematic Catalogue of his Works* (Stuyvesant, NY, 1994), item 12.05).

God) in a less agitated State for some Months past than I have known them to be for Years, the Consequence is, that I have been enabled to bear the Bustle of Society with much less Perturbation of Spirits than heretofore, so that I have frequently mingled in those Sort of public Parties, wherein alone a Man is likely to be talked of *to any Purpose*, that is, where he hath the Opportunity, (if the Will be consentient) of opening whatever there may be of Mind or of Genius belonging to him, & where he is sure of being heard by the candid as well as the envious Critic.—

I attended the first Meeting of the Harmonists Society,[53] (to whom I presented the Glee as you will see by the Title), & Stevens, who is, as Madan[54] would call him, 'a mighty gentlemanly Man' soon after dinner proposed to the President[55] my giving them a Piece on the Piano Forte (which is an unusual Thing at a merely Glee Party) & which Hint was received with a great Fuss of Clapping & the usual Concomitants.—I was in a very good Humour, & played much to my own Satisfaction.[56]

On Sunday last,[57] Carnaby[58] & myself went down together to Parson Barry[59] at Dulwich, where we met the most hospitable Reception.—There were 9 Guests invited besides ourselves, & most of them very sensible, agreeable People. You know what a very clever Musician Carnaby is, & he gave us some vocal Compositions of his which were highly finished, & extremely delightful.—He sang among the *Rest*, one which begins 'Man can thy Lot no brighter Soul allow'[60]

---

[53] A small glee club founded in 1794 by R. J. S. Stevens and three of his friends, which met in alternate weeks during the winter for dinner and glees. The meeting in question was the one on 18 Dec., when SW's glee 'When Bacchus, Jove's Immortal Boy' was performed.

[54] Presumably Martin Madan (1756–1809), son of SW's godfather the Revd Martin Madan (1725–90) (Falconer Madan, *The Madan Family and Maddens in Ireland and England: A Historical Account* (Oxford, 1933), 118–19).   [55] Probably the Duke of Sussex (1773–1843), sixth son of George III.

[56] R. J. S. Stevens recorded this occasion in his *Recollections*: 'Tuesday, Dec. 18th, was the first meeting of the Harmonists Society this Season. Mr Samuel Wesley was one of our Visitors. After dinner, being perfectly collected, and not in the least flushed with liquor (his usual practise at this time of his life) he played on the Piano Forte, some of the most ingenious and astonishing Combinations of *Harmony*, that I ever heard. By way of Finale, *to his Extemporary*, he took the burthen of, *O strike the harp* [a popular Trio by Stevens], and made as simple and pleasing a movement on its subject, that we were all delighted. A rare instance of his wonderful abilities' (Argent, 150, 293).   [57] 11 Jan.

[58] William Carnaby (1772–1839), admitted Trinity Hall, Cambridge (1805), Mus.B. (1805), Mus.D. (1808), was a chorister at the Chapel Royal under James Nares and Edmund Ayrton and was subsequently organist of Eye and Huntingdon before settling in London some time before 1808. He composed a good deal of vocal and piano music (*Grove*[5]; *DNB*; Venn).

[59] Probably Edward Barry, MD, DD (1759–1822), religious and medical writer. The son of a Bristol doctor, he gained his MD at St Andrews, but 'always preferring theology to physic', was later ordained into the Church of England. He was for several years curate of St Marylebone and 'one of the most popular preachers in London'. He was also grand chaplain to the Freemasons (*DNB*). He was probably one of the two Barry brothers mentioned in SW to Street, 18 Oct. 1799.   [60] Not traced.

which he says you much approved, & he boasts every where of your good Word.—He carries himself pretty high among *ordinary* Professors, & there are but few among them by whose Praise he is gratified.

I have promised to go on Sunday next[61] to the Abbey,[62] after which I am to dine with Robt Cooke,[63] the Organist, the Son of the D^r whom you remember.—He is very knowing in Music, & is a pleasant Man when you get at him, tho' he is rather shy & reserved at first.—Callcott having heard that I am to play at the Abbey on Sunday has engaged John Cramer to come too, so that I must mind my P's & Q's in such 'worshipful Society.'—The Touch of the Organ[64] is remarkably good; indeed rather too *light* for me.—It is a complete contrast with St *Paul's*,[65] where you may remember that the Keys are all as stubborn as Fox's Martyrs,[66] & bear almost as much buffetting.

This letter reminds me of the Story of the Man who was asked to sing after Dinner in Company.—He was a long while before he could be prevailed on to comply, but when he began, he continued for six Hours.—

There was a Time when I was very fond of writing long Letters; but it was when I had few of the Cares of this Life to distract or disturb my Attention.—The Heart was light & gay, & every Path was *Bowling Green*:[67] but when the Mind has its Way hedged up with the Thorns & Brambles of Trouble, Disappointment, & Loss, & must often plunge, nolens volens into the *Ruts* of pecuniary Embarrassment, it is Odds but that a great Majority of the Brains become confused, if not oppressed into Stupidity, or sublimated into Madness.

When two Persons, each wishing well to the other, are separated in Distance by Circumstances, epistolary Communication being the only possible one, the Trouble vanishes in the Consideration of a mutual *Agrément*, one to the Writer, & the other to the Reader.

The domestic Occurrences, of Births, Deaths, Marriages, Promotions &c in the Vicinity of Marybone,[68] which have occurred lately, I mean to recount in my Mother's Letter, to whom I shall write, having finished this.[69]

---

[61] 18 Jan. [62] i.e. Westminster Abbey.

[63] Robert Cooke (1768–1814) had succeeded his father Benjamin Cooke (1734–93) as organist of St Martin in the Fields in 1793, and had become Organist and Master of the Choristers at Westminster Abbey (posts his father had also held) in 1802.

[64] By Christopher Shrider, built for the coronation of George II in 1727 (Boeringer, iii. 258).

[65] By 'Father' Smith, *c*.1700 (Boeringer, ii. 152–7).

[66] *Actes and Monuments of these latter perillous days, touching matters of the Church*, popularly known as the *Book of Martyrs*, by John Foxe (1516–87) first published in Strasburg in 1559 and in an English translation in 1563 (*OCEL*).

[67] The source of this quotation or proverbial saying has not been traced.

[68] i.e. Marylebone, where SW's mother, brother, and sister lived. By this time they had moved the short distance from Chesterfield Street to Great Woodstock Street.

[69] SW's letter of this date to his mother is at BL, Add. MS 35012, fo. 15.

Dr Callcott, who is indefatigable in searching out every Information he can obtain concerning Musick, & having conceived a high Notion of me as a *Greek* Scholar (which shows how People may deceive themselves) has besought me to peruse a Greek Author, (Aristoxenes)[70] for the Purpose of discovering if possible whether Rameau[71] is not mistaken in asserting that the ancient Radicals of B, C, D, & E (the Tetrachord) were G, C, G, C, (thus making the Mode *Major*) or whether the Ancients did not consider their Fundamentals to be rather E, A, D, A, & so the Mode was originally Minor.—Whether I shall be able to poke out any satisfactory Intelligence from the Author in question is to me a Doubt, but I have promised him what Assistance I can render, & he is so good a Creature that no one but a morose & savage Mind could bear to refuse him any Request it could reasonably grant.

I went yesterday to Dr Crotch's[72] Lecture:[73] it was upon the distinct Merits of Pleyel,[74] Kozeluch,[75] & Mozart.—The *last* of the three, he much underrated, in *my* Opinion, & the *first*, he much exceeded the Truth in panegyrising.—To Kozeluch he appeared to me to render exact Justice, & impartial Praise.

His playing a Score is very extraordinary.—I cannot understand how he manages to play *all* the Parts of a Symphony of Mozart so that you do not miss the Absence of any one Instrument, whether stringed or wind.

I remain in Haste
(tho' certainly not in *short*)
Dear Charles
Yours very truly,

S Wesley

Camden Town | 15 Jany 1807

[70] Aristoxenus (b. 375–360 BC), Greek music theorist, parts of whose *Harmonics* were included in Marcus Meibomius's *Antiquae musicae auctores septem, Graece et Latine*, 2 vols. (Amsterdam, 1652), from which source SW no doubt intended to study them. For Burney's discussion of Aristoxenus, see *History*, i. 441–5; Mercer, i. 349–52.

[71] Jean-Philippe Rameau (1683–1764), whose *Traité de l'harmonie reduite à ses principes naturels* (Paris, 1722; English trans., London, 1737) and *Nouveau système de music théorique* (Paris, 1737) were both highly influential (*Grove*^{6}).

[72] William Crotch (1775–1847) had begun his musical career as a child prodigy. After early concert tours and a period in Cambridge as assistant to John Randall, the aged Professor of Music, he moved in 1788 to Oxford. He was appointed organist at Christ Church, Oxford in 1790, and on the death of Philip Hayes in 1797 became Professor of Music. Between 1800 and 1804 he gave several courses of lectures on music in Oxford, the success of which led to him being invited to lecture at the recently founded Royal Institution of Great Britain. He moved to London late in 1805, and gave no fewer than five courses of lectures at the Royal Institution in 1806 (J. Rennert, *William Crotch* (Lavenham, 1975); Kassler, 'Lectures', 15).

[73] This was the eleventh of a course of thirteen lectures at the Royal Institution which Crotch had started late in 1806. The texts of Crotch's lectures are at NRO, MSS 11063–77, 11228–33, and Col. 7/43–53 (Kassler, 'Lectures', 15).   [74] Ignace Joseph Pleyel (1757–1831), French composer.

[75] Leopold Kozeluch (1747–1818), Bohemian composer.

To Charles Wesley Junior   Camden Town, 21 March 1807

AL, 4 pp. (Rylands, MA 9787)

> Camden Town
> March 21. 1807.

Dear Charles

I am perfectly convinced that you would not grudge the Postage of a Letter from me, & perhaps it is this very consideration which has rendered me less willing to *extort Money*. The Packet which you formerly received I paid the Carriage for at the White Horse Cellar, Piccadilly, where it was booked, & if they charged you for it, they were Thieves.—I wish to be certified of this Fact.

You know too well the Miseries I have undergone, & the irreparable Losses I have sustained to believe that I am desirous of *Length of Days*. The Jews were great Coveters of Longevity, & David seems dissatisfied with Providence when he says 'behold thou hast made my Days as it were a Span long'[1]—B^p Warburton[2] has gone about to prove that they had no Belief in a State after Death.—I suppose you would not dare to contradict a Bishop!

Whilst I am above Ground I must be employed *wholly*, which is my only Resource against Insanity, & altho' I often am obliged to bustle about with a crazy Carcase, *as if nothing was the Matter*, & am often almost ready to faint with Fatigue, yet these Inconveniences I prefer to the Horrors of reflecting on my Sacrifice of Peace, Liberty, Honour, & Independence to——one of the most unworthy of all Mortals.

I am too far advanced in the Vale of Years to say with any Probability—'forsan & haec olim meminisse juvabit.'[3]—but—

Here endeth the croaking Page.[4]

I am at present engaged in a literary Business with Mr Nares of the Museum[5] (Dr Nares's Son whom you remember of old, who *was* a notable Puppy, peeping

---

[1] Ps. 39: 6.

[2] William Warburton (1698–1779), divine and man of letters, ordained 1727, successively preacher at Lincoln's Inn (1746), Prebendary of Gloucester (1753), King's chaplain (1754), Prebendary of Durham (1755), Dean of Bristol (1757), Bishop of Gloucester (1759), and the author of many works of theological controversy. SW's reference is to *The Divine Legation of Moses* (1738–41), his most celebrated work (*DNB*; *OCEL*).

[3] 'Perhaps one day we will take pleasure in recalling even these experiences' (Virgil, *Aeneid*, 1. 203).

[4] This remark concludes the first page of the letter.

[5] Robert Nares (1753–1829), philologist, BA Christ Church, Oxford (1775), MA (1778), Canon Residentiary of Lichfield (1798), Prebendary of St Paul's Cathedral (1798), Archdeacon of Stafford (1801); Assistant Librarian in the Department of Manuscripts of the British Museum (1795), Keeper of Manuscripts (1799–1807); FSA (1795), FRS (1804). His principal work was his *A Glossary, or Collection*

thro' a quizzing Glass, long before such things were authorised by Custom, & if Report say true, as accomplished a whoremaster as any learned Man of his Times, but is now ranked among the most worthy & enlightened characters, equally admired & respected).[6]—What the Subject is, must not be disclosed until its publication announce the Murder of its own Accord.[7]—If we live a few Weeks longer, the whole will be explained.

My Litany is *fixed* for next Sunday week,[8] (Easter Day) at St Paul's. I shall neither be surprised nor much embarrassed if the Organ Blower should *choose to observe the Sabbath* just at the most interesting Point of the Music.—My dear Sir, I am so hardened *by the great Vexations*, that my Soul is become *Brawn*; you may pull & tear at it with all your Might, but it jerks back again to its old Place, like a Piece of India Rubber.

A Chaunt which I have cobbled up for the Occasion (which very likely will *not* be done, since I had rather it *should*), I here add.[9]

Poor Master Tommy has lost his Brother,[10] who died only a few Hours after his Arrival from Ireland, whence he came, it seems, principally to see him.

About a Fortnight ago, I met our merry S[t] Andrew, La Trobe by Appointment at Beardmores. Master Jacky Owen was with us, who was in excellent Humour, & launched out some shrewd sayings in his old lack-a-dazy Manner.—I know not

of Words, Phrases, Names, and Allusions to Customs, Proverbs, &c. which have been thought to require Illustration in the Works of the English Authors, particularly Shakespeare and his Contemporaries (1822). He was editor of *The British Critic* from its beginning in 1793 to 1813 (*DNB*). For the 'literary work', see n. 7.

[6] James Nares (1715–83), composer, organist, and teacher, organist of York Minster (1735), organist and composer of the Chapel Royal (1756), Mus. D. Cambridge (1757), Master of the Children of the Chapel Royal (1757). He had a 'pleasant but slender talent for composition', chiefly exercised in keyboard and church music, and wrote treatises on singing and keyboard playing (*Grove⁶*).

[7] SW's lengthy anonymous review of Callcott's *A Musical Grammar*, which appeared in *The British Critic*, 29 (1807), 398–407, 597–605. This remark confirms the identification of SW as its author made by A. F. C. Kollmann in *Quarterly Musical Register*, 1 (1812), 5, 129.　　　　　[8] 29 Mar.

[9] This chant also appears fully written out at RCM, MS 4021, fo. 1.

[10] The viola player Francis Attwood (1775–1807) (*BD*).

whether he speaks German, but I rather imagine not, otherwise our Sacerdotal Orpheus would probably have given him a Broadside of Wouchten Sprouchten denderhofften splanchshags, to the great Edification of all the Auditors who could be moved 'by Concert of sweet Sounds.'[11]—We had some Music from his Collection,[12] in the Evening, but Owen cried out that it was desperate dull, for to say the Truth, La T. had selected all the most lachrymose, whining, catterwauling Melodies he could stumble upon, and among both Germans & Italians we know there is great plenty to be found, whenever they can fall foul upon the Words 'Miserere mei Deus'[13] 'Quis est homo qui non fleret,'[14] or any Sense that has Relation either to Penitence or the Crucifixion.

I not only agree with Dr Boyce, that chromatic Subjects produce the worst Fugues, but I go further, I think that they *generally* produce the worst Melodies in *Descant for the Voice.*—The *best* Italian Melodies consist of diatonic Intervals, & unless deep Sorrow or acute Pain are to be expressed, I cannot subscribe to the Propriety of wire-drawing the chromatic Scale, till your Hair stands on end & then calling it *Melody*—As Johnson said of another Subject, 'Sir, you had as well call it Geometry.'[15]

And that *the deepest* Sorrow may be completely expressed without one chromatic Semitone, we need go no further than the Air 'Behold & see', in the Messiah, which I take to be the most finished Specimen of the simple sublime in Melody that ever was produced.

Dr Coghlan,[16] Mr Bowen's Friend is in Town, & wishes my Opinion of a Piano-Forte which is to be disposed of at a Sale.—I have engaged to look at it, but these Things are very hazardous Purchases, just vamped up to serve a present Turn, & falling to Pieces in a Month.—This reminds me of a Story of old Thompson[17] the Music-Seller in St Paul's Church Yard, who, when a Gentleman applied to him to purchase for him the finest Cremona[18] he could procure, said 'Psha, psha, don't

---

[11] *Merchant of Venice*, v. i. 84.

[12] *A Selection of Sacred Music from the Works of the Most Eminent Composers of Germany and Italy*, the first part of which was published in 1806.   [13] 'God have mercy on me', the first line of Ps. 51.

[14] 'Who is the man who would not weep': part of the text of the Stabat Mater, a medieval hymn describing Mary standing at the foot of the cross. It was sung at this time as an Office hymn on the Friday after Passion Sunday, and was a favourite text for more extended musical treatments.

[15] The source of this quotation has not been traced.

[16] Lucius Coghlan (*c*.1750–1833), admitted to Trinity College, Dublin (1768), BA (1773), BD and DD (1797). He was a prominent Freemason, and later principal chaplain of the United Grand Lodge of England (Burtchaaell and Sadlier, *Alumni Dublinienses* (Dublin, 1935)).

[17] One of a family of musical instrument makers, music sellers, and publishers who had a shop at 75, St Paul's Church Yard from around 1746 to 1805 (Grove^6; Humphries and Smith).

[18] i.e. a violin from Cremona, a town in Lombardy famed for the quality of its stringed instruments.

be such a silly Man—a Cremona!—why they ax 50 or 60 Guineas for an old worm-eaten Fiddle, full of Cracks & Joins from Top to Bottom.—No, no—take my Advice—don't be humbugged by any of them Sharpers; do as I tell ye—buy a *New One*, & then you know the *Wear* of it.'

By the Way, having mentioned Melody, do you know *Crescentini's Ariettes* (or Canzonets?)[19]—as poor Jonathan[20] would say, 'Beshrew me, but they are gallant Things.'—but they are very far from *gall*ant: they are however gall*ant*: they are sweet gentle Melodies, & accompanied by much better *Basses* than Italians generally write.—Look at them—I am sure you will find them useful to your vocal scholars.

To George Polgreen Bridgetower

[Camden Town],
15 June [1807][1]

ALS, 1 p. (Upper Room, L-148)
Addressed To | M[r] Bridgtower | John Street | S[t] James's Square | N. 3
Pmk 16 JU 180

Dear Sir

I am extremely sorry that I was under a Necessity of going out on Saturday Evening last,[2] but shall depend upon the Pleasure of your Company *next* Saturday,[3] when I hope you will come early that we may have a long Gossip.—I have been so occupied with correcting the Copyist's Blunders in Barthelemon's Oratorio[4] that I have not been able as yet to do Justice to your Manuscript,[5] which I will examine at the first Leisure Moment with the utmost Attention.—

In full Expectation of seeing you on the Day above-mentioned,

I remain, Dear Sir
most truly yours

S Wesley

Monday June 15

---

[19] *12 Ariette italiane* (Vienna, 1797) by Girolamo Crescentini (1762–1846), Italian mezzo-soprano castrato and composer.   [20] No doubt Jonathan Battishill.

[1] The year is given by 15 June falling on a Monday, the partly legible postmark, and the reference to the forthcoming performance of Barthélemon's oratorio (n. 4).   [2] 13 June 1807.

[3] 20 June 1807.

[4] *The Nativity*, the first part of which was to be performed at Barthélemon's concert at Hanover Square Rooms on 19 June, at which SW played the organ (*The Times*, 19 June 1807).

[5] Not identified.

To [William] Marriott[1]   Camden Town, 3 November 1807

ALS, 1 p. (Rylands, DDWF 15/13)
Addressed   To | Mr Marriott jun^r | Broad Street | Cornhill | Paid 2^d

Sir

I was rather surprized To-Day on applying at the Bank for half a Year's Dividend at being contradicted by the Clerk when I demanded the Interest of £1420—which I believe will be found to be the real Amount of my Due, as I have made no Alteration whatever in my Stock since you last sold out for me.—The first Money was £50, & the second, £30, which I rather think will appear by a Memorandum in your Books.[2]—I am at a Loss to guess how this Mistake could happen, & shall be obliged to you for a Line which may tend to explain it—I knew that Dispute at the Office would *then* answer no good End, therefore accepted £25=7=8 (which I was *assured* was right,) but concerning which being far from satisfied, I though necessary to make this Application to you upon the Subject.—

I remain
Sir
Yours very obediently
    S Wesley

Camden Town | Nov. 3. 1807

To Joseph Payne Street   Camden Town, [9 November 1807][1]

AL, 2 pp. (BL, Add. MS 56228)
Addressed   To | Mr Street | Mark Lane | 17
Pmk   9 No

My dear Sir

My Friend Madan[2] used to maintain in Argument that there is a physical Perverseness in Things, which very frequently crosses & defeats our best arranged Plans, & our most laudable Purposes.—

---

[1] William Marriott junior, a stockbroker and family friend. His father, William Marriott senior (1753–1815), was a close associate of John Wesley and was one of his executors; several letters to him from SW's sister Sarah are at Rylands (Stevenson, *City Road*, 182–3).

[2] Although SW's meaning is not entirely clear, he appears to state that he was expecting to receive £30 as the half-yearly dividend on his £1,420 of stock, £50 being the amount he had received before Marriott had sold some of his holding on his behalf.

[1] The month and year are given by SW's 'Monday morning', the incomplete postmark, and SW's Camden Town address.   [2] Probably Martin Madan (1756–1809), rather than his father.

55

I do not implicitly accede to this Doctrine, but am rather inclined to believe that we are apt to attribute the Cause of our Want of Patience to an existing Deficiency in Rerum Naturâ, & that our general Notions of Good & Evil are mostly settled by our Perceptions of Gratification or Disappointment.—Locke has somewhere said that we estimate Good & Evil by our Sensations of Pleasure & Pain, which by no Means proves that we are truly acquainted with their real & essential Constitution, abstractedly considered.[3]

Pope (or rather Ld Bolingbroke)[4] you know has endeavoured to reconcile us to the *few* Calamities which await us from the Cradle to the Grave, by declaring that it is our Duty to believe.

'All partial Evil, universal Good.'[5]—Which I take to be a very pacifying & convenient Proposition, altho' I have my Doubts whether it may not be more readily acceded to when we have just gained £30,000 in the Lottery, than in a Paroxysm of Gout or Stone.

What could have tempted me to being a moral & metaphysical Essay, I can hardly guess, unless it was this Sheet of *Fool's Cap* Paper which happened first to come to Hand, & which I being too lazy to divide, (for you must know I am writing in Bed) I felt as if it deserved something frightful & tedious to make it look grander.—

However I believe upon second Thoughts that the *Subject* of my Discourse originated in the odd & vexatious See-Saw Engagements we have been mutually making for so long, without as yet having vanquished our opposing Destiny.—To make Matters more agreeable, I have been considerably unwell for these last few Days, & on Saturday Night so very ill as to be precluded from officiating at Covent Garden Church[6] yesterday, as also from performing an Engagement at Brompton, where I was to have passed the Day among some Friends purposely invited to give me the Meeting.[7] I am still very queer & relaxed, & my Progress To-Day must determine whether or no I can have the Happiness of meeting you To-morrow according to your Arrangement & my own Wish.—I will however put the Matter sufficiently out of Dou<bt> to prevent your experiencing any *chronical* Inconvenience.— My Conditions are these:—If it be in my Power to be with you, I will be in Mark Lane as near 4 as possible, & if I should be later than 10 Minutes after, or a Quarter at the outside, you may safely conclude my Incapability of attending you.

I have frequently felt (when much indisposed) so sudden & unexpected an Alteration for the better, just when it has enable me to keep an Engagement I have

---

[3] Locke, *An Essay Concerning Human Understanding*, bk. II, ch. 20, paras. 1–2.

[4] SW's remark reflects the view commonly held at the time that Pope's *Essay on Man* (1734) was inspired by the philosophical writings of Viscount Bolingbroke (1678–1751).

[5] *Essay on Man*, Epistle 1, i. 292.

[6] i.e. St Paul's, Covent Garden, where SW may have been deputizing for Callcott, who was the organist.   [7] The nature and purpose of this meeting are not known.

been loth to forego, that I never sacrifice the Hope of Performance till the Time has failed for attempting it.—I will therefore not despair in the present Instance, & try what Quiet & Nursing will effect To-Day for the Attainment of my Wishes.—

In case I should be disappointed To-morrow, it just occurs to me to enquire if you can obtain Information for me of the exact Address of Lady Dacre[8] (somewhere near Blackheath), the Rev[d] M[r] Lock, who has the Living of Lee;[9]— Sir Francis Baring,[10] & Thomson Bonar Esq[re].[11]—All of whose Residences are doubtless in the Court Guide,[12] of which I am not possest, 'tho it is a Book that every one should have who has any Business in England.—But I will have it for the next Year—if I do not forget to buy it.

I was highly pleased by some Lines of Colman[13] which I read Yesterday in Bell's Weekly Messenger, entitled 'A Reckoning with Time;'[14]—Pray look at them: —I have not for a long while seen a Collection of Verses more *uniformly* witty & pointed.—I am told that they appeared in the Morning Post of the Saturday or Friday preceding, which I can scarcely credit, as I have not met with any Thing in that Paper for six Months past either rational or interesting, except the Details of the Nobility's Routs & Concerts, & the State of the Health & Bowels of the Royal Family. (admitting they have any.)

You have heard of the Gentleman whose Philosophy induced him to blow his Brains out because it was too much Trouble for him to pull his Stocking off.—As I am just now about to put on mine, I will with your Leave meditate upon the *Rationale* of his Conclusions on the Subject, bidding you for a short Time only, (as I hope)

Adieu

Camden Town | Monday Morning 9 <o'Cl>ock

---

[8] Gertrude Brand, Baroness Dacre (1750–1819). In fact, she lived at 2 Chesterfield Street, Mayfair, with a country property at Lee, Kent (*Burke's Peerage*, under 'Hampden'; *GM* 1819[2], 371).

[9] George Lock (1780/1–1864), Rector of Lee, Kent, from 1803 to his death (Foster). He does not appear in the 1807 *Court Guide*.

[10] Sir Francis Baring, Bart (1740–1810), banker and MP, of 33 Hill Street, Berkeley Square (*DNB*).

[11] No doubt Thompson Bonar, who was elected a Governor of the Foundling Hospital on 30 Dec. 1801; at that time he lived at Old Bethlem (Nichols and Wray, 391).

[12] *Boyle's New Fashionable Court and County Guide and Town Visiting Directory* included listings of the upper echelons of society, both alphabetically and street by street. It was thus a useful publication for those soliciting subscriptions or sending out publicity, and SW's enquiry was no doubt for one of these purposes.

[13] George Colman the Younger (1762–1836), playwright and theatre manager. His greatest success was *Love Laughs at Locksmiths* (1808).

[14] Colman's humorous poem 'A Reckoning with Time' ('Come on, old Time—nay, that is stuff') appeared in *Bell's Weekly Messenger* on 8 Nov. (p. 359). SW was misinformed about it having also appeared in the *Morning Post*.

1808

To Charles Burney   Camden Town, 22 March 1808

ALS, 2 pp. (Osborn, MSS 3, Box 16, Folder 1192)

Addressed To | Dr Burney | Chelsea College | Tuesday 22 March. PM 23 MR 1808

Docketed by Frances Burney: ※

Editor's note Burney's reply to this letter, undated but *c*.23 March 1808, and beginning
'Your remembrance, after (I do believe) so long', is at Osborn, MSS 3, Box 5,
Folder 319.

My dear Sir

Although your many and important Engagements & my own necessary Drudgery have denied me the Happiness of a personal Interview for so long an Interval of Time, yet I trust you are assured that my high Respect & cordial Esteem have in no Degree diminished, & I felt extreme Satisfaction in having lately heard that your Health is considerably improved.[1]

I scarcely need say that I shall have great additional Pleasure in congratulating you Vivâ Voce, whenever you can indulge me with an Hour, compatible with your more consequential Concerns.—

I have also to prefer a Petition which if admissible, both myself & your Petitioner will rest always obliged.—Mr William Linley[2] (Brother to the late Mrs Sheridan the celestial Songstress)[3] is exceedingly desirous of the Honour of being introduced to you, & I felt not a little proud in the Privilege of informing

[1] Burney had suffered a slight paralytic seizure in his left hand in early Oct. 1806, but had made a good recovery. In Aug. 1808 his granddaughter Marianne Francis found him 'as young and gay as ever, reading & writing without spectacles, (which he has never used *yet*,) and cheerful and entertaining, and sprightly, and kind, as he had been 23 instead of *eighty three*' (Lonsdale, 460–2).

[2] William Linley (1771–1835), civil servant, theatrical manager, author, and composer, son of Thomas Linley of Bath (1733–95) and one of a distinguished family of musicians. After education at Harrow and St Paul's School, he worked in India for the East India Company between 1790 and 1795 and between 1800 and 1807. In the late 1790s he shared the management of Drury Lane Theatre with his brother-in-law Richard Brinsley Sheridan (1751–1816), and composed two unsuccessful operas. On his return to England from his second Indian tour of duty he was able to devote himself to writing and composition as a gentleman amateur. Among his compositions were several sets of songs and some elegies and glees. He also wrote two novels. His most important musical publication was a two-volume anthology of Shakespeare settings by himself and others (*Grove*⁶, under 'Linley (6)'; *DNB*; Clementina Black, *The Linleys of Bath* (rev. edn., 1971)).

[3] The soprano Elizabeth Ann Sheridan, née Linley (1754–92), sister of William Linley. After early appearances as a singer in Bath and Bristol she made her London début in 1767 and subsequently sang regularly in the London oratorio seasons (1769–73) and at the Three Choirs Festivals (1770–3). She eloped with Richard Brinsley Sheridan (see below) in 1772; they married in 1773. She then retired from singing in public but continued for a while to give private concerts at her home, sometimes accompanied by Burney (*Grove*⁶, under 'Linley (2)'; Alan Chedzoy, *Sheridan's Nightingale: The Story of Elizabeth Linley* (Cambridge, 1997); Margaret Bor and L. Clelland, *Still the Lark: A Biography of Elizabeth Linley* (London, 1962); SW, Reminiscences).

58

him that I was so happy as to have long enjoyed your Acquaintance & good Will. —I also promised him what I now perform, to request of you whether he may expect this Favour upon any Morning when you can with least Inconvenience sacrifice a few Moments.—I will make any Pre-engagement of my own yield to whatever Time you may appoint, & I am very certain that M[r] L. will look forward to it with much Exultation.[4]

With every best Wish, believe me,
My dear Sir,
Your most devoted & faithful Servant,

S Wesley

Camden Town | Tuesday. March 22[d] 1808

To Charles Burney   [Camden Town], 12 April [1808][1]

ALS, 3 pp. (Osborn, MSS 3, Box 16, Folder 1192)
Addressed To Dr Charles Burney
Docketed by Mme d'Arblay: ※

Tuesday Morning
10 o'Clock

My dear Friend

Your kind Letter[2] has reached me only 5 Minutes ago, & it is needless to express to you the Regret I feel in being unable to avail myself of your Permission to attend you this Day. I will immediately communicate your welcome Summons to my Friend Linley, who will rejoice to be informed that he is likely soon to become *Voti Compos*:[3] I sent him your former Letter,[4] which delighted him to Enthusiasm, & the Part of it relative to M[rs] Sheridan he read to his Mother, whom it affected

---

[4] In his reply, Burney explained that his health had been good 'till the March Lion began to roar'. Since that time, however, he had been scarcely out of bed, and he had been advised by his friends to remain in bed until 'the departure of this oriental monster'. When the weather improved, he would be glad to arrange a time to meet SW and Linley.

[1] The year is given by 12 Apr. falling on a Tuesday and SW's continuing discussion of arrangements for him and Linley to meet Burney. Burney's reply to this letter, undated but *c*.13 Apr. 1808, is at NYPL (Berg).

[2] Not preserved: a subsequent letter to Burney's reply to SW to Burney, 22 Mar. 1808, it evidently contained an invitation to SW and Linley to visit Burney and a suggestion that they should choose this day for their visit.   [3] 'To have achieved his wish'.

[4] In his reply to SW's letter of 22 Mar. 1808 (Burney to SW, *c*.23 Mar. 1808), Burney had expressed his delight at having once more heard from SW after 'unwillingly losing sight of each other so long', and reminisced about his friendship with Elizabeth Linley.

in the tenderest Manner, & who is charmed with the delicate & affectionate Panegyric you have bestowed on so amiable & interesting a Personage.[5]

If you will indulge me with a Line, naming any Morning, or Afternoon which might suit you to receive us, in *next* Week, I will make my Arrangements accordingly, & I am sure that M[r] Linley will eagerly embrace the Opportunity he has longed for, & if our westerly Wind continue (as I hope & trust it will) every succeeding Day will probably produce a renovating Effect on your Health, but pray do not venture too soon out, for the Evenings are yet very sharp & wintry.[6]

I have long wished for an Occasion to beg your Opinion & Advice upon a Scheme of which I know not another Friend who can be so competent a Judge.— The Preludes & Fugues of Sebastian Bach[7] are now become exceedingly scarce in England, & almost unattainable: I have for some months past paid much Attention to them, & consider them in the Light which I flatter myself you do, as the highest Stretch of harmonic Intellect, & the noblest Combination of musical Sounds that ever immortalized Genius.[8]—I have frequently played them among Professors, many of whom had never before heard a Note of them, & others who had imbibed such a Prejudice against them, from the false Idea of their being *dry*, *harsh*, & *unmelodious*, that it was really a triumphant Moment to witness their agreeable Surprize.—The Satisfaction which they have generally produced to all the Judges wherever I have had the Honour of performing them, & the Eagerness they seem to shew for the Possession of them, incline me to think that a new Edition of them by Subscription might prove a Work beneficial to the musical

[5] Burney had written: 'I did not know that the first dear M[rs] Sheridan had a brother living . . . But that most charming and accomplished of female beings I adored, and regarded her as an angel, in correctness and form, conversation and voice, indeed I c[d] neither look at her nor listen to her divine breathings, but with extatic rapture.' In a letter to Thomas Twining of 1 Dec. 1778 (Burney, *Letters I*, 265), Burney had remembered Elizabeth Sheridan's voice as having been 'as sweet as sugar'. He had reason to have such pleasant memories: Elizabeth Linley had sung the principal soprano part in a performance of his Oxford D.Mus. exercise 'I will love thee, O Lord, my strength' in Oxford in 1772.

[6] Burney replied: 'the weather for some days past has been truly balmy & amended me much; but your kind advice 'not to venture out too soon, as the Evenings are yet very sharp & wintry' is anticipated: as I have made . . . a firm resolution never again to be in the open air after sunset, by w[ch] I have banished myself for the rest of my life from dinners, public places, private Concerts, conversazioni, and all the delights of society in quiet parties of select friends & persons of learning, worth, & talents.

Any day therefore in next Week from between 12 & 3—or evening from 5 to 8, I can offer you and M[r] L.[—] suppose it were Tuesday—let me but know, & [I] shall be *Sempre* not at Home to any other human creatures. If you individually wish sooner to compare notes ab[t] name some day & hour as convenient as possible to your own engagem[ts] . . .'   [7] The '48'.

[8] As SW was later to explain in his long letter to Jacob of 17 Sept. 1808, he had already written to Burney in Sept. or Oct. 1807 about his enthusiasm for the music of J. S. Bach. In his reply (not preserved: partly summarized by SW in his letter to Jacob) Burney had invited SW to visit him and to play him some examples of Bach's music. SW's letter to Jacob goes on to give an account of this famous occasion.

World, as well as profitable to the Editor.[9]—Even in the Zurich Copy[10] (which I am told is the best) are several little Omissions, if anything ought to be termed little relating to so stupendous a Structure, & I, determining at all Events to have a Copia *Vera*, have not grudged the Labour of transcribing the whole 48 Preludes with their corresponding Fugues, & I believe I can pretty securely affirm that mine is now the most correct Copy in England.

If you judge this Design worth the Attempt, you will extremely oblige me by the most unreserved Communication of your Thoughts upon the Subject.—I remember that in one of your Letters to me some years ago,[11] you remarked that 'Subscriptions are troublesome Things,' but yet, perhaps in the present Instance, no other Mode of Proceeding would be so likely to evite Risk & dangerous Expence, as I certainly would not think of publishing until the Charges for Printing were wholly defrayed.

I am, my dear Sir,
Your ever obliged & affectionate Friend,

S Wesley

April 12

To [Charles Burney] [Camden Town], 14 April [1808][1]

ALS, 1 p. (Osborn, MSS 3, Box 16, Folder 1192)
Addressed To Dr Charles Burney
Docketed by Mme d'Arblay: ※

My dear Friend,

I have sent your Letter[2] to Linley, who will be delighted with the kind Interest you take in his musical Reputation.—He is indeed worthy 'Laudari a Laudato,'[3] as I flatter myself a further Acquaintance with him will convince you.

---

[9] In his reply, Burney wrote: 'If you determine on *immediate* publication, your expedients for saving the expence of newspaper advertisements I think are prudent & in a long shop bill you may dilate on the excellences of the work at any length you please—but to say the truth I would not hazard the expence of printing till you had played and lectured the work into favour; when I have little doubt but that all studious professors & dilettanti male & female will make Sebastian their future Study as Steffani's duets & Leo's Solfeggi won the morning studies of all the great Italian Singers during the early part of the last Century.' The edition of the '48' by SW and Charles Frederick Horn was eventually published by subscription in four parts between 1810 and 1813.   [10] The Nägeli edition.

[11] Not preserved.

---

[1] The year is given by 14 Apr. falling on a Thursday and SW's continuing discussion of the meeting with Linley.   [2] Burney's reply to SW to Burney, 22 Mar. 1808.

[3] 'To be praised by a man who has himself been praised' (and whose praise for this reason carries particular authority): a quotation from Naevius's lost play *Hector Proficiens*, known from a number of quotations in Cicero.

Many thanks for your friendly Cogitations on $\mathbf{\mathcal{9}:}$ 𝄢 .[4] The scheme
certainly claims some previous Deliberation, & I know of no one who is so amply
qualified to anticipate the probable Result as yourself, therefore if you will give
me your best Advice, (which I know to be the best of the best) I will sing

'Nil desperandum **TE DUCE**'[5]

Yours ever faithfully

S W

Thursday 14. Ap.

To [Charles Burney][1]   [Camden Town,
                                              mid-April–mid-May 1808][2]

AL fragment, 2 pp. (Rylands, DDWF 15/8a)
Docketed by Mme d'Arblay: ※
Editor's note Parts of the letter have been crossed through, presumably by Mme
    d'Arblay.

2\<nd>
S\<h>eet

However, having proceeded through half a Dozen bars without Molestation,
Success, by Degrees, begot a sense of comparative Security, & my Tremor began
gradually to subside, till at last I became so temerarious as to give out upon the full
Organ:[3]

---

[4] The four notes spell out Bach's name.
[5] 'No need for despair, if you are leading', adapted from Horace, *Odes*, 7. 27.

---

[1] Burney is identified as the addressee of this letter by his daughter's characteristic docketing.
[2] Although it is clear from internal evidence that this fragment dates from the spring of 1808, its more precise dating and its placing in the correspondence is problematical. SW's description of playing Bach on the organ may relate to his recital at Surrey Chapel on 15 Mar. (see n. 5). What appears to be a fragment of Burney's undated draft reply to this letter, beginning 'but this mornings business more complicated', is at NYPL (Berg). The content of both fragments suggest a dating after the exchange of correspondence between SW and Burney of late Mar. and Apr. 1808. The suggestion of Salomon, quoted here, and of Burney, in his draft reply, that SW should organize a 'Morning Party' at which he would play Bach's music on the organ, was taken up by SW, and resulted in his concert on 11 June (see n. 8). Given all these factors, a date between mid-Apr. and mid-May 1808 seems most probable.
[3] The opening of the C major fugue from Book I of the '48'.

And Fortune favoured the bold, for I continued an inquisitorial Persecution of my Bellows Blower for two Hours at least, without the least Interruption from without.

This long (& I feel tedious) Narrative may incline you to ask 'quorsum haec'?[4] but it is remotely connected with your Scheme of performing the Fugues in public.— Salomon, who was there on that dangerous Day,[5] brought with him two beautiful Women,[6] whose deep Attention conspired not a little to enliven & inspire me; he himself appeared to be excessively pleased, & when I called on him (shortly after) he said finer Things than I have the Impudence to write.—However, one part of his Panegyric I will venture to put down, that altho' he had heard S. B. played by some of the best German Organists, particularly at Berlin, yet he had never witnessed their producing so *smooth* an Effect as on that Morning.—This was the more gratifying to me, as the Organ in the said Chapel[7] has a very deep & a very obstinate Touch. He added—'What a Shame it is that such Music should not be known in this Country, where every Body pretends to be musical! I will tell you what strikes me: if you were to have a Morning Party in some large Room capable of containing a good Organ, & to play some of these Fugues of Bach, interspersed with Voluntaries of your own, & make the tickets 7 shillings a Piece, I am persuaded that you would make Money by it.[8]—The Abbe Vogler did the same kind of Thing here, in *St Paul's* Cathedral, by the private Circulation of Tickets, & by which he cleared at least 200l.'[9]

[4] 'What's the purpose of these remarks?', a locution often used by Cicero.

[5] Possibly 15 Mar. 1808: according to R. J. S. Stevens, SW on this date gave a recital at Surrey Chapel in Blackfriars Road, where SW's friend Jacob was organist (Argent, 156). [6] Not identified.

[7] If SW's reference is to Surrey Chapel, a 1794 instrument by Thomas Elliot (Boeringer, iii. 124).

[8] In his draft reply, Burney advised: 'lay your traps, & bait them so as to catch the country organists in the way Salomon & myself suggested—have your congress assembled of a morning, & I should think the Hanover Square room best, in which there is always an excellent Org. ready erected.' SW took the advice of Burney and Salomon and promoted a concert at the Hanover Square Rooms on 11 June, at which it was announced that he would 'perform on the Organ . . . several admired compositions of the celebrated SEBASTIAN BACH, together with several EXTEMPORANEOUS VOLUNTARIES' (*Morning Chronicle*, 7 June 1808). Burney noted the concert in his diary, and may have been present: 'Mr S. Wesleys morning performance on the Org. Extempore, & on the P. F. Sebastian Bach's preludes and Fugues, in Hanover Square new room.'

[9] Georg Joseph Vogler (1749-1814), German theorist, teacher, organist, pianist, and composer. He was a flamboyant virtuoso performer on the piano and organ, noted particularly for his improvisations. His organ recitals, of which he gave over 2,000, attracted a great deal of attention. He visited London in 1783 and 1790. The performance in St Paul's Cathedral mentioned here has not been traced.

Having previously experienced, in the last named Speaker, more Zeal in planning, than Steadiness in the Execution of his Schemes, altho' I thought his Suggestion worth Consideration, yet I should not have bestowed on it that serious Attention which after what you have written it undoubtedly claims.— With regard to *lecturing* upon the Subject,[10] Q can there be sufficient Time to prepare anything like *a Course* during the present advanced State of the Season? For I should not be fond of producing only rudis indigestaque Moles[11] upon a Work challenging such minute Criticism.—If I live to another Winter I may perhaps be able to form at least an Outline of such a Course,[12]

To [Charles Burney]   [Camden Town], 23 June [1808][1]

ALS, 2 pp. (Osborn, MSS 3, Box 16, Folder 1192)
Addressed To Dr Charles Burney, MusD
Docketed by Mme d'Arblay: ※

My dear Friend,

I cannot advance a Step without your Advice, therefore must pester you (as long as you consent to bear it) as sedulously as a thorough Papist does in cases of Conscience when he has ensured the Heart of his Confessarius.

---

[10] Following the success of William Crotch's courses at the Royal Institution, public lectures on music had recently become popular and fashionable, and were seen by SW as a particularly effective way of promoting the music of Bach. In his draft reply, Burney advised: 'let alone the lecturing till next year— but cease thinking of it: as my daughter [Sarah Harriet Burney (1772–1844)] and I see infinite credit & advantages that must necessarily flow from your diagnosis & we have not the least doubt that you will be called for at the Royal Institution; where after Crotch & Callcott have expended all their ammunition, & though they have performed wonders, they will leave you a rich aftermath.' The reference to Callcott here provides additional evidence for the dating of this fragment: Callcott had agreed to give two courses of lectures at the Royal Institution in early 1808, but had only been able to deliver seven lectures in his first course before a breakdown in his health in early Apr. caused him to withdraw. The lack of mention of Callcott's breakdown should not, however, be taken to indicate that the fragment antedates it, as news of it may not have yet reached Burney.

[11] 'Chaos, a rough and unordered mass' (Ovid, *Metamorphoses*, 1. 7).

[12] This incomplete sentence occurs at the bottom of the page. The remainder of the letter, presumably continued on a subsequent sheet or sheets, is missing. As Burney had predicted, SW was invited to lecture at the Royal Institution in the following season.

---

[1] The year is given by SW's address and the content: SW's reference to 'my Lady Somebody or Other' (n. 3) firmly ties it to the following two letters, both of which also refer to her. It also helps to pinpoint the date of a change of address, or more probably a renumbering of SW's house. SW was at 9 Arlington Street at the beginning of 1808; by the time of his fully dated letter to Burney of 7 July he had moved (or the house had been renumbered) to No. 27. The underlining of '27' here suggests that the move or renumbering was recent.

Yesterday, Mr Griffin junior[2] (an excellent Organist, & a most worthy & amiable Man) informed me, that my Lady Somebody or other,[3] (I have a very plebeian Knack of forgetting Titles) sent to *him* for the Loan of Seb. Bach's Fugues: she had already ransacked every Musick Shop in Town, but in vain; & was accidentally informed that he was in Possession of this invaluable Treasure: —What ought he to do?—However let me tell you what he did.—He felt himself puzzled by the Request, for he is among those who think with me & the Poet, that 'When Women sue, Men give like Gods'[4]—but his Prudence overcame his *Philogyny*, & he had the German Sincerity which extorted from him the unwilling tho' determinate Answer that 'it was true he had the Fugues in Question, but that they were so scarce, and to him so precious, that he never trusted them from under his Roof.'

Here is a Proof of the Truth of your Prophecy, that this admirable Musick might be *played into Fashion:*[5] you see I have only risked one modest Experiment,[6] & it has electrified the Town just in the way we wanted.—Now what I request of you is to give me an Order how to proceed:—Shall I immediately issue Proposals about *lecturing*, or about *publishing* Sebastian with annotations & an explanation?—Or is it too late to make any Noise about it till next Season?[7]—

I know you will give me your kind Counsel, & I also know that 'Nil desperandum est, te Duce.'

SW

27 Arlington Street Camden Town | June 23

---

[2] The composer, pianist, and organist George Eugene Griffin (1781–1863), son of George Griffin (1740/1–1809). He was organist of St Botolph, Bishopsgate from 1805 to 1815, and elected to membership of the Royal Society of Musicians in 1808. He was later a founder member of the Philharmonic Society; a string quartet and a piano quartet by him were performed at early concerts, and he on occasion played the piano (Matthews; Foster, *Philharmonic*, 14, 30, 35, 41, 42).

[3] In fact, Lady Chambers (see next letter).

[4] Slightly misquoted from *Measure for Measure*, I. iv. 80.

[5] In Burney to SW, *c.*13 Apr. 1808: see SW to Burney, 12 Apr. 1808, nn. 1 and 9.

[6] SW's Hanover Square Rooms concert on 11 June 1808.

[7] SW appears to have published no proposals for lectures or editions in the summer of 1808.

To [Charles Burney]¹   [Camden Town], 28 June [1808]²

ALS, 1 p. (Upper Room, L-151).
Docketed by Mme d'Arblay: ※

My dear Friend

As your Words & Sebastian's Notes are to me equally precious, I must request & intreat you to favor me with the Letter you first designed for me upon the Subject of *my Layady*.³—By the Way it was Lady Chambers, the Wife of Sir Willm Chambers, a Knight or *Barrownight* (Baronet) pretty well known.⁴—

I shall strictly follow your Advice upon all Points in which you will condescend to bestow it upon me, and as I was Yesterday raised to the Dignity of a Master Mason at the Somerset House Lodge,⁵ where a solemn Oath of Sincerity is taken, I have no urgent Temptation to break my Word with any one, & particularly with You, who have so kindly & so constantly extended your invaluable Friendship to

    Your faithful

      S Wesley

Tuesday 28th of June

To Charles Burney   Camden Town, 7 July 1808

ALS, 3 pp. (Osborn, MSS 3, Box 16, Folder 1193)
Addressed To | Dr Burney | Chelsea College
Pmk 7 JY 1808
Docketed by Mme d'Arblay: ※

---

¹ Burney is identified as the addressee of this letter by his daughter's characteristic docketing.

² The year is given by 28 June falling on a Tuesday and the reference to 'my Layady', also referred to in the following (fully dated) letter.

³ Not preserved: as is clear from the following letter, Burney subsequently sent it to SW.

⁴ Probably the Lady Chambers listed in the *Court Guide* as living at 43 Mortimer Street East and at Snaresbrook, Essex. She was in fact the widow of the eminent architect Sir William Chambers (1726–96).

⁵ SW's involvement with Freemasonry went back to his early adulthood. He had been initiated into Preston's Lodge of Antiquity on 17 Dec. 1788 and had become Junior Deacon in the following year. Among his fellow lodge members either at that time or later were Samuel Webbe I and II and Robert Birchall. His membership lapsed in 1791 through non-payment of lodge dues, but he rejoined in 1811. His involvement with the Somerset House Lodge (like the Lodge of Antiquity, one with strong musical traditions, and with many musician members) had begun earlier in 1808, when he had been admitted as an honorary member at the lodge meeting on 23 Jan. A number of SW's friends and colleagues were already, or later became, members of the lodge (Oxford).

My dear Friend,

I am just returned from the Cambridge Commencement,[1] to which I went by the joint Request of Professor Hague,[2] & Mʳ Carnaby, who particularly wished me to be present at his taking his Doctor's Degree. He produced a very pretty & correct Anthem[3] which was very well performed: Mʳ & Mʳˢ Vaughan,[4] & Mʳ Leete[5] were the principal Singers.—There was also a Selection from the Messiah, & from the Creation, on another Morning, in which I conducted the Choruses, which gave general Satisfaction, & I assure you that I have worked very hard (particularly on *Sunday*, to the scandal of all good Presbyterians)—For to say the Truth, no sooner had I tired out one Bellows-Blower but they dragged me away to attack another, & when he was *settled*, away to a third, so that I have lived in a perpetual contention of *Fingers versus Fists*, & the Joke of the Thing is that the Odds concluded in Favour of Fingers.

Although my Absence from Home has unavoidably caused two or three little Disappointments (principally such as the immediate Reply to Letters) yet, upon the whole, I by no Means repent having made this Excursion.—The Place (at which I had not been for 20 years before) is infinitely beautiful & interesting.—The Walks, the Quiet of the Streets, the Order, the Neatness, the *Security*, the Magnificence & Antiquity of the Buildings, the elegant Manners of the *elder* Graduates & venerable Masters, are altogether so irresistible, that I never quitted any Sejour, even in the happy Days of Childhood, with more Regret.

By the way, this Journey has also advanced Sebastian Bach's Cause not a little, for I made a Point of playing him (even at their Glee Parties, upon the Piano Forte) wherever an Evening Meeting took place.—Magna est Veritas, et prævalebit:[6]

---

[1] Commencements (i.e. degree ceremonies) at Oxford and Cambridge were occasions for large-scale music festivals. The 1809 Cambridge Commencement opened with a service at Great St Mary's (the University church) on Thursday, 30 July which included contributions from Carnaby and SW, and was followed by evening concerts in the Town Hall on 30 June and 1 July, and a morning concert on 1 July at Addenbrooke's Hall.

[2] Charles Hague of Trinity Hall (1769–1821), English violinist and composer, Mus.B. (1794), Mus.D. (1801), who had in 1799 succeeded John Randall as Professor of Music at Cambridge. After early years in Cambridge he had gone to London in 1786 to study with Salomon and Benjamin Cooke; he and SW would doubtless have met at this time (*Grove*⁶; *DNB*).

[3] Carnaby's Mus.D. exercise (not identified) was performed after a service at Great St Mary's on Sunday, 3 July (*Cambridge Chronicle and Journal*, 25 June, 2, 9 July 1808).

[4] The tenor Thomas Vaughan (1782–1843) and his wife Elizabeth, née Tennant, a soprano. Both were active singers in London and on the provincial music festival circuit, and appeared with SW the following year at the Tamworth Festival (Brown and Stratton; Sainsbury).

[5] Robert Leete (*ante* 1772–*post* 1836), a bass. He was a member of both the Catch Club and the Glee Club, and secretary of the Catch Club from 1828 to 1836 (Brown and Stratton; Argent).

[6] 'Great is truth, and shall prevail', a quotation from Thomas Brooks (1608–80), *The Crown and Glory of Christianity* (1662), p. 407, adapted from the Vulgate's 'magna est veritas, et praevalet' (3 Esdr. 4: 41).

—In the present Case I may say *praevaluit*,[7] for it surprized me to witness how they drank in every note.—Some of the Auditory were frequently Men of considerable musical Talent: a few of them would sit down (between the several Pieces of various Kinds) & try *a few Bars* of one of the Fugues or Preludes, & when they found themselves set fast (which you know could not be very long first) they used to say 'Well!—if I had but these Compositions, I would practise them Night & Day.—I once thought that Handel's were not only the best but the hardest Fugues in the World, but now I find myself mistaken in both Suppositions.'—

So I have now a fresh Instance of the Truth of your Prophecy, that by *playing* them into Fashion, the Avidity for possessing them could be infallibly increased.—

A Friend of mine (a very clever Artist) has nearly finished a *Painting* of Seb. Bach, from a small Drawing lent me by Mr Kollmann,[8] which latter Circumstance I believe I previously mentioned to you.[9]—Quære, would not an Extract, translated from the Life in German,[10] be a good Avant-Coureur to the Fugues, with a Portrait prefixed to the Title?—In this also I shall follow your Advice.

I found on my Return yesterday your petit Billet upon the subject of *my Layady*,[11] for which I am (as always) thankful to you.

I could not resist the Temptation of telling you *all how & about it*:[12] *All* indeed is a Mistake, for there are a thousand *Incidents* which I wish to inform you of relative to this grand Tour, which will be better vivâ Voce, & I shall lose no Time in bringing my Budget of Gossip to Chelsea (between 3 & 5) within these few Days.

Yours, my dear Friend,
as ever

S Wesley

Camden Town. | Arlington Street. 27. | Thursday. 7. July. 1808

---

[7] 'It *did* prevail'.

[8] The composer and theorist Augustus Frederic Christopher Kollmann (1756–1829) moved to London from Hamburg in 1782 and was appointed organist of the Royal German Chapel in St James's Palace in the same year. He was one of the leading figures of the English Bach movement, whose interest antedated SW's own by some years: in his *Essay on Practical Musical Composition* (1799) he included the organ Trio Sonata in E flat, BWV 525, the C major Prelude and Fugue from Book II of the '48', BWV 870 (the first example from the '48' to be published in England), and proposed the publication of an analysed edition of the '48'.

[9] The identity of SW's artist friend is not known, and neither the drawing of Bach lent to SW by Kollmann nor the painting taken from it is known to be extant.

[10] *Über Johann Sebastian Bachs Leben, Kunst, und Kunstwerke* (1802) by the German music historian, theorist, and bibliographer Johann Nikolaus Forkel (1749–1819); for plans for the publication of a complete translation, see SW to Jacob, 17 Oct. 1808.

[11] Lady Chambers: see SW to Burney, 28 June [1808]. The 'petit billet' was presumably the letter referred to there.   [12] A favourite phrase of SW; its source has not been traced.

To Mary Beardmore[1]   Camden Town, 7 July [1808][2]

ALS, 1 p. (London University, ALS 293)
Addressed To | Miss Beardmore | Canonbury Place | Islington | N. 5
Pmk 7 JY 1808

My dear Madam

The Reason of my long Silence & Absence has been my Attendance at the Cambridge Commencement where I have been to assist a Friend upon his taking his Doctor's Degree in Musick, and at which place I have been solicited to remain much longer than I intended in so kind & friendly a Manner that I felt unable to resist so much Importunity.—

I shall hope to be with you on Saturday next,[3] & will procure you some new Musick.

I remember recommending to you a beautiful Song of Bach, from the Opera of Orfeo, which I fear is scarce, but which if I can I will obtain:[4] otherwise I will endeavour to bring some others that may be suitable.—

I remain
My dear Madam
Yours very sincerely
  S Wesley

                                          Camden Town. Thursday July 7

---

[1] Mary Beardmore (1778/9–1838), the elder daughter of Joseph Beardmore; SW also taught her sister Frances (1789/90–1868).   [2] The year is given by the postmark.
[3] 9 July.
[4] Not identified: evidently one of the seven arias composed by J. C. Bach for the 1770 London production of Gluck's *Orfeo ed Euridice*, and published that year by Bremner in *The Favourite Songs in the Opera Orfeo* (C. S. Terry, *John Christian Bach*, rev. 2nd. edn. (1967), 234–5). A later arrangement for organ by SW of one of these ('Obliar l'amato sposa') is at BL, Add. MS 69854, fos. 14–15.

To [Benjamin Jacob]¹   Camden Town, 13 August [1808]²

ALS, 3 pp. (RCM, MS 2130, fo. 23)³

Camden Town 13. Augᵗ

My dear Sir,

I do not profess myself to be so great a Schemer as our late Friend Dʳ Arnold, who, we all know, speculated himself into Mischief too often;⁴ but I have a Plan to propose to you of which I should be glad to have your early Opinion.

It is manifest that Sebastian makes that Sort of Sensation which will in a short Time form a *Party* Business among several societies of musical Pretenders; of those who know & like nobody but Handel, others who swear in only Haydn's, Mozart's, & Beethoven's Words, others who relish only 'Little Peggy's Love,'⁵ 'A Smile & a Tear,'⁶ & similar Sublimities of which you need not be reminded.

---

¹ Benjamin Jacob (1778–1829), organist of Surrey Chapel, friend and collaborator of SW in the promotion of the music of J. S. Bach, and the recipient of an important series of letters from SW, subsequently edited by SW's daughter Eliza and published in 1875 as *Letters of Samuel Wesley to Mr Jacobs, Organist of Surrey Chapel, Relating to the Introduction into this Country of the Works of John Sebastian Bach* (the *Bach Letters*). As a boy he was a chorister at Portland Chapel and studied harpsichord and organ under William Shrubsole and Matthew Cooke, organist of St George's, Bloomsbury. His appointments included the Salem Chapel; Carlisle Chapel, Kennington Lane; and Bentinck Chapel, Lisson Grove. He was invited by Rowland Hill to be organist of Surrey Chapel in 1794, and remained there until 1825. He appears to have been known as (and to have signed himself) Jacobs at the beginning of his correspondence with SW, but soon afterwards to have changed his name to Jacob (*Grove*⁶; Emery, 'Jack Pudding', 306). He lived at Charlotte Street, Blackfriars Road (the western end of the present Union Street), close to Surrey Chapel. Although lacking an address portion, it is clear from the content and present location of this letter that it is to Jacob.

² The year of this letter is not given. It is apparent, however, from the discussion of the 'sensation' caused by Bach's music and SW's proposal for the formation of a Bach 'junto' that it comes from an early stage in SW's promotion of Bach, and that the year is 1808 rather than 1809, as implied by its position in Eliza Wesley's edition.

³ This collection contains all the letters to Jacob subsequently published by Eliza Wesley. Some fragments of other letters to Jacob, not included in the *Bach Letters*, are at Edinburgh.

⁴ Samuel Arnold (1740–1802), composer, organist, editor, and impresario, had a long and varied career. He was at different times composer to both Covent Garden and the Little Theatre in the Haymarket, composer to the Chapel Royal, conductor of the Academy of Ancient Music, director of the oratorios at Drury Lane and the King's Theatre, organist of Westminster Abbey, and editor of the first uniform edition of Handel's works. SW's reference may be to Arnold's disastrous tenancy of Marylebone Gardens between 1769 and 1774, which reputedly lost him £10,000, or to the episode in 1794 when he took a lease of the Lyceum near Exeter Exchange, which he attempted unsuccessfully to establish as a 'combination playhouse and circus', but was forced to give up when he was unable to retain a licence (*Grove*⁶; *BD*).

⁵ The 'Scotch Dance' from the ballet *Little Peggy's Love* by Cesare Bossi (1774/5–1802), frequently performed at this time as a separate item, and popular in arrangements for piano: see *The Celebrated Scotch Air danced by Madam Hilligsberg . . . in Little Peggy's Love, arranged as a Rondo for the Piano Forte by M. P. King* [?1796] (*CPM*).   ⁶ A song by Harriett Abrams.

Now I really think that all those who have the Courage to speak out in Defence of the greatest of all Harmonists ought to coalesce & amalgamate in a Mode which should render their cordial Sentiments & Judgement *unequivocal* in the Face of the World, & that we ought to stigmatize such Hypocrites as affect to be enchanted with Sebastian on one Day, & on the next, endeavour to depreciate & vilify him.

In order to ascertain who are verily & indeed 'the Israelites in whom is no Guile'[7] I can think of nothing more expedient than the Formation of a Junto among ourselves, composed of characters who sincerely & *conscientiously* admit & adhere to the superior Excellence of the great musical High Priest; & who will bend their Minds to a zealous Promotion of advancing the Cause of Truth & Perfection.—Such a society would *at least* produce one happy Effect, that of rendering *thoroughly* public what as yet is but partially so.—I look upon the State of Music in this Country to be very similar to the State of the Roman Church when the flagrant Abuses & Enormities had arisen to such a Height as to *extort* a Reformation.—We know what Wonders were wrought by the Resolution & Perseverance of a single Friar, & that Martin Luther,[8] having *Truth* for his firm Foundation (for this was the Reason of his Success) managed in a very short Time to shake the whole Fabric of Ignorance & Superstition, although sanctioned by the Precedence of many former Ages, & enforced by the most despotic Authority both ecclesiastical & civil.

It is high Time that *some* Amendment should take place in the Republic of Musick, & I know of no Engine equally powerful with the immortal & adamantine Pillars of Sebastian's Harmony.—I really think that our constant & unremitted Question to *all* who call themselves Friends to Excellence should be 'Who is on our Side, who'?[9]—And I have but little Doubt that by the Establishment of a *regular Society* in Defence of the Truth, we should e'er long reap some good Fruits of our laudable Endeavours.—Write me your Thoughts <on> the Subject as soon as convenient,

<and be>lieve me, my dear Sir,
ever truly yours
S Wesley

---

[7] John 1: 47.
[8] Martin Luther (1483–1546), whose nailing of ninety-five theses on the sale of indulgences to the church door at Wittenberg in 1517 instigated the Reformation.   [9] 2 Kgs. 9: 32.

To George Smith[1]   Camden Town, 14 August 1808

ALS, 2 pp. (BL, Add. MS 31764, fo. 24)
Addressed To | —Smith Esqre | Feversham[2] | Kent
Pmk AU 15 1808

Sir

On Thursday last I was informed by your excellent & very extraordinary Daughter, that you have (for the present) waved all Thoughts of her applying to the Organ, as in that Case it would be absolutely necessary for her to practise upon that Instrument, without which it were utterly impossible to acquire the true Style of it, & as I before observed, this is so totally different & contrary to that of the Piano Forte, that the equal Study of *both* would unavoidably disturb & impede the Progress on either.

I am told by Mrs Barnes[3] that you wish Miss Smith to commence private Lessons upon the Piano Forte, & in Consequence of her uncommon Abilities, it appears to me quite sufficient for her to take *these* Lessons only, & to give up the *School* Lessons altogether.[4]—It remains with you to determine whether she shall have *one* or *two* Hours in the Course of the same Week.—If she continue to improve in the Ratio which I have hitherto witnessed, I am of Opinion that one Hour in a Week will do great Things.—At all Events, I do sincerely assure you Sir, my Opinion of your Daughter's musical Talent is so high, & my Partiality to her whole Behaviour so great, that rather than not proceed in endeavouring to make her a first rate Performer, I would sacrifice my Time *gratis* for the Purpose; You may therefore hence conclude that pecuniary Consideration has not much to do with my Proposals of her Advancement, & I shall feel myself peculiarly gratified by being able ultimately to produce my Pupil to the musical Criticks such as I *know* she must prove, if her future Acquirements shall keep Pace with present Acquisitions.

She has considerably surprized me by her rapid Comprehension & Execution of Cramer's first Book of the Studio;[5] the Remainder of which she has so successfully digested during the late Holidays;[6] & the Manner in which she went on

[1] The father of one of SW's pupils; not otherwise certainly identified. He may have been the George Smith elected a member of the Madrigal Society on 10 Dec. 1798, when his address was given as the Navy Office (MADSOC).   [2] i.e. Faversham, near Canterbury, Kent.

[3] One of two sisters, joint proprietors of Oxford House, a girls' school on Marylebone High Street, where SW had taught music since around 1784.

[4] It was evidently possible to take lessons either through the school ('school lessons') or by private arrangement with the teacher ('private lessons').

[5] Johann Baptist Cramer's influential and widely used *Studio per il pianoforte* (1804–10), a collection of piano exercises and studies in all the major and minor keys.

[6] The summer holidays appear to have begun around midsummer, and the new term to have started in early Aug.

Thursday through some of the Examples which she had not acquired previously with me, afforded me extreme Delight, & prophecied so much Perfection, that I really regard myself singularly fortunate in having happened upon a real Genius for the Exertion of very high & rare musical Powers, joined to the very best Disposition for Instruction, as her mild & docile Temper cannot fail to accelerate her Improvement in a Way seldom to be witnessed.

I really could go on to expatiate upon the rare Intelligence of your amiable young Lady, till I might be suspected of Flattery on that Point; but I am so conscious of not exaggerating the Fact, (& having been conversant with great Variety of musical Students from a pretty early Age) that I trust you will acquit me of any Charge but that to which I willingly plead *guilty*, namely, that I contend Miss Smith is, (bonâ Fide) possessed of the most illuminated musical Intellect that I have met with for very many Years.

> I remain,
> With much Respect,
> Sir,
> Yours most obediently,
> & very sincerely
>> S Wesley

Camden Town | Aug. 14. 1808

To [Benjamin Jacob]¹   [Camden Town], 28 August [1808]²

ALS, 1 p. (RCM, MS 2130, fo. 39)

Sunday. 28 Aug.

My dear Sir

Many thanks for your kind Attention: I herewith return a Book which I borrowed on Friday last as a *Compagnon de Voyage*, though he is not the most flattering Friend in the World.—'The Centaur not fabulous'³ is among the

---

¹ Although lacking an address portion, it is clear from the content and present location of this letter that it is to Jacob.

² The year is established by 28 Aug. falling on a Sunday and SW's inclusion of 'kind Respects' from 'Mrs W': he and Charlotte were still living together in 1808, but separated in early 1810.

³ *The Centaur not Fabulous* (1755), by Edward Young (1683-1765). Young was a favourite author of SW's father, and echoes from *Night Thoughts*, Young's most celebrated work, frequently appear in his hymns and poems (J. R. Watson, *The English Hymn* (Oxford, 1997), 251-3).

bitterest of *religious* Satires, & although I believe Dr Young might mean to do good by whatever he wrote, there is always an Asperity of Mind, & a gloomy Cast of Disposition in the Majority of his Works, which seems to have been the Result of either a saturnine Temper, or some disappointed Passion.

I was certainly in very good Humour for playing yesterday Evening.—I know not whether I was not put rather upon my Mettle by my old Rival's Introduction of his two Critical Companions.[4]—That Mr Abbot[5] seems to know something about the Matter, but I guess that he is one who delights to mix among his Praise 'as much detraction as he can.'—

Your Man is in Haste, which renders me equally so to conclude myself

Dr Sir
Yours most truly

S Wesley

Mrs W. desires her kind Respects.

P.S.—I will write to you before Sunday.

To [Benjamin Jacob][1]   [Camden Town], 17 September 1808

ALS, 7 pp. (RCM, MS 2130, fo. 1)

Septr 17. 1808

Dear Sir

I am much obliged by your ingenious & circumstantial Detail of your Success with *Saint* Sebastian,[2] as you very properly term him, & am rejoiced to find that you are likely to regard his Works with me as a musical Bible, unrivalled, & inimitable.

I am grieved to witness in my valuable Friend Doctor Burney's Critique[3] (for he is a Man whom I equally respect and love) so slight an Acquaintance with the

[4] SW's 'old rival' may have been his brother Charles. The 'two critical companions' have not been identified.   [5] Not identified: perhaps one of the 'critical companions'.

[1] Although lacking an address portion, it is clear from the content and present location of this letter that it is to Jacob.

[2] SW's reference to Bach as 'Saint Sebastian' and his extended use of religious imagery when discussing him and his music is characteristic.

[3] Either in the two passages from Burney's *History* quoted below (see nn. 9 and 10), or in his article on Bach in Rees: 'Sebastian Bach is said by Marpurg, in his "Art de la Fugue," to have been "many musicians in one, profound in science, fertile in fancy, and in taste easy and natural;" he should rather

great & matchless Genius whom he professes to analyze: & I have however much Satisfaction in being able to assure you *from my own personal Experience* that his present judgement of our Demi-God is of a very different Nature from that at the Time he imprudently, incautiously, and we may add, *ignorantly* pronounced so rash & false a verdict (altho' a *false Verdict* is a Contradiction in Terms) as that which I this Day read for the first Time, upon 'the greatest Master of Harmony in any Age or Country.'

It is now (I think) nearly a Twelvemonth since I wrote to the Doctor respecting my profound Admiration (& Adoration if you like it as well) of Sebastian:[4] I stated to him that I had made a Study of his Preludes & Fugues, adding that his Compositions had opened to me an entirely new musical World, which was to me at least as surprizing as (when a Child) I was thunderstruck by the opening of the Dettingen Te-Deum at the Bristol Cathedral, with about an hundred Performers: (a great Band in those Days.)[5]—I went into something like a general Description of what I conceived to be his characteristic Beauties, & particularly specified *Air* as one of the chief & most striking.[6]—I have by me the Doctor's Reply to my Letter,[7] although I cannot at the present Moment advert to it, but I fully remember his observing in nearly the following Words, 'In order to be consistent with myself with regard to the great Sebastian Bach, before I precisely coincide with you, I must refer to what I have written at various Times, & in various Places of my History, Travels, &c. in which I had Occasion to mention him, but I shall feel exceedingly gratified in hearing his elaborate & erudite Compositions performed by you (for I never yet *heard* any one of them) & can tell you that I have a very curious & beautiful Copy of *his Fugues*, which was presented to me many years since by his Son Emanuel,[8] & which I shall have much pleasure in shewing you.'

---

have said original and refined, for to the epithets easy and natural many are unwilling to assent; as this truly great man seems by his works for the organ, to have been constantly in search of what was new and difficult, without the least attention to nature and facility.' For Burney's contributions to Rees and the relationship of these to his earlier writings, see Roger Lonsdale, 'Doctor Burney's "Dictionary of Music"', *Musicology* 5 (1977), 159–71.

[4] In fact, it was rather less than six months. As a comment in Burney's letter to SW of *c.*23 Mar. 1808 makes clear (see SW to Burney, 12 Apr. 1808, n.4), SW had only renewed contact with Burney in Mar. 1808, probably with his letter of 22 Mar. The letter referred to here is not preserved; it no doubt dated from early Apr. 1808.

[5] This performance of Handel's 'Dettingen' Te Deum (1743) may have been at the annual Festival of the Sons of the Clergy, held in Bristol Cathedral each Aug.; it presumably took place some time before 1776, when SW moved permanently to London.

[6] A pointed rejoinder to one of Burney's chief criticisms of Bach: see nn. 9 and 10.

[7] Not preserved.

[8] Carl Philipp Emanuel Bach (1714–88), son of J. S. Bach, whom Burney had visited in Hamburg in Oct. 1772 (Percy A. Scholes (ed.), *Dr Burney's Musical Tours in Europe*, 2 vols. (1959), ii. 219–20; Hans-Gunter Ottenberg, *C. P. E. Bach*, trans. Philip Whitmore (Oxford, 1987), 145–6).

When I waited on my venerable Friend, he had been kind enough to previously lay upon his Music Desk the *MS* in Question (together with several other beautiful & superb Works of our immortal Master); but when I came to examine this said rare Present, how much was I surprized to find it so full of *scriptural* Faults, that it was not without some Difficulty I could manage to do Justice to one of the Fugues which I had been formerly the most familiar with, & although I did not *boggle*, yet I played with extreme Discomfort!—My Friend however was extremely delighted, & the very first Part of his Critique expressed his Wonder *how such abstruse Harmony & such perfect & enchanting Melody could have been so marvellously united!*—

What a convincing Proof this is that his *former* Criticism upon our matchless Author was an hasty & improvident Step! I conceive that the Fact stands thus: When Burney was in Germany, the universal Plaudits & Panegyricks upon the Father of *universal Harmony* were so interesting, that it would have been impossible for him to have avoided giving such a Man a Place in his Account of Musical Authors in his General History:[9]—Nevertheless it appears very evidently from the erroneous Sentence he has pronounced therein upon the Comparative Merit of him & Handel,[10] that he never could have taken due Pains to make himself Master of the Subject; otherwise his late candid Acknowledgment would not have been made; and is Proof sufficient that he only wanted *Experience* of the *Truth* to make him ready & willing to own it.

I must also tell you another Piece of News; namely that this imperfect & incorrect Volume, this *valuable & inestimable* Gift of Sebastian's dutiful Son, happens to contain only the *24 first* Preludes & Fugues; all written in the *Soprano* Clef, (to make them more easily understood, I suppose),[11] & the Preludes so

[9] Burney had written: 'Of the illustrious musical family of BACH I have frequently had occasion for panegyric. The great Sebastian Bach, music-director at Leipsic, no less celebrated for his performance on the organ and compositions for that instrument, than for being the father of four sons, all great musicians in different branches of the art . . . If Sebastian Bach and his admirable son Emanuel, instead of being musical-directors in commercial cities, had been fortunately employed to compose for the stage and public of great capitals, such as Naples, Paris, or London, and for performers of the first class, they would doubtless have simplified their style more to the level of their judges; the one would have sacrificed all unmeaning art and contrivance, and the other been less fantastical and *recherché*, and both, by writing in a style more popular, and generally intelligible and pleasing, would have extended their fame, and been indisputably the greatest musicians of the present century' (*History*, iv. 594–5; Mercer, ii. 954–5).

[10] 'Handel was perhaps the only great Fughist, exempt from pedantry. He seldom treated barren or crude subjects; his themes being almost always natural and pleasing. Sebastian Bach, on the contrary, like Michael Angelo in painting, disdained facility so much, that his genius never stooped to the easy and graceful. I never have seen a fugue by this learned and powerful author [i.e. J. S. Bach] upon a *motivo* that is natural and *chantant*; or even an easy and obvious passage, that is not loaded with crude and difficult accompaniments' (*History*, iii. 110; Mercer, ii. 96).

[11] A sarcastic reference to the choice of clef for the notation of the upper stave of the manuscript: the soprano clef would in fact have been *more* difficult to read than the more usual treble clef.

miserably mangled & mutilated, that had I not met them in such a Collection as that of the learned & highly illuminated Doctor Burney, I verily believe that I should have exclaimed, 'An Enemy hath done this';[12] I should have at once concluded that such a Manuscript could have been made only by him who was determined to disgrace instead of promote the Cause of correct Harmony.[13]

Ever since I had the Privilege of so great a Triumph (for I can call it nought else) over the Doctor's Prejudice, he has evinced the most cordial Veneration for our sacred Musician, & when I told him that I was in Possession of 24 *more* such precious Relicks,[14] he was all aghast in finding that there could be any Productions of such a Nature which he had not seen:[15] this again is another proof of his having hastily judged, & also how remiss the Germans must have been, not to have made him better acquainted with the Works of their transcendant Countryman.

I am told by the Revd Mr Picart,[16] (one of the Canons of Hereford Cathedral) that Seb. B. has written Pieces for *three* Organs,[17] & innumerable others which are not sent to England purely from the Contempt which the Germans entertain of the general State of Music in this Country, & which unfavourable sentiment, I am sorry to say, has but too much foundation on the Truth.

You see, that there are others who have as much Cause to apologize for the length of Letters as you, if Apology were at all necessary among Friends, but yours, which I this Day received has given me so much real Satisfaction, as I fully trust that you are determined to defend the cause of Truth & Sebastian (for they are one) against all the frivolous Objections of Ignorance, & the transparent Cavils of Envy, that I safely rely upon you as one of my right hand Men against all the prejudiced Handelians.—It has been said that Comparisons are odious; but without Comparison, where is Discrimination? and without Discrimination, how are we to attain a just Judgement?—Let us always weigh fairly as far as human Powers will allow, & endeavour to divest ourselves of the Propensity which leads us either to idolize or execrate whatever we have been unfortunately habituated so to do, without previous & due Examination.

---

[12] Matt. 13: 28.

[13] For a subsequent account of this meeting, see SW to Charles Butler, 7 Oct. 1812.

[14] i.e. Book II of the '48'.

[15] According to Burney's account of his visit in *Dr Burney's Musical Tours in Europe*, ii. 219–20, C. P. E. Bach had showed Burney *two* manuscript volumes of fugues, which Ottenberg takes to have been both books of the '48'.

[16] Samuel Picart (1774/5–1835), matric. Brasenose College, Oxford (1792), BA (1796), MA (1803), BD (1810), senior master of Hereford School (1803), Prebendary of Hereford (1805), and Rector of Hartlebury (1817–35) (Foster). He subscribed to Novello's *A Collection of Sacred Music* (1811) and to the Wesley-Horn edition of the '48', and was a noted collector of music (Foster; Percy M. Young, *The Bachs, 1500–1850* (London, 1970), 295–6; King, 47).

[17] Picart's reference was presumably to pieces which require three-manual instruments.

I feel great gratification in having been *accessory* to your Study of Sebastian: I knew that you had only to know him to love & adore him, & I sincerely assure you, that in meeting so true an Enthusiast in so good a Cause (& depend on it that nothing very good or very great is done without Enthusiasm) I experience a warmth of Heart which only Enthusiasts know or can value.

That our *Friendship* may long continue, either with or without Enthusiasm (tho' I think a Spice of it even there no bad thing) believe me, is the very cordial wish of

Dear Sir
Yours very faithfully
S Wesley

To Benjamin Jacob   [Camden Town], 17 October 1808

ALS, 3 pp. (RCM, MS 2130, fo. 5)
Addressed To | Mʳ Jacobs | Charlotte Street | Black Friar's Road | Octʳ 17 1808.
Pmk 17 OC 1808

My dear Sir

We are going on swimmingly. Mr. Horn[1] (the Music Master to the Princesses) is furthering the Cause of our grand Hero with Might & Main. He had arranged 12 of the Fugues for 4 Instruments[2] before I had the Pleasure of his Acquaintance, & was longing to find some spirited enthusiast like himself, to co-operate in bringing the musical World to Reason & Common Sense, & to extort a Confession of the true State of the Case against the Prepossession, Prejudice, Envy, & Ignorance of all *anti-Bachists*.

---

[1] Charles Frederick Horn (1762–1830), German-born organist, teacher, composer, and theorist, who had come to England in 1782. He was Queen Charlotte's music teacher from 1789 to 1783, and thereafter taught various members of the royal family, including some of the daughters of George III and Charlotte. He was an important figure in the English Bach movement: in addition to his arrangement of Bach fugues for string quartet discussed in this letter, he was later co-editor with SW of the organ trio sonatas and of the first English edition of the '48'.

[2] *A Sett of twelve Fugues composed for the Organ by Sebastian Bach . . . arranged as Quartettos* (1807); the Preface is dated 1 May 1807. Horn's title reflected the general belief at this time that Bach's keyboard fugues were all written for the organ. Only ten of the set are in fact from the '48': the fugues in C major and C sharp minor from Book I, and the fugues in D major, E flat major, D sharp /E flat minor, E major, G minor, A flat major, B flat major, and B major from Book II; some of these are transposed into keys more convenient for stringed instruments. The remaining two fugues are the organ fugue in D minor, BWV 538 ('The Dorian') and the probably spurious keyboard fugue in B flat on B-A-C-H, BWV 898.

We are (in the first Place) preparing for the Press an authentic & accurate Life of Sebastian, which M[r] Stephenson the Banker[3] (a most zealous & scientific Member of our Fraternity) has translated into English from the German of Forkel, & wherein is a List of *all* the Works of our Apollo.[4]—This we propose to publish by Subscription, as a preparatory Measure to editing the Fugues,[5] & which will naturally cause a considerable Sensation not only in the musical but also in the literary World.[6]—Is not this all as you would have it?—I cannot doubt your Affirmative, & you perceive that I have not been idle.

It appears by the Life of Sebastian, that he was not only the greatest Master in the World, but also one of the most worthy & amiable Characters that ever adorned Society.—I remember often exclaiming when working at him 'I am sure that none but a *good* man could have written thus,' & you perceive that my Conjecture was accurate.

M[r] Horn has a vast Quantity of his Compositions that have never seen the Light; among the Rest, stupendous Trios for the Organ,[7] which he used to play

[3] Edward Stephenson (1759–1833), banker, amateur musician, and collector of music and violins, was a long-standing friend of Horn, and was (with J. P. Salomon) godfather to Horn's son Charles Edward (1786–1849). He and Horn were at this time neighbours: he lived at 29 Queen's Square Bloomsbury, and Horn at No. 25. He has in the past been erroneously identified as Rowland Stephenson (1782–1856), his brother-in-law (*Grove*[6]).

[4] An announcement that SW and Horn were preparing a translation of Forkel's *Über Johann Sebastian Bachs Leben, Kunst, und Kunstwerke* for the press appeared in the Nov. number of the *Librarian* and the Dec. number of *MM* although without identifying Stephenson as the translator. This translation did not appear, and the first English translation (reprinted in *New Bach Reader*, 419–82) was finally published in 1820; the identity of its translator and its relationship to the Stephenson translation are not known (*New Bach Reader*; Walter Emery, 'The English Translator of Forkel', *ML* 28 (1947), 301–2).

[5] i.e. the '48'. In fact, it was not until almost a year later that SW and Horn began to prepare this edition: see SW to [?Horn], [*c*.30 Sept. 1809]. The edition was announced in the Mar. 1810 number of *MM* and was published in four parts between Sept. 1810 and July 1813.

[6] In a letter now lost, SW had written to tell Burney about Horn and their plans to publish Stephenson's translation of Forkel. In his reply of 17 Oct. 1808 (Osborn), Burney had replied: 'I am glad you like Mr Horn; I have never seen him—but from all that I have heard of him, I set him down in my mental list as a worthy, ingenious, & liberal minded professor . . . With respect to your plan of publishing the life of our divine Sebastian jointly with Mr Horn, I shall be extremely glad to have a *talk* with you on so very interesting a Subject; you and your co-partner will confer honour on yourselves by blazoning the powers of our Idol. I have formerly had some dealings with Dr Forkel—I have not the honour of knowing Mr Stephenson—if his translation of the life is well done, it is pity to undertake a new version. I wish you had perused it. Mr Kollmann's Geese, you know, are all Swans.' The implication of the latter part of this quotation may be that objections had been raised by Kollmann to the quality of Stephenson's translation, but that Burney considered them to be exaggerated and not sufficient to justify the commissioning of a new translation.

[7] The six Trio Sonatas for organ, BWV 525–30, an edition of which was published in separate numbers by SW and Horn in 1809. In his Reminiscences SW implied that the editorial work and the authorship of the preface were his alone.

thus: his right Hand played the first Part on the Top Row of the Clavier; his left the 2^d Part on the 2nd Row, & he played the Base *wholly* upon the Pedals. There are Allegro Movements among them, & occasionally very brisk notes in the Base Part, whence it appears that he was alike dexterous both with Hands & Feet.[8]

Horn has a further Design than the mere Publication of our 48 Preludes & Fugues; he wishes to extend the Work to a complete Edition of all his Compositions that are to be found: and if God spare our Health, why should we despair of presenting the World with 'all these Treasures of Wisdom & Knowledge?'[9]

He is as indefatigable as yourself, & has written with his own Hand whole Centuries of Pages which would amaze you.—He has not only transcribed all the 48 Preludes & Fugues, but also written them on Paper ruled for the purpose, capacious enough to contain *an entire Fugue*, however long, upon two Pages only, thus avoiding the Inconvenience of turning over, for which there is hereby no necessity even from the Beginning of the Work to the End.

Mr Kollman in his Essay on Practical Musical Composition 1799 has published one of those Trios above mentioned,[10] towards the End of the musical examples (N. 58).—by this you will be able to judge of the rest; for there is no Inferiority throughout them: all are equally admirable & excellent altho' each in an entirely different Style.

I sadly want to see you, tho' I know not well how to contrive it: St Paul's opens again on Sunday next,[11] & I have promised Attwood to look in there in the Morning: In what part of the same Day should I be most likely to find you?

Yours ever truly

S Wesley

I know not Mr Neate's[12] correct Address; will you therefore be so kind as to forward the enclosed to him immediately?

Do not forget my best Regards to my kind Friend Mrs Jacobs.

---

[8] SW's remarks show how little was known of Bach's organ music at this time, even by musicians: he needed to spell out to Jacob the importance of Bach's pedal parts and the fact that Bach was 'alike dexterous both with hands and feet'.   [9] Col. 2: 3.

[10] The Trio Sonata No. 1 in E flat, BWV 525, which appears as pls. 58–67.

[11] 23 Oct.; the reason for the closure is not known.

[12] Charles Neate (1784–1877), pianist and composer, doubtless the 'Master Neate' who played a piano concerto at Ashley's performance of Haydn's *Creation* performance at Covent Garden on 4 Apr. 1800. He joined the Royal Society of Musicians in 1806 and was a founder member of the Philharmonic Society in 1813, when his address was given as 4 Duke Street, Portland Place (Matthews; Loan 48.1).

To Benjamin Jacob   Camden Town, 19 October [1808][1]

ALS, 3 pp. (RCM, MS 2130, fo. 7)
Addressed To | Mʳ Jacobs | Organist | Charlotte Street | Black Friar's Road.

Camden Town.
Wednesday Evᵍ Oct 19.

My dear Sir,

    I thought you would be gratified in gaining early Intelligence of our Intention to come forward with Memoirs of our matchless Man (if Man he may be called), as I am clearly of Opinion that they will serve as a thorough Defiance of all the Snarlers & would-be-Criticks, howsoever dispersed throughout the British Empire. —Upon the Continent his Fame has been so long circulated & established that they must have for many years past sneered at our Ignorance of such an Author, professing (as we do) to be a Nation attached to Music.—Salomon has said truly & shrewdly enough that the English know very little of the Works of the German Masters, Handel excepted, who (as he observes) came over hither when there was a great Dearth of good Musick, & here he remained (these are his Words) establishing a Reputation wholly Constituted *upon the Spoils of the Continent.*[2]

    This would nettle the Handelians devilishly, however it is the strict Truth, for we all know how he has pilfered from all Manner of Authors whence he could filch any thing like a Thought worth embodying, & altho' it is certain that what he had taken he has generally improved on (not when he robbed the Golden Treasury of Sebastian, by the Way) yet there is such a Meanness in putting even his own Subjects in so many different Works over & over again, vide his Lessons, Concertos, Chamber-Duets, Instrumental Trios, & almost all his Compositions, that I do sincerely think, & am ready to maintain it among sensible unprejudiced Judges, (for it is but time lost to argue with Bigots, which is another Word for Madmen) [that] Handel, for so great a Master, has as little just claim to the Merit of original Genius as the most servile of his Imitators.[3]

---

[1] The year is given by 19 October falling on a Wednesday and SW's Camden Town address.

[2] After an early career in Halle, Hamburg, and Italy, Handel had arrived in England late in 1710 and rapidly established himself as the foremost composer in England.

[3] Handel's borrowings, both from himself and from other composers, were well known in the late 18th cent. (see Burney, *History*, iii. 536, iv. 154, 315; Mercer, ii. 426, 617, 742–3), and were discussed at around this time by Crotch in his lectures. Although Handel was sometimes criticized for lack of originality, he generally escaped the more serious charge of plagiarism: a commonly expressed view was that what he borrowed, he repaid with interest. For a conspectus of attitudes over two centuries to Handel's borrowings, see George J. Buelow, 'The Case for Handel's Borrowings: the Judgment of Three Centuries', in Stanley Sadie and Anthony Hicks (eds.), *Handel Tercentenary Collection* (London, 1987), 61–82.

I am glad you tickled up Gaffer Stevens[4] a Bit: I need not tell *you* that half, & more than half even of such Professors as ought to know & do better, give a Decision hap-Hazard upon sundry Matters which they have never duly considered —I am delighted that you happened to remember Burney's identical Words:[5] your anticipation of what he[6] was about to say must have been not an *agreeable* Surprize, but rather of the confounding Kind.—Just while I think of it let me provide you with immediate Ammunition against the feeble Defence of Handel upon the score of his *clear* & *marked* Subjects. The Doctor's Fugue you have accurately, as also the Judgement Fugue, & what I call the *Saints in Glory*-Fugue, by which I mean that in E Major, 4 ♯♯.[7] Add to this the one hard by it in E♭ Major, & I think these will furnish sufficient for many *Rounds* against such as 'love Darkness rather than Light, because their Eyes & Ears are evil.'[8]

However, as I before observed to you, History & Experience teach us, that the Progress of Truth, however slow, is always infallibly sure.—How many hundreds have been regarded as Hereticks & Atheists (& treated accordingly) for maintaining that the *Earth turns round*, & now, who but Savages & Ideots believe the contrary?—The Affair is this: a great Majority of those who exist, or at least derive Emolument by teaching & governing others, are themselves very incompetent to either: it is natural that they should dread the Detection of their Ignorance, since, as was said of old, 'it is by this Craft they get their Gain.'[9]

You may rely on it that you yourself are looked upon with a thorough envious Eye by your Brother Organists, who instead of endeavouring successfully to

SW was not usually so censorious of Handel: on other occasions he was quick to spring to his defence against anti-Handelians (see SW to Novello, 17 Feb. 1813). The reference in his accusation of Handel's plagiarism of Bach is not clear, unless by 'The Golden Treasury' he meant the '48' and was thinking of the close similarity between the subject of the chorus 'And with his stripes we are healed' from *Messiah* and the A minor Fugue from Book II. But Handel could not have known the '48', and the subject in question is in any case a stock cliché of the period and was no more Bach's property than Handel's.

[4] i.e. R. J. S. Stevens. In his diary entry for 12 Oct., he noted: 'Coffee with [Joseph] Smith. Bradbury Trueman and Jacobs there, who played some of Sebastian Bach's fugues' (Argent, 164). SW is probably referring to this occasion.

[5] Perhaps the comparisons between Bach and Handel in Burney's *History* and his contributions to Rees (see SW to Jacob, 17 Sept. 1808, n. 10).   [6] i.e. Stevens.

[7] i.e. fugues by Bach with 'clear and marked subjects', to counter Stevens's criticism. The 'Doctor's Fugue' and the 'Judgement Fugue' have not been identified. It seems likely from SW's choice of the E major fugue (the 'Saints in Glory Fugue') and the one 'hard by it' in E flat that he is referring here to Book II of the '48'.   [8] John 3: 19.

[9] Acts 19: 25: the reference is to Demetrius and other silversmiths of Ephesus, who derived their income from making shrines to Diana, and whose activities St Paul sought to curb.

imitate your persevering Industry, by which you have accomplished so much, & gained such a clear Insight into the true Style of our Autho[r,] prefer the shorter & easier Way (as they think) of establishing their Pretentions to Criticism by defaming their Superiors.

Your Letter found me this Evening in my Chamber, to which I have been confined all Day, or rather from which I dreaded to go out, having had a severe Touch of a bilious Complaint, to which I am occasionally subject, particularly at this Time of the year: but a Day's nursing & a few grains of Rhubarb & Magnesia or the like, almost always set me to Rights again, & I fully expect to get out To-morrow, of which indeed I should much regret to be disappointed, as I am engaged to a Party[10] where we are to have some Sebastian, arranged by Horn for 2 Violins, Tenor & Bass,[11] & a glorious Effect they produce, as you may guess.— What must they do in a full Orchestra![12]

Even Germans themselves are not free from the Envy of such a transcendant Genius. I will not tell you the Name of the Person till Sunday (for I mean to be with you) neither would you *believe*, & perhaps can hardly credit it on my solemn Asseveration that a Man of real musical Judgement, some Science, & admirable Talent on his own Instrument, compared one of those Fugues which Horn has arranged (which you do not remember as it is not among the 48),[13] to *a Hog floundering in the Mud*.

Thank Heaven that Prejudice & Spite, however prevalent in England, are not solely found here: if it were so, I should wish rather to be ranked among the honest Hindoo Barbarians.

Adieu, I trust to see you on Sunday by 1 o'Clock.

Yours ever truly

    S Wesley

Mrs W. joins in best wishes to Mrs J. yourself & Family.

[10] In Paddington: see SW to his mother, 20 Oct. [1808] (Wesley's Chapel, London).

[11] i.e. from Horn's *A Sett of twelve Fugues*: see SW to Jacob, 17 Oct. 1808, n. 2.

[12] Less than a year later SW included an arrangement of the D major fugue from Book I of the '48' (one of the fugues arranged by Horn) in a revised version of his D major organ concerto which he performed at Tamworth: see SW to Jacob, 25 Sept. 1809.

[13] Either the organ fugue in D minor, BWV 538 ('The Dorian') or the probably spurious keyboard fugue in B flat on B-A-C-H, BWV 898.

To [Benjamin Jacob][1] [Camden Town, ?17 November 1808][2]

ALS, 4 pp. (RCM, MS 2130, fo. 9)

My dear Sir,

I always suspect the Sincerity of sudden Conversions.— Had not my Brother[3] known of your intimate Acquaintance with me, I should have been sooner induced to think that his Heart & his Words went together on Monday Night, but as I know he *can* play Salomon's Tricks (if not upon the Fiddle, yet upon a more dangerous instrument described by S[t] James),[4] I own I am a little of the Sadducee[5] in the present Instance, & am really afraid that (in regard to my Brother's real Opinion of Bach) 'there is no Resurrection.'[6]

I have already repeatedly expressed to you my Regret that a Man of my Brother's very transcendant musical Knowledge & skill should have been so betrayed *by bad Company* into Habits of thinking & acting so diametrically opposite to his Convictions & better Judgement: of course it follows (and I am sure that *you* will give me Credit for it) that whatever I ever have said or ever shall say, which may have an Appearance of Severity, can not be the Result of any worse Principle than the *Grief*, not the *Anger*, I feel in the Perversion & Perversity of such a mind.

Well then, you will not suppose that in what I speak to you confidentially concerning C. W. I have either 'Envy, Hatred, Malice, or Uncharitableness.'[7] The Searcher of all Hearts knoweth the contrary: I think of him with some Pleasure, as to the *native* & *original* Goodness of his Disposition, but with more Melancholy when I consider such a cruel Sacrifice to the Whims & Artifices of designing Persons who have made him the mere Puppet of their base & interested Designs.

Now to more pleasing Reflexions.—I am glad that you brought forward the Hymn Tune[8] for two Reasons, the former (& the better) because I know it is

---

[1] Although lacking an address portion, it is clear from the content and present location of this letter that it is to Jacob.

[2] This date is added on the manuscript in pencil in another hand, and is repeated in Eliza Wesley's edition. It is possible that it was taken from a postmark or a date on an address panel which is no longer extant.

[3] SW's brother Charles had evidently been evincing some enthusiasm for Bach's music. SW was not disposed to trust the sincerity of his words: Charles was an arch-conservative and a staunch Handelian in his musical tastes.   [4] The tongue: see Jas. 3: 1–12.

[5] The Sadducees were the traditionalist Jewish priestly party, noted for their reactionary conservatism.

[6] Matt. 22: 23.   [7] BCP, the Litany.

[8] Possibly SW's 'Might I in thy sight appear' (1807), the opening of which he quotes in his next letter to Jacob.

just in the Style which particularly pleases C. W. (for his best Compositions are pathetic:) & 2[dly] if he should venture to report the Fact to our worthy Sister,[9] she will be extraordinarily chagrined in finding that a Man whom she has represented (these are her own words) as 'destitute of every Sentiment, of Justice, Honour, or Integrity'[10] should have had sufficient Respect to *any* religious Words to think of setting them to Music: I dare say she will add that they are thoroughly profaned by the experiment.

Your playing Bach on Monday set my Brother upon *his Battle-Horse*. I'll answer for it that he made Handel's Harmonies tolerably full.—I never yet found any other Man who seemed so *made* for him.—Kelway,[11] C.W.'s Harpsichord Master (an admirable Musician & perfect Player) was known to have said every where that W. played Handel in a vastly superior Manner even to Handel himself.— Kelway (by the Way) was one of the most accurate Criticks of *Performance* of his (or perhaps any other) Time.—

I can have no possible Objection to acceding to your Request about sitting to M[r] Bacon,[12] but would wish to know how long at one Time he would require my Attendance: it will be extremely agreeable to me to be better acquainted with him, & I wish you to signify the same to him at your first convenient Opportunity.

---

[9] SW's elder sister Sarah (1759–1827). She was involved in a small way in various literary activities and acted as governess to a number of families; by this time she was increasingly involved with the care of her mother, with whom she and her brother Charles continued to live. SW's relations with her and Charles had been strained since his adolescence, and for much of his adult life he had little contact with them except in times of personal or financial crisis. Sarah's many letters to SW (which, untypically, he preserved) are characterized by plain speaking and frequent criticisms of his conduct.

[10] Evidently a quotation from a letter from Sarah: not preserved.

[11] Joseph Kelway (*c*.1702–82), English organist, harpsichordist, and composer, organist at St Michael's, Cornhill (1730) and St Martin's in the Fields (1736). He had been the teacher of SW's brother Charles and earlier of Handel's friend Mrs Delany, who rated him 'little inferior to Handel'. Burney described his playing style as one of 'masterly wildness . . . bold, rapid, and fanciful' (*Grove*[6]; Burney, *History*, iv. 664; Mercer, ii. 1009).

[12] Like his father John Bacon the elder (1740–99), John Bacon (1777–1859) was a highly prolific sculptor who specialized in monuments. After initial training from his father he entered the Royal Academy Schools in 1782. He won a silver medal in 1786 and a gold medal in 1797, and exhibited at the Royal Academy from 1792 to 1824. He was another member of the Wesley–Jacob circle of Bach enthusiasts, and had apparently succeeded in introducing the music of Bach to his own children. In a letter to him of 12 Dec. 1808 (Emory), Jacob remarked: 'It delights me to hear that your children are Bachists! What a convincing proof it is that the subjects are natural and beautiful for otherwise babes would not be able to reach them, and there are several families within my circle, where the divine strains are to be heard from the lisping voices of infants.' Jacob went on to quote a passage from SW's letter to him of 8 Dec. SW sat for his portrait, which was completed and delivered to Jacob in Nov. 1809 (Jacob to Bacon, 18 Nov. 1809 (Emory)). The portrait, which according to this letter was in pencil, has not been traced. For Bacon, see Rupert Gunnis, *Dictionary of British Sculptors 1660–1851* (London, 1953), 28–31.

If he will give me *legal* Notice, by which I mean about the space of a Week, I will wait upon him with much Pleasure; we can then settle a Time for my sitting to him, which I do not think would suit me on any day when I go to Cossens's,[13] as I am always full of crowded Work then from Morning till Night.

Pray inform Mr G. Gwilt,[14] that I shall with great satisfaction attend him on Wednesday:[15] I must cut & contrive how to manage, for this is my Paddington Day, & I must be cunning to *transfer* some of the Business on the Occasion. I fear there is no Possibility of getting previously to your Organ,[16] because it will be no easy Matter for me to get into your Latitude sooner than ½ past 4, & even then I must beg Leave to attend the Brats at a much earlier Hour than usual in order to accomplish this.[17]

You may also tell Elliott[18] that I will dine with him on some Day between the 20th & 27th as desired, altho' I do not love 'a *little* Church Organ.'—Perhaps this is only an Antiphrasis, & that he & you mean a great one.

Remember me in the kindest way to M^rs 𝄢 [music example][19] & all my young Bachists, & I trust that I shall remain, (not only in this, but in a better World,)

Your lasting Friend,

S Wesley

---

[13] Probably the school in Paddington where SW taught on Wednesdays and Saturdays. SW's letters to Bacon are addressed to him at Paddington Green, where Bacon may have had a studio. It may have been suggested to SW that he could conveniently sit for his portrait while in the neighbourhood.

[14] Both George Gwilt (1775–1856) and his brother Joseph (1784–1863) were for a time members of SW's musical and social circle. They were prominent architects, shared SW's interest in the music of J. S. Bach and Gregorian chant, and were Freemasons. George Gwilt was a close neighbour of Jacob: he lived close to Surrey Chapel at 8 (now 18) Union Street (*DNB*; Colvin; *Survey of London*, xxii. 84). For Joseph Gwilt, see SW to Novello, [24 Nov. 1809].   [15] 23 Nov.

[16] At Surrey Chapel.

[17] It was a considerable distance from Paddington to the Blackfriars Road area, where Gwilt and Jacob lived and where Surrey Chapel was situated.

[18] The organ builder Thomas Elliot (*c*.1759–1832) was a close professional associate of SW at this time. He built the organ at Surrey Chapel (1793), supplied the organ for SW's lecture courses at the Royal and Surrey Institutions, and built SW's own house organ. He had evidently offered to demonstrate 'a little church organ' to SW.

[19] i.e. Mrs Jacob. The music example is the opening of the C sharp major fugue from Book II of the '48'; the significance of its use here is unknown.

To Benjamin Jacob   [Camden Town, ?21 November, 1808][1]

ALS, 4 pp. (RCM, MS 2130, fo. 11)

My dear Sir,

Although I fully hope & expect to enjoy your Company on Wednesday next,[2] yet as you ask me a question in your last, concerning a Personage[3] who (as you very truly observe) is an Acquisition to *any* musical Cause that he is determined to espouse, I am pleased in an Opportunity of coinciding with you upon so agreeable a Subject as a candid Confession proceeding from a mind formerly prejudiced, but now (I trust) conquered by the irresistible Omnipotence of Truth.

You ask me what I think—I think with you that my Brother held out as long as he could, but that being so closely besieged by very many Judges of Music who have been so thoroughly & sincerely converted to the Truth of *the Bach Perfection*, he found it impossible to maintain a tenable Post any longer, & therefore wisely made a Virtue of Necessity, for I am yet of Opinion that if he could even now defend the Pre-eminence of Handel, he would; & I have but little Doubt (so long & so well as I have known him) that amongst mere Handelians he will but too readily relapse into Blasphemy.

Now observe, that I do not say this as if I were indifferent on *which* side he enlisted, but am only endeavouring to prove to you, from my own experience, that you will do well not to be too implicit in your Faith, with Regard to his *real* Opinion.—There can be no Question that *while he is hearing* the Sublimities of our Idol, he must prefer them to any other Sounds that could have been conceived: but no sooner does a Temptation to his *besetting* Sin (the blind Worship of Handel) fall in his Way, than he returns 'to his Wallowing in the Mire.'[4]—

Time proves all Things, & I sincerely hope (tho' I much doubt) that it may prove my Conjectures erroneous.

On Wednesday we may appoint a Day for Mr Bacon, & on Saturday[5] I will some how or other endeavour to manage a Meeting at Elliott's—the fact is that

---

[1] This letter is dated 22 Nov. 1808 in another hand. This date, which may have been taken from a postmark on an address portion no longer preserved, is repeated in Eliza Wesley's edition, and its accuracy is accepted here. 22 Nov. was a Tuesday in 1808; SW's reference to 'Wednesday next' (instead of 'tomorrow' or 'tomorrow week') for his meeting with Bacon suggests that he may have written the letter in the evening of Monday, 21 Nov.

[2] Possibly 23 Nov., the same meeting as referred to in the previous letter.

[3] Charles Wesley jun.

[4] cf. 2 Pet. 2: 22: 'The dog is turned to his own vomit again; and the sow that was washed to her wallowing in the mire.'

[5] Possibly 26 Nov., and the meeting at Elliot's premises referred to in the previous letter.

Saturday is one of my Paddington Days, & there is that Nuisance in Society yclept a Dancing Master who usurps my Territory till 1 o'Clock, & I have always 4 Hours work after him. The Governess is not among the most accommodating of her Sex, & often gives herself more Airs than I can very patiently tolerate.— Although upon occasion I can be a Match for saucy people, yet as Litigation always puts me in a Fever (which is a dear Sacrifice for Victory) I would rather prevent Dispute than exert my Power of Defence.—We will however talk this Matter over throughly on Wednesday, or rather perhaps on Thursday Morning, for I shall make Use of my *Blanket Privilege* in Charlotte Street on the preceding Night, unless any Circumstance in your domestic Arrangements may possibly render it inconvenient.

With regard to Lyne's Primer Grammar,[6] I can take it with me when I next part from you.—Charles[7] is quite overjoyed in anticipating the Utility of which I know it will be to him, even *now*, after having waded through Lilly's.[8]— The Method is beautifully simple, & I am persuaded that with *your* Application (which I know not a Parallell unto excepting in John Cramer & S[r] Isaac Newton[9]) I am persuaded that all the Latin you will find occasion for, you will acquire within a few Months.

I have changed my form of salutation this Time—Pray remember me most

kindly to M[rs]  etc. [10] etc.

Adieu,

    SW

---

[6] Richard Lyne, *An Introductory Book for the Use of Grammar Schools: The Latin Primer* (1795), which had evidently supplanted Lily's Primer (see n. 8).

[7] i.e. SW's son. Like his father, he had a lively interest in the classics, and was evidently a precocious scholar: the Apr. 1808 number of *MM* carried a letter from him in which he queried the correctness of the quantity of a syllable used in a Latin epitaph (*MM* 25 (1808), 222).

[8] William Lily (?1468–1522), *A Short Introduction of Grammar . . . for the Bringing up of all those that Intend to Attain to the Knowledge of the Latin Tongue* (1567), the standard Latin primer in England since the 16th cent.   [9] Sir Isaac Newton (1642–1727), English scientist and mathematician.

[10] The opening of SW's 'Might I in thy sight appear' (1807), a setting for solo voice and keyboard of v. 4 of his father's hymn 'Saviour, Prince of Israel's race'. Autographs of SW's setting are at BL, Add. MSS 14340 and 71107; for modern editions, see Geoffrey Bush and Nicholas Temperley (eds.), *English Songs 1800–1860* (*Musica Britannica*, vol. 43) (London, 1979); Robin Langley and Geoffrey Webber (eds.), Samuel Wesley, *Two Sacred Songs* (Oxford, 1997). For SW's later quotation of the text, see SW to [William Hone], 18 Aug. 1825.

To William Crotch

Camden Town, 25 November 1808

ALS, 3 pp. (NRO, MS 11244, T 140A)
Addressed To | Dr Crotch | Dutchess Street | Portland Place | Friday 25th Nov.
Pmk 4 o'Clock 25 NO

> Camden Town
> Nov. 25 1808

Dear Sir

I hope that I shall always feel ready to render any Service to the cause of real good Musick, & of all those who are zealous to promote it, among whom it is known, & acknowledged that you are eminently conspicuous.[1] In answer to your Questions concerning the Date of Seb. Bach's Birth & Decease I cannot at this Moment give you correctly the Year of either, but it will perhaps be satisfactory News to inform you that Mr Horn, Sen^r2 (the quondam Instructor of the royal Family) & myself are preparing for the Press the whole Life of Sebastian together with an accurate List of all his Works which much resemble Handel's for their Multitude & which (not much to the Honour of England) have been as yet totally unknown here, even by their Titles.—This Life was written in German by Forkel, & has been translated by Mr Stephenson of Queen Square, a great Enthusiast in the Cause, & a most excellent Judge of Musick.—If you however have any immediate Occasion to be informed of the exact Dates in Question, I will apply to Mr Horn, who, upon referring to the Life will be able instantly to satisfy you concerning them.[3]

---

[1] For Crotch, see SW to Charles Wesley jun., 15 Jan. 1807, n. 72. This letter is evidently in response to enquiries from him concerning J. S. Bach, no doubt in connection with his work on vol. iii of his *Specimens of Various Styles of Music Referred to in a Course of Lectures read at Oxford & London*, a spin-off from his Royal Institution lectures. Vols. i and ii had been published earlier in 1808; vol. iii was published around Apr. 1809. It included the E major Fugue from Book II of the '48', discussed by SW in the postscript to this letter, as its sole example of J. S. Bach's music. In his Preface, Crotch wrote: 'Sebastian Bach was contemporary with Handel. His most celebrated productions are organ fugues, very difficult of execution; profoundly learned, and highly ingenious . . . The student should be careful not to form a hasty judgment of his character as the riches of his learning are not scattered superficially, but lie too deeply buried to be immediately perceived. In the management of a strict fugue he stands unrivalled, and he seems to be the most scientific of all composers.' In a footnote which helps to establish the date of the preface, Crotch remarked that 'the life and several works of this great composer will shortly be published by Mr. Horn and Mr. Samuel Wesley; to the latter I am much indebted for the use of his valuable and correct manuscript copy of the above work.'

[2] i.e. Charles Frederick Horn, in distinction from his son Charles Edward Horn (1786–1849).

[3] SW's comment reveals that he did not at this time have a copy of Forkel's biography in his possession. SW's copy, apparently acquired later, is now in the Pendlebury Library, Cambridge, and is annotated by him as being 'the gift of my very kind & respected Friend, Mr William Drummer'.

It is known that Bach & Handel were Contemporaries, & that the latter out-lived Bach, who had a high Respect for the Talents of Handel, & made several Efforts to obtain a Conference with him, *which he never could accomplish.*[4]

The Pains you have taken to sift & analyse every Note in the Fugue to which you are justly so partial,[5] convince me that you are fully determined to appreciate his true Worth.—As my *own* Value for him exceeds all Power of Language the less said *by me* perhaps the better, but this I will venture to affirm from my own *Experience* (which I find to be the safest Criterion of Truth) that the more he is studied, understood, & heard, the more he instructs, charms, & affects us. I find new Beauties every Time I take him up, & am always tempted to declare when I shut the book that the last Page I have perused is the most interesting.

Let me advise you as a Friend to burn your London Copy[6] without Delay or Ceremony: it is a Libel upon the great Author it affects to announce, & if an indifferent Judge of Musick were to be asked his Opinion of Bach from such a nefarious Specimen, I think he would be fully warranted in saying that 'his Harmonies are full of grammatical Blunders, & he could not have understood the Rules of Counterpoint.[']

I understand that Wilkinson[7] in the Haymarket is trying to insult the Public with a similar Grub Street Performance,[8] but I shall write him down publickly with a Pen dipped in Gall.—If my Life & Health are spared, you shall see not only the Preludes & Fugues but some other odd Matters of this poor Gentleman who has remained so long incognito to our learned musical Nation, which will not disgrace him.

The Zurich Edition,[9] from which I made my MS. copy is *the only* one, on which any tolerable Dependence can be safely placed, & even in this I have found not fewer than 30 or 40 Faults, such as the Omission or Intrusion of a ♭, ♯, or ♮, which you know in Works of chromatic & sometimes *enharmonic* Modulation, produce very queer & crude Effects.

---

[4] This information was doubtless from Forkel, who described two unsuccessful attempts that Bach made to visit Handel during Handel's visits to Halle (*New Bach Reader*, 460–1).

[5] No doubt the E major Fugue discussed above, which Crotch in his *Substance of Several Courses of Lectures on Music, Read in Oxford and the Metropolis* (1831), 120, described as 'perhaps the best' of the fugues in the '48'.

[6] Presumably the Broderip and Wilkinson edition of Book II of the '48', based on the 1801 Simrock edition and published as *Préludes et Fugues pour le Forte-Piano . . . I Partie.*

[7] Of the firm of Wilkinson & Co., which had succeeded Broderip and Wilkinson earlier in 1808, and had premises at 13 Haymarket.

[8] Presumably a proposed edition of Book I of the '48', which Wilkinson would have titled *II Partie.* According to Johnson's *Dictionary*, 'Grub Street was originally the name of a street near Moorfields in London, much inhabited by writers of small histories, dictionaries, and temporary poems, whence any mean production is called *grubstreet*'.

[9] i.e. the Nägeli edition.

By the way, in the Edition above mentioned, a double ♯ is contradicted, not by a single one, but always by a ♮; this used to puzzle me devilishly for a long Time till I was up to the Rig (to use an elegant Phrase) for I played it the old orthodox white Key wherever it came, which you know made the Harmony delightful, & well confirmed what had been said by People who ought to have known better, that 'Bach had no air', they might have added 'nor Harmony either' in those Circumstances.

Adieu, my dear Sir, forgive my Prolixity, & be assured that I am with Esteem

Yours very truly

S Wesley

P.S. The reason why I think Bach wrote B♮ in the 24th <B>ar, is because before the 6th crotchet in the same Bar, a ♯ is placed in the Zurich Edit. & this had been superfluous had the same Note been sharpened in the first Instance; besides, upon repeated Trials I think you will find that the ♯ B after the ♮ produces an agreeable Variety.[10]

N.B. Bach composed the 48 Preludes & Fugues expressly for the Purpose of making Proficients on the Clavier in all the 24 Keys, & he calls it (I believe) in German, *the compleatly well tempered Clavier*, which you know is alike applicable to Clavichord, Harpsichord, Piano Forte, or Organ but there is no Question that it is only on the Organ their sublime & beautiful Effects can be truly heard.

To [Charles Burney]¹ [Camden Town], 6 December 1808

ALS, 1 p. (private collection of Michael Burney-Cumming; address panel Osborn, MSS 3, Box 5, folder 319)²

Pmk 6 DEC 1808

Docketed by Mme d'Arblay: ※

[10] SW's postscript refers to the E major fugue from Book II of the '48', and is doubtless in response to an enquiry from Crotch about a reading in Crotch's own copy. SW is here arguing for the correctness of the reading in his own manuscript copy and the Nägeli edition on which it was based, both of which have a B♮ at the third crotchet in the bass part of bar 24, followed by B♯ at the sixth crotchet in the tenor. The two other early printed editions have a B♯ in the bass at this point. The reading favoured by SW is adopted by Crotch in *Specimens* and is also in the Wesley–Horn edition. Most modern editions, including the *Neue Bach Ausgabe*, prefer the other reading.

¹ Burney is identified as the addressee of this letter by his daughter's characteristic docketing.

² The address panel also bears Burney's undated draft reply, beginning 'those that seldom go to a concert or Theatre'. The year of the postmark on the address panel was misread by Hemlow as 1802, and the date of CB's draft reply is accordingly given by her as '[*post* 6 Dec. 1802?]' (Joyce Hemlow, *A Catalogue of the Burney Family Correspondence, 1749–1878* (New York, 1971), 45).

My dear Friend

'The Time cries Haste & Speed must answer it'. I do not mean that I need feel hurried in the Preparation of these Lectures,[3] but yet I am so averse from the Probability of being *hard run*, or of doing any Thing (that I can do at all,) in a slovenly Way, I wish to *pipe all Hands* without Delay, & plunge *con Amore*, in Medias Res.

Since I parted from you, I have thought that perhaps the following Subjects for *two* of the Lectures might not be inappropriate; I mean *On the Power of musical Prejudice*, & on the *Power of Musick upon Morals*.[4] Pray tell me whether you approve these as Theses.

But first tell me what you think will be the most *taking* Style of introductory Lecture?[5] My grand Aim is to endeavour to dispel a few of the Clouds of Partiality & Prejudice which certainly have too long overshadowed *Apollo*[6] in this Country.

In a successful Attempt at this, your very sincere & grateful Friend will avow, (& swear if it should be necessary) that he has not lived in vain.

Adieu my dear Sir, you know my Heart, I trust

SW

Decr 6. 1808

To [Benjamin Jacob]   Camden Town, 8 December 1808

ALS, 3 pp. (RCM, MS 2130, fo. 13)

My dear Sir,

Previously to the Receipt of your last kind Letter,[1] which I this Day received, I had resolved to have nothing to do with that infamous Libeller, the

---

[3] As Burney had predicted, SW had been invited to lecture at the Royal Institution. His course was originally planned to begin in Feb. 1809, but was postponed first to 3 Mar. and then to 10 Mar. This was to be SW's first experience of lecturing, and he was understandably keen to ask Burney's advice on how best to proceed. (Kassler, 'Lectures'; Royal Institution of Great Britain, Minutes).

[4] The text of a later lecture on musical prejudice, delivered on 13 Jan. 1830, but possibly incorporating some material dating back to SW's 1809 Royal Institution course, is at BL, Add. MS 35014, fo. 53. The text of SW's lecture on Music and Morals has not been preserved.

[5] The eventual title of SW's first lecture was 'On Music as an Art and as a Science' (see SW to Burney, 20 Dec. [1808]). The text of a later lecture with a similar title, dated 7 Jan. 1828, but possibly incorporating some material dating back to SW's 1809 Royal Institution course, is at BL, Add. MS 35015, fo. 175.

[6] i.e. J. S. Bach.

---

[1] Not preserved.

Satyrist:[2] for any Person either of decent Character or tolerable Education to contend with such a Wretch, would be about as wise as for a General to send a formal Challenge to a Scavenger.

I was informed to Day that I am to expect a Summons from a Friend to a grand Birth Day Anniversary Dinner on the 21st however as it has not yet arrived, I shall consider myself previously engaged to you & Mr Bacon,[3] therefore I hereby commission you to convey my Respects to him, & if *6* o'Clock should not be too late for him (as I cannot get loose from the Manor House[4] till $\frac{1}{2}$ past 5) I will hope for the Pleasure of joining your Party.

I am glad to find that Sebastian is to be heard even 'out of the mouths of Babes & Sucklings':[5] depend on it, there is nothing more necessary to render his divine Strains the chief Delight & Solace of all *truly harmonized* Souls, but an assiduous Cultivation of them.—[6] He was certainly dropped down among us from Heaven.

I am concerned to find that your Friend ἀγωνιζόμενος[7] is not likely to domesticate among us, but yet am rejoiced to find there are Hopes of at least a transient Visit.—He certainly is a very superior man, & as such men are scarce, I am indeed idolatrously covetous of such Society. I am happy in being able to declare that I feel myself supported by the Friendship (the best *human* Prop) of a little Phalanx of such Characters as I do think I may venture to say were 'made only a little lower than the Angels,'[8] & what I most fear is that the Kindness I experience in this World will render me too fond of it, & make me mistake Earth for Heaven.

I am much flattered by the good Opinion which your venerable Friend is pleased to entertain of me, although I have afforded him no *practical* Proof of deserving it, unless in the exercise of my Fingers.—I assure you that I have not felt

---

[2] *The Satirist, or Monthly Meteor*, a monthly periodical published between Oct. 1807 and June 1814, edited first by George Manners and later by William Jerdan. It had attacked the Surrey Institution in Sept. 1808 (pp. 136–9), but the immediate cause of SW's remark was no doubt the heavy-handed 'Hints to Lecturers' in the Dec. number (pp. 508–13), which Jacob may have drawn to SW's attention in his letter (Sullivan, *TRA* 383–6; *The Satirist* 3 (1808), 136–9, 508–13).

[3] Doubtless for a sitting for his portrait.

[4] The Manor House at Paddington Green, where the school at which SW taught was located: see SW to Bridgetower, 23 Feb. 1797, n. 4. The meeting was presumably at Bacon's nearby house or premises (see SW to Bacon, 28 Dec. [1808], n. 3), as there would have been insufficient time for SW to travel from Paddington to Blackfriars.   [5] Ps. 8: 2.

[6] These two sentences are quoted by Jacob in his letter to Bacon of 12 Dec. (see SW to Jacob, [?17 Nov. 1808], n. 12).

[7] 'Struggler': the *nom de plume* of a prominent convert of Rowland Hill, not now identifiable. The story of his conversion was evidently well known at the time. For a letter from him to Hill, see Edward Sidney, *The Life of the Rev Rowland Hill, A.M.* (London, 1833), 217.   [8] Ps. 8: 5.

so much affected by any Harangue from the Pulpit for many years past as I was on Sunday by the honest unstudied natural Discourse Mr Hill[9] gave us: I prefer such a Sermon to all the polished rhetorical Essays in the world, which (most falsely) are called *Preaching*—moralising is the utmost extent of the Term suitable to such cold, dry, lifeless Compositions, & I had rather hear two Pages of John Bunyan's Pilgrim[10] than Folios of such uninteresting Trash.

N.B. I had rather be your joint Organist than your Successor, altho' I am very grateful to Mr Hill for his thinking me worthy the latter Post: I trust that (if it be best for us) we may live some Years yet to be mutually serviceable to the Cause of Music, of Friendship, & of Truth; which I am old fashioned enough to think ought never to be separated, & in the love of the Truth believe me

My dear Sir
Yours faithfully
   S. W.

Mrs W. unites with us all in kindest Regards.

Camden Town | Thursday 8 Decr 1808

---

[9] The Revd Rowland Hill (1744–1833), evangelistic preacher and minister of Surrey Chapel. The sixth son of Sir Rowland Hill, first Baronet, he was educated at Shrewsbury and Eton, and entered St John's College, Cambridge in 1764, graduating BA in 1769. He began his preaching career while at Cambridge; after graduation he sought ordination, but was repeatedly refused on account of his irregular and controversial preaching. He was eventually ordained in 1773 and was subsequently appointed to the curacy of Kingston, Somerset. He remained a controversial figure, and on leaving Somerset was refused a licence by the Bishop of Carlisle. He continued to preach 'wherever he could find an audience, in churches, chapels, tabernacles, and the open air, often immense congregations, and sometimes amid great interruption and violence' (*DNB*). He and his brother Sir Richard Hill, Bt., built Surrey Chapel in 1782 and he became its minister, where his 'earnest, eloquent, eccentric preaching' attracted large congregations. He was also active in the Religious Tract Society, the British and Foreign Bible Society, and the London Missionary Society, and was an enthusiastic advocate of vaccination, carrying out thousands of vaccinations in person (*DNB*; Edward Sidney, *The Life of the Rev Rowland Hill, A.M.* (1833). For Surrey Chapel, see SW to [Jacob], 4 Sept. [1809], n. 13).

[10] *The Pilgrim's Progress* (1678–84) by John Bunyan (1628–88).

To [Charles Burney]¹   Camden Town, 20 December [1808]²

ALS, 2 pp. (Osborn, MSS 3, Box 16, Folder 1193)
Docketed by Mme d'Arblay: ※

My dear Friend

I am eternally pestering you, but you bear my Baiting so patiently, that like the generous Majority of the World, I avail myself of your Non-Resistance, & resolve to put your Philosophy to the extreme Test.

Two more Questions previous to breaking the Ice (which by the Way is no easy Thing to do at present) & I will promise to be quiet until I come to *rehearse* my first Lecture to you at the College.

Although I have been used to play in Public from a Child, & therefore never feel embarrassed if my Tools are good, yet to *speak* in Public is another Affair, & of Course Want of early Habit must naturally create a Diffidence & Uncertainty of Success. Quaere therefore, whether it would not be advisable for me to hatch a little prefatory Apology, previous to the absolute Business of the Lecture, in Order to deprecate that Sort of Censure which might be excited by any Failure in the Manner of Delivery?

The second Point is, whether you think that there seems any real Necessity of adducing practical Examples in the first Discourse, the Subject of which (by your Approbation) will be on Music considered as an Art & as a Science.—This being so broad a Question, & where *general* Observations only appear to me requisite, that I see not well a fair Opportunity of any *manual* Operations, without using some Force towards the Argument, & Purport of the Disquisition.³

Favour me with your early Thoughts on these Topicks my dear Friend

    SW

                                        Camden Town 20 Dec^r

---

¹ Burney's identity as the recipient of this letter is given by his draft reply on the same sheet (see n. 2).

² SW's request for advice on how to proceed with his forthcoming course of lectures at the Royal Institution establishes the year as 1808. Burney's draft reply, dated 20 Dec. with '1808' added in another hand, is on the same sheet; his references to the recent death of his eldest son Richard Thomas and the serious illness of his daughter Esther confirm this dating.

³ Burney replied: 'With respect to your two queries, *pauca verba* will suffice. I approve entirely a prefatory apology and deprecation of severity to a lecturer unpracticed in public speaking with anything but his Fingers. And I am as clearly of opinion that you sh^d keep back your performance till it is necessary to illustrate some remarkably pleasing style of composition wch you have been describing.'

To Charles Wesley Junior

Camden Town,
[*ante* 23 December 1808]¹

ALS, 1 p. (BL, Add. MS 35012, fo. 119)

Dear Charles,

Perhaps you or some of your friends will like to hear my Te Deum, Jubilate, and Litany, at St Paul's, next Sunday, Christmas Day.² They always keep this service of mine for high days and holidays; therefore there is hardly any other opportunity of hearing it but upon the four great festivals.³ The prayers begin at a quarter before ten in the morning.

I am sorry you cannot come to Mr Smith's⁴ on Saturday next, more particularly because I shall have no other day for this month to come vacant. The people at Bath are besieging me perpetually to come down without delay, and Dr. Harrington, Rauzzini, and the rest of the *musickers*, are already making great preparations.⁵ My fingers are so cold I can scarcely hold my pen.

Yours truly

SW

Love to my mother

---

¹ The year is given by Christmas Day falling on a Sunday and by SW's reference to his settings of the Te Deum, Jubilate, and Litany (see n. 2). SW's references to 'next Sunday' and 'Saturday next' imply that this letter was written no earlier than Monday, 19 Dec. and no later than Thursday, 22 Dec.

² For SW's setting of the Litany, composed in 1806, see SW to Charles Wesley jun., 15 Jan. 1807, n. 4. The autograph of the Te Deum and Jubilate (BL, Add. MS 14342) are dated 1808.

³ i.e. Christmas Day, Easter Day, Ascension Day, and Whitsunday.

⁴ Not certainly identified.   ⁵ SW visited Bath in Jan. 1809, returning on 27 Feb.

To John Bacon[1]   Randalls, near Leatherhead,[2]
28 December [1808]

ALS, 1 p. (Emory, Box 6)
Addressed To | —Bacon Esq[re] | Paddington Green[3] | near | The Church
Pmk DE 29 1808

Randalls
Near Leatherhead
Dec[r] 28th

Dear Sir

You must forgive my Non-Attendance To-morrow, by Reason of an Embargo laid upon me by one Richard Brinsley Sheridan,[4] of whom you may possibly of heard, & who detains me here vi et armis[5] a close Prisoner in his strongly fortified Castle.—I have already projected a Plan for breaking Gaol but whether it will not prove abortive in the Execution To-morrow must decide.—The Instant I shall have been so fortunate as to arrive once more at the great City, I will give you immediate Intelligence, mean while

believe me
Dear Sir
Yours very truly
   S Wesley

To John Bacon   Camden Town, 1 January 1809

AN, third person, 1p. (Emory, Box 6)
Addressed To | —Bacon Esq[re] | Paddington Green | near | The Church
Pmk 2 JA 1809

---

[1] For Bacon, see SW to [Jacob], [?17 Nov. 1808], n. 12.

[2] The address at this time of Richard Brinsley Sheridan (see n. 3).

[3] This was probably the address of Bacon's studio and workshop. Jacob's letter to Bacon of 12 Dec. 1808 was addressed to Newman Street, which according to the *Memoir of John Bacon* in the Jan. 1815 number of *EM* was the house in which he was born, and in which he was at that time living.

[4] The playwright and MP Richard Brinsley Sheridan (1751–1816), proprietor and manager of Drury Lane theatre. This is the only reference to him in the correspondence, and it is not known how SW came to be staying with him. SW may have known him through his connections with William Linley, the brother of Sheridan's first wife Elizabeth (*DNB*; Fintan O'Toole, *A Traitor's Kiss: The Life of Richard Brinsley Sheridan* (1997); Linda Kelly, *Richard Brinsley Sheridan: A Life* (1997).

[5] 'By force of arms'.

Mr S. Wesley presents his Respects to Mr Bacon, proposing to have the Pleasure of attending him next Tuesday[1] as near *One* o'Clock as he possibly can.

Camden Town | Sunday Jany 1. 1809

To William Savage[1]   Camden Town, 28 February [1809][2]

AL, third person, 1 p. (Royal Institution of Great Britain)

Arlington Street
Camden Town Feb 28th

Mr Samuel Wesley begs Leave to inform Mr Savage that he arrived in Town last Night, from Bath, where he was unavoidably detained some Weeks longer than he at first expected to be.[3]—He is at present considerably indisposed with a bad Cold, attended with swelled Glands of the Throat, which have rendered him very hoarse, & unable to speak out without much Inconvenience.—On this Account he would wish Permission to fix *Wednesday* next[4] for reading the Lecture, by which Time he hopes entirely to have recovered, and also would be glad to know whether any personal Attendance upon any one of the Managers is customary or expected previous to the Commencement of the Series.

   Mr S. may be assured that Nothing short of Illness should have occasioned this Procrastination, & requests him to communicate this Observation to the Managers.

---

¹ 3 Jan.

¹ William Savage (1770–1843), printer and engraver, was born in Howden in the East Riding of Yorkshire, and had in 1790 set up in business as a printer and bookseller in partnership with his brother James. In 1797 he moved to London, and around 1799 was appointed printer to the newly founded Royal Institution, where he also became assistant secretary to the board of managers, secretary to the library committee, secretary to the chemistry committee, and superintendent of the printing office. He was also in business on his own account from around 1803, and in 1807 printed Forster's *British Gallery of Engravings*, the high quality of which established his fame. His *Dictionary of the Art of Printing* appeared in 1840–1 (*DNB*).

² The year is given by SW's references to his recent visit to Bath and to his forthcoming course of lectures at the Royal Institution.

³ SW had been enthusiastically received and had been much in demand in Bath. In a letter to Sarah of 28 Jan. (Wesley College, Bristol), he wrote: 'I continue here in very good Health and Condition, and the Doubt only is when I shall be suffered to come away, for really the Bath People are most extremely kind & polite . . . I have very hard work to fight off the Invitations by which I am beset from Morning till Night.'

⁴ 8 Mar., instead of Friday 3 Mar. as originally planned. For reasons given in the next letter, SW eventually gave the lecture on 10 Mar.

To Benjamin Jacob

Camden Town, 2 March 1809

ALS, 3 pp. (RCM, MS 2130, fo. 15)
Addressed To | Mr Jacobs. | Charlotte Street | Black Friar's Road
Pmk 2 MR 1809

Camden Town.
March 2. 1809.

My dear Sir,

Here I am once more, and shall rejoice in the first Opportunity afforded me of an Interview after so long an Interval of Separation. You will I know give me full Credit for not having intentionally neglected writing to you: believe me I have been a greater Slave *during the Holidays* than I am when in the Mill-Horse Road of A B C Drudgery:[1] hurried & dragged about from Pillar to Post, and at Times when I most wanted & needed Retirement & Quiet for preparing my first Lecture, which although not designed for a profound or very luminous Composition (which I assure you *bonâ Fide*, that it will not be) yet some previous Meditation was needful, were it only to make a String of Trifles of the same *Tissue*; for nothing you know can be less tolerable than the mere outward & visible Sign of a Discourse without any of the inward & spiritual Grace that ought to attend it.

As Matters have turned out I am all in good Time: My first Lecture, such as it is, has been in Readiness for some Days, & I think I have no very contemptible Skeletons prepared for a second & third, which will make up *half* the course: I also think that I have at least a good *Subject* for a 4th if not a 5th, & if the miracles of Sebastian will not furnish me Ammunition for a 6th, I think I must have rather changed my Faith in him.—By the Way, I have had the Loan of many *Exercises*[2] of his, for the Harpsichord, which are every whit as stupendous as the Preludes & Fugues, & demonstrate him (what every fresh Scrap of his I meet does) the very Quintessence of all musical Excellence. It's droll enough that amongst these is inserted a beautiful Air,[3] which is published along with a Sett of *Emanuel* Bach's Lessons,[4] & which I saw at Bath: I am very much inclined to think that this Son, like many others, made but little Scruple of robbing his Father; and that he was not concerned for his Honor seems plain enough by the vile & most diabolical Copy that he gave

---

[1] This phrase is very reminiscent of Burney: cf. Lonsdale, 296, citing Burney to Twining, 3 Nov. 1786: 'the constant drudgery of a musical ABCdarian'.

[2] From SW's subsequent remarks (see n. 3), evidently Bach's *Clavierübung I* (the six Partitas, BWV 825–30), published by Hoffmeister in 1801–2 as *Exercises pour le clavecin*.

[3] Either the Aria in Partita IV, BWV 828, or in Partita VI, BWV 830. Neither has been found in published editions of C. P. E. Bach's music.

[4] Presumably his *Six Progressive Lessons for the Harpsichord or piano forte in different keys* (*c*.1740), an English edition of the 18 *Probestücke in 6 Sonaten*, (Wq. 63; H. 70–5).

Doctor Burney as a Present,[5] & from which the latter was wise enough to judge of & damn his works (as he thought): but the *Phoenix* must always revive.

I assure you I have long wished to be again among my London Friends, and am not a little revived by feeling myself in the old Saddle again, hard as I must travel;— for *new* Friends, however kind & sincere they may eventually prove, have not the *mellow* effect upon the Mind (if I may so say) as older ones, & it takes some Time to study Peoples' Habits & Inclinations before we can be in that perfectly pleasant *Familiarity* in their Conversation which to me is the most delicious Point in Society. —I trust that my good Friend & generous Hostess, whose name I need not mention, is in good Health; whom I assure you I mean to visit before long, whether you are in the Way or not, so now you have legal Notice, & may take your Measures accordingly.

As my Lecture is not to be read before next Friday week[6] (by the Request of some of the Governors who cannot attend on the Wednesday before, as I had appointed, & who do me the Honor to wish to be present) I shall be able, by Hook or by Crook to see you, & have a Pennyworth of Chat upon the Fun, some Day or other between now & then.—I am given to imagine that the *Squad* (you know whom I mean) had rather that their old Friend the Devil were Lecturer than I.—

Yours ever truly

S Wesley

Remember me to Rowley[7] & all the young Powlies.

To Benjamin Jacob   Camden Town, 3 March 1809

ALS, 3 pp. (RCM, MS 2130, fo. 17)
Addressed To | M[r] Jacobs. | Charlotte Street | Black Friars Road
Pmk 4 MR 1809

> Camden Town.
> March 3. 1809

My dear Sir

I have just received your very prompt Answer to mine,[1] & regret much that I am unable to be with you either To-Morrow[2] or Sunday,[3] but I think that if

---

[5] See SW to [Jacob], 17 Sept. 1808.   [6] 10 Mar.

[7] Jacob's son Rowland George, doubtless named after Rowland Hill. His manuscript book, noted by him as being a gift from his father in 1813 and giving his date of birth as 7 Dec. 1800, is at RCM, MS 4583a. He died in 1817. The 'young Powleys' were presumably Jacob's other children, who included his daughters Mary Lucretia and Elizabeth Ann, both baptized in 1804.

[1] Not preserved.   [2] 4 Mar.   [3] 5 Mar.

Wednesday next[4] would suit, I could manage to get to you by 5 o'Clock, tho' I fear not sooner. I wish as speedy a Line as you can give me on the Subject.

To your Query respecting Sebastian, I at once reply in the Affirmative: his Works would furnish Materials for 600 as easily as for 6 Lectures, & were all or half which he has written to be critically analyzed & duly animadverted upon, I doubt much whether the longest Life would not prove too short for the Task.—

But we must for the present confine & repress our Inclination to publish *too hastily* our Creed in the transcendant Merits of this marvellous Man: it will all go on well by slow Degrees, and the Instance you give of Stevens's beginning to revoke his Blasphemies, may be considered as a very strong & extraordinary Proof of it.—

I am glad you like Linley: he is a great Favourite of mine, & indeed I should be peculiarly ungrateful were I not attached to him, as I have every reason to think his Regard very sincere—He is a man of much musical Talent, as I dare say you soon discovered.

I have not forgotten having left your Book of Bach's Lutheran Hymns[5] at John Cramer's House: I will get them back at the first Opportunity: I was reminded particularly of the Circumstance two Days ago, when I found a Trio or two among the Exercises which I immediately remembered having played with you from your own Book.

I am about to put the *1ˢᵗ Trio* of the Six lent me by Horn,[6] into the Engraver's hands almost immediately—the best Way will be unquestionably to print them singly.

Remember me very cordially to Mʳˢ J. and all the young Fry—all here join in kind

Respects with
Dear Sir
Yours ever sincerely
  S Wesley

---

[4] 8 Mar.

[5] Presumably *Joh. Seb. Bachs vierstimmige Choralgesänge*, ed. J. P. Kirnberger and C. P. E. Bach, 4 vols. (Leipzig, 1784–7); or possibly the *Choral Vorspiele* mentioned in SW to [Jacob], [?26 Apr. 1809] below.

[6] The Sonata in E flat, BWV 525, the first of the six organ Trio Sonatas, BWV 525–30. The edition by SW and Horn appeared as single numbers at intervals in 1809; in his Reminiscences SW stated that it was prepared from a manuscript copy supplied by Horn.

To [William Savage]¹   Camden Town, 16 March [1809]²

ALS, 1 p. (Royal Institution of Great Britain)

Dear Sir

Having heard nothing from you to the contrary, I conclude that the Day on which I appointed to read, which was *next Wednesday*,³ is agreed to, & will hold myself in readiness accordingly.—The Subject of the Lecture will principally relate to *the Improvement of the Chromatic Scale, evinced in the Construction & Effects of the Patent Organ, designed by Willm Hawkes Esqre and built by Mr Elliot*.⁴

Perhaps this will serve as a sufficient Syllabus

I remain
Dear Sir
Yours truly
   S Wesley

Thursday 16 March

To George Polgreen Bridgetower   Camden Town, 25 March [1809]¹

ALS, 2 pp. (Emory, Letter 61)
Addressed To | Mr Bridgetower | John Street | 3. | Pall Mall | Saturday Afternoon
Pmk 27 MR 1809

Camden Town
25th of March

---

¹ The preservation of this letter in the correspondence files of the Royal Institution leaves no doubt that it was written to someone there. In the light of SW's letter to him of 28 Feb., William Savage is the most probable recipient.

² 16 Mar. falling on a Thursday and SW's reference to his forthcoming lecture establish the year of this letter.   ³ 22 Mar.

⁴ This lecture caused considerable controversy. SW used it to demonstrate the Hawkes–Elliot patent organ, which sought to overcome the problems of intonation encountered on conventionally tuned instruments in some keys by the provision of additional pitches controlled by a pedal. SW's action in promoting a commercial product and his alleged disingenuousness in omitting to point out some of the new system's imperfections were the subject of repeated attacks in *NMMR* from May 1809 on. The text of a later and considerably revised version of this lecture is at BL, Add. MS 35014, fos. 2–16. For a more extended discussion of the controversy, see Philip Olleson, 'The Organ-builder and the Organist: Thomas Elliot and Samuel Wesley', *JBIOS* 20 (1996), 116–25.

---

¹ The year is given by the postmark.

Dear Sir

I need not multiply Words (I trust) to assure you that I am much disappointed by the Necessity of deferring the Pleasure of your Visit on Monday next:[2] when I made the Engagement, it did not occur to my Remembrance that I am obliged to dine with the Somerset House Lodge on Account of adding my Vote to the Ballot for a most deserving Acquisition to the Society.—If Friday next,[3] commonly called Good Friday be a Day on which you have no Scruples concerning the Lawfulness of a Major or Minor Key, I shall be quite chez moi & most happy to receive you at 4 o'Clock to *fast* with me.—You know that an Englishman's Religion in Lent consists in eating *salt* Fish instead of *fresh*, and I find no particular Mortification in conforming to this pious Custom upon solemn Occasions.

Yours ever truly
S Wesley

To George Polgreen Bridgetower

Camden Town,
14 April [1809][1]

AL, third person, 1 p. (Rylands, DDWF 15/14)
Addressed Mr Bridgetower | John Street | Pall Mall
Pmk AP 15 1809

S Wesley is compelled to inform Mr Bridgetower that Mr Novello[2] has put off the Party at the Portuguese Chapel[3] for to morrow, all the Priests being engaged in absolving their Penitents from the Crime of slandering the Duke of York's Reputation.[4]

Friday 14th April | Camden Town

---

[2] 27 Mar.   [3] 31 Mar.

[1] The year is given by the postmark.

[2] Vincent Novello (1781–1861), organist, choirmaster, composer, and publisher, later to become SW's closest professional associate, and the recipient of over 170 letters from him between May 1811 and Dec. 1825. As a boy he had been a chorister at the Sardinian Embassy Chapel, where he also received lessons from Samuel Webbe I. He was appointed organist of the Portuguese Embassy Chapel at the age of 16 in 1797 or 1798, and SW had probably known him from this time, if not earlier.

[3] The chapel of the Portuguese Embassy, in South Street, off South Audley Street, Mayfair, where Novello was organist. It was a leading centre for Roman Catholic worship, with a long and distinguished musical tradition. The nature of the 'party' has not been discovered; it was perhaps a recital, conceivably the 'Portugueze fun' mentioned in SW to Jacob, [?26 Apr. 1809].

[4] Frederick Augustus, Duke of York (1763–1827), the second son of George III and Queen Charlotte and younger brother to the future George IV, had formed an ill-advised liaison with Mary Anne Clarke, described by *DNB* as 'a handsome adventuress'. She exploited her relationship with the Duke, who was Commander-in-Chief of the Army, by 'promising promotion to officers, who paid her for her

To George Smith

Camden Town, 23 April [1809][1]

ALS, 2 pp. (BL, Add. MS 31764, fo. 20)
Addressed To | George Smith Esqre | Feversham | Kent | 24th of April

Camden Town
April 23^d

Sir,

I feel it my Duty to apprize you of a very extraordinary Derangement that has taken Place at Oxford House Marylebone.—The Mesdames Barnes, after my Services at their School for 25 Years, have at length thought proper to engage another Master,[2] under the Pretence of my allowing the Pupils too small a Portion of Time for each Lesson, to advance them in a musical Progress.

It is rather an extraordinary Circumstance that no such Remonstrance has ever been made at four other Schools,[3] two of which I now continue to attend, and the other two I quitted, one because the Number was not of sufficient Consideration to render it worth the Trouble, and the other on Account of the Governess's quitting the Concern & retiring altogether from Business.—

I received some Weeks ago, an exceedingly flippant & ungenteel Letter from Mrs B. in which she observed that 'Mr Smith would be extremely angry, when he should know that his Daughter had been so much neglected by me.'—this neglect (as she falsely termed it) was merely my Continuance at Bath, for a Fortnight longer than I had originally designed to do, during which Time Mrs B. had not the slightest Pretext of Reason to complain, since Mr Cooke,[4] a most able Master & excellent Musician constantly attended the School in my Absence: but I did not commission him to instruct Miss Smith, as I did not consider myself in Honour authorized to depute a private Master[5] in that Instance without having previously consulted your Inclination upon the Subject: but I fully resolved at my Return to supply all

recommendations'. The matter was raised in the House of Commons on 27 Jan. 1809 and referred to a Select Committee. The Duke of York resigned his position as Commander-in-Chief on 28 Mar. 1809, and the allegations of corrupt practices were in time dropped (*DNB*; Fulford, 51–60).

[1] SW's references to his recent absence in Bath and his dismissal from the Barnes's school establish the year of this letter.

[2] SW's replacement was William Horsley (1774–1858). SW had in fact been dismissed over a month earlier: Horsley's diary entry for 21 Mar. had noted: 'Wesley finally rejected by Mrs Barnes. School offered to me at Midsummer' (Oxford, Bodleian Library, Horsley Papers (MS Eng e. 2134)).

[3] The two schools at which SW was teaching at this time were at Turnham Green and Paddington; the identity of the other two is not known.

[4] Probably Matthew Cooke (1760/1–1829), organist of St George's, Bloomsbury, and former teacher of Jacob.

[5] Cooke had evidently been teaching SW's 'school' pupils in his absence, but not his 'private' pupils. For the distinction between the two, see SW to Smith, 14 Aug. 1808, n. 4.

the Deficiency which might possibly have been the Consequence of my Detainder, & have done this fully, by giving Miss Smith an Hour's Lesson in several Instances, as will appear when the List of her Lessons shall be transmitted.—Indeed I have always felt so warmly interested for her Improvement that I am conscious of having at all Times exerted every Effort which I conceived could be efficacious to promote it; and the immediate Occasion of my troubling you with this Letter is to enquire whether it is your Wish that she should continue my Pupil, or whether she is to be turned over to whatever Master whom the Governesses (who know not a Note of music) shall think proper in their weighty Judgement to appoint in my Stead.—

I have the Pleasure to acquaint you that your Daughter is at every Lesson gaining much ground, especially in *reading* Music she has not seen before: & this Facility gives very cordial Delight & Satisfaction to

Sir,
Your obliged & obedient Servant
   S Wesley

To [Benjamin Jacob][1]   Camden Town, [?26 April 1809][2]

ALS, 3 pp. (RCM, MS 2130, fo. 19)

My dear Sir

I am a great Fool—I forgot whether I desired you to bring with you To-morrow my two Books of Bach.[3]—Whether I did or not, let me now request you to bear it in mind.—I do *not* forget that your Choral Vorspiele[4] is (or ought to be) in Cramer's Possession; but rather than you should be *bilked* out of it, you should have my Copy[5] to all Perpetuity, if there were never another in the *varsel* World.—

I hope & expect an happy Day To-morrow; but 'who knoweth what a day may bring forth'?[6]—How every Hour proves that 'in the Midst of Life we are in Death'![7]—but it is well we are assured of whom we may seek for Succour.

[1] Although lacking an address portion, it is clear from the content and present location of this letter that it is to Jacob.

[2] This date is added in pencil on the manuscript in another hand and is repeated in Eliza Wesley's published edition. It is possible that it was taken from a postmark or a date on an address panel which is no longer extant.   [3] Not identified.

[4] *J. S. Bachs Choral Vorspiele für die Orgel mit einem und zwey Klavieren und Pedal*, 4 vols. (Breitkopf, 1806).

[5] SW's copy of vols. 1 and 2 of the *Choral Vorspiele*, inscribed as having been given to him by Joseph Gwilt in 1809, is now at the RCM.

[6] cf. Prov. 27: 1: 'Boast not thyself of to morrow; for thou knowest not what a day may bring forth.'

[7] BCP, Burial Service.

Sermonizing[8] having become now a Part of my Profession, I will make no Apology for what some of the fine Bloods & Bucks would call Canting: but you & I know better Things:—I have much to say to you, but I fear that there will be but little Time to-Morrow to talk, save and except with our Fingers.—

I will bring To-morrow the Vorspiele, if it be only to electrify my Brother with[9]

The Portugueze Fun[10] is not settled yet: we will give all the stiff Handelians & Wolfians[11] a Death Wound to their Prejudice & their Impudence or there is no Truth in

SW

To [George Smith][1] Camden Town, 26 April [1809][2]

ANS, 1 p. (Emory, Letter 60)

Sir

Frankness on one Side demands it on the other: and as you are of Opinion that your Daughter is more likely to improve with Mr Cramer than with myself, I recommend to you the immediate Engagement of him, and shall directly apprize him of your Intention; remaining,

Sir,
Your very obedient Servant
S Wesley

Camden Town. | Wednesday 26 April

---

[8] i.e. lecturing.

[9] The opening of Bach's chorale prelude 'Wir gläuben all an einen Gott', BWV 680, contained in vol. 1 of the *Choral Vorspiele*. SW's quotation of the opening is incorrect: the first two notes ought to be joined with a tie. The passage is correctly given in the *Choral Vorspiele*.

[10] Not identified: perhaps a projected recital at the chapel, and possibly the 'party' discussed in SW to Bridgetower, 14 Apr. [1809].

[11] Possibly the supporters of the German music teacher and composer Georg Friedrich Wolf (1761–1814); but the point of the reference is not clear.

---

[1] The content of this letter establishes Smith as the recipient.

[2] The year is given by 26 Apr. falling on a Wednesday and SW's Camden Town address.

To George Smith   Camden Town, 9 May [1809]¹

ALS, 3 pp. (BL, Add. MS 31764, fo. 22)
Addressed To | George Smith Esqre | Feversham | Kent | May 9th

Camden Town
Tuesday May 9th

Sir

As I am not conscious of having 'acted any Part' either towards yourself or Mrs Barnes that can justly be considered as incorrect, I am not only willing, but desirous to enter into the most unequivocal Explanation of my Conduct relative to the Misunderstanding at Oxford House.

During my Stay in the West² I engaged a professional Man of real Worth & Talents (who is now my Assistant at another School) to attend the Pupils regularly until my Return, & I regret that I did not apply to you for Information whether it would have been agreeable to you that Miss Smith should also take her separate Lessons of him; if I had, it is probable that as you appeared at that Time to have a thorough Confidence in my Judgement & Opinion, you would have acceded to the Proposal, & in that Case, all these unpleasant Consequences would have been evited.—It is a most unaccountable Affair to me, that Mrs Barnes, who upon my Arrival in Town, expressed the highest Approbation of Mr Cooke's Attention & Punctuality, & who, it was to be expected, would have rather felt an Increase than a Diminution of favourable Sentiments towards the Person who recommended him, should have suddenly, & without any Kind of reasonable Pretext that I can assign, inform[ed] me that it was their Intention to engage another Master after the Midsummer Holidays;³ and whether this was a becoming Behaviour towards one who had been their constant Servant for nearly 30 Years,⁴ I leave to all dispassionate & unprejudiced Persons to judge.

With Regard to the individual Case of your Daughter, it appears to me, that if you were as well satisfied with her Progress now (which has been certainly a very rapid one) as you formerly seemed to be, I cannot guess why you should have wished to remove her into other Hands: you certainly have an unquestionable Right to engage as many Masters as may suit your Inclination, & to change them as often: but after having so strongly expressed your complete Approbation of my Instructions, & seemed so fully to rely upon my Advice relative to the Choice of her Music, &

---

¹ The year is given by 9 May falling on a Tuesday and SW's Camden Town address.

² i.e. at Bath.

³ Horsley noted in his diary that he started teaching at Oxford House on 10 Aug.

⁴ In his letter to Smith of 24 Apr., SW had stated that he had taught at the Barnes's school for twenty-five years.

Manner of Study &c I own I could not but consider your subsequent Intention as inconsistent with that Reliance on my Candour which you formerly professed.

I have no Inclination to disguise to You that I have always felt considerable Zeal to render your Daughter an excellent Player, & have used my utmost Efforts towards the Accomplishment of it.—This being the Truth, I did always suppose it your Intention that I should have the full Credit due to my Exertions in her Favour, & that she should be considered *exclusively my* Pupil.—The Friendship which subsists between me and Mr Cramer will at all Times prevent the Possibility of his suspecting me of an Atom of Jealousy as to the Eminence of his Abilities, and I do not retract a Word of my Opinion given you that I consider him as 'the Prince of Piano-Forte Players,' or I <may> add the *Emperor*, for the Word Prince <has> deservedly fallen into some Disrepute.[5]—At the same Time, I know (& he knows) that I understand the *Principles* of Piano Forte playing as well as himself, & after having taught it for 30 Years, with the compleat Knowledge of a very superior Instrument, it would reflect Disgrace on me if I did not.—

I have only to add, that if you should choose Miss Smith to go on *with me*, I would make no Objection whatever to attend *her*, whatever Master Mrs Barnes may employ to instruct the other Pupils: the Favour of an early Answer on this Question will oblige,

Sir
Yours very obediently
S Wesley

To William Crotch [Camden Town], 15 May [1809][1]

ALS, 1 p. (RCM, MS 3073)
Addressed To | Dr Crotch | Dutchess Street | Portland Place | N. 2

Dear Sir

I am much obliged by your Attention concerning Bach.—The Choral Vorspiele I had obtained some Months ago, & am truly glad to find that you have gotten hold of it, as I am sure it must afford you great Delight. If you have not had Time as yet to examine it throughout, I particularly recommend to your Notice the Numbers 8 (page 18). 10 (26) 15 (p. 5 2^d Book) 18. 19. 20.[2]

---

[5] A reference to George, Prince of Wales, who in 1810 became Prince Regent and in 1820 George IV, and whose excesses were notorious.

[1] The year is given by 15 May falling on a Monday and Crotch's address.

[2] 'Allein Gott in der Höh sei Ehr', BWV 676; 'Wir gläuben all' an einen Gott', BWV 680; 'Wer nur den lieben Gott lässt walten', BWV 691; 'Liebster Jesu, wir sind hier', BWV 706, 633, and 634; 'Allein Gott in der Höh sei Ehr', BWV 711; and 'Allein Gott in der Höh sei Ehr', BWV 664.

You are (I presume) aware that the German Titles to the several Pieces, are the first Words of certain Lutheran Hymns to which Sebastian added all that florid Counterpoint in Fugue & Canon which you meet with, & which I need not tell you produces on the Organ the most magnificent Effect.—

I am again unlucky, for I fear I cannot have returned from Turnham Green[3] To-Morrow in Time for your Lecture,[4] mais *je ferai mon possible*.[5]

Adieu & believe me,
most truly Yours

S Wesley

Monday Morning | 15th of May

To [Benjamin Jacob][1] [Camden Town, *c.*15 May 1809][2]

AL, 4 pp. (Edinburgh) Damaged.

Editor's note This letter consists of a single sheet, folded in half so as to form four pages. The bottom of the sheet has been irregularly torn away so that the last few lines of each page are lacking in their entirety and parts of four lines immediately above the tear are also missing. The missing text has been conjecturally restored where possible.

Dear Sir

I am told (how truly I cannot answer) that my Antagonist & your Correspondent[3] is M[r] Purkis the blind Organist:[4] if this be so, your having called him as blind

---

[3] A hamlet in the north of the parish of Chiswick, west of London, where one of SW's schools was situated.

[4] 16 May: one of a course of lectures on 'The Rise and Improvement of Scientific Music' that Crotch was currently giving on Tuesday and Friday afternoons at the Hanover Square Rooms (*GM* 1809[1], 252; *The Times*, 30 Mar., 8 Apr. 1809).   [5] 'I will do what I can.'

---

[1] Although lacking an address portion, it is clear from the content and present location of this letter that it is to Jacob.

[2] The approximate date of this letter is established by the reference to SW's Hanover Square Rooms concert on 3 June (see n. 11). SW's reference to the Epsom race meeting (18–20 May) suggests that it was written at the beginning of that week.

[3] A reference to the attack on SW by an anonymous correspondent signing himself 'J.P.' that had appeared in the May number of *NMMR* following SW's Royal Institution lecture of 22 Mar. 1809, in which SW had demonstrated and recommended the Hawkes–Elliot patent organ (see SW to [Savage], 16 Mar. [1809], n. 4). An extended controversy followed in subsequent numbers. SW here identifies 'J.P.' as John Purkis; in a later letter to Jacob he identifies him as the Hon. George Pomeroy (SW to Jacob, 28 [?Sept.] 1809; Emery, 'Jack Pudding'; Philip Olleson, ' "The Perfection of Harmony Itself": The William Hawkes Patent Organ and its Temperament', *JBIOS* 21 (1997), 108–28).

[4] John Purkis (1781–1849), organist of St Clement Dane's and St Olave, Southwark. He regained his sight in late 1810 or early 1811, and subsequently became the principal performer on the Apollonicon, the giant organ built by Flight and Robson and exhibited by them at their premises in St Martin's Lane (Dawe; Matthews; *Grove*[5]).

as a Bat will be a little unlucky; & as being capable of a personal Construction, which however he deserves for fighting *in the Dark*: had he given us his real Name, we might have managed the Contest in a more secure Manner.—As it is, Facts confute him, & these are the most powerful of all Weapons.—I should be glad to be thoroughly certain that Purkis is the Man: I *know* however that lately, when he was told that I defended the new Tempera<ment he> said 'Does he?—I w<ish I could> hear him, I w<ould wager a pound> or two that < . . . >

[p. 2] You find that my Lecture[5] hangs an A——e,[6] as the genteel saying is.—They pretend that they did not get my Heads of it soon enough for the Cards to be distributed.—It happens well, for all the Fools of Fashion, which you know constitute a large Majority of my Audience, are all running helter-skelter, pell-mell to the Epsom Races,[7] & leaving the Lecture Room as empty as their own Heads. Only two Lectures are < . . . > this Week, the one by < . . . , the o>ther by Davy,[8] but < . . . > be my last, & the < . . . > to prepare < . . . >

[p. 3] I beg you many Pardons for disappointing you of the Trios.—The D—l of the Matter is that your Carrier's Beat does not extend so far south as your Domain.[9]—I will send them at a Venture by him to Clementi's[10] with a Note directed to you—surely they will reach you safely thence.—

On Saturday 3ᵈ of June I have fixed to have my Morning Party.[11]—Horn has lent me a divine Mottett of Sebastian for 5 Voices,[12] which I am adapting to Latin Words:[13] the Original ones are German, always *harsh*, & mostly unintelligible to an English Audience.—I hate the Language as much as I respect the People.

The Reason that the *Cards* announcing the Trio[14] were not delivered is b<ecause> there is a Rule (it see<ms>) not to issue out < . . . > or Scheme<s . . . >

---

[5] At the Royal Institution.   [6] 'Is delayed'.

[7] The Epsom race meeting was held from 18 to 20 May.

[8] The chemist Sir Humphry Davy (1778–1829), who was giving a course of lectures at the Royal Institution at this time. The other lecturer has not been identified.   [9] i.e. Blackfriars Road.

[10] Clementi and Co. had premises at this time in Tottenham Court Road.

[11] The concert was at the Hanover Square Rooms. According to a newspaper advertisement quoted in Edwards, 654 (original not traced), the programme included 'several compositions of Sebastian Bach, among which a grand sacred Motetto for five voices'.

[12] 'Jesu, meine Freude', BWV 227.

[13] 'Jesus, decus meus'. SW presented a copy of this motet in Latin translation to the Madrigal Society on 24 Apr. 1810 when he attended one of its meetings as a visitor (BL, MADSOC F5 (Attendances and Transactions, 1785–1828)).

[14] One of the Bach organ trio sonatas in the edition by SW and Horn: see SW to Jacob, 3 Mar. 1809, n. 6.

[p. 4] I am informed that it will be advisable for us to print the Numbers of Croft & Greene[15] upon less expensive Paper, otherwise that the Concern is by no means likely to answer: I should like much to have a Meeting upon the Subject, & shall summon Page[16] for the Purpose, whereat if you can manage to join, & as 'in the Multitude of Counsellors is safety',[17] I have hopes of an Improvement in our Arrangements.—I have To-Day received 5 Subscription Names from a Dean & Chapter, <and am pr>omised 5 More from < . . . > ecclesiastical < . . . > cathedrals take < . . . > more, it will < . . . > Singers < . . . >

To Tebaldo Monzani[1]   Camden Town, 26 May [1809][2]

AN, third person, 1 p. (Kassler)

Mr S. Wesley desires Mr Monzani's Acceptance of the enclosed Tickets,[3] & should any more be required than the 24 he has sent for Sale, he will thank Mr M. to drop him a Line p^r Post, which shall be immediately attended to.

Friday May 26th | Camden Town

---

[15] A paragraph in *MM* for Dec. 1808 had announced: 'One of the most desirable treats ever offered to the musical public is preparing for the press by Mr S. Wesley and Mr. John Page, vicar choral of St. Paul's Cathedral, in the publication of the transcendant Anthems of Dr. Croft and Dr. Green [*sic*], of which a new edition has long been wanted.' This was no doubt an edition of selections from *Musica Sacra: or Select Anthems in Score* (1724; 2nd edn. as *Cathedral Music, or Select Anthems in Score*, 1780) by William Croft (1678–1727) and *Forty Select Anthems* (1743) by Maurice Greene (1696–1755). The first volume appeared probably in Jan. 1809, and was reviewed in *MM* for Feb. 1809; no copies have been traced. SW's comments presumably relate to a projected second volume, for which at this time insufficient subscriptions had been received; no copies have been traced, and it is likely that it was never published.

[16] John Page (*c*.1760–1812), cathedral musician and editor. His *Harmonia Sacra* appeared in ninety separate numbers, making up three volumes, and was complete by 1800. It was intended as a supplement to Arnold's *Cathedral Music* (1790), which itself was conceived as a supplement to Boyce's title of the same name (3 vols., 1760–73). Apart from two examples it did not go back beyond the Restoration, but it was a useful compendium of music by Blow, Purcell, Croft, Greene, and Boyce, and also contained music by SW ('I said, I will take heed'), Battishill, and others (*Grove*[6]).   [17] Prov. 11:14.

---

[1] Tebaldo Monzani (1762–1839), Italian flautist, instrument maker, composer, and publisher of sheet music, who had settled in England around 1787. He had gone into partnership with Giambattista Cimador around 1800, and at the time of this letter was in partnership with Henry Hill in the firm of Monzani and Hill at 3 Old Bond Street (*Grove*[6]; Post Office Directories).

[2] The year is given by 26 May falling on a Friday and SW's Camden Town address.

[3] For SW's Hanover Square Rooms concert on 3 June, obtainable from Monzani and Hill, and from other music shops.

To [Benjamin Jacob][1] [Camden Town, ?29 May 1809?][2]

ALS, 1 p. (RCM, MS 2130, fo. 40)

Monday Morning

My dear Sir

You must play the Trio,[3] *will ye nill ye* so no more on that subject.—I cannot fix Thursday[4] positively till the Day of our grand vocal Rehearsal be settled, & this depends upon Mrs Vaughan and the Rest of the Lungs to be exerted in the Proof of Sebastian being no *mere Organist.*[5]

I find that the *Cerberus*[6] has been known to say '—Yes—we allow Bach to be a good Writer for the *Organ*, but what strange Stuff his attempts at *vocal* Music would have been'!

Y^rs^ in Haste

S Wesley

To Willoughby Lacy[1] Camden Town, 20 June 1809

AN, third person, 1 p. (Kassler)

Mr Samuel Wesley will have the Pleasure of calling on Mr Lacey *To-morrow* between 11 & 12, for the Purpose of examining the State of the Organ at the Room in the Haymarket[2]

Camden Town | Tuesday 20 June | 1809

---

[1] Although lacking an address portion, it is clear from the content and present location of this letter that it is to Jacob.

[2] The date is suggested by SW's 'Monday' and the discussion of the preparations for his Hanover Square Rooms concert on 3 June 1809, featuring choral music by J. S. Bach to demonstrate that Bach was 'no mere organist' (see n. 5).

[3] One of Bach's organ trios, which Jacob and SW would have performed together as a duet; probably the one most recently published.

[4] 1 June: perhaps for a rehearsal with Jacob which could not be confirmed until the date of the vocal rehearsal for the concert on 3 June had been fixed.

[5] A reference to the inclusion in the programme of 'Jesu meine Freude'.

[6] See SW to Charles Wesley jun., 15 Jan. 1807, n. 28.

---

[1] Willoughby Lacy (1749–1831), actor and theatrical manager, and former associate of Garrick and Sheridan (*BD*).

[2] i.e. the Concert Room at the King's Theatre, where SW was to play an extempore organ voluntary at Lacy's benefit concert on 22 June (*The Times*, 22 June 1809).

To Benjamin Jacob   Camden Town, 24 July 1809

ALS, 3 pp. (RCM, MS 2130, fo. 21)
Addressed To | Mr Jacobs | Charlotte Street | Black Friar's Road
Pmk JY 26 809

My dear Sir

The Reverend Canon Picart hath a most unhappy Mode of endeavouring to explain himself, but if we can make him out together (& it is not always two Laymen that are a Match for one Priest) we may think ourselves luckier than if we lived in the Times when one Priest could get 100 Laymen burnt *without Benefit of Clergy*.

Our modern Melchisedech[1] writeth thus: 'I am sorry my confused expressions have occasioned you so much Trouble. I meant Paper ruled with Scores of six staves,—or Scores of four Staves in a Page.—This Arrangement I thought would cover Scores of any Number of Staves from six to three.'—

He means I think *a Score* of 6 or 4 Staves, *as often repeated* in one Page, as the Length or Breadth of the Paper will admit. What think you.

My dear Mr Jacobs, this is very cheap Paper, I do own—but it costs a dear deal of Trouble to write upon it.—The Ink will not penetrate, all I can do, & as to the present Sheet, I know & admit that it is greasy (tho' from what Cause I know not)—*Vide* the Top of this and the last Page.

I however shall find good Account in employing it upon other Occasions, although not for writing Letters, either of Ceremony or Friendship—the former ought to be written *fair* and the latter *fast*—and I defy any Man to do either one or the other upon this.—

Yet it is useful Paper—It is good for making a Memorandum of a Debt to one's Tallow Chandler, or one's Butcher, which one would rather do *at Leisure*, & for which greasy Paper is not ill calculated when we consider the above Professions.

I have been so put out of Humour by two or three vexatious & impudent Things,[2] news of which I received when I returned to Day, that I was glad to have an Opportunity of getting into a less saturnine Vein by the circumstance afforded me by our Sacerdotal Bachist *Picart* of assuring you again how truly I am

ever yours

S. Wesley

Camden Town | Monday. July. 24th 1809

---

[1] Melchizedek, king of Salem and high priest (Genesis 14: 18), also mentioned in the Vesper Psalm 'Dixit Dominus' (Ps. 110), a text set three times by SW.

[2] Possibly a reference to the continuing controversy in *NMMR*: the Aug. number contained a further attack on SW by 'J.P.'.

To John George Graeff   [Camden Town], 28 July [1809]¹

ALS, 1 p. (BL, Add. MS 60753, fo. 121)
Addressed To | J. G. Graeff Esqre
Watermark 1808

Friday
Afternoon. 28th July

My dear Sir

You will excuse my asking you upon a Sheet of Coarse Copy Paper whether you shall be at Leisure this Evening, & whether I may expect the Pleasure of a Call from you? As I have nothing in Particular to employ me, I think we may amuse ourselves one Way or other—I know you have no Taste for the Sublime or Beautiful in Music,² otherwise I would give you some of Pucitta's Operas,³ or Von Esch's Divertimentos with *Triangular* Accompaniments;⁴ but as the Matter is, I must bear to drudge through some of old Bach's humbug dismal Ditties, all so devoid of Air, Taste, Sentiment, Science, or Contrivance, that I am astonished how a sensible Man like yourself could ever have held up such an Impostor to Admiration—It only shews what ignorant Pretenders to musical Knowledge *you Germans* are.

Notwithstanding which, I am truly yours

S. Wesley

---

¹ The year is given by 28 July falling on a Friday, the reference to Pucitta's operas (see n. 3), and the 1808 watermark.

² Two of the three categories into which Crotch divided music in his system of aesthetics, as propounded in his lectures. This taxonomy closely followed the one formulated by Sir Joshua Reynolds for the visual arts.

³ An ironic reference. After an early career in which he wrote at least seventeen operas for the theatres of Milan and Venice and a period as director of the Italian opera in Amsterdam, Vincenzo Pucitta (1778–1861) was from 1809 to 1814 composer and music director of the King's Theatre. His career was closely associated with that of the soprano Angelica Catalani, for whom he wrote a number of operas and other compositions. No fewer than three of his operas had their premières at the King's Theatre in 1809: *I villeggiatori bizzarri* (31 Jan.), *La caccia di Enrico IV* (7 Mar.), and *Le quattro nazione* (11 July).

⁴ Little is known about Louis Von Esch (*fl. c.*1786–1825) beyond the music he wrote. According to Sainsbury, who described him as 'a celebrated German instrumental composer', he published harp and piano music in France from 1786 onwards; many of his compositions were published in London between around 1800 and 1825. The 'piece with triangular accompaniments' may have been the *Divertissement Turque* for piano, written at around this time; or it may have been one of his divertimenti with accompaniments for flute, violin, and cello.

To Mary Beardmore   Camden Town, 31 August [1809]¹

ALS, 1 p. (London University, ALS 293)
Addressed To | Miss Beardmore | Canonbury Place | Islington | N 5.
Pmk SP 1 1809

Camden Town
August 31.

Dear Madam

I delayed answering your last obliging Letter² in Hope that it might have been in my Power to arrange my Engagements in a Way that would have allowed me the Opportunity of attending yourself & Sister at Canonbury according to your Wish, but really I am concerned to state that I fear I cannot manage it at all regularly, as my Days are at present too much occupied to render it possible for me to command 3 Hours in a Morning: I know of no better Proposal to offer than that of waiting upon you at some Place appointed within half an Hour's Journey of Camden Town, & of your receiving your Lessons there:—this I think might be done, should it happen to suit your Convenience, & in this Case I will make a Point to secure a Piano Forte at some musical Friend's Abode, where you shall be sure to be uninterrupted.—I will look out some Music for you without Delay & convey it to Milk Street;³ remaining, with best Regards to all your Family

Dear Madam
Your obliged & faithful Servant
S Wesley

To [Benjamin Jacob]¹   [Camden Town], 4 September [1809]²

ALS, 3 pp. (RCM, MS 2130, fo. 25)

My dear Sir

I omitted to observe to you either on Saturday or Sunday that I am all aground for Music Paper, & I was not wise enough to take down the Direction to the Person from whom you procure that necessary Article to us Minstrels, so good & so cheap.

---

¹ The year is given by the postmark.   ² Not preserved.
³ Off Cheapside: the business premises of Joseph Beardmore, Mary Beardmore's father.

---

¹ Although lacking an address portion, it is clear from the contents and present location of this letter that it is to Jacob.
² The year is established by 4 Sept. falling on a Monday and SW's reference to his forthcoming visit to Tamworth (see n. 3).

—If you should have an Opportunity of soon going that Way, & will kindly bear my present Distress in Remembrance, you will do me a real Benefit, for I want to compleat the Parts of my Concerto[3] without Delay, that I may have nothing else to do but pack up my Awls[4] & whirl away to Tamworth[5] at the appointed Time.

I have just received a Letter from D[r] Burney,[6] an extracted Portion of which will not be uninteresting to you.

'I believe M[r] Salomon is now out of Town; but when I saw him last, in talking of *our great Sebastian*, he said you were in Possession of some sonatas of his *divine Manufacture*, with a very fine Violin Part to them,[7] which he wished me to hear.—I have no Violin in Order; but when I return home (Dr. B. is now at Bulstrode, the Seat of the Duke of Portland)[8] & you are both at Leisure, I wish you would prevail on him to fix a Day, & to send one of his own Violins any time before 2 o'Clock.—While you are charming me with two Parts, I shall act in a triple Capacity & play the parts of Pit, Box, & Gallery, in rapturously applauding the Composition & Performance.—'

You see one is never too old to learn, & here is an Instance that it is never too late to mend!—What more could the D[r] have said, even had he *originally* been the like Enthusiast with ourselves in the Cause of Truth.—

His *Repentance* (tho' he does not profess it yet in Words) seems so evident from the *zealous* Expressions he uses, that I really think we must cordially forgive the past, for we can hardly expect him when tottering over the Grave,[9] & having attained (whether justly or otherwise) a Reputation for musical Criticism, *publickly* to revoke what he advanced at so Distant a Period of Time,[10] & when perhaps he thinks that his Strictures are forgotten or at least overbalanced by his present Acknowledgement of the real State of the Fact.

---

[3] The Organ Concerto in D, which SW was to perform on 22 Sept. at the Tamworth Music Festival. The autograph score of the original version (BL, Add. MS 35009) is dated 22 Mar. 1800, and was probably the organ concerto that SW had played at Salomon's performance of Haydn's *Creation* at Covent Garden on 21 Apr. of that year. For the performance at Tamworth he rescored the concerto for a substantially larger orchestra and inserted his own arrangement of the Fugue in D from Book I of the '48' before the concluding Hornpipe. [4] i.e. in a punning sense, his 'alls' (*OED*).

[5] A thriving manufacturing town of some 3,000 inhabitants, thirteen miles from Birmingham on the Warwickshire–Staffordshire border. The festival, held on 21 and 22 Sept., involved over 130 performers and also included performances of *Messiah* and *The Creation* (Lightwood, 150–3; Philip Olleson, 'The Tamworth Festival of 1809', *Staffordshire Studies* 5 (1993), 81–106). [6] Not preserved.

[7] The six sonatas for violin and harpsichord, BWV 1014–19, an edition of which had been published by Nägeli in 1800. SW had only recently acquired his copy: inscribed 'bought at Escher's music shop for Eighteen Shillings' and dated 11 Aug. 1809, it is now at the RCM.

[8] William Henry Cavendish-Bentinck (1738–1809), third Duke of Portland, Prime Minister from 1807 until his death. Burney was a frequent visitor at Bulstrode Park, Buckinghamshire, his family seat (Lonsdale, 469). [9] This was premature: Burney did not die until 12 Apr. 1814.

[10] Burney's *History* was published between 1776 and 1789.

As soon as I can command an Hour, I will set about my deliberate Opinion on the *various* & inimitable excellencies of **the Man**,[11] which I think will settle the Business at least as decisively as our Challenge to **J—ACK P—UDDING**.[12]

Adieu for the present,—we must contrive one more Pull at Surry[13] before I hyke over to Staffordshire.

Kindest regards to all,
from
Your sincere Friend,

S Wesley

Monday | 4 Sept[r]

[Enclosure][14]

J.P.

Tho' J.P. refuses to give up his Name
To muffle his Malice a Hood in,
The Matter amounts to exactly the same,
For his Nonsense proclaims 'tis J-ack P-udding.

To Charles Burney   Camden Town, 4 September 1809

ALS, 3 pp. (Osborn, MSS 3, Box 16, Folder 1193)
Addressed To | D[r] Burney
Docketed by Mme d'Arblay: ※

Camden Town
Sept[r] 4 1809

[11] Bach.

[12] A buffoon, clown or merry andrew (*OED*), in allusion to the attack on SW by 'J.P.' in the pages of *NMMR*.

[13] i.e. Surrey Chapel, where Jacob was organist: an octagonal building on the north-east corner of Blackfriars Road and Union Street. It was built in 1782 by Rowland Hill and his brother Sir Richard Hill, Bt., as a chapel for the Countess of Huntingdon's Connexion. Rowland Hill became its first minister and Jacob was appointed organist there in 1794. After it closed as a place of worship in 1881 the chapel was used for a time as a factory, and later for boxing, when it was known as 'The Ring'. It was badly damaged during the Second World War and was subsequently demolished (*Survey of London*, vol. xxii: *Bankside (The Parishes of St Saviour and Christchurch Southwark)*, 119–20 and pl. 85, showing its exterior in 1798 and interior in 1812).

[14] The following four lines of doggerel are written on a separate sheet, but they were evidently enclosed with this letter.

My dear Friend,

I am glad to find that your welcome Letter[1] which I have but 5 Minutes ago received bears Date from the Country,[2] as I am in Hope that notwithstanding our topsy turvy Season fine Air & the Attentions of your noble Host will gradually renovate your Health & Spirits.—You will perhaps indulge me with another Line e'er you leave Bulstrode, by which I shall be enabled to look forward to the desirable Moment of Meeting to enjoy the lovely Sonatas which Mr Salomon has described to you.—They will confirm an excellent & true Observation which you made upon hearing some of the Preludes, that 'they are as new, & as modern, as if composed only yesterday.'—I am not averse from being called an Enthusiast in the Cause of Sebastian, but I really do think, even *coolly*, & in my calmest Judgement, that never was such Variety of Style met with in any other Composer, at least in any that has ever come within my Observation.

The Mottivo of the Allegro in the 1st Son.[3] is of a very original *plaintive* Cast, as you will perceive—ex pede Herculem.[4]

I used to play the Violin very well some 30 Years ago, but having had the Mischance of losing a favourite one in a Hackney Coach,[5] & never since having

[1] The letter referred to and partly quoted in the previous letter; not preserved.

[2] i.e. Bulstrode: Burney remained there until the middle of Sept. (Lonsdale, 469).

[3] The opening of the second movement of the Sonata No. 1 in B minor, BWV 1014.

[4] 'From the foot of Hercules': Burney will be able to gauge the character of the whole from the short extract quoted by SW. SW's allusion is to a story in Aulus Gellius, *Noctes Atticae*, 1.1.1–3, which cites a lost life of Hercules by Plutarch stating that Pythagoras was able to calculate the size of Hercules from the size of his foot.

[5] SW had lost his violin, an Italian instrument from Cremona, in or around Dec. 1783. In a letter now lost, Mary Freeman Shepherd had suggested to SW that he should place an advertisement in the newspapers offering a reward for its return, to which he had replied: 'I will tell you the Truth—I am a little superstitious with regard to the Cremona: I am no Jansenist and yet I believe it was predestinated to be lost: the means I have used for its recovery proved successful to others that have had the like mischance, therefore I cannot but think that infinite wisdom intended it so to be: I assure you that for these three weeks I have given up all hopes of recovering it, and made myself entirely easy on that account . . . Depend upon it Madam—the Violin is in the hands of a person who knows its value, otherwise a guinea would surely have been an object to a Hackney Coachman or Pawnbroker. Whoever possesses the Instrument is well acquainted with the Treasure he has been so fortunate to obtain, and nothing but that scarce Virtue honesty will prevail on him to part with it' (SW to Mary Freeman Shepherd, 26 Dec. [1783] (Paris, Archives de France, S4619; copy at BL, Add. MS 35013, fo. 8)).

met with another that suited my Hand & Fancy as well, I turned sulky at the whole *Genus,* which you will say was acting very like an Ideot, & I readily admit it; but lo! these same Sonatas have regenerated my liking of the Instrument, & I have taken up my wooden Box once more in Order to master the Obligato Part designed for it, & can now play them through without much Difficulty or Blundering, so that even if we should not readily manage to fix Salomon for an early Trial at Chelsea Coll. yet I could bring with me a good Man & true to execute the Piano Forte Part, while I attempted the Accompaniment.[6]

The Author of the Words of the Oratorio of Ruth[7] was D[r] *Haweis,*[8] who is yet living, & about 72 or 3. He is a Clergyman in the late Lady Huntingdon's Society,[9] & an excellent Judge of Music, as well as a very accomplished *Flautist* in Time past.—Smart[10] was indeed a very superior Man: If I mistake not, he wrote the Oratorio 'The Cure of Saul' which was set by D[r] Arnold, & was at one while a Favourite when he[11] carried on Oratorios at Covent Garden.[12]

In Expectation of another kind Word from you when your Leisure & Inclination permit, I rest, my dear Friend, with the most sincere & unalterable Regard

Yours ever faithfully

S Wesley

---

[6] SW's doubts about Salomon's availability were evidently well founded: by the time of SW to Jacob, [?30 Sept. 1809], the plan was for SW to play the violin and Jacob the piano.

[7] Either Giardini's oratorio (1768), which received annual performances at the Lock Hospital between 1768 and 1790, or SW's own early oratorio: the words of both were by Haweis (Simon McVeigh, 'Music and the Lock Hospital in the 18th Century', *MT* 129 (1988), 235–40.

[8] The Revd Thomas Haweis (1734–1820) had been appointed chaplain to Selina Hastings, Countess of Huntingdon, in 1768. She appointed him her trustee and executor, and after her death in 1791 he was responsible for all the chapels in her Connexion. He was a close friend of Martin Madan, SW's godfather, and was for a time his assistant at the Lock Hospital chapel. He was the composer of the hymn tune 'Richmond', usually sung to the words 'City of God, how broad and far'. SW was mistaken about Haweis's age: he was 75.

[9] The Countess of Huntingdon's Connexion, a branch of Methodism founded by Selina Hastings, Countess of Huntingdon (1707–91).

[10] The poet Christopher Smart (1722–71). Although he was the author of an oratorio text (*Hannah,* 1764) and of metrical versions of the psalms, he did not write the words of *The Cure of Saul,* a pasticcio by Arnold first performed at the King's Theatre on 23 Jan. 1767. According to *Grove*[6], they were by J. Brown (1715–66), Vicar of Newcastle upon Tyne. [11] i.e. Arnold.

[12] SW's memory appears to have played him false. Arnold was composer at Covent Garden from 1764 to 1769, and may also have managed the oratorio seasons there at this time. There is no evidence of any performances of *The Cure of Saul* at Covent Garden during this period. Arnold also managed oratorios at Drury Lane in the 1790 and 1793 seasons and at the King's Theatre in the 1798, 1799, 1801, and 1802 seasons, but no performances of *The Cure of Saul* are recorded for this period at either house.

To Benjamin Jacob   Birmingham, 25 September 1809

ALS, 3 pp. (RCM, MS 2130, fo. 27)
Addressed To | Mr Jacobs | Charlotte Street | Black Friar's Road | London |
25 Sept^r

Birmingham
Monday 25 Septr 1809.

My dear Sir,

I have the Comfort of acquainting you that my Tamworth Excursion has proved most unexpectedly serviceable to my *corporal* Sensations, for I have been on the mending Order ever since my Arrival there,[1] & I am now in very good Condition at the Place above dated,[2] whence however I must set out To-morrow Morning,[3] & I mean to travel in the Oxford two Day Coach, to prevent over Fatigue, which I was obliged to submit to in the first Instance, from the Necessity of going *at Night*, which constantly disagrees with me; & if you remember the Weather on Monday Night last (or rather Tuesday Morning) you must know that the Situation of Coach Travellers, whether inside or out, could not be over & above eligible, especially as we were troubled with a restless Companion who was continually jerking the Windows up & down for what he called *Air*, but which was a furious Wind & pelting Rain, so that it was next to a Miracle I did not take a Cold *for the Winter*, but yet I escaped, to my no small Surprize.

You will wish to hear how the Performances were received; & I wish you had been among us to have witnessed the Delight they afforded to the whole Audience, who (when at the Church) seemed to long for the Privilege of clapping & rattling their Sticks.—Even as it was, there was a constant Hum of Applause[4] at the Conclusion of every Piece, & there never could have been more strict & flattering Attention any where, than was manifest throughout the whole.

The Choruses went off *spank*, slap bang, like a Cannon, or Mr Congreve's Rockets.[5]—Notwithstanding I sat at a great Disadvantage, for the New Choir

---

[1] SW had travelled to Tamworth on the night of 18–19 Sept. The festival concerts comprised performances of *Messiah* and *The Creation* in the parish church of St Editha on the mornings of 21 and 22 Sept., a miscellaneous concert in the theatre on the evening of 21 Sept., and a concluding 'Grand Selection of Sacred Music' in the church on the evening of 22 Sept.

[2] SW had presumably travelled the thirteen miles to Birmingham on 23 Sept. in time for his concert there that evening.   [3] 26 Sept.; SW presumably arrived back in London on the following day.

[4] i.e. general approbation: hand-clapping was evidently not permitted in the church.

[5] William Congreve (1772–1828), who had in 1808 invented the rocket which bears his name (*DNB*). SW's piano piece *The Sky-rocket: A Jubilee Waltz* [1814] is dedicated to him.

Organ[6] compleatly obstructed all Possibility of seeing any Part of the Orchestra but a Violin or two on my right & left Wing, so we were obliged to have a Mirror in Order that I might see Frank Cramer,[7] as it was *just as well* that he & I should start together, & this was managed pretty well, save & except that the Necessity of hanging the Glass so high proved a sad Annoyance to my unfortunate Neck, which was obliged to stretch till I thought I should never be able to reduce it to its common Length again.—

The Concerto[8] was excessively praised, & the Fugue of our Sebastian produced a glorious effect with the Instruments.

I promised Buggins[9] to conduct his Concert here (at Birmingham) which was very well attended at the Theatre,[10] & the Fantazia I played on the Piano Forte I concluded with 'Roly Poly Gammon & Spinach,'[11] which tickled the Tobies[12] of the Button Makers[13] at such a Rate, that I thought I never should have gotten off the Stage, at least till I had broken my Back with Bowing.—The Noise was absolutely *confounding*, & if I had not that valuable Stock of Impudence belonging to me, of which you have had numerous Demonstrations, the Weight of the Welcome must have overpowered my Nerves, & I really think that even such a Jack-Gentlewoman[14] as Mother Storace,[15] would have been tempted to make a thorough Faint away of it.

---

[6] As a contemporary print shows, the organ was in the west gallery, a considerable distance from the orchestra if it was placed (as seems likely) in the crossing. As SW's reference implies, and as the print confirms, the new choir organ (by Thomas Elliot) was a *Rückpositif*, positioned at the organist's back as he sat at the console, and thus considerably obscuring his view even when a mirror was used. For the organs of Tamworth, see Boeringer, iii. 69–71; David C. Wickens, *The Instruments of Samuel Green* (1987), 147–8.

[7] Francis Cramer (1772–1848), the leader of the orchestra, son of the violinist Wilhelm Cramer (1746–99) and the younger brother of Johann Baptist Cramer. He was taught the violin by his father and started to appear in concerts from 1790. He was a prominent orchestral musician who led the orchestra at the Ancient Concerts and later at many concerts of the Philharmonic Society.

[8] SW's Organ Concerto in D.

[9] Samuel Buggins, a Birmingham trumpeter and impresario who played second trumpet in the orchestra at Tamworth, and whose son Simeon was the treble soloist in the performance of *Messiah* there.

[10] The Theatre Royal, New Street. The concert, on 23 Sept., featured many of the Tamworth performers and included much of the same music (*Aris's Birmingham Gazette*, 18 Sept. 1809).

[11] i.e. the refrain of the popular song 'A frog he would a-wooing go', alluded to in the postscript to SW to Jacob, 2 Mar. 1809. SW's use of 'fantazia' suggests an improvisation; for the autograph of an undated rondo for piano by SW on this tune, see BL, Add. MS 35006.   [12] The buttocks.

[13] The manufacture of buttons was one of Birmingham's principal industries.

[14] A woman of low birth or manners who makes pretensions to be a gentlewoman; hence an insolent woman or an upstart (*OED*).

[15] Nancy (Ann Selina) Storace (1765–1817), the sister of the composer Stephen Storace (1762–96), was the first Susanna in Mozart's *Le nozze di Figaro* in Vienna in 1786. According to *Grove*[6], 'her short, plumpish figure made her ineffectual in the serious opera, but she was inimitable in the comic ones that

I long to see all our Sebastian Squad, & I trust we shall soon meet. Remember me most kindly to all yours, & tell Mrs Jacobs that even the *Brums* are beginning to venerate our Orpheus—at Tamworth the effect of the Fugue among the Orchestra was such, that they were perpetually humming the Subject whenever I met any of them in the Streets, either by Day or by Night.

Adieu, my good Friend, excuse this hasty Rhapsody, but I knew you would accept in good Part any rough hewn Pot Hooks & Hangers from your very sincere &

cordial Mess-Mate

S Wesley

To Benjamin Jacob [Camden Town], 28 [?September] 1809[1]

AL fragment, 3 pp. (Edinburgh)
Editor's note The surviving portion of this letter, written on a single sheet folded once, consists of the lower part of three pages and forms roughly half of the original.

Addressed Benjamin <Jac>obs

[p. 1] < . . . > you.—There are many Reasons for my urging a *speedy* Explanation upon the Subject.

I was yesterday informed in the most confident Manner (but I vouch for the Truth of scarce any Intelligence) that our J. P. is not less a Personage than the *Honble* Mr Pomeroy.[2]—I remember the Man, & always extremely disliked him as a most conceited Pretender to musical Criticism.

---

constituted most of the Vienna repertory.' On her return to England with her brother in 1787, she sang at the King's Theatre until it burnt down in 1789, and then joined the Drury Lane company, where she sang in almost all of her brother's operas. Following his death she left the Drury Lane company and in 1797 went on a foreign tour with the tenor John Braham (1774–1856). They became lovers and had a son, Spencer, in 1802. By this time, she was singing again in the London theatres; she retired from the stage in May 1808 (*Grove*[6]; *BD*; Jane Girdham, *English Opera in Late Eighteenth-Century London: Stephen Storace at Drury Lane* (Oxford, 1997)).

[1] SW's dating of 'Thursday 28th 1809' at the foot of the letter points to either Sept. or Dec. Either date is possible, but Sept. is the more likely on grounds of content.

[2] The Hon. George Pomeroy (b. 1764), son of Arthur Pomeroy (1723–98), 1st Viscount Harberton, an amateur musician associated with Joseph Kemp, the editor of *NMMR* (*Burke's Peerage*; Kassler, *Science of Music*, 424, 657, 674, 699–700, 1061, 1181–2).

[p. 2] < . . . > the Mind, increases the Indisposition of the Body.

I have enclosed the 7s. which I am ashamed of not having sooner transmitted upon the trifling Account of the Cards you were so good as to get executed.[3]—I so much approve the Style in which your Printer manages these Matters, that I shall again trouble you on a similar Account.—I think you will approve of the Proposals annexed,[4] which I long to see floating about in the World without further Loss.

[p. 3] I regret that it will not <be> possible for me to come towards your Quarter on Sunday next;[5] but will give you the earliest Notice I can, when it will be likely for me to accomplish it.

With best Regards to Mrs J. & all your<s>,
I am
My dear Sir
Sincerely Yours
   S Wesley

Thursday 28th 1809

< . . . > the Proposals when < . . . > Expedition to < . . . >

To [?Benjamin Jacob][1]   [Camden Town,
                                           ?30 September 1809][2]

ALS, 2 pp. (RCM, MS 2130, fo. 37)

Dear Friend

I am in the utmost Distress, & there is no one on Earth but yourself who can help me out of it.—Dr Burney is stark staring mad to hear Sebastian's Sonatas, & I have told him all how & about your adroit Management of his Music in general.

---

[3] Evidently publicity materials which Jacob had had printed on SW's behalf, perhaps for SW's forth-coming lecture course at the Surrey Institution.   [4] Not identified.

[5] 1 Oct.

[1] Although this letter is included in the same collection as other letters to Jacob, it bears no address portion or other unequivocal indications that it is to him. It is possible that it is to another recipient, perhaps Vincent Novello.

[2] This letter continues the discussion of arrangements to perform Bach's violin sonatas to Burney, first raised in SW's letter to Jacob of 4 Sept. Burney's absence from London until around the middle of the month (Lonsdale, 469) and SW's visit to Tamworth and Birmingham rule out most dates in Sept. SW's reference to Burney's 'second Excursion into the Country', planned for early Oct., and the need to fit in the performance before his departure, suggests that it occurred on 2 Oct. The date of Portland's letter of invitation to Burney (see n. 4), which Burney could not have received until 29 Sept., and other internal evidence in the letter suggest 30 Sept. as its most probable date.

He was immediately resolved on hearing you on the *Clavicembalum* & me on the Fiddle at them.—He has appointed *Monday next*[3] at 12 o'Clock for our coming to him, as this is the only Time he has left before a second Excursion into the Country.[4] —You see it is an extreme Case—I had appointed three private Pupils for Monday, but shall put them all off to Tuesday—Would to Heaven you may be able to do the like.—The Triumph of Burney over his own Ignorance & Prejudice is such a glorious Event that surely we ought to make *some* sacrifice to enjoy it.—I mentioned young Kollmann[5] as quite capable of playing the Sonatas, but you will see by the enclosed[6] (just received) that he prefers you.—Pray comply in this arduous Enterprize— Remember our Cause, 'Good Will towards Men' is at the bottom of it, & when Sebastian flourishes here, there will be at least more musical 'Peace on Earth.'[7]

You see we are utterly ruined unless you come forward To-morrow.[8]—Think of what we shall have to announce to the Public; that Dr Burney (who has heard almost all the Music of other Folks) should be listening with Delight at almost 90 years old,[9] to an Author whom he so unknowingly & rashly had condemned! Only imagine what an Effect this must have in confounding & putting to Silence such pigmy puerile Puppies as Williams[10] & Smith[11] & a Farrago of other such musical Odds & Ends.

I can't dine with you To-morrow, but will breakfast with you at $\frac{1}{2}$ past nine, & bring the Sonatas under my *Oxster*[12] (as the Scots call it) for you will like to have a previous Peep.—You see I make sure of you on Monday.—I think I see & hear you saying 'Yes, you may.'

> Love to all
> Yours (in *no* Haste as you perceive) ever truly
> S. W

---

[3] 2 Oct.

[4] Portland's letter to Burney of 28 Sept. (Osborn) contained an invitation for Burney to visit him for a second time at Bulstrode (Lonsdale, 469).

[5] George Augustus Kollmann (1789–1845), pianist, composer, and inventor, son of A. F. C. Kollmann. He was taught the piano by his father, whose piano concerto he performed at the New Musical Fund concert on 15 Mar. 1804. His compositions included a set of piano sonatas (1808), an air with variations (1808), and a set of waltzes (*Grove*[6]).

[6] Evidently a letter from Burney, presumably written on receipt of Portland's invitation, and requesting a performance without delay; not preserved.

[7] Both quotations are from the Gloria of the Anglican communion service.

[8] Presumably for a rehearsal.   [9] In fact, Burney was 83.

[10] Probably George Ebenezer Williams (1783–1819), organist at the Philanthropic Chapel and deputy organist of Westminster Abbey; in 1814 he was appointed organist there (Shaw; *Grove*[6]).

[11] Probably John Stafford Smith (1750–1836), at this time one of the organists of the Chapel Royal, and Master of the Children there. He was also a noted musical antiquarian (Shaw; *Grove*[6]).

[12] His armpit.

To [?Charles Frederick Horn][1]   [Camden Town,
                                                ?*c*.30 September 1809][2]

ALS, 3 pp. (RCM, MS 2130, fo. 35)

Huzza!—Old Wig[3] for ever, & confusion of Face to Pig-Tails & Mountebanks!—
Chappel[4] at Birchall's tells me that the People teaze his Soul out for the *Fugues*:
that the eternal Question is, 'when does Mr Wesley intend to bring forward the
Fugues in all the 24 Keys? ['] I can plainly perceive that Chappell would be not
a little glad to get the Concern into his own & his Master's Hands, but I think
we shall be too cunning to suffer that.—He says he is convinced that it would be
advisable to publish *12* of the 1st Sett as soon as possible, & he *must* be sincere in
this Instance I think, because he stopped me Yesterday in the Street (when I was
very much in Haste) & dragged me Vi & Armis into the Shop, to communicate
his Complaints.—

Now, what say *you* to making a strict Revision of the 12 first Preludes & their
Correspondent Fugues, from my Copy[5] (which you have) & causing them to be
transcribed in a capital & correct Manner for the Press, without delay?[6]

[1] For Horn, see SW to Jacob, 17 Oct. 1808, n. 1. Because of the inclusion of this letter in the same
collection as other letters to Jacob, it has hitherto been assumed that it is to him. SW's discussion of the
preparation of a collaborative edition of the '48', however (see n. 6), gives strong grounds for concluding
that the addressee was in fact Horn.

[2] Although the content of this letter clearly indicates a date some time in 1809, its more precise
dating is problematical. In his letter to Jacob of 3 Mar. 1809, SW announced that he was about to send
the first of the six Bach organ trios to the engraver, and that it would be best to issue them singly; his
reference here to the sale of copies of the second trio of the set points to a date somewhat later in the year.
The conjectural dating proposed here is consonant with what is known of the chronology of the
Wesley–Horn edition and with SW's reference to Williams and Smith, also mentioned in SW to Jacob,
[*c*.30 September 1809].

[3] An ironic reference to J. C. Bach's dismissive name for his father: see SW to Novello, 25 Sept. [1824].

[4] Samuel Chappell (*c*.1782–1834), music seller and publisher, at this time employed by Birchall. On
3 Dec. 1810 he set up in partnership with Johann Baptist Cramer and Francis Tatton Latour to form the
firm of Chappell (*Grove*[6]). The Wesley–Horn edition of the '48' was eventually published by Birchall.

[5] Presumably the manuscript copy made by SW from Graeff's copy of the Nägeli edition: see SW to
Graeff, 21 May [?1806].

[6] Plans for the Wesley–Horn edition of the '48' had first been discussed almost a year earlier: see
SW to Jacob, 17 Oct. 1808. At that stage, no further progress appears to have been made on the edition,
possibly because SW and Horn subsequently decided to publish the organ trio sonatas first. From the
time of the present letter, Wesley and Horn moved quickly: the advance announcement for the edition
appeared in the Mar. 1810 number of *MM*, and the edition itself appeared in four parts between Sept. 1810
and July 1813.

'Strike the Iron while 'tis hot' is among the good proverbial Advices, & I see not why we should not take every Advantage *instantly* of the good Disposition of the Public, which may by Degrees lead to the solid & permanent Establishment of truth, & overthrow of Ignorance, Prejudice, & Puppyism with regard to our mighty Master.—Chappell has sold 6 Numbers of the 2^{d7}—& wants *6 more directly*, together with *all the Copies* of my Voluntaries printed by Hodsoll[8] which I can rake out for him.—

'The Organ is King, be the Blockheads ever so unquiet'[9]—I really cannot sufficiently express my Thanks to that Power 'which ordereth all Things well' for making me an humble Engine of bringing into due Notice that noble Instrument, by which so many Minds are brought to attend to Truths upon which their present & future Happiness depend.

It is also very remarkable (and seems to be providential) that the Contriver of these exquisite Pieces of Art, so calculated to awaken the noblest & most solemn Ideas, should himself have been an exemplary Instance of unaffected Piety, & of the mildest Christian Virtues.—How much additional Value, & what Lustre does it not put upon his divine Effusions!

'Speed the Plough'[10] must really be the Order of the Day.—Let us remember that we 'have put our Hand to it,' & I think we have no Temptation to 'look back'—Let us lose not an Hour in forwarding such Harmony on Earth as has the direct Tendency to bring us to the *celestial*, & really such Men as Williams & Smith may be considered as Satan's Implements to thwart the Designs of Providence.—I do not think I am too severe in this Observation: I assure you I think it the literal Fact. Write to me about this Matter, & by all Means crack it about every where how vehement the Demand for Bach is *at the most brilliant Music Shop* in *London*.

I purpose to come from Paddington after the School to you on Saturday Evening, & will endeavour to be with you by *8* o'Clock. Adieu,

SW

[7] i.e. the second of the Bach organ trio sonatas.

[8] SW's Voluntaries, Op. 6, were composed over a period of years and were published individually between 1802 and 1817. Full details of their composition and publication history are not known, but by this time the first nine of the twelve had been published (Robin Langley, 'Samuel Wesley's Contribution to the Development of English Organ Literature', *JBIOS* 17 (1993), 102–16; review of Op. 6 No. 1 in *MM* 13 (1802), 601).

[9] Adapted from BCP, Ps. 99: 1: 'The Lord is King, be the people never so impatient: he sitteth between the Cherubins, be the earth never so unquiet.'

[10] An old expression, and the title of a recent comedy (1798) by Thomas Morton (?1764–1838).

To Tebaldo Monzani   Camden Town, 4 October [1809]

Wesley's Chapel, London (LDWMM 1997/6603)
Editor's note The text of this letter was not available for consultation.

SW asks Monzani if he wishes to purchase the copyright of his 'little burlesca'[1]
which he thinks has 'every chance of becoming popular'.

To Benjamin Jacob   [Camden Town], 5 November [1809][1]

ALS, 1 p. (RCM, MS 2130, fo. 29)
Addressed To | Mr Jacobs | Charlotte Street | Black Friar's Road
Pmk NO 6 1809

My dear Sir,
    Enclosed is the Card[2] I promised.—I trust that you will manage (by Hook or
by Crook) to look in at the Surrey[3] on Tuesday Evening, as altho' the principal
Body of the 1st Lecture[4] is an old Story to you who have both heard & read it, yet
I have added two or three Touches, I think for the better, of which I should like
to have your Opinion.—I shall find my Way to the Lock-up House after I have
finished my Sermon, when we will confabulate all how & about *a-many Things*,

---

[1] Probably SW's undated 'I walked to Camden Town' (autograph RCM, MS 4021), thus described
by SW on the autograph. No copies of a printed edition have been traced.

[1] The year is given by the postmark.

[2] Not certainly identified: probably an admission ticket for SW's course of lectures at the Surrey
Institution, due to start on 7 Nov.; or perhaps a card advertising the edition of the Bach organ trio sonatas,
also mentioned in SW to Jacob, [24 Nov. 1809].

[3] On Tuesday, 7 Nov. SW was to give the first of a course of six lectures on music at the Surrey
Institution, one of several such bodies founded around the beginning of the 19th cent. in emulation of
the Royal Institution. It occupied the Rotunda in Blackfriars Road, originally built in 1788–9 for James
Parkinson to house the natural history collection of Sir Ashton Lever, including the tropical and other
curiosities collected by Captain Cook on his voyages. It contained a lecture theatre, reading and conversation rooms, a chemistry laboratory, offices, committee rooms, and living accommodation for the
Secretary. The reading rooms had opened on 1 May 1808 and lectures on chemistry, mineralogy,
natural philosophy, and other subjects had started in Nov. of the same year. The lecture theatre, which
could hold an audience of over 500, was illustrated in Ackermann's *The Microcosm of London*. (*Survey
of London*, vol. xxii: *Bankside: (The Parishes of St Saviour and Christchurch, Southwark)* (1950), 115–17
and pl. 81b; Rudolph Ackermann, *The Microcosm of London*, 3 vols. (1808–11), iii. 154–60.) It survived
until after the Second World War but has now been demolished.

[4] Not certainly identified, but very probably 'On Music Considered as an Art and Science', with
which SW had opened his course at the Royal Institution on 10 Mar.

especially upon your Party at the Chapel,⁵ & the immediate Promulgation of *the Man*,⁶ (which expression I now prefer to any Epithet of *'great'* or *'wonderful'*, &c. which are not only common, but *weak*, as is every other Epithet applied to one whom none can sufficiently praise)—

My services to the Scarlet Whore of Babylon To-Day⁷ were very gratefully & handsomely received.—If the Roman Doctrines were like the Roman *Music* we should have Heaven upon Earth.

Yours in Haste
ever truly,

S. Wesley

Sunday Night. 5 Nov.

To [Benjamin Jacob]¹   Camden Town, [6 November 1809]²

ALS, 1 p. (RCM, MS 2130, fo. 41)

My dear Sir

You will think me sufficiently stupid in not recollecting when I wrote you last Night, that I have some Intention (if I can but manage it) of coming to you in the Course of To-morrow previous to my mounting the Rostrum, for as you bespoke me to return to Charlotte Street³ after *Sermon*, it will be very snug & commodious to put on a Pair of Shoes at so near a Distance from the Place of Execution.—You see how *ceremonious* I am with my Friends, & I'll tell you another Secret, which is that if I feel very hungry when I arrive, I shall ax for somewhat to eat, look ye d'ye see? But I cannot appoint my Hour for certain, therefore I insist on your making no preparation or *Spreadation* for

Yours in Haste

S. Wesley

Monday Evᵍ | Camden Town

⁵ Doubtless the concert being arranged for 29 Nov. and referred to in SW to Jacob, [24 Nov. 1809].
⁶ Bach.
⁷ i.e. the Roman Catholic Church: SW had presumably been playing for a service, probably at the Portuguese Embassy Chapel, where Novello was organist.

¹ Although lacking an address portion, it is clear from the content and present location of this letter that it is to Jacob.
² SW's 'Monday', and his references to his letter to Jacob 'last night' and his lecture on the following day, give the date.   ³ Jacob's house, off Blackfriars Road, close to the Surrey Institution.

To Benjamin Jacob   [Camden Town and] Turnham Green,
                                         [24 November 1809]¹

ALS, 3 pp. (RCM, MS 2130, fo. 31)
Addressed To | Mʳ Jacobs | Charlotte Street | Black Friar's Road | Friday 2
Pmk 24 NO 1809

My dear Sir,

I wish your Opinion of delivering each person *who presents a Ticket*, one of the
Cards announcing the Trios of Bach: I should conceive that Mʳ Hill² could not urge
any Objection against this, & that it is almost too trifling a Circumstance to render
a Consultation upon it *with him*, necessary.—However, as you know his *Ins* &
Outs so much better than I, the Matter is left to your Decision—I will bring with me
a good jolly Lot of the said Cards To-morrow,³ which at all events will be in as good
(or a better) Train of Distribution than when facing Primrose Hill, as at present.⁴

I think there can be no Question that the Circulation of them on Wednesday,⁵
would push on the Cause of the Trios materially.

I have not sent M. P. King⁶ a Notice of Wednesday, & will leave it to you.—

¹ SW's '2 o'Clock Friday' and the postmark give the date of this letter: SW evidently started it at
home in Camden Town and continued it at Turnham Green, where he had a teaching engagement
(nn. 4 and 18).

² i.e. Rowland Hill. It is evident from this reference and from SW's later comments that the cards were
to be distributed at the concert at Surrey Chapel on the following Wednesday, 29 Nov. (see n. 5).

³ 25 Nov., when SW and Jacob were evidently to meet, probably to rehearse for their forthcoming
concert.   ⁴ i.e. at SW's house in Camden Town.

⁵ At the concert at Surrey Chapel on 29 Nov. The concert was designed to stimulate interest in
Bach's music, and was almost certainly the one referred to by SW in his Reminiscences: '[Jacob] planned
with me a Selection from the works of Bach and Handel as a matter of grand Morning performance at
Surrey Chapel, with the consent and approbation of the Revᵈ Rowland Hill. Among the organ pieces
were inserted two of Bach's beautiful and brilliant Sonatas with a Violin accompaniment [i.e. two of the
Sonatas for Violin and Harpsichord, BWV 1014–19]. I had been a fine Performer on that instrument
many years before, but had long disused it. However on the present occasion I resolved on resuming it,
and accordingly set to practise these pieces so as to be completely qualified for a public performance of
them. Mr Jacobs [*sic*] caused a list of every article to be printed and circulated in every Quarter where
the Tickets of admission were deposited; and as the Performance was entirely gratuitous, the invitations
were readily enough accepted. The chapel was very numerously attended and the performance occupied
to the best of my recollection from three to four hours. The whole was executed with accuracy and
Precision, and the hearers professed themselves universally gratified and satisfied with every portion of
it.' A similar account is given in the entry for Jacob in Sainsbury, compiled directly from information supplied to Sainsbury by Jacob in a letter of 15 Jan. 1824 (Glasgow University Library, Euing Collection).
According to Jacob, the performance lasted four hours, and the audience numbered '3,000 persons of
the highest respectability, also many in the first rank of professors and amateurs'.

⁶ Matthew Peter King (*c*.1773–1823), theatre musician, teacher, and composer, principally of dramatic and vocal music (Brown and Stratton).

I have exhausted all the Ammunition brought by your Messenger,[7] & have sent to Hoare,[8] Wright,[9] & some other Bankers of Consequence (Hammersley for Instance)[10] all of whom are musical, & will *prate* about the Thing, which you know is all we want at present: & if a Majority happen to be pleased (which we may without much Presumption conclude) we shall have no bad Chance of being *paid* for our Work at a future Opportunity.

I think if you can borrow a Court Guide, or List of Lords, Ladies, Bucks, & other Blackguards, we may meet with a few Names that we shall be unwilling to have omitted, when the grand Day is over.

I long to know what you have written to my Brother, & whether you have given him a coaxing Word or two.—I fear that setting **J. C. B.**[11] before **G. F. H.** will in Spite of all good Endeavours on your Part, be regarded as an unpardonable Sin—I believe that no *Lecture on Prejudice*[12] will ever eradicate his—What a grievous Circumstance for a Mind intended for *Expansion* equal to its *Conceptions* which certainly *are great* & extraordinary.—I have repeatedly told you my high respect for his powers of musical Criticism—Alas that one who feels the merit of '**the MAN**' as much every whit as *we* do, will not do *himself* the Honour of acknowledging it.

It appears to me that we shall save Trouble by borrowing Mr Jos. Gwilt's[13] Zurich Fugues,[14] as the fewer References from one Book to another, the more Time we shall save, & consequently render the Auditory more patient.—In this Case, perhaps you will secure the said Book for our Rehearsal To-morrow as well as the Fiddle de dee from Professor Perkins.[15]

---

[7] i.e. publicity for the concert.

[8] Probably the Hoare mentioned in SW to Charles Wesley jun., 15 Jan. 1807, and n. 49.

[9] Probably Thomas Wright of the banking firm of Wright, Selby, and Robinson, and possibly the 'Mr Wright' mentioned in SW to Street, 18 Oct. 1799.

[10] Presumably the Hammersley who was a partner in the banking firm of Hammersley, Greenwood, Drew, and Brooksbank.

[11] A slip of the pen for 'J.S.B.' This correction is made without comment by Eliza Wesley in her edition.

[12] One of SW's Royal Institution Lectures, probably repeated as part of his course at the Surrey Institution, had been entitled 'On Musical Prejudice': see SW to Burney, 6 Dec. 1808.

[13] Like his elder brother George (see SW to Jacob [17 Nov. 1808]), Joseph Gwilt (1784–1863) was an architect, an amateur musician, and a member of the Wesley–Novello circle. He was evidently a wealthy man: in 1811 he offered to meet the expenses of an ambitious project to publish a collected edition of harmonized Gregorian chant (see SW to Novello, 11 Nov. [1811], 27 June [1812]) and in 1813 underwrote the cost of publishing SW's madrigal 'O sing unto mie roundelaie' (see SW to Novello, 17 Feb. [1813]). He had strong antiquarian interests, and is known to have purchased many items at the sale of Burney's library in 1814. He also shared the enthusiasm of SW and Novello for the music of J. S. Bach, and his second son, born in 1811, was christened John Sebastian after him. Like his brother, he was a neighbour of Jacob (*DNB*; Colvin; King, 28, 134, 136).   [14] i.e. the Nägeli edition of the '48'.

[15] No doubt the violinist James Marshall Perkins of 75 King Street, Westminster (Doane).

Unless that same Straduarious[16] be kept in high Order, I have many Doubts of its answering our Purpose as well as my own tender Stainer[17]—however, you know me not over-given to condemn without a Hearing.

Forgive my boring you thus, but the Subjects in this Billet seemed to me of some Importance.

Adieu
till *as near* 6 as the Fates will allow.
Yours ever truly
    S. Wesley

Turnham Green,[18] | 2 o'Clock Friday

To [Benjamin Jacob][1]   Camden Town, [?2 December 1809][2]

ALS, 2 pp. (RCM, MS 2130, fo. 38)

Saturday

My dear Sir

Many Thanks for your early & kind Attention—The Numbers[3] you have sent will be sufficient for my Purpose, as that containing the *Commencement* of the Attack, is of the most Importance in the series of my Cannonade.—

We shall have Fun alive next Tuesday,[4] & if you can by hook or by crook, get J. P. & X. Y. Z. (who I believe one Person) to come, I think I shall have some Murder to answer for, which is a great Comfort to any delicate Conscience.—

---

[16] Evidently Perkins's violin, by Antonio Stradivari (1644–1737) (*Grove*[6]).

[17] SW's own violin, by the Austrian maker Jacob Stainer (?1617–1683) (*Grove*[6]).

[18] SW had apparently started this letter at his house in Camden Town and completed it later in the day at Turnham Green, where he had a teaching commitment.

---

[1] Although lacking an address portion, there can be no doubt from the content of this letter and its present location that it is to Jacob.

[2] The content of this letter (see n. 3) links it to SW's controversial lecture 'On Musical Deception', which he delivered as part of his course at the Surrey Institution, which ran for six weeks from 7 Nov. The suggested dating assumes that SW gave this lecture on 5 Dec., and that the 'feast' referred to in the letter was the Surrey Chapel concert of 29 Nov.

[3] No doubt the May, Aug., and Oct. numbers of *NMMR*, which contained the criticisms of 'J.P.' and 'X.Y.Z.' In a letter to the editor of *NMMR* dated 9 Oct. and published in the Nov. number, SW publicized his forthcoming course of lectures and announced his intention of replying to his critics, stating that 'if J.P., X.Y.Z., or any other such LITERARY Gentlemen, choose to attend, they may hear their gross ignorance, and defamatory falsehoods, duly exposed'.

[4] See n. 2. SW's lecture, entitled 'On Musical Deception', was evidently planned to be a robust attack on his critics.

Mrs. Billington has sent me a Letter of Thanks for the Feast on Wednesday,[5] inviting me to one of the *Alderman* Sort at her House.

Adieu—
Y^rs ever
S. Wesley

Turn Over

Linley writes to say that he will be glad of his two Books as soon as they can conveniently be sent.—If an Opportunity should occur between now & Tuesday perhaps you can contrive to get them handed over to him.

To [Knight Spencer][1]   [Camden Town], 9 December 1809

ALS, 3 pp. (RCM, MS 2130, fo. 33)

Decr 9. 1809

Sir

I have received the Favour of your Letter,[2] & am obliged to you for the Motive which you express as having actuated you to write it.—Had I considered the Controversy, (the Introduction of which you seem so much to condemn) as a merely private & personal Matter between the two anonymous Antagonists[3] & myself, I should have coincided with you in Opinion that it was not a Subject of sufficient Importance to propose as a prominent Feature in a Lecture: but as the Authors (or *Author*, for I am inclined to believe the double signature only a Pretence) attacked not only *myself* but *the whole Body* of musical Professors together, in the most scandalous Style, denominating them no better than a Banditti of Pick-Pockets, I should have considered myself an unworthy Deserter of the Profession to which I belong, to suffer it to lie under the base Imputations attributed to them by a malevolent Opponent, when so fair an Opportunity

---

[5] The Surrey Chapel concert on 29 Nov.

[1] This letter is included in Eliza Wesley's edition of the *Bach Letters*, where she states that it is addressed to Spencer. The identification derives from a pencil note (not in Eliza's hand) on the manuscript, probably taken from an address portion which has since been discarded or destroyed. The identification of Spencer as the addressee is undoubtedly correct: he was at this time Secretary of the Surrey Institution.

[2] Not preserved. Spencer had evidently written to SW to complain about the personal nature of the lecture in which SW had attacked his *NMMR* critics, and to suggest that SW should deliver an additional lecture to make amends.   [3] i.e. 'J.P.' and 'X.Y.Z.'.

offered itself of confuting his Assertions, & vindicating their Cause: Besides Sir, if you reflect for a Moment, that the Subject I chose for my Lecture was that of 'musical Deception' so flagrant & flagitious an Instance of it came immediately & most naturally within the scope of my general Design, & I am sure a stronger & more disgraceful Proof of it, could not ever be brought forward.

With regard to 'making Amends' for an Act which I cannot consider in the Light of an Offence, you must excuse my differing from you as to its Necessity.— That my 'recent Conduct' (by which of Course you mean my vindication of the Profession assaulted by an anonymous Assassin) should have given cause to 'unpleasant Remarks,' either 'universally' or partially 'excited,' I am thus far sorry, because I was persuaded in my own Mind, not only of the Sincerity of my Intentions to do good, by exposing Imposture, but also, flattered myself, that my Motives would have been as favourably construed as I am conscious that they deserved to be.

Having engaged to read no more than *Six Lectures* in the present Season, the Composition of a supernumerary one, would be attended with a Consumption of Time, which my very close Pressure of Engagement, I regret to observe, will render impossible.

I remain, with Respect, & gratitude, Sir,
Your obliged
& very obedient Servant
S Wesley

To John Langshaw Junior[1]   Camden Town, 26 December 1809

ALS, 2 pp. (Emory, Wesley–Langshaw Letters)
Addressed To | Mr Langshaw | Organist | Lancaster
Pmk 27 809
Endorsed Decr 26 1809

[1] John Langshaw jun. (1763–1832) had been sent in 1778 as a boy of 15 to London by his father John Langshaw sen. (d. 1798) to study with Benjamin Cooke, organist of Westminster Abbey. Finding Cooke inadequate as a teacher, he quickly transferred to SW's brother Charles, and became a frequent visitor to the Wesleys' home, where he was made welcome and treated as one of the family. He returned to Lancaster in the winter of 1780–1, and apart from a visit of three months to London in early 1784 had remained there ever since. He succeeded his father as organist of Lancaster parish church on the latter's death. This letter is one of a collection of thirty-two letters written over a period of forty-nine years by Charles Wesley to John Langshaw sen. and by his two sons to John Langshaw jun. (Wainwright).

Dear Sir

Although you may not have entirely forgotten my Name, yet so long a Time has elapsed since any epistolary Communication between us has occurred, that I should not wonder at the Surprize this hand Writing may for a Moment occasion.—

Therefore altho' John Langshaw & Samuel Wesley have not very lately met either in Person or in black & white, I nevertheless am of Opinion that some Tidings of the *Existence* of each will be acceptable to both.—

The present Occasion of my immediate Application to you, relates to an *Organ*, which it seems is to be constructed for your Quarter of the World,[2] & I understand that several Estimates have been, or are about to be delivered in, from various Makers on the Subject.—

I therefore have taken the Liberty of suggesting to You, that *in my Opinion*, there is no Organ Builder in England whose Work would do him more Credit than *Elliott*, in the present Instance, & should you approve of his Proposals, without being pre-engaged in Favour of some previous Applicant, I do not hesitate to promise that you will not be disappointed in your Choice nor I in Danger of any Disgrace by my Recommendation.[3]—

My own Organ is built by him, & notwithstanding its Limitation to *three* Stops (to which I consented, for the Advantage of an Octave of *double Base* Pedals) the Tone of it is such as to much delight all the Judges who have heard it.[4]

I have not the Pleasure of being known to any of your Family *personally*, excepting your late worthy Father & Brother; but in presenting them my best Respects & Wishes, you will oblige

Dear Sir
Your old (& yet I trust not wholly forgotten)
Friend & Servant

S Wesley

Camden Town | near London | Dec[r] 26th 1809

---

[2] i.e. for Lancaster parish church. The organ was eventually built in 1811 by George Pike England (Boeringer, ii. 95).

[3] SW's concern was far from altruistic. If his recommendation had resulted in a firm order to Elliot, he would have received a substantial commission.

[4] Nothing more is known about this instrument.

To Charles John Smyth[1] Camden Town, 10 January 1810

ALS, 3 pp. (BL, Egerton MS 2159, fo. 68)
Addressed To | The Revd C. J. Smyth | Norwich | Norfolk
Pmks JA 11 1810, JA 11 810

> Camden Town
> January the 10th 1810

Dear Sir

I am sorry that I have not sooner had an Opportunity of complying with your Request upon the Subject of Mr Elliot's Organ, constructed upon Mr Hawkes's Plan of Temperament,[2] but as I was desirous to afford you as satisfactory an Explanation as I could, (which could not be without a previous Consultation with Elliot) I delayed writing until this had taken Place; & I now trust that the few following Observations may partly remove what has hitherto seemed to you objectionable.

In your Letter to our Friend Linley,[3] you enquired 'whether the Organ on which I exhibited at the Royal Institution had compound stops?'[4]—It had but three Stops in all, namely two Diapasons & Principal.[5]

You observe (very truly) that 'the Beatings of an imperfect Consonance are doubled by the Principal & quadrupled by the Fifteenth,' and proceed,—'Heaven knows how these Beatings would be multiplied by the Compounds,' adding that you are 'persuaded the Thirds ought to be good, or Compounds excluded.'

I will now transcribe what Elliot communicated to me in Elucidation of his Mode of tempering, previously remarking your Observation of being 'charmed with the Beauty of the Chords in Places where you least expected to find it.'—

---

[1] The Revd Charles John Smyth (1760–1827), matric. New College, Oxford (1777), BA (1781), MA and Fellow (1786), rector of Great Fakenham, Norfolk and chaplain to Lady Bayning (1803), Vicar of Calton, Norfolk, Rector of St George's, Colegate, Norwich, and minor canon of Norwich Cathedral (1811). He was an amateur musician, music theorist, and composer, who contributed a number of articles to *MM* and *Philosophical Magazine*; he also published pamphlets on music and composed a morning and evening service (Foster; Kassler, *Science of Music*, 955–60).

[2] The Hawkes–Elliot organ, as used by SW at his Royal Institution lectures in early 1809. SW had subsequently used the same organ, or a similar one by Elliot constructed on the same principles, at his Surrey Institution lectures. For a more extended discussion of the organ and its construction, and of the technical points raised in this letter, see Philip Olleson, ' "The Perfection of Harmony Itself": The William Hawkes Patent Organ and its Temperament', *JBIOS* 21 (1997), 108–28.

[3] Either William Linley, or possibly his brother Ozias (1765–1831), who was with Smyth a minor canon at Norwich Cathedral. For Ozias, see SW to Novello, 5 Oct. 1814, n. 9.

[4] i.e. mixtures, consisting of a number of ranks.

[5] i.e. two eight-foot stops and one four-foot stop.

I presume that you allude to the Keys of E♭ Major, A♭ Major, D♭ Major, E♮ Major, B♮ Major, F♯ Major.[6]

These, by the Addition of real Pipes,[7] certainly produce an Effect, which when compared with the false old Temperament in which E♭ & D♯ passed for *the same Tone*, A♯ for B♭, F♯ for G♭, & G♯ for A♭, & vice versâ, renders the latter quite intolerable, but the former highly delightful.

Now in regard to the other Keys, Elliot thus observes:

'The Thirds, when sharpened, scarcely one Fourth of a Comma,[8] beat, when properly in Tune, so as to be hardly perceptible to the Ear, & by which Means the Fifths are improved, & the extreme Keys are rendered much more agreeable.'

'The compound Stops, when well voiced, will so combine together as not to be distinguishable from the same Tone, as in the simple ones; & a Chord taken with them is no more unpleasant to a nice Ear than when taken on a single Stop.— For although the Beats multiply in the acute Tones, yet they are so faint that the most critical Ear cannot distinguish them from perfect, which is not surprizing, when it is considered that they are only the 40th Part of a Tone too sharp.'

The Truth of this Statement I can vouch for by various Experiments which I made at Elliot's House[9] two Days ago, on Purpose to be able to give a safe Opinion upon the Subject.—Indeed, if we only reflect upon the monstrous Crash of Dissonance which *really* exists in every Chord upon an Organ, (*tuned any possible Way*) when the compound Stops are employed, & which, if we take a compound Stop singly (Sesquialtera[10] for Instance) becomes execrable & intolerable, & yet consider how wonderfully all this is chastened & subdued by the fundamental *Diapason*, so as to form one rich & harmonious *Amalgam* (if I may so express it) we shall easily account for the Evanescence of the more inconsiderable Dissonances, upon which you have animadverted, which really become imperceptible.—You well know Sir, that we may always refine upon Theory beyond what can ever be reducible to Practice, & it appears to me, that if Harmony on an Organ can be sufficiently improved by Temperament to entirely remove objectionable Sounds, & to bring every Chord, if not to absolute Perfection, yet to a very fair Proportion of it, we ought to

---

[6] As is apparent from a description of the Hawkes-Elliot instrument by John Farey in *Philosophical Magazine* for May 1811, Elliot's temperament was a form of sixth-comma mean tone. The keys listed by SW here are those which are most out of tune in the quarter-comma mean tone temperament in general use at the time and referred to by SW as the 'false old Temperament'.

[7] The additional pipes of the Hawkes system, giving separate pitches for C♯ and D♭, D♯ and E♭, F♯ and G♭, G♯ and A♭, and A♯ and B♭. The performer was able to select either all sharps or all flats by means of a pedal.

[8] i.e. between 5.38 and 5.91 cents or hundredths of a tone, depending on which one of three possible commas was meant. In fact, the major thirds in Elliot's system were tuned sharp by 3.77 cents.

[9] At 12 Tottenham Court, New Road, where he also had his workshop. SW lived next door at 13 Tottenham Court in 1812–13.

[10] The normal diapason chorus mixture stop in England at this time, consisting of three ranks (17–19–22).

rest contented.—I think that Hawkes's Scheme has effected this in the extraneous Keys, & that Elliot's Temperament has sufficiently improved the others.—

I remain, with much Respect
Dear Sir, your obliged & obedient Servant,
    S Wesley

To Sarah Gwynne Wesley[1]   [Camden Town], 18 January 1810

ALS, 3 pp. (Rylands, DDWes 6/55)

Dear Mother

I hope that you did not wait Dinner for any of my People nor provide any extraordinary Food on that Account.—It was quite impossible for me to come to you yesterday, & I had no Opportunity of letting you know this in Time: little Emma[2] has the whooping Cough, but is much better, & suffers far less than the Generality of Children in that Disorder, so that I trust she will soon be recovered. —Your Intelligence came too late for me to Breakfast with Miss Coope:[3] I think her Direction is N. 14 New North Street Bloomsbury—I am however not sure of the Number tho' I am of the Street & therefore if you will leave out the right Address, I will call or send for it at the first Opportunity.—

You must give me 3 or 4 Days Notice when you wish me to dine with you next, as I am so *widely distributed* almost from Morning till Night, that Letters very frequently arrive too late for a commodious Answer to them.

Remember me to my Brother, & tell him that if he is minded to go to St Paul's on Sunday next[4] to the Afternoon Service, he will hear that Fugue in three Movements (in three Flats)[5] which he assisted me in playing the other Evening, & which he was so delighted with, upon that noble Organ with the double Base,[6] which makes a magnificent Effect.—The Service begins at $\frac{1}{4}$ after 3.

I am
Dear Mother
Very affect^{ly} Yours
    S Wesley

Thursday Jan. 18th 1810

[1] Sarah Gwynne Wesley (1726–1822), SW's mother. She lived with SW's brother Charles and his sister Sarah.   [2] Emma Frances (1806–65), SW's daughter.
[3] Not identified.   [4] 21 Jan.
[5] Bach's Prelude and Fugue in E flat, BWV 552 (the 'St Anne').
[6] A reference to the 16-foot pedal pipes of the St Paul's organ.

To Charles Wesley Junior   [Camden Town], 3 February 1810

ALS, 2 pp. (Emory, Letter 68)

Saturday Morning
Feb 3. 1810

Dear Charles

You have often heard in the Gospel of the two Personages, one of whom promised to work in the Vineyard, & afterwards retracted his Determination; & the other who was at *first* unwilling to make himself useful, & yet took a different Turn afterwards, & went.[1]—Now, if I am rightly informed, you resemble the latter Gentleman; for after my having received from you a Letter, stating that an Engagement which was to withhold you from appearing at the Theatre on Tuesday last, either you, or your Ghost, was observed in a lower Box, listening with much seeming Satisfaction to the Concerto which you had previously expressed some Wish to hear.—[2]

If it was your Ghost, I would by all means have you think seriously of this Intelligence for I am credibly assured upon the Veracity of several Welsh Clergymen & a great Majority of Irish Roman Catholic Priests (none of whom are ever known to lye) that although if a Man's Spirit be seen in the Day-Light, it betokens him to be very vivacious, yet the Matter is quite the contrary when such a Phenomenon appears after Dark, or at Candle or Lamp-Light; & if such observations be *orthodox*, (& where should Orthodoxy be found, if not among the Clergy) you must feel extremely alarmed at this Intelligence, which perhaps it may have been a little imprudent in me to communicate: but as *Memento Mori* has been sometimes found an exceedingly useful advice, especially to rich lazy Misers who have not made their Wills, you will I trust not deem my entering upon so important a Subject as a Matter of Impertinence or idle Curiosity.

If you really shall be able to prove that you yourself in propria persona were the Object of Vision, & that it was no Phantom, you must necessarily consider such an Event extremely consoling to your Friends, especially those of the more religious sort, since these (if not lost to all proper Sense of Respect & Confidence due to the sacred Order) cannot for a Moment hesitate to regard your Life in great Danger, after their solemn Prophecy in similar Cases.

---

[1] Matt. 21: 28–30.

[2] SW had played the organ in a performance of *Messiah* at Covent Garden on 30 Jan., where he was also soloist in his own Organ Concerto in D (*The Times*).

Trusting however that you can shew demonstratively that *you were yourself & Nobody else* on Tuesday Night, I am

Dear Charles,
both in *Substance* & *Spirit*,
Yours very truly
    S Wesley

To Charles Wesley Junior

ALS, 1 p. (Fitzwilliam)
Addressed To | Charles Wesley Esqre | Great Woodstock Street | Nottingham Place

Friday 16th Feb.

Dear Charles

I send you a divine Scrap of 'the old Wig'—[3] it is upon an old Lutheran Tune which I remember having heard many Years ago[4] at the Savoy Chappel:[5] I went into the Place about 10 in the Morning, & afterwards to some other Places of Worship: (poor Hugh Reinagle[6] was with me) after rambling about for two Hours & more, we returned by the Strand & popped into the Chappel again, where we found the Congregation & the Organist (who was Baumgarten)[7] hard *at the same Tune.*—It is always sung while the People are receiving the Sacrament.—

---

[1] SW's request at the end of the letter (see n. 7) indicates that he was probably using James Ball's business premises at 27 Duke Street, Grosvenor Square as a postal address following his separation from his wife Charlotte and his departure from Camden Town.

[2] The year is given by 16 Feb. falling on a Friday and the address of Charles Wesley jun.

[3] J. S. Bach's organ chorale prelude 'Schmücke dich, O liebe Seele', BWV 654. SW also relates this anecdote in an annotation on the page containing this chorale prelude in his own copy of Bach's *Choral Vorspiele* (now at RCM).

[4] From the reference to Reinagle (see n. 5), it is clear that the incident must have occurred in or before 1784.   [5] i.e. the Lutheran Chapel at the Savoy, in the Strand.

[6] The cellist Hugh Reinagle (1758/9–85) was one of the four sons of the Austrian trumpeter Joseph Reinagle. He studied the cello under John Crosdill and Joseph Shetky. In 1783, at the time of his admission to the Royal Society of Musicians, he described himself as a professional musician of at least seven years' practice. He was consumptive, and in Dec. 1784 ten members petitioned the RSM for financial assistance for him. By this time he had moved to Lisbon in an attempt to improve his health, but he died there shortly afterwards.

[7] Karl Friedrich Baumgarten (*c.*1740–1824), German composer, violinist, and organist, who settled in London around 1758. In addition to his post at the Savoy Chapel he was active as an orchestral violinist and as a composer of music for the stage. He also wrote organ and chamber music.

I am busy in arranging a Plan which *must* deliver me from many Vexations, & which if longer delayed would eventually cause me to *look through a Grate* for life.—I have been a Dupe & a Slave too long to the most unworthy of Women.[8]

Y[rs] truly

SW

Direct to me at Ball's: Duke St[r], Grosv. Sq[re].[9]

To George Polgreen Bridgetower

[?Adam's Row][1],
29 March [1810][2]

ALS, 1 p. (BL, Add. MS 56411, fo. 9)
Addressed To | M[r] Bridgetower | N. 2 (or 3) | John Street | S[t] James's Square *crossed out and replaced by* 51 Chancery Cross
Pmk 30 MR 1810

Thursday
29 March.

Dear Sir

I much regret having been unable to fix a Moment hitherto for our Meeting: I now offer you a *tempting Evening*, no other than next Sunday,[3] when a few of the *orthodox Harmonists* will meet at M[r] Stephenson's,[4] Queen Square N. 29 (think) for the Purpose of celebrating the Natal Day of *Sebastian Bach*.[5]—I am commissioned to invite all thorough Enthusiasts in such a Cause to be present—among whom I think I am not much mistaken in enumerating you.—

Pray come, & believe me, with much Regard,

Yours faithfully

S Wesley

[8] Probably a reference to arrangements SW was making for a formal separation from his wife Charlotte following the breakdown of his marriage and his removal from the family home; for the circumstances, see Biographical Introduction.

[9] Ball's business premises were at 27 Duke Street. SW appears to have rented a teaching studio there.

[1] Following his separation from Charlotte in early 1810, SW set up house with his former housekeeper or servant Sarah Suter at 11 Adam's Row, Hampstead Road, close to its junction with the New Road (now Euston Road). SW is known to have been at this address in July 1810, but it seems likely that he had moved there earlier in the year and that he was there at the time of this letter.

[2] The year is given by the postmark.   [3] 1 Apr.

[4] i.e. Edward Stephenson (1759–1833): see SW to Jacob, 17 Oct. 1808, n. 3.

[5] Bach was born on 21 Mar. (OS) or 1 Apr. (NS) 1685.

To [Charles Burney]¹   Adam's Row,² 17 July 1810

ALS, 1 p. (Osborn, MSS 3, Box 16, Folder 1193)
Docketed by Mme d'Arblay: ✳

My dear Friend,

I am right glad to find that upon Examination you are rid of the Apprehension that my Legerdemain Tricks might break your House down, & really when you stated the possible Danger resulting from only the Weight of one additional Instrument, I myself had my Fears that some late Delapidation might have been the Cause: However I think we are now en bon Train for a Trial of 'the comical Pieces' in Question:³—I expect to see my Friend Novello either To-Day or To-morrow, & as you leave us the Choice of Time, we will endeavour to fix on that which may least interfere with your more important Concerns.—I think that *12* is the earliest Hour that suits you, but perhaps *1* may be yet more convenient, & therefore will not besiege you sooner.⁴

¹ Burney is identified as the addressee of this letter by his daughter's characteristic docketing.

² This is the first letter from SW to bear his Adam's Row address. He lived here until late Mar. or early Apr. 1812, when he moved the short distance to Tottenham Court, New Road.

³ This letter is in reply to Burney to SW, [*ante* 17 July 1810] (LC, Moldenhauer Collection). In late June, Burney had invited SW and Novello to visit him at Chelsea College (Burney to SW, 27 June 1810 (BL, Add. MS 11730, fo. 33, quoted in Percy A. Scholes, *The Great Dr Burney*, 2 vols. (London, 1948), ii. 217–18)). In a subsequent letter (not preserved) or in a conversation, SW suggested that he and Novello should take the opportunity of their visit to perform Bach's *Goldberg Variations*; in the absence of the necessary two-manual harpsichord in Burney's apartment, they would play them on two pianos, using Burney's own Broadwood grand and another instrument which they would arrange to have transported there for the purpose. Burney initially demurred on the grounds of lack of space and the possible damage to his apartment that such a procedure might cause, suggesting instead that SW and Novello might instead like to find a suitable piano shop where they could play the Variations. The drawback to this arrangement, as Burney subsequently recognized, was that he would have no part in it, as he had made up his mind never again to go out 'into the open air'. On further reflection, however, he decided that his desire to hear the *Goldberg Variations* outweighed any worries about damage to his apartment, and that there was after all sufficient room in his parlour, 'when unbe-littered', for two pianos. The description of them as 'comical pieces' is Burney's. See Philip Olleson, 'Dr Burney, Samuel Wesley, and Bach's *Goldberg Variations*', in Jon Newsom (ed.), *The Rosaleen Moldenhauer Memorial: Music History from Primary Sources: A Guide to the Moldenhauer Archives* (Washington, 2000), 169–75.

⁴ Novello's and SW's visit was finally arranged for 11 a.m. on Friday, 20 July, the additional piano having been delivered to Burney's apartment earlier on the same day to allow time for it to be tuned and settle in. In making final arrangements for this visit, Burney wrote to SW: 'While the weather continues warm, I had rather wait on ye at 11, than 12 or 1—I am now entirely for the performance of the 30 Wariations *de suite*; as you two virtuous gemmen, doubtless, are so *parfet* in all these pretty *chunes*, that you'll go on as swimming from beginning to end, as if wind and tide were both strongly in your favour. I think the forte, i.e. fortés, may begin to storm the works of Engineer Bach, before 12. And if we have any time to spare, after being played over, we can *talk* them over—or (what wd be shtill petter auch coot) if little i were to say *bis* there might, may-hap, be time for a Da Capo.' (Burney to SW, 19 July 1810 (BL, Add. MS 11730, fo. 35)).

Now with regard to your Plan of Decimation[5] I cannot but think that as it is always a cruel one in the military Sense, so it would be partly, in our small musical Regiment of 30.—The whole Series will not employ much more than *one* Hour to pervade, & I must say, that I fear a considerable Degree of the immediate Contrast between the several Sections, would be diminished by a Chasm.—As the Variations are all upon *one* Theme, & that Theme is every where felt throughout, at least as strongly as the Characteristic Letter in a Greek Verb, there is no Probability of *your* letting any Part of them run to Waste.—However, the Permission to attend you *thrice* instead of *once* is a Temptation outweighing my Objections, & therefore you shall have just as few or as many of these queer *Chunes* (as we say at Bristol) as you may find palatable.

Adieu for the present, my good Friend.

SW

11 Adam's Row. Hampstead Road | Tuesday 17. July 1810

To [Joseph Payne Street]¹   Adam's Row, 11 October [1810]²

ALS, 2 pp. (BL, Add. MS 56228)

Adam's Row. Hampstead Road.
11th of Oct^r

My dear Sir,

I have this Day experienced a little Disappointment, in the Alleviation of which if you can conveniently assist, I am persuaded that you will.—About 12 Months since, an Acquaintance (for there is some Difference between this & a Friend) obligingly accommodated me with the Loan of £20, which when I returned him, he very politely said, that upon any similar Occasion, he would come forward with equal Promptitude.—Upon the Strength of this Declaration (which was given with that Sort of Energy that at least *sounded* sincere I applied to him Yesterday

---

⁵ i.e. to divide them into three sets of ten variations. Burney had suggested: 'Suppose we decimate the 30 variations, and divide them into 3 decads, performing 10 once, or twice, if we like or dislike them much, each day? which will allow us time to breathe, digest and judge' (Burney to SW, [*ante* 17 July 1810] (Osborn)).

¹ Although this letter lacks an address panel, it is clear from its provenance and inclusion with other letters to him that it is to Street.

² The year is given by SW's Adam's Row address and his reference in his postscript to his 'migration' there from Camden Town.

in Consequence of his *volunteer* Proposal, for the Loan of £50. on whatever Terms he might consider not only safe but even advantageous with Regard to the Interest. The Plea for Refusal was that he had lately advanced a large Sum on Account of a *Brother*,[3] (& I am glad to find that these rare fraternal Acts exist in our Metropolis) therefore that although he should feel peculiarly happy to oblige me, yet &c &c—the Rest all a Farrago of Cant & Lies.

If *you* can lend me £20 on the present Occasion, I know you will: & if you can, I should also wish you to fix the Time when you want it returned, that I may at once tell you whether I can remunerate *to the very Day*.

Upon a Supposition that this Favour might be inconvenient to yourself, yet it is not impossible that among your numerous & respectable City *Monde* (sufficient Security being given) you could negotiate this Matter for

Your's ever truly

S Wesley

P.S. I much wish to have a Tête a tête Talk with you, in a confidential Way, upon many Matters which have conduced to my Migration from Camden Town to my present Place of Abode.

To [Knight Spencer][1]   Adam's Row, 3 January [1811][2]

ALS, 2 pp. (Private collection)

Hampstead Road
Thursday Evening. Jan 3.

Dear Sir

I have received the Favour of your Letter,[3] & am concerned to find that there can be no postponing of the Day of my first Lecture,[4] as I fear I shall be not a little pressed for Opportunity to prepare it in the Way I formerly had done, before the very unfortunate Accident which has so thoroughly frustrated my original Plan of

---

[3] i.e. a fellow Freemason.

[1] Although lacking an address portion, it is clear from its date and content that this letter is to Knight Spencer.

[2] The year is given by 3 Jan. falling on a Thursday and SW's Hampstead Road address.

[3] Not preserved.

[4] SW's new course of lectures at the Surrey Institution had been advertised to start on 14 Jan. It is apparent from SW's letter to Spencer of 1 Feb. that its start was later postponed.

Proceeding.—As it is, I will endeavour to produce a Discourse partly similar to that which has 'fallen among Thieves,' although I much Doubt whether I shall do it with half the Satisfaction to my own Mind which I should feel in being able to bring forward the one first intended.[5]

It is necessary to state, that upon re-considering Matters, I shall find requisite not *two* Piano Fortes, but one only, with the same Organ that was engaged last Season;[6] & as a large Portion of the Lecture in Question will be devoted to Temperament, to illustrate this in the Manner I wish, there must be made an Alteration in the Management of the Pipes of the Organ which Elliott informs me will be attended with the additional Expense of five Pounds: the Experiment is indispensible, therefore I trust it will not meet Objection, as there is no other Alternative in order to render clear a Doctrine in the Distribution of the musical Scale which is of the utmost Importance in the Improvement of Harmony on keyed Instruments.[7]

Elliott wishes for as early an answer as possible, for he tells me that he must work hard to compleat what is wanted, before the 14th Instant.[8]—His Address is Tottenham Court, new Road near the Turnpike.[9]—Elliott, Organ Builder is placed both on the Wall of the House, & on the Street Door.—

I remain with Respect
Dear Sir
Yours very obediently
    S Wesley

[5] SW had hoped to reuse a lecture previously given at the Royal Institution and subsequently at his Surrey Institution course the previous year, but it had been lost or stolen. His replacement lecture (BL, Add. MS 35014, fos. 2–16), annotated 'the first lecture of the second Course', bears the same date as this letter. Entitled 'The most eligible Method of acquiring a Command of Keyed Instruments—Tuning— Old & new Method—Equal Temperament', it recommended keyboard players to become proficient at playing in all keys, and discussed the respective merits of different forms of temperament. The version preserved bears marks of extensive alteration and revision over the many years that SW delivered it, and it is evident that some of the text as delivered in 1811 has been discarded. It is nonetheless apparent from the lecture's title, its contents, and the discussion later in this letter that it covered much the same ground as the controversial lecture originally delivered at the Royal Institution on 22 Mar. 1809 which gave rise to the *NMMR* controversy.

[6] By Thomas Elliot; it had evidently incorporated the Hawkes–Elliot patent mechanism.

[7] Elliot's modification was perhaps to allow SW to compare different methods of temperament, including equal temperament, in his lecture.   [8] The day fixed for the first lecture.

[9] On the present Euston Road, near its junction with Tottenham Court Road and Hampstead Road, and very close to Adam's Row.

To Knight Spencer   Adam's Row, 1 February 1811

ALS, 1 p. (Princeton, John Wild Autograph Collection (C0047) vol. 13, leaf 103).
Addressed To | Knight Spencer | Surrey Institution | Black-Friars | Friday 1ˢᵗ of Febʸ
Pmk 7 O'Clock 1 FE 1811

Adam's Row Hampstead Road
Friday Feb 1ˢᵗ 1811.

Dear Sir

When I called on Wednesday last[1] at the Surrey Institution, I was informed that you were not in Town, but speedily expected: the chief Purport of my Visit was to enquire how far my Privilege extends of obliging some of my Friends with Tickets of Admission to the musical Lecture; & as I should be very loth to exceed due Bounds in that Instance, must request as soon as possible, having been almost teazed already by several who are rather importunate to become Auditors.

The Theme of my 1ˢᵗ Lecture may be announced as follows;

'On the most eligible Method of acquiring an easy Command of keyed-Instruments.'[2]

I remain, with Respect,
Dear Sir
Yours very obediently

S Wesley

To [Knight Spencer][1]   [Adam's Row] 7 April [1811][2]

ALS, 1 p. (BL, Add. MS 56411, fo. 25)
Docketed April 7ᵗʰ 1811. S Wesley

Dear Sir

I have written to Mʳ Spagnoletti,[3] desiring an immediate Answer to the general Request of the Subscribers to your Institution concerning Wednesday

---

[1] 30 Jan.

[2] As is clear from this letter, the start of SW's course of lectures had been postponed, possibly to 4 or 11 Feb. At the date originally advertised for the beginning of the course, SW was in Tunstall, Suffolk, visiting his friend Christopher Jeaffreson, who was vicar there: see SW to Sarah Suter, 6 Jan. [1811], [*post* 6 Jan. 1811], and 15 Jan. 1811 (BL, Add. MS 35012, fos. 30, 32, and 36).

[1] Although lacking an address portion, it is clear from its content that this letter is to Knight Spencer.

[2] The year is given by 7 Apr. falling on a Sunday and the docketing.

[3] Paolo Spagnoletti (1768–1834), Italian violinist, resident in England from about 1802 to his death. He was at different times leader of the orchestras at the King's Theatre, the Pantheon, the Lenten oratorio seasons at the King's Theatre, the Antient Concerts, the Philharmonic Society, and for numerous benefit concerts. The 'general request' was probably for him to perform at the final lecture of the course on 10 Apr.

next,[4] & hope that his Answer will be favourable.—Perhaps you were not present in the Theatre when I announced at the Conclusion of my last Lecture, that my Close of this Course would regard the Necessity of establishing a Standard Pitch for all keyed Instruments, & the Propriety of teaching Beginners on *good* Instruments, & not on Rubbish picked up at the Shops of Brokers, apparently cheap, but eventually very dear.[5]

I am,
Dear Sir
Yours very obediently
    S Wesley

Sunday 7th of April

To an unidentified recipient[1]   Adam's Row, 21 May [1811][2]

ALS, 1 p. (Rylands DDWF 15/24A)

Hampstead Road
Tuesday Ev[g] 21st May

Sir,

Upon consulting the State of my Engagements about the Time you mentioned as most likely for your musical Meeting to take Place, I find that the very lowest Terms I can propose without Detriment to my Business in London will be forty Guineas, & which I have fixed at that Rate merely in Consideration of your having represented the Concern as being at present rather a Matter of Experiment than of absolute profitable Certainty to the Promoters of it.

I remain, with Respect,
Sir,
Yours very obediently
    S Wesley

---

[4] 10 Apr.
[5] SW's lecture may have included some recommendations for specific makers. It is not included among the texts of his lectures at BL, Add. MS 35014–15.

---

[1] This letter is evidently in reply to an enquiry from the organizer of a provincial music festival, who had written to ask about SW's availability and fee.
[2] The year is given by 21 May falling on a Tuesday and SW's Hampstead Road address.

To Vincent Novello[1]   [Adam's Row], 22 May [1811][2]

ALS, 1 p. (BL, Add. MS 11729, fo. 3)

Wednesday 22^d May

Dear N,

You may have been probably informed by a Lady with whom I dined in Company on Sunday last that I looked in yesterday morning at 240 O S[3] to enquire whether you expected me to mount the *Box* for you (such it literally is you know) To-morrow at 11?[4]—I was answered in the Affirmative, therefore will certainly so do, *Deo volente*, as they used to say, (& as if any Thing *could* be done *without* God's Will.)—A Circumstance has occurred which renders my being at the Chapel from 11 till 1 (but perhaps there will be no Sermon) not quite so commodious as I thought it would have been when I volunteered, but it is so easily gotten over, that I desire you to maintain all your *didactic* Arrangements in Statu quo.

I must also desire to know exactly what is to be performed; for I am an aukward Devil when hurried, & you will acknowledge that there are very sudden Stage-Tricks played in your Choir with Regard to immediate Reversions of original Intentions, & which if not methodized a little for *me* who am not up to your very clever Harlequin Jumps from a Kyrie on the Desk to another at the Bottom of a Well, or to be fetched from Mr Fryer's[5] in S. Audley Street, while they are singing the Gloria of the Introit, then the Mass must stand still in a very decorous & edifying Manner to the Congregation.

---

[1] For Novello, see SW to Bridgetower, 14 Apr. [1809], n. 2. This is the first surviving letter to him, part of a collection of over 170 that he presented to the British Museum in 1840. At the time of this letter, SW and Novello had known each other for some years: probably since Novello's boyhood, or at least from the time of his appointment as organist of the Portuguese Embassy Chapel in 1797 or 1798. Their closer relationship appears to have followed SW becoming Novello's assistant at the Portuguese Embassy Chapel at around this time.

[2] The year is given by 22 May falling on a Wednesday and by SW's references to his edition of the '48' (see nn. 8 and 9).

[3] Novello's house at 240 Oxford Street. The site is now occupied by part of Marble Arch underground station.

[4] i.e. to play the organ at High Mass at the Portuguese Embassy Chapel on the following day, which was Ascension Day.

[5] The Revd William Victor Fryer (1768–1844), Principal Chaplain of the Portuguese Embassy Chapel. He was an amateur musician and the dedicatee of Novello's first publication, *A Collection of Sacred Music, as performed at the Royal Portuguese Chapel* [1811]. He was godfather to several of Novello's children, and Novello's eldest daughter Mary Victoria (later Mary Cowden Clarke) was named after him (Anstruther, iv. 197–8; Clarke, *My Long Life*, 10–11).

You will see that my Reason for all this prosing is to prevent my doing you more Disgrace than I can reasonably avoid; therefore will not be 'angry even unto Death' (which the Prophet Jonas told God Almighty he had a *Right* to be)[6] because I am prolix in the Endeavour to bar choral Accidents.

Leave M^r F's 2^d Vol. of the Zurich[7] out for me, & he shall have my 2 first Numbers[8] with all Expedition & my 2 latter,[9] please Heaven I live to edite them, otherwise my Debt to him for the 24 remaining shall be paid by my Executor, & if not, by my Executioner.

SW

To Charles Stokes [Adam's Row], 6 June [1811][1]

ALS, 1 p. (Boston)

Doctor Stokes! Sir!

I am neither 'a liar,' nor 'the Son of Darkness,' as one Dr Falstaff was wont to say,[2] though I doubt whether *every* Son is not rather in the Dark before he's born.—If I said that I had *written* repeatedly, I retract the Assertion: that I have *called* repeatedly, your honoured Mother, if she has a Tongue in her Head, will tell you, upon due & respectful Enquiry.—We will talk about the Trio[3] when we meet: the *Business* I alluded to concerned it: I think both you, Novello, & myself may make a few Guineas *in the approaching Holidays* by performing the same

---

[6] Jonah 4: 9.

[7] Fryer's copy of Book II of the '48' in the Nägeli edition, the accuracy of which SW had earlier commended to Crotch (see SW to Crotch, 25 Nov. 1808), and which he used as the basis of the edition he prepared with C. F. Horn. SW's request here for the loan of Fryer's copy (which would have supplemented his own manuscript copy of the Nägeli edition (now BL, Add. MS 14330)) indicates that he was about to start work on Part 3 (the first twelve preludes and fugues of Book II). Proofs of this part were sent to SW for correction in late Sept. (see SW to Novello, 27 Sept. [1811]) and it was published by the end of the year. For the publication chronology of the Wesley–Horn edition, see Edwards, 655–6.

[8] Parts 1 and 2 of the Wesley–Horn edition, comprising the twenty-four preludes and fugues of Book I.   [9] Parts 3 and 4, comprising the twenty-four preludes and fugues of Book II.

[1] The year is given by 6 June falling on a Thursday and the reference to Salomon's concert (n. 5).

[2] 'If they speak more or less than the truth, they are villains, and the sons of darkness' (*1 Henry IV*, II. v. 173).

[3] SW's Trio for Three Pianofortes, which Stokes, Novello, and SW had premièred at SW's Hanover Square Rooms concert on 27 Apr. R. J. S. Stevens, who was present, described it as 'a noisy composition, not what I expected to hear' (Argent, 179).

to some of the Sea Fish,[4] who being all deaf, can find no Fault either with the Counterpoint or Execution.

I am to take the Piano Forte for Salomon on Monday next:[5] will you turn for me?—I give you Time enough to prepare, you see, & if you could manage to come to the Rehearsal at 11 next Saturday at the Rooms (were it but for half an Hour,) we might settle several Operations.—

Let me know *directly* whether you can come to me on *Sunday* Evening next,[6] as I shall arrange (to-morrow) accordingly.

Yours in the Truth
    SW

Thursday June 6

To Vincent Novello   [Adam's Row], 3 July [1811][1]

AL, 1 p. (BL, Add. MS 11729, fo. 4)
Addressed To | Mr Novello | Oxford Street | N. 240.
Pmk 7 o'Clock 3 JY 1811

Muster N.

Read (if you can, for 'tis a funny Hand) the Piece of Paper inside.[2]—If you have any Self-Love remaining, I think you can hardly withstand such a pretty Way of coaxing a Gentleman.—

Perhaps in Consequence of the horrid disagreeable Evening we passed at Gwilt's[3] on Sunday Last, you will refuse to dine in my Company on the next Lord's Day: however, Linley is impatient to know the worst.—He hangs out at N. 11. Southampton Street Strand, whereat I counsel thee to pelt him with two penny Worth of Pot-Hooks and *Hangers* forthwith.—He will inform me of your Answer:—I mean to be with you at Vespers on Sunday:[4] I have appointed a very intelligent young Man,[5] (who is taking a few hints in Organ Practice, & who

---

[4] Although the precise meaning of this remark is not clear, it evidently had to do with plans for one or more further performances of the Trio.

[5] On 10 June, when Salomon gave his annual benefit concert at Hanover Square Rooms; the programme included one of Bach's solo violin sonatas and the first British performance of Cherubini's *Chant sur la mort de Joseph Haydn*. SW is not mentioned in the advertisement, which appeared in *The Times* on the day of the concert.   [6] 9 June.

---

[1] The year is given by the postmark.   [2] Not preserved.
[3] It is not clear if Joseph or George Gwilt is referred to here.   [4] 7 July.
[5] Not identified.

comes from Birmingham) to come & hear your paltry Whistle-Box.—Hoping at all Events that you will come to hear Linley's *Antim*[6] which is to be criticized (& hyper-criticized if needful) at N. 11. Adam's Row, on the next Sunday Evening as ever was, is, or shall be, & as you will find true *by these Presents*, with my Duty to honoured Madam[7] & all enquiring Friends I rests

Your umble Sarvant
two cumhand

Wednesday | Jule-High | the thurd

To Vincent Novello   Adam's Row, 12 August [1811][1]

AL, 2 pp. (BL, Add. MS 11729, fo. 5)
Addressed To | M[r] Novello | Oxford Street | N. 240 | Monday Morning | 12th of August.
Pmk 4 o'Clock 12 AU 1811

Dear No

I have been groping in my Scapula's Lexicon[2] for the Welbeck Street Greek,[3] & believe I have fumbled it out at last.—You did not tell me of what Nature the Building was, over which these Pagan, ungodly & unchristian Characters are engraven, to the Shame & Scandal of all devout Protestants & Jews.—By the Meaning of the Word in Question, this here same Place must have (or ought to have) Relation either to a Hospital or a House of Correction in the Cold Bath Fields Line like.[4]—**Diatalaiporeo** is a Verb of which the Sense is '*I suffer Labours & Misery, I am oppressed by Sorrow & Bitterness of Soul*,' which you know may be well applied to the Inhabitants of either Domain above mentioned: but I cannot find this Word in Form of a Substantive with the Preposition διa put before it; therefore I do must humbly conceive that the Gentleman or Gentlemen who have made this grand *Swell* of their Larning, chose to give the Preposition Gratis, & without Authority, for Scapula's Lexicon is well known to contain all the Primitives & Derivatives, i.e. all the Roots & Branches of heathenish Greek.

---

[6] Not identified.   [7] Novello's wife Mary Sabilla, née Hehl (*c*.1789–1854).

[1] The year is given by the postmark.

[2] Scapula's *Lexicon Graeco-Latinum Novum*, first published in 1580, and still the standard Greek lexicon at this time.

[3] From SW's later remarks, evidently an inscription on a building in Welbeck Street.

[4] The House of Correction at Cold Bath Fields, on a site in Farringdon Road currently occupied by the GPO Mount Pleasant Sorting Office (*Encyclopaedia of London; London Encyclopaedia*).

—**Talaiporos** means a wretched Person—a miserable Being: of which the Genitive Case is **Talaiporo*u***, the Termination given to it on the Wall we have been exploring: so that the Sense remains thus, 'Of a wretched or miserable Being'—*Why* this Genitive Case should have been chosen, in Preference to a Nominative one, is a Point which renders my Confidence in the Author's Skill in Greek not a little problematical.—And there is another Circumstance which strongly confirms my Suspicion of his being an *Amateur* only: for the first *O* in the Word should not have been a short but a long one: not an O-*micron* (little) but an O-*mega* (great, or long) the Word should have stood thus, to make it *look* like real Greek;

ΔΙΑΤΑΛΑΙΠΩΡΕΟΥ

How often do I think of old Madan's[5] shrewd Saying to his Son: 'Martin, what a lamentable Thing it is, that one Half of the World are not contented to be Fools, but they must let the *other* Half know it.'—

I think (by the Way) that his giving *Half* the World Credit for *not* being Fools, had more Charity than Truth in it; but then we must remember that he was a *Parson* of the *reformed* Church, & therefore had a Right to put not only *Popery*, but *Consistency* at Defiance.—

Let me know whether you want me at 11, or at 3, on Thursday,[6] as soon as you can.—Come tomorrow if possible—or rather, *make* it possible.

To Vincent Novello   [Adam's Row], 3 September [1811][1]

ANS, 1 p. (BL, Add. MS 11729, fo. 7)
Addressed To | Mr Novello

Dear Novvy

I saw J. Elliott[2] at Paddington Yesterday, who threatens you with a Visit this here Evening, at a *Wenture* like.—I in my Return from the School will call (probably between 7 & 8) & should you be at Home, I shall try whether you are *good-natured* (as the Wenches say).—If you sh^d be out, or dead, or any Thing of that, you know there's no Harm done.

    SW

3d of Sep^tr | Tuesday

---

[5] i.e. The Revd Martin Madan (1725–90), 'SW's godfather.

[6] The coming Thursday, 15 Aug., was the Feast of the Assumption, when there would have been a High Mass at 11 a.m. and Solemn Vespers at 3 p.m. at the Portuguese Embassy Chapel.

---

[1] During the period of SW's correspondence with Novello, 3 Sept. fell on a Tuesday in 1811, 1816, and 1822. 1811 is the most probable year.   [2] The singer James Elliott.

To Vincent Novello   [Adam's Row], 12 September [1811][1]

ALS, 1 p. (BL, Add. MS 11729, fo. 8)
Addressed To | Mr Novello | Oxford Street | 240
Pmk 2 o'Clock 12 SP 1811

S. Webbe[2] called on me Yesterday Evening, to whom I mentioned your Intention of going to his Father[3] To-morrow Evening, but he told me that *Friday* is a
less convenient Day than *Sunday* next would be, & if you will go on Sunday, he
will meet you, which would render the Visit I think more generally pleasant.—
Perhaps you will send him some Answer upon the Subject.—On Reflexion, I am
always so jaded on Fridays after the Turnham Green Expedition,[4] that I should
also wish the Sunday substituted for the first named Day. I purpose being with
you at Vespers, where Webbe said he would be also.—

Mr Gwilt,[5] with whom I was till Yesterday *Noon*, is very desirous of possessing
a handsome Breviary: I told him that I was in Treaty upon the disposal of one with
Mr Fryar, who had not yet transmitted his ultimate Decision.—Will you therefore
be so kind as to signify this Circumstance to Mr F. without Delay, as *sometimes*
the best People change their Minds on a sudden, not that I have any Reason to
suspect my Friend G. of the Weather Cock Principle.

I have much to say to you, but there seems some unaccountable Barrier
(I know not where & how) to our more frequent Conference.

Adieu,
In haste
Yours in Truth
SW

Thursday | 12th of Sept^r

---

[1] The year is given by the postmark.

[2] i.e. Samuel Webbe II (1768–1843). Like his father (see n. 3), Webbe was an organist, pianist,
and composer of glees and Roman Catholic church music. He and SW had known each other from
their boyhoods. He had moved to Liverpool around 1798, and had only recently returned to London
(*Grove*[6]; *DNB*).

[3] Samuel Webbe I (1740–1816), Roman Catholic organist, composer, and teacher, and the most
important and influential figure in Roman Catholic church music in London in the late 18th cent. He
wrote a great deal of music for Catholic worship, mainly for the chapels of the Portuguese and Sardinian
embassies, where he was organist. At the Sardinian Chapel he also gave lessons free of charge 'to such
young gentlemen as present themselves to learn church music'; his pupils included Vincent Novello and
almost certainly SW. In the 1780s and early 1790s he was involved with the publication of three volumes
of Roman Catholic service music, much of it by himself. He was also prominent and highly respected as
a composer of glees.   [4] One of SW's schools.

[5] Joseph Gwilt, who had a keen interest in the Roman Catholic liturgy.

To Vincent Novello   [Adam's Row], 27 September [1811]¹

ALS, 1 p. (BL, Add. MS 11729, fo. 31)
Addressed To | Mr Novello
Endorsed at end Witness my hand Josephus Majorini²

Dear N,

Chappel³ has very *conveniently* sent me *all* the Preludes & Fugues of the 3^d Book,⁴ & as I am going off at *three* this Afternoon,⁵ of Course I have plenty of Time to revise them.—But without Joke, I must beg you to lend me here as in other Matters a helping Hand or rather a helping Eye, or more properly both, otherwise the Engraver will be glad of a Pretext to neglect them.—Excuse this, from your very truly

    S Wesley

Friday 27th of Sept^r

---

¹ The year is given by 27 Sept. falling on a Friday and the reference to Part 3 of the Wesley–Horn edition of the '48' (see n. 3).   ² i.e. Joseph Major: see SW to Novello, 16 Aug. [1812], n. 2.

³ Samuel Chappell (*c.*1782–1834) had been employed by Birchall but had left in Dec. 1810 to set up in partnership with Johann Baptist Cramer and Francis Tatton Latour as Chappell and Co. Parts 3 and 4 of the Wesley–Horn edition of the '48' were published jointly by Birchall's and Chappell's.

⁴ i.e. proofs of Part 3 of the Wesley–Horn edition of the '48', for SW to correct.

⁵ SW was about to set off for Birmingham, where he was to be musical director of the music festival. It began on 2 Oct. with the customary church service in St Philip's (now Birmingham Cathedral), followed by choral concerts in the church on the mornings of 3 and 4 Oct. and evening concerts at the Theatre Royal; SW would have needed to have been in Birmingham for the general rehearsal on Monday 30 Sept. His engagement for the festival no doubt was a consequence of his success at the Tamworth Festival in 1809 and his appearance at a concert in Birmingham immediately afterwards. In Nov. 1810 he had made what appears to have been a private visit to Birmingham, probably to discuss details of the programme with the festival's organizer, Joseph Moore: see SW to Sarah Suter, 7 Nov. 1810 (BL, Add. MS 35012, fo. 29).

To Vincent Novello [Adam's Row], 11 November [1811][1]

ALS, 3 pp. (BL, Add. MS 11729, fo. 10)
Addressed To | Mr Novello

Dear N

I conclude by your not looking in last Night that you doubted my Resolution of accompanying you to the Foundling Chapel:[2] indeed if I had gone it w^d have been solely for some Chat with you.—I was hard at Rousseau[3] for some Hours, & I think with some Advantage.—If I could have your Gradual *To-morrow* I can make two or three Extracts before Saturday, & take Care that the Book shall be returned *on Saturday*, which as there is no Holiday this Week which will put it in Requisition till Sunday next, will be Time enough to prevent any Disappointment.

I am balancing in my Mind where to begin, for the Idea of harmonizing all the Introits, Tracts, Offertories, Post Communions, Antiphons & Hymns is such a gigantic Affair, that I must ensure the life of a *Struldbrug*[4] for the Purpose of accomplishing it: moreover it would run up to the Magnitude of the Encyclopædia Britannica or some such Work, & become so costly as to frighten 9 10^{ths} of the Gregorians all over Europe.—It was for such Reasons that I wanted to have more Conversation with you about it all, hoping that we might together hit upon some Medium which would render the Undertaking valuable & attractive without making it unwieldy & too sumptuous.—Gwilt insists on its being a *Quarto*, & indeed I therein agree with him, as a *less* Size would become inconvenient by the Multitude of Turnings. Will you contrive somehow to let me know without Delay, whether I can have Access to the Gradual, & how—Could it be left at Mr Blacket's[5] or at your House, or where?

Perhaps you will call in this Evening.—I wish you would, for instance between 6 & 8 o'Clock, or between 8 & 10: I shall be sure to be within, & we might do much in a short Time, the Plan being once settled.—

Somebody gave me a Hat after Vespers appertaining to some other Skull: I discovered it the Instant I got down Stairs, but was unwilling to disarrange your

---

[1] The year is given by 11 Nov. falling on a Monday and SW's discussion of harmonizing Gregorian chant.   [2] Perhaps for a concert or a special service; not identified.

[3] The philosopher, author, composer, and music theorist Jean-Jacques Rousseau (1712–78), who wrote extensively on music and whose views on music were highly influential. SW may, however, be referring to one of Rousseau's non-musical works.

[4] The Struldbrugs were the race of immortals in Swift's *Gulliver's Travels* (1726).

[5] Not identified: presumably a member of the congregation of the Portuguese Embassy Chapel who lived nearby.

Choir preparing for Action.—The Hat in Question covers my Head about as compleatly as a Saucer would a Porridge Pot, consequently is very commodious & becoming.—

If you come to me To Night which I trust you will, perhaps you may report to me the Complaints of the right Owner, who will probably state that my Hat fitted his Head as well as the Cupola of St Paul's.

Yours as usual[6]

SW

Monday 11th of Nov^r

The feast of St Martin, Patron of the Butchers: why I know not, as he is reported to have been a quiet Body, hurting neither Man nor Beast.[7]

P.S. I suppose you have heard nothing of Importance *touchant l'Etablissement de l'Ambassadeur*,[8] or you w^d have dropped me a hint thereof.—I should much like to know whether there be *really* a Prospect of Success or not.—Suspense is an uncomfortable State, even upon the Gallows.

To Vincent Novello[1] [Adam's Row], 9 December 1811

ANS, 1 p. (Edinburgh)
Addressed To | Mr Novello | 240 | Oxford Street | 9th of December
To Catholick Choirs & Organists.

An erroneous Manner of terminating the *sixth* Tone of the Psalms having obtained, in consequence of not distinguishing it rightly from the *first*, (which it nearly resembles with Respect to Intervals;) it becomes advisable to state that the Chants of the *four* former of the 8 Ecclesiastical Modes[2] ought always to be

---

[6] As SW was later to comment (see SW to Novello, 5 July [1815]), Novello's 'own way of concluding'.

[7] Martin of Tours (*c*.316–397).

[8] The Portuguese ambassador, Dom Domingeus de Sousa Countinho, Conde do Funchal (1760–1833). The significance of this remark is not clear.

[1] Although this statement is not specifically addressed to Novello, it is preserved with an address wrapper to him of the same date. It is probable that there was originally a covering letter or note to Novello which has not been preserved.

[2] It is clear from the discussion and the appended examples that SW is discussing the terminations or *differentiae* of the psalm tones (the recitation melodies used for singing psalms during the Office), pointing out that some need to be harmonized as if cadencing on the third degree of a minor key, and others as if cadencing on the tonic of a major key, according to their mode (*Grove*[6], under 'Psalm', II. 2. iii and 'Evovae').

accompanied with a Minor *third* upon their *final* Note; and the four latter with a *Major* third.

The enclosed MS shows the Difference between the Termination of the 1ˢᵗ and 6ᵗʰ Tones, as also the proper Accompaniment to each.

I shall be glad if this Explanation prove useful towards producing Correctness & Uniformity in this Point of the Evening Church Office, which has long needed Observation & Amendment.

S. Wesley

Monday | Decʳ 9ᵗʰ 1811

[Enclosure]

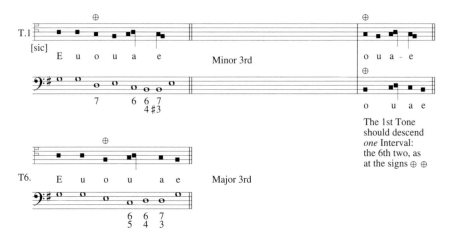

To Vincent Novello   [Adam's Row], 24 [December 1811][1]

ALS, 1 p. (BL, Add. MS 11729, fo. 111)
Addressed To | Mʳ Novello | Tuesday Morning

Dear N.

I hope you remembered to remind Mʳ G.[2] of our having *forgotten* to carry back our Xtmas Carol,[3] & that he has engaged to let us have it in Time for mounting at high Mass To-morrow.

---

[1] The month is given by the reference to Christmas Day and the year from 24 Dec. falling on a Tuesday and the reference to Salomon, who died in Nov. 1815.   [2] Probably Joseph Gwilt.
[3] Not identified.

I thought it unnecessary for *me* to write also to him, as I know your usual Exactness where public (especially Church) Matters are concerned.

I will be in good time To-morrow, be the Weather what it may.

Yours as usual

SW

Tuesday 24th

Our Friend Salomon was in prime Order on Sunday: n'est il pas vrai? He is a wonderful old *Eagle*.

To Vincent Novello   [Adam's Row], 8 February 1812

ALS, 1 p. (BL, Add. MS 11729, fo. 12).

Dear N

Gwilt is engaged out To-morrow, but wishes us to dine with him on the following Sunday,[1] to which I neither feel nor see an Objection.

As I cannot be with you at high Mass,[2] having promised to meet Master Beale upon *his* Perch at S[t] James's, Clerkenwell,[3] & not being *quite* certain of being able to come to Vespers, I think right to send you the enclosed, as in Case you have a Rehearsal, something may be done for its Furtherance on your Compline Evenings, & it is one of the sweetest Descants on the 6th Tone that I know.[4]—

If I can, I will be with you at *three* To-morrow,[5] & I wish, *in that Event* (as the Slang goes) that you could manage to return to my Den, & chat, or so, from another Motive than my innate Love of Idleness.

SW

Saturday. 8th of Feb[y] 1812

[1] 16 Feb.   [2] Presumably on the following day, 9 Dec.

[3] Probably William Beale (1784–1854), a pupil of Samuel Arnold and Benjamin Cooke, who was a gentleman of the Chapel Royal from 1816 to 1820 and became organist of Trinity College, Cambridge, in 1820 (Brown and Stratton; Matthews); or perhaps Robert Beale (1792–1860), who at the time of his application for membership of the Royal Society of Musicians in 1818 was the deputy organist of Bow Church, Cheapside. The organ at St James, Clerkenwell, built in 1792 by George Pike England (*c*.1768–1815), was noted for its octave and a half of pedals (Boeringer, ii. 284–5).

[4] Not identified: evidently a piece suitable for use at the evening Office of Compline, celebrated at the Portuguese Embassy Chapel at 4 p.m. on Wednesdays in Lent. As is clear from a remark in SW to Novello, 7 July [1812], Novello's choir rehearsals were after Vespers on Sundays.

[5] i.e. at Vespers.

To Vincent Novello [Adam's Row], 27 March [1812]¹

ALS, 1 p. (BL, Add. MS 11729, fo. 13)
Addressed To | Mr Novello | favoured by Mʳ Swan²

Dear N

I could not meet you this Morning, but wish to know whether you will be at the Chapel this evening at 5—if you intend it, I will endeavour to be *under the Portico* at a quarter before 5 in South Street (the late Lord Denbigh's, whose, now, I know not) where the Steps are,³ & agree *where* to be together, at the Service.— You spoke of having remained *below* Stairs⁴ on Wednesday, for which I will answer that you had some good Reason, which I should like to be acquainted with.—I will bring with me the 1ˢᵗ Nocturn of the Officium Defunctorum,⁵ in some of which Responses the Melody admits of such Harmony, as really surprizes me.—

In haste,
Yours as always

S Wesley

I could not be in Time for the Rehearsal Yesterday.

Friday. 27th March

*Technically, Feria sexta in Parasceve*⁶

---

¹ The year is given by 27 Mar. falling on a Friday and SW's 'Feria sexta in Parasceve' (see n. 6).

² Not identified.

³ The portico at 71 South Audley Street, on the corner of South Audley Street and South Street, provided a sheltered meeting place conveniently close to the Portuguese Embassy Chapel. The house had belonged to Basil, 6th Earl of Denbigh and Desmond (1719–1800) and was at this time occupied by his widow. The house and its portico still stand (*Burke's Peerage*; *Survey of London*, xl. 305–6 and pl. 80a).

⁴ i.e. in the body of the church rather than in the gallery, where the organ was situated; possibly because the service was unaccompanied by the organ.

⁵ i.e. the section of Mattins for the Dead usually used in choral services. It included three psalms, three lessons, and three responsories.

⁶ i.e. Good Friday. During the period of SW's correspondence with Novello, Good Friday fell on 27 Mar. only in 1812.

To Vincent Novello   [Adam's Row], 31 March 1812

ALS, 2 pp. (BL, Add. MS 11729, fo. 14)
Addressed To | Mr Novello | Oxford Street | N. 240 | 31st of March.
Pmk 31 MR 1812

Vigil of April Fool Day 1812

Dear N

Your Organ at South Street[1] is certainly 'strong in the Faith',[2] but I suspect your Bellows of Heterodoxy; for 'not having the Fear of God before his Eyes, but being moved by the Instigation of the Devil, he did traiterously & of Malice aforethought,' contrive, determine & resolve to be seized by a sudden Fit of Asthma, which the most experienced *practional Hands* could not relieve by the most *sudorific* Administrations & energetic Efforts.—The Consequences were such as might be naturally expected, namely, a Chord & a Puff, a Puff & a Chord, sometimes a Chord & no Puff, & then, a Puff & no Chord: however, this Circumstance had the good Effect of reminding me of my biblical Researches of old, where in the Pentateuch, the Priest is ordered by the grand Architect of the Universe & 'the supreme Disposer of all Events' to wear not only on his Vestment 'a Bell & a Pomegranate,' but also a 'Pomegranate & a Bell.'[3] So that the Parallel will be much in this Guise:

Bell versus Pomegranate
Pomegranate versus Bell.

In the new Law, & under the Christian Dispensation,

Puff versus Chord:
Chord versus Puff.

Which I take to be a compleat & satisfactory Solution of all the Difficulties attending the Reconciliation of the Jewish & Xtian Churches.

---

[1] The original organ at the Portuguese Embassy Chapel in South Street was a one-manual instrument of eight stops by Abraham Jordan (d. 1755 or 1756), presumably dating from around the time when the Embassy moved there in 1747. It was rebuilt and substantially enlarged in 1808 by George Pike England, who added extra stops to the Great and added completely new Swell and Choir divisions (Boeringer, iii. 253–4). [2] Rom. 4: 20.

[3] Exod. 28: 31–4: 'And thou shalt make the robe of the ephod all of blue . . . a golden bell and a pomegranate, a golden bell and a pomegranate, upon the hem of the robe round about.'

I was informed that the High Mass To-Day was not dis-, but un-organized.—per contra, the Vespers were not un-, but dis-organised. I can tell you.

O! England! England!
Wherefore art thou England?[4]

I know one Matter at least, about England as a *Mister*; that if I were an Ambassador, being able to afford the keeping of such an Organ in Tune for half a Guinea a Week (and this would be plenty of Money for the Purpose) I should think myself below any Pretension to the Dignity of the Gallows were I to hesitate a Moment to advance double the Sum for such a Purpose.

Friday the 5th of June is the *Day*, & will be the *Night*.[5]—Catalani[6] has written by her Amanuensis (a French Priest, therefore there can be no Doubt of Fidelity)[7] that I am authorized to announce in the Papers her Determination to come forward in aid of a forlorn (& nearly blind) Organist,[8] & has offered him his Victuals Gratis into the Bargain, next Sunday as ever is to be.—I am recommended to speak to her on the Bertinotti Question[9] after her half Pint of Madeira.

SW

Have you heard any Tidings of the Umbrella *minus*? *Mine* (at present) is certainly *yours* not my own. Don't let us be robbed at Church & in the Choir, among the holy ones, without making out who's who.

---

[4] cf. *Romeo and Juliet*, II. i. 75 ('O Romeo! Romeo! Wherefore art thou Romeo!'), in allusion to George Pike England, who evidently had the maintenance contract for the organ.

[5] The date of SW's forthcoming benefit concert at Hanover Square Rooms.

[6] Angelica Catalani (1780–1849), the foremost operatic soprano in London at the time. After an early career in Italy, Portugal, and France, where she sang before Napoleon, she came to England, where she made her London début in Portogallo's *Semiramide* at the King's Theatre on 13 Dec. 1806. She subsequently sang there in the seasons of 1808 and 1810–13 (*Grove*[6]).   [7] Not identified.

[8] Presumably a humorous reference to SW himself.

[9] After an early career in Italy, Germany, Austria, and possibly Russia, the Italian operatic soprano Teresa Bertinotti (1776–1854) came to England, where she appeared at the King's Theatre from 1810 to 1812; she subsequently sang at Lisbon, Paris, and in Italy, and retired in 1820. With Elizabeth Billington, she was one of Catalani's principal rivals in London at this time. She and others had recently seceded from the King's Theatre and had set up a rival company at the Pantheon. For SW's high opinion of her singing, see SW to Novello, 6 May [1812]. The 'Bertinotti question' may have concerned her participation in SW's concert on the same platform as Catalani (*Grove*[1], under 'Pantheon'; *Grove*[6]; Fenner, 78).

To Mr Freeling[1]   Tottenham Court,[2] 26 April [1812][3]

AN, third person, 1 p. (Osborn, File 39.340)
Endorsed 26 Apr | Tottenham | S. We | Rec^d

Mr Samuel Wesley presents his best Respects to Mr Freeling, & will be happy in accepting his obliging Invitation To-morrow which he has been informed by his Friend Linley is the Day that is now appointed for the Pleasure of attending him.

13. | Tottenham Court | New Road | Sunday 26th April

To Vincent Novello   [Tottenham Court], 6 May [1812][1]

ALS, 3 pp. (BL, Add. MS 11729, fo. 16)
Addressed To | Mr Novello | Oxford Street | N. 240 | Wednesday Evening
Pmk 7 MY 1812

Wednesday 6th of May

My dear N,
    I am in great Tribulation & Discomfort until we meet, for Reasons manifold & weighty.—Imprimis, you may possibly have heard that Catalani has already played me one of her Devil's Tricks, pretending that in Consequence of a new Arrangement (or rather Derangement) with Taylor,[2] she is under a Prohibition, to sing nowhere else in Public than at the Opera House.[3]—How can this be, when

---

[1] Not identified: probably one of SW's pupils.

[2] Within the previous month SW had moved from Adam's Row to 13 Tottenham Court. His new house was next door to the premises of his friend the organ builder Thomas Elliot. This is the first letter to bear the new address.

[3] The year is given by 26 Apr. falling on a Sunday and SW's Tottenham Court address.

---

[1] The year is given by the postmark.

[2] William Taylor (*c*.1753–1825), the proprietor of the King's Theatre. His long involvement with the theatre, dating back to the 1781–2 season, was characterized by a series of disputes with his artists and subscribers arising from his high-handedness and bad financial management. The establishment of the rival company at the Pantheon earlier in the year was the latest expression of the dissatisfaction of artists with his management; although the venture failed, it is said to have cost Taylor £6,000 in lost receipts. By the date of this letter he was in growing financial difficulties, and in Dec. 1813 was removed from the management of the King's Theatre by the Lord Chamberlain (*BD*; Daniel Nalbach, *The King's Theatre, 1704–1867: London's first Italian Opera House* (1972), 94–7).   [3] The King's Theatre.

she is announced for Ashley's[4] Benefit on Whitsun Eve,[5] & continues to sing at Harrison's[6] every Friday?—I am told that Taylor has threatened to with-hold £1300 if she keeps *her Word* with any one but himself. Be it how it may, if she persevere in forfeiting her Promise to SW in the present Instance, I will expose the whole Transaction in the News Papers, in which Resolution I am encouraged by every one who has heard the State of the Case.—Vallebreguez's[7] Language in his letters to me is so positive & unequivocal, that the public Appearance of the Letters must excite universal Reprobation, & although I am not fond of hostile Proceedings wherever there remains a Chance that mild Measures will be successful, yet, in a Cause of absolute Exigency, which requires my clearing myself from the Imputation of Deception, surely the Censure ought to fall on the right Object. What think you of a personal Interview with Vallebreguez, previous to an open Rupture? Sometimes oral has better Effect than *plumean* Agency, & by his Manner of Behaviour when I dined at his House, I had every Reason to suppose that *no Consideration whatever* would have operated to induce a Disappointment.[8]

You mentioned to me several Weeks since that you thought you should have Influence enough to obtain Bertinotti's assistance for *Love*, without *Money*.— You know *my* real Opinion of her Superiority to every Thing but Billington in this Country, therefore (as Burney once wrote me) 'for my own private Eating'[9] she is a Dish worth a whole *Course* of Catalanis: the Curse of the Matter is that pudding-headed Johannes Bull judgeth, (or rather misjudgeth) otherwise, which will necessarily make a Difference in the Receipts of the *ragged* Trash passing for gold, à present.—

---

[4] There were four Ashley brothers involved with the Covent Garden oratorios at this time. General Christopher Ashley (1767–1818) led the orchestra and managed the concerts with his cellist brother Charles Jane (1773–1843). Another brother, John James (1772–1815), played the organ, and a fourth, Richard Godfrey (1774–1836), played the violin, viola, and timpani. 'General' was the eldest Ashley's forename, and not a nickname or a military rank; *Grove*[6] and *DNB* erroneously give his forename as Charles and 'General' as a nickname, and give his date of birth incorrectly. SW's reference is probably to him: but see n. 5. (*BD*; Matthews; *Grove*[6]).

[5] SW's information was doubtless from *The Times*, which on this date carried an advertisement for 'Messrs Ashley's' benefit concert at Covent Garden on Whitsun Eve, 16 May. Catalani did not in the end sing in this concert: her withdrawal, 'in consequence of a difference respecting her engagement at the Opera', was announced in *The Times* on the day of the concert.

[6] The series of concerts organized by the tenor Samuel Harrison (1760–1812). Catalani was advertised to sing at Harrison's benefit concert in the Great Room at the King's Theatre on Friday 8 May (*The Times*, 27 Apr., 5, 7, 8 May 1812), and did in fact do so: for a review, see *The Times*, 11 May 1812.

[7] Paul Valabrègue, Catalani's husband and manager (*Grove*[6], under 'Catalani, Angelica').

[8] Catalani did not sing at the concert: the advertisement in *The Times* on 3 June noted that 'the same misunderstanding which was assigned by Mr Bartleman for withdrawing the name of Madame Catalani must be offered as a reason upon the present occasion'.   [9] Burney's letter has not been traced.

Pray give me an immediate Line, & another upon your *Line of Conduct*. How goeth the Symphony[10] on?—I am up to the A——e in all Manner of omnium Gatherum: what with signing Tickets, teaching those never meant to learn, see, hear, or understand; looking after Scrapers & Chorus-Bawlers, answering & *honouring* Bills for such as have done *me* the Honour to ruin me;[11] laying a *musical* Siege to Badajos for Mr Preston;[12] (& for Bread & Cheese;) collecting Ammunition for the 5th of June, & snatching every Moment to write a *Bar* at a time (not more) of the Duet[13] for the same Occasion; that by the Brains of Locke, Newton, & Mugnié![14] my Sconce is so bewildered & *betwattled* (as the Wenches say) that it is odds but I shall break down like a winded Post-Horse before the Day shall arrive.—

Gwilt's Wife[15] is in the Straw,[16] & I am to dine with him Tête à Tête on Sunday next[17] after opening the Organ at Christ Church, Black Friars.[18]—Cannot you manage to call in the Evening?, say at 8 o'clock, or 9: we could then confer, & would walk home like good Masons together: Music, of course will not be had, but there may be such a Thing as Harmony in Conversation, as well as (what there always is) Discord among Musicians: you know that he[19] is always happy to see you, & I will prepare him that your Call will be upon *me*, & upon *Business*,

[10] Novello's arrangement for organ duet and orchestra of J. S. Bach's Prelude in E flat, BWV 552 (the 'St Anne'), the autograph of which (Vienna, Gesellschaft der Musikfreunde) is dated 28 May 1812, and which was first performed at the concert under discussion here. According to Novello's note on the autograph, SW and Novello 'played the obbligato organ part as a Duett on that occasion, each filling in the harmonies according to the feeling of the moment, and endeavouring to enrich the effect to the utmost, for the sake of Master Sebastian'.

[11] Principally Charlotte, to whom under the terms of a recent Deed of Separation he was paying maintenance of £130 *per annum*.

[12] SW's piano piece 'The Siege of Badajoz', published later in the year by Preston, celebrated the siege and eventual capture on 6 Apr. 1812 by the British of the Spanish town of Badajoz.

[13] The Organ Duet in C; the autograph (BL, Add. MS 14344, fo. 39) is dated 24 May 1812 and was annotated by Novello as having been 'written on purpose for me to play with Mr. S. Wesley at the Hanover Square Rooms'.

[14] An ironic juxtaposition of the distinguished and the undistinguished. Locke and Newton are the philosopher John Locke (1632–1704) and the mathematician Sir Isaac Newton (1642–1727); about Jean Mugnié little is known, except that he was a minor composer of the time, chiefly of popular piano music.

[15] Luisa, wife of Joseph Gwilt.

[16] i.e. in childbed. The child was probably Sophia, who was baptized at Christchurch, Blackfriars on 13 May 1813 together with her elder brother John Sebastian (1811–90) (Parish baptismal records).

[17] 10 May.

[18] In Blackfriars Road, close to the Surrey Chapel and Institution, and the parish church of the Gwilts. The new organ, by Thomas Elliot, had one octave of pedals and was the only church organ known to have incorporated the Hawkes patent device (Boeringer, iii. 116–17).   [19] i.e. Gwilt.

imminent & urgent, so there will be no shock possibly rendered to that universal human & troublesome Concomitant 'L'Amour propre'.—

Yours (in Purgatory)
SW

To Vincent Novello   [Tottenham Court], 22 June [1812][1]

ALS, 1 p. (BL, Add. MS 11729, fo. 20)

Dear N

I have written the annexed[2] for Wednesday, which is S[t] John Baptist's Day you know, & if you can get another Copy of it made out, we can roar it in Style as well as a jolly Song.—It appears to me an appropriate Idea to cobble up something of the sort for the Occasion, & you will best know how to choose such Workmen as will be likely to hit it off smoothest among the Choir.—I of Course will lend my Bellows (such as it is) in Aid of the Cause.

Yours in Haste
as usual
S Wesley

Monday 22[d] of June

P.S. Will you call on me on Wedn[y] at 3 or ½ past? Let me know.

To Vincent Novello   [Tottenham Court], 24 June [1812]

AL, 1 p. (BL, Add. MS 11729, fo. 18)
Addressed To | M[r] Novello | who hath not as yet received this same.

SW feels the **UT**most Satisfaction in **RE**turning his Acknowledgements for the **MI**nute Mention of the Circumstances attending his Tune, in which there

---

[1] During the period of SW's correspondence with Novello, 22 June fell on a Monday in 1812 and 1818. The year 1818 is ruled out as at that time SW was still convalescing at Blacklands House following the breakdown of his health the previous year.

[2] Presumably SW's setting for three male voices of the hymn 'Ut queant laxis' (autograph RCM, MS 4025), proper to the feast of St John the Baptist (24 June).

is not discoverable any Trait of the **FA**stidious Disposition of most musical Criticks, which is as clear as **SOL** at Noon Day: the Author however fears that the Partiality of Friendship may have operated to pronounce too favourable an Opinion of a Composition which many may perhaps consider only **LA**-la after all.[1]

24th of June

To Vincent Novello [Tottenham Court], 25 June [1812][1]

ALS, 1 p. (BL, Add. MS 11729, fo. 21)
Addressed To | M[r] Novello | Oxford Street | N. 240 | Thursday | Afternoon
Pmk 25 JU

Muster Nov

You are a very fine Spark upon my say so.—first you send me a Letter full of your vitty Pribbles & Prabbles,[2] & then you depute M[r] Boyle[3] to come & tell me that you are engaged to the little Jack of Trumps[4] to conduct his Concert forsooth.—So we got to Jack Straw's Castle[5] when the Folk had three parts dined, & were obliged to have all the Pease & Potatoes hauled back upon the Table, to the great Scandal of all devout Christians present: then I must be set down to accompany Te-Deums (by the Way *one* of them was not worth a T—D—) at Sight, hit or miss, with a Gallon of Bucellas[6] in my Sconce.

Deus propitius esto *tibi* Peccatori![7]

S Wesley

13 Tottenham Court | New Road | 25th of June

---

[1] SW here uses the syllables derived from the opening syllables of the first six lines of the hymn 'Ut queant laxis' ('ut', 're', 'mi', 'fa', 'sol', and 'la'): these include all five vowel sounds and six different consonants, set to successively higher pitches, and formed the basis of the medieval and Renaissance solmization system. The melody of the hymn is traditionally ascribed to Guido of Arezzo (*c*.1000) (*Grove*[6], under 'Solmization', I. 1).

[1] The year is given by 25 June falling on a Thursday and SW's Tottenham Court address.

[2] *Merry Wives of Windsor*, I. i. 50.

[3] Not identified; perhaps the J. Boyle who was a subscriber to Novello's *A Collection of Sacred Music*.

[4] Not identified.   [5] A celebrated inn on Hampstead Heath.

[6] A sort of Portuguese white wine, named after a village near Lisbon (*OED*).

[7] 'God be merciful to you, a sinner': adapted from Luke 18: 13.

To [Vincent Novello][1]   [Tottenham Court], 27 June [1812][2]

AL, 4 pp. (BL, Add. MS 11729, fo. 94)

Saturday 27th of June

I am concerned to state that there is very discouraging News to communicate concerning the Progress of Gregorian Harmonization:[3] which you will agree to be the Case when I have informed you of what passed To-Day at the Dirge.[4]—My first Proposition to M[r] Fryer was to have accompanied all the Psalms & Anthems, Responsoria &c of the *Office*, with the Organ, to which M[r] F's objection was two-fold: first, he thought (& the Event has shewn that he thought justly) that there might possibly be some such essential Variations in the large Choir Book, from the Text of the small one of his, copied by Wade[5] (& from which I have harmonized all the Parts of the Office hitherto as far as I have gone) that considerable Confusion might ensue between my Copy & the other in general Use: & secondly, that it might be more prudent not to introduce this Mode of performing the Office with the Organ *all at once*, because there might be certain scrupulous Characters disposed to oppose & censure it as a *Novelty*, inasmuch as at the usual Dirges, the Organ is employed in the Mass only.

I immediately perceived the good Sense of this Caution, & we agreed Yesterday that the Organ should be silent until the Commencement of the Mass: & here I fully depended that the great & the little Book were in Unison together: but no such Thing.—In the Tract 'Absolve Domine,' although the Tone was marked the same (2[d], which I gave out in G minor) the Passages differed so much & so materially that I regretted having embarked with the Voices, & was obliged to go through three Parts out of four, by following the Melody at a Venture, & sacrificing all Reliance upon the Book before me.—Even in the Dies Iræ where one might have reasonably expected perfect Uniformity & *Uniphony*, were Variations of considerable Importance, & upon comparing the Offertorium of the 2 Copies together, I found that had I attempted to accompany

---

[1] Although lacking an address portion or salutation, it is evident that this letter is to Novello.

[2] The year is given by 27 June falling on a Saturday and by SW's discussion of harmonizing Gregorian melodies.   [3] See SW to Novello, 11 Nov. [1811].

[4] i.e. a Requiem Mass at the Portuguese Embassy Chapel.

[5] John Francis Wade (1710/11–86), a copyist of plainchant manuscripts, 'perhaps the most significant figure in the history of plainchant of the eighteenth-century English Catholic church' (Bennett Zon, 'Plainchant in the Eighteenth-Century English Catholic Church', *Recusant History*, 21 (1993), 361–80).

from mine, the *Regulations from St John Baptist's Hymn*[6] would have been wholly ineffectual to preserve the Truth; the Fa's & Sols &c being continually quarrelling.—The same was the Fact concerning the Sanctus & Agnus; in neither of which I was able to use the Organ without perpetual Discord.—The Verse at the Communion[7] was almost a solitary Exception: the Books therein tallied accurately, & I therefore played it through with good Effect.—O meritum Passionis, at the Elevation was also correct, & was a beautiful Strain.—The 'Libera me Domine' (the final Responsory) was also tolerably though not strictly correct in each Copy.—

Now you directly perceive that these Anomalies are a ten-barred Gate against my successful Proceeding, for if I am to expect such radical Inconsistencies among the Books, it would be utterly lost Labour to attempt a Work of general Utility where such Contradictions in the different Copies reduce it to a *Penelopean*[8] Experiment: for to what Purpose would it be to publish a Gregorian Gradual, Vesperal, &c for the universal Use of Choirs, when perhaps they could be of no Service to more than three or four, whose Books might *by a lucky Chance* happen to correspond throughout with mine?

I can devise no other Scheme of ascertaining the only Mode of determining whether it be necessary to abandon the Enterprize or not, than that of examining *all the fairest Copies* of the several Chapels; & comparing their Agreement & Irregularity: this alone is a Task of no easy Accomplishment; & as Time at my Period of Life does not become *less* valuable; before the final Determination takes Place, I must be enabled to calculate *safely* upon the ultimate Advantage accruing in Reward of my Toil: for altho' Mr Gwilt's[9] Offer of entire Indemnity as to the Expence of Printing, Paper &c is *thoroughly liberal*, yet this you must feel would be by no Means an Equivalent for so tedious a Job, as it must infallibly prove, even with my most expeditious Efforts.

I wish to have your most explicit Sentiments upon this Matter;—after having consulted & compared a few of the Church Books, I may shortly be able to make up my Mind respecting the *Practicability* of it, which must of Course precede any Attempt at a Calculation of the Profit, certain, probable, or possible.

---

[6] i.e. 'Ut queant laxis' (see SW to Novello, 22 June [1812]). SW's reference is to the traditional rules of solmization.   [7] 'Lux aeterna luceat eis'.

[8] An allusion to Penelope, the wife of Odysseus, whose nightly unpicking of the weaving she had done during the day was a proverbial example of ceaseless and futile labour.   [9] i.e. Joseph Gwilt.

To Vincent Novello [Tottenham Court, ?2 July 1812][1]

ALS, 3 pp. (BL, Add. MS 11729, fo. 26)

Thursday
Morning

Dear N.

An unexpected Obstacle (which however is likely to be followed by a good Consequence) will prevent our Meeting at Kirkman's[2] To-morrow: if you can fix Saturday[3] instead at 7, I will attend. Do not let the Opera[4] prove the Veto; you can hear that with more frequent Convenience than the 30 Variations.[5]

Bridgtower is to be with us: by the Way, he called at your House last Week to know whether the Mass of Mozart[6] was to be done on Sunday last, & not having heard from you, concluded in the Negative, so I suppose you never obtained the Message.—So much for the Fidelity of Servants.

Pray can you tell me who writes the musical Critique in Akerman's Magazine?[7]—He has puffed my Deserter's Meditations[8] to the Size of M[r] Sadler's

---

[1] It is apparent from the reference to the review of his 'Deserter's Meditations' (see n. 8) that SW wrote this letter around the beginning of July 1812. His 'Thursday', combined with references to Sadler's balloon (see n. 9), and 'throats being cut on the continent' (see n. 11) suggest 2 July as the most probable date.

[2] The showroom of the Kirckman family of harpsichord and piano makers, where an informal performance of the *Goldberg Variations* was evidently to take place. [3] 4 July.

[4] Mozart's *Le nozze di Figaro*, which had on 18 June received its British première at the King's Theatre, and was to be performed again on 4 July. It had several further performances in July.

[5] The *Goldberg Variations*, which were no doubt to be played on two pianos, as at Burney's apartments in July 1810.

[6] Not positively identified: Novello performed many Masses by Mozart at the Portuguese Embassy Chapel.

[7] *The Repository of Arts, Literature, Commerce, Manufactures, Fashion and Politics*, published between 1809 and 1828 by the fine-art publisher and bookseller Rudolph Ackermann (1764–1834). The reviews of music were written by Lewis Engelbach: see John Ford, *Ackermann 1783–1983: The Business of Art* (1983), 77–83.

[8] The review of SW's piano piece *The Deserter's Meditations* in the July 1812 number of *The Repository of Arts* stated: 'In this small publication we meet with ample traces of the mastery of its author. It is not a rondo patched up out of a few common-place turns and chords, just to be played once and then to be consigned to the heap of modern musical rubbish. Mr W. has taken up a common subject, and treated it in a manner which becomes an adept in the science of harmonies. The theme makes its appearance in a variety of protean shapes and keys, constantly diversified by the hand of sterling art. We are at one time entertained with neatly fuged contrivances, at another some masterly counterpoint claims our attention. Every bar partakes of the spirit of the subject, while it displays the skill of the composer. To the true connoisseur this rondo will afford a high treat, and to such only we wish to recommend it, as it would be thrown away upon an ear vitiated by the ephemeral song-products of the day.'

Balloon,[9] & I should have been tempted to much *internal* Inflation upon it, had he not wasted as many Gallons of Gas in Laud of some of M[r] Mugnie's Sublimities.[10]

If I hear no more betwixt now & To-morrow Noon, I shall conclude that you expect me at K's.

Adieu.

Yours as usual

SW

P.S. By the Paper there seems to have been quite a sufficient Number of Throats cut lately on the Continent[11] to warrant a solemn Thanksgiving to God on so lively a Subject, so I suppose we shall get up our Te Deum shortly.[12]

To Vincent Novello [Tottenham Court], 7 July [1812][1]

ALS, 1 p. (BL, Add. MS 11729, fo. 23)

Tuesday.

7th of July

Dear No!

I send you a Twopenny Tune,[2] which mayhap you may think too dear by all the Money.—Should you however judge it worth half, namely one Penny of lawful copper Coin you will perhaps order it to be drilled on Sunday next[3] post Vesperas, & I will attend to ascertain its Fate.—

---

[9] James Sadler (d. 1828), the first English aeronaut, had made his first ascent from Oxford on 4 Oct. 1784, less than a year after the first manned ascent by de Rozier and d'Arlandes in Paris. He retired from ballooning in 1785 but returned in July 1810 for a series of well-publicized ascents culminating in Oct. 1812 in an unsuccessful attempt to cross the Irish Sea. An ascent from Manchester was reported in *The Times* for 2 July and may have prompted SW's remark (L. T. C. Rolt, *The Aeronauts: A History of Ballooning 1783–1903*, (1966), 79–81, 99–102).

[10] The review of Mugnié's piano piece 'L'Amour piqué par une abeille' was similarly effusive.

[11] *The Times* for 2 July carried a report of the battle of Bornos on 1 June, in which there were 1,000 enemy casualties.

[12] The singing of the Te Deum traditionally celebrated victory in battle.

[1] The reference to the 'twopenny tune' (see n. 2) establishes the year.

[2] SW's setting of 'Ave verum corpus', dated 6 July 1812 (autograph BL, Add. MS 14340, fo. 29); it was later published in Novello's *A Collection of Motets for the Offertory*, i. 24. SW's description of it as a 'twopenny tune' alludes to the cost of its postage as an enclosure in a letter.   [3] 12 July.

The upper Part I have designated for Lanza:⁴ the Motivo is at least 32 Years old,⁵ but I have put a few *Furbelos* to suit this jimcrack Age, & I think it may please some of your half-in-half Musickers, such as call the Gregorian, gothic, antique, humdrum, & the Rest of the polite *H*epithets.

I shall call to-day upon your jolly Priest,⁶ & try whether you have given me a faithful Report of his Jocundity & Festivity, by hazarding a Joke or so, if an Opportunity happen.

I wish you would look in here this Evening instead of going to that devilish Opera House:⁷ I want to shew you a Stave of the Lozenges & University Caps, I mean ■ ■ & ◆ ◆ ⁸ N.B. I promise that if you come, you shall not be annoyed by Women, Children, Rats, or any other Vermin.

SW

To Vincent Novello   [Tottenham Court], 24 July [1812]¹

ALS, 1 p. (BL, Add. MS 11729, fo. 24)
Addressed To | Mʳ Novello | Oxford Street | Nº 240
Pmk 24 JY 1812

24ᵗʰ of July
Friday

Dear Cocky

I can meet you at *4* & stay till 5 at Davis's,² if that will *shute* (as we say at *Brister*)³ but I suppose this would not do for Clementi.⁴—The Cause of my failing you

---

⁴ Evidently a boy treble: no doubt one of the large family of Italian composers and singing teachers of this name active in London and Naples at the time, and probably a son of Gesualdo Lanza (1779–1859) (*Grove*⁶; Sainsbury).

⁵ SW's earlier version, for two treble voices and organ (autograph BL, Add. MS 31222, fo. 26), is in fact dated 11 May 1781.   ⁶ Not identified.

⁷ The King's Theatre, where the performance that evening was again of *Le nozze di Figaro*.

⁸ i.e. Gregorian chant.

---

¹ The year is given by the postmark.

² The organ builder James Davis (1762–1827), whose premises were at 14 Francis Street, Tottenham Court Road (*Grove*¹; *The New Grove Dictionary of Musical Instruments*, ed. Stanley Sadie, 3 vols. (1984)).   ³ i.e. Bristol.

⁴ Muzio Clementi (1752–1832), composer, pianist, teacher, music publisher, and piano manufacturer, whose reputation as a composer during his lifetime has been described as being exceeded only by Haydn and Beethoven. He had been brought to England from his native Italy by Peter Beckford in late 1776 or early 1777 and lived initially at Beckford's country estate in Dorset, moving to London in 1774. He toured abroad as a piano virtuoso from 1780 to 1783. On his return to London he achieved great eminence as a

To-Day was very unexpected.—Lord Oxford[5] is negotiating a Business which is likely to be eventually of much Importance to me, & has particularly wished me to dine with him To-Day, it being the *only* Day he could fix before his going out of Town, which will be in the Beginning of next Week. You *know* if he had not been *a Lord* I should not have cared for his Services.

In haste, Y^{rs} truly

SW

I shall call at Davis's at a Venture.

To Robert Glenn[1]   Tottenham Court, 24 July [1812][2]

ALS, 2 pp. (BL, Add. MS 35013, fo. 52)
Addressed To | Mr Glenn | Steward Street | Spital Fields
Pmk 25 JY 1812

Tottenham Court. New Road
24th of July

Dear Sir!

I think that we had a little Conversation the other Night upon the Subject of an Organist to be appointed for Huddersfield, & that you observed there was an Objection to the Election of any one deprived of Eyesight: but not being quite certain whether you stated the Objection to be totally insurmountable, & having promised Mr Grenville[3] (who called on me since you were with me) to use what

pianist, composer, and teacher, and later as a publisher and piano manufacturer. He was abroad again from 1802 to 1810. Among his many 'professional' pupils were Johann Baptist Cramer, John Field, August Alexander Klengel, and Theresa Jansen (*Grove*[6]; Plantinga). The significance of SW's remark is not clear, but it may refer to his misgivings about the suitability of meeting at the premises of one of Clementi's rivals.

⁵ Edward Harley, 5th Earl of Oxford and Earl Mortimer (1773–1848). The nature of the 'business' has not been established.

¹ The organist Robert Glenn (1776–1844) was to become one of SW's closest friends and professional colleagues and the recipient of over twenty letters from him. He was organist of St Margaret Pattens from 1805 to 1844 and music master at Christ's Hospital School from 1810 until his death. SW's youngest child, born in Nov. 1830, was named after him. On 26 May 1834 he married SW's daughter Rosalind (Dawe; Argent).   ² The year is given by the postmark.

³ The blind organist Tom Grenville (?1744–1827) was organist of the Foundling Hospital from 1773 to 1798; he himself had been a foundling. Little is known about his movements between 1798 and 1816, when he was reported as being in financial distress and was granted an annuity of £10 by the Foundling Hospital. He appears not to have been successful in his application for the Huddersfield position (Nichols and Wray, 233–5, 244).

Influence I could with you in his Favour, I feel it incumbent on me to make the Application, that he may receive *authentic* News in the Matter.

I must say, that it appears to me, the Person who so long officiated at the Foundling Chapel as Organist, & who has ever borne an entirely respectable & unexceptionable Character, both as a Professor & a Man, has no inconsiderable Pretension to the Situation of an Organist either in the Country or in *London*; & I can safely declare him thoroughly competent as a Musician to undertake the teaching Branch of the Profession.

Whenever you can favour me with a Call upon the Subject, (as I presume that the Matter must be decided shortly) I shall be glad to report to Mr Grenville your Communication, as I am desirous he should be convinced of my having performed the Promise I made him of undertaking his Recommendation to you.

I am generally within till 10 o'Clock in the Morning, excepting on Tuesday & Friday.[4] In the Evenings I am not certain of being at Home, unless by Special Appointment.

> Believe me,
> Dear Sir,
> Your obliged
> & sincere
>   S Wesley

To Vincent Novello   [Tottenham Court], 11 August [1812][1]

AL, 1 p. (BL, Add. MS 11729, fo. 28)
Addressed To | Mr Novello

11th August Tuesday

Dear N

I have lately heard that there are two different Opinions concerning the Circumstance of the Prince Regent's Order for the Execution of *two Criminals**[2] upon his *Birthday* (To-morrow):[3] One is that he has issued it for the express Purpose of increasing his universal Popularity; & the other, that it is intended as the *most appropriate* Method of celebrating so sacred & hilarious a Festival.

---

⁴ The days when SW taught at Turnham Green.

¹ 11 August falling on a Tuesday and the reference to the execution of the two criminals (n. 2) establish the year.

² For a report of the public execution at Newgate of Catherine Foster and J. Woolman Thompson, see *The Times*, 13 Aug. 1812.   ³ The Prince Regent was born on 12 Aug. 1762.

I should like to have your Notions upon the Subject, as also Mr Fryer's, if they can be had 'without disturbing his devotions.'—

Apropos of Devotion, I wish to know by *Thursday*, whether there be any Necessity of my doing your dirty Work on Saturday next,[4] or in other Words, whether you want me to ascend the Gregorian Altar at 11 & 3 on the said Day?[5]—You are not to guess hence, that I am reluctant so to do, only I must cut & contrive accordingly.

I sent to Stokes, from whom if you have had no Answer, it is not the Fault of [musical notation][6]

How *do* you *do*? (N.B. An elegant Pleonasm, belonging to John Bull *par Excellence*.

*One of them a Lady, in Honour of the Sex.

To Vincent Novello   [Tottenham Court, *c*.13 August 1812][1]

ALS, 3 pp. (BL, Add. MS 11729, fo. 43)
Addressed To | Mr Novello.

My dear Doctor of the Sorbonne—(Sorebone I fear is the more correct Reading in your Case)—

I think that if you will condescend to *re*-think, you will not find the Phrase of 'increased universal Popularity'[2] altogether such stark staring Nonsense as you suspect: for may not a Person become popular in the Opinion of *every* Individual (which you know includes the Idea of Universality) & yet may not this Popularity be *increased* in each Individual by some new Action deserving still more Esteem & Consideration than that which first excited them?—There is no Quibble in this Explanation.—It is recorded of St Charles Barromæus[3] (one of the noblest Cocks in the Calendar) that he daily gave a sumptuous Meal to very many poor people: this Conduct *alone* of course insured him *universal* Popularity; but how much was this increased, when it was discovered that he himself made his own Dinner upon mere Bread & Onions, or the like!—

---

[4] On 15 Aug., the feast of the Assumption of the Blessed Virgin Mary.
[5] i.e. for High Mass and Vespers.   [6] The significance of this allusion is not clear.

[1] SW's reference to Novello's criticism of a phrase SW had used in his letter of 11 Aug. (see n. 2) and his continuing discussion of arrangements for the Day of Obligation on 15 Aug. (see n. 4) together establish the date of this letter as around 13 Aug. 1812.

[2] See SW's comment in his previous letter that the Prince Regent had ordered the execution of the two criminals 'for the express Purpose of increasing his universal Popularity'.

[3] Charles Borromeo (1538–84) (Farmer).

I am obliged to you for excepting against what seemed to you illogical, because it shews that you think me worth Criticism, which I believe is more than some others do whose Judgement I value much less.

Although I am not *obligated* on the approaching Day of Obligation[4] consarning the Hawgin (this is the true Cockney Pronunciation, *by Cock & Pie*—by the Way, the origin of the Oath I believe to be *by God & Pix*, as 'I'll do this, please the *Pigs*,' is a Corruption of please the *Pix*—there was also a Book of religious Ceremonies & Prayers in Q. Elizabeth's Time, called the *Pie*, as intricate at least as the Breviary; this may therefore possibly be the Pie mentioned immediately after *God*, being connected thus closely with Religion.)—

Now, Sir, if you hate Parenthesis, in what Degree of Estimation must I stand with you as a Writer by this time?

Therefore, to begin my Sentence again, I say, that notwithstanding you have no great Need of me on Saturday, yet I should somehow like to take down the Introit & Alleluia, both which I know to be prime for the Feast dont est la Question.[5]— (I believe Question is Feminine in French, but never mind.)—And there is now no Time to be lost about that there *same little bit of Business* (as the Fellow called the Murder he happened to commit, one Day).—If the Gradual could be left at Mr Blackett's early on Saturday Morning, I would call at 10 o'Clock & scratch out the above in Mr Fryer's Apartment, if he could spare the House-Room.

Indeed, I will take my Chance of this, & depend on your giving a Signification thereof to Mr *Polisson*[6] or any other Dignitary qualified to transport the square Notes to South Audley Street for an Hour or two.

I have not seen Mr Archer,[7] for I have been unable to call on him: I shall probably manage this some Time between now & Monday.

Charles Butler[8] the sublime hath transmitted unto me a gorgeous Invitation to a smoking Haunch on *Monday next* at 6 o'Clock: I must therefore rehearse some

---

[4] i.e. 15 Aug.

[5] The introit was 'Signum magnum apparuit in caelo'; the Alleluia verse was 'Assumpta est Maria in caelum'.

[6] Not certainly identified, but presumably one of the Portuguese Embassy Chapel priests: SW refers to him in a later letter as 'the Reverend Mr Polisson'.

[7] The Revd James Archer (1751–1834), Principal Chaplain of the Bavarian chapel 1780–1826, later Vicar General of the London District. He was a subscriber to Novello's *A Selection of Sacred Music* (Anstruther, iv. 10–12).

[8] The eminent Roman Catholic lawyer and writer Charles Butler (1750–1832), nephew of Alban Butler (1710–73), author of *Lives of the Saints*. He was a member of the Portuguese Embassy Chapel congregation, a keen amateur musician, and a staunch advocate of Gregorian chant. He later wrote perceptively on Roman Catholic church music in England in his *Historical Memoirs of the English, Irish and Scottish Catholics since the Time of the Reformation*, 4 vols. (1819–21), ii. 354–9, and in 'Music of the English Catholic Chapels', *Catholic Gentleman's Magazine*, 1 (1818), 573–4.

of my best Behaviour calculated to render me worthy of such worshipful Society, & I think that Swift's Polite Conversation⁹ is the Book of all others that I ought to study for this grand Purpose.

I wish you a good night, Muster No-Well-O, desiring you to be *well* with all convenient Expedition.

Pray do you know the famous *amphiberous* Animal as can live neither upon Land nor Water?

Euouae¹⁰

To Vincent Novello   Tottenham Court, 16 August [1812]¹

ALS, 1 p. (BL, Add. MS 11729, fo. 30)
Addressed To | Mʳ Novello
Endorsed by Major: Dear Novello I am rejoiced to find you are so much better and lament
I don't see you this evening. Truly yours, J Major.

Dear N

I am sorry that I cannot have the Gratification of meeting at Major's² this Evening, who has nailed me to dine with him at a Friend's House of his, & whence we may not probably make our Escape before 11 o'Clock.

The Necessity of shaving, Dressing, & some of the other 'Blessings of this Life'³ prevent my coming to South Street⁴ this Evᵍ, as I otherwise should, but I shall certainly be with you on Wednesday Morning,⁵ *Deo Volente*.

You remember the Parish Clerk's Psalm of *his own composing*, upon the Arrival of King William, after James's shabby runaway Trick.⁶

---

⁹ Swift's *A Complete Collection of Polite and Ingenious Conversation* (1738).

¹⁰ The name for a Gregorian cadence, derived from the vowels in 'seculorum Amen', the concluding words of the doxology 'Gloria Patri' (*Grove⁶*).

¹ During the period of SW's correspondence with Novello, 16 Aug. fell on a Sunday in 1812 and 1818. The reference to the singing of the Te Deum (nn. 5 and 6) gives the year.

² The composer, arranger, publisher, organist, viola player, and teacher Joseph Major (1771–1828), a close friend and professional associate of SW. At the time of his application for membership of the Royal Society of Musicians in Sept. 1794, he was organist of Knightsbridge Chapel, a viola player, and a teacher at two schools. His compositions, mainly of vocal and piano music, were published between 1796 and around 1825. SW gave his own copy of the '48' (BL, Add. MS 14330) to him in 1811 (Doane; Brown and Stratton; Matthews).   ³ BCP, the General Thanksgiving.

⁴ The Portuguese Embassy Chapel.

⁵ 19 Aug., probably for a special service of thanksgiving to celebrate Wellington's victory at the Battle of Salamanca on 22 July, news of which had appeared in the London papers the previous day.

⁶ A reference to the landing in England of William of Orange (later William III), following James II's ignominious flight to France on 11 Dec. 1688.

> 'Britons rejoice! I say rejoice!
> King William is come:
> Therefore sing we, with Heart & Voice
> The hymn that's called **Te Dum**'[7]

SW

Sunday 16th Aug[t]

To George Polgreen Bridgetower   Tottenham Court, 4 September [1812][1]

ALS, 1 p. (BL, Add, MS 56411, fo. 11)
Addressed To | M[r] Bridgetower | Little Ryder Street | Piccadilly | N. 9
Pmk 4 SP

Dear Sir

I have appointed a few Friends to meet me To-morrow Morn[g] at 11 o'Clock in Francis Street, Tottenham Court Road (very near Clementi's Manufactory[2]) at Davis's the Organ Builder, whose name is on the Door & who has built an excellent Instrument for a Church at Surinam in the West Indies.[3]

Mr Logier (a German Professor, & the principal Music Seller in Dublin)[4] is very desirous of hearing *the whole* of the Preludes and Fugues,[5] and I have

---

[7] The author of this extempore anthem was the parish clerk of SW's grandfather, Samuel Wesley of Epworth. The anecdote was evidently a cherished piece of family history: see John Wesley's version in his *Remarks on Mr Hill's Farrago Double-distilled* (1771) (repr. in John Telford (ed.), *The Works of John Wesley*, 14 vols. (London, 1872), xiv. 445). SW's retailing of this story was doubtless in connection with the singing of the Te Deum at the forthcoming service of thanksgiving.

[1] The year is given by 4 Sept. falling on a Friday and SW's Tottenham Court address.

[2] Clementi at this time had premises in Tottenham Court Road.

[3] The organ has not been traced.

[4] Johann Bernhard Logier (1777–1846), German pianist, teacher, inventor, author, and composer. He moved to England in 1791 and joined the band of the Marquis of Abercorn's regiment as a flautist, later being promoted to director of music. After the regiment was dissolved in 1807 he moved to Ireland and directed a band in Kilkenny and at the Royal Hibernian Theatre, Dublin. He opened his music shop at 27 Lower Sackville Street, Dublin, in 1810. He also taught the piano and was the inventor of the chiroplast or 'hand director', 'a laterally sliding frame for the hands fitted above the keyboard' (*Grove*[6]), which he patented in 1814. The first edition of his *An Explanation & Description of the Royal Patent Chiroplast* (1814) contained testimonials from Johann Baptist Cramer, J. T. Latour, William Shield, and SW, and SW commented favourably on his *Companion to the Royal Patent Chiroplast* (*c.*1815) in a review in the Mar. 1815 number of *EM*. In late 1816 or early 1817 he opened a music academy at 20 Bedford Place, Russell Square, where he was later joined by Samuel Webbe II. His teaching methods, involving the use of the chiroplast and group teaching, gave rise in 1817 and 1818 to a major controversy amongst his fellow musicians (see SW to Glenn, 23 Mar. 1818). He moved to Germany in 1821 (*Grove*[6]; Kassler, *Science of Music*, 702–23).

[5] The '48'.

promised to *attempt* them all through, altho' really I have lately had so little Opportunity of playing, that I do not expect to do them much Justice. I shall, however, be glad of the Company of so *candid* a Hearer as yourself, who I know will make due Allowance for the Want of Practice.

I am always,
Dear Sir
Yours most truly
    S Wesley

Tottenham Court. | New Road | Friday 4th of Sept^r

To Vincent Novello — Ramsgate,[1] 1 October [1812][2]

ALS, 3 pp. (BL, Add. MS 11729, fo. 33)
Addressed To | Mr Novello | Oxford Street | London | N. 240 | Octr 1st

Ramsgate.
Harbour Street. 7.
Thursday Octr 1

My dear N

I abstained from laying Siege to you by Post, until I felt qualified to give you a true and particular Account of our Intentions, *Contentions*, & Operations. I mention contention because my Coadjutor[3] & myself have been retarded in our public Advancement by the Whimsies & Stupidity of two black Crows in the Shape & Guise of *Parsons*; one of them a Blockhead & the other a Brute.— The story is this.—Mr Webbe Senior suggested to his Son that he conceived it would be advisable, previous to our issuing public Notice relative to anything like a Concert, to obtain the Permission of performing some select Pieces on the Organ at a Church, or Churches (if deemed more eligible to attract *Customers*) & to give the Entertainment Gratis, in a Morning, thus rendering ourselves known

[1] A seaside resort on the Isle of Thanet, a peninsula on the east coast of Kent. Because of their position close to London and their accessibility by river as well as by road, Ramsgate and its larger neighbour Margate were favourite holiday resorts for Londoners, and attracted large numbers of visitors. SW's visit seems to have been a speculative venture, undertaken without any local knowledge or contacts. He had travelled with Samuel Webbe II to Ramsgate by river on Thursday 18 Sept., and described his journey in his letter of the same date to Sarah Suter: 'I could not be sick for the soul of me, but kept eating & drinking all day with 30 people spewing round me' (BL, Add. MS 35012, fo. 40).

[2] The year is established by 1 Oct. falling on a Friday and by SW's presence in Ramsgate.

[3] Samuel Webbe II.

not only as Artists, but as Lads of some Liberality & obliging Propensity.—The Clergyman of Ramsgate[4] was afraid of offending the tight-laced Part of his Congregation by this Novelty, & therefore refused us; & the Hottentot of Margate[5] upon our Application sent a most impudent vulgar Answer stating our request to be so 'highly indecorous & improper that he hesitated not a Moment to give it his decisive Refusal.'—In Consequence of these Pros & Cons, the Time which might & would have been profitably employed in Preparations for our intended Party was unavoidably expended (not to say wasted) in waiting the Sentence of these drivelling old Puts,[6] & we were not able to announce our Day &c until Saturday Evening last.[7]

Added to these Delights, there has been not a little Debate concerning the most opportune Season for our Exhibition, some advising the Morning (or Noon) & others the Evening.—The Advocates for the Morning argued the great Probability of *Loungers* employed at that Time in quest of 'something new & strange'[8] as an Inducement to fix the Meeting then; but to this was opposed the Fact of all the fine Folk *being in the Habit* of prancing about on their Palfries, & bowling about in their Tumbrils for 2 or 3 Hours after scrubbing their mangey Carcases in the Sea, which would quite do away any reasonable Expectation of their coming to hear our Quaverings before Dinner Time.—

The Arguments in favour of the Evening have ultimately prevailed, & we have *at length* determined on Saturday Evening next, Oct'r 3'd at 8 o'Clock.[9]—We have met with some very kind & active Friends, who are making whatever Interest they can in our Favour, & I think that we have a tolerably good Prospect—but you know that *my* Expectations of Success in any Undertaking are not generally presumptuous, & I shall not murmur in the least, provided we depart hence without burning our Fingers, & I rather think we may rationally hope as much as that.[10]—

[4] Richard Harvey (1768/9–1836), matric. Corpus Christi College, Cambridge, 1785, LL B (1790), Deacon (1789), Priest (1793), Curate of St Laurence, Ramsgate (1791); Vicar (1793–1836) in succession to his father (Venn).

[5] William Frederick Baylay (1778/9–1845), matric. Emmanuel College, Cambridge, 1800, BA (1802), MA (1805); vicar of St John's, Margate (1810–28) (Venn).

[6] 'A stupid man, silly fellow, blockhead, duffer'; a 'country put' was a bumpkin (*OED*).

[7] 26 Sept.   [8] Possibly an allusion to *The Tempest*, I. ii. 404 ('something rich and strange').

[9] 3 Oct. The concert was in the Assembly Rooms at Ramsgate: see SW to his mother, 6 Oct. 1812 (BL, Add. MS 35012, fo. 21).

[10] SW's caution was well founded. In his letter to his mother of 6 Oct., he reported: 'when all Accounts are balanced, we shall just have saved ourselves harmless in the Payment of the Room, Singer, Advertisements &c but the having established a Reputation there among the People of the Place, who are all of the first Order & Consequence in Rank & Title, is a Point of no little Importance, & I trust may lead to future & permanent Advantage.'

We have engaged Miss Stephens[11] (who is at Margate) as our Singer: I think you told me she was to have sung at the Thanksgiving Business[12] in your Chapel: she has a very sweet Voice, & sings in a pretty Style: there is no one else hereabout that can be endured by any but French Ears.—

We mean to be very modest in our Pretensions, of the vocal Sort especially; Miss S. is to sing two Songs, & Webbe & I intend joining her in two Glees. furthermore, also & moreover, I shall attempt to fiddle the Accompaniment of Pleyel's Sonata, [13] which may be done without broken Bones I trow; at least it is 'devoutly to be wished'.[14]

My Compeer will also give one of Dussek's most stately Pieces as a Solo: the Duet of 'the Sisters'[15] will also make its Appearance, according to your Advice: another of Clementi (a Rattler)—& a Fantasia,[16] with some St Giles's Ditty or other[17] for the Delight & Edification of the learned Critics now resident in the Isle of Thanet, & who rank pretty much with the Majority of those in London, touching Judgement & Acumen, but that you know is neither *here* nor *there*.

Pray, Sir, do me the Favour to accept my 'humble & hearty Thanks for all your Goodness & loving Kindness to me'[18] & my School Mistress to the North of Oxford Street.—As we doubt being able to set forth sooner than Monday,[19] of Consequence I must once again intreat your Assumption of the magisterial Chair on that Day, & you shall have very speedy Intelligence of our Arrival, whenever that shall be brought about, which I trust will be in the Course of Tuesday.

I forget whether you are as devout an Adorer of the main Ocean as I, but if I were a Gem'man like, I would always live within a Hop, Skip & Jump thereof.—I am convinced by my present Experience that it would secure me a Perpetuity of Health, which I am singular enough to esteem a greater Blessing than long Life.—

---

[11] The soprano Catherine Stephens (1794–1882), later one of the most popular English singers of her generation, but at this time at an early stage in her career (Sainsbury; Brown and Stratton; *Grove*[6]).

[12] Perhaps the service on 19 Aug.

[13] The opening of the first movement (Allegro molto) of No. 3 of Pleyel's *Six Sonatas for the Pianoforte, with an Accompaniment for the Flute or Violin and Violoncello, composed & dedicated . . . to . . . the Queen of Great Britain* (1788) (Rita Benton, *Ignace Pleyel: A Thematic Catalogue of his Compositions* (New York, 1977), 188–9). For Pleyel, see SW to Novello, [4 Feb. 1814].

[14] *Hamlet*, III. i. 64–5.

[15] Possibly 'Two daughters of this aged stream are we' from Purcell's *King Arthur*.

[16] i.e. an improvisation by SW, perhaps on a popular song, similar to the one on 'A Frog he would a-wooing go' that he had played at his Birmingham concert in Sept. 1809.

[17] SW's allusion is perhaps to the notorious slums of the St Giles area of London.

[18] BCP, the General Thanksgiving. Novello had evidently taken over SW's teaching engagements during SW's absence in Ramsgate.

[19] 5 Oct. In the event, SW and Webbe arrived back in London in the evening of that day: see SW to his mother, 6 Oct. 1812 (BL, Add. MS 35012, fo. 21).

Mr W. & I appear about every other Day in Puris Naturalibus[20] upon the Coast, to amuse the Fish & the Ladies.[21] We scorn wooden Machines, where there is neither Prospect nor Sea Room; irksome Obstacles to aquatic Animals.

Yours as ever

S Wesley

P.S. Horsley[22] & his Spouse Elect, Callcot's eldest Daughter,[23] with her Mother[24] are down here, & we met them Yesterday by Accident on the Coast, just as we were about to strip.—Miss C. said she should have known me at *any* Distance by Sight, & she had a narrow Chance of exercising her Memory in my *birthday* Suit.

P.S. We meet at Margate & Ramsgate the most perfect Piano-Forte Artists you can imagine: they play uniformly in 5^{ths} & Octaves. I see your Name as a Subscriber to Mr Panormo's Concerto,[25] & I am sure by the Specimens of his Compositions I have seen, that you have a great deal to *learn* yet.

To Charles Butler   Tottenham Court, [7 October 1812][1]

ALS, 2 pp. (Rylands, DDWes 9/20)
Addressed To | Charles Butler Esqre | Lincoln's Inn | Wednesday Evening
Pmk 8 OC 1812
Docketed Octr 1812 Mr Wesley

---

[20] 'In an unadorned state of nature'.

[21] Annotated by Samuel Webbe II at this point: 'fine *scurvy* objects to amuse the Ladies'.

[22] William Horsley (1774–1858), organist, composer, and musical theorist. He had been assistant to Callcott at the asylum for female orphans, and had succeeded him as organist there in 1802. He was not a close friend of SW, although they moved in much the same professional circles, and had taken over SW's teaching at Mrs Barnes's school after SW's dismissal in 1808. His chief distinction was as a glee composer, and he was described by Baptie as 'one of the most elegant, learned and artistic of all the excellent glee composers our country has produced' (Grove^6; David Baptie, *Sketches of the English Glee Composers* (London, 1895), 82). Two of his hymns ('Belgrave' and 'Horsley') are still sung today. He appears prominently in SW's letters of 1825 following his hostile review in *QMMR* of SW's Service.

[23] Elizabeth Hutchins Callcott (1793–1875), daughter of John Wall Callcott; they married on 12 Jan. 1813.

[24] Elizabeth Mary Callcott, née Hutchins.

[25] Either by Francesco Panormo (1764–1844) or his son Ferdinand Charles, both of whom published large quantities of piano music at this time. A 'Mr Panormo' promoted a concert at the Argyll Rooms on 13 June 1813, at which he performed a piano concerto by himself, possibly the one described here. No copy has been traced (Sainsbury; Brown and Stratton; *The Times*, 8 June 1813).

[1] The date is given by SW's 'Wednesday Evening' and the following day's postmark.

Dear Sir

I have just now received your Letter,[2] & and cannot possibly feel the smallest Objection to a Summons from the accomplished and venerable Doctor.—I trust therefore to give you the Meeting on Sunday,[3] & to ascend the 'Gradus ad Parnassum,'[4] as near Noon Tide as the *Uncertainty of our next Moment* may permit.

Entre nous, our worthy Friend produced a Set (in MS.) of the former 24 Preludes and Fugues of S. Bach which was a Present from his Son Emmanuel Bach, & which D[r] B. imagined to have constituted the *Whole* of that Work; whereas the Fact is, that these are only the first *Half*.—Of this I soon convinced him, by bringing forward the other 24, & performing some of them before him, with which he was highly delighted.[5]—I instance this, only as a Proof that the good Doctor has been *occasionally* (tho' certainly not very frequently) precipitate in his Decision upon a few musical Matters, & our joint Opinion concerning his slight Knowledge of the Gregorian Note seems justly to authorize such a Conclusion.

I believe that I mentioned to you the general Wish that seems to prevail of introducing the Gregorian Melodies properly harmonized for the Organist.[6]—I am perfectly convinced that such a Work would become universally valuable, & feel both ready & desirous to undertake it, specially if after your having obtained the Intelligence of which you are in search, you would give a prefatory Essay upon the Subject.—

I am,
Dear Sir,
Very respectfully & sincerely Yours
    S Wesley

13. Tottenham Court.—New Road | Wednesday Evening

---

[2] Butler's letter to SW of the same date (BL, Add. MS 11729, fo. 36), which conveyed a request in a note from Burney that Butler and SW should ' "mount his [i.e. Burney's] lofty apartment next Sunday about 12 at noon, & let him hear from you, a thorough Bach of the great Sebastian's golden grain".' SW enclosed Butler's letter in his next letter to Novello; Burney's note to Butler is not preserved. For Butler, see SW to Novello, [*c*.13 Aug. 1812], n. 8.   [3] i.e. to meet Butler on 11 Oct.

[4] 'Steps to Parnassus': i.e. the stairs leading to Burney's apartments in Chelsea College, with an allusion to the term's frequent use as a title for musical instruction books: J. J. Fux (1660–1741) used it for his celebrated counterpoint treatise (1725), and Clementi was later to use it for a collection of piano studies (1817–26).

[5] See SW's earlier reference to this occasion in his letter to Jacob of 17 Sept. 1808.

[6] In his letter, Butler had written: 'I am so serious about the Gregorian Note, that I have sent to Paris for [a] work respecting it.'

1812

To Vincent Novello [Tottenham Court], 11 October [1812][1]

ALS, 1 p. (BL, Add. MS 11729, fo. 35)
Addressed To | Mr Novello

Dear N

The enclosed[2] will account for my not being with you this Morning, which I fully designed to have accomplished, had it not arrived, & a Summons from a Man of 90 years may not happen in his *91*st[3]

I also fear that I cannot be in your Latitude this Afternoon, as after the Meeting I must see Linley in Southampton Street Strand,[4] but I will contrive to get at you shortly.—

If the Gregorian Books could be left for me, on *Wednesday*, I think I can get Time to scribble out a rough Copy of the Mass which we revised in the Course of the Week.—There is no Holiday requiring high Mass, I believe before Sunday next.—

Yours most truly,
    S Wesley

Sunday 11th of Oct^r

To Vincent Novello [Tottenham Court], 24 October 1812

ALS, 1 p. (BL, Add. MS 11729, fo. 37)
Addressed To | Mr Novello | Saturday Afternoon

Saturday 24th of Octr 1812

Dear N

There seems to be some Prevalence of Incantation in the Matter of the Church Books:[1] I was unable to call at the Chapel till one of the Clock this Day & unfortunately could make no one hear, therefore after repeated Tattoos I was unwillingly obliged to make a Retreat.—I wished to have been able to scribble

---

[1] The year is given by 11 Oct. falling on a Sunday and the reference to the 'summons' from Burney.
[2] Butler's letter.   [3] SW was mistaken about Burney's age: he was 86.
[4] William Linley's address.

[1] Presumably the Graduale and the Antiphonale, containing the chants for the Mass and the Offices.

out the Antiphon for the Vespers To-morrow[2] (as well as the Gregorian Mass)[3] & I think this may yet be done, if you can so manage as to get the two Books conveyed to M[r] Blackett's by 9 o Clock To-morrow Morning, in which event I would call at his House, & do the Job (if he will give me House-Room during the Time necessary for the Purpose) & I would take Care to return the Books in Time for high Mass,[4] as I know I could compleat what I want in about an Hour.—At all Hazards I will take my Chance of your Endeavour to negotiate this grand Concern.—I like not abandoning a Design from such teazing Obstacles. Sam. Webbe[5] & Gwilt[6] I expect to come to Vespers, & *the latter* you know would be pleased by hearing the Antiphons sung with a Base on the Organ.—

Adieu for the Moment,

Yours as ever,

SW

P.S. I leave M[r] Fryer's & the Organ Book of Vespers &c.

To Vincent Novello   [Tottenham Court], 29 October 1812

ALS, 3 pp. (BL, Add. MS 11729, fo. 39)

M[r] No Well O.

I spell it so on Purpose for I don't hold with your Pie-Crust sort of Promises.— Pray Sir, did you not appoint, & all but swear that you would bring your Body corporate & corporeal hither last Tuesday as ever was?—And pray Sir, what kind of an Alibi do you mean to set up in Arrest of Judgement?—You did not know before, but now you will know that I squatted my A——e upon a *Stool* (a Musick Stool I mean) for three blessed Hours long, straining my thieving Irons as if they had been so many Strips of India Rubber, to claw hold of supple Jack's woundy Exercises,[1] all on Purpose not to affront your Doctorship's *acumenous* Ears, when you should have brought your scientific Backside to an Anchor at N. 13.[2]—

---

[2] 25 Oct., the twenty-third Sunday after Pentecost, when the Magnificat antiphon at Vespers was 'At Jesus conversus, et videns eam, dixit: confide, filia: fides tua te salvam fecit, Alleluia.' SW is presumably referring to a harmonization of the plainsong.

[3] Presumably part of SW's harmonization of the plainsong Mass VIII (the *Missa de Angelis*), on which he was evidently still working. The completed autograph (BL, Add. MS 17731) is dated 21 Dec. 1812; the Kyrie had been published the previous year in Novello's *A Collection of Sacred Music*.

[4] At 11.00 a.m.   [5] Samuel Webbe II.   [6] Joseph Gwilt.

[1] Not identified, unless SW is referring to J. S. Bach.   [2] SW's house at 13 Tottenham Court.

If these Arraignments are not for mortal Sins, & you do not humbly plead guilty to them, depend upon it that the Sacrament of Penance will stand you in no Stead, & you may as little expect to join in the Chorus Angelorum[3] hereafter, as to find Judas Iscariot there chaunting Hallelujahs.

However, as while there is Life, there are Hopes, let me, with that Charity which distinguisheth all us good Catholicks, humbly trust that your speedy Repentance, & the Satisfaction I shall require of you, will ultimately save you from the bottomless Pit. What that same Satisfaction may be, is at present a Secret, not to be disclosed before the Feast Day of All Saints, between the Hours of 11 & 12, & where, you may (with the Assistance of a general Council convened expressly for the Occasion) be possibly able to guess.

I had yesterday the beatific Vision of the Reverend M[r] Polisson, who answered me in that *upright* Manner by which he is so justly characterized:—'You may go up, Sir.'—

I loves Helegance, *I* does.

So we are all to be merry after our 'sad Solemnity & black' on Monday next.[4]— I hope Gastang[5] will be there, as I have a great Curiosity to see him eat Plum Pudding.—Besides, I want to hear him sing 'Sweet Bird', & 'The Soldier tired',[6] both of which I am informed he executes equally well.

I am hard at [7]
[sic]

If I can get a little Bit ready by Monday I will, but do not reckon upon it with that Sort of Reliance that I *once* had on your bonne Foi.

SW

Thursday Evening | Oct[r] 29th 1812

P.S. I sends a silly Piece of defiled Music Paper.[8]

---

[3] 'The choir of angels': like SW's later reference to the 'bottomless pit', a quotation from the text of the Requiem Mass.

[4] The celebration of the Requiem Mass on 2 Nov., the feast of All Souls, when black vestments would have been used.   [5] Not identified: evidently a boy treble.

[6] Two popular soprano solos: 'Sweet bird' is a soprano recitative and aria from Handel's *L'Allegro, il Pensieroso ed il Moderato* (1740); 'The Soldier, tir'd of war's alarms', is a celebrated bravura aria from Arne's *Artaxerxes* (1762).

[7] The opening of Credo III, implying that SW was working on a harmonization of this part of the Mass.   [8] Not preserved.

To [?Johann Peter Salomon][1] Tottenham Court,
5 November 1812

ALS, 1 p. (Boston)

Dear Sir

I beg you to accept my Apology for not having sooner thanked you for the Letter, Book, & Invitation which I received several Days since, but as I fully designed to call at N. 70[2] between now & Sunday & fix upon Operations with you vivâ voce, I less felt the Necessity of a Post Man's Assistance.—I intend to be at the Vespers according to Mr Turner's[3] Desire, & to proceed thence to the Feast of Philosophy[4] with you.—The Service will detain us till nearly $\frac{1}{2}$ past 4, I *believe*, on Examination of the Office of that Particular Day,[5] in which are to be Scraps of 'Pribbles & Prabbles' (as Sir Hugh[6] says) for one lousy Saint or another,[7] which will extend the Time a Quarter of an Hour extra at least, I fear.

However, amongst philosophical Qualities, having been told that *Patience* used to be enumerated; our sage Deroise Stewart[8] we must hope, will forbear his Wrath, even should the Fish be overdone by 4 or 5 Seconds, in Consequence of the Delay occasioned by holy Mother Church.—

Yours, dear Sir,
Very truly
    S Wesley

13. New Road | Thursday Night | 5 Nov[r] 1812

---

[1] For Salomon, see SW to Street, [3 May 1800], n. 7. The identification of him as the probable addressee of this letter is from the reference to 'no. 70' (see n. 2).
[2] 70 Newman Street, Salomon's house.   [3] Not identified.
[4] Not identified: possibly a masonic function.   [5] 8 Nov.
[6] i.e. Sir Hugh Evans, the Welsh priest in *Merry Wives of Windsor*, I. i.
[7] Cybi, the Four Crowned Martyrs, Gerardin, Tysilio, and Willehad (Farmer).
[8] Not identified.

To James Asperne[1]   32 Cornhill,[2] 14 November [1812][3]

AL, third person, 1 p. (Rylands, DDWF 15/42)

Saturday Night. 14. Nov[r]
Cornhill. 32

M[r] S. Wesley called on M[r] Asperne to solicit his Indulgence for his apparent Neglect in not having much sooner acknowledged the polite Attention he received from him several Days ago.[4]—He wishes to assure M[r] Asperne that he feels not the least Objection to accede to his Proposal regarding the Portrait, & begs Leave to inform M[r] A. that he has one in his Possession which *was* considered a good Likeness at the Time it was taken, but this being *15 Years* ago, there can be little Doubt that the Furrows of Age have been so much increasing in *Indenture* that a Fac-simile might appear somewhat ridiculous at the present Period.[5]—At all Events S. W. will most readily agree to M[r] Asperne's Wish, & although he cannot instantaneously fix a Moment for sitting to the Artist he mentions, he will be happy to name an early Day for that Purpose, in Consequence of M[r] A's Desire.— With Respect to any Memoir of himself, he knows not well how to negotiate it: S. W. is not only averse but incapable (from many Considerations) to become his own Biographer.

[1] James Asperne (d. 1821), the publisher and proprietor of *EM* from 1803 until his death (Sullivan, *AAAJ* 106–12).

[2] The publishing offices of *EM* since 1802. SW had evidently called on Asperne and left this note for him on failing to find him there.

[3] During the period 1802–21, when the premises of *EM* were at Cornhill and Asperne was its publisher, 14 Nov. fell on a Saturday in 1807, 1812, and 1818. 1812 is the most probable year, given by SW's reference to his portrait (see n. 5).

[4] Asperne had evidently approached SW with a suggestion that he should include a biographical memoir of him in *EM* and had enquired if SW would be willing both to sit for a portrait and to write the memoir himself. Neither the memoir nor the portrait appeared.

[5] Probably a reference to the portrait by 'Mr Robinson', described in SW's *MW* Obituary as having been painted when SW was 'about thirty' (i.e. around 1796), and generally regarded at the time as a good likeness. Robinson was probably R. Robinson, a miniature painter who in 1797 exhibited a portrait of a gentleman at the Royal Academy of Arts which conceivably could have been of SW.

To Vincent Novello   [Tottenham Court], 5 December [1812][1]

ALS, 2 pp. (BL, Add. MS 11729, fo. 41)

Saturday
5. Dec^r

Dear N

I leave with you the prior Piece of the Sanctus,[2] which may now be easily connected with the latter Part.—I have nearly done with the Mass of the 5th Tone,[3] after finishing which, I shall not in Haste bother myself with Gregorian; not at least for the Sake of *Honour*, & I see not at present any bright Prospect of Profit for my Labour.—I shall hawk about the Mass in D[4] when concluded, which I will rather suffer to moulder in a Chest than sell for a *Song*; but have very little Expectation of an adequate Price offered for the Copy-Right.—As the Gregorian is beginning to be proscribed *by the Clergy themselves*, it is plainly an unfavourable Epoch to reckon upon its Encouragement, even when presented with florid Advantages, & had I been aware of the sudden & silly Revolution taking Place in your Choir,[5] I should certainly have employed much of my Time otherwise, which I now consider as imprudently and incautiously sacrificed.

By the Way, have the Kindness to gather up all the Scraps of Square Notes which I have scratched out, as soon as you conveniently can, & make a Bunch of them, not to burn, but to restore to their old faithful Master

SW

P.S. The Antiphone at Magnificat for the 5th Sunday after the Epiphany is, Colligite primum zizania, & alligate ea in fasciculos *ad comburendum*: triticum autem congregate in horseum meum, dicit Dominus.[6]

'Scrape together all the Gregorian Masses & Anthems, & bundle them all up for a good Bonfire on the 5th of November,[7] but make a correct Copy on vellum Paper of all Mr Webbe's[8]

---

[1] The year is given by 5 Dec. falling on a Saturday and the continuing discussion of harmonizations of Gregorian chant.   [2] Probably another part of SW's harmonization of the *Missa de Angelis*.

[3] The incomplete four-part *Missa de Sanctissimo Trinitate, Tono Quinto* (BL, Add. MS 35001).

[4] The *Missa de Angelis*.

[5] Although the details of the 'sudden and silly revolution' are not known, SW's subsequent remarks imply that it was directed against Gregorian chant, and involved the replacement of chant by polyphonic settings.

[6] 'Gather ye together first the tares, and bind them in bundles to burn them: but gather the wheat into my barn, saith the Lord' (Matt. 13: 30).

[7] The anniversary of the gunpowder plot in 1605, when a group of Roman Catholic conspirators headed by Guy Fawkes (1570–1606) made an unsuccessful attempt to blow up the Houses of Parliament; the foiling of the plot has subsequently been commemorated by the lighting of bonfires and the burning of effigies of Guy Fawkes.

[8] i.e. Samuel Webbe I, whose settings of the Mass and other church music still formed a major part of the repertoire of the London Roman Catholic chapels.

& David Perez's[9] Church Music, together with all other Pieces for divine Service by Portugueze authors, who have uniformly & happily defied the hacknied Rules of Counterpoint adopted by Handel, Haydn, Mozart & such old fashioned tight-laced Pedants.[']

N.B. The said latter Compositions are to be kept always in the Sacristies of the several Chapels in England (except when actually required for Use) among the sacred Vestments, Pyxes, Chalices & c.

N.B. If you have Pluck enough shew this to M[r] Fryer.

To Vincent Novello   [Tottenham Court], 14 December 1812

ALS, 1 p. (BL, Add. MS 11729, fo. 42)
Addressed To | M[r] Novello

Dear N.

M[r] Picart has again been assailing me for the Symphony you arranged of S. Bach,[1] & for my Organ Duet.[2] You have a very clear Copy of the latter made by yourself, from which he could make a better than from my Original: therefore I shall be much obliged by your making as early a Rummage as you can, which will save me from further Persecution.—M[r] P has been so very liberal (in his Accommodations respecting Music) to me that I cannot consistently or decently refuse him a Request of the present Kind: otherwise I am not fond of letting MSS get wandering abroad, for some Reasons, sufficiently cogent to *me,* & among the rest, the Probability of their being erroneously transcribed is a weighty one.

I am convinced that you will (as soon as you possibly can) make a Muster of my sanctified Shreds & Patches,[3] of which I am desirous to effect somewhat of an orderly Arrangement, whether they shall ever appear in Print or not.—And when you have copied the Sanctus in B,[4] I shall be glad of it, as I wish to scratch it out in a bound Book.

Yours very truly,

S Wesley

14th Dec[r] 1812 | Monday

[9] David Perez (1711–78), Italian composer of Spanish descent. At the invitation of Jose I of Portugal he became in 1752 *maestro di cappella* to the Portuguese court and music master to the Portuguese royal princesses. His church music was frequently performed at the Portuguese Embassy Chapel, and Novello included some pieces by him in his *A Collection of Sacred Music.*

[1] i.e. Novello's arrangement of Bach's 'St Anne' Prelude: see SW to Novello, 6 May [1812].

[2] The Duet in C, first performed on 5 June 1812.

[3] A near-quotation from *Hamlet,* III. iv. 93: i.e. SW's arrangements of Gregorian chant.

[4] Not identified.

To [?Muzio Clementi][1]   [Tottenham Court], 6 January 1813

ALS, 1 p. (BL, Add. MS 31764, fo. 26)
Endorsed Wesley 6 Jany 1813

Dear Sir

Since I saw you last I have received full Authority to determine all relative to the Piano-Forte in Question, & the Instrument at 42 Guineas is the one that is to be packed off directed for W. Williams Esqre Barrister at Law, Weymouth, Dorset:[2] a Set of Strings &c will be also required, & I should suppose a tuning Hammer; in short, whatever, may be considered necessary, & what is usual in an Order of a similar Kind for the East Indies.—The Instrument will not be unpacked during the Voyage, which I was desired to mention.

I should conceive it proper to add a Line directed to Mr Williams (with whom I am not acquainted) who first applied to my Friend W. Linley of Southampton Street to procure such a Piano Forte for his Daughter, & Linley made over the Commission to me.—It seems that he is a very old Acquaintance of the Latter, who would not (I am sure from Experience) recommend any one without the fullest Conviction of his Honour & Responsibility.—I believe the Order is wished to be compleated without any Delay that can be avoided: how soon there may be a Ship sailing for India I know not, but of Course you will easily ascertain: I should like Linley to see the Instrument before its Departure if it can be conveniently managed.

I am
Dear Sir,
Your sincerely
   S Wesley

P.S. I have not yet obtained any Copies of my Tune with Variations,[3] which I expected this Morning at the latest.

Tottenham Court. New Road. | Wednesday Night. Jan. 6. 1813

---

[1] It is apparent from the content of this letter that its addressee was in business both as a piano manufacturer and a music publisher. The identification of SW's 'tune with variations' as his Variations on 'The Bay of Biscay' (n. 3) adds weight to the conjecture that the addressee was probably Muzio Clementi or someone in his firm. For Clementi, see SW to Novello, 24 July [1812], n. 4.

[2] William Williams, second son of Robert Williams of Birchin Lane, City of London, who was admitted to the Inner Temple on 22 Nov. 1792 and called to the Bar on 23 Nov. 1798. He had chambers at 6 Pump Court and practised at the Wiltshire Sessions and on the Western Circuit, of which Dorset was part (*Law Lists*; Inner Temple records).

[3] No doubt SW's Variations on 'The Bay of Biscay', dedicated to and published by Clementi, and reviewed in the Feb. 1813 number of *MM* (p. 69).

To Vincent Novello [Tottenham Court], 12 January [1813][1]

ALS, 1 p. (BL, Add. MS 11729, fo. 47)
Addressed To | Mʳ Novello | Oxford Street | 240 | Tuesday Morning
Pmk 12 JA

Tuesday Janʸ 12

Dear N

In Consonance with your Wish I give you the earliest Intelligence that Charles Ashley & I have struck (or stricken, in *Strictness*) a Bargain concerning the Roritoris,[2] & he has acceded to my Terms in a very civil gentlemanly Way.[3]

I gave him a friendly Hint that Smart[4] had signified his Design of introducing some of the sacred Music of the more modern Composers, & that as this will certainly prove a Novelty, probably attractive, it were worth Ashley's Consideration whether it would not be advisable to bring forward a Counterpoize of a similar Kind at Covent Garden.—To this however he objects on the Score of the *Trouble & Expence.*—I wish he may not repent of his Parsimony.—These are the silly Means by which the Progress of Science is obstructed, & we justly become the Scorn of the musical World upon the Continent.

Adieu, believing me
always truly yours,
S Wesley

[1] The year is given by 12 Jan. falling on a Tuesday and SW's discussion of his negotiations about the terms of his engagement as organist at the Covent Garden oratorio concerts (n. 2).

[2] i.e. the Lenten oratorio concerts at Covent Garden, at which SW was to appear as regular organist for the first time. 'Roritoris' is a Wesleyan coinage, punning on 'oratorio' and 'rory-tory' (or 'tory-rory') meaning 'boisterous'.

[3] In his Reminiscences SW recorded that he was paid six guineas per concert, or ten guineas if he played a concerto.

[4] The conductor and impresario Sir George Smart (1776–1867), the director of the rival series of oratorio concerts at Drury Lane. He was a founder member of the Philharmonic Society in 1813 and conductor of many of its concerts, and during a long career was one of the most influential figures in English music, both in London and in the provinces. Among the new sacred works he introduced at Drury Lane were Beethoven's *Christ on the Mount of Olives* in 1814 and his Mass in C in 1815 (*Grove⁶*; Ehrlich, *Music Profession*, 37–42; Young).

To an unidentified recipient[1]   Tottenham Court, 12 January [1813][2]

ALS, 2 pp. (Rylands, DDWF 15/17)

13 Tottenham Court.
Tuesday 12 Jan[y]

Dear Sir

I have just received a Letter[3] from our good Friend Jeaffreson,[4] who in Consequence of my having hinted to him in another which I wrote since I had the Pleasure of seeing you last, that you would have liked to give me the Meeting[5] during my Stay at Tunstall, desires me to inform you without Delay, that he would be extremely glad if you would consent to come down *with me* thither, & pass a few Days.—In Consequence of my Confinement, I have been hitherto unable to *appoint* any Day for the Journey, but my Knee is now so much on the mending *Hand*, that I think two or three Days more will render me sufficiently sound in Limb to bear the whirl and jumble of a Stage Coach.[6]

If you have any Thoughts of complying with J's Wish, have the Kindness to give me a Call either this or To-morrow Evening, or should either or both be inconvenient, favour me with a Line upon the Subject; believing me mean while

Dear Sir
Very truly yours
S Wesley

---

[1] Conceivably Zebedee Tydeman, described in Sainsbury as a pupil of Callcott and a teacher of violin and piano. He was the son of a Suffolk farmer and later taught at Framlingham, not far from Jeaffreson's home at Tunstall. He is mentioned in SW to Sarah Suter, 20 Jan. 1811 (BL, Add. MS 35012, fo. 38), written from Tunstall, and was evidently a mutual friend of SW and Jeaffreson.

[2] The year is given by 12 Jan. falling on a Tuesday and SW's Tottenham Court address.

[3] Not preserved.

[4] The Revd Christopher Jeaffreson (1769/70–*c.*1847), matric. Pembroke College, Cambridge (1788), BA (1792), MA (1799); ordained deacon (1792), priest (1793), Curate of Tunstall and Iken, near Woodbridge, Suffolk (1792), Vicar of Longborough, Glos. (1813–46). He had probably first met SW on a visit to London: SW had given music lessons to Jeaffreson's wife in late 1809 (see SW to his mother, 9 Dec. [1809] (Rylands, DDWF 15/15)), and had subsequently visited the family in Tunstall in Jan. and July 1811.   [5] i.e. to have accompanied SW on his visit to Tunstall.

[6] It is not known if SW made this visit. If he did, he would have needed to have returned to London by 30 Jan., when the Covent Garden oratorio season began.

To Vincent Novello   [Tottenham Court, 13 February 1813]¹

ALS, 1 p. (BL, Add. MS 11729, fo. 49)
Addressed To | M͏ʳ Novello | Oxford Street
Pmk 15 FE 1813

Saturday Evening

Dear N

I suppose you mean to eat Victuals somewhere or other on Monday next² as ever is to be, & if you were to do so with me I am much inclined to believe that they would not choak you in *particklers.*—I meditate to dine at 4 o'Clock without Wine or Women, but shall substitute Bread & Cheese & Punch in the Bargain for them; so you see what you have to depend upon.

N.B. If you are very good indeed, you may play the 104ᵗʰ Psalm³ after Dinner, & the Black Joke⁴ upon the Horgins.⁵

SW

P.S. Glenn will be with me: he is a sensible modest Man, Qualities very repugnant to your Feelings!

To Vincent Novello   [Tottenham Court], 17 February [1813]¹

ALS, 2 pp. (BL, Add. MS 11729, fo. 51)

Wednesday
17ᵗʰ of February

Dear N

I cannot exactly determine whether your Reason for non appearance on Monday² here ought to be regarded as a sufficient one, till I see you To-morrow Evening, when we are likely to have the Point argued in a true parliamentary Manner by our Friend Sam Webbe,³ who you know has been a celebrated Man in Matters

---

¹ The date is given by SW's 'Saturday evening' and the postmark.   ² 15 Feb.

³ Probably an arrangement of the tune 'Hanover', sung at this time to a metrical version of Ps. 104.

⁴ A popular Irish tune, also known as 'Black Joak' and 'Black Jock'. SW's reference may be to the set of piano variations on this theme by Clementi (1777) (*CPM*; Plantinga, 40–2).

⁵ i.e. on SW's house organ.

---

¹ The year is given by 17 Feb. falling on a Wednesday and the content.

² 15 Feb: the meeting discussed in the previous letter.   ³ Samuel Webbe II.

of political Discussion,[4] which in the Reign of Tom Paine[5] he carried so far, that he narrowly escaped, himself, from *being carried* into Quarters at least as uncomfortable as those of the Messieurs Hunt.[6]

The said Sam I thoroughly expect To-morrow (*Thursday*) at 6, & I mean to have all the dull & dolorous Ditties[7] ready for your Solace, as required: among them will be the Madrigal which lost the Prize, as I expected it would; for I could not prevail upon myself to scrawl absolute Nonsense, even for a silver Cup.[8] Gwilt[9] *will* have it printed for his own Fun, & Skarratt[10] is about it now: I think however it will not be *illegible* (from the Engraver's Defilement) in the MS. by Thursday: 'it must do as well as it can.'[11]—

There appeared in 'the Times' of the Monday after the Oratorio,[12] a Thing intended as a Critique, upon the Performances at both Houses;[13] in Virulence against *Handel & true* Music surpassing that of old Pope Pius in his Bull against Queen

---

[4] In his autobiography, the radical reformer and member of the London Corresponding Society Francis Place recorded that he regularly borrowed French books in 1797 and 1798 from one of his fellow members, a 'Mr Webbe', whom he identified as a musician (*The Autobiography of Francis Place*, ed. Mary Thale (Cambridge, 1972), 176, cited in Deborah Rohr, 'A Profession of Artisans: The Careers and Social Status of British Musicians, 1750–1850', Ph.D. diss., University of Pennsylvania, 1983, 356). On the question of the membership of the London Corresponding Society of Webbe and his father, see also Ann Beedell, *The Decline of the English Musician, 1788–1888* (Oxford, 1992), 61 and n. 90.

[5] Thomas Paine (1737–1809), English radical author. Between 1774 and 1787 he was in America, where he wrote a series of pamphlets encouraging opposition to English rule and advocating American independence. He returned to England via France, and in 1791 published the first part of his *The Rights of Man*, written in response to Burke's *Reflections on the Revolution in France*. The threat of arrest following the publication of the second part in 1792 caused him to flee to France. His 'reign' was presumably his time in England between 1787 and 1792 (*DNB*; *OCEL*).

[6] The brothers John (1775–1848) and Leigh Hunt (1784–1859), co-editors of the weekly newspaper *The Examiner*, who on 4 Feb. had been fined £500 each and sentenced to two years' imprisonment for a libel on the Prince Regent printed in the *Examiner* of 22 Mar. 1812. Leigh Hunt was a friend of the Novello family and a frequent visitor at Novello's house.

[7] Evidently a collection of glees and catches or the like.

[8] In Dec. 1811, to celebrate the seventieth anniversary of its foundation, the Madrigal Society offered a silver cup worth 10 guineas to the composer of the best madrigal 'in not less than four or more than six parts . . . after the manner of madrigals by Bennett, Wilbye, Morley, Ward, Weelkes, Marenzio and others' (*Grove*[3]). Entries were to be submitted by 24 May 1812, and the prize was eventually awarded in Jan. 1813 to William Beale's 'Awake, Sweet Morn'. SW's unsuccessful entry was 'O sing unto mie roundelaie' (MADSOC; *Harmonicon* 3 (1825), 134).   [9] Joseph Gwilt.

[10] The music engraver Robert Thomas Skarratt (Humphries and Smith).

[11] SW later identifies this as a favourite saying of A. F. C. Kollmann: see SW to Novello, 22 Feb. [1825].   [12] 1 Feb.

[13] There had been performances of *Messiah* at both Covent Garden and Drury Lane on 30 Jan., the anniversary of the execution of Charles I. SW took part in the Covent Garden performance, where he was also the soloist in one of his own organ concertos. The anonymous review in *The Times* contained a lengthy attack on Handel's music, and there was a further review on 6 Feb.

Elizabeth:[14]—I have had it copied out, & have lent it to Webbe, who was anxious to peruse it: I have determined to trim the Gentleman in the next Month's Magazine,[15] & you can hardly believe what funny Opportunities he affords of so doing.—

More of this & other Affairs To-morrow, till when I rests

Your Uncle Sarjent

SW

P.S. I have great Hopes that through the former Interest with Mr Essex[16] when he was only Mus. Bac. I can even now procure you his Assistance in his Doctorial Capacity, & that he will not refuse you Instruction concerning the Chord of the 7th upon the moderate Terms of a Guinea per Lesson.

To Vincent Novello [?Tottenham Court], 1 March [?1813][1]

ALS, 1 p. (BL, Add. MS 11729, fo. 52)

Dear N

If you can manage at such short Notice as this Time to the present Evening to look in upon me, I shall be very glad to see you.—I expect honest James Ball of Duke Street, & no-one else whom I know of, & shall give Orders that we be not interrupted by any Interloper whatever.

You have a Book into which you copied some of my Pot-Hooks & Hangers, & as the Originals are a little astray in different Corners of my Palace if you will tuck the said Book under your Arm, we may calculate how much Time you have submitted to sacrifice to the Whimsies of

Yours most truly

S Wesley

Monday March 1st

St Taffy's Day as it were[2]

---

[14] The Bull 'Regnans in excelsis', issued in 1570 by Pius V (1504–1572), which excommunicated Elizabeth I.

[15] It is not clear which magazine SW was referring to here, and no such article has been traced in monthly periodicals. Samuel Webbe II later wrote to Leigh Hunt enclosing a copy of the article in *The Times* and suggesting that Hunt might like to attack it and its author in the *Examiner*: see Webbe to Hunt, 4 Mar. 1813 (BL, Add. MS 38108, fo. 74).

[16] Timothy Essex (c.1765–1847), organist and choirmaster of St George's Chapel, Albemarle Street. He had been awarded an Oxford B. Mus. in 1806 and a D. Mus. in 1812 (Foster).

---

[1] During the period of SW's correspondence with Novello, 1 Mar. fell on a Monday in 1813, 1819, and 1824. This letter could have been written in any of these years, but 1813 is the most probable.

[2] St David's Day.

To Vincent Novello   [Tottenham Court], 30 March 1813

ALS, 1 p. (BL, Add. MS 11729, fo. 57)
Addressed To | Mr Novello

Dear N

You will readily give me Credit for the Regret I experienced in disappointing you Yesterday, particularly when you reflect upon the Cause.—The dear little Infant left *this blessed & happy* World last Night between 9 & 10 o'Clock—& I think that no-one in his Senses who has lived to *half* of either mine or your Age would wish her back again.[1]—

I was under the Necessity of giving up my Engagement with George Gwilt, at whose House[2] (in the Borough) I was to have dined, & should have requested you to accompany me, as I am well assured that you would have been at least as welcome a Guest as myself.—

So firm was my Intention of being at St Paul's, that I had transposed the three Fugues from D♯, G♯ & B♭ Minor into the more commodious Keys,[3] & there were Hopes of a favourable Crisis of the Disorder until Yesterday Morning, otherwise I would have apprized you in Time to have prevented your unsuccessful Call for

Your sincere friend

S Wesley

Monday[4] | 30 March. 1813

To Robert Glenn   Tottenham Court, 31 March [1813][1]

ALS, 1 p. (Duke).
Addressed To | Mr Glenn | Steward Street | (N. 4) | Bishopsgate | Paid | Wednesday
    Evening
Pmk 1 AP 1813

New Road 31st of March
Wednesday

---

[1] The first name of this daughter is not known. She was presumably the child whose impending birth is mentioned in SW to his mother, 12 Nov. [1812] (Fitzwilliam), where he states that his 'poor Companion is in absolute labour'.   [2] In Union Street, Blackfriars Road.

[3] SW's manuscript containing his transpositions of the Fugues in D sharp, G sharp, and B flat minor from Book II of the '48' into D minor, G minor, and B minor is at the RSCM.

[4] In fact, Tuesday. SW's reference in the following letter to the death of his daughter 'on Monday night' confirms that he had mistaken the day rather than the date.

---

[1] The year is given by the postmark.

My very good Friend

I am deeply concerned to inform you that I am unavoidably precluded from the Pleasure I fully purposed myself of joining the agreeable Society to-Morrow at your Friend Mr Savage's[2] House, in Consequence of a domestic Misfortune which occurred only on Monday Night last; the Death of my dear little Child, who you know was lately inoculated with the *small* Pox. (instead of the *Cow*, which latter I wished, but the Mother would have her Way)—Poor Sarah[3] is indeed very ill at present, & I feel it my Duty to remain with her as much as possible.—On Friday Evening[4] I *must* be at my Post,[5] of Course, & shall therefore hope you will call at 5 o'Clock here. I shall immediately write to Mr Savage, but yet I should wish you to let him know without Delay of this unfortunate Obstacle to my Gratification, lest any Accident may possibly delay the Receipt of my Letter as soon as I could wish it to arrive.—

God bless you, my kind Friend, & believe me always whether *in* or *out* of Affliction

Your most sincere and cordial

S Wesley

P.S. You may negotiate with Mr S. respecting another Day: should Matters at Home go on smoothly, I could probably wait upon him on some Day in the course of the next or the following Week.

Excuse this *Copy* Paper: it was the first that came to Hand, & I am desirous of expediting this.

To Vincent Novello   [Tottenham Court], 31 March 1813

ALS, 1 p. (BL, Add. MS 11729, fo. 59)

Dear N

Herewith is a Tune,[1] put together in Sorrow of Heart, consequently not in the merriest Style; but you will like it, & therefore I have made for you a Copy somewhat fair to look upon.

---

[2] Not certainly identified: perhaps William Savage, Printer to the Royal Institution and the addressee of SW's letters of 28 Feb. [1809] and 16 Mar. [1809].

[3] i.e. SW's partner Sarah Suter (1793/4–1864), here mentioned for the first time in these letters. For further details, see Biographical Introduction.   [4] 2 Apr.

[5] i.e. at the organ at the Covent Garden oratorio concert. The programme for this concert must have appeared particularly poignant: it included the 'Dead March' from Handel's *Saul*, in which SW played the obbligato organ movement, and the chorus 'When the ear heard her' from his *Funeral Anthem for Queen Caroline* (*The Times*, 2 Apr. 1813).

---

[1] SW's understandably gloomy four-part setting of 'Ecce panis angelorum', the autograph of which (BL, Add. MS 14340) is dated 31 Mar. 1813.

Should you be unengaged, & disposed to meet me at Major's, on Sunday[2] after the Vesper Hour (suppose 6 o'Clock) I could come, & whether he be at Home or out, we might have a little Chat, & a Touch upon his Piano: I mention *his* Place, because I cannot have any Music at Home at present: there has been Danger of a Brain Fever in the Mother of the little Infant.

Adieu till we meet, which I hope may be on Sunday.

Yours as usual

S Wesley

Wednesday Night March 31ˢᵗ 1813

To Vincent Novello   [Tottenham Court, 2 April 1813][1]

ALS, 1 p. (BL, Add. MS 11729, fo. 60)
Addressed To | Mʳ Novello | Oxford Street | 240 | Friday Evening
Pmk 3 AP 1813

Dear N

I guessed that my Ditty[2] would suit your Complaint in this here Quadragesimal[3] Time, & I really believe that I am obliged to my low Spirits for the Melody, but I am not in Haste to purchase another upon the like Conditions.

I know not whether I shall be able to see Mʳ Picart between now & Sunday,[4] but fear I cannot *To-morrow*, as I must go early to Turnham Green, & on Sunday Morning he is likely to be engaged in *his* Trade.

On Friday next (the concluding Oratorio)[5] I have nailed you down fast to assist me in your Arrangement of Sebastian's Symphony,[6] & I could wish you to attend the Rehearsal, which is most probably to take Place on the Friday Morning.—I mention this, because it is so likely for you to be *out* at the Performance; not that you or I can have any such Apprehension for the *Wind* Instruments, which you know are *always so correct*, that a Rehearsal is a kind of

---

² 4 Apr. Major lived in Carmarthen Street (see SW to Novello, 4 Jan. 1814).

¹ The date is given by SW's 'Friday 5 o'clock' at the end of the letter, his 'Friday evening' on the address portion, and the postmark bearing the following day's date.   ² The motet 'Ecce panis'.

³ i.e. Lenten.   ⁴ 4 Apr.

⁵ 9 Apr., the last Covent Garden oratorio concert of the season.

⁶ Novello's arrangement of Bach's 'St Anne' Prelude for organ duet and orchestra (see SW to Novello, 6 May [1812], n. 10), inaccurately described in *The Times* advertisement for this concert as 'a Fugue of Sebastian Bach's, arranged as a symphony for a full orchestra, interspersed with solos for two performers on the organ' (*The Times*, 9 Apr. 1813).

Affront to them: I shall nevertheless insist upon it, as a sine quâ non of bringing forward the Piece at all.

Yours ever truly
SW

Friday 5 o'Clock

To Vincent Novello [Tottenham Court], 14 [April 1813][1]

AL, 1 p. (BL, Add. MS 11729, fo. 87)
Addressed To | Mr Novello | 240 | Oxford Street

Wednesday
14th (Holy Week N.B.)

Sur,

I says as how that I owes you three Pints of Beer, three Pound Bank Notes,[2] & a Lamentation of Jeremias[3]—I knew a Man, who spelled it Jerry-my-A—e, which was indecorous, some says.—

Now as to the 3 Pints, I will pay them To-morrow Night, if you behaves your-self in a cocky-like Mander—& it will be the old Priest his Fault, if I do not give Tongue in **Aleph**, **Beth**, **Gimel**, **Zain**, & the rest of that French Lingo.[4]—

The three Pound like must stand over till after my *Benefit*,[5] by which as all the World witnesses, I always *lose*. **Viva la Musica!**

A pretty *Diaboliad* they made of Don Juan t'other Night, but Griffins may do any Thing, being non-descript Honey-Mills.[6]

---

[1] The month and year are given by SW's 'Holy Week' and the content.

[2] No doubt in payment for Novello's participation in the Covent Garden oratorio concert the previous Friday.

[3] i.e. a musical setting of parts of the verses of mourning of the prophet Jeremiah, sung in the Roman Catholic liturgy as lessons for the first Nocturn of Mattins on Maundy Thursday, Good Friday, and Holy Saturday (*Grove*[6]).

[4] The first letters of the Hebrew alphabet, prefixed to the individual verses of the Lamentations, and included in musical settings.   [5] SW's forthcoming concert at the Argyll Rooms on 4 May.

[6] This puzzling remark appears to allude to an otherwise unrecorded private concert performance of Mozart's *Don Giovanni*, one of several which are known to have preceded the London stage première at the King's Theatre on 12 Apr. 1817. One such was the benefit concert for George Eugene Griffin at the Hanover Square Rooms on 23 May 1809. SW's remark here implies that Griffin was also involved in this performance. For Griffin's activities in promoting Mozart's operas in London, see Rachel Cowgill, 'Mozart's Music in London, 1764–1829: Aspects of Reception and Canonicity' (Ph.D. diss., University of London, 2000), 175–88; see also A. H. King, 'Don Giovanni in London before 1817', *MT* 127 (1986), 487–93.

To Vincent Novello [Tottenham Court], 30 April [1813]¹

ALS, 1 p. (BL, Add. MS 11729, fo. 61)

Friday Morn^g
30th of April.

Dear N

Mr Glenn & myself were disappointed at your Nonappearance on Sunday last,² especially as you had manifested considerable *Empressement* for the Spectacle—however we concluded that the bad State of the Weather proved the Lion in the Way.³

I find that it would be very incommodious to perform the Piano Forte Trio;⁴ the Orchestra at the Argyll Rooms⁵ cannot contain three of these Instruments without extreme Inconvenience, especially since the Organ⁶ will occupy so much of the Space—there will be Plenty of P. F. without that Piece, as you may perceive by perusing the enclosed.⁷—

Bartleman⁸ prevents his Boy (King)⁹ from singing for me, or rather for Willm Linley, who much wished one of his Songs¹⁰ (a very good one) to be sung by him.—The Disappointment to me is none, as I did not want him for any Thing, any more than his very silly Master.

¹ The year is given by 30 Apr. falling on a Friday and the references to arrangements for SW's forth-coming concert at the Argyll Rooms (see n. 5).   ² 25 Apr. The nature of this event is not known.

³ Prov. 25: 34: 'The slothful man saith, there is a lion in the way: a lion is in the streets.'

⁴ i.e. at SW's concert on 4 May.

⁵ The concert rooms on the corner of Argyll Street and Oxford Street where SW's concert was to take place; the Philharmonic Society's concerts were also held there. The Argyll Rooms were demolished in 1818 to make way for the building of Regent Street and were replaced in 1820 by the New Argyll Rooms, a short distance away on the corner of Little Argyll Street and Regent Street (*Grove*¹; *Grove*⁶, under 'London', VI, 5 (iii); *Encyclopaedia of London*).

⁶ The preliminary announcement for the concert (*The Times*, 22 Apr. 1813) had promised that 'a capital organ will be erected expressly for the occasion'. A later advertisement (1 May, repeated 3 May) gave full details of the programme and performers and a more detailed description of the organ, which was by Flight and Robson and was to have a 'general swell throughout all the Stops, and Double Base Pedals'.

⁷ Presumably the draft programme or running order for the concert: not preserved. Included in the programme, according to the advertisements in *The Times*, was the first performance of a new piano concerto by SW (now lost), played by SW's pupil Charles Wilson.

⁸ The bass James Bartleman (1769–1821). He was a chorister at Westminster Abbey under Benjamin Cooke and made his début at Covent Garden as a boy treble on 24 Apr. 1784. His adult début was at the Concert of Ancient Music in 1788, and he sang at Covent Garden from 1791. In the same year he joined Harrison and Knyvett's Vocal Concerts. He was one of the leading basses of his day and frequently appeared in oratorio concerts and at the Academy of Ancient Music; he was also a founder member of the Glee Club and a member of the Concentores Sodales. He retired in 1818 (*DNB*; *Grove*³; Argent, 287).

⁹ A boy treble pupil of Bartleman's, no doubt the 'Master King' whose benefit concert took place at Willis's Rooms on 3 June. He may have been the son of the composer Matthew Peter King (Brown and Stratton).   ¹⁰ Not identified: evidently the canzonet mentioned in the following letter.

I am somewhat bothered to make up my instrumental Orchestra, Tuesday being an Opera Night:[11] howbeit there are who say that Opera on Tuesday there will be *none*.[12]—

Could I know this for certain To-morrow, I might yet go on Bowling Green.—

Y[rs] ever truly

SW

I will apprize you of the Rehearsal when I can get enow of People to make one up.

To Vincent Novello   [Tottenham Court, ?1 May 1813][1]

ALS, 1 p. (BL, Add. MS 11729, fo. 62)

Dear N

I should have liked to perform the Organ Duet, but the Organ which I am to have, although very excellent, has only one Rank of Keys, consequently we could not play the Andante, which is some of the best of the Fun, but which you remember has some Criss-Cross Work in it which cannot possibly be done without a 2[d] Clavier.[2]

We have both enough upon our Hands at this moment, Faith & Troth: I am however the worse off of the two by Reason of the Puzzlement I am in to make

---

[11] SW's concert clashed with an opera performance at the King's Theatre, and members of the opera orchestra were therefore unavailable to play for him. An undated letter to Glenn concerning the violinist Arthur Betts may also relate to SW's difficulties in recruiting players for this concert: see Appendix, Letter 8.

[12] An allusion to the troubled situation at the King's Theatre, where Catalani was in dispute with William Taylor about the non-payment of her salary. On Tuesday, 27 Apr. she was billed to appear in Ferrari's *L'Eroina di Raab*, a replacement for a previously advertised performance of *Le nozze di Figaro* which was postponed to Thursday, 29 Apr. At a late stage Pietro Carlo Guglielmi's *Due nozze e un sol marito* with Mrs Dickons was substituted, Catalani's refusal to sing being given as the reason. The promised performance of *Figaro* on 29 Apr. did not take place, and the advertisements for Pucitta's *La caccia d'Enrico IV* for Saturday 1 May announced that Catalani had 'withdrawn her services from this theatre'. Her non-appearance occasioned a riot, described in a lengthy report in *The Times* on 3 May as 'one of the most extraordinary disturbances, in all its circumstances, which we ever knew in a place of public entertainment'. In consequence, the advertised performance of *La caccia d'Enrico IV* at the King's Theatre on 4 May was cancelled. SW's remark suggests that the riot was not entirely unexpected (*The Times*; Fenner, 78).

---

[1] This letter, discussing arrangements for SW's concert 'next Tuesday', appears from its contents to post-date SW's letter to Novello of 30 Apr. The absence of any mention of the riot at the King's Theatre in the evening of 1 May suggests that it was written before then, or at any rate before news of the riot had reached SW.

[2] The slow movement of the Organ Duet includes some passages of hand-crossing between the players ('criss-cross work'), which make its performance on a single-manual instrument impossible.

out my Orchestra, on account of the Opera on Tuesday: I was led to a Persuasion that there would be no Difficulty in obtaining a good Band independently of the Opera People:—This however is quite otherwise, & I am obliged almost to do as the Gospel relates upon another Occasion, 'go forth into the Highways & Hedges & compel them to come in, *that my House may be filled.*'³—

Bartleman prevents his Boy from singing, in his usual obliging & Christian-like Style of Conduct. *I* have not the least Disappointment from it, therefore the Brute has failed in his Attempt to distress *me*, but *Linley* I know feels hurt, because he was to have sung a Canzonet of his, which is now consequently withdrawn.—

You will of Course *take a Hand* with me in the Symphony of Bach:⁴ I wish you would look in at Flight & Robsons,⁵ as I think you will like the Pedals, & your Concern being the Base, in that Piece, you will have the Opportunity of giving good Effect in that Quarter, or rather *Half.*

I would write more, willingly, but am very much in Actæon's Predicament; who you remember was torn in Pieces by his own Dogs:⁶ only mine is a worse Case, because his were not musical ones.

SW

To Benjamin Jacob   [Tottenham Court], 10 May 1813

ALS, 1 p. (RCM, MS 2130, fo. 46)
Addressed To | Mʳ Jacob | Charlotte Street | Black Friars Road

Dear Sir

I have the Pleasure to inform you that I have arranged a Plan with Birchall, which will enable me to bring out the 4ᵗʰ Number of the Preludes & Fugues¹ by the 1ˢᵗ of July next, & shall give a public Notice of it within a few Days hence.—

---

³ Luke 14: 23.

⁴ Novello's arrangement of the 'St Anne' Prelude, in which SW was evidently to take the *Primo* part and Novello the *Secondo* and the pedals.

⁵ The builders of the organ. Benjamin Flight (*c.*1767–1847) had set up in partnership with Joseph Robson (d. 1876) around 1800 in premises in Lisle Street, Leicester Square. By this time they were at 101 St Martin's Lane. The partnership continued until 1832 (*Grove*⁶).

⁶ According to Greek myth, the hunter Actaeon had chanced upon the goddess Diana as she bathed naked. To prevent him from relating what he had seen, she turned him into a stag, whereupon he was eaten by his own hounds. SW was most probably familiar with the version of the story in Ovid, *Metamorphoses*, 3. 128–252.

---

¹ The final part of the Wesley–Horn edition of the '48', consisting of the second half of Book II. No copy of the 'public notice' has been found. Inexplicably, an anonymous review of all four volumes of

Dear Sir

I have the Pleasure to inform You
that I have arranged a Plan with
Birchall, which will enable me to
bring out the 4th Number of the
Preludes & Fugues by the 1st of
July next, & shall give a public
Notice of it, within a few Days hence. —
The Subscribers in general have
been exceedingly remiss in their Ap=
=plications for their 3d Number, which
has been one Reason (& the chief one)
for the remaining Book being so long
delayed. — I was however always re=
=solved, ... at all Hazards, to per=
=form my Engagement in this Business
with the Public, which I would have
much sooner done, could I have coaxed
the Engravers into better Humour before.
With best Wishes to Mrs Jacob &
Family, I remain   Dear Sir

                        very truly Yours
Monday
10th of May.
                                    Wesley
1813.

Samuel Wesley to Benjamin Jacob, 10 May 1813. *By courtesy of the
Royal College of Music, London*

The Subscribers in general have been exceedingly remiss in their Applications for their 3^d Number,[2] which has been one Reason (& the chief one) for the remaining Book being so long delayed.—I was however always resolved, at all Hazards, to perform my Engagement in this Business with the Public, which I would have much sooner done, could I have coaxed the Engravers into better Humour before.

With best wishes to Mrs Jacob & Family, I remain
Dear Sir
Very truly yours,
    S. Wesley

Monday 10th of May 1813

To Robert Glenn   [Tottenham Court], 18 May [1813][1]

ALS, 1 p. (BL, Add. MS 35013, fo. 58)
Addressed To | Mr Glenn | N. 4 | Steward Street | Spitalfields

Tuesday Morning 18th of May

My dear Sir,
    Mr Novello & myself have appointed to meet *on Thursday*[2] at St Paul's Cathedral, in the Afternoon, & at the Commencement of the Service, after which we intend to rattle some of the old Boy's Fugues upon the Organ.—We hope you will come, & perhaps you would like to bring a Friend or two with you, *if you think there will be Room enough in the Church.*

Adieu till we meet, believing me
Ever truly yours
    S Wesley

the Wesley–Horn edition had appeared in *GM* for Jan. 1813, but SW's remarks here and a comment in his letter to Novello of 23 June 1813 put it beyond doubt that the final volume was not published until July.

[2] The third part of the Wesley–Horn edition of the '48', consisting of the first half of Book II, had been published late in 1811: see SW to Novello, 27 Sept. [1811], which discusses the correction of the proofs.

[1] The year is given by 18 May falling on a Tuesday and the discussion of the visit to St Paul's Cathedral on 20 May, also mentioned in the following letter.   [2] 20 May.

To Vincent Novello   [Tottenham Court], 26 May 1813

ALS, 1 p. (BL, Add. MS 11729, fo. 63)
Addressed To | Mr Novello | Oxford Street | N. 240 | Wednesday
Pmk 26 MY 1813

Dear N.

I find all the Papers that we took to St Paul's, right, excepting the Organ Duet, which, if not in your safe Keeping, I confess I shall be at a Loss where to search for:—however I consider this as the least valuable of the MSS. & shall not vex myself much in the Event of its being lost.—If you can make Time to send me a Line upon this momentous Point, soon after you obtain this, it will settle my Notions one Way or the other, which are rather *muddled* on the subject at this present Writing.

Webbe[1] was very indignant at our not apprizing him of the Meeting on Thursday last:[2] I had but little to say in Way of Apology: he has however invited me to come to him on *Saturday* next[3] at 7, for the Purpose of my learning my Lesson, that is to say, his Duet.[4]—I wish you would meet me there: we should walk a good Scrap of the Way homeward together.

Adieu—
Yours most truly
SW

26th of May | 1813. | Wednesday

To Vincent Novello   [Tottenham Court], 21 June [1813][1]

ALS, 2 pp. (Osborn, File 39.332)
Addressed To | Mr Novello | Oxford Street | N. 240 | Monday Afternoon
Pmk 1813

Dear N

I am concerned to report unto you a twofold Disappointment: first, that it is utterly impossible for me to meet you this Evening, inasmuch as the

---

[1] i.e. Samuel Webbe II.   [2] At St Paul's Cathedral on 20 May.
[3] i.e. 29 May. Webbe lived at 13 Howard Street, Strand, between Somerset House and the Temple (Philharmonic Society Foundation Book (Loan 48.1)).   [4] Not identified.

[1] The year is given by the postmark.

Song[2] *dont il est Question* is unluckily placed in a Position which would render me too late for the Philharmonic,[3] unless I were to leave the Gardens before its Performance, (which would defeat the only Purpose of my going to them) or if I were to be present at even the Beginning of *your* Concert, I must then arrive too late at Vauxhall[4] for the said Song.—therefore my Dilemma is compleat, you see.

The 2ᵈ Miscarriage is touching the Wednesday Meeting,[5] which I'm truly vexed to say cannot take Place: for I find so much to do previously to the Possibility of my leaving Town this Week, that I almost question whether I shall be able to quit the *Lovelies of London* until another Sunday shall have over-taken us.—I will however advertize you of my *Movements* which I am loth to own are not likely to be *musical* ones (Copyings excepted) until I get into the Country among the Minstrels.[6]

I believe you have made up your Mind to take Things quietly as they are, rather than fret & chafe because they are not as we could wish them: I know no other Receipt for avoiding Fevers & Suicide & such like Trifles.

I will get your 2 Chunes[7] done at all Adventures previously to my Peregrination, tho' I cannot at this Moment promise for the very Day on which they will be ready.

Yours as usual

SW

---

[2] As is clear from the following letter, a song to be performed by a female pupil of SW that evening at a concert at Vauxhall (see n. 4); the identity of neither the piece nor the pupil is known. The concert was advertised as a 'Grand Gala', to be attended by the Prince Regent and to include a firework display (*The Times*, 21 June 1813).

[3] i.e. the Philharmonic Society's concert. The Society, a group of professional musicians working in London who wanted 'a regular platform for serious, predominantly instrumental and orchestral music' (Ehrlich) had been founded in Feb. 1813 and had promoted eight concerts in its first season. Novello was one of the original members; the concert under discussion was the last of the season (Ehrlich, *First Philharmonic*, 2–6). For the early history of the Philharmonic Society, see also Foster, *Philharmonic*, 5–59; Elkin, 9–20.

[4] Vauxhall, in Lambeth, was one of the London pleasure gardens, where there were regular concerts during the summer months (*Grove⁶*, under 'London, 5'; J. G. Southworth, *Vauxhall Gardens: A Chapter in the Social History of England* (1941); Wroth, 286–326.

[5] Presumably on the coming Wednesday, 23 June.

[6] SW was preparing to go to Ipswich, where on 6–8 July he was to 'preside at the organ and pianoforte' at the festival organized by his friend Charles Hague; he set off on 25 June (see next letter). In his *Diary of a Lover of Literature*, Thomas Green recorded that on 27 June he went to the Tower Church in Ipswich with Charles Hague and SW, where SW extemporized for them for over an hour; on the following evening Green had dinner with SW, and gives an entertaining account of SW's conversation. SW recorded his experiences in Ipswich in his letters to Sarah Suter of 6 and 9 July (BL, Add. MS 35012, fos. 45 and 46); he returned to London on 11 July. His introduction to Ipswich may have come about through Hague, or through his friend Jeaffreson. For a report of the festival and of SW's performances, see *Suffolk Chronicle* and *Ipswich Journal*, 10 July 1813.

[7] i.e. tunes. Not identified: SW enclosed them with his next letter to Novello.

P.S. I have had an unpleasant Piece of News To-Day, my Mother has had the Touch of a Complaint which we fear is of the Paralytic Kind: what renders it more likely is that she is nearly 86 Years old.[8]

Monday 21 June

To Vincent Novello [Tottenham Court], 23 June 1813

ALS, 2 pp. (BL, Add. MS 11729, fo. 64)
Addressed To | Mr Novello | Oxford Street | 240
Pmk 24 JU 1813

Dear N.

Herein are the Tunes required, written at a Mail Coach Pace, & therefore very probably containing some Inaccuracies: these however you can examine, & substitute what shall be the right Thing whenever the wrong may happen to occur.—

My Girl was very well received at Vauxhall: encored, & so on; & the Manager[1] seemed pleased: if he only *please* to engage her, we shall all be pleased.—I doubt however if this will take place during the present Season, as there seem Singers enow without her.—

Jemmy Hook[2] to whom I had the Impudence to introduce myself, & to whom I never before spake in my Life, surprized me not a little by his extreme Courtesy, & still more by informing me that he had just published a Voluntary at Bland & Weller's,[3] inscribed to my own Honor's Worship & Glory.—Of course, I was very reconnoissant: he desired me to take up *any* Number of Copies I might be disposed for: I have taken three, & have given one to little Joey[4]—I assure you that the Stuff is none of the worst, & the Fugue much more in the Shape of one than

---

[8] In fact, she was nearly 87.

[1] George Rogers Barrett (Wroth, 316).

[2] James Hook (1746–1827), pianist, organist, teacher, and composer. He moved to London from his native Norwich around 1763–4 and rapidly established a reputation as a piano teacher and as a composer of 'light, attractive entertainment music'. He was appointed organist and composer at Marylebone Gardens around 1768–9, and held the same appointment at Vauxhall from 1774 to 1820 (*Grove*[6]).

[3] Piano makers, music sellers, and publishers, with premises at 23 Oxford Street. No voluntary by Hook dedicated to SW and published by them has been traced, although one answering SW's description was published by C. Wheatstone. This may well have been the piece in question, subsequently sold to Wheatstone and republished with a new title page. For a modern edition, see Robin Langley (ed.), *English Organ Music: An Anthology from Four Centuries in Ten Volumes*, vol. 6: *From John Keeble to Samuel Wesley* (Sevenoaks, 1988), 15–20.   [4] i.e. Joseph Major.

any Thing I ever yet heard Crotch do upon the Organ.—Hook's Præludium at the Opening of the Acts was also exceedingly good: in thorough Organ Style, & with knowing Modulation.—I was never more agreeably surprized altogether.

I intend to start hence on Friday,[5] by 5 of the Clock in the Morning.—therefore if you have any Inclination to see me once more before John Ketch Esquire[6] does me & my Country Justice, your better Way will be to look in here, at the condemned Hold in the course of To-morrow Evening.—

I will also shew you the Woluntary, & should like to have your candid Opinion thereof & thereon.

Yours as usual

SW

P.S. Birchall's People promise to send the Bach Proofs[7] to you, but nevertheless have the Charity to jog some of their heavy-arsed Memories.

Wednesday. 23[d] of June 1813

To Vincent Novello   [Tottenham Court], 18 August [1813][1]

ALS, 1 p. (BL, Add. MS 11729, fo. 68)
Addressed To | M[r] Novello. | Oxford Street. | N. 240
Pmk 7 o'Clock 18 AU 1813

Aug[t] 18th

Dear N.

I shall expect you, selon votre Promesse (you loves French like, you does) next Saturday[2] as ever is to be & as near unto the Hour of 7 after Mid-Day as the Fates & Gods, or whatever other Commodities of that Sort exist, will permit. I shall endeavour to coax Bridgtower to bring forward his 'Catguts & Horsehair,' & scrape us out one of the old Humbug's Country Dances.[3] I think this will not be negatived by any shew of Hands.

---

[5] 25 June.   [6] The hangman.
[7] i.e. the fourth and final part of the Wesley–Horn edition of the '48'.

---

[1] The year is given by the postmark.   [2] 21 Aug.
[3] An ironic reference to one of J. S. Bach's Partitas for solo violin, which are in the form of dance suites: see next letter.

Mr Webbe Senr has been very earnest for my Intercession with you to procure, if possible, a Deputy for his Sardinian Organ:[4] he states, that the Salary is certainly very inconsiderable, only £10, or Guineas, per Annum.—I gave him my Word that I would report his Request, & ventured to add that I doubted not your Promptitude to make diligent & early Enquiry about it.—

I intend to ask Sam Webbe[5] to come on Saturday, & you will then have an Opportunity of confabulating a little *sur le Sujet*—(entendez-vous, mon Ami?). What a Flat[6] you must be for not loving French Musick, when the Language itself is such divine Melody!—

So, Cocky Wellington[7] has been sarving it out to 'em again.[8] Frenchmen are not fond of the Bayonet, which is very extraordinary you will say.—Of an *Irishman* I have heard it observed that nothing puts him sooner into a bad Humour than running a red hot Poker into his——

    SW

Bring a Stave or two of y^r own on Saturday, Dottore Vincenzo

To Vincent Novello   [Tottenham Court], 3 September 1813

ALS, 1 p. (BL, Add. MS 11729, fo. 70)
Addressed To Mr Novello

Dear N

On Tuesday next[1] Friend Webbe & I mean to commit our Carcases to the Mercy of the Winds & Waves,[2] & I want to know whether you be minded to realize the Intention you hinted, of accompanying us?—I am also about to admonish you

---

[4] The Roman Catholic chapel in Duke Street (now Sardinia Street), Lincoln's Inn Fields. This remark suggests that Samuel Webbe I was still nominally in post as organist, although by this time he was in poor health and housebound, and that his duties were undertaken by one or more deputies. Formerly the chapel of the Sardinian Embassy, it was now a public place of worship, but it remained under the patronage of the King of Sardinia and was still known as the 'Sardinian Chapel'.

[5] i.e. Samuel Webbe II.   [6] 'A person easily taken in . . . a duffer, simpleton' (*OED*).

[7] Arthur Wellesley (1769–1852), later 1st Duke of Wellington, Commander-in-Chief of the British forces in the Peninsular War.

[8] A reference to the report by Wellington and others of the Siege of St Sebastian of 21–7 July, published in the *Gazette Extraordinary* for 16 Aug. and reprinted the following day in *The Times*. SW's comment is heavily ironic: this was not a successful operation, and allied losses were heavy.

---

[1] 7 Sept.

[2] SW and Webbe were evidently about to set off on a journey by river, probably to Margate and Ramsgate. Nothing is known about this visit.

of your kind Promise to lend me a helping Hand & Ear at Paddington during my Days of Banishment, which are not likely to exceed 10 at the most, I think.— There are but eight young Yahoos to drill there, & therefore the Job will not be intolerably laborious, & I guess that *three Times* will be the utmost Extent of necessary Attendance.—*Thursday* next will be the first, requisite, & Monday is the other Day.

If your Hawgin plays again now, it is likely that my long Snout may insinuate itself into your Cock Loft on Sunday[3] at 11.—If *otherwise*, let me know, that we may make some other Arrangement for meeting.

Yours truly
  S Wesley

Friday Sept' 3 1813

To Robert Glenn   Gower Place,[1] [10 October 1813][2]

ALS, 1 p. (Emory, Box 6)
Addressed To | M' Glenn | Steward Street | Spitalfields | N° 4
Pmk 12 o'Clock 11 OC 1813

Sunday Evening

My dear Sir,

I have been very much longing for a Call from you, & began to be anxious lest Illness should have been the Cause of your Absence, when I was informed by my Brother that you & he dined together very lately at M' Sykes's[3] in the City, of which if I had had any Notice & M' S. had favoured me with a Line to meet you, I should have felt particularly gratified in joining the Party, which I understand was an extremely *jocund* one.—Pray let me see you soon, as I have much to say to you on divers Points, & wish to communicate some of my intended Operations for the ensuing Season.—Besides, I want you to see my new Habitation, more pleasant, more neat, & more cheap than the dark Hole in Tottenham Court: it is

---

[3] 5 Sept.

[1] As SW states in this letter, he had recently moved the short distance from Tottenham Court to 5 Gower Place, Euston Square. This is the first letter to bear the new address. He was to live here until 1818 or 1819, when he moved to Euston Street (now Melton Street), Euston Square.

[2] The date is given by SW's 'Sunday evening' and the following day's postmark.

[3] Not identified.

N. 5 Gower Place, Euston Square, very near the same Side of the New Road as the former House.—

I am ever
My dear Sir,
Your obliged & faithful
    S Wesley

To the Governors of the
Foundling Hospital

Gower Place,
8 November [1813]¹

ALS, 1 p. (Foundling Hospital, A/FH/A06/001/071/19/1)
Docketed 1813 Mʳ Wesley

My Lords and Gentlemen!

Having this day been informed that the Place of Organist at the Foundling Chapel is just now become vacant by the Death of the late & worthy Mʳ William Russell,² I most respectfully beg Leave to offer my Services in the said Department, & should I be so fortunate as to obtain your Approbation, Patronage & Support, it will be my earnest & constant Endeavour to merit the Honour conferred on

My Lords and Gentlemen
Your very obedient
& very devoted humble Servant
    S. Wesley

5. Gower Place | Euston Square | Monday 8ᵗʰ of Novʳ

¹ The year is given by SW's reference to the death of William Russell, and the organist's post at the Foundling Hospital.

² William Russell (1777–1813) was the son of the London organ builder Hugh Russell and a pupil of John Groombridge and Samuel Arnold. From 1800 to 1804 he was pianist and composer at Sadler's Wells Theatre and composed around twenty pantomimes; from 1801 he was the accompanist to John Braham, Nancy Storace, and Elizabeth Billington at Covent Garden. He held various organists' appointments. He was appointed organist to the Foundling Hospital Chapel on 1 Apr. 1801, following the dismissal of John Immyns. SW was misinformed about Russell's demise; although his death was imminently expected at the time of this letter, he did not in fact die until 21 Nov. (*Grove*⁶; Gillian Ward Russell, 'William Russell 1777–1813: An Enquiry into his Musical Style', 4 vols., Ph.D. diss., University of Leicester, 1994).

To [?Robert Glenn][1]   [Gower Place], 9 November [1813][2]

ALS, 1 p. (Rylands, DDWF 15/17A) Mounted

Editor's note This letter is firmly mounted on a card, and the verso is inaccessible. On the reverse of the card are mounted two fragments, one of which reads 'Mr Saml Wesley | Candidate as Organist | to | Camden Chapel', the other 'S. Wesley | Euston Street | Euston Square'. Both are from a later date and are unconnected with this letter.

My dear Friend[3]

Will you take a Beef Steak with me To-morrow at 2 o'Clock, & afterwards saunter on to Deptford?[4] Pray do.—at all events dine with me.

I have started for the *Foundling*, & am told that I have no bad Chance.— However, nothing *now* disappoints

Yours sincerely

S Wesley

Tuesday | 9th of Nov^r

To Christopher Idle[1]   Gower Place, [*c.*10 November 1813]

Printed canvas letter, 1 p., with autograph salutation and signature and note of recommendation from William Kitchiner (Rylands, DDWF 15/17B).[2]

Addressed (in hand of William Kitchiner)[3] Christopher Idle Esqr | Adelphi Terrace

---

[1] The conjecture of Robert Glenn as the addressee of this letter is strengthened by SW's intimate form of salutation (see n. 3). Another possibility is William Kitchiner: the letter is preserved with SW's printed canvas form for the organist's position at the Foundling Hospital (see next letter), bearing Kitchiner's note of support and the following day's date.

[2] The year is given by 9 Nov. falling on a Tuesday and SW's discussion of his candidacy for the post of organist at the Foundling Hospital.

[3] SW's first letters to Glenn address him as 'dear Sir'; by this time, SW had moved to 'my dear Sir', and 'my dear Friend'.

[4] Possibly to the parish church of St Paul, where John Nightingale (see SW to Glenn, 25 Nov. [1813], n. 3) was organist.

---

[1] A governor of the Foundling Hospital, appointed 1 Jan. 1800 (Nichols and Wray, 390).

[2] Kitchiner added: 'Dear Sir, Allow me to recommend to your patronage my old friend Saml Wesley who is a worthy man, and an incomparable Organist.'

[3] William Kitchiner, MD (1775–1827), a wealthy man of science, inventor, musician, epicure, and eccentric, who wrote on optics, music, and cookery. He was famed for his dinner parties, the guests at which included Sir Joseph Banks, John Braham, George Colman the Younger, William Jerdan, Charles Kemble, Charles Mathews, Sir John Soane, and the Prince Regent; his most celebrated cookery book was *The Cook's Oracle* (1817). Doubts have recently been cast on the accuracy of the account in *DNB* of his education at Eton and his medical degree from Glasgow (*DNB*; Tom Bridge and Colin Cooper English, *Dr William Kitchiner: Regency Eccentric* (Lewes, 1992)). According to Lightwood, 92, Kitchiner had also supported SW's candidacy for the Foundling Hospital position in 1798.

1813

Sir

Understanding that the place of Organist to the Foundling Hospital is now become vacant by the death of MR WILLIAM RUSSELL, I very respectfully beg leave to offer my services for the same situation, and should I be so fortunate as to obtain your approbation, it will be my study to merit the honour conferred on

Sir
Your very obedient
And devoted Servant
    S Wesley

No. 5 Gower-place | Euston-square

To Vincent Novello   [Gower Place, *c*.10 November 1813]¹

AL, 1 p. (BL, Add. MS 11729, fo. 77)
Addressed To | Mʳ Novello | By Favour of the Autograph

Dear N.

You will give me Credit (I think) for not intentionally bothering *any* Body, & hardly suspect me of intentionally teazing *you*; but being pretty well aware of your hostile Disposition to Doctor Samuel Weasel-Eye, therefore I presumes like, upon your Remembrance of your Word given to the said outlandish unaccountable excommunicable omnium-gatherum Son of the Whore of Babylon's great great Grandson, that you will not be *over slack* upon the Business relative to the *Bottom* of a certain printed Paper, very generally circulated in Times like the Present.²— I have no other particular Reason for pressing the *Motion*, than that the Point gained would prove a knock-down Blow to a few malicious Opponents who (by the way) are likely to be worsted either with or *without* Privilege.

If any Objection remain, I am sure that you will candidly state it to me.

[sic]

---

¹ SW's Gower Place address indicates a date of between around Oct. 1812 and 1818–19 for this letter. The conjectural dating here assumes that SW's request related to his 1813 application for the post of organist at the Foundling Hospital.

² i.e. a canvas letter, identical to the one endorsed by Kitchiner, for the Foundling Hospital appointment. SW presumably enclosed it with this letter or had previously given it to Novello, and here asks him to add his personal recommendation.

³ The opening of the Tonus Peregrinus, the psalm tone used exclusively for the Vesper psalm 'In exitu Israel' (Ps. 114).

Ask Jack C—[4] to put a Base to this, or to read the Treble, which is Tenor, which is Counter Tenor, which is Base, which is **Gregorian**.

To Samuel Compton Cox[1]   Gower Place, 24 November 1813

AL, third person, 1 p. (Foundling Hospital, A/FH/MO1/001/104)
Addressed To | Samuel Compton Cox Esq[re]
Endorsed 1813 M[r] Sam[l] Wesley

M[r] Samuel Wesley presents his Respects to M[r] Cox, desiring to observe, that if there be no present existing Objection, he would very willingly undertake the Organ Duty at the Foundling Chapel, *on Tuesday next*,[2] either in the Morning, or Evening, or both, if more agreeable.—

Should this Offer be acceptable, & if any previous Rehearsal with the vocal Performers be required, M[r] W. will readily attend for that Purpose, at any Hour on Saturday most convenient for M[r] Cox to appoint.

5. Gower Place. Euston Square | Wednesday 24th of Nov[r] 1813

To Robert Glenn   Gower Place, 25 November [1813][1]

ALS, 1 p. (BL, Add. MS 35013, fo. 59)
Addressed To | M[r] Glenn | Steward Street | Spitalfields | N. 4 | Paid | Thursday Night.

My dear Friend,
You are long ere now informed of poor Russell's Dissolution. Of Course I can now exert my Interest without any just Charge of supplanting or forestalling: I have not been inactive since the News transpired, & have seen M[r] Treasurer Cox, who spoke very *darkly & cautiously*, but whom I think to be in the Interest of another Candidate.—I offered my Services to the Duty at the Foundling next Sunday,[2] which was declined, it being *asserted* that Nightingale[3] (who had been so long Russell's Deputy) is to perform it on that Day: Now the Drummers[4] tell

---

[4] Not identified.

[1] Samuel Compton Cox, a prominent lawyer. He was a governor of the Foundling Hospital from 1798, Vice-President 1805–6, and Treasurer 1806–39 (Nichols and Wray, 314–15).

[2] 30 Nov., the feast of St Andrew.

[1] The year is given by 25 Nov. falling on a Thursday and SW's Gower Place address.

[2] 28 Nov.   [3] John Charles Nightingale (1790–1833) (Dawe; Matthews).

me they know he will be at his Deptford Church[5] on Sunday next; so that there is some Chicanery afloat already.[6]—

I saw, & spoke with the Duke of Sussex[7] yesterday Evening, at the Grand Lodge, who said 'I will certainly do what I *can* for you.'—(meaning in Regard to the Election.)—If he be sincere, I may have a good Chance.—At all events I shall not fret, however the Matter goes: I know by long Experience that I can bear Disappointment with a much better Grace than Buonaparte.[8]

Let me hear from you soon, or rather *see* You. On Saturday Evening I will be sure to be at Home.

Yours faithfully

S Wesley

5. Gower Place | Thursday Ev^g 25 Nov^r

To Vincent Novello   Gower Place, [23 December 1813][1]

ALS, 1 p. (BL, Add. MS 11729, fo. 75)
Addressed To | Mr Novello | Oxford Street | 240 | Paid | Thursday Ev^g
Pmk 24 DE 1813

Thursday Ev^g
Gower Place
Euston Square

My dear N

I know your Readiness to adopt the Gospel Advice of lifting 'an Ass out of a Pit,'[2] whether on a Sabbath or a Xtmas day.—I am in considerable Distress at the Moment for want of Time to complete a new MS. which *must* appear from the Mouths of sundry Musicians *next Monday*,[3] which is the Day of the solemn

---

[4] William Drummer and his wife Lucy were personal friends of Russell and his wife Mary Ann. They were witnesses at the Russells' wedding, and after Russell's death William Drummer helped Mary Ann Russell to sort out her late husband's affairs.

[5] Nightingale had been appointed organist at St Paul's, Deptford, in Dec. 1812.

[6] Nightingale was evidently the favoured candidate to succeed Russell. He was appointed on 9 Dec., and remained in post until 1833.

[7] Augustus Frederick, Duke of Sussex (1773–1843), sixth son of George III. He was a patron of the arts, amateur musician, and leading Freemason, who as Grand Master of England had created SW Grand Organist on 13 May 1812.

[8] A reference to Bonaparte's reverses in the final stages of the Napoleonic Wars following his defeat at the Battle of the Nations on 16–19 Oct.

---

[1] The date is given by SW's 'Thursday evening' and the postmark.   [2] Matt. 12: 11; Luke 14: 5.

Meeting of Reconciliation between the antient & modern Free Masons,[4] & for which, I have, by the Command of the R. W. M.[5] the Duke of Sussex[6] *half* composed an Anthem:[7] but it will be impossible for me to finish the Chorus Parts without the charitable Assistance of some kind Christian or Jew, (for I am not particular as to the Preference excepting where the *Transcript* is concerned).—Can you help me?—I could get 20 good natured *Blockheads* to scribble for me, but that Cock won't fight you know.—I will come to high Mass on Saturday,[8] but yet wish you to give me an instant Line that I may stir my Stumps accordingly.—

Yours as ever

SW

The Foundling goes on rather in Favour of the long-nosed Man.[9]

To Vincent Novello [Gower Place, 26 December 1813][1]

ALS, 1 p. (BL, Add. MS 11729, fo. 76)
Addressed To | Mr Novello | N. 240

Dear N.

The Bearer will convey the MS.[2] safely. I have been such a Fool as to omit writing out any 2^d Tenor, so I have all that Job to do as soon as I get hold of the Score.—

I know not yet how or where a Rehearsal is to take Place.—I am now just going to Perry[3] to make *some* Arrangement—if it be *possible*, I will apprize you of what is settled, but the Time runs so very short that I almost doubt being able to send you the Result.—I have however already endeavoured to get the Rehearsal either between 1

---

³ 27 Dec.

⁴ The Union of the two Grand Lodges of England, which took place at Freemasons' Hall and the Crown and Anchor Tavern. For a lengthy report of the ceremony, see *EM* 65 (1814), 6–12, 49–52.

⁵ Right Worshipful Master.

⁶ The Duke of Sussex had succeeded his brother George as Right Worshipful Master when George had become Prince Regent in 1811.

⁷ A setting, not preserved, of 'Behold, how good a thing it is', a metrical adaptation of Ps. 133, and a text of particular masonic significance. The words are included in the *EM* account, which also gives the names of the performers. ⁸ On Christmas Day.

⁹ Unidentified: a puzzling remark, as the Foundling Hospital appointment had been made on 9 Dec.

¹ The date is given by SW's 'Sunday morning Festum Sancti Stephani' (see n. 4) and by the further discussion of arrangements for the copying and rehearsal of his anthem.

² Of SW's anthem 'Behold, how good a thing it is'.

³ A masonic official involved with the organization of the music of the event; his name is included in the *EM* account as having written (i.e. copied) the vocal parts.

& 3, or *after* 5, on your Account, so that my *Will* is good, if my Power be restrained.

Yours ever truly,

SW

Sunday morning | Festum Sancti Stephani[4]

To Vincent Novello [Gower Place], 4 January 1814

ALS, 1 p. (BL, Add. MS 11729, fo. 79)

Tuesday M^g
4. Jany 1814

Dear N.

I am sorry we did not better understand each other about the Meeting at Major's.—I was prevented from calling before Dinner upon him, by a new Scholar who detained me in *Jaw* for an extra half Hour: you said you would certainly *wait* for me in the Evening, & I speeded towards you as soon as it was possible.—Pokey[1] dined with me, & was obliged to be off soon after 5: we went away together, & I throughly reckened (I can't spell) reckoned upon finding you in Carmarthen Street,[2] & brought Bach's Mottets[3] & my MS. Book[4] on the Strength of this 'sure & certain Hope.'[5]—

As it is, '*it must do as well as it can.*'—

This used to be one of your Leisure Evenings: will you come & take a Quartern[6] of Gin with old rubicond-faced Sam?—Perhaps you are not aware that I am cruelly in the Dumps at having missed the *Certainty* of being kicked & cuffed about by the worthy Governors of the Sunday Bawdy House![7]—I met Immyns[8] to-Day, & we had Fun alive.—He congratulated me on my *Escape*, telling me

---

[4] The Feast of St Stephen (26 Dec.).

[1] Not identified. From subsequent references it is apparent that he was a keyboard player.

[2] i.e. at Major's house.

[3] No doubt the edition published by Breitkopf in 1803: it contained 'Singet den Herrn ein neues Lied', BWV 225, 'Der Geist hilft unsrer Schwachheit auf', BWV 226, 'Jesu, meine Freude', BWV 227, 'Fürchte dich nicht', BWV 228, and 'Komm, Jesu, komm!', BWV 229.

[4] Not identified: possibly the 'green book' mentioned in SW to Novello, 14 Sept. [1814], which was presumably the same volume as the 'green fat book' of SW to Novello, 11 Dec. [1816].

[5] BCP, Burial Service.   [6] A pint.   [7] i.e. the Foundling Hospital.

[8] John Immyns (1764–*post* 1818) had himself been organist of the Foundling Hospital. He had been appointed in 1798 (see SW to Seward, 16 June 1798, nn. 2 and 3). He was dismissed in Mar. 1801 following complaints about his unpunctuality and slovenly dress; he was succeeded by Russell. He continued to deputize for Russell on occasion, and therefore had first-hand experience of conditions at the chapel (Nichols and Wray, 222).

that I should not have been a Fortnight in the Situation without spitting in Mʳ Treasurer Cox's Face.

Pray come this Evening: I shall be sure to be at Home, & have much to say to you: some perhaps not uninteresting.

Yʳˢ ever (in *Masonic* Fidelity)

 SW

To George Polgreen Bridgetower

Gower Place,
24 January [1814][1]

ALS, 1 p. (BL, Add. MS 56411, fo. 12)
Addressed To | Mʳ Bridgtower | Chapel Street | Grosvenor Place | N. 20 | Monday
 Morning

Gower Place.
Euston Square.
Monday 24ᵗʰ Janʸ

Dear Sir,

I saw my Friend Linley on Monday last,[2] who will be happy to join the Party on Thursday[3] *if* possible: the **If** (not always a 'Peacemaker' maugre Sir John Falstaff)[4] is in Consequence of a Dinner on his Birth Day, which happens to fall on this very approaching Thursday,[5] but he yet hopes to break the Bands of Ceremony & mix afterward in *our* little *Band*, which I know he infinitely prefers.

I apprized him of your Intention to call on him, & he speaks of you as quite an old Acquaintance with whom he should hope that no Formalities would be deemed requisite.—

Novello I saw yesterday, & who will make a Point of attending.—I believe that the Death of his Wife & Children would hardly prove an Obstacle.—He is really the most compleatly φιλομους[6] among my professional Friends, tho' I think I must add yourself as equally so.

Believe me Dear Sir,
very sincerely Yʳˢ

 S Wesley

---

[1] The year is given by 24 Jan. falling on a Monday and SW's Gower Place address. [2] 17 Jan.
[3] 27 Jan. As the following letter makes clear, it was to be at Bridgetower's house.
[4] In fact Touchstone, in *As You Like It*, v. iv. 100. [5] Linley was born in 1771.
[6] 'Music-loving'.

To Vincent Novello [Tottenham Court, 28 January 1814]¹

ALS, 1 p. (BL, Add. MS 11729, fo. 69)

Dear N

I fear that something serious has been the Cause of your failing us last Evening: I therefore hasten to be informed thereof:—Bridgtower was apprehensive that you required a more explicit Invitation, but I felt so confident of the Contrary that I was every Moment expecting your Approach at N. 20 Chapel Street Grosvenor Place,² from 7 o'Clock till 10.—We had a luxurious Treat of Harmony.—Among the Tunes were a Trio of Mozart, two of Purcell, one of S. Bach, another arranged from the 1ˢᵗ Prelude & Fugue of the 2ᵈ Book (or *my* 3ᵈ)³—the Ciacone, & the Fugue in C from the Solos⁴

& *so on*. All these Pieces were admirably given by our Host, & indeed the whole was the most classical Affair in the Crotchet & Quaver Line that I have witnessed for a long Period.—

If *any* Thing could be termed a Desideratum it was either Beethoven's pastoral Symphony⁵ or Webbe's 'Cantantibus Organis'⁶—

Yours as ever
(& in some Anxiety)
    S Wesley

---

¹ The date is given by the reference to Bridgetower's party on the previous evening, 27 Jan., arrangement for which were discussed in the preceding letter. Novello's non-attendance is further discussed in the following letter. ² Bridgetower's house.

³ i.e. the Prelude and Fugue in C, from Book II of the '48'.

⁴ i.e. from the Sonatas and Partitas for solo violin, BWV 1001–6: the Chaconne is the final movement of Partita II, BWV 1004; the Fugue is the second movement of Sonata III, BWV 1005.

⁵ The first attested English performance of Beethoven's Symphony No. 6 (1808) was at Mrs Vaughan's benefit on 27 May 1811, but it may have been performed earlier at one of the concerts of the Harmonic, a concert-giving organization founded by City merchants around 1800 which died out some time before 1813, and which gave concerts at the London Tavern (Nicholas Temperley, 'Beethoven in London Concert Life, 1800–1850', *MR* 21 (1960), 207–14).

⁶ By Samuel Webbe I, published in his *A Collection of Motetts or Antiphons* (1792).

To Vincent Novello   [Gower Place], 31 January [1814][1]

ALS, 1 p. (BL, Add. MS 11729, fo. 80)
Addressed To | Mr Novello | N. 240 | Oxford Street

Monday Morn^g
Jany 31.

Dear N

You were so good as to say (some Weeks ago) that you had still the Privilege of a Nomination for a Subscriber to the Philharmonic Society this Year.[2]—The Lady[3] who was so anxious to obtain one has been successful for herself through the Means of Attwood, but is still extremely desirous (if there be a Possibility) of getting one for her eldest Daughter.—I told her of your obliging Offer to me, & promised to use my Interest with you sur le Sujet.—If she be not too late (for I believe this is the closing Day of Subscription) pray favour me with the Message I am to convey to her.—I fear that she ought to have applied to me sooner in this second Instance.—I told her I expected to meet you on Thursday last,[4] & she was sadly vexed to find that I was disappointed, when I informed her thereof on Saturday last.[5]

Yours very truly
(in Haste)
S Wesley

To Vincent Novello   [Gower Place, 4 February 1814][1]

ALS, 2 pp. (BL, Add. MS 11729, fo. 81)
Addressed To | Mr Novello | Oxford Street | N. 240
Pmk 5 FE 1814

Friday Night

---

[1] The year is given by 31 Jan. falling on a Monday and SW's discussion of a subscription to the Philharmonic Society concerts, also mentioned in the following letter.

[2] From the start, the Philharmonic Society aimed at social exclusivity, and restricted the number of its subscribers. As full members, Novello and Attwood had the privilege of nominating subscribers; SW, who was at this stage only an associate member, did not. The first concert of the new season was to be on 14 Feb. (Ehrlich, *First Philharmonic*, 13–14; Foster, *Philharmonic*, 13).

[3] Mrs Tyndale: see next letter.   [4] 27 Jan., the evening of Bridgetower's party.

[5] 29 Jan.

---

[1] The date is given by SW's 'Friday night' and the postmark.

Dear N

From the Threat in your last I fully expected to have seen you this very Evening. —On Sunday[2] three of my Friends, the Drummers & M[r] Street are to pass the Day with me here, & we purpose to besiege your holy Citadel[3] at 11 o'Clock on the same Forenoon.—They would be much gratified in hearing the 1st Mass of Haydn in B,[4] I am very certain, & perhaps you will so order it, if so be as how that the *Concavities* will unite with the *Convexities*[5] in the Choir that Morning—Vous m'entendez bien.—

I have done a good Piece of your Missa Defunctorum.[6]—I wish you could dine with us on Sunday, but can hardly expect it, as we dine between 3 & 4.[7]—Perhaps also it is Gwilt's Day for 'hallooing & singing of Anthems.'[8]—Otherwise you may surely manage to come in the Evening. You will find the right People & some of the right Stuff in Matter of *Breve* if not of *Breviary*.

Y[rs] as usual

S Wesley

Turn over the book Mister.

P.S. Mrs Tyndale[9] (that is *her* Name) is quite bursten-bellied with Thanks for your having managed to squeeze one of her Progeny among the Phils.—She is a Sort of a blue-Stocking Worthy (in the ABC line) & much about the Size of a moderate Grampus; if you ever saw such a Christian animal: but she knows Music *like any Thing*, I promise you, & is not to be taken in by Pleyel[10] or Reeve,[11] or Beethoven in his Inanities.[12]

Have you peeped at the European Magazine for January?[13]—

---

[2] 6 Feb.   [3] The Portuguese Embassy Chapel, where High Mass was celebrated at 11.00 a.m.

[4] Presumably the *Missa Sancti Bernardi von Offida* ('Heiligmesse') in B flat of 1796, first published by Breitkopf in 1802. It later appeared as No. 1 of Novello's edition of Haydn masses of 1823–5 and was generally known as Haydn's 'First Mass' in 19th-cent. English editions.

[5] Novello's choir evidently contained both men and women.

[6] Presumably SW's harmonized plainsong *Missa Defunctorum* (BL, Add. MS 14342).

[7] At this time, Novello would be playing for Vespers at the Portuguese Embassy Chapel.

[8] *2 Henry IV*, I. ii. 189.   [9] The lady referred to in the previous letter: not otherwise identified.

[10] Ignace Joseph Pleyel (1757–1831), Austrian composer, music publisher, and piano manufacturer, whose music was immensely popular at this time (*Grove*[6]).

[11] William Reeve (1757–1815), described in *Grove*[6] as 'a prolific theatre composer of negligible talent'.

[12] Perhaps a reference to a collection of dances for piano recently published in London as *Six Country Dances and Thirteen Waltzes*, which SW reviewed in highly unfavourable terms in *EM* in May 1814.

[13] The report in *EM* of the Union of the two Grand Lodges of England on 27 Dec. 1813 had included an account of SW's contribution as Grand Organist and as the composer of the anthem 'Behold, how good a thing it is'.

I have finished the slow Movement of my Sonata;[14] much to my Mind.—I obtrude my Egotisms, because you are *always uncommonly* impertinent to know whether I am as idle as Pinto.[15]

To Robert Glenn   [Gower Place], 8 March [1814][1]

ALS, 1 p. (BL, Add. MS 35013, fo. 61)
Addressed To | Mr Glenn | Steward Street | Spitalfields | N. 4 | Tuesday Morning
Pmk 12 o'Clock 8 MR 1814

My dear Sir

I am in a Dilemma concerning Mr Savage.[2]—Novello was so good as to help me in copying the Concerto[3] till one in the Morning last Sunday, & considers as his *Reward* the Privilege of being near me To-morrow when it is played.—*You* of Course I expect, but you know that the Ashleys[4] object to more than *two* Persons near the Organ, & indeed with Reason.—Perhaps Mr Savage will therefore consent to go on another Night when a Concerto is given.—Pray negotiate the Matter in your best Manner.—I hope he will not be offended, for you see I cannot help

---

[14]   No sonata written by SW in 1814 is known.

[15]   The English violinist, pianist, and composer George Frederick Pinto (1785-1806). He had in fact produced a large output in the space of little more than three years before his early death, and was widely admired by his contemporaries: Salomon remarked that 'if he had lived and been able to resist the allurements of society, England would have had the honour of producing a second Mozart'. After Pinto's death, SW edited his *Four Canzonets and a Sonata* (Edinburgh, 1808), and remarked of him in his Reminiscences that 'a greater musical Genius has not been known'. His dissipation and idleness are mentioned in several contemporary accounts (*Grove*[6]).

---

[1]   The year is given by the postmark.

[2]   SW had evidently invited Savage to turn pages for him at the oratorio concert at Covent Garden on the following day, at which he was to give the first performance of his new organ concerto. This arrangement would have enabled Savage to hear the concert without charge.

[3]   Doubtless the Organ Concerto in C, the autograph score of which is dated 5 Mar. 1814 and which was first performed at the Covent Garden oratorio concert on 9 Mar. The score was sold at Sotheby's on 21 Nov. 1978 and is now in private ownership; some orchestral parts are at BL, Add. MS 35009, fo. 162. This was presumably the 'new concerto, composed expressly for these performances' advertised for the previous concert on 4 Mar., and postponed because it was not ready in time. The statement in a note by H. J. Gauntlett dated 23 Sept. 1843 on the score that the concerto was written for the Birmingham Festival is erroneous.

[4]   General Christopher Ashley and Charles Jane Ashley, the managers of the Covent Garden oratorios: see SW to Novello, 6 May [1812], n. 4.

myself, & it would be scandalously ungrateful to deny Novello after his essential Service on the Occasion.—

> Yours ever truly
> S Wesley

Tuesday | 8th of March

To Robert Glenn [Gower Place], 16 March [1814][1]

ALS, 1 p. (Rylands, DDWF 15/18)
Addressed To | Mr Glenn | N. 4 | Steward Street | Spitalfields | Wednesday morning | Paid
Pmk 16 MR 1814

March 16
Wednesday

My dear Sir

I trust that you are not displeased at my not having come to you at the Chapel last Sunday, but I assure you that I could not well leave the Party without becoming highly indecorous.—The Ladies had but just retired from the Table, & there was a very interesting Conversation commencing upon a literary Subject, in which I was *opposed* by a sensible old Lawyer, who nevertheless was in the wrong about the Argument, as was proved upon the Production of a Latin Dictionary.—You will own that this was an aukward Moment to be summoned from the Scene of Conflict, & Mrs Foote[2] seemed so thoroughly unwilling to let me slip (even for half an Hour) I felt, that all Things considered I had better sacrifice my short Visit to you, relying on your Indulgence when you should receive my Explanation.—I fully intend being in Houndsditch[3] to-morrow by 5, where of Course I shall have the Satisfaction of meeting you, & where I promise myself a very pleasant Day.—Adieu for the present, believing me my dear Friend Yours ever truly

> S Wesley

---

[1] The year is given by the postmark.   [2] A family friend, and evidently the hostess of the party.
[3] In the City, near St Paul's Cathedral; the purpose of SW's projected visit there is not known.

To Vincent Novello

[Gower Place, 17 March 1814][1]

ALS, 1 p. (BL, Add. MS 11729, fo. 83)
Addressed To | Mr Novello | Oxford Street | N. 240 | Thursday Morning
Pmk 17 MR

Dear N

The Cramers & Horsley have appointed to meet me at Chappel's on Saturday Evening next,[2] at 8 precisely, & we hope you will join us.—Sam Webbe I have also nominated as a very eligible Man to become one of the Committee on Russell's Business, & I shall immediately apprize him of the Meeting.[3]

Let me know whether you intend to be with me at the Theatre To-morrow,[4] as I must cut & contrive accordingly: You would hardly believe how I am bothered by Applications from *Overturners*.[5]

If you call on Joe Major between now & Sunday, he will shew you the Review of the last Month's European: there is one funny Blunder in the Print, instead of 'a side Drum', they have spelt it *a sick Dream*.—I have desired the Editor to notice it by an Erratum in the next Number.[6]

Adieu till we meet
Yours ever truly
S Wesley

P.S. I told Ashley[7] I should like to perform Bach's Prelude[8] with your Arrangement, which he readily agreed to, but it *must* be rehearsed.

---

[1] The year is given by SW's 'Thursday', the incomplete postmark, and by internal evidence (see nn. 3, 4, and 6).   [2] 19 Mar.

[3] The meeting was of the committee set up to arrange a performance of William Russell's oratorio *Job* for the benefit of his widow and children; it comprised SW, Attwood, John and Francis Cramer, Horsley, Nicks, Novello, and Samuel Webbe II (*The Times*, 9 May 1814). As is clear from the next letter, the meeting did not take place.

[4] On 18 Mar. at Covent Garden, where SW was to play the organ in an oratorio concert.

[5] i.e. page-turners.

[6] The Feb. 1814 number of *EM* included a review by SW of Johann Baptist Cramer's *Rousseau's Dream: An Air with Variations for the Pianoforte* which contained the misprint in question: 'the 4th variation, in which the imitation of a sick dream is given, has an attractive and enlivening effect.' It was corrected in the Mar. number. SW continued to contribute a monthly column of music reviews to *EM* until Dec. 1816 (Olleson).   [7] Either General Christopher or Charles Jane Ashley.

[8] i.e. the 'St Anne' Prelude.

To Vincent Novello [Gower Street], 23 March [1814][1]

ALS, 1 p. (BL, Add. MS 11729, fo. 85)
Addressed To | Mr Novello

Dear N

J. Cramer informs me that Horsley had undertaken to acquaint the Parties that our Meeting could not take place last Saturday[2]—this however the Event proves that he neglected to do.—It is proposed to meet *To-morrow* Evening (Thursday)[3] at 7, & at Chappell's.—I wish too well to the Cause to suffer any Rudeness from an Individual to obstruct its Success, as far as I am concerned, & therefore shall make a Point of being there.—Act as you feel right, but I promised to let you know of the Circumstance, & trust that you feel as I do.—I much regret being wholly unable to be with you on Sunday last[4] either Morning or Evening: when the Oratorio Shop is shut I shall be less a Slave to Hours.[5]—I dare say you were pleasantly managed at George Gwilt's.—

Yours my good Friend
very cordially

S Wesley

Wed^y Morn^g | 23. March

To Vincent Novello [Gower Place], 13 [April 1814][1]

ALS, 1 p. (BL, Add. MS 11729, fo. 89)
Addressed To | Mr Novello | Oxford Street | N. 240
Pmk 14 AP 181

Dear N.

Your Note to the Committee[2] convinced us all that you have *no Notes beside* to attend unto: when will the Te-Deum[3] be performed?—Can I help you in copying? —I mean what I offer: Stress of Business shall not easily pre-occupy the Interest I

---

[1] The year is given by 23 Mar. falling on a Wednesday and the reference to the meeting at Chappell's, also mentioned in the previous letter. [2] 19 Mar.

[3] 24 Mar. [4] 20 Mar.

[5] The final concert of the Covent Garden oratorio season was on 11 Apr.

---

[1] The month and year are given by SW's '13th Wed^y', the incomplete postmark, and by internal evidence.

[2] Not preserved: no doubt conveying Novello's apologies for non-attendance because of another commitment. [3] Presumably the Te Deum referred to in the following letter.

feel in a Friend harassed for Time as I know you must be at the present Moment.—Pray be candid—(though this Requisition is I own next to an Affront).

Harry Smart[4] will let us poke our Snouts into the Orchestra at all godly Opportunities.—Kean's Richard is a Monday Go.[5]—On next Monday[6] he has previously promised Horseley (I think he says, tho' I rather imagine this was said for the Magnificence of *obliging* a **Bac. Mus. Oxon**[7]—i.e. a *Mouse* on an Ox's Back).—Monday Week is Linley's *Do*,[8] so we must postpone, & be good patient Xtians in this vicked Vurld.

    Yours (with tolerable Truth)

    SW

13th | Wed[y]

To Vincent Novello   [Gower Place], 20 April [1814][1]

ALS, 2 pp. (BL, Add. MS 11729, fo. 90)
Addressed To | M[r] Novello | Oxford Street | 240 | Wednesday Evening | 20th of April.

Dear N

    If the Report from the Papers be true, Louis XVIII[2] is off on Sunday next;[3]—either then he will not be present at the Te Deum Affair,[4] or it will be performed

---

  [4] Henry Smart (1778–1823), the brother of Sir George Smart, was leader of the orchestra at Drury Lane, and thus in a position to allow free admission to the orchestra to SW, Novello, and others (*Grove*[6]).

  [5] The acting of Edmund Kean (?1787–1833) in three Shakespeare plays at Drury Lane was currently the talk of London. He had made his London début as Shylock in *The Merchant of Venice* on 26 Jan. 1814; his first appearances in *Richard III* (in Colley Cibber's version) and in *Hamlet* followed on 12 Feb. and 12 Mar. respectively. Thereafter, he gave one performance of each per week. Performances of *Richard III* were advertised for Mondays 18 and 25 Apr. (*The Times*; Raymund FitzSimons, *Edmund Kean: Fire from Heaven* (1976)).   [6] 18 Apr.

  [7] Horsley had been awarded an Oxford B.Mus. in 1800.

  [8] A concert on 25 Apr. at the Hanover Square Rooms for the benefit of the Queen's Lying-in Hospital, where most of the music was by Linley's father Thomas Linley senior (*c*.1733–1795). SW directed the performances and played an organ voluntary and concerto (*Morning Chronicle*, 18 and 22 Apr. 1814).

---

  [1] The year is given by 20 Apr. falling on a Wednesday, the reference to Louis XVIII's departure (see n. 2), and the account of the meeting of Russell's committee.

  [2] Louis-Stanislas-Xavier, Comte de Provence (1755–1824), younger brother of Louis XVI (1754–93), king of France by title from 1795 and in fact from 1814 to 1824. After the French Revolution he had fled France, and had been living in England (at Hartwell, Bucks.) since 1807. His return to France to take up his throne followed the fall of Napoleon.

  [3] *The Times* for 20 Apr. contained details of Louis's forthcoming departure for France on 24 Apr. following the downfall of Napoleon.

  [4] Evidently a service of thanksgiving, currently being arranged.

on, or before or after Sunday.—As you promised to give me Notice of the Matter, I guess that it is most probably postponed, but am desirous of early Intelligence, that if possible I may square Things so as to be at the Solemnity.—

On Monday, the ill-Humour of my Guts (which were about as regular in their Movements, as Mr Hawes[5] is logical in his Arguments) prevented my hearing what the knowing Kids tell me was a very bad Concert:[6] I therefore think that my Cholic was extremely well *concerted.*—Fiddlers love Puns like!—

So you were all alone & nobody with ye last Night but Mr Windsor[7] & Pokey & many &c &c perhaps!—Pray Doctor Know-well-o did not Chappell give you a Line to say that our Committee were to *sittee* at 7 last Night as ever was?—F. Cramer, Webbe, Horsley, Attwood, *Elliott* & I were all there, & we went through two Acts of poor Russell's (I am sorry to say) poor Oratorio.—We are all agreed (in Masonic Secresy) that it can never be publickly performed but *once*, & that it is lucky the Place fixed is a Chappel, for that in a Room or Theatre, there would be certainly serpentine Symptoms.[8]

If your grand *Do*[9] is not fixed for Friday, I shall depend upon you *à dextris meis*[10] at the Rehearsal.—At all Events let me know about Things in the Course of To-morrow.—I dine with the Jeaffreson Family on that Day, & they live in Lodgings at N° 41 Duke Street Manchester Square; perhaps you will call on me there, & will be sure to find me from 6 in the Evening till 11 at Night.—Pray let us settle these weighty Concerns.

On Friday the Committee meet to go over the 3^d Act, at $\frac{1}{2}$ past 8 at Night.— I hope you will be with us.

---

[5] William Hawes (1785–1846), English singer, conductor, and composer. He began his musical career as a chorister in the Chapel Royal (1793–1801), subsequently becoming a violinist in the Covent Garden theatre orchestra, deputy lay vicar at Westminster Abbey (1803), Gentleman of the Chapel Royal (1805), Master of the Choristers at St Paul's Cathedral (1814), and Master of the Children of the Chapel Royal (1817). In 1824 he became musical director of the English Opera House at the Lyceum Theatre, where he was responsible for English adaptations of (*inter alia*) Weber's *Der Freischütz*, Mozart's *Così fan tutte* (1828), and Marschner's *Der Vampyr* (1829) (*Grove*[6]).

[6] The Philharmonic Society concert on 18 Apr. (Foster, *Philharmonic*, 15).

[7] James W. Windsor (1776–1853), composer, organist, collector of music, and music teacher (Brown and Stratton). Manuscripts owned by him, including some containing music by SW, are at the BL and RCM.

[8] The performance of *Job* took place on 15 June at the Foundling Hospital Chapel. The occasion also included a performance by SW and Novello of an arrangement by Novello of Bach's 'St Anne' Fugue for organ duet, preceded by a newly composed Prelude by SW. The autograph of SW's Prelude is at BL, Add. MS 14340.

[9] Presumably the 'Te Deum affair' mentioned in the previous letter.

[10] 'At my right hand' (Ps. 110: 1): i.e. to turn pages.

Windsor you find to be a sensible Man: he is also very modest, & knows almost as much of Harmony as **Bartleman.**—*Chorus Singers* never can be Harmonists, selon *le grand Roi*: (**Anglicè Great-o-Rex.**)

SW

To Robert Glenn   [Gower Place, 14 May 1814][1]

AN, 1 p. (BL, Add. MS 35013, fo. 64)
Addressed To | Mr GLENN | Steward Street | Spitalfields | N° 4 |
Pmk 10 o'Clock 14 MY 1814
Editor's note This entire letter is written in large printed characters.

My Dear Friend Glenn!
  Pray are you alive or dead? If the *latter*, I am sure that you will feel it your Duty to come & see me without Delay.

  W.S.

To Robert Glenn   Gower Place, 25 May [1814][1]

ALS, 1 p. (BL, Add. MS 35013, fo. 66)
Addressed To | M[r] Glenn | Steward Street | Spitalfields |
Pmk Noon 26 MY 1814

Gower Place
Wednesday 25th May

My dear Friend,
  I shall most willingly attend you on Sunday[2] to meet M[r] James,[3] but you must inform me of your dining Hour.—I presume that as you go to the Hospital[4] you will dine early.—Should you be disposed to return hither with me & take your Bread & Cheese I shall be happy in your Company.
  Adieu, for the present, believing me as ever

My dear Friend
Your obliged & faithful

  S Wesley

---

[1] The date is given by the postmark.

[1] The year is given by the postmark.   [2] 29 May.   [3] Not identified.
[4] Presumably Christ's Hospital School, where Glenn was music master.

P.S. Will you turn for me on Saturday Evening?[5]—I rather think Novello will come too, therefore cannot well accommodate any one *else*, without cross Looks from the rascally Ashleys.

To Vincent Novello   Gower Place, 26 May [1814][1]

ALS, 1 p. (BL, Add. MS 11729, fo. 92)
Addressed To | Mr Novello | Oxford Street | N. 240 | Thursday | 6 o'Clock
Pmk 27 MY 1814

Gower Place
Thursday 26th of May

Dear N

I have but just now received your Letter arriving too late for me to think of dining with the Gentlemen at Hampstead.[2]—As you seemed dubious whether this were what is called 'the <u>Fine</u> Dinner,' or only a *fine* Dinner upon some other Account, I did not hold myself in much Preparation to be invited; & Mr Wilkinson's[3] individual Summons would certainly not have induced me to thrust my Snout (perhaps unwelcomely) into the Party.

Beside, as Mr Fryer signified no Wish to *you* of my making one among them, nothing could have appeared more aukward than the Presentation of my Person in so very *extemporaneous* a Mode.—

I believe you know that I wish not to resemble the Gentleman in Hudibras[4]

> 'Who thrusts his Nose in all Affairs,
> As Pigs in Hedges do by theirs.'[5]

I have asked Glenn to be with me on Saturday Evening,[6] but you are pretty well aware that I consider either your *dexter* or *sinister* Support valuable.—Pray therefore let me have the Honour of obtaining for you an 'oblique Regard' of General Ashley, & his transcendent Brothers.—Will you call & take Coffee with me at ½ past 5 on Saturday?—

SW

---

[5] On 28 May at the Ashleys' annual Whitsun Eve benefit concert at Covent Garden, at which SW was to play the organ (*The Times*, 26 May 1814; *Morning Chronicle*, 28 May 1814).

[1] The year is given by the postmark.

[2] Unidentified: the gathering may possibly have been at Jack Straw's Castle (see SW to Novello, 25 June [1812]).   [3] Unidentified: probably the 'qui tam attorney' of SW to Novello, 25 June [1816].

[4] The satirical poem by Samuel Butler (1613–80), published in 1663.

[5] Misquoted from *Hudibras Part II: An Heroical Epistle of Hudibras to Sidrophel*, ll. 1315–16: 'That makes your way through all affairs | As pigs through hedges creep with theirs'.

[6] On 28 May, at the Ashleys' benefit concert.

To Vincent Novello [Gower Place], 1 July [1814]¹

ALS, 1 p. (BL, Add. MS 11729, fo. 96)
Addressed To | Mʳ Novello | Oxford Street. | N. 240 | Friday Evening
Pmk 2 JY 1814

Dear N

I have not been yet successful in discovering the 'whereabout' of the original Score of the Trio,² but shall not give over Search, in Hope of getting at it by Sunday.³—Meanwhile there can be no violent Immorality in your just enquiring for me of Webbe whether he may not possibly have it among his MSS. I am pretty sure that he wished for a Copy, which it was not likely that I would refuse.—Put the worst to the worst, there is no Impossibility of making a third Copy from either yours or Stokes's, & tho' this cannot be accomplished by Sunday (unless one of us could afford Time to do nothing else) yet we may make something of a Shift to get a *Sort* of Practice of it by peeping over each other's Books.—At all Events, let us meet as intended, at 5.—

I have written to Pokey, & desired him not to fail, & I think he will not.—

Yours in Haste.

S Wesley

1ˢᵗ of July. | Friday

To George Polgreen Bridgetower Gower Place, 1 July [1814]¹

ALS, 1 p. (Add. MS 56411, fo. 14)
Addressed To | Mʳ Bridgtower | Chapel Street | Grosvenor Place | N. 20 |
    Friday Evening
Pmk 2 JY 181

My dear Sir,

Being now comparatively a disengaged Animal to what I was when the Performance of Linley's & Russell's Musick was in Preparation² (in both of

---

[1] The year is given by the postmark.
[2] i.e. the Trio for Three Pianofortes. The autograph score was sold at Sotheby's on 21 Nov. 1978; it is now in private ownership.   [3] 3 July.

[1] The year is given by 1 July falling on a Friday and SW's reference to 'Linley's & Russell's music' (see n. 2).
[2] The performances of Linley's father's music at the Hanover Square Rooms on 25 Apr. and of Russell's *Job* at the Foundling Hospital Chapel on 15 June.

which Affairs I had a great Deal of Trouble) I beg Leave to inform you that I shall be happy to know, when & where I am to make good my Promise to my Brother of hearing you execute the exquisite Solos of Bach.—If you will name any Evening within a Week hence, I (for myself) will *make* it convenient to attend your Appointment, & upon obtaining your Answer will immediately acquaint my Brother.—Novello sorely regretted his Loss, originating in an idle Mistake of mine in the former Instance,[3] but I trust you will suffer him to be of the Party, as you cannot have an Auditor more capable of highly relishing the Exertion of your uncommon Talent upon the most expressive of all musical Instruments.

> Believe, me, my dear Sir,
> With unfeigned Regard,
> Most truly yours
> S Wesley

Gower Place | Euston Square | July 1. Friday

To Vincent Novello [Gower Place], 9 July [1814][1]

ALS, 2 pp. (BL, Add. MS 11729, fo. 66)
Addressed To | Mr Novello | Oxford Street | N. 240

Dear N.

I mounted Guard, selon ma Promesse for you yesterday.[2]—We could not get up any thing very magnificent, because your Honour's Worship & Glory had omitted to leave the Key of your Bum-Fiddle Box.[3]—We therefore determined

---

[3] A reference to Novello's non-attendance at Bridgetower's party on 27 Jan. 1814: see SW to Novello, [28 Jan. 1814].

[1] 9 July falling on a Friday initially suggests 1813 as the most probable year for this letter. On this date in 1813, however, SW was in Ipswich (see SW to Sarah Suter, 6 July and 9 July 1813 (BL, Add. MS 35012, fos. 45 and 46)). SW's references to his reviewing for the *European Magazine* (see n. 8) and to the Day of Thanksgiving on 7 July (see n. 11) establish 1814 as the correct year, while the reference to the service at the Portuguese Embassy (see n. 2) suggests that SW had mistaken the day of the week rather than the date.

[2] 8 July was the feast of St Elizabeth of Portugal and was marked by sung High Mass at the Portuguese Embassy Chapel.

[3] Presumably a music-stool with a lockable compartment for music under the seat.

upon Webbe's grand Chromatic Mass in G. Major,[4] which was accordingly carried to Execution.—Little Prina,[5] however, in his Zeal for the good of the Church, would resolve (in Spite of my Veto) to run to your House for the Key, which he did, & brought it, but we had done with the Gloria first, (I think) & your Brother[6] judiciously observed that it were better to do what was easy with a *small* Choir (as was the Fact) than risk the spoiling excellent Music requiring a large one.—

Asperne, the Editor of the European Magazine,[7] scruples to pay me for my Review[8] until he has ascertained what other musical Reviewers exact & obtain in similar Cases.—You once reviewed in a Magazine.[9]—Pray tell me what were your Terms?—I had rather have a round Sum *per Annum*, than go higgling about *Sheets* &c—I should think 25 Guineas for the Year not out of the Way.[10] Apropos of Magazines—as soon as you have done with mine, of April, I will thank you for it.

I shall probably see you on Sunday, either Morning or Afternoon.—I hope your aquatic Affair[11] turned out well; I was right glad to be all Day out of the Reach of the Royal Blackguard, who I hear was hissed all the Way in a jolly Style.[12]

Give me a Line, as my rascally Bookseller waits to know my Requisition.— What Cattle they are!

Mais—il faut manger.[13]—

SW

9th July | Friday[14]

---

[4] Ironic: Samuel Webbe I's Mass in G, from his *A Collection of Sacred Music as used in the Chapel of the King of Sardinia* (*c*.1785), is a notably plain work.

[5] John Francis Prina (1798–*ante* 1841), a junior member of the Portuguese Embassy Chapel choir (Matthews; Sainsbury).   [6] Francis Novello (b. 1779), who sang bass in the choir.

[7] In fact, its publisher and proprietor; the editor was Stephen Jones.

[8] i.e. SW's monthly column of reviews of music, which he had been contributing since Feb. 1814.

[9] Not identified.

[10] Payment was usually calculated by the sheet, and any attempt SW may have made to negotiate payment on an annual basis was evidently unsuccessful: see his letters to Jones, 15 Feb. and 26 Dec. 1816.

[11] Not identified.

[12] A day of thanksgiving to celebrate the ending of the Peninsular War had been held on 7 July; it had included a procession to St Paul's headed by the Prince Regent and Wellington, and had been widely reported. For the hissing of the Prince Regent, see the *Examiner*, 10 July 1814.

[13] 'One must eat'.   [14] In fact, Saturday.

To Vincent Novello [Gower Place, 19 July 1814]¹

ALS, 1 p. (BL, Add. MS 11729, fo. 98)
Addressed To | Mʳ Novello | 240 | Oxford Street.
Pmk 20 JY 1814 8 o'Clock MR

Dear N.

I have compleated the Transcript of the Trio,² & therefore now the only remaining Point is the Settlement of a Time for performing it in 'worshipful Society.' *Sunday*, I think, all Matters considered, <is> not the most eligible Day, especially as we are to assemble in rather a public-looking Place;³ added to this, two or three People whom I mean to invite, & who are worthy Guests, are more punctilious about the Ceremony of Sunday than you & I.—What say you to Monday next?⁴—I shall be disengaged from *One* o'Clock on that Day, & will attend at any Hour from that till 12 at Night, which perhaps might be considered *rather late.*—Pray turn all this over in your cogitating Sconce, & let me know without unnecessary Delay how you can cut & contrive:—Salomon is much agog to be among us: I would strain a point to accommodate him as to Time.—Clementi has promised to come.—The Cramers I shall invite, although of J. B. I have no hope, *especially* as I think it probable that he has heard (by some side Wind) how *well* Wilson can play his Musick.⁵

The selected Mass⁶ went in very prime Stile on Sunday, notwithstanding the Absence of Lanza.—Miss Bowyer⁷ & her Mamma were all in the Raptures.—Indeed all went nicely, & the 'Vitam Venturi'⁸ they roared out with becoming Enthusiasm, in which I joined, & made young Lᵈ Petre⁹ laugh thereat, which comforted the Cockles of my Heart amain.—

    SW

---

¹ The date is given by the following morning's postmark.
² The Trio for Three Pianos: SW's lost manuscript had evidently not been found.
³ As the following letter states, the performance was at Clementi's premises in Tottenham Court Road. ⁴ 25 July.
⁵ Charles Wilson (b. 1796) had first performed in public as a child of 7 in 1803 at the Hanover Square Rooms. He was taught for a time by William Beale, but in 1812 became a pupil of SW. He gave the first performance of a new piano concerto by SW (now lost) at SW's Argyll Rooms concert on 4 May 1813, when according to a newspaper report 'the amateurs and professors who were in the room were unanimous in declaring, that he will be one of the most accomplished performers on the pianoforte which this country has ever produced.' Despite the success of this and other early appearances, his 'natural diffidence, and a repugnance to the gaze of the many' led him to withdraw from public performance and to devote himself to composition and private teaching (Sainsbury).
⁶ A compilation of movements by Durante, Pergolesi, Mozart, Perez, Perti, Novello, and others in vol. 2 of Novello's *A Collection of Sacred Music.* ⁷ Not identified.
⁸ The concluding section of the Credo of the Mass: a lively fugal movement by Giacomo Antonio Perti (1661–1756). ⁹ William Henry Francis, Baron Petre (1793–1850).

To Robert Glenn   [Gower Place], 22 July [1814][1]

ALS, 1 p. (BL, Add. MS 35013, fo. 68)
Addressed To | M[r] Glenn | Steward Street | Spitalfields | Friday Evening
Pmk 8 o'Clock 23 JY 1814

22[d] of July
Friday

My dear Friend

You remember that when Moses went upon his Expedition to Mount Sinai, the Israelites became impatient for his Return, & besought Aaron the high Priest to make them Gods for (said they) 'as to this Moses we wot not what is become of him.'[2]—Now this latter Sentence is so applicable to yourself, as to my Ignorance of your Situation about Healthy Engagements &c that I have been waiting in vain to know by a Line (which I flattered myself you would have given to me long ago) what hath become of *you?*

On Monday next at *6* in the Evening, we shall have a little Piano Forte Music at Clementi's Manufactory in Tottenham Court Road.—Wilson will play Cramer's Concerto in D minor,[3] & we shall also have my Piano Forte Trio—if you have nothing better to do, come amongst us: I have summoned some of the great Guns, Cramers, Clementi, Kollmann,[4] *La Tour*[5] &c.

Yours most sincerely,

S. Wesley

N.B. No *4*[6] Gower Place | Euston Square

---

[1] The year is given by the postmark.   [2] Exod. 32: 1.

[3] Either the Concerto No. 2, Op. 16 (1797) or No. 3, Op. 26 (*c*.1801).

[4] Probably George August Kollmann.

[5] J. T. Latour (1766–1840), French pianist and composer, pianist to the Prince Regent, and an associate member of the Philharmonic Society (Sainsbury; Foster, *Philharmonic*).

[6] SW's earlier letters from Gower Place had been addressed from No. 5; by this time either SW had moved or his house had been renumbered.

To Vincent Novello [Gower Place], 29 July [1814]¹

ALS, 1 p. (BL, Add. MS 11729, fo. 100)
Addressed To | Mr Novello | Oxford Street | N. 240 | Friday Afternoon | July 29
Pmk 4 o'Clock 29 JY 1814 EVE

Dear N.

I am not yet certain whether you will esteem Two Pence² much over the Value of the enclosed Bagatelle:³ if you think it worth the Money perhaps you will let it be sung on Sunday next:⁴ I believe that upon narrow Inspection you will find the Choir will not need more than a Dozen Rehearsals, which you will accordingly call between now & Sunday, as there is so much Time to spare for the Purpose.

I fully intend being with you at high Mass to know the Fate of this abstruse Piece of Counterpoint.

    Yours as usual

      S Wesley

Friday. 29th July

To Vincent Novello [Gower Place], 11 August [1814]¹

ALS, 1 p. (BL, Add. MS 11729, fo. 101)
Addressed To | Mr Novello | Oxford Street | N. 240 | Friday Morning
Pmk AU 1814

Thursday Night
11. Aug

Dear N

I was not at Vickery's² on Tuesday Evening³ in Consequence of having been severely attacked on Monday by a plaguey bilious Colic, which confined me, maugre moi même to the House until Yesterday Morning, when I ventured abroad

---

¹ The year is given by the postmark.
² i.e. the price that Novello would have to pay in postage. ³ Not identified. ⁴ 31 July.

¹ The year is given by the postmark.
² The Revd Francis William Johnson Vickery (1787/8–1866), matric. University College, Oxford (1803), BA (1809), MA (1812), who had been elected to membership of the Madrigal Society on 21 Sept. 1813; at this time he lived at 33 Theobalds Road (Foster; MADSOC). ³ 9 Aug.

to Business, although against my Doctor's Consent.—I am now considerably recovered, intending to see you at 3 on Sunday next:[4] Vickery called to enquire about me To-Day, stating that you did not join the Party on Tuesday: I told him he was therefore to conclude that you were not returned to Town.—He wants to hear the South Street Organ, & means to meet us on Sunday at the Vespers.—He also wishes to be possessed of your two Volumes of Church Music,[5] & as I did not know whether Phipps[6] is commissioned to sell them, I told him that I would learn from yourself the best Way of obtaining them.

The Mass on Sunday[7] went remarkably well, I thought.—I found Fryer's Mandate for *Mozart's*,[8] to which I could feel no very grand Objection.—He subjoined in his petit Billet 'No Alteration'; which indeed I was not disposed to make, & of which he needed not to suspect me.—I have not yet found my harmonized Gregorian 'De Angelis.'—Perhaps you may not yet be infallibly certain that I did not lend it to you—if I *did*, I know it safe; & if I did not, I hope it so.—It was <ra>ther a favour<it>e *foster* Child, which I should be sorry to lose altogeth<er a>s I cannot give *another* of the Sort, so good an Education, I fear.

Y^{rs}

SW

To Vincent Novello Gower Place, 14 September [1814][1]

ALS, 1 p. (BL, Add. MS 11729, fo. 102)
Addressed To | Mr Novello | Oxford Street | 240 | Wednesday | 1 o'Clock

Gower Place
Wednesday Noon 14 Sept^r

Dear N,

It was ridiculous in me to conjecture that the Musick was not returned from Gwilt's, when Part of the *same* Cargo was conveyed *by us* <af>terwards to the

---

[4] 14 Aug. [5] *A Collection of Sacred Music.*

[6] The proprietor of Phipps and Co., music and musical instrument sellers and publishers of 25 Duke Street, Grosvenor Square, *c.*1810–1818; he was formerly a partner in the firm of Goulding, Phipps and D'Almaine (Brown and Stratton; Humphries and Smith). [7] 7 Aug.

[8] Not identified.

---

[1] The year is given by 14 Sept. falling on a Wednesday and the addresses of SW and Novello.

Islington Chapel[2] on the Saturday when we were so unfortunate as to displease M[r] Purkis[3] by pleasing every Body else.—I am now however very anxious concerning the *Green Book*,[4] which was certainly taken to the Chapel with the rest, & you may remember that England's young Man[5] engaged to convey my Books to my House: the Book containing the Choral Vorspiele[6] (in which also is the triple Mass)[7] I have found, but not the other.—England sent the young Man to me, who declares solemnly that he brought back *two* bound Books; one of which ought assuredly to have been my MS. of the Exercises & Organ Pieces.—If you can lend me any Clue to unravel this Mystery, for God's Sake do it quickly, otherwise I shall be obliged to have Recourse again to M[r] Picart & undertake the Drudgery of copying it all a second Time, with the added Mortification of the Book having perhaps fallen into some Blockhead's Hands, who may wrap up his Candles in the Leaves.

Pray have you yet found out, from the Intelligence of 'the Examiner' that you are 'a young Man of great *Promise*?'[8]—If he had termed you a Man of great Performance, he would have been nearer the Mark.

Do write me a Line on the Receipt of this, & don't forget to come to me on Friday.—How did Pokey get on, Sunday *Ater* Noon? (as M[r] Cox classically terms it.)

Y[rs] as usual

SW

---

[2] i.e. St Mary Magdalene, Holloway Road, consecrated on 17 Aug. 1814. The occasion (of which no record has been found) may have been a recital by SW and Novello to open the organ, which was by George Pike England and said to have been the last one built by him (Boeringer, ii. 282).

[3] The significance of this remark is not clear. Purkis may have been the organist of the church and may have resented the success of SW and Novello.

[4] Evidently a treasured volume of manuscript organ music, containing pieces by Bach. Not certainly identified: probably the same volume as the 'green Fat-Book' mentioned as mislaid in SW to Novello, 11 Dec. [1816].   [5] i.e. an employee of George Pike England.

[6] The 1806 Breitkopf collection (see SW to Jacob, [?26 Apr. 1809], and n. 4).

[7] The Mass in G for three choirs, BWV Anh. III 167, ascribed to J. S. Bach and published by Breitkopf in 1805; it is now thought to be by Johann Ludwig Bach or Antonio Lotti. The volume under discussion here is now at the RCM.

[8] In a letter in the *Examiner* for 11 Sept. 1814 (pp. 591–2) headed 'Are the English a Musical People?', an anonymous correspondent signing himself 'Mark Minim' singled out SW and Novello as leading musicians of the day. SW was referred to as 'the finest organist in the kingdom', while Novello was described as 'a young man of very considerable promise'. This was part of a continuing correspondence which had begun with a letter from 'Musicus' in the 29 May number (pp. 351–2), followed by a reply from 'Tallis's Ghost' on 21 Aug. (p. 543).

To Vincent Novello   Gower Place, 28 September [1814][1]

ALS, 1 p. (BL, Add. MS 11729, fo. 103)
Addressed To | Mr Novello | Oxford Street | N. 240 | Wednesday | Night 8 o'Clock
Pmk 29 SP 181

Wednesday Night
28 Sept^r

Dear N

Fully expecting you To-Night according to your Promise, I intended to have given you the enclosed,[2] which at all Events I feel it my Duty to transmit: I received it at 3 o'Clock today, & (as you will find) contains an Invitation from my Friend Kingston to meet me To-morrow at an unceremonious Dinner in Weston Street, Borough N° 16, at half past 3 o'Clock, where the Repast consists principally of Beef Steaks, cooked in what is called the *Stoke Hole* of a Brewery, & which, in its Way, is certainly a very prime Concern.—Good Wine & good Conversation in the Party, I can very securely promise you, from multiplied Experience.[3] I know that you spoke of an Evening Engagement at Cristall's,[4] but even supposing that this cannot *possibly* be given up (of which however you must allow me to doubt the Impossibility) you might pass at least from 3 to 4 Hours with us, & yet arrive at your prior Quarters in very fair & decent Time: I very much wish you to come, as I am persuaded that you will like the Thing, & the Style of the Invitation which is annexed would I think rather prepossess you to strain a Point for the Purpose.

Yours as usual

S Wesley

N.B. Weston Street Brewery. N. 16—*Probyn*[5] is the Name of the Master of the Concern— Kingston has nothing to do with it but is Probyn's Friend, Inmate, & Confident for some 10 or 12 Years past.

---

[1] The year is given by 28 Sept. falling on a Wednesday and Novello's Oxford Street address.

[2] A letter from William B. Kingston, written the previous evening (BL, Add. MS 11729, fo. 104), containing the invitation which SW goes on to summarize here.

[3] Kingston had expressed a particular desire to make Novello's acquaintance. He wrote: 'will a brew-house Beef-Steak & a cordial welcome (which you can assure him) tempt him to dispense with a more ceremonious invitation? If not, say nothing about it: tho' if he be one to stand upon etiquette . . . he's not the man I take him for. At any rate, I should think, the pleasure of your society would outweigh all considerations of ceremony in this case.'

[4] Not identified: presumably the 'Mr Christall' who was a subscriber to Novello's *A Collection of Sacred Music*.

[5] Not identified: evidently the owner or manager of the brewery. A Miss Probyn of Union Place, New Kent Road, possibly his daughter, was in 1824 among the subscribers to SW's Service in F; she may have been the Eliza Kingston Probyn who was organist of St Bartholomew from 1825 to 1864 and of St Stephen's, Walbrook from 1825 to 1868 (Dawe).

To Vincent Novello [Gower Place], 5 October 1814

ALS, 1 p. (BL, Add. MS 11729, fo. 105)
Addressed To | Mr Novello | favoured by Mr Moore[1]

London. Wednesday
Octr 5. 1814

Dear N

You will probably be surprized at my besetting you at a Moment when you are in the Thick of old Handel's best Psalm Tunes,[2] quavered by the best Psalm Singers in England (excepting those in Italy my Honey). On Thursday (or more intelligibly *To-morrow*) I mean to throw my Carcase into the Norwich Mail,[3] & I wished also to have taken with me your very clear Copy of mine Organ Duet in C,[4] & also that of S. Bach which we played at the Foundling.—I did my best for you on Sunday, & a few Friends of mine were highly delighted with all they heard.— We had Mozart's Kyrie, & Gloria, the Credo of the Selected, & the Agnus of Moz: *your* Tantum, & a Sacrum—both excellently done.[5]—I assure you, I begin to think myself a very tolerably Deputy on the Hawgin for the bloody murdering Popish Papishes.—

---

[1] Joseph Moore (1766–1851), the organizer of the Birmingham triennial music festivals from 1802 to 1849. The 1814 festival was on 5–7 Oct. SW presumably gave this letter to Moore in London for him to deliver to Novello in Birmingham.

[2] Novello was playing the viola in the orchestra for the festival (*Aris's Birmingham Gazette* advertisements), and evidently also helping with choral rehearsals.

[3] SW had been engaged to perform in a concert of organ and vocal music at St Peter Mancroft, Norwich, originally arranged for 12 Oct., but subsequently postponed to 20 Oct. for the reasons stated later in this letter. The concert was advertised as including 'the most celebrated Organ Compositions of the first Masters, as well as Extempore Voluntaries and Organ Duetts' (*Norwich Mercury*, 1, 8, 15 Oct. 1814). The name of SW's partner for the organ duets is not given in press advertisements, but may well have been John Charles Beckwith, organist of St Peter Mancroft and of Norwich Cathedral (see SW to Pettet, 5 Oct. 1815, n. 3). SW's visit probably came about through his friendship with William Linley, who accompanied him, and whose brother Ozias (see n. 9), was a minor canon at Norwich Cathedral. SW's letters to his mother of 12 Oct. (Emory, printed Lightwood, 174–5) and to Sarah Suter of 16 Oct. (BL, Add. MS 35012, fo. 48) give further details of this successful and enjoyable visit: SW was introduced by Ozias Linley to all the principal members of Norwich society, was given a special dinner at the Assembly Rooms on 15 Oct., and played for services at the Cathedral on at least three occasions. He returned to London on 22 Oct.

[4] SW's reference to his Organ Duet 'in C' is to identify it as the duet of 1812 and to distinguish it from the earlier duet (now lost) mentioned in SW to Burney, [Feb.–May 1802].

[5] SW had deputized for Novello at High Mass at the Portuguese Embassy Chapel on 2 Oct., and here lists the music performed: the Kyrie, Gloria, and Agnus Dei from a Mass by Mozart, the Agnus Dei (by Durante) from the 'Selected Mass' in vol. 2 of Novello's *A Collection of Sacred Music*, and settings by Novello himself of 'Tantum Ergo' and 'O Sacrum Convivium', probably those from the same publication.

Now, Sir, the Fact is thus:—the Norwich *Do* in the Church[6] is postponed, principally on Account of the Assize Week,[7] which will not be until the 20th Inst. & partially because the most effective vocal Performer (a M[r] Tayler)[8] having lost a near Relation, he cannot with Decency appear in Public so soon as Wed[y] next.— Now my dear Cocky, let me have a Letter from thee, on thy Return to London, *immediately*, & send me also the Duets, dont il y a Question, directed for me at the Rev[d] Ozias Linley's, Norwich.[9]—

God bless you, & I wish you (what I need not) merry & wise.

SW

P.S. Pray do not neglect the Advantage you now have of learning how to *conduct* a Chorus.

P.S. Prina told me he was ordered by you to take sundry Organ MSS. out of the Box & convey them to your House: supposing it likely that some of my Gear was among them, I directed him to search, but he writes to say that neither of the Duets is *findable*.

To Robert Glenn [Gower Place, 27 January 1815][1]

AL, 2 pp. (BL, Add. MS 35013, fo. 54)
Addressed To | Mr Glenn | at M[r] Banks | Kirby Street | Hatton Garden | Friday Evening.
Pmk 30 JA 1815

My dear Friend

If not pre-engaged, I shall be glad of your Company to take a Chop with me on Monday next previously to the Oratorio,[2] & shall be also glad of your Assistance at my right Hand, should you feel disposed to give it me.—

---

[6] St Peter Mancroft.

[7] Concerts and other entertainments were often scheduled to coincide with assize weeks, when a large number of visitors could be expected. The Norwich City Sessions were on 18 Oct. and the County Sessions on the following day.

[8] The bass Edward Taylor (1784–1863), a prominent member of Norwich musical society. He moved to London in 1825, where he made his début at a Covent Garden oratorio concert on 28 Mar. 1827; he also sang at various provincial festivals. He was appointed Gresham Professor of Music in 1837. For a memoir of his life, see 'The late Professor Taylor', *Norfolk News*, 28 Mar. and 4 Apr. 1863, repr. in Thomas Damant Eaton, *Musical Criticism and Biography* (1872), 210–55.

[9] Ozias Thurston Linley (1765–1831), 'organist, clergyman and practical joker' (*Grove*[6]) had been a minor canon of Norwich Cathedral since 1790. In 1816 he was appointed a junior fellow and organist at Dulwich College, where he remained until his death (Lightwood, 175–6; *Grove*[6]; Foster).

---

[1] The date is given by SW's 'Friday' and the just legible postmark.

[2] On 30 Jan., the anniversary of the execution of Charles I, when SW was to play the organ at a performance of *Messiah* at Covent Garden.

I know not what Ashley's Arrangements may be relative to Admission into the Orchestra, & therefore in this first Instance it will be safest for me not to take any one *beside* yourself, as I should not well brook either a Denial, or saucy Looks on the Occasion.

To Robert Glenn [Gower Place], 13 February [1815][1]

ALS, 1 p. (BL, Add. MS 35013, fo. 56)
Addressed To Mr Glenn | Kirby Street | Hatton Garden

My dear Friend

I had quite forgotten that Tonight is the first Meeting of the Philharmonic Society,[2] & I am obliged to shew my long Nose there, on which Account I am very unwillingly deprived of the Pleasure I promised myself in your Company this Evening: I was also summoned to attend the Somerset House Lodge Dinner to Day, which must be given up for the above-named Reason.

If you can, come & take a Chop with me on Wednesday next at 4, previous to our Oratorio Business.[3]

Yours ever truly,

S Wesley

Gower Place. | 13th of February

---

[1] The year is given by the reference to the first concert of the Philharmonic Society (See n. 2) and to SW's mention of the 'oratorio business' (See n. 3).

[2] The opening concert of the season was to be given that evening (advertisement for whole season in *The Times*, 11 Feb. 1815; Foster, *Philharmonic*, 18). SW had been elected to associate membership in late 1813, and was taking an increasing interest in the affairs of the Society. He was elected to full membership in June 1815, and became a director in the following Nov.

[3] The Covent Garden oratorio concert on 15 Feb., at which SW was to play the organ.

To Robert Glenn   [Gower Place], 4 March [1815]¹

ALS, 1 p. (BL, Add. MS 35013, fo. 70)
Addressed To | Mʳ Glenn | Mʳ Barkers | Kirby Street | Hatton Garden
Pmk 12 o'Clock Noon 4 MR 1815

Saturday
4ᵗʰ of March

My dear Friend
    I have been reflecting upon the Circumstances of the Vacancy for Organist
to Lambeth Church,² & having been informed that the Place is worth £70 per
Annum, am of Opinion that it is not to be disregarded.—You will much oblige me
by making a diligent Enquiry upon the Subject among your numerous & respectable Acquaintance.—Several of my Friends are clearly of Opinion that were I
to volunteer my Services to the Church Wardens, it would at once terminate the
Idea of any Competition.—Of this however I am not convinced at present but
shall be happy to have your friendly & candid Judgement thereupon, remaining
as ever

    Yours most cordially
        S Wesley

To Vincent Novello   [Gower Place], 5 July [1815]¹

ALS, 3 pp. (BL, Add. MS 11729, fo. 113)

My dear N.
    There certainly is a *Devil*, which I prove thus: when I sent to old Horn² for the
30 Variations, I received the annexed Answer.³
    I expect you at 6 To-morrow. Sam. Webbe will be with us. Bring us some Tune
of your own, 'that's my Bawcock'.—NB Shakspeare.⁴

---

¹ The year is given by the postmark.   ² Doubtless the parish church of St Mary.

¹ The year is given by 5 July falling on a Wednesday and SW's reference to his forthcoming trip to
Great Yarmouth (see n. 7).
    ² i.e. Charles Frederick Horn, rather than his son, the tenor Charles Edward Horn (1786–1849).
    ³ Not preserved; in it, Horn presumably declined to lend his copy of the *Goldberg Variations*.
    ⁴ *Henry V*, IV. i. 45; see also *Twelfth Night*, III. iv. 111.

Salomon says he will try & get off his Engagement to go with Parson Blomberg[5] to the Opera,[6] & come to us instead.—I think we shall have some Fun.—I am summoned to Yarmouth,[7] & must throw myself into the holy Protection of the Coachman on Sunday next at 2 o'Clock, therefore cannot have a Reiteration of the *Pleasure* we experienced in the Fugue on Sunday last.—Miss Harington,[8] who is not much less of a Gossip than the Generality of that Species of Animal constituted by Nature to carry about it a *Receiver* general, has told me that your Irish genius the Organ *Stopper*[9] ran after her on Sunday, swearing by Jasus that he would not have so many Masters—that 'One was his Master, even' Mr Fryer.

The quotation is from St Paul,[10] whose Epistles, as you have them by Heart, it is quite insultive in me to hint about.

Put me in Mind to give you the French Essay I transcribed To-morrow.

N.B. I did not transcribe it *To-morrow*: my Ordo Verborum is I own often very obscure & perplexed, & reminds me of that droll & just Remark by one of the Characters who criticises the Manner of Delivery of a Speech in the Mock Play, in the Midsummer Night's Dream.—The Speaker makes all his Stops wrongly, & runs one Sentence into another most ridiculously, upon which is observed 'his Speech was like a tangled Chain, nothing impaired, but all disordered.'[11]—

Yours as usual

(your own Way of concluding)

S Wesley

4. Wednesday. July 5

[5] The Revd Frederic William Blomberg (1761–1847), Prebendary of Westminster Abbey (1808–22) and of St Paul's Cathedral (1822–47). He was closely associated with the royal family, and was supposed by some to have been a natural son of George III (Venn).

[6] On 6 July the King's Theatre mounted a special gala evening to mark the victory over the French at Waterloo on 18 June, for the benefit of the widows and children of British soldiers killed in action. The programme included Beethoven's 'Battle' Symphony, conducted by Smart, one act of an unspecified 'grand serious opera', and *Caesar's Triumph over the Gauls*, a 'ballet cantata' with music by Laverati (*The Times*).

[7] SW had been invited by John Eager, organist of St Nicholas, Great Yarmouth, Norfolk, to give a concert with Charles Smith at the church on 12 July (advertisement *Norwich Mercury*, 8 July; report 15 July). This was part of an ongoing programme of musical activities at Great Yarmouth: the reopening of the organ at St Nicholas in 1812 had been marked by two recitals by William Russell, and a music society giving weekly concerts had been founded in Mar. 1814 (A. H. Mann, Notebooks on Music in East Anglia (NRO); *Norwich Mercury*). For Eager, see SW to Novello, 18 July 1815, n. 9.

[8] Not identified: evidently a member of the Portuguese Embassy Chapel congregation. She was a subscriber to Novello's *A Collection of Sacred Music*.

[9] Not identified: presumably the organ-blower at the Portuguese Embassy Chapel.

[10] In fact, from Matt. 23: 10.

[11] Theseus, commenting on the Prologue's speech in the mechanicals' play in *A Midsummer Night's Dream*, v. i. 125.

N.B. Bring a Trio or two of Bach: we can then have them in their right Way. I have them all bound in one Volume.[12]

To Vincent Novello   Great Yarmouth, 18 July 1815

ALS, 3 pp. (BL, Add. MS 11729, fo. 115)
Addressed To | Mr Novello | Oxford Street | London | N. 240 | July 18th
Pmk JY 19 815

Yarmouth
Tuesday, July 18th 1815

Dear N

I was informed that you expected me to write from this Place, & I almost believe that you said as much to me yourself: if therefore I am mistaken in both Instances, your Duty will be to make me refund the Postage at our next Meeting.[1]

We have had a 'kind of as it were' here, to use Mr Prior's[2] very clear Definition of a stupid married Pair's Condition; or to use more common Language, I & my Coadjutor Charley Smith[3] have had a Mixture of good Air, good Bathing, good Company, good Cheer, good Music & cold Attendance at the last Article:[4] it seems that this young Bridegroom (he has lately wedded Miss Booth of Norwich[5]) did not speculate with the Policy & Precaution requisite for any good Success, as to the Time fixed: Our Party ought to have taken Place in the Week of the Races, when the Town is always sure to be full, & the People all mad for *any* public Fun, from an Oratorio down to Punch.[6] However the People who *did*

---

[12] Presumably the organ trio sonatas, in the Wesley-Horn edition. SW's request for Novello to bring his own copies, and his statement that they could then play them 'in their right way' suggests that they were intending to play them on two separate instruments rather than as a duet on one.

[1] SW set off for Great Yarmouth on Sunday 9 July (SW to Novello, 5 July [1815]).

[2] Not identified.

[3] Charles Smith (1786–1856), singer, organist, and composer. He was a treble in the Chapel Royal choir under Edmund Ayrton, sang as a treble at Ranelagh and was later articled for five years to John James Ashley. At the time of his application for membership of the Royal Society of Musicians in 1812 he was organist of Welbeck Chapel and taught at four schools. He moved to Liverpool in 1817 (Brown and Stratton; Matthews).

[4] The concert given by SW and Charles Smith on 12 July was the concluding item in a week of entertainments which also included a 'water frolic' on Breydon Water on 7 July and a cricket match on the following day. For a report of the concert, see *Norwich Mercury*, 15 July 1815.

[5] A teacher of piano and singing who also played the pedal harp, and had performed with SW at his concert in Norwich on 20 Oct. 1814. She and Smith had married on 26 June (*Norwich Mercury*, 15 Oct. 1814, 1 July 1815).   [6] The race week was not until the week ending 23 Sept.

attend appeared all very much delighted, & some of them (especially the Visitors from Norwich) were good Judges, & of course much tickled with such a Row as we gave them upon the most magnificent Organ[7] I have yet heard, & in which I think you would agree with me. Your MS. Music Book has been of special Service to us: the Triple Fugue in E♭,[8] was received with the same kind of Wonder that people express when they see an Air Balloon ascend for the first Time: Smith I believe planted two or three Spies to watch the Effects of such Sounds upon their *Countenance*, & consequently *Mind*.

The 30 Variations we mean to try tomorrow upon the said Organ—this will be a Treat to Mr Eager[9] the Organist, at whose House I am staying, & who wishes to be introduced to you on his Arrival in London, which he expects to be in the next Christmas Holidays. You will find him rather an extraordinary Man, & knowing several Things well.—As a Musician, he has had no Advantages whatever but from his own industrious & persevering Assiduity: he has thereby attained a pretty fair Proportion of *dry Theory*, having fagged at more Treatises than have done him much good, which you know is very easy to do: he is a bad Player on the Organ, a tolerable one on the Piano, & a very good Leader on the Violin; has studied several wind Instruments, viz Horn, Trumpet, Flute, Clarinett, Oboe & Bassoon, & can play them all tolerably: he is moreover a Maître de Ballet, & teaches all the young Wenches to exercise their Legs & Haunches in the most eligible Attitudes to get Husbands.—He has read a good Deal, & is a good Grammarian in French & Italian, & has made his eldest Girl of 11 years, an extremely good Piano Forte Player, so that you ken, my gude Mon, that this 'mine Host of the Garter'[10] is not to be sneezed at, & I assure you he is quite agog for an Introduction to you, which I rather wonder at, after my giving him *my* Opinion.

I purpose, with God's Blessing, & a little of the Devil's Assistance (or the Coachman's which is pretty much the same) to be in London on Friday Morning[11]

---

[7] The three-manual 1733 instrument by Byfield, Bridge, and Jordan had been repaired and enlarged in 1812 by George Pike England, who raised the compass throughout to F, added a double diapason on the pedals and a two-rank mixture on the choir, and provided new keys and pedals (Boeringer, ii. 345–6). The opening recitals by William Russell on 8 and 10 Sept. 1812 had included music by Handel, Mozart, and J. S. Bach.   [8] The 'Saint Anne' fugue in Novello's arrangement.

[9] John Eager (b. 1782), organist of St Nicholas, Great Yarmouth. The article on him in Sainsbury also emphasized his versatility, stating that 'there is scarcely an instrument he does not play, or has not taught professionally' (Sainsbury; Brown and Stratton).

[10] An allusion to the landlord of the Garter Inn in *The Merry Wives of Windsor*.

[11] 21 July. SW subsequently postponed his return to London to allow him to perform at two concerts in Norwich. On 27 July he played a voluntary at the Anniversary Sermon at Norwich Cathedral for the benefit of the Norfolk and Norwich Hospital, where the music also included Boyce's Te Deum (advertisement, *Norwich Mercury*, 22 July; report, 29 July 1815). On the following day he gave a concert with Charles Smith at St Peter Mancroft (advertisement, *Norwich Mercury*, 22 July 1815).

by 9 o'Clock: it is highly probable that I shall look in at your Shop either in the Morning or Evening of Sunday, when we may talk over some of my Yarmouth Pranks more *ad longum*.

I did not mention the Amount of our Receipts: we share £22, which is better than losing as much, you know.

Adieu for the Present, believing me as always
Yours most cordially
   S Wesley

To Alfred Pettet[1]   Gower Place, 31 July 1815

ALS, 3 pp. (Rylands, DDWF 15/19)
Addressed To | A. Pettet Esqre | near | The Castle Hill | Norwich | Augt 1st.
Pmk 1 AU 1815

London. July 31st 1815
Gower Place

Dear Sir,

You will perhaps be a little surprized at this unexpected & unrequested Volunteer of a Letter, however when I have acquainted you with my Reasons for writing you will readily excuse my seeming Indecorum.

Imprimis, I felt a little Regret that we could not obtain some more snug Conversation before my Departure:[2] you are however fully aware that I remained continually occupied (not to say rather harassed) by the several Points of Requisition in which I stood, both privately & publickly: this Circumstance will I trust exonerate me from any Suspicion of *Inattention* to you (& which would exceedingly hurt me to reflect on) & I therefore rest an hearty Reliance on your Candour, & I will venture to add your *Experience* of me not to believe it either probable or possible.

Next, I have to express my Mortification at not having secured an Opportunity of transcribing the Disquisition[3] which I had the Pleasure to lend you, & which

---

[1] Alfred Pettet (*c.*1785–*c.*1845), assistant organist at St Peter Mancroft, Norwich. He was also active in Great Yarmouth, where he presided at piano and organ in the concerts of the Music Society, established the previous year. He was unsuccessful in his application for the post of organist at Norwich Cathedral on the death of John Charles Beckwith in 1819, but succeeded him in the same year as organist at St Peter Mancroft. Around 1825 he published *Original Sacred Music*, a compilation of church music by various composers, including SW (Sainsbury; Brown and Stratton).

[2] Presumably on 29 or 30 July, following SW's concert on 28 July at St Peter Mancroft.

[3] Not identified.

for its Strength & Originality must be certainly a very valuable Fragment both to you & me.—As I have no other Copy of it but that in your Hands, I am consequently rather anxious to attain one with the least Delay that shall suit Convenience.— N.B. It is not to *every one* that we ought to confide such an *exagitating* MS.

A third Statement you must allow me to make is that our Friend Sharp[4] (who I presume is now at Yarmouth) promised me the Words of that excellent funny Song of the *Noachic Procession* into the Ark,[5] which has caused such great Disorder & Dismay amongst your *thorough orthodox* Sacerdoticals.[6]—As soon as you can acquaint Sharp of my Impatience on the Subject I am persuaded that he will put the Affair *en bon Train.*

Fourthly & lastly (to conclude the Heads of my stupid & troublesome Sermon) I must request a Portion of your Advice & Assistance upon the different Mode of being managed which I experienced *to* Yarmouth, & *from* Norwich.—The fare I paid in Town when quitting London was only £2 = 10, (with the Exception of the Shillings exacted by the Guard & Coachman), & no Charge whatever was then made for my Luggage:—When I took my Place in the Norwich Mail to return hither, £2 = 15 were demanded, which Sum was accordingly paid, & when I alighted at Charing Cross, *6 shillings more* were demanded for Luggage; making the Charge of £3 = 1, & with the Douceurs to the above named Worthies £4 = 6.

Now if you can inform me why this different Arrangement takes Place, I shall be glad, for although I should blush to be shabby, I have an utter Hatred to *Imposition,* & will ever persevere in my Determination to oppose it, whether in Art, Science, or *Meum & Tuum,* in all of which, God knows there is a most exuberant Abundance.

When I know whether I have been humbugged in this Business or no, I shall proceed accordingly, for it were idle to embroil oneself wantonly for the Trifle of a few Shillings.—I think it was observed that the Coach in which I travelled to Ipswich[7] was not the regular Mail, but an Expedition Coach;[8] this might *possibly* account for Luggage not being charged in the first Instance.—Of this, however, I wait your Instructions, upon which alone I shall be regulated.

Upon my Return hither, I found some 12 or 14 letters on Business waiting my Answer, & soon after comes in Novello requesting me to do his popish Drudgery for two Sundays to come at the Portugueze Chapel:[9] so you see I must pay a little dearly for my Freak to your County.—I in no Degree regret it; on the contrary I never could feel more pleasantly independent of Cares & Restraints than in so

---

[4] Not identified: presumably a member of Pettet's musical circle.   [5] Not identified.

[6] Presumably a sardonic reference to Ozias Linley and Robert Elwin: see SW to Pettet, 22 Sept. 1815.

[7] Presumably a slip of the pen for 'Yarmouth'.   [8] i.e. an express service.

[9] An undated letter to an unidentified recipient, possibly Glenn, may also refer to this request: see Appendix, Letter 9.

friendly & chearful Society as I have had a *reiterated* Proof of, in this my second & most satisfactory Visit.

With best Wishes to Mrs P. & Regards to all enquiring Friends, believe me,

My dear Sir,
With great Esteem,
Yours most cordially
S Wesley

To Vincent Novello [Gower Place], 1 September [1815][1]

ALS, 2 pp. (BL, Add. MS 11729, fo. 117)
Addressed To | Mʳ Novello | Oxford Street | N. 240 | Friday | Morning
Pmk 1 SP 1815

Dear N

Since we parted on Wednesday Night[2] I have been seriously ill with what the larned Physickers call the Cholera Morbus, but what plain unadulterated Christians like you & me denominate a damned violent Cholic.—I got little or no Rest all that Night, & am yet very weak, but am venturing (in a Coach) to Turnham Green, whence I shall come back by a similar Conveyance.—I could not stir out all Yesterday, but the Confinement afforded me an Opportunity of writing a good Deal, & answering Correspondents who had been too long waiting.—If we consider fairly, we shall find that all Evils have some opposite Good responsive to them, & People would be less discontented if they would balance their Ups & Downs in Life.

As I am ordered to keep myself very quiet, & not venture among any Bustle whatever till my Intestines shall have been again screwed up at least to Concert Pitch, I must sacrifice the Idea of going to see the Jugglers[3] To-morrow, but I hope to be sufficiently stout on Sunday to be with you either in the Morning or Afternoon, meanwhile believe me always

Dear N
Yours faithfully,
S Wesley

Friday Septʳ 1, the first of Massacre among Partridges &c.[4]

---

[1] The year is given by the postmark.   [2] 30 Aug.
[3] Probably the troupe of Indian jugglers who were performing at the Minerva Repository, 28 Leadenhall Street (advertisements in *The Times*, 12, 15, 25, 31 Aug.).
[4] i.e. the first day of the partridge-shooting season.

To William Shield[1]   Gower Place, [13] September 1815[2]

ALS, 3 pp. (BL, Egerton MS 2159, fo. 70)
Addressed To | William Shield Esq[re] | Berners Street.

Gower Place Euston Square
Wednesday 12th of Sept[r] 1815

My dear Sir

I have repeatedly besieged your Mansion since your Sejour in the Country, to the great Annoyance (I fear) of your Portress, who however bore my Importunity with most exemplary Patience.—At my last Call but one I was agreeably informed of your Arrival in Town, & in Consequence of this good News I left Word that I would look in *this Morning* about 11 o'Clock, an Hour at which I was told you would be likely to be found within. However I had not that fortunate Result from my Visit.—The Damsel who opened the Door, (& whom I had not seen before) declared you to be from Home.—I accordingly left my Card in Hope of better Luck *ultimately*.—I have been informed by Flight & Robson that M[r] Fuller[3] came one Day from the Country, for the express Purpose of hearing the Music I prepared for his Organ,[4] & although the Barrel had not been corrected (for he was there before I had heard a Note of it myself) he manifested the most unequivocal Signs of perfect Approbation.—This News was of course very welcome to me, especially as I felt conscious that his Satisfaction was certain to be increased when he should listen to the Pieces in their castigate unexceptionable State.—

---

[1] William Shield (1748–1829), violin and viola player and theatre composer. A pupil of Avison in Newcastle upon Tyne, he came to London around 1773 and played in the orchestra of the King's Theatre for eighteen years, first as a violinist and later as a viola player. He wrote over thirty operas between 1778 and 1807, both full-length works and afterpieces, of which the most successful was *Rosina* (1782). He was a founder member of the Philharmonic Society, and was appointed Master of the King's Musick in 1817. He was also a noted collector of music, and both *An Introduction to Harmony* (1800) and *The Rudiments of Thoroughbass* (1815) are in fact anthologies drawn from music in his own library. *An Introduction to Harmony* included the D minor Prelude and Fugue from Book I of the '48', BWV 851, the first piece from the '48' to be published anywhere.

[2] This date corrects SW's 'Wednesday 12th of Sept[r]': 12 Sept. was a Tuesday in 1815.

[3] John Fuller of 36 Devonshire Place (*Court Guide*).

[4] As SW's later remarks make clear, the music that SW was arranging included extracts from Bach's motets. The organ was presumably a barrel and finger organ (i.e. a barrel organ which could also be played in the conventional way). Flight and Robson built a number of such organs: for details of two later instruments, dating probably from the 1830s, see Nicholas Plumley, 'Two Flight and Robson Barrel Organs', *JBIOS* 1 (1977), 101–11.

I must now request the Favour of a Line instructing me whether the said worthy Gentleman is at present in Town, as I feel it a Duty, after his very polite & hospitable Reception in Devonshire Place, to pay my Respects at as early a Moment as possible.—He was partly expected to come & hear the Organ on the Day that several Professional Men were invited: the Meeting was afterwards noticed & described in the News Papers very soon afterward, & I doubt not that you perused the Paragraph.[5]—

Pray have the Kindness to say whether I left in your safe Keeping the *Credo* of Seb^n Bach,[6] which I remember having *brought* with me to Berner's Street, but rather think I did *not* take away when I did the Book of Motetts[7] from which the Movements prepared for the Organ have been selected.

I am meditating a Publication of the former noble Work, if I can only secure *seventy* Subscribers, which I think you will judge to be no very arrogant expectation.—My Design is not that of pecuniary Profit: I want merely to clear my Expences, & this cannot be done under from 60 to 70l:—even with the best Economy.[8]

Although hitherto so 'ill-starred' I shall again make an early Effort for a vivâ Voce Conference, until which wished-for Event believe me, & at all Times,

My dear Sir,
Your truly obliged
& <grate>ful

S Wesley

---

[5] The newspaper account of this demonstration has not been traced.

[6] i.e. the Credo of Bach's B minor Mass. SW's copy has not been identified. It may have been the one now at the Pendlebury Library, Cambridge, made in 1811 by J. Barber, probably from the copy dated 1788 in the Royal Library (now BL, RM 21.e.7); a mid-18th-cent. copy in the hand of John Christopher Smith is at the Bodleian Library, Oxford (MS Tenbury 1230). Burney and Picart are known to have possessed copies, to which SW may have had access; they were included in the sales of their libraries on 8 Aug. 1814 and 10 Mar. 1848 respectively (*Catalogue of the Music Library of Charles Burney, sold in London, 8 August 1814*: facsimile edn. with an Introduction by A. Hyatt King (Amsterdam, 1973); Percy M. Young, *The Bachs, 1500–1850* (1970), 296; King, 32, 47, 133, 136).

[7] Presumably the volume referred to in SW to Novello, 4 Jan. 1814.

[8] Although the Kyrie and Gloria of the B minor Mass had been published by Nägeli in 1801, there was at this time no edition of the Credo, and SW's projected edition would have been the first. In fact SW was not able to secure enough subscriptions to proceed, and the edition did not appear at this time. SW made at least one further attempt to publish it: the 'English and Foreign Literary Intelligence' section of the *English Musical Gazette* for 1 Jan. 1819 announced that it was 'soon to be published by subscription' and was 'in a forward state of preparation for the press, under the immediate superintendence of Mr Samuel Wesley'. There are no copies extant of this edition, and it must be assumed that it was never published.

To Alfred Pettet [Gower Place], 22 September 1815

ALS, 1 p. (Harvard)
Addressed To | Alfred Pettet Esqre | Norwich | (favoured by Mr Linley)[1]

London, Septr 22. 1815

Dear Sir

Our Friend W. Linley franks this to you together with the Composition for Mr Taylor,[2] to whom I beg you to present my kind Respects with many Thanks for his obliging & spirited Promotion of the Cause of the *Credo*, which I really now begin to think is likely to come forth into the World, to the Wonder & Delight of true Musicians & the Confusion of some of our Doctors, & would-be-Criticks.

I hinted to Linley, with whom I passed the last Wednesday, that in Consequence of the very cordial & warm Reception I have in two Instances met in your ancient & honourable City,[3] I feel it a Pleasure, as well as a Duty, to lend my Services whenever in my Power, upon any patriotic public Occasion: I therefore suggested to him, that I should have much Satisfaction in assisting at the Charity Meeting about to take Place for the Benefit of the Blind,[4] & if my Offer be accepted, I shall expect no other Remuneration whatever, beside merely my travelling Expenses.—Whether after having been so recently at Norwich, this Proposal may possibly wear the Appearance of *Supererogation*, & if pushing myself into Notice uncalled & unrequired, I leave to be considered & determined by the higher Powers: I can only say that I am conscious that the Offer is made from a Motive of Gratitude not of Vanity, & therefore I leave the Matter to be canvassed & the Event decided as shall seem most prudent & eligible on all Sides.

Please to thank Mr Sharp for the Song,[5] which however was transcribed (I guess) at such a Mail-Coach Pace, that some of the Words reminded me of a certain Writing some Time ago which made one King Belshazzar's Hair stand on

---

[1] William Linley presumably took the letter with him on a visit to his brother Ozias in Norwich.

[2] Either Edward Taylor or the blind Norwich organist James Taylor (1781–1855), who later contributed to *QMMR*. For James Taylor, see Thomas Damant Eaton, 'Some Account of the Life and Doctrines of Mr James Taylor, Organist' in his *Musical Criticism and Biography* (1872), 256–90. The composition has not been identified.   [3] In Oct. 1814 and July 1815.

[4] The Charity Concert for the Indigent Blind, to be directed by Pettet at St Stephen's church on 19 Oct. during the Michaelmas Sessions Week. As is clear from SW's letter to Pettet of 29 Sept, SW's offer came too late for him to take part in the programme.

[5] 'The Noachic Procession' (see SW to Pettet, 31 July 1815). No copy has been traced.

End.[6]—however I puzzled it out rightly I *believe*, at last.—It's a mighty funny Thing, & I think perfectly innocent, maugre Friend Ozee's[7] wry Faces at it.—To be sure one ought to be cautious not to sing it in Presence of *Bob Elwyn*.[8] By the bye, when next you see that learned, ingenious, & facetious Limb of the Church militant,[9] pray convey my best Regards, & tell him I am perfectly convinced that the Recollection of some of his Jokes will cause the Detention of my outward Man in this wicked World, for some Years longer (at least) than if I had missed making his Acquaintance.

I shall spend this Evening with Novello, & will spur him on: indeed he seldom needs Stimulus whenever he has an Opportunity of doing a friendly or obliging Turn of any Kind.—You may rely upon having the Parts you require, in good Time.[10]—He however says that he is ashamed of his Name being mentioned *for the first Time* in your County upon so trivial an Occasion as adding a few *puffing* Auxiliaries to a paltry Tune; but I told him that his Name is better known in Norfolk already than he is aware.

Upon the Subject of my Proposal in the first Page,[11] you will oblige me by as early Intelligence as you conveniently can.—

Believe me, with true Esteem,
My dear Sir
Yours very faithfully
   S Wesley

P.S. My Book (MS) in which the Chimney Sweepers' Song[12] is, I am waiting for, from the Hands of the Binder.—I shall send to blow him up on the Strength of his unwarrantable Laziness, for he ought to have returned it a Month ago.

---

[6] The writing on the wall which appeared at Belshazzar's feast and announced the fall of his kingdom: see Daniel 5: 1–30.   [7] Ozias Linley.

[8] Robert Fountain Elwin (1783–1853), adm. Gonville and Caius College, Cambridge (1801), BA (1805), ordained deacon and subsequently priest (1807); he was at this time Rector of Wilby and Hargham, Norfolk, near Norwich (Venn).   [9] i.e. Ozias Linley.

[10] Of an arrangement by Novello of 'Adeste Fideles' ('O come, all ye faithful', also known as the Portuguese Hymn): see SW to Pettett, 5 Oct. 1815.

[11] i.e. to play at the forthcoming charity concert.

[12] 'The Chimney Sweepers', a humorous glee [*c*.1795] by John 'Christmas' Beckwith (1750–1809), father of John Charles Beckwith. SW's manuscript book has not been preserved.

To George Polgreen Bridgetower

Gower Place,
22 September 1815

ALS, 1 p. (Emory, Letter 56)
Addressed To | Mr Bridgetower | Chapel Street | Grosvenor Place | N. 20 | Friday
   Morning
Pmk 22 SP 1815

Gower Place
Euston Square
22^d of Septr 1815.

Dear Sir,

Will you favour me with a Line, just to inform whether I had not the Pleasure of lending you Bach's Violin Solos[1] some time since? I have been searching diligently, though hitherto in Vain, but I shall be delighted to learn that they are in your safe Keeping.—In the Event of the Worst, that they are really lost (& then I know they must have been stolen out of my House) I would immediately resolve upon copying them again propriâ Manu,[2] from the first Edition I could obtain the Loan of.—As Salomon *gave* me the Copy in MS. to which I allude, I cannot very decorously acquaint him with my present Tribulation: he has a printed Copy, which I have seen, & which I fancy is the same Edition as your own.[3]

Believe me
very sincerely
Yours
   S Wesley

---

[1] i.e. SW's manuscript copy of the Sonatas and Partitas, BWV 1001–6.   [2] 'In my own hand'.
[3] The Simrock edition (*Tre sonate per il violino solo senza basso*, Bonn, [1802]), which was in fact the only complete edition at this time.

To Alfred Pettet   Gower Place, 29 September [1815]¹

ALS, 3 pp. (BL, Egerton MS 2159, fo. 74)
Addressed To | Alfred Pettet Esqre | Norwich | Norfolk | 29th of Sept^r

London
Gower Place. 29th of Sept^r

My dear Sir

I should have not thus *instantaneously* pestered you with another Letter, had it not been for the Desire expressed in yours of receiving an early Account of the Fate of your obliging Present, which arrived safely Yesterday, in *good* Condition, which in Regard to Game is in my Estimation very far preferable to *high* Condition, although this Confession compleatly destroys my Reputation as an Epicure, who I believe values Articles of the Sort usually in Proportion to their *Putrescence*.— I however may boast of one (& I believe the only) Epicure in my Family who was a first Cousin by my Mother's Side,² & whom I heard say that 'nothing was so delicious as a stinking Haunch of Venison save & except a rotten Woodcock.'

Accept my cordial Thanks for your Zeal in the Cause of the Credo, & I have this Day received a List of 4 additional Names to the *Hall Concert*,³ who I understand have at the Instance of Mr E. Taylor⁴ come forward in a very spirited Stile upon the Occasion: by the Way I think it both proper & respectful to insert the Names of these Gentlemen composing it, *severally* & alphabetically with the Rest.—Perhaps therefore you will at a convenient Opportunity favour me with the Nomenclature of these my Patrons.

I much regret not having sooner volunteered my *digital* Services on Account of your approaching Meeting,⁵ & can only say that upon any other similar Occasion I shall hold myself in Readiness, whenever there may be a Chance of thereby benefiting the Concern.—As to the Circumstance of the Price of Admission not being high, this to me would not furnish the smallest Reason to object, because the Cause of Charity being of itself the noblest in Nature, the Respectability of it is (in my Mind) not in the least affected or diminished by putting it in the Power of *more* Individuals to be serviceable to it, than could happen were the Means more costly.

Will you have the Kindness to inform our Friend W. Linley that I went to Preston's in Quest of the Music Book required, & have at Length obtained it, *after*

---

¹ The year is established by SW's references to subscriptions for the Credo and to the negotiations between the Professional Concerts and the Philharmonic Society (see n. 9).

² Not certainly identified: probably one of the children of Howell Gwynne (1711–80) or of Marmaduke Gwynne (1722–72), brothers of SW's mother (Theophilus Jones, *History of Brecknock*, 3rd edn., ii. 238–40; iv. 248, 269–70).   ³ A series of Norwich subscription concerts.

⁴ Edward Taylor.   ⁵ The charity concert on 19 Oct.

some Days' Delay, but that now I shall go to Work almost immediately according to Instructions contained in his last Letter.[6]

Will you also, at the first Opportunity you may have of communicating with M[r] Pymer of Beccles,[7] return him my best Thanks for a Leash[8] of excellent Birds & also make my most cordial Respects to him & Family.

This may be called bothering you with Commissions, but I too well know your Promptitude to oblige to believe that you may consider me too importunate.

I have no musical News of Importance to *import*, unless you may think it of any that the Persons stiling themselves the *professional* Concert,[9] in Contradistinction & indeed in *Opposition* to the Philharmonic have (through Viotti,[10] whom I consider as an Arch Hypocrite) made what I believe to be no better than a mock Proposal towards an Union with the Society whom the former so treacherously left: in consequence of this a Committee has been appointed to examine the Nature & Extent of their Propositions, & a Meeting upon the Business is about to take Place very shortly: my present Opinion & Apprehension is that no real solid Agreement will be effected between the two Fraternities, & that the Feuds between them will rather be increased than diminished, so that the ultimate Result will be the Annihilation of both.[11]

---

[6] Probably an edition of the *Music in Macbeth* falsely attributed to Matthew Locke, which SW was arranging for Linley, and which appeared the following year as the Appendix to Linley's *Shakspeare's Dramatic Songs* (*CPM*). Linley was presumably staying in Norwich with his brother Ozias.

[7] Thomas Pymer (or Pymar) (*c*.1764–1854), organist of St Michael's, Beccles, Suffolk, and a member of Pettet's musical circle. He was a subscriber in 1824 to SW's Service and in 1826 to Novello's *Fitzwilliam Music*, and sent gifts of game to SW on other occasions.   [8] i.e. three (*OED*).

[9] The original Professional Concert had been established in 1783 by professional musicians including Clementi, Wilhelm Cramer, and Salomon, and without the support of wealthy amateurs. It had been discontinued in 1793, but a new series of Professional Concerts had recently been launched in direct competition with the Philharmonic Society.

[10] The violinist and composer Giovanni Battista Viotti (1755–1824), a founder member of the Philharmonic Society, now involved with the Professional Concerts.

[11] Anxious about their future, the organizers of the Professional Concert had approached the Philharmonic Society to discuss a possible merger of the two societies. The matter was discussed at a Philharmonic Society committee meeting on 27 Sept. chaired by SW. A subcommittee consisting of Attwood, Horsley, and Webbe was set up to examine the proposal and to meet with representatives of the Professional Concert; they reported back to the committee meeting of 9 Oct. Negotiations about the possibility of a merger continued for some time but without any outcome, and the matter was eventually dropped (Ehrlich, *First Philharmonic*, 9; Loan 48.3/1). The Professional Concerts seem to have lasted no longer than the 1816 season: according to a memoir of Salomon in the *Harmonicon* for Feb. 1830, 'in 1815, an attempt was made by a party . . . to propose and extinguish the Philharmonic Concerts. They gave the hapless name of "Professional Concerts" to their performances in 1816. After a short existence these concerts yielded up the ghost, without exciting the least commiseration for their richly-deserved fate.' The Philharmonic (now the Royal Philharmonic) Society continues to this day, albeit in much changed form.

This I own I regret, but it gives me much less Uneasiness that were you to cease to believe me

my dear Sir
most truly & cordially yours

S. Wesley

Goose Day[12] I vow! & forgot this great Festival till this Moment.

To [Alfred Pettet][1]   Gower Place, 5 October 1815

ALS, 1 p. (SMU)

London
Gower Place Oct[r] 5. 1815

Dear Sir

With this will arrive (I trust) a spiritual & a convivial Dish, by which I mean the Hymn 'Adeste Fideles',[2] & the Chimney Sweepers' May Day Adventure.—

Novello desired me to observe, that when you have made such Transcript as you wish, he will be glad to have the Score returned at the first convenient Opportunity.

You will oblige me by mentioning to M[r] Beckwith,[3] when you next see him, that I feel indebted for his last Letter, & very friendly Attention relative to my Subscription for the Credo, & also by telling M[r] Linley that my Score of the Songs &c[4] is in great Forwardness, & will be shortly compleated.

I regret that I am too much pressed for Time to lengthen this Letter, although probably *you* may have great Reason to thank your Stars that I do not longer trespass on your Patience.

With best Wishes to all yours,
believe me always
Dear Sir
Your sincere & faithful

S Wesley

---

[12] i.e. Michaelmas Day, when it was traditional to eat goose.

[1] It is clear from the date and content of this letter that it is to Pettet.

[2] An arrangement of 'Adeste fideles' had appeared in Novello's *A Selection of Sacred Music*. This was presumably another arrangement.

[3] John Charles Beckwith (1788–1819), who had in 1809 succeeded his father as organist of Norwich Cathedral. He was also organist of St Peter Mancroft (*Grove*[6]; Shaw, 205).

[4] i.e. SW's arrangement of the *Music in Macbeth*.

To George Polgreen Bridgetower

[Gower Place],
11 November [1815]¹

ALS, 1 p. (BL, Add. MS 56411, fo. 16)
Addressed To | Mʳ Bridgetower | Chapel Street | Grosvenor Place | Nº 20. | Saturday
   Morning
Pmk 11 NOV 1815

Gower Place
Euston Square
Saturday Nov. 11.

Dear Sir

Mʳ Ball, of Duke Street, informed me that you have a new *great Gun* in the
musical Way, to whom you wish me to be introduced, & I am inclined to think,
from the Description of his Stile of Performance, that it is the Gentleman whom
Clementi proposed lately to become an Associate of the Philharmonists this
Season, & which Motion I had the Pleasure of seconding.²—Pray let me know as
soon as convenient, when the Meeting can be managed, & I will endeavour to
arrange my Odds & Ends accordingly.

(By the Way) I directed a Letter to Chapel Street, some *Months* ago, which I
conclude never reached you.³—In it I expressed a Solicitude concerning my MS.
Copy of Bach's Violin Solos, which I *hope* that I lent to you, because in that Case
I know them to be safe: I have searched diligently for them, but hitherto without
Success.

Believe me
Dear Sir
Very truly yours
   S Wesley

¹ The year is given by the postmark.
² The pianist August (Stephan) Alexander Klengel (1783–1852), a pupil of Clementi who had
travelled extensively with him on the continent. Following their successful visit to St Petersburg in 1805,
Klengel remained there until 1811. He had arrived in London earlier in 1815 and was proposed for associate membership of the Philharmonic Society on 16 Oct. at a meeting chaired by SW. His quintet for piano
and strings was performed at a Philharmonic Society concert on 26 Feb. 1816.
³ SW to Bridgetower, 22 Sept. 1815.

To Vincent Novello   [Gower Place], 7 December 1815

ALS, 2 pp. (BL, Add. MS 11729, fo. 122)

Thursday
Dec[r] 7. 1815

Dear N

I regret that I shall not be able to see you at the Chapel on Sunday next, but perhaps you will be at the Philharmonic shortly, as our Meetings become continually more frequent.—To-morrow is fixed for another of the Directors.[1]—I gave my Vote for your Honour on Monday, but as you foretold, they have elected Naldi.[2]—Let me have the Magazine in a Day or two, otherwise I may come too late with my Answer to the Gentleman who does not like me & M[r] Jackson.[3]—I have nearly finished your Masses,[4] & have taken one or two Liberties with *my own*,[5] which I rather trust you will not much disapprove.

Yours always truly

S Wesley

P.S. Where you see the Blots, they were made by my sneezing on the Paper, for I have a vile Cold.

---

[1] There were general meetings of the Philharmonic Society on 13, 16, 22, 27 Nov. and on 4 Dec.; the dates of directors' meetings at this time are not known. SW had been elected a director on 22 Nov. (Loan 48.3/1).

[2] The election at the meeting of 4 Dec. was to fill the directorship left vacant by the death of Salomon on 28 Nov. The bass Giuseppe Naldi (1770–1820) was elected with seventeen votes, Novello and Dragonetti each receiving one vote.

[3] The Nov. 1816 number of *EM*. The Sept. number (pp. 218–19) had included a polemical epistolary article by SW under the *nom de plume* 'Philomusicus' which quoted with approval a passage from the essay 'On Gentlemen-Artists' in William Jackson of Exeter's *The Four Ages, together with Essays on Various Subjects* (1798), attacking the pretensions of amateur musicians. The 'gentleman who does not like me and M[r] Jackson' was 'HW' (unidentified), whose reply to SW's article had been published in the Nov. number (pp. 399–400). SW's subsequent reply to 'HW' appeared in the Dec. number (pp. 486–8) (Olleson, 1103–4).

[4] i.e. SW's arrangements of two Gregorian masses, later published in Novello's *Twelve Easy Masses*, 3 vols. (1816).   [5] SW's *Missa in duplicibus* (1789) in the same publication.

To Vincent Novello   Gower Place, 9 December [1815][1]

ALS, 1 p. (BL, Add. MS 11729, fo. 123)
Addressed Mr Novello | Oxford Street | N. 240 | Saturday Decr 9
Pmk 9 DE 1815

Gower Place
Saturday 9th of Dec^r

Dear N

Among other prudential Arrangements, it was determined last Night[2] that a certain Number of Members competent to correct & superintend the Copies of Parts from the several Scores in MS that may be brought forward at the Concerts be chosen, & among them your Name was of course immediately proposed: I believe there will be no Doubt that you will be appointed President in the said Department, & it is particularly <w>ished that you be present at the general Meeting on Monday next,[3] of which I presume you have before now had legal Notice.—I hope you will not object to the Office in Question, as I am convinced your Acceptance of it will prove a most material Benefit to the Concern, & greatly tend to the Perfection of the Performances, several of which it seems have suffered exceedingly in their intended Effect from the Incorrectness of the Copies.

I was sorry I could not avail myself of the Invitation to meet you this Evening at Robertson's:[4] I have been pre-engaged at Islington for 10 Days past, otherwise would most willingly join the Party.—Pray make my Respects to Mr R. & his Brother, explaining the Circumstance.

Yours always truly

S Wesley

P.S. I want the Magazine as soon as you can let me have it.

---

[1] The year is given by the postmark.

[2] Presumably at a directors' meeting of the Philharmonic Society. No minutes of directors' meetings from this time have been preserved, and it is probable that none were taken.

[3] On 11 Dec., when the matter was further discussed and the committee was formally constituted: it consisted of Novello, Cipriani Potter, Burrows, Carnaby, Walmesley, and Williams, and had as its remit the 'revisal of the library, and the examination of all works copied for performances at the concerts' (Loan 48.3/1).

[4] Henry Robertson, Treasurer of Covent Garden Theatre, who subscribed to Novello's *A Collection of Sacred Music* and was a member of the Novello circle (Clarke, *Life and Labours*, 11). The name of his brother is not known.

To Vincent Novello [Gower Place], 18 December [1815][1]

ALS, 1 p. (BL, Add. MS 11729, fo. 124)
Addressed To | Mr Novello | Oxford Street | 240 | Monday Evening

Dear N,

You vanished some how at the Chapel Door yesterday, & I lost you altogether.
—I wished to have told you that there is a blind Man[2] who is desirous of establishing himself as a Tuner; & he is also desirous of being admitted to tune the
Pianofortes of some of our professional *Heads*, for the Purpose of gaining some
Reputation from their Report of his Work.—He tells me that he has several Times
tuned John Cramer's Piano, & he tuned mine some Weeks ago very well.—He asked
me if I thought you would let him tune yours, which I ventured to say you were not
likely to refuse.—He will call at your House To-morrow or Wednesday, & therefore
you will be so good as to leave some Message for him in Case of your Absence.

Yours always truly
SW

Monday Evening | 18th of Dec^r

P.S. I forget his Name, but that is not yet material.

To Vincent Novello [Gower Place], 30 December [1815][1]

ALS, 2 pp. (BL, Add. MS 11729, fo. 125)
Addressed To | Mr Novello | Oxford Street | N. 240 | Saturday Morning
Pmk 0 DE 181

Dear N.

The Somerset House Lodge does not meet on Monday next,[2] but I am otherwise engaged, therefore let us name *Tuesday* for being with Banks:[3] if you write

---

[1] The year is given by 18 Dec. falling on a Monday and by Novello's address.
[2] Not identified.

[1] The year is given by 30 Dec. falling on a Saturday and by Novello's address.   [2] 1 Jan. 1816.
[3] The Revd John Cleaver Banks (1765/6–1845), originally John Banks Cleaver, educated Harrow,
admitted Clare College, Cambridge (1783), LL B (1789), ord. deacon (1791), priest (1805), curate of East
Retford, Notts. (1805). He was the dedicatee of Clementi's *Three Trios for Pianoforte, Violin, and Cello*,
Op. 35 (1796) and of his Sonata in E flat, Op. 41 (1804). He lived at 5 Park Row, Knightsbridge (Venn;
Court Guide; Alan Tyson, *Thematic Catalogue of the Works of Muzio Clementi* (Tutzing, 1967), 75, 81).

to him immediately, directing to the Revd Cleaver Banks, Knightsbridge, near the Barracks, the Odds are in Favour of his coming to the Chapel on Sunday morning: at all Events, he will return you a timely Answer.

Yours as ever

S Wesley

PS I was *axt* yesterday what was the true Translation of '*Pot-pourri*,' & whether it was not a *Hodge-Podge* of Inconsistencies?—I said, my best Conjecture of the Origin was *Popery*. 'Catafalco, an Italian Term, literally signifying Scaffold.—It is chiefly used for a Decoration of Architecture, Sculpture, & Painting, raised on a timber Scaffold, to shew a Coffin or Tomb in a funeral Solemnity.'

Chambers's Cyclopædia, *sur l'Article* 'Catafalco',

Mown Seer N.B.

Saturday morning 30th of Dec^r

To Vincent Novello   Gower Place, [15 January 1816][1]

ALS, 1 p. (BL, Add. MS 11729, fo. 127)
Addressed To | Mr Novello | Oxford Street | N. 240 | Monday Morning
Pmk 15 JA 1816

Gower Place
Monday Morning

Dear N

We cooked the Hash yesterday as well as we could without you, & I think the Mass went very well: we had Ricci's Kyrie, Gloria, Sanctus, & Agnus, & the selected Credo, & Roman Domine:[2] Miss Stamp[3] (who is intimate with Miss Harington) was introduced into the Choir, & certainly would be an Acquisition to you, were she engaged as a Fixture.—The Feast was 'of the Name of Jesus,'[4]

---

[1] The date is given by the postmark.

[2] SW describes the music sung in Novello's absence at the Portuguese Embassy Chapel on the previous day: the Kyrie, Gloria, Sanctus, and Agnus from the two-part Mass in G minor by Francesco Pasquale Ricci (1732–1817), first published in Samuel Webbe I's *A Collection of Masses* (1792) and subsequently in Novello's *A Selection of Sacred Music*; the Credo from the 'Selected Mass' in the same publication, containing sections by Franki, Perez, dos Santos, Mozart, and Perti; and an unidentified setting of the prayer for the monarch 'Domine salvum fac'.   [3] Not identified.

[4] Celebrated in the Roman calendar at this time on the second Sunday after Epiphany (6 Jan.).

& Turle[5] & Prina sang 'O Jesu Pastor bone,'[6] that fine treacly Lollypop of old Webbe, but it had quite a ravishing Effect, upon the *Ladies* especially.

The Hymn 'that's call'd Te *Dum*'[7] is to be hallood out next Thursday[8] it seems, & your *Nightingales* want a Rehearsal, & wished me to inform you & suggest that perhaps *Wednesday* Evening might suit you to drill them.—I promised to give you this Intelligence.

I enclose the Hymn of the Feast Yesterday,[9] which of Course you will harmonize among the Rest.—It is a very nice one.

Yours in great Haste

S Wesley

I suppose you had a roaring Day with Hunt[10] yesterday.

To [Benjamin Jacob][1]   Gower Place, 15 February 1816

ALS, 1 p. (RCM, MS 2130, fo. 47)

4 Gower Place Euston Square.
Thursday. 15th of Feb. 1816.

Dear Sir

You are perfectly welcome to the Psalm & Chant annexed,[2] if they will suit your Purpose: I have also added a few Proposals for a Work[3] which from the Name of the Author, I guess you will find no Inclination to decry: My Object

---

[5] James Turle (1802–82), a boy treble in the chapel choir. Born in Taunton, he had begun his musical education as a chorister in Wells Cathedral choir from 1810 to 1813. He was later organist of Christ Church, Blackfriars (1819–29) and of St James's, Bermondsey (1829–31). He was Greatorex's assistant at Westminster Abbey, and succeeded him as organist and master of the choristers on Greatorex's death in 1831 (Shaw, 336–7). He directed the Abbey choristers at SW's funeral.

[6] 'O Jesu Deus magna pastor bone dulcis agne', by Samuel Webbe I, from his *A Collection of Motets or Antiphons* (1792).   [7] The Te Deum: see SW to Novello, 16 Aug. [1812], n. 7.

[8] On 18 Jan., a day of general thanksgiving and public holiday for the birthday of Queen Charlotte (*The Times*).   [9] 'Jesu, dulcis memoria'.

[10] Probably Leigh Hunt, a regular member of Novello's circle.

---

[1] Jacob is identified as the addressee from SW's best wishes to his wife in the postscript. This is SW's first surviving letter to him for some time, and suggests that they were by this time in only infrequent contact. It was doubtless in response to a request from Jacob for SW to contribute to his *National Psalmody* (see n. 2).

[2] Presumably 'He's blest whose sins have pardon gained' (a metrical setting of Ps. 32) and a chant for the Te Deum, which Jacob subsequently included in his *National Psalmody* (1817).

[3] As is apparent from SW's later comments, the Credo of the B minor Mass.

in publishing it is not Emolument, which indeed is seldom to be expected in this Town from any *masterly* musical Productions, but my chief View has been to manifest to English *real* Judges of the Art, how mistaken & false was the Report of those who have impudently pretended to prove that the great Sebastian Bach could not compose truly *vocal* Music.—I mean also that the present Work be regarded as a Study for *Masters* in orchestral Composition, & such indeed it will be found.—I want merely to cover the Expenses of the Publication, which I find cannot be done by less than 70 Subscriptions at a Guinea each: at present I have about *40*, so that *30* more are required.—I need not add much as Panegyric upon *any* grand Production of the matchless Man, but I will only just observe that even you, who have been familiar with sundry of his Compositions, will be surprized at some of the gigantic Features of the admirable Credo in Question.

I remain
Dear Sir
Sincerely Yours
S. Wesley

My best Respects to Mrs Jacob.

To Stephen Jones[1]   Gower Place, 15 February 1816

ALS, 1 p. (Rylands, DDWF 15/20)
Addressed To | Mr Jones | Printing Office | N. 103 | Shoe Lane | Fleet Street | Thursday
Night
Pmk 16 FE 1816

Dear Sir
As the Examination of 'a Sonata by Wm Beale' did not appear in the January Number, I presume that the annexed Pages united with it will be quite sufficient for the next, & I shall be obliged by your sending me the Proof Sheet as in the former Instance when printed.[2]—I mentioned in my last a Wish that you would

---

[1] Stephen Jones (1763–1827), the editor of *EM* since 1807. He had previously been editor of the *Whitehall Evening Post* (from Mar. 1797) and was responsible for the revision of *Biographia Dramatica* (1812). He was a prominent Freemason, and for some years edited the *Freemasons' Magazine* (*DNB*).
[2] SW's review of Beale's *A Second Sonata for the Pianoforte with an Accompaniment for the Violin* duly appeared in the Feb. 1816 number of *EM* (p. 144), together with reviews of R. Williams's set of variations on 'Begone, dull Care' and Hook's song 'Far o'er the Swelling Seas', the copy for which presumably constituted the 'annexed pages' referred to here.

be so good as to calculate the Account of the Pages of the Musical Review from Midsummer to last Xtmas 1815, & perhaps you will send it together with the Proof Sheet.—Should this be too troublesome as a general Request, if you will candidly tell me so, I will not encroach upon your Time on this Subject in future.

> I remain
> Dear Sir
> Very truly Yours,
>> S Wesley

Gower Place | Euston Square | Thursday. 15th of Feb. 1816

P.S. How do you get on with Thelephthora?[3]

To Vincent Novello   [Gower Place], 22 February [1816][1]

ALS, 3 pp. (BL, Add. MS 11729, fo. 129)
Addressed To | Mr Novello | N. 240. | Oxford Street | Thursday Night
Pmk 23 FE 1816

Thursday Evening
22^d Feb^y

Dear N.

I think you will *not* conclude, that from neither seeing nor hearing from me so long, I did not give you full Credit for the solid Reasons you brought forward for your Absence on the Evening when we expected the Pleasure of your Company: We were disappointed, certainly, but *Pokey* very opportunely came in, & furnished a Substitution for your good Offices in the Matter of Bach's Sonatas,[2] several of which he got through very respectably, I endeavouring to help the 'Sheep's Guts & Horsehair' Part of the Concern as well as I could.—

---

[3] *Thelyphthora, Or, a Treatise on Female Ruin, in its Causes, Effects, Consequences, Prevention, and Remedy, Considered on the Basis of the Divine Law* (1780) by SW's godfather Martin Madan, which SW had perhaps lent or recommended to Jones. For the influence of Madan's controversial views on marriage and his advocacy of polygamy on SW's own thinking, see Biographical Introduction.

[1] The year is given by the postmark.
[2] J. S. Bach's Sonatas for Violin and Harpsichord, BWV 1014–19.

I must say, that altho' our Party was in my own Nutshell of a House, every one seemed to enjoy himself thoroughly, & I have seldom witnessed a Meeting where universal Satisfaction more prevailed.—I trust that *before Lent be over* we may have another such a pleasant merry Bout, even should the Day be one of those whereon eating Flesh becomes damnable.

I suppose you are apprized of the Rehearsal To-morrow Evening at the Argyll Rooms,[3] named for 6, & at which I hope we shall meet: I shall make a Point of being there, & expect *some* Entertainment, with a mixture of Disgust, if this *Sextuple Citharian* Humbug[4] is to be practised.—I am told that Attwood had the Honour of suggesting this grand Novelty, but I suspect that he is only the Puppet, & that the *real Fundamental* was the mountebank Knight.[5]

An Acquaintance & Pupil of mine who subscribes to both the Phil. & the Prof. tells me that he was present at both Concerts of the latter:[6] the Attendance was but indifferent on the first Night, but on the second, far worse, & the *Sort* of Company into the Bargain. As to the Performance, he says it appeared to him that Lindley's[7] Violoncello was designed for the chief Attraction, & as to Vaccari,[8] he seemed to be playing on a very inferior Violin.—The Critic above has good musical Taste, & I have no Cause to suspect that this Representation is in the least Degree exaggerated.

I was obliged to go with Sam Webbe last Sunday Morning to the Bavarian Chapel,[9] why, I will explain to you when we meet, but otherwise I should have been at your Shop.

Yours always truly,

S Wesley

---

[3] For the Philharmonic Concert on Monday 26 Feb. In fact, as the postscript to SW's next letter explains, the rehearsal was later postponed to the following day.

[4] Ferdinand Ries's *Bardic Overture*, scored for six harps and orchestra, which received its first performance at the concert under discussion.

[5] Sir George Smart, who had purchased his knighthood in Dublin in 1811: a procedure which had cost him nearly £200, but which he evidently considered worth the expense for the added prestige it brought. For this episode, which predictably failed to impress SW, see Young, 6–7; Ehrlich, *Music Profession*, 40.

[6] The concerts of the Philharmonic Society and the Professional Concerts alternated on Monday evenings at the Argyll Rooms. The first two concerts of the Professional Concerts were on 5 and 19 Feb.

[7] Robert Lindley (1776–1855), the leading English cellist of his generation.

[8] Either N. Vaccari, one of the original associate members of the Philharmonic Society, or Francesco Vaccari (b. 1773), an Italian violinist who was briefly in England in 1815–16 (*Grove*[5]).

[9] The church of Our Lady of the Assumption and St Gregory, Warwick Street, which had opened in 1790 on the site of the former Bavarian Embassy Chapel. Like the former Sardinian Embassy Chapel, it was by this time a public place of worship, but it still retained many of its links with Bavaria and was still generally known as the 'Bavarian Chapel'.

P.S. Du Bois[10] (the Author of 'my Pocket Book & <c'>) said to me a few Days ago, that Braham's late Prank with Wright's wife, instead of being an Instance of Immorality, is a direct Proof of the contrary, inasmuch as he plainly prefers a matrimonial Alliance to the state of Fornication.[11]

To Vincent Novello [Gower Place], 25 February [1816][1]

ALS, 3 pp. (BL, Add. MS 11729, fo. 132)

Sunday Morning
25 Feb

Dear N.

I communicated the Contents of your Letter[2] to Ayrton,[3] & indeed suffered him to read it himself, which I thought the best Evidence of Candour in the Affair: this was during the Rehearsal Yesterday.[4]—He seemed to feel the general Justness of the Remonstrance, but in Objection urged that 'the Institution of the correcting Committee[5] was originally for the purpose of lightening the Expense to such of those Members as declined performing gratuitously in the Orchestra,' & he added that a great Majority of the Band were now paid, so that very few remained who had

---

[10] Edward Dubois (1774–1850), 'wit and man of letters' (*DNB*), predecessor to Stephen Jones as the editor of *EM*, and the author of the satirical pamphlet *My Pocket-book* (1807).

[11] The tenor John Braham (1774–1856) had recently left his long-standing partner Nancy Storace and had run off to the continent with the wife of Wright, a family friend at whose house he had often lodged after performances in London, and who as a purser in the service of the East India Company was often away from home. Braham's desertion of Storace attracted a good deal of adverse publicity and led to him being hissed at a performance of *Israel in Egypt* on 16 Mar. Wright subsequently sued Braham for criminal conversation and was awarded £1,000 damages. Braham's conduct is said to have hastened Storace's death in 1817 (*BD*; *The Times*, 24 July 1816).

[1] The year is given by 25 Feb. falling on a Sunday and the content, from which it is clear that this letter is the one referred to and enclosed in SW's letter to Novello of the following day.

[2] A letter to SW, not preserved, in which Novello evidently discussed his involvement in the Correcting Committee of the Philharmonic Society (see n. 5) and set out issues for SW to raise with Ayrton at the next directors' meeting. Novello appears to have protested about the lack of any reward for this work and to have suggested that an appropriate recompense would be complimentary tickets for the Society's concerts.

[3] William Ayrton (1777–1858), composer, writer, and impresario, youngest son of the organist Edmund Ayrton (1734–1808), FSA (1807), FRS (1837). He was a founder member of the Philharmonic Society, Treasurer 1813–14, and at this time a director. He was manager or director of the Italian opera at the King's Theatre in 1817 and 1821, when Mozart's *Don Giovanni* and Rossini's *La gazza ladra* received their London premières. He wrote reviews of music and literature for the *Morning Chronicle* (1813–26) and *Examiner* (1837–51) and edited and contributed to the *Harmonicon* (1823–33).

[4] On 24 Feb., for the concert on 26 Feb.

[5] For the setting up of this committee, see SW to Novello, 9 Dec. [1815].

the Privilege of a Ticket in the Way you have instanced.[6] However he recommended me to come forward with the Proposition, not as immediately from *you* nominally, but as from the Committee collectively, which I did, but could not carry the Motion upon the liberal (& I think the 'logical' Principle you wished to establish; but it was agreed that *one* Ticket should be granted for *each* of the Members of the Committee to accommodate a Friend, in the way of Loan, that is, that each Member take in Rotation during the Period of the Concerts to lend the said Ticket to his individual Friend, so that *one* of the Committee will have the Opportunity of admitting a Friend to *two* of the Concerts in the Course of the Season.[7]

The meeting of the Directors yesterday was (on account of so much to be done in a very short Time) far from satisfactory to me, but I am only one among 12, & I am the youngest among them, in reference to my *Time* of Election,[8] altho' (except Clementi) the oldest in Point of Age.

I was obliged to hasten to the Glee Club,[9] for I left them sitting at past 4 o'Clock, & had just time to secure a Place at the Table: I should not have gone had I not promised Linley to preside at the Performance of a Glee of his, & indeed I would have immediately gone from the Directors Meeting *home*, but for this Promise, for I have a very severe Inflammation in my right Eye, which is the Cause of my not being at your Sanctum this Morning.—I was to have gone to Pokey this Evening, but must nurse this said game Eye for Fear of not being at my Post To-morrow.[10]—Of course I shall not go to the Lodge.[11]

Perhaps you will look in here To-night when you may be sure of finding me within.

Yours ever truly

S Wesley

PS Watts's[12] summons was for *Saturday*, so that the Friday Rehearsal was countermanded I presume: I fear you were disappointed but I had not Time to let you know of the Change.

---

[6] Under the original rules of the Philharmonic Society, no member or associate member was permitted to receive a fee for performing in the Society's concerts, and the implication of SW's remark here is that they received a complimentary ticket in lieu. This self-denying ordinance was soon abandoned. For the early history of the Philharmonic Society, see Ehrlich, *First Philharmonic*, 1–14.

[7] As there were eight concerts in the season, this implies that the Correcting Committee had reduced from its original six to four members.

[8] SW appears to have forgotten about Naldi, who was in fact the most recently elected director.

[9] The Glee Club, one of many similar societies originating in the later 18th cent., had met regularly since 1783 to dine and sing madrigals, glees, catches, and canons. Its members over the years included Samuel Arnold, Samuel Webbe I and II, Callcott, and Bartleman. In a membership list of 1820 SW is described as among the club's Perpetual Visitors: this was presumably a category of honorary membership (*Grove*[1]; *Grove*[6]; Anon, 'Catch and Glee Clubs', *QMMR* 2 (1820), 324–31).

[10] i.e. for his teaching commitment.

[11] The Somerset House Lodge, which was to meet the following day.

[12] W. Watts, Secretary of the Philharmonic Society, 1815–1847 (Elkin, 135).

To Vincent Novello   [Gower Place], 26 February [1816]¹

ALS, 1 p. (BL, Add. MS 11729, fo. 131)
Addressed To | Mʳ Novello | 240 | Oxford Street | Monday Morning | Paid
Pmk 26 FE 1816

Dear N.

The enclosed² was designed to have been given into your Hand at your Sortie
from Vespers Yesterday, but as this was to have been done by a *Female*, I had not
the Brutality to send her out at so rainy a Period as three o'Clock happened to be.

We are I trust likely to meet this Evening:³ when you read the *envelloped* you
will see that this might have been very problematical only.

Yours as usual
   SW

Monday Morning 26ᵗʰ of Febʸ

To Vincent Novello   [Gower Place, 4 March 1816]¹

ALS, 1 p. (BL, Add. MS 11729, fo. 133)
Addressed To | Mʳ Novello | Oxford Street | N. 240 | Monday Evening
Pmk 5 MR 1816

Dear N.

There seems Fatality against my ever hearing the grand Battle Symphony,² &
my learning how to conduct Choruses from the noble Knight-man, for this Morning
arrived a Summons from the grand Lodge to attend the Quarterly Communication on Wednesday next,³ when I am obliged to dine with my Brother Officers at 5,
& afterwards to take my Station at the Organ for the Remainder of the Evening, &
the Business is never over before 11, so you see I am properly check-mated.

---

¹ The date is given by 26 Feb. falling on a Monday and Novello's address.
² The previous letter.   ³ At the Philharmonic Society concert.

---

¹ The date is given by SW's 'Monday evening' and the following day's postmark.
² Beethoven's 'Battle' Symphony (1813) had received its first London performance on 10 Feb. 1815 at
a Drury Lane oratorio concert directed by Sir George Smart. Smart included it in several subsequent
concerts in the 1815 season, and at all of his Drury Lane oratorio concerts in 1816. SW's reference is to the
performance at the concert on 6 Mar., which he had evidently hoped to attend. As the organist for the
rival Covent Garden oratorio concerts, SW would not normally have had the opportunity to attend
Drury Lane oratorio concerts.
³ 6 March; SW was required to attend in his capacity as Grand Organist.

Do if you can, come & comfort me To-morrow Evening, for you may think I need some Balance against these ✝ Events.

I shall be at Home from 6 o'Clock, & yours entirely after, therefore if you have any Compassion 'in Visceribus tuis'[4] in Lent time (a powerful Stimulus to you on the Occasion) pray come & save from Despair & Death &c.

Y^rs

SW

To [William] Ayrton[1]   [Gower Place], 10 April [1816][2]

ALS, 3 pp. (National Library of Scotland, MS 2207, fo. 188)
Addressed To | T. Ayrton Esqre | James Street | Buckingham Gate | Wed^y Evening
Pmk AP 1816

> Gower Place Euston Square
> Wednesday. 10th of April

Dear Sir,

I have just now received a Letter from our Friend W. Linley, in which he states extreme Regret that he is positively precluded the Possibility of attending at the Argyll Rooms on Saturday Evening, as he fully intended, for the Purpose of hearing the Trial of his Music,[3] which it seems is to be brought forward on that Evening, but of which Circumstance I was not aware until the Arrival of his Letter.—The Cause of his Absence is simply this: Saturday is the Beef-Steak Club[4] Day, & there is some special Business to be settled on Saturday *next* (13th) upon which the Duke of Sussex has particularly requested that every Member be present: *Cela etant*,[5] poor Linley cannot help himself without the Danger of a royal Rap on the Knuckles, which he seems more apprehensive of, than in his Circumstances I think I should be, but this by the Way.

---

⁴ 'In your bowels'.

¹ This letter is addressed to 'T. Ayrton', apparently in error. The address is that of William Ayrton (see SW to Novello, 25 Feb. [1816], n. 3).

² The year is given by a just-legible postmark and by internal evidence.

³ Linley's pieces were to be tried out at the Philharmonic Society rehearsal on 13 Apr. They were not performed at the following concert on 15 Apr.

⁴ The Beef Steak Society, otherwise known as the Sublime Society of Beefsteaks, a club of twenty-four men of noble or gentle birth founded by John Rich in 1735. They met for a beef-steak dinner every Saturday from Nov. to June, and at this time numbered the Prince Regent and the Dukes of York and Sussex among their members. Linley had been elected to membership in Feb. 1810 (*Encyclopaedia of London*; *DNB*, under 'Linley, William').   ⁵ 'That being so'.

Now our said worthy Wight, (Bill Linley hight)[6] has commissioned me to make the most respectful Apology possible for a Failure so totally unwilling & unexpected, & particularly wishes me to become his Locum tenens, quoad the Trial of his Shaksperian Ditty, or *Ditties*,[7] for I find that there are two Pieces submitted to Inspection, & I believe his Wish is that *both* be tried.—He shewed (in his Letter) rather more Solicitude for the Success of 'Tell me where is Fancy bred' than for the other.—*We* must endeavour to be candid concerning both.

A Quotation is the fairest way of letting you know what he would be at. e=g=

'I must now, my Friend summon you *with the Voice of a Friend* to attend the Practice of my Piece on Saturday at the Philharmonic, & speak & act for me there.—I do not know which of the two I have sent in, they will try, or whether both but certainly they will try one.—In regard to the Dirge "Pardon Goddess," the Duet Part may be sung by a Soprano & a Tenor; but better as two Sopranos.—The rest is Chorus, but if there are not Voices sufficient, it may be done as a Quartetto, doubling the Parts.'

'The little Ode "Tell me where is Fancy bred," I could wish to be sung as it was at Smart's Oratorio.[8]—The Soprano (Mrs Dickons)[9] asking the Question, & the Tenor (Mr Braham) answering it.—Then the Chorus following, sung first as a Quartetto, & repeated in Chorus.'

These are my Injunctions, & perhaps you had best keep this Paper, lest I should mislay the original, or omit to bring it on Saturday, for really the fact is that satis satago Rerum mearum[10] without rushing into Responsibility for other Folk,—however Linley is so excellent a Fellow, so clever a one, & so thoroughly a Gentleman, that to treat him or his with Coldness or Indifference would be absolute Brutality, which I trust that neither he nor any other Man (much less Woman) will ever meet from

Dear Sir,
Yours sincerely
With much Esteem

S. Wesley

[6] An allusion to the epitaph on Thomas Tallis in Greenwich church, quoted in Boyce's *Cathedral Music* and Burney, *History*, iii. 75 (Mercer, ii. 68): 'Enterred here doth ly a worthy wyght | Who for long tyme in Musik bore the bell | His name to shew was Thomas Tallis hyght | In honest vertuous lyff he dyd excell.'

[7] Linley's settings for duet and chorus of 'Tell me where is fancy bred' (*Merchant of Venice*, III. ii. 63) and 'Pardon, goddess of the night' (*Much Ado about Nothing*, V. iii. 12), which had been included in vol. 1 of his *Shakspeare's Dramatic Songs*, published the previous Aug.

[8] Presumably one of Smart's Drury Lane oratorio concerts. It has not been possible to identify the concert: Linley's composition does not appear in any of the printed programmes or advertisements for either the 1815 or 1816 season, and was probably a last-minute addition to the programme.

[9] Maria (Martha Frances Caroline) Dickons, née Poole (1774–1833), singer, actress, harpsichordist, composer (*BD*). [10] 'I've really got my hands full with my own affairs'.

To Vincent Novello [Gower Place, 13 May 1816][1]

ALS, 2 pp. (BL, Add. MS 11729, fo. 135)

Dear N

As you did not call according with your Intention, on Friday,[2] I take the first Opportunity of informing you that we mean to have our Trio *on Saturday next*[3] *at Noon*, in Kirkman's Room.—Stokes cannot be one, as he pleads particular Business on the *Score* of *some Score* which he is to get a little Money by: but Joey Major is studying his Part, & I think will be able to do it Justice: I have managed to get rid of *half* the Scholars on Friday, on Purpose that we may have a Rehearsal in the Evening at Kirkman's.—

Pray find me out between the Acts this Evening:[4] I will wait for you in the gossiping Room for 10 Minutes.

The Quebec Business[5] yesterday went on very agreeably.—I never knew an Affair where *Singers* were concerned more smoothly negotiated.—They were very obedient, & tolerably correct.

Yours as usual

S Wesley

P.S. Clementi tells me he shall strain a Point to come, saying (handsomely enough) that 'whenever he has heard a good Thing once, he likes to hear it twice, & that three Times are better, & so on in Proportion.'

I have invited Kalkbrenner.[6] Cramer[7] of course is too grand for us; we must be contented with the attention of Clementi, *his Master*.—By the Way, I hear that Cramer's Performance on Thursday[8] was extraordinarily great: but I suspend any Assent till I have your Opinion.

---

[1] The correctness of this dating, added in another hand, is confirmed by the contents of the letter.

[2] 10 May. [3] 18 May. [4] i.e. at the Philharmonic Society concert.

[5] Not identified: possibly an event at the Quebec Chapel, Portman Square.

[6] Frédéric Kalkbrenner (1785–1849), French pianist and composer, who had come to England from Paris at the end of 1814 and had rapidly risen to fame as one of the leading pianists of his day.

[7] i.e. the pianist Johann Baptist Cramer rather than his violinist brother Francis. His lessons with Clementi, in 1783–4, 'were decisive in forming his artistic character' (*Grove*[6]).

[8] At the Cramers' benefit concert at the King's Theatre on 9 May. The programme included solo items by both brothers (*The Times*, 9 May 1816).

To Vincent Novello   Gower Place, [22] May [1816]¹

ALS, 3 pp. (BL, Add. MS 11729, fo. 136)
Addressed To | Mr Novello | Oxford Street | N. 240. | Wednesday Evening | Paid
Pmk 23 MY 1816

Dear N.

When we parted on Saturday,² we did not notice the former Intention of going together to Mrs Elliston's³ Ball: perhaps you were there, but I was really too much fatigued to budge, when I had once reached Home at 8 o'Clock, especially as there must have been a Renewal of Dressing &c, & I was sufficiently satisfied with the Dressing of my Dinner.

You were saying that you would hint to Leigh Hunt a word of Annuntiation concerning the Oratorio on Saturday Week.⁴—If you persevere in this Intention, no Time should be lost as if the Notice should appear on Sunday *the 2^d of June* (one Day after the Performance) it would appear very much like the State of good Music in this Country, manifestly going backward.

I met Picart pelting down St James's Street To-Day, who was hoping to run off with some of the old Boy's Tunes from the Sale.⁵—he feared *you* most, he said, knowing your Contempt of the Author.

I have had a charming Hour with Klengel⁶ to-Day, whom I hawled into Guichard's Shop,⁷ & got him to sit down to a Piano Forte, whereon he played delightfully.—I think he *must* be a good Organist, from the Firmness & Equality

---

¹ The year is given by the postmark. The date corrects SW's misdating.   ² 18 May.

³ No doubt Elizabeth Elliston, née Randell or Rundell (1774/5–1821), the wife of the actor and theatrical manager Robert William Elliston (see SW's letter to him of 19 May 1820). A former dancing teacher, she had married Elliston in Bath in 1796. In 1810 she contributed music to a production of *The Beaux' Stratagem* and an adaptation of *A Bold Stroke for a Wife*. She lived at 9 Stratford Place (*BD*; *GM* 1821¹, 380; Court Guide).

⁴ The 'word of Annuntiation', was for SW's and Charles Jane Ashley's benefit concert at Covent Garden on 1 June, and would have needed to appear in the *Examiner* on the coming Sunday, 26 May. No such announcement appeared.

⁵ The sale of Johann Baptist Cramer's library at White's was on 21 and 22 May; it contained many items by J. S. Bach (King, 25–6).   ⁶ See SW to Bridgetower, 11 Nov. [1815], n. 2.

⁷ The premises of the music seller and publisher C. Guichard at 100 New Bond Street. Guichard was also a member of the Portuguese Embassy Chapel choir, and Novello's successor as organist there (Humphries and Smith; *The Times*, 30 Apr. 1827).

of his Touch: he gave a Toccata of his own, quite in the great Man's *best Style*:[8] We must not compare Ries[9] with him, much less Kalkbrenner.

He will come to the Chapel on Sunday Morning, & was commending the Arrangement of the Fugue we are to play,[10] which *Charles Smith* shewed him, & of which I gave him (Smith) a Copy at Norwich: I told him that the Arrangement was *yours*, on which he behaved very properly, for he expressed *no Surprize* after that Intelligence.

In Consequence of the decided Disapproval I discovered in you, of noticing the Trio[11] in the Newspapers I have given up the Idea of any Advertisement about it; & on more mature Deliberation I do not conceive that much Advantage would thence accrue, as the Piece will not be performed on the Night of the Benefit.[12]

I long to hear whether you have pounced upon a Stave of Sebastian extra.[13]— Perhaps you will write on the Subject between now & Sunday.

Yours as usual

S Wesley

23^d of May. Wednesday. | Gower Place

---

[8] i.e. that of Clementi, Klengel's teacher. SW was possibly thinking of Clementi's *Sonata for the Piano and a famous Toccata*, Op. 11 (1784).

[9] Ferdinand Ries (1784–1838), pianist and composer, a pupil and secretary of Beethoven. He came to London in the spring of 1813 and lived in England for 11 years. He first appeared at the Philharmonic Society on 14 Mar. 1814 and his works frequently appeared in its concerts (*Grove*[6]).

[10] No doubt Novello's arrangement of the 'St Anne' fugue, which SW and Smith had played as a duet at their recital at Great Yarmouth on 12 July 1815 (see SW to Novello, 18 July 1815).

[11] It appears from this that SW had proposed to send in a report of the performance of the Trio at Clementi's the previous Saturday, which would mention that it was to be repeated at his benefit on 1 June. Novello's disapproval may have had to do with the dubious propriety of SW using a report of this private performance to publicize his forthcoming benefit. [12] i.e. on 1 June.

[13] i.e. at Cramer's sale.

To Vincent Novello

[Gower Place], 1 June [1816][1]

ANS, 1 p. (BL, Add. MS 11729, fo. 138)
Addressed To | M[r] Novello | Oxford Street | 240 | Sat[y] Morn[g]
Pmk 1 JU 1816

Dear N

Pray come & take your Coffee with me at 5 exactly this Afternoon: I want to advise with you concerning the Distribution of the Stops in the last Movement of my old new Tune.[2]

Yours as usual

S Wesley

Gower Place | Saturday Morning. | June 1st

To Vincent Novello

[Gower Place], 25 June [1816][1]

ALS, 1 p. (BL, Add. MS 11729, fo. 140)
Addressed To | M[r] Novello | Oxford Street | N. 240 | Tuesday Morning

Dear N

As you are concerned in the enclosed,[2] I must trouble you with a *Line*, as the Hangman said to the Malefactor, & you will find that I cannot return a satisfactory Answer to Picart without your Authority.—

The Vespers went very smoothly on Sunday,[3] & I bespoke the Litanies, like a good Catholic Xtian, as all the World knows I am, instead of David's humdrum

---

[1] The year is given by the postmark.
[2] A reference to SW's performance of an organ concerto by him at his benefit concert at Covent Garden that evening. According to press advertisements and a handbill for this concert (Duke), the concerto was a new one, in which, 'in allusion to the Glorious First of June' (i.e. the celebrated British naval victory over the French at Ushant on 1 June 1794) SW was to introduce 'the National Air of "Rule Britannia" with the full orchestra'. In fact, it was almost certainly the Concerto in C, first heard on 9 Mar. 1814 (see SW to Novello, 8 Mar. [1814]), with the set of variations on 'Rule Britannia' replacing the original finale.

[1] The year is given by 25 June falling on a Tuesday and SW's reference to Picart (see also next letter).
[2] A letter from Picart (not preserved), also discussed in the following letter.   [3] 23 June.

Ditty of 'God bless us' &c[4] which you have hacked to Rags & Tatters, according to the correct Account of M[r] Wilkinson, the *Qui tam* Attorney.[5]

I had moreover another Reason for tipping them Kyrie Eleison, namely to shew my Zeal & Veneration towards Virginity, for which I fear you have not a due Respect, not even when a Virgin conceives & bears a Son.

Yours &c

S Wesley

Tuesday Morning 25th of June

P.S. I shall be at Major's from $\frac{1}{2}$ past 8 till $\frac{1}{2}$ past 10 this Evening, perhaps 'illuminabis Vultum tuum super nos, et miseriaris nostri.'[6]

To Vincent Novello   [Gower Place], 28 June [1816][1]

ALS, 1 p. (BL, Add. MS 11729, fo. 141)

28th of June
Friday evening

Dear N.

I am rather desirous to send an Answer to Picart which I cannot do in a satisfactory Way until you inform me whether you can lend him the Stabat Mater of D'Astorga[2] which he mentions in the Letter I enclosed to you.—I purpose coming to your Transubstantiation Manufactory on Sunday Morning,[3] whereat you will probably signify what shall be said in Picart's Case.—There is a Music Master from Norwich[4] who I believe means to come to hear your Whistle Box at my Instance.—Major has left town, but also my Brace of *Pages*, or rather of Leaves

---

[4] Not identified: perhaps a setting of part or all of Ps. 67 ('God be merciful unto us and bless us; and cause his face to shine upon us') by David Perez.

[5] Not certainly identified: *Clarke's New Law List* for 1816 includes John Wilkinson of 13 Southampton Street, Bloomsbury and Richard Wilkinson of 32 Queen Street, Cheapside in its list of London attorneys. The significance of SW's description of him as a 'qui tam' attorney, implying that he was an informer (*OED*) is not clear.

[6] 'You will cause your face to shine upon us, and be merciful unto us': adapted from the Vulgate of Ps. 67: 1.

---

[1] The year is given by 28 June falling on a Friday and SW's references to his 'Waterloo Song' and his voluntaries (see nn. 5 and 6).

[2] The Stabat Mater by Emanuele d'Astorga (1680–?1757), popular from about 1760 and published several times in the early 19th cent. (*Grove*[6]).   [3] 30 June.

[4] Not identified.

which you shall have at my first possible Moment.—I have finished my Cut Throat Waterloo Song,[5] & am writing little tiney nimminy Pippiny Voluntaries[6] like any Doctor of Music.—I will bring you two or three on Sunday, for your Improvement & Illumination in common Chords & $^{6}_{4}$'s &c.

Y[rs] as usual

S Wesley

To Vincent Novello [Gower Place], 15 July [1816][1]

ALS, 1 p. (BL, Add. MS 11729, fo. 142)

Monday.
15 July.

Dear N

I could not send the accompanying Parcel till now, or would have done it, as you will believe, & have seen you into the Bargain.—I am summoned to Norwich,[2] & by *what I am told* much may be done at Yarmouth in the Week following that of the Assizes.[3]—One must make the Experiment, & '*it must do as well as it can*' as our old phlegmatic German[4] said.

Pray call in soon.

Yours as usual

S Wesley

All the Voluntaries are done.[5]—I must send them to Clementi in a Hurry, so if you value *MSS* you must make Haste.

---

[5] Not preserved, but evidently SW's 'Waterloo Battle Song', ('As on fam'd Waterloo the lab'ring swain') to words by the Revd J. Davies, performed by the bass Thomas Bellamy (1770–1843) at the New Musical Fund concert on 24 Apr. 1817 (programme at BL, New Musical Fund Concert Bills, shelfmark C 61 g.20). For the circumstances of composition of this song, celebrating the British victory at Waterloo on 18 June 1815, see SW to unidentified recipient, 23 July 1816.

[6] SW's *Twelve Short Pieces for the Organ with a Full Voluntary Added*, published by Clementi later in the year.

[1] The year is given by 15 July falling on a Monday and SW's reference to his impending visit to Norwich.

[2] SW had been engaged to play a voluntary at the Anniversary Sermon in Norwich Cathedral for the Norfolk and Norwich Hospital on 15 Aug. (*Norwich Mercury*, 3, 10, 17 Aug. 1816).

[3] SW's reference is to the Norwich assizes, which were on 15 Aug.

[4] A. F. C. Kollmann: see SW to Novello, 22 Feb. [1825].

[5] The *Twelve Short Pieces*: the autograph (RCM, MS 4025) is dated 10 July 1816.

To an unidentified recipient[1]   Gower Place, 23 July 1816

ALS, 3 pp. (Emory, Letter 57)

Gower Place
Euston Square
Tuesday July. 23^d—1816.

Dear Sir

As I have a sincere Confidence in the Reality of your Candour & the Coolness of your Judgement, I am consciously convinced that I cannot find any of my Friends or Acquaintance more properly qualified, or more readily disposed to give a free, liberal, & just Opinion of a late Transaction, which I will briefly state, as to the Facts only, leaving the Commentary entirely to your dispassionate Reflexion.

About six Weeks ago, I received an Application from a Revd Mr Davies,[2] of Brompton Row, to whom I was till then a Stranger, but who I find is a Clergyman of high Respectability, & a most extensive Acquaintance in the first Circles of Society.—He wished me to set some Stanzas which he had written upon the memorable Victory at Waterloo: We immediately agreed concerning Terms &c & he then enquired of me, *whom* I considered as the most eligible *Tenor* Singer to bring the Song forward on the Stage?—As Braham was out of the Question, in regard to a Summer Theatre, Mr Horn[3] seemed the properest Person possible to engage for the Purpose: I therefore recommended Mr Davies to see M^r H upon the Subject, which he speedily did, & Mr H. very handsomely volunteered his Services, adding that he 'should take great Pleasure in exerting his best Abilities for the Success of any Composition of S. Wesley.'—Accordingly a Time was fixed for our Meeting, & Mr Horn came to my House on Friday Morning last, by the Appointment of Mr Davies & myself, having previously expressed his Intention of bringing the Song forward as *this Evening* (Tuesday 23^d)[4]—He heard

---

[1] The identity of the recipient is not known, but Picart is a possibility in view of his appearance in other letters around this time.

[2] Named in the programme of the New Musical Fund concert of 24 Apr. 1817, at which the 'Waterloo Battle Song' was performed, as the Revd. J. Davies, AM; not otherwise identified.

[3] The popular tenor and composer Charles Edward Horn (1786–1849), son of SW's former collaborator Charles Frederick Horn (*Grove*[6]).

[4] At the Lyceum Theatre (The English Opera House), where Horn regularly sang, and where that evening's performance was of *The Devil's Bridge* and *A Man in Mourning for Himself*. The song was not advertised, and would presumably have been introduced as an additional item.

the Song, & professed to be highly delighted with it, & as a Proof that his *then* Resolution was to sing it on the Night named, he suggested to S.W. that it might be advisable to omit certain Bars in the latter Movement, lest there might be the least Probability of its being deemed too long for an English theatrical Audience.—This Proposal was instantly complied with, & Mr Horn departed with S.W.'s Score in his Hand, & an energetic Observation that 'the Copyist must be immediately set to Work, as not a Moment ought to be lost.'—Mr Davies, upon the Strength of these Preparations, apprized many of his Friends & Acquaintance that the Performance would take Place, in Consequence of which a large Party of Persons of Rank & Fashion agreed to attend the Theatre.—Yesterday Morning I received a Letter from Mr Horn, declining to bring the Song forward according to his Promise, & offering as an Excuse, Reasons (or rather Evasions) which if alledged at all, ought surely to have been alledged in the first Instance, in the very Outset of the Business, & before the Public were taught to expect the Introduction of the Piece in Question. (For this Remark I must crave your Pardon, because I had previously declared my Intention of leaving all the Comment to yourself).

I must however beg Leave to propose the following Queries.—

Putting yourself in my Place, would you not have reckoned securely on Mr Horn's Performance upon the Evening of his own Appointment, in Consequence of his Eulogium & uncommon Promptitude in the Affair?

Is it not a fair Conclusion, that either Mr Horn must be considered as an unstable Character, or that some undiscovered Influence must have been unfairly used to induce him to break his Promise?

Has not only Mr Davies (the Author of the Poetry) but also Mr Arnold (the Manager)[5] been unhandsomely treated? the former, by being misled into the Belief that the Song was forth-coming, which induced him to muster a grand Party in its Support; & the latter, by causing to be with-holden from the Public, a Piece which even the *Subject* of Waterloo must have attracted considerable Numbers to the Theatre *out of mere Curiosity*, & if well received would have secured a Repetition of full Attendance in future?

Your unreserved Notions on the above will much oblige

Dear Sir
Yours very sincerely
   S Wesley

---

[5] Samuel James Arnold (1774–1852), son of Samuel Arnold, the manager of the Lyceum Theatre.

To [Vincent Novello]¹   [Gower Place, *post* 27 July 1816]

AL, 1 p., (BL, Add. MS 11729, fo. 143)

A Dialogue which happened on Saturday, July 27ᵗʰ 1816 in Chappell's Music Shop, between Mʳ Jones,² the Welsh Harper & Antiquarian, Mʳ Ayrton, the philharmonic Orator³ & Legislator & S. W.

Jones.—'Mʳ Wesley, how came you not to be at White's last musical Auction,⁴ where several of Sebastian Bach's Works were sold & some of them, which I think you know nothing of?' S.W.—'I saw the Catalogue previous to the Sale, & found no Pieces of Bach with which I was not before acquainted.—I am at Present in Possession (as a Loan) of six curious & grand Preludes & Fugues, with an additional Base Line entirely for the Pedals.⁵—' Ayrton—'I think these were sold at Salomon's Auction.⁶—' SW—'I am inclined to believe the Contrary & I know them to be very scarce in this Country—I doubt whether there be another Copy here.—' Ayrton: 'I'm *sure* 'tis no such Thing—there were several Manuscripts of Bach in Salomon's Library which I did not think worth bringing forward, & rather think this Work was among them.' SW: 'I wonder at this Omission of yours, as every Note of this Author is valuable.' Ayrton (with a Sneer): 'To *you* they may be so, but very few are of your Opinion.' SW: 'All those are of my Opinion who deserve the Name of either Musicians or Judges of Music.—Bach's Works are the finest Study possible for *all* our musical Doctors in this Country.—Were he living he would stare not a little to find *how they had ever acquired their Title*.'*

[Exit SW, Jones and Ayrton staring mutually at each other and at an humble untitled *Mister*'s Hardihood, which of Course they dubbed to be Impudence.—

---

¹ This sheet is preserved with other letters to Novello. Although not in the form of a conventional letter, it appears to have been written for Novello's information and amusement, and may have been accompanied by a covering note, no longer preserved.

² Edward Jones, known as Y Bardd y Brenin or the King's Bard (1752–1824), Welsh musician, antiquarian, and author. He first appeared in London in 1775 as a harpist, and gained a high reputation as a performer and teacher. He was appointed bard to the Prince of Wales (later the Prince Regent and George IV) in 1783. Among his many publications were *Musical and Poetic Relicks of the Welsh Bards* (1784); vol. ii: *The Bardic Museum of Primitive British Literature* (1802); vol. iii: *Hén Ganiadau Cymru: Cambro-British Melodies, or the National Songs and Airs of Wales* (1820) (*DNB*; *Grove*⁶).

³ i.e. William Ayrton, who was at this time a director of the Philharmonic Society.

⁴ The sale of Samuel Webbe I's extensive library on 4 July, following his death on 25 May (King, 133).

⁵ Presumably *Sechs Praeludien und SECHS FUGEN für Orgel oder Pianoforte mit Pedal* (Vienna and Pest, 1812), comprising BWV 543–8, or the 1814 Vienna reissue by Riedel: this was the only collection of Bach's organ preludes and fugues to have been published at this time. No copy has been traced in the UK.

⁶ Salomon died on 28 Nov. 1815; no details of a sale of his library have been traced.

N'importe.—I came away in high good Humour with myself, and I guess you are not much out of Humour with me for *sarving* it out handsomely to these Vermin.][7]

*N B Ayrton's Father[8] was a Doctor of Music, & one of the most egregious Blockheads under the Sun.

To Alfred Pettet   [Gower Place], 29 July 1816

ALS, 3 pp. (BL, Egerton MS 2159, fo. 72)
Addressed To | Alfred Pettet | near Castle Hill | Norwich | Norfolk | 29th of July

London July 29th 1816

My dear Sir

Your obliging Letter[1] reached me Yesterday, for which I return you my sincere Thanks, as also for your strenuous Exertions upon *Turkey-ish* Topics.—I really think (setting my Loss out of the Question) that a severe Example ought to be made of these Inn-keeping Scoundrels, & I dare say that your Friend the Counsellor will put you in a Way of making the Dogs remember Turkies & Concertos.

I anticipate with Pleasure my Jaunt to your part of the Island, & think of setting forward in the Middle of next Week:[2] with Regard to my *whereabout* I must give you the Trouble of some little Arrangement with our Friend Beckwith upon the Subject.—He was so kind as to wish me to make his House my *entire* Home, but this I could not with Decency do, after your friendly Offer of House Room at your Quarters: I therefore felt the more *equitable & conscientious* Proceeding to be splitting the Difference, and propose to make myself a joint Concern between you: the mode of Distribution must be left to yours and M[r]. B's Decision.

Mister Eager
I must beleagure:

he has not sent me a half-penny Worth of Answer to my Letter dispatched to him a Week ago, or thereabouts.

---

[7] The square brackets are SW's.

[8] Edmund Ayrton (1734–1808), organist and *Rector Chori* at Southwell Minster (1755), Gentleman of the Chapel Royal (1764), vicar-choral of St Paul's Cathedral (1767), lay vicar at Westminster Abbey and Master of the Children of the Chapel Royal (1780). He took a Cambridge Mus.D. in 1784 and possibly an Oxford D.Mus. in 1788 (*Grove*[6]; Shaw, 277).

---

[1] Not preserved: presumably detailing Pettet's efforts to trace the lost parcel, which had evidently included a turkey and the manuscript of a concerto by SW.   [2] i.e. around 7 Aug.

I will inform Novello of your honest Principle upon the Matter of 'Adeste Fideles.'—by the Way he as much merits the Title of one of the *'faithful'* (in the Roman Catholic Sense, which always signifies a bigotted Papist) as you or I, for he believes not a Word of Purgatory, Priestly Absolution, Transubstantiation, Extreme Unction, nor any other Extreme of such extreme Absurdities.

Beckwith informed me that Eager was *eager* in my Cause: you remember that Charles Smith's Wrong-headed-ness (a *newish* Sort of a Word) prevented some good at Yarmouth in the former Instance:[3] Mʳ E. manifested great Candour & good-Nature notwithstanding Smith's shameful Neglect consulting him, & I bear this in Mind with very cordial Gratitude, as also his uniform Hospitality during my Stay at Yarmouth.—Indeed I feel myself particularly obliged to him for his uncommonly respectful & friendly Conduct.

And now, I believe my best Relief for your Trial of Patience is shortly to add God bless you & yours, as in Duty bound your Petitioner shall ever pray.

  S Wesley

P.S. I paid poor Braham a Visit of Condolence To-Day.—the little Gergashite seems not to relish the 'slight Contribution levied upon him'—he looks (to use an elegant Metaphor) as if he had been eaten & spewed up again.[4]—Don't tell this to Mʳˢ P.

To Vincent Novello   [Gower Place], 1 August [1816][1]

ALS, 2 pp. (BL, Add. MS 11729, fo. 144)
Addressed To | Mʳ Novello | Oxford Street | N. 240 | Thursday Afternoon | Paid
Pmk AU 1816

          Thursday Aug 1

My good friend N.

I purpose leaving Town on Saturday week[2] at the furthest, & am trying to cut & contrive how to oblige my Friends in the Country without offending those who are here.—I have no extreme Doubts that if you can lend me a helping Hand you will, but my Conscience would not permit me to subject you to Inconvenience on

---

 [3] Smith's ill-advised choice of dates for their visit to Great Yarmouth in 1815: see SW to Novello, 18 July 1815.

 [4] On 23 July the jury had found for Wright in his criminal conversation suit against Braham and awarded him damages of £1,000. For the background to the case, see SW to Novello, 22 Feb. [1816], n. 11.

 [1] The year is given by the postmark.

 [2] On 10 Aug.: SW needed to be in Norwich for the rehearsal on 12 Aug.

my Account, & much less to any Loss.—You must therefore be quite Candid sur le Sujet, telling me point blank the existing State of your Morning Engagements. —I shall write also to Wilson,[3] upon whom I have a Claim, without asking any Favour, but of course your Name will be the more welcome at Turnham Green: there are only *two* private Scholars in town, & them I shall make wait for me, without bothering you or any body else.

If you cannot look in here To-morrow Evening between 7 & 9, give me a Line, & I will at all events endeavour to see you on Sunday either in the Morning or Afternoon.

Yours in Haste
Most truly
S Wesley

To Vincent Novello [Gower Place], 7 August [1816][1]

ALS, 1 p. (BL, Add. MS 11729, fo. 146)
Addressed To | Mr Novello | Oxford Street | N. 240 | Wed^y Ev^g

Wednesday Evening
7th of Aug^t

My dear N

Our little Boy[2] is in so precarious a State that I much fear I must sacrifice the Pleasure I anticipated of meeting you at Surrey Chapel To-morrow at one o'Clock.—However, should any favourable Change take Place, I will be with you.—I *must* attend two Pupils in the neighbourhood of Cheapside, whatever may occur at Home; but still I should feel ill disposed, or more properly totally disqualified for any musical Exertion of Energy, if Death should happen.

---

[3] Charles Wilson, who evidently also deputized for SW on occasion.

[1] The year is given by 7 Aug. falling on a Wednesday and SW's reference to the grave illness of his son (see n. 2).

[2] There are no details of the date of birth or the name of this child. His death, within a day or two of this letter, triggered the onset of SW's most serious period of depression, and led ultimately to his breakdown the following May. Although SW set off for Norwich as planned, he was taken ill on the way and was not able to complete his journey and carry out his projected engagements there (Sarah Wesley to W. B. Kingston, 26 Aug. 1817 (Emory)). In a letter of 28 Aug. 1816 to Charles and Sarah (Rylands, DDWes 6/44), SW claimed that his collapse had cost him £100 in lost fees, and that he faced financial ruin as a result.

—Howbeit, I will hope for the best, & *if possible* will appear at the Chapel Door by *One* punctually.—At all Events I trust *you* will meet Jacob, who of course has written to you according to his Promise.

Yours, always truly

S Wesley

PS I have your Key of the Music Box: Pray call in the Evening of To-morrow, you will be sure to find me within. Adieu!

To Vincent Novello   [Hampstead],[1] 3 October 1816

ALS, 1 p. (BL, Add. MS 11729, fo. 147)
Addressed To | M[r] Novello

My good Friend,

I called yesterday in Frith Street[2] to apologize for not meeting you on Sunday evening.[3]—Mr K[4] was out, but I left a Card. I really could not have relished any Music, & therefore should have been worse than Nobody as a Participator; & *Samson*[5] is an Oratorio which *especially* revives unpleasant Recollections! All, *Weakness*, you will say—& justly.

To-morrow I shall trust for your kind Substitution,[6] & *for this once* must beg you to undertake the whole Burthen for me: I have taken a Lodging at Hampstead for a few Days, & mean to go over this Afternoon, returning to & fro *as I can*, & think to stay till Saturday Morning in the first Instance.

The annexed Roll[7] you will be so good as put in your Pocket tomorrow.— A Miss Cresswell[8] is to begin something of Handel from Clarke's Selection:[9] the

---

[1] As SW explains later in the letter, he had taken temporary lodgings in Hampstead. The address is not known.

[2] Doubtless premises of the Kirckman piano firm; Joseph Kirckman (ii) (*c*.1790–1877) (*Grove*[6]) is known to have started his business at 67 Frith Street in 1822, and these premises may have been used by his father prior to this date. They were also the first business premises of J. A. Novello & Co., the publishing firm established in 1829 by Novello's eldest son.   [3] Probably Joseph Kirckman (ii).

[4] 29 Sept.

[5] By Handel. SW was perhaps thinking of the recent death of his son ('Sam's son').

[6] i.e. for SW's teaching commitments at Turnham Green, where he taught on a Friday.

[7] Presumably some music for one of SW's pupils; not preserved.

[8] Evidently one of SW's pupils; not certainly identified, but possibly a daughter of Richard Cresswell of 39 Great Coram Street (*Court Guide*).

[9] Presumably a collection by John Clarke-Whitfeld (1770–1836): not identified.

Choice of the Piece I leave entirely to you.—I know not how to attempt an Excuse for the Toil & Trouble occasioned you by your sincere & grateful

    S Wesley

Thursday Octr 3. 1816

P.S. I am sorry to be obliged to press the Governess's Requisition of a Quarter of an Hour to each Brat.

To Vincent Novello   [Hampstead], ?10 October [1816][1]

ALS, 1 p. (BL, Add. MS 11729, fo. 148)
Addressed To | Mr Novello | 240 | Oxford Street.
Docketed S. Wesley 1816

My dear Friend,

    I fear that I shall not be able to reach Hammersmith before 12 at soonest to Morrow: Can you therefore help the Ass in the Pit without *much* Inconvenience? —Entre nous (*only*) I have been sadly nervous since Tuesday, maugre Hampstead Air, but 'it must do as well as it can' however it be.

    Should you be able to reach Turnham Green by *about 11*, we can manage to come away together perhaps.—

    My *Confiteor*[2] to you ought to be a long one!—it is very sincere, for I am thoroughly ashamed of the tiresome Test to which I put your Friendship.—

    Adieu, in Haste,
    most (& always)
    cordially your
    obliged
      S W

Thursday 11th Oct^r

---

[1] It is evident from the reference to 'Hampstead air' and SW's request to Novello to deputize for him that the year of this letter is 1816. 11 Oct. did not fall on a Thursday in this year, and SW appears to have mistaken either the day of the month or the day of the week. His reference to meeting Novello at Turnham Green on the following day suggests that the correct date should probably be 10 Oct., which was a Thursday.   [2] His confession.

To Vincent Novello [Gower Place], 11 December [1816]¹

AL, 3 pp. (BL, Add. MS 11729, fo. 150)
Addressed To | Mʳ Novello | Oxford Street | 240 | Wedʸ Aftⁿ
Pmk 11 DE 1816

My good Friend,

I am informed that you mean to call here To-morrow between *one & two* o'Clock, which I hope is true, as I will make a Point of being ready to receive you: I have also a special Reason for wanting your Presence, as I *must* prevail on you to help me in the Review for the approaching Month,² & *how*, I will fully explain when we meet: the *20ᵗʰ* is the last Day when the Printer can *receive* Communications, therefore, no Time can be spared in Preparation: I will do *the little* I may be able in Conjunction.—Let this remain *in Petto*,³ & indeed I doubt not that this would be so without a Hint.—

Yours always

P.S. Perhaps you can inform me of a lost Sheep of mine: I mean the *green Fat-Book*⁴ as you used to term it; I am unable at present to discover it among the few Music Books I value: wherever it was played from *last*, I am pretty sure that you were with me, therefore I have the better Chance, from your good Memory, than from my now (comparatively)

---

¹ The year is given by the postmark.

² SW's column of reviews of music for the Dec. number of the *European Magazine*, due to appear at the end of the month, for which copy needed to be written. This column consisted of a continuation of the review of Novello's *Twelve Easy Masses* begun in the Nov. number and a review of SW's own arrangement of the *Music in Macbeth* which formed the Appendix to William Linley's *Shakspeare's Dramatic Songs*. SW's remarks suggest that Novello may have had a hand in this column; if so, it is most likely that the review of the *Music in Macbeth* was by him (Olleson, 1102–3). After the Dec. number the column was discontinued by Asperne: see SW to Jones, 13 Jan. 1817.   ³ 'Within your breast'.

⁴ This evidently celebrated volume was singled out for special comment in 'Our Musical Spring', a lengthy article, unsigned but almost certainly by Edward Holmes, on music in London in the years leading up to the Great Exhibition, which appeared in *Fraser's Magazine* for May 1851 (pp. 586–95). It included an extended tribute to the important role of SW in introducing the music of Bach into England: 'There came into moderate circulation here [i.e. in London] a volume containing some of Bach's organ music, and a part of his *Suites de pièces* for the Clavier. The organ music was a treasury of full harmony, spread out over the whole extent of keys and pedals, in a manner that our Kelways and Worgans had never dreamed of, and indeed which had never been seen in the works of Handel or Scarlatti. This volume contained beautiful things. There were the Kyries—fugues on a Canto Fermo in soprano, tenor, and bass; the noble prelude for the full organ in E flat, and the fugue with various counterpoint on the melody of St Ann's tune; it had likewise several choice trios for two claviers and pedal on sacred chorals.

bad one.—However this Quality of Memory still serves me for an accurate reminiscent Statement of almost all the useless, mischievous, disastrous & distressing Events in my Life *hitherto*, & for the keen, tormenting & insupportable Consciousness of whatever Goods, & felicitous Events are passed, never more to return in similar or other Shape.

If you *cannot* be with me between 1 & 2, immediately inform me, & also fix *when* you can, I hope it will be at all Events in the course of To-morrow.

G. P.[5]

Wednesday Decr 11

To [Stephen Jones][1]   Gower Place, 26 December 1816

ALS, 1 p. (Rylands, DDWF 15/22)

Dear Sir

You will much oblige me by an Estimate of the Pages from Midsummer to the present Xtmas in the European (Musical Review).—& an early Communication will be esteemed a Favor by Dr Sir

Yours
very truly
S Wesley

P.S. I must beg your Indulgence for giving you this Trouble.

Gower Place | 26 Decr 1816

Wesley held this book also in the greatest reverence, and taught others to love it too. Whoever had a copy of his own thought himself happy; while those who could only borrow one began industriously to write out its chief contents. We think, with a smile, that in our youth this book used to be known by us as the "green fat" book, for so Wesley familiarly named it with aldermanic gusto.' Nothing less than a metaphor inspired by the full contentments of a City feast would do complete justice to the overflowing pleasure of the scientific ear in this music' (p. 591).

[5] The significance of these two letters is not known.

[1] Although lacking an address portion, there can be no doubt from its contents that this letter is to Jones.

1817

To Stephen Jones   Gower Place, 13 January [1817]¹

ALS, 1 p. (Kassler)
Addressed To | Mʳ Jones | Pratt Place | Camden Town | N. 10
Pmk JA 13 1817

Dear Sir

Mʳ Asperne has informed me that it is his Intention to *discontinue* the Musical Review in his Magazine: whether he means that he rejects only *my* Services, but purposes to employ those of others, I cannot say,² but the above Notice will account to you for not receiving any Matter for the Press from *me* in this Month as heretofore. — if he thinks that he can put it into abler Hands, of Course he is in the right to do so, but I cannot but consider the *short Warning* as far from handsome Treatment. — With sincere Thanks for your kind Assistance on all Occasions, believe me

 Dear Sir
 Yours very truly
  S Wesley

Gower Place. | 13ᵗʰ of Janʸ | Monday

To [Vincent Novello]¹   [Gower Place, ?early 1817]²

ANS, 2 pp. (BL, Add. MS 11729, fo. 153)

My dear friend,

You guess the Purport of this: I am again your importunate Applicant for a Lift *To-morrow*: My upper Story is still far from in *patient* Order, & I feel that you have a Right to add the same Observation in Consequence of my thus molesting you. — However you have kindly *forbidden* my Apologies, & I will therefore not augment your Trouble by them.

 Ever yours,
  S W

Tuesday Mornᵍ

---

¹ The year is given by the postmark.

² In fact, the column was discontinued. Whether Asperne's decision was on purely journalistic grounds or arose from a dissatisfaction with SW's performance is unknown.

¹ Although lacking an address portion, there can be no doubt that this letter is to Vincent Novello.

² The content and distressed tone of this undated note suggest that it was written at some time during SW's decline in health between Aug. 1816 and his breakdown in May 1817, probably in early 1817.

286

I request your candid & unreserved Opinion delivered to me delivered *in* your own Hand & *by your own Hand*, of my *whole* present State, both mental, public, & domestic, freely delivering your Sentiments as far as you have been able hitherto to judge of the probable, possible, or more immediate Causes of the general & permanent Discomfort you have so long witnessed.—Be assured that I shall take *every Thing* you may observe in good Part, if not immediately according with my exact Notions at the present Moment, & at all Events it will serve to strengthen Reflexions which I am continually induced & obliged to make upon *Ways & Means of every Kind.*

To Vincent Novello [Chapel Street],[1] 31 May 1817

ALS, 1 p. (BL, Add. MS 11729, fo. 154)
Addressed M‹r› | Novello | 240 | Oxford Street | Sat‹y› Morn‹g›
Pmk 31 MY 1817

Sat‹y› 30‹th›
May 1817[2]

My dear Friend

Here I am in the greatest Agonies of Mind and Body too, tho' the latter are the less[3]—*All forsake me*: why is this?—If you think you *ought* not to come and comfort me I must submit, but I trust this is not so.—O come my dear Novello, and leave me not utterly in my deep Distress.—My Prayer is unavailing, else how do I long for a Release from my offended Maker!—It is *hardest* that even my little ones are with-holden from seeing me. Alas, alas, Despair is for ever in Prospect.

Will you come this Evening. Do, for Pity's sake.

S W

---

[1] According to Charles Wesley jun.'s diary (Rylands, DDWF 23/15), SW was 'removed' to an address in Chapel Street on 23 May 1817 on the order of his doctors.

[2] This date is incorrectly given by SW: 30 May was a Friday in 1817. The correct date is confirmed by the postmark.

[3] On 4 May the mental health problems that had been assailing SW since the death of his infant child the previous Aug. came to a head. Thinking to escape his creditors, he 'flung up the window, and himself out of it—25 feet deep, on stones', as Sarah recorded in a letter of *c.*12 May to William Wilberforce (Emory). For further information on SW's collapse and its aftermath, see Biographical Introduction.

To William Hawes[1]   [Blacklands House, Chelsea],[2]
                                                   28 November 1817

ALS, 1 p. (BL, Loan 79.10/3)
Addressed To | Willm Hawes Esqre | N. 7 | Adelphi Terrace | Strand
Endorsed (?by Hawes): Wesley concerning the admission of his son

Dear Sir

Pray accept my best Thanks for *your extremely kind Offer* relative to my little
Boy.[3] He is a very apprehensive Child & very *fond* of Music; how far he may have
Talent & Voice sufficient to do Credit to your valuable Instructions Experiment
will best shew: his Temper & Disposition I believe to be good, wanting only due
Direction, & I know him to be susceptible of Kindness, which with *You* I am
confident he will meet.[4]—My good Friend Glenn will doubtless confer with you
fully upon Points of necessary Arrangement, meanwhile I trust you will believe
me to remain with much Esteem & cordial Gratitude

My dear Sir
Your greatly obliged
S Wesley

Friday 28th of Novr 1817

---

[1] For Hawes, see SW to Novello, 20 Apr. [1814], n. 5.

[2] Blacklands House, the private lunatic asylum in which SW was placed following his breakdown; it
was in Chelsea, roughly where Lennox Gardens is now. It had formerly been a celebrated girls' school,
and Burney had taught there at the time of writing his *History* (A. G. l'Estrange, *The Village of Palaces; or,
Chronicles of Chelsea*, 2 vols. (1880), i. 180; Burney to SW, 17 Oct. 1808 (Osborn)). SW remained there
under the care of Mrs Bastable, its proprietress, and Dr Alexander Sutherland, its consultant physician,
until late June 1818.

[3] SW's son Samuel Sebastian (1810–76): Hawes had been appointed Master of the Children at
the Chapel Royal earlier in the year and had evidently offered to take Samuel Sebastian as a chorister.
Samuel Sebastian was to remain there for the next seven years. After leaving, he assisted Hawes with the
music at the Lyceum Theatre, and was organist at St James's Chapel, Hampstead Road (1826), St Giles,
Camberwell (1829), St John, Waterloo Road (1829), and Hampton Parish Church, Middesex (1831),
holding some of those posts concurrently. In 1832 he was appointed to Hereford Cathedral and began his
long career as a cathedral organist. He subsequently held appointments at Exeter Cathedral (1835–41),
Leeds Parish Church (1842–9), Winchester Cathedral (1849–65), Winchester College (1850–65), and
Gloucester Cathedral (1865–76) (*Grove*[6]).

[4] SW's confidence in Hawes may have been misplaced: he is described in *Grove*[6] as 'a harsh dis-
ciplinarian and a confirmed pluralist . . . too much engaged in other pursuits to devote himself to the
boys' education and welfare, though they lived at his house.' Later letters contain disparaging references
to Hawes's exploitation of Samuel Sebastian's fine treble voice by hiring him out to sing at concerts.

To Robert Glenn

[Blacklands House, Chelsea],
3 January 1818

ALS, 1 p. (Rylands, DDWF 15/23)
Addressed To | Mʳ Glenn | No 6 Kirby Street | Hatton Garden | (by favour of
  Dʳ Sutherland)[1]

My dear Sir

Upon Examination, the little Book you were so kind as to bring me, is not the one I wanted—it should have had this Latin Title 'Ordo recitandi officii Divini.'[2] If you ask for a *Latin Directory* they will give you the right one, and *you must apply soon for it or all the Copies will be gone.* I am very sorry to be thus troublesome, but your great Goodness will excuse it: the Book you brought is kept quite clean, so that I have no doubt they will change it without Expense: I know not how to convey it till I see you: I wish I could send it.—I long for *the great Music Book,*[3] which would much gratify me *at present.—Pray* manage it for me if possible.—I am *sure* you will do me all the good you can in *every* Way.—I have composed a Movement as you desired.[4]—Do *if you possibly can,* make your kind Visit sooner in the Week than Friday—do try to come to me on Wednesday, but absent or present believe me my dear Friend

Your devoted & grateful

S Wesley

N.B. The *little* Book might be easily sent to me by the Stage without Delay.

Saturday 3ᵈ of Janʸ 1818

---

[1] Alexander Robert Sutherland, FRCP, FRS, FGS (?1781–1861), a leading authority on the treatment of mental illnesses, who was looking after SW's treatment. He had been appointed Physician at St Luke's (London's main hospital for mental illnesses) in Mar. 1811, and was appointed Consulting Physician there in Mar. 1841. He had been involved in SW's treatment since early in 1817, and SW had known him socially at least since Mar. 1809, when Sutherland was admitted to the Somerset House Lodge. At the time of this letter SW was still at Blacklands House under Sutherland's professional care, and this letter was evidently entrusted to him with a request to deliver it to Glenn.

[2] 'The Order of Reciting the Divine Office', the annual publication which contained the local rubrics for the services of the Roman Catholic Church for the year.

[3] Perhaps the 'green fat Book' referred to in SW to Novello, 11 Dec. [1816].

[4] Not surprisingly, SW was composing little at this time, but a Walza in D dated 1818 (RCM, MS 4022) may be the piece referred to.

To Robert Glenn

[Blacklands House, Chelsea],
23 March 1818[1]

ALS, 1 p. (BL, Add. MS 35013, fo. 73)
Addressed To | Mr Glenn | N 6. | Kirby Street | Hatton Garden. | Monday 23^d of March
Pmk 23 MR 1818

My dear Friend

I trust that you will give me the Comfort of a Visit as soon as you possibly can: and that you received the Psalm[2] safe, which I committed to the Charge of Mr Kingston[3] who promised to forward it immediately several Days ago.—I wish it may be good enough to answer your Purpose.

This is Holiday Week you know! and I am sure you will not refuse to grant me a Holiday, by your Presence.[4]—

Wednesday will be the 25th—Q^r Day. 'A Word to the Wise'—you will, (I humbly hope) bring the poor Prisoner some good News.—

I see that *Logier* has raised a Hornet's Nest about him.[5]—At this I do not wonder for several Reasons.

Of *him*, & of more important Persons & Things to *me*, when we meet, which I will not now teaze you by *begging* may be without Delay, but rely on your speedy

Kindness to
Your ever obliged Friend

S Wesley

Monday. March 23^d 1818

---

[1] SW is known to have had an attack on this date: two pages of autograph sketches and memoranda, dated by SW and evidently written in delirium, are at RCM, MS 4025, fo. 30.   [2] Not identified.

[3] William Kingston, a long-standing friend who nonetheless appears only occasionally in the letters. He was one of the small group of SW's musical and masonic friends who took charge of SW's financial affairs and treatment during his illness. In a letter to Novello of 17 Feb. 1849 (BL, Add. MS 17331, fo. 36), he stated: 'during a long period, I believe myself to have had his entire confidence; & that, in our numerous private conversations, he more fully revealed himself to me his *inner* Man, than to any other human Being.'   [4] SW was writing on Easter Monday.

[5] A reference to the recent controversy caused by Logier's system of group music teaching. In Nov. 1817 Samuel Webbe II had arranged a demonstration by his pupils of Logier's system to members of the Philharmonic Society. An anonymous paragraph in *The Times* for 18 Nov. 1817 stated that 'the experiments were received by the distinguished professors before whom they happened with marks of very great approbation'. The Philharmonic Society took exception to the endorsement of Logier's system that this implied, disputed the validity of Logier's teaching methods, accused Webbe of authorship of the paragraph, and impugned his professional integrity for publishing a false account of the demonstration. After several letters of accusation and counter-accusation in *The Times*, Webbe in a letter to the Society of 12 Dec. resigned his membership. The controversy continued in a number of pamphlets in early 1818 (Kassler, *Science of Music*, 711–14).

To Vincent Novello   [Gower Place or Euston Street],[1]
                                          17 November [1818][2]

ALS, 2 pp. (BL, Add. MS 11729, fo. 106)
Addressed To | Mʳ Novello.

Dear N

Will you call to meet at Ball's[3] on Thursday next,[4] between 12 & 1?—I am quite
surprised at the *Terms* Chappel mentions for the Trouble of scoring such a teazing Concern as a Symphony: indeed I thought that Sʳ G. Smart had intended a
civil & different Kind of Engagement by nominating me for the Job. *18 Pence* a
Sheet is no more than has been charged for *common Copying* many Years ago in
my Recollection.[5]—

Hélas! pour les Benedictions de la Musique.—

Thanks for your Present: surely you think of the Proposal about the Score as
I do—or I very much mistake.

Yours truly
& in Haste
SW

Tuesday. | 17 of Novʳ

I think if my Legs were what they used to be, I could get a dozen Fold more by running
Errands than arranging Scores on such Terms.—

---

[1] Because of the small number of letters surviving from the period of SW's illness, it is difficult to
know when he moved the few yards from Gower Place to Euston Street (now Melton Street), near the
present Euston Station. The first letter to bear the new address is dated 5 June 1819, but it is likely that he
moved there some time earlier, and he may well have been there at the time of this letter.

[2] The discussion of SW undertaking scoring at low rates (see n. 5) establishes the year.

[3] At 27 Duke Street, Grosvenor Square, where SW appears to have rented a teaching studio.

[4] 19 Nov.

[5] Smart's recommendation was to the Philharmonic Society, and was no doubt intended as a helpful
gesture to SW in his still convalescent and impoverished state. Novello evidently complained to the
Society about the rate, and it was doubled (Loan 48, Directors' Meeting Minutes, 15 Dec. 1818).

To Edward Hodges[1]   Duke Street, February 1819

Source Faustina Hasse Hodges, *Edward Hodges* (New York, 1896), 199–200.
Endorsed by Edward Hodges: From Mr. Samuel Wesley about my Typhus Pedal.[2]
Editor's note Faustina Hasse Hodges (1823–95), who included this letter in her memoir
   of her father, is known on occasion to have altered the punctuation and even the
   wording of the letters she transcribed; this transcript may not therefore be a verbatim
   copy of the original.

London, 27 Duke St., Grosvenor Sq.
February, 1819

In answer to the favour of your letter, for which I return my thanks, I wish to
observe, that your new invention appears to me exceedingly ingenious, and a
great increase of grand effect will be produced in the hands of a complete master
of Modulation and of the Organ:—but that it is only in such hands that this end
is likely to be attained; how far therefore it is of general utility may possibly be a
question, for I am sure I need not inform you that the number of performers who
understand the entire management of an organ is comparatively few.

I beg leave to add that I shall feel most ready to receive any future communication upon the subject you may judge proper to make to

Sir, Your obliged and obedient servant,

S. Wesley

---

[1] Edward Hodges (1796–1867) was born and grew up in Bristol. From Apr. 1819 he was organist
of St James's church, where SW was baptized and had his first organ lessons, and from 1821 also of
St Nicholas. From an early age he was interested in improvements to the design of organs. In 1821 he
was responsible for the inclusion of an iron pedal-board in an organ built by John Smith of Bristol for
St Nicholas, and in the following year supervised the building of the organ for the new Clifton church
by the same builder. He and Smith also remodelled the organ at St James's in 1824. He was awarded
a Mus.D. from Cambridge in 1825. It is unlikely that Hodges knew SW at this time, but they become
friends later, probably through their mutual friend Daniel Guilford Wait. SW stayed with Hodges during
his visit to Bristol in Oct. 1829, and Hodges left a memorable eyewitness account of SW's playing at
that time. In 1838, frustrated by his lack of advancement in England, Hodges emigrated to Canada, where
he had been offered the post of organist at St James's Cathedral, Toronto. Early in 1839 he moved to New
York, where he became organist of Trinity Church (*Grove*[6]; J. Ogasapian, *English Cathedral Music in
New York: Edward Hodges of Trinity Church* (Richmond, Va., 1994)).

[2] Hodges's 'improvements' to the design of organs were sometimes of dubious value. The typhus
pedal, perhaps his strangest invention, was 'a device whereby a group of notes, probably outlining a given
harmony, was mechanically sustained as a pedal point' (Ogasapian), or as Hodges's daughter Faustina
put it, 'a contrivance whereby any number of keys may be held down for an indefinite length of time'.
Hodges seems to have been alone in his enthusiasm for the idea: see Ogasapian, *English Cathedral
Music*, 32.

To Robert Glenn   [Gower Place or Euston Street],
                                              17 March [1819]¹

ANS, 1 p. (BL, Add. MS 35013, fo. 74)
Addressed To | Mr Glenn
Watermark 1817

Dear Sir

If it be agreeable for you to assist me on Friday next, I will expect the Pleasure of meeting you in that odious Den of Banditti, the Green Room, at half past 6 on the said Evening.²

A Line by the Lad will much oblige.

Yours most truly

S Wesley

                                              Wednesday 17 March

To Richard Mackenzie Bacon¹   Euston Street,² 5 June 1819

ANS, 1 p. (Cambridge, Add. MS 6247/130)
Addressed To | R. M. Bacon Esqre | Norwich
Pmk 5 819
Endorsed To Mr Bacon from Mr Wesley the celebrated Organist

---

¹ The year is given by 17 Mar. falling on a Wednesday, the reference to the oratorio concert on 19 Mar. (see n. 2), and the 1817 watermark.

² By the time of this letter SW had recovered sufficiently to have regained his old position as organist for the Covent Garden Lenten oratorio concerts. His request was for Glenn to turn pages for him at the performance of *Messiah* on 19 Mar. (*The Times*).

¹ Richard Mackenzie Bacon (1776–1844), Norwich newspaper owner and editor, and publisher of *QMMR* (see n. 4). He was the only son of Richard Bacon (1745–1812), proprietor of the *Norwich Mercury*, and took over from his father as proprietor in 1804. He was active in Norwich musical circles, and was largely instrumental in founding the Norwich triennial festival. He founded *QMMR* in 1818 and was one of its main contributors (*DNB*; *Grove*⁶; Langley, 194–216).

² This is the first dated letter from Euston Street. SW was to live there until Mar. 1830, when he moved to Mornington Place.

1819

Sir

Having been informed by Mr Horsley[3] that you are desirous of an Auxiliary in your musical Publication,[4] & as he has been so obliging as to recommend me in the Affair, I shall esteem myself favoured by your transmitting whatever Plan of Negotiation you may have formed upon the Subject, which will meet due Attention from

Sir

Yours very obediently

S Wesley

16 Euston Street. Euston Square | Saturday June 5. 1819

To Vincent Novello   Euston Street, 28 October [1819][1]

ALS, 1 p. (BL, Add. MS 11729, fo. 71)
Addressed To Mr Novello | Oxford Street | N. 240

My good Friend

The enclosed will perhaps prove some Apology for sending to your House to enquire after Birds: My dear Sir, the Letter I received on *Monday last*, & I did not advert to the *Date*, which you will see is *Septr 26*, so that it was kept at Mr Ball's (if correctly delivered) for *one* Month.—It certainly relates to Birds which I formerly received from Mr Pymer & which were sent to Balls, I dare say *from you*, according to his Desire to forward them towards me.

Detaining letters is not very excusable: the Loss of Life, or of the Means of Life may be a frequent Consequence thereof.—My broken Thumb must account for my Writing being so wretchedly bad.

Adieu, & pray forgive the manifold Faults & Blunders on sundry Occasions committed by poor

SW

28th of Octr Thursday. | Euston St E Sq. 16

---

[3] Horsley was closely involved with *QMMR*; he contributed many articles to it and acted as Bacon's chief source of information on music in London (Langley, 253–61).

[4] Presumably Bacon's projected dictionary of music, currently in the planning stage. *QMMR* reported in 1820 that it was in preparation, and a prospectus identifying SW as one of the contributors was included with the Dec. 1822 number. No copies have been traced, and it appears not to have been published (Langley, 216–81; Kassler, *Science of Music*, 48–9).

[1] The year is given by 28 Oct. falling on a Thursday and the addresses of SW and Novello.

To Vincent Novello   [Euston Street], 3 December [1819]¹

ALS, 3 pp. (BL, Add. MS 11729, fo. 73)

Friday Morn.
3 Dec

My dear N

I have long since done with all musical Controversy, but I think that in Regard to your Norwich Nibbler,² the best & shortest Way will be to refer him to Burrowes's Primer³ for Instruction about the 5ᵗʰˢ, & as to the other Point, since he seems not to know yet the Difference of an Octave and a Unison, it will be but an act of Xtian Charity to tell it him. When your Note came I was dining out in the Neighbourhood with my old Friend Parson Jeaffreson & his Family.⁴—I am so glad that you & *Linley* have understood each other about the Shakspere Book:⁵ who could have made the Mischief? What a vile Chaos is this World!—I hope, & *firmly believe* there is a better. Linley is a *very excellent Man*, & has the highest Respect for you.—I want sadly to see you.—

Behnes,⁶ the Artist in Newman Street wishes to be known to you (with whom you exchanged a Message or the like about me some Months ago: you wrote to him I think, upon Recollection).—You would find him & the

---

¹ The year is given by 3 Dec. falling on a Friday and the reference to the 'Norwich Nibbler' (see n. 2).

² The Norwich organist James Taylor (see SW to Pettet, 22 Sept. 1815, n. 2), had contributed a long and generally respectful review of Novello's *A Collection of Sacred Music* to the current number of *QMMR* (2 (1819–20), 15–22). Novello had taken exception to Taylor's remarks about 'one or two instances' of consecutive fifths and octaves, which Taylor considered insignificant but nonetheless felt obliged to mention. He subsequently replied to Taylor: his letter, in which he attempted to refute the 'unfounded charge' made against him, is not preserved, but is mentioned in Taylor's second article, dated 27 Dec. 1819, which appeared in the following number of *QMMR* (2 (1819–20), 167–70).

³ The *Thorough Base Primer* (1819) by John Freckleton Burrowes (1787–1852), organist of St James, Piccadilly, and a pupil of Horsley.

⁴ The family may still have been in the lodgings at 41 Duke Street, Manchester Square that they had occupied in 1814: see SW to Novello, 20 Apr. [1814].

⁵ Presumably Linley's *Shakspeare's Dramatic Songs*.

⁶ William Behnes (?1795–1864), who lived at 31 Newman Street, off Oxford Street. The son of a piano tuner from Hanover, he was brought up in London, where he worked for his father. He entered the Royal Academy Schools in London in 1813 and later set up as a portrait painter. In 1822 he executed a bust of Walter McGeough (see SW to McGeough, 11 Nov. 1822, and n. 2) (*DNB*). Newman Street was celebrated as a street of artists, and many artists lived or had studios there.

Brothers⁷ sensible Lads: I call there almost daily; they are excessively kind & friendly.—

I have been told that you have Thoughts of residing towards Camden Town: is this true?⁸—

Will you give me some early Intelligence about our Meeting? Consultation concerning a Concert (*if I am to attempt one*) is now necessary, & you must condescend to advise me:—F. Cramer, Braham, & Vaughan have promised their Help.⁹—

Yours ever truly

SW

What an *independent* enviable Group are the Inhabitants of a Church Yard! How they mock the wretched Scramblers over their Heads!

To Vincent Novello   Euston Street, 9 December [1819]¹

ALS, 1 p. (BL, Add. MS 11729, fo. 296)
Addressed Thursday 9 Dec^r | To | Mr Novello | 240 | Oxford Street |
Pmk 9 DE

16 Euston Street
—Sq^re

Dear N

The following are my Notions about the Progression objected to.—²

---

⁷ William Behnes's brothers Henry (later Henry Burlowe) (d. 1837) and Charles (d. 1840), who were also artists.

⁸ Novello may have been considering a move at this time, but when he left Oxford Street the following year it was for 8 Percy Street, off Tottenham Court Road. In 1823 he moved out of central London to Shacklewell Green, but moved back to Bedford Square, Covent Garden, in 1826.

⁹ No record of this concert has been traced, and it is not known whether or not it took place.

¹ The year is given by 9 Dec. falling on a Thursday, the addresses of SW and Novello, and the continuing discussion of the *QMMR* review.

² Taylor had not given specific instances of alleged consecutives in his *QMMR* review, but did so in his second *QMMR* article, no doubt in response to a challenge in a letter from Novello; he may also have communicated this information to Novello privately. Two of the passages he instanced were from SW's own contributions to Novello's collection, and one of these may be under discussion here.

First, I think the Effect by no means harsh or unpleasant to the Ear, & when a Transition is not so, even if it be not according to an old strict Rule (or in other Words a License) I do not see a Necessity for rejecting it.

2dly there certainly are numerous Instances of the same Progression in some of the best Writers, as you truly observe.

3dly the very same occurs in Handel's Song 'Ev'ry Valley,' Messiah

I was taught that a perfect & imperfect 5th in Succession were allowable, when not put in the extreme Parts, the highest & lowest.—I have no more to say.

Will you meet me at M^r De la Fite's,[3] on *Saturday evening*, N° 40, Clarendon Square, Somers Town, near the Catholic Chapel,[4]—I will stay for you from 6 till 8. He is a very kind Friend to poor

SW

PS If I am to try for a few Halfpence by a Concert, ought Time to be trifled with? *Pray come on Sat*[5]

[3] The Revd Henry Francis Alexander Delafite (1772/3–1831), matric. Trinity College, Oxford (1794), BA (1798), MA (1805), for thirty years evening lecturer at St Paul's, Covent Garden, foreign secretary of the Royal Society of Literature. His *GM* obituary noted that his family had settled in England following the revocation of the Edict of Nantes in 1685, that Delafite's mother had been governess to the daughters of George III, and that this connection had led to his education at Oxford. He was a friend of the French geologist De Luc, and published an English translation of his *Elements of Geology* in 1812. At his death he had just completed a new edition of De Luc's *Letters on the Physical History of the Earth* (Foster; *GM* 1831[2], 90).

[4] Somers Town, lying north of the present Euston Road between Euston and St Pancras stations, was the home of many French refugee families. Clarendon Square, now demolished, lay south of the present Polygon Road, part of which formed its north side. In a later letter SW gives Delafite's address as 35 Clarendon Square. The Roman Catholic chapel was the church of St Aloysius, built by the Abbé Carron in 1808, on the south side of the present Phoenix Road, part of which originally formed the south side of Clarendon Square (*Survey of London*, xxiv. 120, and Pls. 4 and 86).   [5] 11 Dec.

To Vincent Novello [Euston Street], 23 December [?1819][1]

ALS, 1 p. (BL, Add. MS 11729, fo. 45)
Addressed M[r] Novello | 240 | Oxford Street | Thursday

Dear N

No news from Miss S.[2] Perhaps a little more Urgence for an Answer might not have been superfluous.—I do not like to write again, but it is teazing to be trifled with where *Bread* is the Question.

Pray hand me your kind Cobble of my blunderbuss Canon.[3] Will you send it or leave it for me at Behnes's as soon as may be? for I shall be thought neglectful otherwise I fear.—Of what am I now most worthy in the Line of *Donation*?—What think you of a Sarcophagus? The Ambassador's Letter[4] (ie mine to him) has been committed to safe Hands.—Would it may produce Justice to the right Party.

Y[rs] ever truly
SW

23[d] Dec

To Robert William Elliston[1] Euston Street, 19 May 1820

ALS, 1 p. (Bristol)
Addressed To | R. W. Elliston Esq[re]
Annotated in another hand M[r] Goadby's Address is N° 60 Skinner Street Snow Hill

Dear Sir

Concerning young M[r] Goadby,[2] the Bearer, I beg Leave to inform you that he has attended and drilled many of Corri's Pupils in his House for nearly three

---

[1] During the period of SW's correspondence with Novello, 23 Dec. fell on a Thursday in 1813 and 1819. The reference to Behnes, also mentioned in other letters of this period, and the existence of a letter from SW to Novello of 23 Dec. 1813 on an entirely different topic, suggest that 1819 is the more probable year.

[2] Possibly Catherine Stephens, in response to an enquiry from SW about her availability for his projected concert: see SW to Novello, 3 Dec. [1819], and n. 9.   [3] Not identified.

[4] Presumably to the Portuguese Ambassador, Dom Pedro de Sousa Holstein, Duque de Palmela (1781–1850); not preserved.

[1] Robert William Elliston (1774–1831), actor, singer, manager, and playwright, who had recently become the licensee of Drury Lane Theatre (*DNB*; *BD*; Christopher Murray, *Robert William Elliston* (1975).   [2] Not identified.

Years: his own Voice, which is a low Tenor, is but indifferent, and not sufficiently smooth for Glee singing, but he reads music with Facility, and has some well-grounded Knowledge of the Piano Forte, with a Firmness of Finger, and I really think that you would find him useful in assisting choral Practitioners.—By placing him *somewhere* in your musical Department you will truly oblige

Dear Sir
Yours most sincerely

S Wesley

16. Euston Street. E. Sq. | New road | Friday 19 of May 1820

To Vincent Novello   Euston Street, 29 August [1820][1]

ALS, 2 pp. (BL, Add. MS 11729, fo. 156)
Addressed To | Mr Novello | Percy Street
Endorsed by Novello: From dear Sam Wesley

My dear N

It is as false as mischievous to tell you that I never enquire after you: I have not gone to Ball's for many Weeks, because I do not like Insult added to the Train of my Miseries.—Major is the only Person of whom I can learn concerning you, and him I seldom see more than once in a Month or 6 Weeks.—I most truly and deeply sympathized on the News of your most afflicting Loss:[2] *several* times have I known its Bitterness by Experience.[3]—I have always considered you among the *very* few who care what becomes of me, and have been ever alive to your Kindness for me.—My Views of any Peace of Comfort on Earth have long since terminated, and could I only secure a Probability that my poor Children would not exist in Wretchedness, I could perhaps drag out the sad Remainder of my melancholy Journey in less Horror and Agitation.—To be starved one's self is dismal enough, but to become the Cause of similar Destruction to others, and worst of all to those we do and ought to love, is insupportable by any but a Heart of Adamant.

---

[1] The year is given by 29 Aug. falling on a Tuesday and the addresses of SW and Novello.

[2] The recent death of Novello's son Sidney, born in 1816. For Novello's devotion to Sidney and his depression and ill health following his death, see Clarke, *Life and Labours*, 22–4.

[3] Three of SW's children had died in infancy or early childhood. In addition to the two children whose deaths in Mar. 1813 and Aug. 1816 feature in these letters, a daughter born in Nov. 1794 had died in Dec. 1797.

I am very low and ill, but would most willingly meet you, anywhere but in Duke Street.[4]—The Music at the Chapel is too overwhelming for me to stand.— Behnes's in Newman Street is always open to me, and where I wish you to address any Communication to your sincere (tho' now decayed and perishing) old Friend and Companion

    SW

29th of Aug.—Tuesday | Euston S[t] Eust[n] Sq[re]

To Vincent Novello   Denmark Street,[1] 20 November [1820][2]

ALS, 1 p. (BL, Add. MS 11729, fo. 158)

Endorsed by Novello: I wish to place this affecting Note on record, as an eternal disgrace to the pretended Patrons of good music in England, who could have the contemptible bad taste to undervalue & neglect the masterly productions of such an extraordinary Musician as Sam Wesley, and who had the paltry meanness of spirit, to allow such a real Genius (who, like Purcell, was an honor to the Country where he was born) to sink into such poverty, decay and undeserved neglect, as to be under the necessity of seeking employment as a mere drudging *Copyist* to prevent himself from starvation!

The behaviour of the *rich Patrons* of Wesley in *England*, reminds me of the equally despicable behaviour of the self-styled nobility among the cold-blooded, selfish and beggarly-proud Scotch, towards their really illustrious countryman, *Burns*.

May such unfeeling brutes meet their just reward.

Nov. 20
Monday Noon

My good Friend N

Can you give or obtain for me, any *Copying*, literary or musical? Either of them would be very acceptable at present, and the Terms I must leave to your Consideration, remaining always

    My dear Friend,
    Most cordially yours,
      S Wesley

---

[4] i.e. at Ball's.

[1] Rimbault's house (see postscript and n. 3).

[2] The year is suggested by 20 Nov. falling on a Monday and by SW's request for copying work.

P S I write this at Mr Rimbault's,[3] N. 9 Denmark Street, Soho, where I call almost daily, and should receive an early Line speedily, with which I hope you will oblige me.

I have not forgotten your Desire of the *Ossian* Recit:[4] *have Patience with me*: whenever I write it, I must do it from Memory, for I have not the Book where it is.—M^r De la Fite is in the Country—I *think* he has it in his Trunk locked up.

To Lord Calthorpe[1]   Euston Street, 4 August 1821

ALS, 1 p. (Hampshire Record Office, 26M62/F/C285)

To the Right Honble Lord Calthorpe

I trust that I shall not be deemed too presumptuous in addressing your Lordship as a Candidate for the Situation of the New Church of St Pancras.[2]

In the fortunate Event of being honoured with your Lordship's Vote and Interest, my best Exertions will not be wanting for the Fulfilment of the Duty with Attention and Punctuality.

I have the Honour to be,
With all due Respect,
My Lord,
Your Lordship's most obedient
and devoted Servant

Samuel Wesley

Euston Street | Euston Square | Aug. 4. 1821

[3] Stephen Francis Rimbault (1773–1837), organist of St Giles in the Fields. He was the father of Edward Francis Rimbault (1816–76), who in later life achieved eminence and some notoriety as a musical antiquarian and as a collector and editor of music (*Grove*[6]).

[4] Possibly SW's 1784 setting for voice and orchestra of 'Alone on the sea-beat rock' ('Arnim's Lamentation'), the autograph of which is at BL, Add. MS 35005.

[1] George, 3rd Baron Calthorpe (1787–1851) (*Burke's Peerage*). As the owner of the Calthorpe Estate, occupying a large area in the St Pancras parish, he was an influential member of the Select Vestry, whose support could be important to SW in obtaining the position of organist at the new church.

[2] St Pancras, Euston Road, by H. W. and W. Inwood, consecrated on 7 May 1822 (*GM* 1822[1], 462–3). An undated note in SW's hand noting his candidacy for this position is at BL, Add. MS 35027, fo. 3. The organist eventually appointed, in the following Feb., was T. W. Henshaw (Minutes of Church Trustees, St Pancras Church Lands Trust Minute Book, St Pancras Church, 21 Feb. 1822).

To Vincent Novello [Euston Street], 2 October [1821]¹

ALS, 1 p. (BL, Add. MS 11729, fo. 159)
Addressed Mr Novello

Dear N.

Will you tell me whether the short Magnificat² you require may be composed like one of Webbe's,³ in little Duets & Solos with an occasional Chorus,⁴ & for what Voices I had best set it?—

I fear my *best* will be but a very poor Job, for all the inventive Spirit of my Brains has alas! long evaporated.

Favor me with your specific orders by Bearer if possible.

> Your afflicted
> & grateful Friend
>   SW

2^d of Oct. Tuesday

To Vincent Novello [Euston Street], 9 October 1821

ALS, 1 p. (BL, Add. MS 11729, fo. 160)
Addressed To | Mr Novello

Dear N.

If any Thing I can write please you, it is well:—I shall never more write any Thing that will please *myself*.¹

---

¹ The year is given by 2 Oct. falling on a Tuesday and SW's reference to his setting of the Magnificat (see n. 1).

² A setting by SW of the Latin text of the Magnificat. The autograph, dated 6 Oct. 1821, is at Austin; a copy dated 1821 in the hand of Novello is at BL, Add. MS 65455. Novello's request was presumably for a contribution to a printed collection he was planning.   ³ i.e. Samuel Webbe I.

⁴ SW was perhaps thinking of the setting in his *A Collection of Music as used in the Chapel of the King of Sardinia* (*c*.1785), which answers this description.

¹ SW's remark was presumably in response to some appreciative comments by Novello on his Magnificat setting.

I am sorry I cannot trace the 'Whereabout' of my poor Confitebor, because it is (*altogether*) the least incorrect of my musical Scrolls, and *might* have had a Chance of becoming profitable (if published) to some of my unfortunate Progeny, when my Carcase shall be in the Churchyard (should it obtain Xtian Burial of which I am *most cordially conscious* that it is in all Respects & on all Accounts totally undeserving.)—

I am always
D^r N
Very truly yours
(& nothing else worthless belongs to you)
   SW

Octr 9.—1821

To Vincent Novello   Euston Street, 27 November [18]21

ALS, 1 p. (BL, Add. MS 11729, fo. 162)
Addressed To | Mr Novello | Percy Street | Rathbone Place

Dear N
Can you recommend me to a Pennyworth of Writing of any Sort, whether of Music or Words in the transcribing Way? As a *Composer* I am a Cripple, but in copying I believe I remain as correct, tho' certainly not so expeditious as heretofore.—You will perhaps give me a speedy Line upon the Subject, and I hope believe me always

Your obliged Friend
   SW

16 Euston Street. Tuesday 27 Nov.—21

To [Walter McGeough]¹   Euston Street, 11 May [1822]²

ALS, 1 p. (Argory)

Dear Sir

I rely much on your Indulgence to pardon the Liberty I take upon the present Occasion: the Truth is, that an Acceptance³ for £12 having become due this Day, which an unexpected Disappointment prevents my being prepared to honor, I am therefore induced to presume upon your Kindness in this Exigence, which will be gratefully considered as a most reasonable Assistance, by

> Dear Sir
> Your truly obliged
> and very devoted Servant
>
>   S Wesley

16 Euston St. | Euston Sq^{re} | Saturday 11th of May

To Lord Burghersh¹   Euston Street, 2 September 1822

ALS, 1 p. (Kassler)
Docketed 2nd Sep 1822 | Mr Samuel Wesley

---

¹ The Irish landowner Walter McGeough (1790–1866), whom SW knew through musical and possibly also masonic circles in London. Later in the year SW was involved in the commissioning of a large finger and barrel organ for The Argory, the large house overlooking the River Blackwater near Moy, Co. Armagh that McGeough was currently having built; it is now in the possession of the National Trust. The notable organ commissioned by McGeough remains there, and is still in playing order: for a description of its appearance, mechanism, and operation, see Bicknell, 221. Although this letter is not addressed to McGeough by name, it is preserved with SW's other letters to McGeough at The Argory, and is undoubtedly to him.

² The year is given by 11 May falling on a Saturday and SW's Euston Street address.

³ A bill of exchange or promissory note that SW had issued at some time in the past.

---

¹ John Fane (1784–1859), 11th Earl of Westmorland from 1841, soldier, politician, and amateur musician. He was educated at Trinity College, Cambridge (MA 1808) where he studied music with Hague. In the course of a long military career he served in various campaigns in the Napoleonic Wars, was at one time aide-de-camp to Wellington, major general (1825), lieutenant general (1838), and general (1854). He was MP for Lyme Regis (1806–10), Privy Councillor (1822), British envoy in Florence (1814–30), resident minister in Berlin (1841–51), and ambassador to the Imperial court at Vienna (1851–5). Most of his spare time was devoted to music, and he was a good amateur violinist and a prolific composer. He was the founder of the Royal Academy of Music and its President until his death (*DNB*, under 'Fane, John'; *Grove*⁶ under 'Burghersh, John Fane').

My Lord

Permit me to return my grateful Acknowledgements to your Lordship and the Committee of the Royal Academy of Music,[2] for the very flattering Manner in which you are pleased to announce the Insertion of my Name among the Members of so honourable an Establishment,[3] and to assure your Lordship and the Society that I shall feel most happy in the Opportunity of proving myself not unworthy the signal Attention conferred on My Lord,

> Your Lordship's very obedient
> and devoted Servant
>
> S Wesley

Euston Street. | Monday Sept[r] 2. 1822

To Walter McGeough   Euston Street, 12 October 1822

ALS, 2 pp. (Argory)
Addressed W. M[c]Geough Esq[re] | Drumsilla | Armagh | Ireland | 12th of Oct[r]
Pmk OC 12 1822
Docketed 12 Oct 1822 the Organ

> London. Euston Street. Euston Squ[e]
> Saturday 12th of Oct[r] 1822

Dear Sir

I feel it my Duty to explain to you the State of Matters respecting your Organ,[1] in that Department of its Construction which has been allotted to *me*.[2] I Therefore beg Leave to inform you that out of the 33 Pieces set down in your Papers, for Arrangement, *Eleven* of them are found to be alone quite sufficient

---

[2] Founded in 1822, the Royal Academy of Music accepted its first intake of students in 1823.

[3] SW had been invited to become an honorary member, a position which involved no duties but granted 'the privilege of personal admission to the concerts, rehearsals, and examinations' of the Royal Academy. Fifty-seven such members were elected at the Royal Academy's foundation ('The Royal Academy of Music', *QMMR* 4 (1822), 370–400, 516–26: pp. 378, 518–19).

[1] The commission for the organ had been placed at SW's recommendation with the organ builder James Davis (see SW to Novello, 24 July [1812], n. 2). Davis had recently been left £12,000 by his elder brother David (also an organ builder), who had died on 9 Jan. 1822. By the end of 1822 he had decided to retire, and passed on the commission for the Argory organ to James Bishop, who built it and delivered it to McGeough in Sept. 1824 (Elvin, 97–100; Michael Sayer, 'James Davis and the Lancashire Organ Builders', *MT* 111 (1970), 645–7, 649). For Bishop, see also SW to Bishop, 28 Feb. [1824].

[2] SW had been contracted to arrange the music for the barrels.

to occupy the whole of *Eight Barrels*, which are two Barrels more than your original Order included:[3] consequently, to accomplish the Completion of your Wish, we must have Authority from you to increase considerably the Number of Barrels; and therefore request the Favour of your immediate Injunctions upon the Subject, that Things may proceed *en bon Train*; and I trust that I shall be then enabled to prepare all the Remainder of the Pieces to your Satisfaction.

I am concerned to add but uncomfortable News with regard to myself, suffering not only from bodily Infirmity, but being also harassed by tormenting Applications in Consequence of vexations & unexpected pecuniary Disappointments.—Among the most pressing of them is a Bill for £15, which the Holder refuses to retain any longer; threatening me with immediate legal Hostility, which his Severity of Character will too certainly commence, without the *Prompt* Remittance of the Sum.—Others, who have some just Demands on me, are not altogether so rigorous and urgent; but yet, I cannot *in Safety* pursue my ordinary and necessary Avocations, without a little timely assistance from my Friends, at the present Juncture, and I trust, my good Sir, that you will kindly pardon the Liberty I venture to take in making to you this confidential Communication, and that you will continue to believe me, with most cordial Respect,

Your devoted and very grateful Servant

S. Wesley

P.S. Davis[4] desires me to signify to you his Intention of writing to you in the Course of a Week hence.

To Walter McGeough   [Euston Street], 11 November 1822

ALS, 3 pp. (Argory)
Addressed To Walter MᶜGeough Esqʳᵉ Drumsilla | Armagh | Ireland | Nov 11
Re-addressed 17 Eccles Sᵗ | Dublin
Pmks 11 NO 822, 13 NO 1822

London Nov. 11. 1822

---

[3] Bishop's final estimate and specification for the organ, dated 3 Mar. 1824 (The Argory) provided for only six barrels; any additional barrels ordered were to be charged at £15 each (Elvin, 99).

[4] i.e. James Davis.

My dear Sir

Pray forgive me for not having more immediately returned my very cordial Thanks for your extremely kind Letter,[1] which, together with its Contents was safely received, and proved a very material Benefit and seasonable Assistance.

I have of Course made an early Point of seeing the Behnes's, and Davis upon the Subjects you required, and from the former I am commissioned to acquaint you that they would write to you *very speedily* respecting the Bust &c.[2] and I presume that by the Time *this* arrives you will most probably obtain their Intelligence upon that Business: at all Events, I beg you to rest assured that I have punctually executed your Commands in that Quarter.

From Davis I am directed to say that he will certainly write to you either to-Day or tomorrow, and I *trust* that he will give an explanatory and satisfactory Account of a Silence which I own appears to me very reprehensible.[3]

Now as to myself, I will forthwith give the List of what I have already arranged, which amounts to *14* Pieces upon Examination 1. Wesley's March.[4] 2. Hornpipe.[5] 3. Gramachree.[6] 4. Scot's wha hae.[7] 5. Overture to Artaxerxes.[8] 6. See the Conq'ring Hero.[9] 7. Before Jehovah's awful Throne.[10] 8. Hallelujah Chorus.[11] 9. March in the Zauberflöete.[12] 10. Queen Mary's Lamentation.[13] 11. March in Scipio.[14] 12. Overture to Anacreon.[15] 13. Overture to the Zauberflöete.

---

[1] Not preserved: presumably in response to SW's letter of 12 Oct.

[2] McGeough had commissioned a portrait bust of himself from William Behnes. It was executed in 1823 and is still at The Argory. SW was evidently an intermediary in the affair.

[3] Davis's letter is not preserved.

[4] Probably the March from the Overture to SW's *Ode to St Cecilia*, which also appeared in an arrangement for organ in his *Voluntary* dedicated to William Drummer of 1828.

[5] Probably the popular Hornpipe from SW's D major Organ Concerto (1800), which had been published separately as a piano piece in 1820 (*CPM*).

[6] Grammachree Molly ('As down on Banna's Banks I strayed') a popular Irish air first published in 1774 (*CPM*).

[7] 'Scots wha' hae with Wallace bled': Robert Burns's battle-song, representing Robert Bruce's address to his army at Bannockburn, had first appeared in James Johnson (ed.), *The Scots Musical Museum*, 6 vols. (Edinburgh, 1787–1803). It was available in the 1820s in a number of different versions and arrangements, and a set of variations on it by SW was published in 1824 (*CPM*).

[8] By Thomas Augustine Arne (*c*.1740–86).   [9] From Handel's *Judas Maccabaeus* (1747).

[10] The popular hymn tune 'Denmark', by SW's godfather Martin Madan.   [11] From *Messiah*.

[12] The March of the Priests, which opens Act II of Mozart's *Die Zauberflöte*.

[13] 'I sigh and lament me in vain', by Tommaso Giordani (*c*.1733–1806).

[14] From Handel's opera *Scipione* (1726).

[15] The overture to *Anacréon, ou l'Amour fugitif* (1803) by Cherubini (1760–1842), a particularly popular orchestral piece of the day: see Ehrlich, *First Philharmonic*, 6.

14. Fischer's Minuet with Mozart's 12 Variations.[16] None of these have been yet *set* upon Barrels, the Reasons which Davis promises to explain to you in a clear intelligible Manner, and I trust that he will do so without further Delay.— As I have now obtained the correct Division of the *Time* of each Piece by the Metronome, he will con-sequently be able to judge accurately the Number of Barrels which the whole 14 pieces would occupy, but it still remains with you to decide whether you would *exclude* any of them on account of their occupy-ing more than 6 Barrels, especially as there are several other Pieces which you seem desirous should be inserted, and which are not yet arranged, on account of those already prepared having exceeded the *original* Extent to which your Order was limited.[17]—

Therefore, my dear Sir, you see I must wait for your Commentary upon Davis's Report to you which when I have the Pleasure to obtain, I shall be most ready and desirous to proceed in any Way which shall be comfortable to your Wish, whether by *Augmentation* or *Substitution* of Matter for the Barrels. You readily perceive that for the Completion of the *whole* List with which you favoured me, a *considerable* Increase of the Barrel Work will be indispensable and here both Davis and myself must be regulated by the Result of your Determination: which, whatever it be, I flatter myself that you will find me zealous to do my best, and to prove to you with what Respect and grateful Sense

I consider myself at all Times
My dear Sir
Your much devoted Servant
    S Wesley

[16] Mozart's popular set of keyboard variations on the minuet which forms the finale of the Oboe Concerto No. 1 by Johann Christian Fischer (1733–1800), K. 179/189a (1774).

[17] It is not known how many barrels McGeough commissioned, or what music they contained. Only three of the barrels originally supplied survive, the remainder probably having been destroyed in a fire at The Argory in 1898. They contain the following items, all of which are included in SW's list: Fischer's Minuet with Mozart's Twelve Variations; the Overture and March from Mozart's *Die Zauberflöte*; the Overture to Arne's *Artaxerxes* and 'See the Conqu'ring Hero Comes' from Handel's *Judas Maccabaeus*. For the innovative registrations, presumably by SW himself, see Bicknell, 221.

To Vincent Novello

ALS, 1 p. (BL, Add. MS 11729, fo. 164)
Addressed To | Mr Vincent Novello

My dear Novello

My old Friend, M[r] Jos. Barret,[1] (No 50. Upper Berkley Street, Edgware <Road>) a sensible, worthy, conscientious and feeling Character, has given me his solemn Promise, that should he outlive me, which I most cordially hope and trust he will, I may safely depend upon his energetic Endeavour to fulfil my Request and gratify my earnest Desire of having my poor Remains deposited as near as can possibly be contrived to the precious Relicks of my transcendent and inestimable Friend[2] in the Church Yard of Paddington:—and I have stated to the said J. B. my firm Persuasion that you will readily & heartily co-operate with him towards the punctual Accomplishment of this my anxious Wish, long cherished, & unceasing.

I own that you would much gratify me by consenting to an Interview with him upon the Subject, and which I am positive you would not afterwards regret, as you would find him a perfectly well bred Man, possessed moreover of the unaffected Delicacy which belongs to a *genuine* Philanthropist, therefore you need not apprehend from him the slightest future Encroachment on your Time by a vivâ voce Agreement & Stipulation to perform a tender Act of Charity to him who was once

S Wesley

Euston Street | July 4th 1823

---

[1] Not identified: according to SW in his letter to Novello of 14 June [1824], he had been his friend for twenty years, and was not a musician.

[2] Anne Deane, the daughter of Mrs Deane of The Manor House, Paddington, mentioned in SW to Bridgetower, 23 Feb. 1797. SW had a love affair with her around 1799 which appears to have precipitated his temporary separation from Charlotte in late 1801 and to have estranged him from his sister Sarah. Little is known in detail about the incident. Anne Deane died in Jan. 1806 and was buried in Paddington churchyard on 26 Jan. of that year (Paddington burial records (London Metropolitan Archives)).

To Vincent Novello Euston Street, 26 November [1823]¹

ANS, 1 p. (BL, Add. MS 11729, fo. 166)
Addressed To | Mʳ Novello | Shacklewell Green | Stoke Newington | Paid
Pmk 26 NO 1823

Dear N.

Pray give me a Line informing me when and where we could meet for half an Hour's confidential Chat.

I want your Advice upon a Point relative to a Society consisting of Fools, Knaves, and Musicians,² which last Personages you know full well are always a Mixture of both.

Yours as always

S Wesley

26ᵗʰ of Nov. | Euston Street | 16

To Vincent Novello [Euston Street], ?4 December 1823¹

ALS, 1 p. (BL, Add. MS 11729, fo. 168)
Addressed To | Mʳ Novello | Shacklewell Green | Stoke Newington | Paid
Pmk DE 1823

Dear N

Tell me promptly & bluntly whether you approve the annexed.²

Since we met, I have been thinking that an Improvement in our Mode of Adieu on Wednesday³ would be made by your submitting for once in a way to sleep for that Night in that Quarter of the world aptly termed by Byron 'the Devil's Drawing Room,' or London, (in a word less appropriate)⁴—In this Case we shall

---

¹ The year is given by the postmark.
² No doubt the Glee Club: see SW's draft letter to Richard Clark, enclosed with the following letter to Novello.

---

¹ This letter is misdated: 6 Dec. was not a Thursday in 1823. The correct date should probably be Thursday, 4 Dec. ² The draft letter to Clark below.
³ 10 Dec., when SW and Novello apparently had a social engagement together. The reference later in the letter to Chalk Farm, which was evidently to be on their homeward route, suggests that it may have been at the house of James Harding at Kentish Town (see SW to Novello, 18 Sept. [1824]), or with the Burgh family in Hampstead (see SW to Novello, 13 Sept. 1824).
⁴ i.e. at SW's house in Euston Street. Novello had moved earlier in the year out of central London to Shacklewell Green, Hackney, and it would have been more convenient for him to stay overnight with SW after an evening engagement than to return home immediately. The original source of the description is in fact Smollett's *Roderick Random* (1748), ch. 18.

be enabled to brave Danger together, and if both murdered any where about Chalk Farm, the Advantage of such an Event *in Company* is too great to be rationally slighted by two such stoical Philosophers as you and

    SW

Thursday. 6th of Decr 1823

[Enclosure:][5]

To Mr Secretary Clark[6]

Sir

As I no longer now attempt to sing (although in Years past I found singing an Amusement) I feel conscious that I can afford no Assistance in this way to any vocal Society; moreover, the Truth is, that in growing old, I suspect I grow also somewhat fastidious, acknowledging that I am a little weary of musical Chords in the shape of Glees.—You have successfully obtained for the Club[7] a skilful extemporaneous *Pianist*,[8] therefore no Chasm in you usual series of Performances can be occasioned by my future Lack of Attendance.[9]

---

[5] BL, Add. MS 11729, fo. 169.

[6] Richard Clark (1780–1856), secretary of the Glee Club, composer, arranger, and author, had begun his career as a chorister at St George's Chapel, Windsor; he was later lay clerk at St George's Chapel and at Eton College (1802–11), lay vicar of Westminster Abbey and vicar choral of St Paul's (1811), and Gentleman of the Chapel Royal (1820). In 1814 he published *The First Volume of Poetry . . . The Most Favorite Pieces as Performed at the Noblemen and Gentlemen's Catch Club, the Glee Club and all Public Societies*, which also included a brief history of these societies. He was described in an article on the Catch and Glee Clubs in *QMMR* 2 (1820), 324–31 as 'a gentleman of learning and research'.

[7] The Glee Club: see SW to Novello, 25 Feb. [1816], n. 9.

[8] Not identified, but evidently a replacement for SW. The 1820 *QMMR* account recorded that the performance of glees was 'sometimes interspersed with extemporaneous playing on the piano forte by Mr Wesley, whose erudition and execution are so universally the object of admiration'.

[9] Included with SW's letters to Novello at BL, Add. MS 11729, fo. 304 is a scrap of paper in SW's hand with the following four lines of doggerel, no doubt connected with this letter:

> I forbear with the Glee Club in future to dine
> Tho' the Members are all so respectable
> Bad singing, bad Viands, false Friends, & bad Wine
> Are to me (I confess) not delectable.

With this short Statement of simple Fact I add a sincere Wish that the Prosperity of the Society may continue equally secured by fresh Acquisition of Talent, and uninterrupted Permanence of Unanimity; remaining

Sir,
obediently yours
SW

To Vincent Novello   [Euston Street], 19 December 1823

ALS, 1 p. (BL, Add. MS 11729, fo. 171)
Addressed To | Mr Novello | Shacklewell Green | near | Stoke Newington
Pmk 1823

Dear N

As a formidable Bench of musical *Amateurs* are to sit in Judgement upon my Magnificat & Nunc Dimittis on Thursday next,[1] you will oblige me by putting it into your Pocket on Sunday, when if you will leave it in Percy Street[2] I shall be able to get at it in good Time.—I hope you have performed your Promise of putting out or in any Note you have found could be changed for the better.—I think that among my manifold Sins & Infirmities you will not impute to me pretended Humility, for there is not another professional Man in England, Scotland, or Ireland, whose Emendation would be worth a Button in the Opinion of

Yours truly
SW

19th of Decr 1823. | Friday

---

[1] A reference to the projected performance of SW's settings of the two evening canticles, composed the previous year, at St Paul's Cathedral on Christmas Day. These completed his Morning and Evening Service, which he was to publish the following year; it also included his 1808 settings of the Te Deum and Jubilate from Matins and his 1806 setting of the Responses to the Commandments and the Sanctus from the Communion Service. Discussion of the arrangements for further performances of the service, its publication and its critical reception, loom large in the letters of 1824 and 1825.

[2] Novello's former address, which he perhaps retained as his business premises following his move to Shacklewell Green.

To Vincent Novello   Euston Street, 17 February [1824][1]

ALS, 1 p. (BL, Add. MS 11729, fo. 173)
Addressed To | Mr Novello | Shacklewell Green | Stoke Newington | Tuesday 17 Feb.
Pmk 17 FE 1824

16 Euston Street
17. Feb.

Dear N

'The Gossip, Report' is seldom 'an honest Woman of her Word,'[2] & therefore I want to know from you whether she has lyed in declaring that you are to be an Umpire in the approaching digital Contest among the Psalm Tune Combatants at St George's Hanover Square.[3]—I have been talked into becoming one Fool among many, and to appeal to learned Hearers whether at 58 years' old I can resolve $\frac{6}{4}$ with equal Certainty as Mr Mather,[4] Mr J. Sale[5] and a numerous Host of more fashionable Opponents than your old Friend.

You will easily believe that my past Experience renders me *tolerably philo-sophical* as to what may be the Event, but I choose to disprove the Falsehood which has been pretty successfully circulated, that *I am averse from all musical Employment*, tho' that I hate Music as a Source of great Misery is unquestionably true.—

Let me hear, *when* I can get half an Hour's Chat with you.

Y^rs as ever,

   SW

---

[1] The year is given by the postmark.   [2] *Merchant of Venice*, III. i. 6–7.

[3] i.e. the election for the post of organist, for which SW was a candidate. SW was unsuccessful in his application; the identity of the successful candidate is not known.

[4] George Mather, the blind organist of St Bride's, Fleet Street from 1821 until his death in 1854 (Brown and Stratton; Dawe).

[5] John Bernard Sale (1779–1856), bass singer, composer, and organist, chorister at St George's Chapel, Windsor, and Eton College (1785), lay vicar at Westminster Abbey (1800), gentleman of the Chapel Royal (1803), organist of St Margaret's, Westminster (1809); later organist of the Chapel Royal (1838), and music teacher to Queen Victoria (Shaw).

To James Bishop[1]   Euston Street, 28 February [1824][2]

ALS, 1 p. (Argory)
Addressed Mr Bishop | Organ Builder | York Buildings

Euston St. Euston Sq 16
Saturday Feb 28

Sir

I presume you are already informed that the Organ to be finished for M[r] M[c]Gough *by you* in Consequence of M[r] Davis having declined proceeding with it himself, was bespoken by me originally, I having recommended M[r] Davis to M[r] M[c]G among the various Builders to whom he had previously applied.—Mr D agreed to pay me a Premium of 50 Guineas for the Commission, and I scarcely need to add, that as the Job is now in *your* Hands (which are very good ones) of Course the Settlement of my Bargain with *him* is made over to you and that when the Organ is compleated you alone will be the Party to whom I must look for the stipulated sum.[3]

I thought right to state the Fact to you, that no future Mistake upon the Subject may arise, and shall be obliged by a Line in Answer, remaining

Sir,
Y[rs] obed[tly]

S. Wesley

---

[1] James Bishop (1783–1854), organ builder, who founded the firm that bears his name at around the end of the 18th cent. (*Grove*[6]; Elvin).

[2] The year is given by 28 Feb. falling on a Saturday and the content (see also SW to Novello, 8 Mar. 1824).

[3] The practice of organ builders paying commission to organists for recommending their work was widespread, but (as SW knew all too well), builders frequently refused to pay commission due. As SW's letter to Novello of 8 Mar. shows, this is what happened in this case. The 50 guineas commission originally agreed between SW and Davis may have represented 10 per cent of the original estimated cost. If so, this would have been in line with the rate usually paid in these circumstances: Bishop's estimate of 3 Mar. 1824 for the Argory organ was for £600. For the commission system and its abuses, see Nicholas Thistlethwaite, 'The Hill-Gauntlett Revolution: An Epitaph?', *JBIOS* 16 (1992), 50–9; p. 51.

To Alfred Pettet   Euston Street, 8 March [1824]¹

ALS, 2 pp. (BL, Egerton MS 2159, fo. 76)
Addressed To | Alfred Pettet Esqʳ | Professor of Music | Norwich | March 8
Pmk 8 MR 1824

Euston Street.
Monday March 8.

Dear Sir

I am aware that I ought (in friendly Propriety) to have much sooner acknowledged your *former* Letter² & obliging Present, but you will hardly believe me when I assure you that Letter Writing, which was once an Amusement & Gratification, (and in numerous Instances is an indispensable Duty) has now become rather an irksome Task:—I do not love to write a Tirade of careless Nonsense, and am grown so fastidious with myself as to suspect myself often of producing in general very little better.

There is a little Anthem of mine in 4 Parts, composed originally to the two first Verses of the 65ᵗʰ Psalm, with Latin Words,³ but which are transferable into English *with equal good Effect in the Music*: the Anthem has never been heard but among select Friends, and therefore (tho' written Years ago) will in Public appear as a Novelty.—I mean to adapt the English Words without Delay, and flatter myself that it will suit your Purpose *at least as well* as a Collect: you have already *three* of this Sort, and therefore it strikes me that a short *full* Anthem will not be only equivalent, but as welcome to the *Eye* by its Title.⁴

I am preparing in my old Days to pester the World with another Dose of Egotism, in thrusting forward a Morning & Evening Service, viz, Te Deum, Jubilate, Sanctus, Kyrie eleeson, Magnificat, and Nunc dimittis;⁵ for which Proposals are already issued,⁶ and the said Tunes are promised to make their

---

¹ The year is given by the postmark.

² Not preserved: it evidently contained a request for SW to contribute a composition for inclusion in the collection of sacred music that Pettet was compiling. This was *Original Sacred Music*, published probably in 1825. The 'obliging present' was no doubt the 'Epicurean Treat of rich *unadulterated* Sausages' sent by Pettet's wife and mentioned in SW's postscript.

³ SW's 1798 setting of 'Te decet hymnus' (autograph at RCM, MS 4020).

⁴ SW's adaptation of 'Te decet hymnus' to English words appeared in *Original Sacred Music* as the full anthem 'Thou, O God, art praised in Sion' (autograph at RCM, MS 4028).

⁵ The Kyrie Eleeson and Sanctus in fact belong to the Communion Service. SW explained his unorthodox spelling of 'eleison' as being a more correct transliteration of the Greek.

⁶ Proposals had apparently been issued by 24 Feb, SW's birthday: on this date Charles Wesley jun. recorded in his diary that he had written on SW's behalf to Lord Hampden and 'Mr Edgcumbe' (Lord Mount-Edgcumbe), presumably to elicit subscriptions for the Service (Stevenson, *Memorials*, 464).

Appearance for *Judgment* & *Execution* in the Month of May.[7]—Some of my partial Friends, and among them Novello have said very encouraging Things about them, and I am inclined to trust that the Publication will be at all Events not a Matter of Loss, which however we know to be the very frequent Case with the Works of the most meritorious Pretensions.

If you choose to know *all how & about it*, I will send you some Proposals, together with your Book, and the Anthem in Question, requesting you to inform me in what Way it will be most agreeable to you for me to forward them.

> Believe me to remain
> My dear Sir
> Very faithfully yours
> S Wesley

My best Comp^{ts} and Thanks to Mrs P. for her Epicurean Treat of rich *unadulterated* Sausages: an Article unattainable in the pestilential Pork Shops of lovely London!

To Vincent Novello [Euston Street], 8 March 1824

ALS, 1 p. (BL, Add. MS 11729, fo. 175)
Addressed To | Mr Novello | Shacklewell Green | near | Kingsland
Pmks 9 MR 1824 MR 9 1824

> Monday 8. March. 1824.

Dear N

I hasten to forward the enclosed:[1] let me know what Number of them you wish to have in Addition: the Matter is rather en bon Train as to Publicity, inasmuch as Attwood manifests a Desire to perform the Pieces at St Paul's, on *a Sunday*; when the most Auditors are likely to be present, and consequently the better chance of catching Ears, and if the Sixpences can be caught together with them, so much the better for the Concarn.

Honest Messrs Davis & Bishop together have just swindled me out of 50 Guineas:[2] You will perhaps say, what else could I expect of a *Bishop*? but the Marvel is that such a Philosopher as Davis, (a worthy Wight who is not so vulgar as to believe in a God, or a Devil) should do such a Thing.

---

[7] In fact, the Service was not published until late Oct.

[1] Not preserved: presumably the proposals for the Service.

[2] The commission for the Argory organ, which Davis and Bishop had evidently declined to pay.

Little Evans[3] (whose Veracity we all know to be unquestionable) tells me that you have formally delivered in your Resignation of the South Street Drudgery:[4] and yet I wish a Confirmation of the Fact from yourself before I give any decisive Answer to Enquirers.

Yours as ever

SW

To Alfred Pettett [Euston Street], 18 March 1824

ALS, 1 p. (Drew, Wesley Family Letters, Samuel Wesley (1766–1837) series)
Addressed A. Pettet Esq

Euston Street.
March. 18. 1824

Dear Sir,

I thank you for your kind Letter,[1] regretting at the same Time that I cannot *at this Writing* send the MS. which I design for you,[2] but which shall be ready shortly.—from your former Letter I understood that a Month from that Date would be sufficiently soon to suit your Purpose; so that I did not proceed so promptly to the Adaptation I explained to you as I should have done had you named an earlier Period.

I transmit herewith the Prospectus of my intended Publication,[3] nothing doubting that you will aid its Progress in your Part of the World by a good Word, and I think my good friends Egar[4] and Pymar will feel similarly disposed.

The Service is soon to be performed at S[t] Paul's, so you may supposed me in dread Anxiety for the Verdict of the learned Canons, Vicars-Choral, Vergers, Bellows Blower &c.

With best Respects to M[rs] P.
believe me, my dear Sir,
most truly yours,

S. Wesley

---

[3] Charles Smart Evans (1780–1849), alto singer, composer, teacher, and organist. As a boy he was a chorister at the Chapel Royal and studied under Edmund Ayrton. He was appointed joint organist with Callcott at St Paul's, Covent Garden in 1798, and in 1808 became a Gentleman of the Chapel Royal. He was the composer of more than twenty glees (*Grove*[1]; Baptie; RSM).

[4] i.e. the organist's position at the Portuguese Embassy Chapel.

---

[1] Not preserved.

[2] 'Thou, O God, art praised in Sion', SW's contribution to Pettet's *Original Sacred Music*.

[3] The Service.   [4] i.e. John Eager of Great Yarmouth.

To Vincent Novello [Euston Street], 23 March [1824][1]

ALS, 1 p. (BL, Add. MS 11729, fo. 53)
Addressed To | M[r] Novello

23 March

Dear N.

Thanks.[2]—Do you chuse that the Words 'Organist to the Portuguese Embassy' shall stand in the *printed* List after your Name?[3]

I am puzzled how to dub the Folk aright, and who are to be ycleped Squires, & who only plain Misters.—I want to evite all *Qui pro quo* that I can, but the Mischief is that they who have the *least* Right to the Title of *Armigeri* are the *most* likely to be offended without it.

Pray counsel me upon this momentous Matter.

The Service is to be rehearsed on *Saturday* next[4] at S[t] Paul's: at least *so I am told*, but I depend upon Nothing—if you like to take your Chance, do.

Y[rs] in Haste

SW

To Vincent Novello [Euston Street], 25 March [1824][1]

ALS, 1 p. (BL, Add. MS 11729, fo. 55)
Addressed M[r] Novello | To the Care of Miss Campbell[2]

Dear N

Attwood has postponed the Day of Trial to Saturday week (Ap. 3), & I think for a sensible Reason: he says that as that is the Day of rehearsing the

---

[1] The year is given by the reference to the rehearsal of the Service (see n. 4).

[2] Doubtless for Novello's agreement to subscribe for six copies of the Service.

[3] SW was anxious to establish how Novello wished to be described on the subscription list, as he had by this time announced his resignation from the Portuguese Embassy Chapel. The subscription list does in fact describe Novello in this way, and it appears that he retained his title even after formally giving up the post: he is described thus on the title pages of *The Fitzwilliam Music* (published in late 1825 or early 1826) and *A Periodical Collection of Sacred Music* (?1826).

[4] i.e. on 27 Mar. The performance was later postponed to 3 Apr. (see next letter).

---

[1] The year is given by the references to the Service and the rehearsal for the Philharmonic Society concert (see n. 3).   [2] Not identified.

Philharmonic Concert,[3] many of his Friends will be in Town *on that Account*, & will come to St Paul's *before*, & perhaps *after* the Rehearsal too.*

Moreover, an Anthem of his own is also to be sung.[4]

Y^{rs} as usual

    SW

Thursday. | March 25

* I mean that they will probably attend the Afternoon as well as the Morning Service.

To Robert Glenn   Euston Street, 1 April [1824][1]

ANS, 1 p. (BL, Add. MS 35013, fo. 80)
Addressed R Glenn Esq. | Kirby Street | Hatton Garden | Thursday.
Pmk 1 AP 1824

Dear Sir

My Service is to be tried at St Paul's on Saturday next (3^d Inst.) in the Morning and Afternoon—

I felt it *my Duty* to inform you thereof, and remain (in Haste)

most truly yours

    S Wesley

Thursday Ap. 1. | Euston St.

To Alfred Pettet   Euston Street, 6 April 1824

ALS, 1 p. (Drew, Wesley Family Letters, Samuel Wesley (1766–1837) series)
Addressed To | A. Pettet Es^q | Norwich

Dear Sir

There is a good Latin Proverb, 'He who gives promptly, gives twice:' [Bis dat, qui citò dat][1] and which ought to make me ashamed of having detained you in

---

[3] The Philharmonic Society concert was on the following Monday, 5 Apr.   [4] Not identified.

[1] The year is given by the postmark.

[1] Attributed to Publilius Syrus (*fl.* 1st cent. BC). The square brackets are SW's.

such tedious Expectation of my Minims and Crotchets:[2] however, at last here they are, and I yet trust will arrive in Time to save you and your Engraver from serious Inconvenience: I thought you would prefer the Canto Part written in the G rather than the C Clef (as it originally was) the Generality of female Amateurs not being so well versed in the Use of the Latter.[3]—

The sole Reason of your not obtaining the Anthem earlier has been the Necessity I have been under of transcribing the Voice Parts of my Service for the Choir at S¹ Paul's, where it was performed for the first Time on Saturday last, and for (a *Coup d'Essai,*) very respectably: it will soon be repeated on a Sunday,[4] for I am pleased to say that the Dons were mightily tickled with it.

With kind regards to M ᵣˢ P. believe me remaining

Dear Sir
very sincerely yours
S. Wesley

Euston Street | Tuesday. 6ᵗʰ of Ap. | 1824

To Vincent Novello [Euston Street], 19 April 1824

ALS, 1 p. (BL, Add. MS 11729, fo. 177)
Addressed To | Mʳ Novello | Shacklewell Green | Kingsland Road | Monday 19ᵗʰ of April
Pmk 19 AP 1824

Dear N,

On Sunday next (25ᵗʰ) it is purposed among their High-Mightynesses Dean & Chapter with sundry other subaltern Dignitaries (such as Canons, Bellows-Blower &c) to repeat my Morning & Evening Service.—If Report be correct, you were to play your last high Mass at South Street (*professionally*) yesterday, so that you may probably be sufficiently at Leisure to risk a Cold in that comfortless Paragon of empty Magnificence either in the Morning or Afternoon

---

² 'Thou, O God, art praised in Sion'.

³ The choice of clefs for vocal music was a much-debated issue at this time. Novello in his *A Collection of Sacred Music* had used the traditional C clefs for the soprano, alto, and tenor parts, justifying his decision in his Preface, but there was a growing movement towards the use of the treble clef instead of the soprano clef for the top part. This practice was adopted in Pettet's publication and also in SW's own Service.

⁴ This performance, planned for 25 Apr., may have not taken place: see SW to Novello, 19 Apr. and 23 Apr. 1824.

of Sunday.—At all events I judged that you would choose to be informed of the Circumstance.

I sadly want a little Confab with you.—Cannot you pass an Evening with Joey M.[1] and stay for *one* Night in lovely London?

Yours ever truly

SW

Monday | 19th of April. 1824

To Vincent Novello [Euston Street], 23 April 1824

ALS, 2 pp. (BL, Add. MS 11729, fo. 180)
Addressed To | Mr Novello | Shacklewell Green | near | Kingsland | 23 April
Pmk 23 AP 18

Dear N

Voici des Propositions![1]—You have indeed been very generally successful in the Distribution of the former:—If more are necessary, perhaps the better Way now will be to leave a little Parcel at Major's for you.—I believe you frequently call or send thither.

By the bye you mention nothing of any Intention to meet me there for an Evening.—I should like to know soon, that I may contrive not to be prevented by any *less* pleasant Requisition of Attendance elsewhere.

There has been a little *friendly* manoeuvring among the vocal Operators at St Paul's to cause a Disappointment on Sunday next, in which Negotiation I suspect 'that worthy Man Mr Hawes'[2] to have added his strenuous and laudable Endeavours; so that I shall not be a Whit surprized if the whole Performance of *my* Service should be superseded on that Day.—Perhaps *you* will believe that my only Source of Chagrin would be the having announced it to *those* who will consider the Failure *a Loss*: for my own Part, I am sure that unless it be sung with a little more Feeling & Precision than before, I had rather it never were heard *there*.

In a Choir made up of half-schooled Musicians and dignified Parsons, a Composer has not an infallible Certainty of hearing his own Tunes to the best

---

[1] Joseph Major.

[1] 'Here are some proposals': presumably for the Service.

[2] In addition to his other positions, Hawes was Master of the Choristers at St Paul's.

Advantage, and when one among them incapable of doing much good, but whose Ability and Inclination to do Mischief are *great* and *equal,* nothing *less* than one of Prince Hohenloe's Miracles[3] can save the poor Artist from a Butchery of his Productions.

Well well! 'It must do as well as it can,' as our phlegmatic *Theorist*[4] once said to console Jacob for a Pile of Houses constructed to darken his Day-Light.

'Wishing, of all Employments is the worst', Young (I think it is Young) observes,[5] and there is a quaint Advice of some Sage or other, *almost* as easy to give as to take; videlicet,

'Never grieve at any Thing which you can, or cannot help!'
Fine talk.

Yours as always
   SW

Friday 23[d] of April. 1824

To Vincent Novello   [Euston Street], 26 April [1824][1]

ALS, 1 p. (BL, Add. MS 11729, fo. 182)
Addressed To | M[r] Novello | favoured by M[r] Gibson[2]

Dear N.

Is the second Chord in the enclosed Scrap[3] a false Harmony or not?—If it *is,* give me the true Reason why it is, and if not, what is the proper figuring to be placed to the Intervals?

---

[3] The alleged faith-cures wrought by Prince Alexander von Hohenlohe-Langenburg-Schillingfurst (1794–1849), various acccounts of which had been published in 1824.

[4] A. F. C. Kollmann (see SW to Novello, 25 Mar. [1825]).   [5] *Night Thoughts*, iv. 71.

[1] The year is given by 26 Apr. falling on a Monday and SW's reference to the disputed progression in his Service (n. 3).

[2] Not identified: possibly the 'Mr Gibson' who was a subscriber to the Service.

[3] An outline of the harmony of the Gloria Patri section of the Jubilate, bars 16–18, suggesting that the Service had in fact been performed at St Paul's the previous day, and that this passage had occasioned comment. It was later quoted in the review of the Service in the *Harmonicon* in Jan. 1825: of the offending chord, the anonymous reviewer commented that 'we meet with the chord of the 7th and the 2nd in an extremely bare, crude, state, and to our ears very cacophonous, though Dr. Blow might have enjoyed it much' (p. 11).

Yours in Haste

SW

[enclosure]

[sic]

26th of April. | Monday

To Vincent Novello   [Euston Street], 12 May 1824

ALS, 3 pp. (BL, Add. MS 11729, fo. 183)

Wednesday 12th May. 1824

Dear N

You know there is much Squabbling at Present in the Courts of Law about a right Definition of Blasphemy;[1] but I fear that you have incurred the Guilt of musical high Treason in the Estimation of another Court, perhaps not less formidable to those who can *flatter* for *Bread*: What think you of the *King's* Court? (par Excellence).—You are not aware that among those whom you denominate 'plodding Pedants,' and 'tasteless Drones,' you have unluckily included a Personage high in Royal Favour and musical Office,[2] and to whom, although I cannot but apply what Voltaire[3] did to Father Adam, that he is not 'le premier des Hommes,' yet he must be confest to hold a *literary Priority* even to Johnson, Porson, and Tooke; for his name commenceth with **A**, and I do believe that if you guess, you may be right to a **T** in the next Letter.

---

[1] Probably a reference to the forthcoming trial for blasphemy on 8 June at the Old Bailey of William Campion, one of Thomas Carlile's shop men, for selling the works of Thomas Paine and other similarly seditious books.

[2] Thomas Attwood, whose fortunes at court had revived following the accession of George IV in 1821. He composed the anthem 'The King shall rejoice' for the coronation, and was shortly afterwards appointed organist to George IV's private chapel at the Brighton Pavilion. His royal connections made him the subject of much ridicule in SW's letters.

[3] Pseudonym of François-Marie Arouet (1694-1778), French satirist, novelist, historian, poet, dramatist, polemicist, moralist, critic, and correspondent (*OCEL*). The source of this quotation has not been traced.

Although but by a few Years my junior (therefore no Chicken), yet I am assured by many that he is even now only a *chopping Boy*—upon the Organ.[4] Well then, be it known unto you (and to all the World for what I care,) that this is the ponderous Authority that has laid all its Weight upon my unfortunate (and I thought inoffensive) Apoggiatura, which however I nevertheless consider very effectually rescued from Suffocation by your timely Interference; and your general Observations upon *the Insufficiency of Rule*, to render harsh Sounds pleasant, or pleasant Sounds harsh, are so thoroughly incontrovertible, that finding the Chord which did not shock me, does not shock *you*, them whom it does shock I shall leave to recover at their Leisure.

It is usually thought a great Recommendation to a man aiming at Advancement and Celebrity, that *he has been under the Tuition of some very eminent Master*:[5] but still this Plan will not infallibly succeed: I remember the Circumstance of an amateur Performer on the Violin (and a Nobleman, be pleased to remember), boasting in a large musical Society in the Presence of Giardini,[6] that he had *learned* to play the Violin under him for a series of Years:— Giardini replied—'I beg your Pardon my Lord—it is true dat I did *try to teach you* for about *ten* Years, but you never never did *learn* any Ting, O no no! Notting at all'!—

I do not mean to determine whether this Story has any remote Reference to Criticisms and Choppings, and great **A**'s.

Yours truly,
and as you will not see me, let me see your Writing
  SW

---

[4] In fact, Attwood was born in Nov. 1765, and was thus SW's senior by only a few months. He was said to be an indifferent performer on the organ, notwithstanding his position as organist of St Paul's.

[5] A reference to Attwood's studies with Mozart in Vienna between 1785 and 1787.

[6] The Italian virtuoso violinist and composer Felice Giardini (1716–96) had settled in England in 1750 following an early career in Italy and a succesful European concert tour. Described by Burney as 'the greatest player in Europe', he was much in demand both as a performer and as a teacher. He left England for Naples in 1784, returning for an unsuccessful comeback in 1790. The identity of the nobleman who is the butt of this anecdote is not known.

To Vincent Novello   [Euston Street], 20 May [1824]¹

ALS, 1 p. (BL, Add. MS 11729, fo. 185)
Addressed Mr Novello

Dear N

I never more regretted the *Difficulty* of being in two Places at the same
Moment than now—for I must be out of Town both To-Day & *to morrow*, otherwise would willingly have accepted the Challenge *on St Ann's Account*.²—

I have scarcely a Minute left to tell you what you know without it, that I am as
always,

Y^rs

SW

Thursday 20th of May

To Vincent Novello   [Euston Street], 14 June [1824]¹

ALS, 4 pp. (BL, Add. MS 11729, fo. 187)

Dear N.

The Words of the vocal Ditty herewith² were nearly the last that my excellent
Father uttered to me very shortly before his Death, and I have for some Time
wished to give them Sounds a little congenial with the Sentiment.³—Your Opinion
of this Tune, and all other musical Matters is nearly the only one I consider worth
a Thought, so I leave it with you in the rough State, not having yet made any other
Copy.⁴—

---

¹ During the period of SW's correspondence with Novello, 20 May fell on a Thursday in 1813, 1819,
and 1824. The most probable year is 1824.

² Perhaps an allusion to a suggested performance by SW and Novello of Bach's 'St Anne' Prelude and
Fugue.

---

¹ The year is given by 14 June falling on a Monday and SW's discussion of his *Carmen Funebre*.

² SW's *Carmen Funebre*.

³ The words, taken in part from Ecclesiastes 2: 11, 20, are: 'Omnia vanitas et vexatio spiritus, praeter
amare Deum et illi soli servire' ('All is vanity and vexation of spirit, except to love God and to serve Him
alone'). This account is repeated in SW's obituary in *The Times*.

⁴ This rough copy does not appear to have survived. An autograph fair copy score, annotated by
Novello as being the 'original manuscript', is at Austin; another autograph score, annotated by Novello
as being a copy in SW's hand, is at RCM, MS 4022.

Should you outlive me, which I hope & trust you will, by many Years, I can now please myself with the Notion of your regarding this Scrap as what I have entitled it, Carmen Funebre applied to myself, and a Testimony of my Veneration for the Dictates of a Parent whose Value was utterly unknown to me till he was translated to Society alone worthy of him!

You will not term this preaching and croaking, knowing that I only disclose genuine Feelings; for I have long regarded as an Axiom, a very unfashionable and nearly exploded Doctrine in our enlightened Nation, to which I however shall adhere with determined Tenacity, namely, that Nothing is worth a Lye.—This *Prejudice* (as Courtiers and Time-Servers term it) has always stood in my Way to that Preferment which so many *call* Honour; and Veracity is pretty well known to be no Road to Riches, and so little is it successful in making *Friends*, that one Dr Terence,[5] (who lived rather before your or my Time) has remarked that it leads to just the contrary Result, for says he

Obsequium Amicos, *Veritas Odium* parit.[6]

Tho' I never could 'boo to golden Calves,' yet I have learned to bend to old Age with tolerable Contentedness, so certain that a few Days or Years will set *all strait* in the Grave.

I must obtain your Consent to introduce my Friend Barret to you, solely on one Account: and as this concerns a last Request of mine,[7] I do reckon upon your not opposing it:—be assured he is not among those who will annoy you by leaving at your Door a Pack of Cards (with his name in German Text), or with teasing Solicitations to visit—: in short, I will pledge 20 Years Experience of his Character that he will be no more troublesome to you in *Future* than he is *now*.

He is moreover a sensible Man: and yet perhaps *some* will doubt this, for he knows nothing of Music!

Y^rs in Truth,
SW

Monday. 14 June

---

[5] The Latin dramatist Publius Terentius Afer (*c*.190–159 BC).

[6] 'Compliance procures friends, and frankness procures animosity' (*Andria*, 41).

[7] To be buried in the churchyard at Paddington near to Anne Deane: see SW to Novello, 4 July 1823.

To Vincent Novello   [Euston Street, *post* 14 June 1824]¹

ALS, 2 pp. (BL, Add. MS 11729, fo. 192)
Addressed Mr Novello

Dear N

Herewith are the separate Parts of the Carmen Funebre,² and I think that as the
Motett 'Exultate Deo'³ is quite familiar of old to our Friend Street, and the present Tune somewhat of a Novelty (never having been sung at all) it will be as well
to put it into the Hands and Mouths of your well-drilled Corps, to be produced
on the Evening when you wish me to join your vocal Party.

As soon as I can I will make a Score for *you*, as I promised.—Perhaps you may
be able to *sketch* out sufficient Score from the Parts to rehearse it a little with those
whom you judge the least likely to be quite steady and correct.

It is lucky that Mad^me Catalani is not the 1st Canto, as she must first have learned
the 116 Bars *par Coeur*, requiring therefore a longer Lesson than would be quite
agreeable to give.

The text of Scripture which declares that one 'who *runs* may *read*'⁴ does not
appositely apply to our vociferous Heroine: We all know that she *runs* longer and
faster than any Mortal of musical Taste can tolerate, but the *reading* Remainder of
the Text is quite 'another Part of Speech.'—*

Yours,

SW

* Banti⁵ was another of these vocally voluble Dunces, who made the Band attend
24 Rehearsals for one Opera, never having studied so vulgar a Portion of singing
as the Gamut *on Paper*. She was however one of the best Singers, the finest
Actress, and the stoutest Swallower of Brandy in the operatic Annals of England.

---

¹ The reference to the inclusion of the parts for the *Carmen Funebre* with this letter suggests a date
shortly after SW's letter to Novello of 14 June.
² Three of the five individual parts, in SW's hand, are at BL, Add. MS 35003.
³ SW's elaborate five-part setting of Exultate Deo dates from June 1800, and Street would have known
it from that time.
⁴ Habbakuk 2: 2: 'And the Lord answered me, and said, Write the vision, and make it plain upon
tables, that he may run that readeth it.'
⁵ Brigida Giorgi Banti (*c.*1756–1806), Italian soprano, described in *Grove*⁶ as having been at an early
stage in her career 'a very bad singer with a very beautiful voice, and so lazy that she could not be taught'.
After establishing her reputation in continental Europe in the 1780s and early 1790s she made her
London début in 1794 in Bianchi's *Semiramide*. She continued as principal soprano at the King's
Theatre until her retirement in 1802. SW's high opinion of her voice and acting abilities was shared by
Mount-Edgcumbe, who called her 'by far the most delightful singer I ever heard' (*Grove*⁶).

To Vincent Novello [Euston Street], 1 August [1824]¹

ALS, 2 pp. (BL, Add. MS 11729, fo. 189)
Addressed To | Mʳ Novello | Shacklewell Green | Kingsland

Sunday 1 Augᵗ

Dear N

I know not whether the sudden Death of your Maître d'Hotel² may have deranged your musical Meeting in this Week,³ but I write to apprize you that I had not forgotten it, and would have come to you had I not engaged to leave London till Saturday next.⁴

Herewith is a Score of the Carmen Funebre⁵ which I promised, and also the Parts in Case you choose to give it a second Trial with your Choir.⁶ You may let me have the Parts back any Time within a Fortnight that may suit your Convenience.

I was vexed to learn that you felt any Thing like Disappointment at not being apprized of the Day when the new ecclesiastical Theatre was opened:⁷—Had I had the least suspicion that such a clumsy Mimickry of the Mass would have entertained you, I should most certainly have given you legal Notice, but I could not suppose that the Bawling of Brats in a Psalm Tune would be worth your walking a Step out of your Way.—You need not be told that whenever you feel

---

¹ The year is given by 1 Aug. falling on a Sunday, the reference to the *Carmen Funebre*, and Novello's address. ² Not identified: evidently a member of the Classical Harmonists (see n. 3).

³ A meeting on 5 Aug. of the Classical Harmonists, a private concert-giving society founded in 1821 by Novello. It met on the first Thursday of each month at the Crown and Anchor tavern.

⁴ 7 Aug. SW was about to go to Margate with Samuel Sebastian, but needed to be back in London on the following Sunday, 8 Aug., so as to carry out his duties at Camden Chapel (see n. 7), where he had recently been appointed organist. He then intended to return to Margate. In his letter to Sarah Suter of 3 Aug. [1824] (BL, Add. MS 35012, fo. 51), written from Margate, SW outlined these plans and requested Sarah to send to the engraver Skarratt for the proofs of his Service, which he proposed to correct when in London and return to Skarratt on the following Monday morning.

⁵ Probably the score now at Austin.

⁶ Three of the five parts referred to here may be the ones at BL, Add. MS 35003. The score and parts, together with this letter, probably constituted the 'letter and parcel for Novello' mentioned in SW's letter to Sarah Suter of 3 Aug., which he presumed she had sent on to him.

⁷ Camden Town Chapel (later known as All Saints, Camden Street) had been consecrated on 15 July (*GM* 1824², 489–90). SW had been appointed organist at a salary of £63 p.a. on 20 May (Minutes of Church Trustees, St Pancras Church Lands Trust Minute Book, St Pancras Church). For the building, by W. and H. Inwood, see *Survey of London*, xxiv: *St Pancras Part 4*, 136–7 and pls. 90–1. Its first minister, the Revd Alexander d'Arblay (1794–1837), was the son of Burney's daughter Frances (Madame d'Arblay). For an account of the consecration service, at which SW played the organ, see Mme d'Arblay to Mrs Barrett, [*c*.16] Aug.–2 Sept. 1824, in Joyce Hemlow *et al.*, *The Journals and Letters of Frances Burney (Madame d'Arblay)* (Oxford, 1984), xi. 543–9.

disposed to kill an Hour on a Sunday (either Morning or Afternoon) the Organ Loft and Organ are always at your Command.

Adieu, and if it suit you, I should like to find a Line from you here on Saturday.

SW

To Vincent Novello [Euston Street], 1 August 1824

ALS, 1 p. (BL, Add. MS 11729, fo. 191)
Addressed To | Mʳ Novello | Shacklewell Green | near | Kingsland

Sunday Evening
Aug. 1. 1824:

Dear N

Since I wrote the enclosed¹ there is a young Person who has applied to me for a few Hints upon the Organ:² his Stay in Town is only a Fortnight, the Time I mean to get for my Holidays.—I encouraged him to petition you in my Name: he is a perfect Stranger to me, but introduced himself at the Porch of the Chapel To-Day after the Service in a very prepossessing Manner: so do as you feel right.

The torn Billet will explain my being at this Moment rather in Haste.

Yours always
SW

To Vincent Novello Euston Street, 13 September 1824

ALS, 3 pp. (BL, Add. MS 11729, fo. 194)
Addressed To | Mʳ Novello | Shacklewell Green | near | Kingsland | Monday | 13 Sepᵗʳ
Pmk 13 SP 1824

Dear N,

From my Smattering in Latin I just venture to guess at a line of Italian, as far as an Opera Song goes, but having no Dictionary I steer without Rudder or Compass, only by the *Stars* of the Latin Roots.—You ask what's all this about?

¹ The previous letter.   ² Not identified.

Why I am putting Chords to Handel's 13 Duets[1] for the Accommodation of the Country Ladies and Gentlemen, under the divine Authority of the Royal Harmonic Institution,[2] and at the Solicitation of that royal quondam culinary Artist, but now the supreme Disposer of Minstrelsy and Minstrels in 'the Devil's Drawing Room;' (—Byron's name for London—) and whose Name I need not spell at length to *you*.[3]—You may remember something of him at the House of Jos. Gwilt Esq[4] that Mirror of irradicable Friendship & Constancy.—Now I like to understand the Words with which I meddle whether by *Choice* or *Necessity*: the latter is the Case at Present, and I shall feel it very kind if you will just sketch me out the Meaning of the Lines annexed in English.—I daresay I have classed them aukwardly, but if they are wrongly spelt it is the Fault of the Copy, as I was very careful in my Transcript.

I was much disappointed at not meeting you at Hampstead on the Day that Burgh[5] gave me great Hopes of your coming.—I believe I know your principal Objection to visiting there, namely the vitriolic and acetous qualities of the Hostess, whom I no more delight in than yourself, but I have learned to make her quite a secondary or more truly no Consideration, and there is so much of amiable Frankness and Cordiality in your Pupil that it more than compensates *me* for the Gothic Inhospitality of Mamma.—Moreover Burgh himself is so odd a Fellow,

---

[1] *Thirteen Celebrated Italian Duets, accompanied with the Harpsichord or Organ* (1777). SW's arrangements were published in individual numbers in late 1824 as *A Collection of Duets, by Handel, Steffani, Clari, Jommelli, Marcello &c. &c arranged with an accompaniment for the Piano Forte by S Wesley*. Twelve duets were published, all by Handel, of which eleven were from the *Chamber Duets*: for further details, see SW to Charles Wesley jun., 6 Nov. 1824, n. 2. SW's discussion here and the publisher's plate numbers, which also indicate a publication date in late 1824, correct the publication date of 1820 given in *CPM* (*CPM*; Neighbour and Tyson).

[2] The Royal (originally Regent's) Harmonic Institution was formed in 1819 by twenty-three professional musicians, of whom SW was one, as a joint-stock company to finance the reconstruction of the Argyll Rooms in Regent Street by the publication of music and the sale of music and musical instruments. Many investors soon withdrew, and by spring 1823 Welsh and Hawes were the principal shareholders (D. W. Krummel and Stanley Sadie (eds.), *Music Printing and Publishing* (1990), under 'Regent's Harmonic Institution').

[3] Not certainly identified: possibly William Kitchiner (see SW to Idle, [*c.* 10 Nov. 1813], n. 3). He had acquired the nickname 'royal cook' from entertaining George IV when Prince Regent.

[4] As this and subsequent remarks show, there had evidently been a cooling in the relationship between SW and Gwilt: see also SW to [Hawes], 29 Mar. [1828].

[5] The Revd. Allatson Burgh (b. 1769/70), matric. University College Oxford (1787), BA (1791), MA (1794), vicar of St Lawrence Jewry, author of *Anecdotes of Music, historical and Biographical; in a Series of Letters from a Gentleman to his Daughter* (1814). He was a subscriber to Novello's *A Collection of Music* and lived at Hampstead. Novello's pupil, referred to later in this letter, may have been Burgh's daughter Caroline, the addressee of the letters in the *Anecdotes of Music*; she was also no doubt the Miss Burgh of Hampstead who subscribed to SW's Service (Foster).

that he diverts me at least as much as Matthews[6] or Punch.—(N.B. I have always regarded the latter as by far the greatest Comedian of any Age or Country).—

But after all, no one can justly direct the Conduct, because he cannot possess the individual Consciousness of another, therefore not feel *identically* with him; but I cannot help thinking that had you been with us that Evening, you would have found antidote to the Poison over and above, the former being scarcely perceptible.

I am about arranging the Names of my Customers[7] alphabetically.—Will it be too much Trouble to you to give me (in *Condensation*) the List of those whom you have sent to my Shop?—

I am teazing *other* Friends in the same Way, so that my Excuse is that I have the Impartiality to torment more Benefactors than yourself.

Yours as always

S Wesley

13th of Septr 1824 | Euston Street | Monday

To Vincent Novello   Euston Street, 18 September [1824]^1

ALS, 3 pp. (BL, Add. MS 11729, fo. 196)
Addressed To | Mr Novello | Shacklewell Green | near | Kingsland | Saturday Ev^g
Pmk 20 S 1824

Euston Street.
Saturday 18 Sept^r

Dear N

For the first Time in my Life I do not believe your Word, and am fully persuaded in my Mind that there are but few (if any) Passages in Dante or Petrarca that would puzzle you. Remember, I only want a literal Translation of the Sense of those Bagatelles, but if you pertinaciously refuse to make one, perhaps your Brother[2] has more charitable Feeling (who has been habituated for so many Years to Operatic Versification,)—and possibly you will hand him over the Lines at your Leisure.

---

[6] The comic actor Charles Mathews (1776–1835). He was at this time appearing in 'The Trip to America', a one-man show which he first performed at the Lyceum Theatre on 25 Mar. 1824 (*DNB*).

[7] i.e., the list of subscribers for SW's Service, in preparation for its impending publication.

---

[1] The year is given by the postmark.   [2] Francis Novello.

Now for Wednesday!—John Harding of Kentish Town,[3] my *Friend* (not *Acquaintance*) is an extreme & unpretending Lover of the Organ; neither is there any Invitation which he so gratefully receives as that to a good Performance thereon.—The Savoy Church Organ[4] I have always praised highly to him, & promised that on the first Day I could appoint a Meeting there he should surely be apprized. I know that you agree with me about the excellent Qualities of the Whistles in that there Box, and presuming also that your Relish of such Sounds hath not diminished (tho' I should lie if I did not own that mine has) I have called on Dr Steinkoffph,[5] who is out of Town but have seen the Minister[6] (whose Name, equally euphonious, I have forgotten) and who informed me that *he* knew of nothing to obstruct our Access to the Organ on Wed^y next[7] but it was needful to consult the Clerk, (who is also the Organist)[8] to ascertain whether there be a clear Course on that Day, and that he would apprize me in the Course of Monday next, & I shall wait the Event with some Impatience, as yourself & Harding ought to receive the News as nearly together as Distance of Place will admit.—

Moreover my Friend requested me to express his Hope & Trust that you will accompany me to dine with him after our musical *Dose* (n.b. he is a medical Man) and I think I may promise that you will not regret your Acquiescence. I doubt whether there will be any Persons beside *our three selves* & his Assistant, a very modest unassuming Man, whilom a Sailor, beaten by the Waves of *Fortune* among the rest, and generously encouraged by our worthy Host, who has found him deserving & grateful.—Should any 5th Individual be invited (which I very much doubt) I will warrant that he shall be neither a foolish nor a disagreeable Addition; for as Harding is acquainted with *all Manner of People*, and a Man of Sagacity (without Pretension to Learning, out of his Profession) he is sure never to make heterogeneous Mixture at his Table: In short he is one of the very few in whose House I can securely say to you 'here we are—at Home.'

I am almost ashamed of so long a Preamble, but I know you are punctilious, & so am I, & would not make a similar Proposal, were I not *so sure* of my Ground. If you find me wrong, do not trust me again.

---

[3] Little is known of SW's friend John Harding beyond the warm description of him here and some scraps of information in later letters. In early 1822 he helped SW in his attempt to secure the St Pancras church appointment, and was the dedicatee of two sets of organ voluntaries by SW published at around this time. As SW notes later in this letter, he was a doctor (Harding to Sarah Wesley, 16 Jan 1822, (Rylands, DDWF 26/58)).

[4] The organ at the Lutheran church in the Savoy, by John Snetzler (?1767), was famous for being one of the first organs in England to have independent pedals (Boeringer, iii. 237).

[5] Carl Friedrich Adolph Steinkopf (1773–1859), Lutheran minister. After training in Theology at Tübingen University he came to England in 1801 as pastor to the Lutheran church in the Savoy. He was the first foreign secretary of the British and Foreign Bible Society from 1804 to 1826 (*DEB*).

[6] Not identified.   [7] 22 Sept.   [8] Not identified.

A Mr Dowling,[9] whom I met at H's and who is at present his Patient, I found to be one of the most intelligent and delightful of Companions.—I fear he is not equal to dining out.—Would to Heaven he were: he is abounding in inventive Wit, Anecdote, Learning, general Intelligence, devoid of all Shadow of Pedantry, and on all points most singularly good-humoured.

I have told Harding many a Time that if he suffers him to die I shall be hanged for killing his Doctor.

Expect to hear from me on Tuesday at all Events.

Yours as always

S Wesley

To Vincent Novello   [Euston Street], 20 September [18]24

ALS, 2 pp. (BL, Add. MS 11729, fo. 198)
Addressed To | Mr Novello | Shacklewell Green | near | Kingsland | Monday Evening
Pmk 20 SP 1824

Monday
Evening
20 Sept^r—24

Dear N

On Wednesday, at 12, the Clerk of the German Church will be in Readiness to receive us about the Premises.

Will you bring with you some Scraps of the musical Leviathan?[1]—Suppose the 30 Variations?[2]—I will bring the Sonatas with the Violin Accompaniment,[3] which form a nice Trio, and moreover the Effect on the Organ will be somewhat novel.—

I hope & trust that the Rest of the Arrangement for the Day (which was the very best I could devise) will be palatable to you.—Harding is not without Hope that Dowling may be well enough to come to us.—I know *he* wishes *you* to be pleased, whatever I may do.

---

[9] Not identified.

[1] J. S. Bach.   [2] The *Goldberg Variations*.

[3] i.e. the six Sonatas for Violin and Harpsichord, BWV 1014–19. Unlike most sonatas for violin and keyboard of the period, which are for violin and basso continuo, these sonatas have a fully written out harpsichord part, and are thus in a trio sonata texture (hence SW's use of 'trio'). SW was no doubt intending to perform them with Novello as an organ duet, in the same way as they performed the organ trio sonatas.

Anything of Mozart or other such pygmy Composers you like to bring, pray do, but do not *overstuff* your Pockets with Rossini.[4]

Yours (en attendant)
   SW

P.S. If, instead of returning to Shacklewell at Night, you will venture yourself Home with me, I can promise you a dry and *uncontaminated* Bed.—Do as you will, or I'll make you.[5]

To Vincent Novello   [Euston Street], 25 September [1824][1]

ALS, 1 p. (BL, Add. MS 11729, fo. 200)
Addressed To | Mr Novello | Shacklewell Green | near | Kingsland | Sat^y 25 Sept^r
Pmk 26 SP 1824
Watermark 1819

Dear N

I learn that the perambulating Biographers at the Abbey whose Trade it is to prate to the Public about the Tombs and the Wax Work Royalties, object to the *Noise* of the Organ out of Church Hours, as interruptive of their Oratory. Now I guess that you would not relish much Impertinence from such Quarters, and I have therefore agreed with Mr Cooper[2] to meet at his Church (St Sepulchre's,[3] clumsily so christened) on Wednesday at Noon, where I think you will not disapprove of the Organ, and where we shall experience no Chance of Disturbance.—He will bring some Tunes of the *old Wig* (as John X^{tn} B. dutifully called his Father) which

---

[4] The music of Rossini, long popular in London, was enjoying a particular vogue at the time of this letter, and Rossini himself had only recently returned to Paris after an extended stay in London. He had arrived in late 1823, and a programme of his operas was arranged at the King's Theatre. His first concert, at Almack's, was on 14 May 1824, and a second, of sacred music, followed on 11 June. He returned to Paris by 1 Aug. For the popularity of Rossini's music in London, see contemporary reports in *Harmonicon* and the daily press and Fenner, 145–57.

[5] As identified by SW in his letter to Novello of 20 Jan. [1825], a favourite saying of SW's father.

[1] The year is given by the postmark.

[2] George Cooper (*c.*1783–1843), organist of St Sepulchre, Holborn from the death of his father (also George Cooper) in 1799 until his death; he was also assistant organist of St Paul's Cathedral until 1838, when he resigned the post in favour of his son (also George Cooper).

[3] St Sepulchre-without-Newgate, Holborn. The organ was a 1676 instrument by Thomas Harris, enlarged by Byfield in 1739 and Gray in 1817 (Boeringer, ii. 206–7; Plumley, 123–6).

will render it less necessary for us to overload ourselves with Books, but I hope that Holmes[4] will bring & play his Fugue that you mentioned.

I was very glad that you relished your Evening at Kentish Town:[5] Harding *feels* all the Hospitality which he shews, and is no faint Antithesis to our old Host in Stamford Street:[6] little *Profession*, but genuine *Cordiality*.

Yours as usual
  SW

25 Sept[r] | Sat[y]—

P.S. I need not add that the Church aforesaid is hard by to Newgate.

To [John Harding][1]   [Euston Street], 27 September 1824

ALS, 1 p. (Gloucester)[2]

Dear Sir,
  I find that those Vagabonds who shew the Tombs & Royalty in Wax Work at the Abbey, object to the *Noise* of the Organ, out of Church Hours, and as we should not much relish an Altercation with the said Orators errant, I have settled with Cooper to meet at S[t] Sepulchre's Church on Wednesday at 12 where the Organ is excellent, and no Interruption whatever will be likely.

---

[4] Edward Holmes (1799–1859), organist, teacher, critic, and author, who after a period of apprenticeship to R. B. Seeley, a Fleet Street bookseller, was taken as a music student into Novello's home, where he came to know Shelley, Hazlitt, Leigh Hunt, Charles Cowden Clarke, and Charles and Mary Lamb. He became a highly influential writer on music: he was music critic for the *Atlas* from 1826, and also wrote for *Fraser's Magazine*, the *Spectator*, and, from 1845, for *MT*. He wrote extensively on Mozart, and his *Life of Mozart* (1845) was the first biography of the composer in English. He was a subscriber to SW's Service, where he was described as organist of the New Church, Poplar (*Grove*[6]; Clarke, *Life and Labours*, 15).

[5] i.e. at Harding's house.

[6] Presumably Joseph Gwilt; he lived at 8 Stamford Street, Southwark, between 1810 and 1812.

---

[1] For Harding, see SW to Novello, 18 Sept. [1824], n. 3. This letter, the counterpart to SW's letter to Novello of two days earlier, lacks an address portion. There can be little doubt from its contents that it is to Harding.

[2] See H. Diack Johnstone, 'Treasure Trove in Gloucester: A Grangerized Copy of the 1895 Edition of Daniel Lysons's History of the Three Choirs Festival', *Royal Musical Association Research Chronicle* 31 (1998), 1–90.

If you will be so good as to apprize our Hampstead Host[3] of this Arrangement, leaving it of Course entirely at his Option to join the Auditory, you will oblige me.

I hope you dine with us on Wednesday.[4]

Yours ever truly

    S. Wesley

Monday | 27. of Septr 1824

P.S. Novello was delighted with his Day at Kentish Town.[5]

To Vincent Novello   [Euston Street], 28 September [1824][1]

ALS, 2 pp. (BL, Add. MS 11729, fo. 202)
Addressed Tuesday Morning | To | Mr Novello | Shacklewell Green | near | Kingsland
Pmk 28 SP 1824

Tuesday 28 Sept^r

Dear N

Your letter has quite *metagrobolized*[2] me (as Rabelais might call it) for I am quite at a Loss what to do for the best. You have doubtless some good Reason for avoiding Cooper, which I am the more sorry for, as I have frequently heard him speak of you in the Terms that he *ought*.

Having fixed to meet him at his Church To-morrow at 12, and he having moreover promised to bring Music on Purpose, I cannot without that Incivility which I am sure you would avoid, decently annul the Engagement.—The enclosed[3] will shew what a Pull there is *another* Way, and how to hedge the Business (as the Gamesters say) is now the Question.

To split a Difference is often as hard as to split a Hair, and I know no very comfortable Mode of Arrangement here so as to please all Parties.

---

    [3] Burgh.   [4] 29 Sept.   [5] i.e. at Harding's house.

    [1] The year is given by the postmark.

    [2] i.e. mystified. The word is much used by Rabelais in his *Pantagruel* (1532 or 1533) and *Gargantua* (1534), which SW would probably have read in the English translations by Urquart and Motteux.

    [3] Not preserved.

Harding has been informed of the Meeting at the Church, and I know will strain a Point to attend: I must now acquaint him of this Contre Coup, leaving to his Option what Movement to make as to *his* individual Disposal at the Hour named.—

Upon tumbling this Chapter of Accidents over in my Mind, perhaps the most decent Mode of making the best of unfortunate Necessity will be for me to get to M[r] B.'s[4] as near 4 o'Clock as I can, which Plan will leave Time for a Compliance with any Fancy your fair Pupil may choose to suggest to us: they never dine sooner than 5, (often at 6) therefore there will remain Opportunity of walking, talking, and *organizing* before Dinner, if such should be the Order of the Moment.—

I much regret missing a Walk with you, but I think you will not consider me wrong in not breaking my Word.

Yours ever truly

S Wesley

To Vincent Novello [Euston Street], 18 October 1824

ALS, 1 p. (BL, Add. MS 11729, fo. 204)
Addressed To | M[r] Novello | Shacklewell Green | near | Kingsland | Monday
Pmk 19 OC 1824

Dear N

I trust that Illness was not the Occasion of your disappointing us all at Kentish Town last Sunday Week.[1]—Rainy Weather I am sure would not have done it.

That Eye Sore to our royal Composer (my Church Service) means to be troublesome to him (& perhaps to others) in the course of next Week.[2]

Yours as usual

SW

What is to become of my 'Carmen funebre'?

18 Oct[r] 1824

---

[4] Burgh's house, where Novello was presumably due to teach Burgh's daughter.

[1] 10 Oct., presumably at a music party at Harding's. [2] i.e. it was about to be published.

To Thomas Simpson Cooke[1]   Euston Street, 19 October 1824

ALS, 1 p. (BL Add. MS 33965, fo. 103)
Addressed To | T. Cooke Esqre

Dear Sir,

You will much oblige me by an immediate Line of Information, whether Mr Fuller[2] (whom I recommended to Mr Elliston as a useful Member in your theatrical Chorus) may or may not consider himself as positively engaged for that Department; remaining

Very truly yours
S Wesley

19th of Octr 1824 | Euston Street. Euston Square

To Charles Wesley Junior   Euston Street, 6 November 1824

AL, incomplete, 1 p. (Emory, Letter 58)

Euston Street
Nov. 6. 1824.

Dear Charles,

At last you herewith receive the long promised Copies of my Church Service, and I think you will say that the Engraver has performed his Task well, although at the eleventh Hour.

I must request you to lend me for two or three Days the Italian duets of Handel:[1] I have been affixing an Accompaniment (in Lieu of the Figured Bass) to the whole Set, which is now complete excepting the last Page of the 13th Duet,

---

[1] Thomas Simpson Cooke (1782–1848), Irish tenor, violinist, and theatrical composer, had come to London after an early career in Dublin, where he was leader of the orchestra and an occasional actor at Crow Street Theatre. He was an exceptionally versatile musician. He composed music for a number of operas produced at Drury Lane, sang tenor roles there for some twenty years, and played several instruments: at one of his benefits he performed successively on the violin, flute, oboe, clarinet, bassoon, cello, double-bass, and piano. From 1823 to 1828 he was the leader of the Drury Lane orchestra; in 1825 he moved from the orchestra pit to the stage to play the part of Adolph [i.e. Max] in the theatre's English version of Weber's *Der Freischütz*. He was the manager of Vauxhall Gardens from 1828 to 1830, for many years the principal tenor at the Bavarian chapel, led the orchestra on occasion at Philharmonic Society concerts, and was a celebrated teacher of singing (*Grove*[5]; Fenner, 463–6, 656).

[2] Almost certainly not the Fuller mentioned in SW to Shield, [13] Sept. 1815; probably the Fuller who delivered SW's letter to Novello of 25 Mar. [1825].

[1] The *Thirteen Celebrated Italian Duets*, to the 1777 edition of which Charles had subscribed.

and which was deficient in the Score from which I had to arrange them, so that your Accommodation will very speedily set all to rights.[2]

I have had much Employment from the Harmonic Institution in similar Jobs of arranging a Multitude of the Oratorio Songs from the Scores,[3] and I believe they are now put into a more practicable and useful Form than they were heretofore.—Few persons (comparatively) possessed the Scores, and perhaps fewer could accompany aright merely from the Figures, and the Editions of Bland[4] and other quack Publishers were quite futile & contemptible.

To Vincent Novello   [Euston Street], 12 November [18]24[1]

ANS, 1p (BL, Add. MS 11729, fo. 206)
Addressed To | Mr Novello | Shacklewell Green | near | Kingsland | Friday Morning

Dear N

Harding called yesterday to tell me that neither he or the Burghs can come To-morrow to the Church of St Lawrence, Jewry,[2] therefore I think you will agree with me that the Meeting will be best deferred.—What say you to the Saturday following? (21st Inst.)[3]—give me an early Line.

Yours as always

SW

P.S. Your Copies have been in King Street,[4] several Days past.—I believe you have heard from Linley.

Friday 13th of Nov^r—24

---

[2] The manuscripts of twelve of these arrangements (nos. 1–12 of the 1777 published edition) are at RCM, MS 4026. The edition published by the Royal Harmonic Institution contained twelve duets: 'Tra amplessi innocenti' from the cantata 'Cecilia, volgi un sgardo' (no. 1) and nos. 1–11 of the 1777 edition (nos. 2–12). No arrangement by SW of the thirteenth duet ('Se tu non lasci amore') has been traced.

[3] The manuscripts of SW's arrangements of several numbers from Handel's *Acis and Galatea*, *Joshua*, *Judas Maccabaeus*, and *L'Allegro, il Penseroso ed il Moderato* are at RCM, MS 4026. Each bears a four-digit number which was evidently its plate number and indicates that they were published in late 1824 and possibly early 1825. Published copies of only two of these arrangements have been traced.

[4] Thomas Bland (*c*.1750–*c*.1840), music seller, instrument dealer, and publisher, who had retired in 1795 after a highly successful career. For Bland's association with Haydn, see *Grove*[6]. SW's reference is no doubt to his cheap editions of many of Handel's works.

[1] This corrects SW's erroneous date of Friday 13 Nov.

[2] Burgh's church, in Gresham Street in the City of London. The organ was by Renatus Harris (1686), subsequently enlarged by him in 1706 and by John Byfield in 1752. Earlier in 1824 Hugh Russell had added pedals and a new Cremona stop (Boeringer, ii. 181–2; Plumley, 82–5).   [3] In fact, 20 Nov.

[4] King Street, Holborn, the address given for Joseph Major in the subscription list to SW's Service.

To Vincent Novello   Euston Street, 23 November [1824]¹

ALS, 1 p. (BL, Add. MS 11729, fo. 208)
Addressed To | Mᴿ Novello | Shacklewell Green | near | Kingsland | Tuesday 23ᵈ of Nov
Pmk NO 23 1824

Euston Street
Tuesday 23 of Novᴿ

Dear N

I know that you are not much frightened at Rain where your Promise is concerned, & therefore am rather at a Loss to account for not having found you at Sᵗ Lawrence's Church on Saturday last:² I was there soon after 12, and waited till near 1, when I thought I was defensible in despairing of your Appearance.—I fear that one of your cruel Head Akes was the Obstacle.—

Pray write me something about the real Fact: perhaps you will make one in the Organ Loft on Sunday next:³ I need not add how welcome you will be to your old faded Friend

SW

To Vincent Novello   [Euston Street], 29 November 1824

ALS, 2 pp. (BL, Add. MS 11729, fo. 210)
Addressed To | Mᴿ Novello | Shacklewell Green | near | Kingsland | Monday Morning
Pmk NO 29 1824

Monday 29 Novᴿ 1824

Dear N

Sam¹ shall have Mᴿ Holmes's Composition² to study as soon as possible, and I have a Request to make of you trusting to meet no Objection.

---

¹ The year is given by the postmark.
² 20 Nov: the meeting arranged in SW's previous letter to Novello.
³ 28 Nov., at Camden Chapel.

¹ Samuel Sebastian.
² Perhaps the fugue mentioned in SW to Novello, 25 Sept. 1824; not otherwise identified.

Sir Robt Peat^3 is an old Acquaintance, & I may even say Friend of mine. He is the Parson of Brentford,^{4} a good Scholar, a very *feeling* Lover of Music, a Man of superior Manners, & what *we* think better than all these, his Heart is warm and sincere.—He is all agog to hear my Service: he knows you well by Reputation, & moreover has frequently heard the Performances in South Street.—When I was last with him (a Fortnight since) he expressed his earnest Wish that we should muster up the said Service and indulge him with it at the Parsonage: I promised to suggest the Matter to you, & the Plan which seemed to me easiest of Execution was that I should bring Sam, and you and I engage an assistant Voice a-piece for Alto & Tenor; I undertaking the Bass and you becoming our Maestro at the Piano Forte, he having no Organ in his House, altho' a very tolerable one at his Church close by.^{5}

He will secure *safe* Beds for the Party, and therefore no Inconvenience can arise about the general and often perplexing Inconvenience of going Home at a late Hour when at a long Distance.

I know your Dislike of forming new Acquaintance; but I did not mislead you in the Introduction to Harding, and I much mistake if you will find the present Proposal a disagreeable Campaign.

If you *bite*, the Appointment of a Day rests with you, and you will furnish me with an Answer for Peat on Thursday Evening.^{6}

Yours as usual

SW

Your Copies are at Major's, who is also invited to join us in the Brentford Party, being also an old Acquaintance of our Parson.

---

^{3} Sir Robert Peat (1771/2–1837), admitted as a 'ten-year man' to Trinity College, Cambridge (1795), DD Glasgow (1799), Perpetual Curate of St Lawrence, New Brentford (1808–37), Chaplain to George IV (Venn; *GM* 1837^2, 209, 662). ^{4} Then, a village west of London.

^{5} A two-manual instrument by one of the England family (before 1814) (Boeringer, ii. 238).

^{6} On 2 Dec., no doubt at the monthly meeting of the Classical Harmonists.

To Vincent Novello   Euston Street, 3 December [1824][1]

ALS, 1 p. (BL, Add. MS 11729, fo. 212)
Addressed To | Mr Novello | Shacklewell Green | near | Kingsland | Friday | 3 o'Clock
Pmk 3 DE 1824

Friday Afternoon
3^d Dec^r

Dear N

I much fear that the same Cause of your Absence from Lisle Street[2] yesterday Evening was that which prevented my seeing you To-Day in Brunswick Square.[3] —My Brentford Arrangement of Course is as yet at a Standstill; but Mr Robertson (last Sunday at Street's) chearfully volunteered himself for *Wednesday next*,[4] and certainly you could not name 'a more sufficient Man' than James Elliot for Accuracy of Intonation.—He was not at the Concert last Evening, so that unless you may have first appraized him of the Scheme, he has not (to speak Masonically) yet 'seen the Light.'

I trust that *this* finds you in better Order: if so, give me an immediate Line, unless you prefer being a very good Boy at Church with me next Sunday.—

Yours in Truth
SW

Euston Street

To Vincent Novello   Euston Street, 6 December 1824

ALS, 1 p. (BL, Add. MS 11729, fo. 214)
Addressed To | Mr Novello | Shacklewell Green | near | Kingsland | Monday Morning
Pmk DE 6 1824

Euston Street
Monday 6th of Decr 1824.

---

[1] The year is given by the postmark.

[2] Probably at the premises of the Royal Society of Musicians (*Encyclopaedia of London*). As SW's later reference makes clear, this was evidently a concert; no details of it have been found.

[3] According to Clarke, *Life and Labours*, 21, Novello taught for twenty-seven years at a school in Brunswick Square.

[4] 8 Dec.

Dear N

I wish you could have given me a better Account of your *Corporality*, which I trust is now in high Improvement.—How would next Thursday Week[1] suit you? I shall not write to Brentford until you and I have settled the Day.—Your Proposal of Mr Frank's[2] Assistance is much to my Mind, and I shall surely act upon it.— The only *Hitch* is the Probability of our worthy Friend Hawes's Interference, who will not suffer Sam to budge from his Prison on any Day that he can rob him of a Guinea.[3]

Pray give me (toute suite) the Names of *all those who have now received* their Copies[4] from *you*, and *Places of Abode.* You will hardly believe what Work I have to secern those who *have* had their Books from them who have not.

The Moment you give me your Answer about Thursday I shall write to our Parson—(one of those at whom I think you will not scoff).—

SW

To Vincent Novello [Euston Street], 12 December [1824][1]

ALS, 1 p. (BL, Add. MS 11729, fo. 216)
Addressed To | Mr Novello | Shacklewell Green | near | Kingsland | Monday Morning
Pmk DE 13 1824 EVEN

Sunday Evening 12th of Dec^r

Dear N

I did not answer you sooner, because I could not: last night I received a Letter from the Parsonage, Brentford.—Our Host expects us on Wednesday week (22^d). He leaves to my Decision the corporal Disposition & Deposition of his Guests, stating that he can secure Vehicles *at almost any Hour* for such as should be obstinately determined to quit Brentford before Sun Rise; *or* provide Beds for *all* at their Option. I have replied that I much prefer the *latter* Plan, and I hope that you do so too.—

---

[1] 16 Dec.   [2] Not identified.

[3] Samuel Sebastian was still under Hawes's charge at the Chapel Royal, where Hawes evidently took every opportunity to hire him out for concerts and to take the fee for himself.

[4] i.e. of the Service.

---

[1] The year is given by the postmark.

Having asked James Elliot to take a Part in a ludicrous Trio prepared for the next Meeting of the Somerset House Lodge,[2] (where by the bye you ought to be present to hear it) I would rather that *you* should propose his joining the Brentford Party, for otherwise he might consider me perhaps unwarrantably importunate in a double Request. (so speedily following the first.) Think, & give me your speedy Answer. Will you take early Care of the repeated Invitation to Robertson?—The Proposal of your Brother's Help is *an Octave of Pedal Pipes.*—Pray secure him, with the Addition of my best Thanks.

Yours (necessarily in Haste)
SW

To Vincent Novello   Euston Street, [13 December 1824][1]

ALS, 2 pp. (BL, Add. MS 11729, fo. 218)
Addressed To | Mr Novello | Shacklewell Green | near | Kingsland | Monday Morning
Pmk DE 13 1824 NOON

Euston Street
Monday Morning

Dear N

Your second Letter reached me soon after I had delivered my Reply to your former one into the Hand of a Friend who promised to forward it by the earliest Post this Morning, it will therefore probably arive much sooner than this.

I am not a little vexed at your News concerning your Health, the Pace of which I however trust will soon proceed to 'Allegro di Molto,' if your medical Advisers mind their Business.—By the Way, I have great Confidence in the Skill & Honesty of *Abernethy*.[2]

Linley has had from me De la Fite's Address some 6 or 8 Times over.—The Truth is that being a Gentleman at Ease he has but little Occasion for an Exertion of Memory: but here is the Direction once more—*Revd Henry De la Fite, 35 Clarendon Square, Somer's Town.*

---

[2] Probably on 27 Dec: according to the Lodge's byelaws passed on 23 May 1814, it met on the fourth Monday in Dec. (Oxford). The trio has not been identified.

---

[1] The date is given by the postmark.

[2] The eminent surgeon John Abernethy, FRS, FRCS (1764–1831). He was appointed assistant surgeon at St Bartholomew's in 1787 and consultant surgeon in 1815. He was the founder of the medical school at St Bartholomew's and lectured there from 1791 on anatomy, physiology, and surgery (*DNB*).

You would do me wrong in supposing me likely to refuse you any Trifle of mine which you might think worth having. I waited for your Description of the Things you want. There is a little Duo of mine (about 40 years old) for 2 Cantos, (an Ave Regina Cælorum)³ which I guess may suit your Purpose as a Matter of easy Execution: when you inform me the exact Nature of any other Bagatelles you would have, I will rake among my Dunghill of MSS. & if I can find any thing above Contempt you shall have it.

It seems (all Matters considered) more prudent to defer the Brentford Party altogether until you are sufficiently convalescent to make one, for Parson Peat much wishes an Introduction to you, & the Meeting without you would be like the Tragedy of Hamlet, *his* Character being omitted.

You must oblige me however with a Line upon this, for I have (you will find) appointed the 22ᵈ, and of Course expect an early Reply from Sʳ Robert.

Yours faithfully

SW

P.S. The Money came all safe. Gratias tibi.

To Vincent Novello

Euston Street, 20 December [1824]¹

ALS, 2 pp. (BL, Add. MS 11729, fo. 220)
Addressed To | Mʳ Novello | Shacklewell Green | near | Kingsland | Monday Decʳ 20ᵗʰ
Pmk DE 20 1824

Euston Street
Monday 20ᵗʰ of Decʳ

Dear N

I have resolved to defer the Brentford Expedition until we can reckon more securely upon you without whom the whole Affair would be to me Insipidity & Disappointment.—Elliot is engaged elsewhere on Wednesday next,² so that here is another Reason for Postponement, & I have not applied to Mʳ Robertson, therefore no Aukwardness occurs from counter Proposals.—If you should be

---

³ The autograph of the original version, for two sopranos and continuo, and dated 1781, is at BL, Add. MS 31222; the autograph of the later version is at BL, Add. MS 65454. Novello subsequently included it in vol. 2 of his *Convent Music*.

---

¹ The year is given by the postmark.   ² 22 Dec.

au fait by Wednesday Week,[3] perhaps that Day would not be objectionable to you.—I shall write toute suite to Sr Robert, naming that as a *possible* Time for our Rendezvous, stating also the unpleasant Occasion of our Mutations, which I am certain he will regret together with myself: he is a Person endowed with no common Delicacy of Mind, & with him Friendship is something more than 'a Name.'

I send herewith the tiny Piece I wrote about in my last.[4]—You are right welcome to the others you enumerated.—If I remember truly, 'Ecce panis'[5] is in D minor, and I also recollect that I omitted *one* Line in the Hymn itself which must be supplied to render it all *orthodox*, a Term for which I know you have the most profound Veneration.

When I get Peat's answer I must pester you with the Post Man again.—As Xtmas is so near I shall expect you to bring in your Bill on *Boxing Day* (26th) [(]or rather on the *27th*, the former falling on Sunday) for the Lot of threepenny Letters[6] I have lately worried you withal; an Account I shall readily liquidate if you will send me good News of yourself & your Doctor.

Every one joins me in my Worship of Abernethy's Acumen & Sagacity.—He is a *rough* Diamond, but one of the most brilliant Water.[7]—I wish you could be induced to give him a Turn.—N.B. He is no Friend to an Apothecary's Shop established in the Guts of his Patient.

> Adieu (pour ce Moment)
>   SW

To Vincent Novello   Euston Street, 21 December [1824][1]

ALS, 2 pp. (BL, Add. MS 11729, fo. 222)
Addressed To | Mr Novello | Shacklewell | near | Kingsland | Tuesday Night
Pmk 22 DE 1824

> Euston Street
> Decr 21. Tuesday

---

[3] 29 Dec.   [4] The revised version of 'Ave regina caelorum'.
[5] SW's 1813 setting of 'Ecce panis angelorum'. As his remarks in subsequent letters show, his fears about the missing line proved groundless.   [6] i.e. the cost of postage to Shacklewell Green.
[7] Abernethy was famous for the roughness of his manner. *DNB* describes him as 'a man of blameless life, highly honourable in all his dealings, generous to those in need of help, incapable of meanness or servility. His blunt independence and horror of "humbug" were doubtless among the factors of that rudeness and even brutality of manner for which he was notorious, and of which many strange stories are told.'

[1] The year is given by the postmark.

Dear N

By the enclosed[2] you will find that the Party could not have been assembled To-morrow; but you will also find that our reverend Host is in Expectation of a Day fixed in the next Week.—I have written to him to say that I should propose Wednesday 29th to *you*, observing too, that you were at present sufficiently indisposed to render an *absolute Promise* somewhat temerarious.—Your Reply to this will determine my Mode of Statement to the *be-knighted* Priest, and if you think there is a tolerable Chance of your being *up* to going *down* to Brentford on the said Day, perhaps you will apprize your Brother and Mr Robertson of the same.— Elliot told me Yesterday that he knows of nothing likely to prevent *him*, so that if the other Points shall be secured, we may venture to make a final Arrangement altho' 'with Fear & Trembling,' as your favourite St Paul the Apostle expresses it.[3]

As I wish to give my Friend as early an Account of existing Circumstances as may be, pray indulge me with a Line as speedily as you conveniently can and mind you do not omit some Comment, (I expect a satisfactory one) upon my Motion for consulting Abernethy.

Yours always

SW

To Vincent Novello [Euston Street, 22 December 1824][1]

AL, 3 pp. (BL, Add. MS 11729, fo. 225)
Addressed To | Mr Novello | Shacklewell Green | near | Kingsland | Wednesday Night
Pmk 23 DE 1824

Dear N

Your sending me your last, *postpaid*, induces me to suspect that with all your deep Skill in Rabelais you do not yet understand Banter, or that you wilfully blink it on the last Occasion, for I will not believe (for one Second of Time) that you could think me the *Chesterfield*[2] who would insinuate contrary Meaning about *Threepences*.

---

[2] Peat to SW, 19 Dec. [1824] (BL, Add. MS 11729, fo. 223), deferring the visit on account of an injury to his back that he had sustained when getting out of a hackney coach while on his way to London the previous Friday.

[3] A favourite phrase of St Paul, used in 2 Corinthians 7: 15, Ephesians 6: 5, and Philippians 2: 12.

[1] The date is given by SW's 'Wednesday' and the following day's postmark.

[2] i.e. Lord Chesterfield. The source of this allusion has not been traced.

I am glad you are going to Cambridge,[3] for sundry Reasons. You will (Imprimis) make Change of Air, which is generally beneficial: then, you *like* the Experiment, which all the Faculty agree to be worth three Fourths of their Advice and Drugs: again, you will be gratified by an Examination of the numerous Curiosities in the Libraries: again, I think you told me you have not yet visited the Place, and you will have to witness a Miracle (which with your great Predilection for Miracles must be peculiarly gratifying). I mean that marvellous Structure of King's College Chapel, wherein is an Organ of *Avery*[4] (the best Builder since old Smith)[5] and the *only* one which he ever had Honesty (or Shame) enough to compleat entirely. There is however one Point on which I counsel you to be strictly on your Guard; which is the deep *Learning* of the Librarians, of which take the following instance.

When I was at Cambridge the first Time,[6] I was introduced to the Librarian of Trinity College,[7] and with so especial a Recommendation, as to be admitted to a Peep at such choice Books as are not produced to ordinary Visitants.—Among them the erudite Antiquarian handed me a Volume with 'Sir, this is a most curious MS Missal.' I pored over two or three Pages when Conscience (an over-match here for Politeness) forced me to observe, 'Sir you must excuse me when I tell you that this is *not a Missal.*' The learned Clerk, all astonied at my Ignorance and Impudence, exclaimed 'What Sir! Do you question a Fact which has been confirmed by the Testimony of Centuries?'—'Sir (said I) the Service of the Roman Church is not made up all of the Mass or eucharistic Part of it;—There are Orisons termed Canonical Hours, divided into Portions called Mattins, Lauds, Prime, Terce, Sext, None, Vespers & Compline—now this Book has none of the Mass in it, nor is a Missal the proper Name for it, but a *Breviary*, which upon

---

[3] Novello was about to go to Cambridge to inspect the collection of music bequeathed to the University by Richard Fitzwilliam, 7th Viscount Fitzwilliam of Meryon (1745–1816), and housed at this time at the Perse School. On 8 Dec. the University had set up a syndicate to consider how best to deal with the riches of the collection, and Novello subsequently offered to inspect it and report on it (King, 36–7; F. G. E[dwards], 'The Fitzwilliam Museum, Cambridge', *MT* 44 (1903), 158–63, 228–32; Cambridge, Grace Book N, 1823–36).

[4] It is not clear whether this organ was an entirely new instrument, or a substantial enlargement of the existing 1687 Renatus Harris organ, undertaken by John Avery (1738–1808) in 1803. The Sperling notebooks in the Royal College of Organists refer to it as 'Avery's last instrument', a description which is supported by SW's remarks. SW was mistaken in saying that Avery completed the organ: whatever the status of the work he carried out, the organ was left incomplete at his death in 1808 and had to be completed by Elliot in 1810 (Boeringer, i. 212–13).   [5] 'Father' Smith (*c.*1630–1708).

[6] In the late 1780s: see SW to Burney, 7 July 1808, where SW stated that he had not been to Cambridge 'for twenty years before'.

[7] Either Thomas Green (1737/8–88), matric 1756, scholar (1759), BA (1760), MA (1763), Professor of Geology (1778), librarian until his death, or his successor John Clark (b. 1759/60), matric. 1780, BA (1784), MA (1788), Librarian from 1788 (Venn).

Enquiry you will find to be the Truth.' 'Well' (said my infallible Showman) 'I was always given to understand that a Mass Book & Breviary were both one and the same'.—'Sir *then* you were given only to misunderstand.'

Upon this he looked bloody malicious, which I not only did not wonder at, but could easily & heartily forgive, inasmuch as there were several Cantabrigiensian Dons around, witnessing a giant *of 24 Letters*, for once capsized by a pygmy of *seven*.

If you have Time enough, give me a line before you go.—I mean to take Sam (only) with me on Wednesday next to Brentford. Peat has never seen him, and loves children dearly, so that the size of the Boy & his Voice combined will (I think) render him no Incumbrance for a Night.

Adieu!
Now do write

Wednesday night

As above said I see You upon Revision.

To Vincent Novello   Euston Street, 8 January 1825

ALS, 3 pp. (BL, Add. MS 11729, fo. 227)
Addressed To | Mr Novello | Shacklewell Green | near | Kingsland | 8th of Jan^y | Saturday Night
Pmk 10 JA 182

Euston Street
Saturday 8th Jany 1825

Dear N

Mr Holmes gave me much Gratification on Wednesday in reporting that your Journey to Cambridge has been beneficial.[1]—I yet wish extremely that you would see Abernethy.—I hate the Faculty almost as I hate Lawyers, but he is a splendid Exception of Honesty and Skill—try him, I conjure you—Even his Gothic Manner would probably amuse you, and even by *that*, do you good.

---

[1] It is not known when Novello returned to London. While in Cambridge he examined and catalogued the manuscripts in the Fitzwilliam collection, and in a long letter of 27 Jan. to the Senate set out the various ways in which selections might be published. His catalogue (not preserved) and letter were presented to the Senate on 18 Mar., as a result of which it was immediately decided that he should be granted permission to transcribe and publish at his own expense any selections he should choose (Cambridge, CUR 30.1; Grace Book N, 1823–36).

Moreover, Holmes said he believed that Indigestion is one chief Cause of your corporal Discomfort, & it is universally acknowledged that if ever a Man knew what was going on in another's Stomach, without being actually in it himself, it is Abernethy.[2]—This I know, that *all* the medical Men I interrogate about him are unanimous in Confession of his indisputable Superiority, & 'Envy, & the Tongue of Loss' can only spit out 'He's a great Brute in his Manners.'

The Rats have been nibbling at my poor Service in the Harmonicon.[3]—I feel obliged to accommodate them with a Kick, not merely out of Respect, but because it is a Pity that the *innocent* part of the musical World should be humbugged and insulted by Lies, hypocritically forwarded to it as Truth & Candour.[4]

I need not add that I shall be happy in some News of yourself, *from* yourself.

Yours as always

S Wesley

P.S. I have pronounced the new Organ at Camden Chapel[5] a very imperfect one but my Word (as a Madman) not being considered *orthodox*, Mr Adams[6] and honest Mr Davis[7] the Organ Builder are fixed to tell the real Truth about it on Wednesday next.[8]

P.S. 2^d I had thought it best not to be present at this solemn Mockery of common Sense, but if *you* will go with me on Wednesday next, I shall be delighted at the Fun, therefore give me an instant Line, yea or nay.—the Conclave are to assemble at 12 o'Clock.—If you go, call on me soon after 11: if you do not, I think I shall not go myself.

---

[2] Abernethy was a specialist in the treatment of digestive illnesses, from which Novello evidently was suffering. According to Sir James Paget, cited in *DNB*, Abernethy in his lectures 'seemed to hold that all local diseases which are not the immediate consequence of accidental injury are the results of disorders of the digestive organs, and are all to be cured by attention to the diet, by small doses of mercury, and by purgatives.' The Abernethy biscuit is named after him.

[3] A reference to an unsigned review of SW's Service which had appeared in the Jan. 1825 issue of the *Harmonicon*; it was almost certainly by William Ayrton, the journal's editor.

[4] For a summary of SW's repeated attempts to have a reply printed, see Biographical Introduction.

[5] The organ was said to have been an old instrument by an unidentified maker, repaired and fitted with a new case by John Gray (d. 1847) (Boeringer, ii. 239).

[6] Thomas Adams (1785–1858), organist and composer. He studied under Busby and was organist at Carlisle Chapel, Lambeth (1802), St Paul's, Deptford (1814), St George's, Camberwell (1824), and St Dunstan-in-the-West, Fleet Street (1833); he held the two last posts until his death. He was one of the most prominent organists of his generation.

[7] SW was no doubt remembering Davis's refusal to pay the commission that SW considered his due for recommending him as the builder of Walter McGeough's organ for The Argory (see SW to Novello, 8 Mar. 1824). [8] 12 Jan.

To Vincent Novello   [Euston Street, 17 January 1825][1]

ALS, 3 pp. (BL, Add. MS 11729, fo. 229)
Addressed To | Mr Novello | Shacklewell Green | near | Kingsland | Monday Evening
Pmk 17 JAN 1825

Monday Evening

Dear N

Your sudden Reverse of Purpose yesterday prevented the Opportunity which
I promised myself of uttering sundry (not Sunday) Words to you upon several
Matters.—Harding's first Question was 'Where's Novello'? said with a Look
that swore Disappointment: I could only say that the aquatic Change of Cloud
had operated to render a further Excursion from Shacklewell Green an Exploit of
more Courage than Prudence, & that I was authorised to 'report' this Reverse of
'Progress.'

He took it all in good Part, adding a Wish that you would look in at the first
Time that Leisure & Inclination might allow you; & I ventured to promise such
a Probability.

I wanted to mention to you that I must have the 'Ecce Panis' before I can supply
the deficient Line, for it will not answer well to do as the Parson did who having
lost two Leaves of his Sermon, found that the former Leaf ended with the text
'It is better to go into the House of Mourning than into the House of Feasting,'
and the Beginning of the next Page was 'And again I say unto you—Rejoice.'

I have seen Linley this Morning, whom I felt anxious to assure that the
Circumstance of a black Ball against him was altogether a Mistake:[2] I told him
moreover that he might expect a speedy Line from you to the same Effect, which
manifestly comforted the Cockles of his Heart (by the Way I don't know their
exact anatomical Position.)

He solemnly disclaims all Knowledge & even Suspicion of my sapient Judge,[3]
and yet expressed an excessive Solicitude lest I should reply in other than gentle
Terms: this I cannot well account for: He even goes on to declare as his firm
Persuasion that the Critique (so misnomored) was written with evident Marks of
friendly Intention.[4]

---

[1] The date is given by the postmark.
[2] The details of this episode are not known; Linley was elected shortly afterwards (see SW to Novello,
[15 Feb. 1825]). It is clear from subsequent references that the society was the Classical Harmonists.
[3] i.e. the author of the review of SW's Service in the *Harmonicon*.
[4] The *Harmonicon* review was in fact by no means as harsh as SW suggested.

Now *we* know that Linley once upon a Time considered me as a fit Inhabitant of D[r] Sutherland's Mad House,[5] but his Decision in the present Instance almost tempts me to enquire of the Doctor whether he has a Vacancy left for *one* in his hospitable Asylum.

That *Friend* who clumsily compliments a Man upon his Sufficiency of Brains (in one Breath) and then tries to prove him ignorant of his Trade, (in another) I think may be enumerated among Gay's many Friends of the *Hare*.[6]

I shall go on to finish what I have thought sur le Sujet, which when done, I shall require your *impartial* Notions upon it.—Whether I have the *Candour* of the Archbishop[7] or not may be questionable, but unless you will consent to be Gil Blas,[8] you will use me still worse (if possible) than you have done hitherto.

I am about to write to Brentford.—What shall I say about you?—

Linley's Lust for the *Fête* at Dulwich[9] (a Party of fusty Batchelors) is quite insatiable.—It's absolutely a *Furor Cœlibum*,[10] and *bum* is rather an aukward Syllable in a Batchelor's Propensities.

Write soon.

SW

To Vincent Novello   [Euston Street], 20 January [1825][1]

ALS, 2 pp. (BL, Add. MS 11729, fo. 231)

Thursday Morning 20th Jan[y]

Dear N

I discover that after all, I have been hypercritical upon myself, (which however is a Fault on the right Side): Upon consulting the Missal, I found, that the Line I imagined I had omitted is nevertheless inserted in my Tune, so that there is no Chasm needing a Replenish.

---

[5] A reference to Linley's part in the decision by SW's family and friends in 1817 to send him for treatment to Blacklands House.

[6] In 'The Hare and many Friends', one of the *Fables* (1727) by John Gay (1685–1732), all of the hare's friends refuse to help her to escape from pursuing hounds.

[7] Presumably Edward Harcourt (1757–1847), Archbishop of York 1807–47, who was a director of the Ancient Concerts; the import of this remark is not clear.

[8] The eponymous hero of the picaresque novel (1715–35) by Alain-René Lesage (1668–1747), translated into English by Tobias Smollett in 1749, and a large influence on 18th-cent. English literature (*OCEL*).

[9] Presumably at Dulwich College, where Linley's brother Ozias was fellow and organist.

[10] 'A frenzy of bachelors'.

---

[1] The year is given by 20 Jan. falling on a Thursday and the content.

You asked me about the Commentary upon my Monitor in the Harmonicon: I am not over anxious in general to take up the Cudgels: there are so few Points in this World worth quarrelling about, & still fewer People worth quarrelling with, that Time is almost always to be better employed than in Controversy.— Nevertheless I own with you that to be wholly passive when unfairly attacked operates as an encouragement to a repeated Act of Injustice, and therefore a Check to the Aggressor is defensible in a moral Sense.

I told you that I should submit what I mean to write, to your Inspection when finished, which I think will be by the End of the Week.—I cannot invite you to that Box of Catcalls at the Chapel[2] on Sunday, but if you could meet me after *the Drop* has fallen, we could lounge away to Hardings & examine Notes together.

I want to hear 'a full true & *particular* Account' of all the Raree Shows they regaled you at Cambridge withal, and what Sort of Chaps you fell in with there:— Certainly good Society is to be had in such a Place, but when I was there, I was rather annoyed by a few of the geometrical Dandies, some of whom made it the Forfeit of a Bottle (or a Dozen) to quote Latin or Greek: so that *they* among others are ashamed of their Trade: but I must say there were some valuable unaffected Scholars among the *older* Members of the University whose Converse abundantly compensated for the Fooleries of the Popinjays.

With regard to Sunday next, I close this with my dear Father's frequent Command to me, 'Sam, do as thou wilt, or I'll make thee.'

Adieu

SW

To Vincent Novello
Euston Street, 27 January [1825][1]

ALS, 3 pp. (BL, Add. MS 11729, fo. 233)
Addressed To | Mr Novello | Shacklewell Green | near | Kingsland | Thursday Evening 27 Jan^y
Pmk 27 JA 1825

Dear N

Should you be minded to take a Stroll to Kentish Town[2] on Sunday,[3] you know when & where to pick me out, & I shall most willingly jog on with you, provided you will excuse my Pace being somewhat less than that of winged-footed Achilles.

---

² i.e. Camden Chapel.

---
¹ The year is given by the postmark.   ² Presumably to visit Harding.   ³ 30 Jan.

The Apology for all my mortal Sins committed against holy Counterpoint in my Church Service[4] being now made, as well as I could manage it, the same shall be presented to your Supervision if you will meet me on Sunday.

I am pretty sure that the Gentlemen of the Harmonicon will say to me in other Words 'Depart from us, for we will have none of thy Ways.'[5]—With all my Heart: I don't like theirs, and if they *should* insert the Paper from Apprehension of what must be the Construction put on their Refusal, still I have resolved to have nothing more to do with them: they are evidently a Junto of mere book-making Blunderers, interspersed with a few half-in-half Musicians with just Knowledge enough to betray their Ignorance.

I am authentically informed that M[r] Ayrton, of operatical Notoriety,[6] is one of the head-Pigs at the Trough, and I nothing doubt that our royal & metropolitan Organist[7] is like unto him in the Dignity of musical Jurisdiction.—I think Crotch could hardly write such nonsense as the others, but as he loves Money better than real Reputation, every Lye may have its Price in this noble Army of Wiseacres.

Prince Hohenloe's Miracles have been very fashionable:[8] I have lately worked one myself, which (strange to say) I can put in my Pocket: it has been already in the Ears of many, & I hope will be in the Tongues of more, & there is a great deal of useful Transubstantiation attached to it.[9]

If you will come on Sunday, I will try to prove my Words true.

Yours as always

SW

P.S. I think Elliston's Brains (if he have any) ought to be blown out. He it seems would have extorted £2000 from poor Kean if he had not risked his, & 5000 more Peoples' Lives on Monday Night.[10]

---

[4] SW's reply to the *Harmonicon* review of the Service.   [5] Job 21: 14.

[6] In addition to editing the *Harmonicon*, Ayrton also wrote the reviews of opera. Alternatively, SW's allusion may have been to Ayrton's difference of opinion in 1817 with Waters, the lessee of the King's Theatre, about his remuneration for managing opera there. A well-publicized court case ensued in which Ayrton sued for £1,200, and notwithstanding the testimony of Sir George Smart and Attwood that he deserved not less than £1,000, was awarded only £700.

[7] Attwood, in allusion to his position as organist to George IV and of St Paul's Cathedral.

[8] Hohenloe's alleged miracles had been widely reported. One of them had been the pretext for a satirical letter in *The Times* for 21 Jan. which employed much the same conceit as that used by SW here.

[9] The hymn 'Ecce panis angelorum', which SW described on the autograph as a 'transubstantiatorial hymn'.

[10] A reference to the events which followed the widely reported criminal conversation case on 17 Jan. in which Kean had been sued for £2,000 by Robert Albion Cox for adultery with his wife Charlotte. The jury found for Cox and awarded him £800, a verdict which had shown 'that although they did not consider Cox to be entirely blameless they believed Kean to be very guilty' (Raymond FitzSimons, *Edmund Kean: Fire from Heaven* (1976), 192). Kean's arrogance and openly immoral behaviour had long made

P S 2ᵈ Do you think that the Proposal of copying & arranging *six* Pages of MS. for a Guinea (throughout a Work) is too much, or too little, or neither?

To Vincent Novello [Euston Street], 31 January 1825

ALS, 1 p. (BL, Add. MS 11729, fo. 236)
Addressed To | Mʳ Novello | Shacklewell Green | near | Kingsland | Monday Morning
Pmk 31 JA 1825

Monday.
Jan. 31. 1825.

Dear N

Harding has desired me to request that you will dine with him after my Work of Penance on Sunday Afternoon next:[1] I told him I thought nothing else than a Pre-Engagement would be likely to prevent you: I hope I was right.

I purpose to bring on Thursday my Apology to the Harmonicon for my high Crimes & Misdemeanors in the Mismanagement of holy Tunes, & think you will find it less exceptionable than before your Hints.

I shall try for Sam on Thursday Evening,[2] but you know that Mʳ Hawes is Mʳ Hawes: to say any Thing more of him that is *true* would be libellous.

Yʳˢ as always

SW

P.S. I should like to look at Graun's Te Deum[3] before Thursday, as my Eyes do not grow much younger.

---

him unpopular with the public, and the details of his conduct revealed in the trial aroused widespread condemnation, to the extent that the government feared that if he were to appear as advertised in *Richard III* at Drury Lane on 24 Jan. there would be a riot, and attempted unsuccessfully to have the performance cancelled. SW's information that Kean had been forced by Elliston to appear no doubt came from the report in *The Times* on 25 Jan., but was in fact incorrect: Elliston had attempted to dissuade Kean from appearing, but Kean insisted on doing so. The £2,000 mentioned by SW was an inaccurate reference to a supposed penalty clause in Kean's contract for his non-appearance; his reference to Elliston endangering the lives of '5,000 people' was an exaggeration: the capacity of Drury Lane at this time was 3,100. For a full account of the affair, see FitzSimons, *Edmund Kean*, 185–200.

[1] 5 Feb. [2] 3 Feb., doubtless for the forthcoming Classical Harmonists concert.
[3] The Te Deum (1757) by Carl Heinrich Graun (1703/4–1759), evidently to be performed at the Classical Harmonists concert.

To [?John Harding]¹   [Euston Street, 31 January 1825]²

ALS, 1 p. (Kassler)

My dear Sir

I have just received the enclosed,³ which I am quite sure is written in the Spirit of Sincerity, of which you have the Opportunity to judge *adequately*, as the Autograph speaks for himself, and therefore I cannot (if I would) dilute or garble his Sentiments.

You find that he meditates an Afternoon Call with me at Kentish Town on Sunday.⁴

Yours faithfully
  S Wesley

Monday Evening | Feb. 1 1825

To Vincent Novello   [Euston Street, 15 February 1825]¹

ALS, 1 p. (BL, Add. MS 11729, fo. 237)
Addressed To | Mʳ Novello | Shacklewell Green | near | Kingsland
Pmk 15 FE 1825

Dear N

I trust that your Daughter² is out of Danger, & am encouraged in this by the Report of a Friend who saw you reading in Tranquillity on Friday last in Brunswick Square.

You must give me your early Opinion on the enclosed,³ which however I guess will not be far discrepant from my own, but I shall not proceed any how till you have written to me.

---

¹ The identification of Harding as the addressee of this letter is suggested by SW's reference to his projected visit to Kentish Town on the following Sunday.

² SW has misdated this letter; the correct date should probably be Monday 31 Jan.

³ Not preserved: perhaps a note from Novello expressing his apologies for not being able to meet Harding some time in the coming week.   ⁴ 6 Feb.

---

¹ The date is given by the postmark.

² Not identified: Novello had seven daughters living at this time.

³ Not preserved: perhaps another draft of SW's reply to the *Harmonicon* review of the Service.

Linley is in high Spirits upon his Election to your Society,[4] & wants *your Society* in another Sense, (of which he has apprized you) I mean of feeding on his Beef Steaks & his Brother's Music[5] (which is very good) at Furnival's Inn,[6] whenever you can name a convenient Day.

You know what it is to have to do with *Vocal Excellence* in the form of She-Singers.—I am inclined to think that some of the Songs in Judas Macchabæus[7] are likely to suffer no slight *Metagrobolization* (as your Friend Rabelais might say) from our Defect in the Article of female Infallibility.—And yet it is affirmed there was a Pope Joan.

Adieu

SW

To Vincent Novello   [Euston Street], 22 February [1825][1]

ALS, 1 p. (BL, Add. MS 11729, fo. 239)

Tuesday.
22[d] Feb.

Dear N

I shall expect you to take some Coffee in my Rabbit Hatch of a Parlour, To-morrow, exactly at half past 5.[2]

I think the Arrangement of the Bill sufficiently injudicious: we all know that Mozart's (as the best Music) ought to come *last* in the true Order of Things, but the Creation (being much lighter *Materiel*) should have formed the 2[d] not the first

[4] The Classical Harmonists, who had earlier blackballed Linley (see SW to Novello, [17 Jan. 1825]).

[5] Either that of Ozias, some of whose chants and anthems survive at Dulwich College, or of Thomas (1756–78), whose promising career as a composer was cut short by his early death in a boating accident.

[6] Linley's apartments. Furnival's Inn, on the north side of Holborn, was originally one of the Inns of Chancery, affiliated to Lincoln's Inn. The Inn was dissolved in 1817, and a new residential building with the same name (but without any legal connections) was erected on the same site. Charles Dickens lived there in 1834–5 and started *The Pickwick Papers* there (*London Encyclopaedia*, under 'Inns of Chancery').

[7] The first of the Covent Garden oratorio concerts, on 18 Feb., included portions of *Judas Maccabaeus*; the female soloists were Miss Paton, Miss Love, and Miss Graddon (*Harmonicon* 3 (1825), 47). Unusually, this concert was not advertised in *The Times*.

[1] The year is given by 22 Feb. falling on a Tuesday and the reference to the forthcoming Covent Garden oratorio concert (see n. 3).

[2] Doubtless before going on to Covent Garden for the evening's oratorio concert, at which SW was to play the organ and piano, and Novello was to turn pages.

Part: for I will answer for plenty of serpentine Notices from above long before the 'Lux æterna' comes on.[3]—

I however hope that there will not be an entire Havoc of that divine Tide of Harmony, but my Fears are altogether paramount.

Well—there is nothing more philosophic than Kollman's phlegmatic motto, 'It must do as well as it can.'—Bawling & Braham for ever![4]

I have had the Mulligrubs, justly attributable to a refreshing Stream of cold Air rushing in front of the Organ for 4 Hours unremittingly on Friday Night.[5]—

O the Glories of theatrical Slavery!—

Thank Heaven I can beg my Bread a better Way.

Adieu

SW

To Robert Glenn   [Euston Street], 17 March [1825][1]

ALS, 1 p. (BL, Add. MS 35013, fo. 82)
Addressed To | Robt Glenn Esq. | Kirby Street | Hatton Garden | Thursday Morning
Pmk 17 MR 1825

Thursday Morning March 17

My dear Sir

I hope that this finds you quite recovered from the unpleasant Sensations you appeared to labour under when we last parted, & that I shall be favoured with your Company & Assistance To-morrow Evening:[2] Coffee will be in readiness at 5, & if you can be with me then *punctually* we may swallow it without scalding our Throats.—The Messiah (you find) is our Evening Task, of which I think, *while we can hear* we can never be tired, as we never can be, of *Bread, while we can eat.*

Yours faithfully

S Wesley

---

[3] The programme for the concert consisted of extracts from *The Creation* as Part I, Mozart's *Requiem* as Part II, and 'A Grand Selection of Modern Music' as Part III.

[4] Braham was the tenor soloist in this concert.

[5] i.e. at the Covent Garden oratorio concert on 18 Feb.

---

[1] The year is given by the postmark.

[2] To turn pages at the Covent Garden oratorio concert, where SW was to be the organist in a performance of *Messiah*.

To Vincent Novello [Euston Street], 25 March [1825]¹

ALS, 1 p. (BL, Add. MS 11729, fo. 240)
Addressed To | Mʳ Novello | (by Favour of Mʳ Fuller)²

Friday 25ᵗʰ of March.

Dear N

Your Cambridge Business³ is of urgent Importance: I therefore lose no Time in returning your Letters.—

If my Animadversions on Mʳ Ayrton's Nonsense are to appear at all, it is high Time they should: I think you said that Insertion in the Examiner must be given up: Monthly Publications are often greedy of Controversy (I mean the Publishers of them:)—What Print do you guess will be the most ready to receive my Farrago? I am told, that the Gentleman's Magazine (wᶜʰ is the most antient of them all) refuses nothing, good, bad, or indifferent, & therefore *now* has lost much of its pristine Respectability & Consequence:⁴ but (according to our *infallible Dogma* of the infallible Lutheran Pope Kollman) 'it must do as well as it can'—the Query is, what is the best it can do? Write—

    SW

Attwood was at Cov. G. on Friday,⁵ bestowing high Encomium upon Von Weber's Sublimities.⁶ I hope he was equally complimentary upon the Profundities of Mʳ Wade.⁷ Hawes & Attwood are sworn conscientious Brothers.⁸

---

¹ The year is given by 25 Mar. falling on a Friday, SW's continuing discussion of his reply to the *Harmonicon* review, and other topical references.

² Not certainly identified: probably the man whom SW recommended as a singer to Thomas Simpson Cooke (see SW to Cooke, 19 Oct. 1824), or possibly John Fuller of 36 Devonshire Place (see SW to Shield, [13] Sept 1815. One of these men (probably the former) was a friend of SW and Novello, and is mentioned in many of SW's family letters of the period.

³ Doubtless a reference to the decision of the Senate of the University of Cambridge a week earlier to allow Novello to transcribe and publish music from the Fitzwilliam collection.

⁴ *GM*, first published in 1731, was by the early 19th cent. generally regarded as old-fashioned and of little consequence (Sullivan, *AAAJ* 136–40). For an indulgent view of its character at this time, see William Hazlitt, 'The Periodical Press', *Edinburgh Review* 38 (1823), 369, quoted in Sullivan, *AAAJ* 138–9.

⁵ i.e. at the performance of *Messiah* on 18 Mar., in which the choristers from St Paul's had taken part.

⁶ Following the first London performance of *Der Freischütz* on 22 July 1824, the music of Carl Maria von Weber (1786–1826) had become extremely popular in London, and extracts from *Der Freischütz* appeared frequently in concert programmes in late 1824 and in 1825 (Warrack, 310–11; Percival R. Kirby, 'Weber's Operas in England, 1824–6', *MQ* 32 (1946), 333–53. SW's remark is ironic.

⁷ The theatre composer Joseph Augustine Wade (1796–1845) had written an oratorio, *The Prophecy*, in 1824; his comic opera the *Two Houses of Granada* was produced at Drury Lane in 1826, and *The Pirate of Genoa* at the English Opera House in 1828 (Brown and Stratton; Fenner, 493–4).

⁸ Both Hawes and Attwood were Freemasons and belonged to the Lodge of Antiquity, SW's former lodge. SW is doubtless also referring to their close professional links.

To Vincent Novello   [Euston Street], 29 March [1825]¹

ALS, 2 pp. (BL, Add. MS 11729, fo. 242)

Dear N

I have deposited my Panegyric upon the Harmonicon Criticks with Mʳ Pouchée, the Publisher of 'the News of Literature & Fashion'² in whose Paper first appeared 'the Ghost extraordinary'³ which was written evidently by some occult Friend, whom I conjectured to be Du Bois, which however was denied by Pouchée, who declines acknowledging the real Author.

I apprized him that there were several musical Quotations requiring Types, at which he seemed not at all discouraged from forwarding the Paper, in Case of general Approval, & of which I desired him to give me the earliest Notice.

I think that without the Quotations adduced immediately to the Eye, the Argument would have suffered some Evaporation, for there are comparatively few who would spend their Time in consulting the Scores of Boyce's Volumes:⁴ besides, the Appearance of the Quotations actually in the musical Characters *looks all so larned like.*

I hope you are dodging your Head Akes & all other Akes that are dodgeable.

In Haste Yʳˢ
    SW

Tuesday 29ᵗʰ of March

---

¹ The year is given by 29 Mar. falling on a Tuesday and SW's continuing discussion of his reply to the *Harmonicon* review.

² Edward Dixon Pouchée. The *News of Literature and Fashion* appeared between 1824 and 1828.

³ This humorous article in the *News of Literature and Fashon* for 16 Oct. 1824 was occasioned by an entertaining correspondence in *The Times* during the previous week between SW and the publishers of Sainsbury's recently published *Dictionary of Music*. The entry for SW in the *Dictionary* stated that he had died 'around 1815'. In a letter in *The Times* for 12 Oct., SW humorously pointed out the error, at the same time taking the opportunity to publicize the imminent appearance of his Service. In an ill-advised reply, the publishers of the *Dictionary* attempted to explain and excuse their error. This elicited a second letter from SW, which in its turn occasioned a further response from the publishers. The entire correspondence was then reprinted in the *News of Literature and Fashion* alongside the 'Ghost Extraordinary' article. SW's reply, entitled 'A Voice from Charon's Boat', appeared in the following week's number. The entire *Times* correspondence and the two *News of Literature and Fashion* items were also reprinted in *Harmonicon* 2 (1824), 210–12. See also Lawrence I. Ritchey, 'The Untimely Death of Samuel Wesley; or, The Perils of Plagiarism', *ML* 60 (1979), 45–59.

⁴ i.e. his *Cathedral Music*, 3 vols. (1760, 1768, and 1763). SW's 'argument' was to justify his harmonic practice in the Service by the citation of examples drawn from pieces in Boyce's collection.

To Vincent Novello
Euston Street, 12 [April 1825]¹

ALS, 1 p. (BL, Add. MS 11729, fo. 243)
Addressed To | Mr Novello | Shacklewell Green | near | Kingsland | Tuesday
Pmk 13 AP 1825

Euston Street
Tuesday Morning.
12th

Dear N

So I am to have the Honour of firing the first three-penny Pop Gun,² after your safe Return to 'these Regions of Smoke.'³—

Major told me of your Presence at the Concert last Night,⁴ & I shall now wait for early Intelligence of your Academick Discoveries.—He also shewed me a Number of the last Norwich Musical Review,⁵ which I had not Time to peruse regularly (as he told me you were in a Hurry for it) but from which I learn that in meddling with Church Musick I have mistaken my Talent; & I cannot resist the Temptation of returning the Compliment to the Authors of the Remark.

Pouchè, the Editor of the ['] News of Literature & Fashion' has but one Objection (& that a very fair one) to insert my Reply to the Harmonicon; that *it is too long for a News Paper*: Joe Street jun^r⁶ tells me he will forward it in one of the Monthly Journals.

Swift somewhere says that 'a brave Man may *necessarily* submit to be devoured by a Lion, but who is he who would tamely consent to be gnawed in Pieces by Rats'?⁷

Adieu pour le Moment

SW

---

¹ The date is given by SW's 'Tuesday morning 12th' and the following day's postmark.

² Another reference to the cost of postage to Shacklewell Green.

³ As SW's later remarks make clear, Novello had been in Cambridge examining and transcribing music in the Fitzwilliam collection. The description of London is from a song in Arne's and Bickerstaffe's *Love in a Village* (1762). ⁴ The Philharmonic Society concert on 11 Apr.

⁵ The Apr. number of *QMMR*, which on pp. 95–101 contained a lengthy critical review of SW's Service.

⁶ Joseph Edward Street, one of the sons of SW's old friend Joseph Payne Street, and possibly the child to whom SW stood godfather on 22 Aug. 1801 (see SW to Street, 18 Aug. 1801). He is probably the 'Street jnr', frequently mentioned in R. J. S. Stevens's *Recollections*, who sang in music parties as a boy treble (Argent). Like his father, he was active in the Madrigal Society and was for many years its secretary, being succeeded in due course by his own son O. W. Street.

⁷ The source of this quotation has not been found.

To [Mary Ann Russell][1]   Euston Street, 16 April 1825

ALS, 3 pp. (BL, Add. MS 11729, fo. 245)
Endorsed by Novello: Addressed to the Widow of M[r] Russell, Org[t] of the Foundling
relative to the Oratorio of 'Job'

Euston Street.
Saturday 16th of April 1825

My dear Madam

I delayed an earlier Reply to the Favour of your Letter[2] only because I was desirous of giving due & mature Consideration to its Contents, determining to deliver to you my most candid Sentiments.

As I find that the Publication of the Oratorio[3] is finally resolved upon, of Course it becomes a Point of the greatest Importance to forward the Work with all possible Expedition: that an Arrangement of the Score for the Piano Forte is absolutely requisite for general Convenience is indisputable, & that this Operation demands considerable Judgement & Attention is equally so.—I conceive that the Task could not be adequately executed by *one Person* in less than a Month *at least*, supposing that his principal Exertions were directed to that Object: I mentioned my Persuasion of this Fact to my Friend Drummer[4] this Day, adding also as my Opinion, that since the present is among the numerous Cases in which 'the Affair cries Haste, & Speed must answer it,' no Measure could be adopted so likely to promote this desirable Expedition as to commit the said necessary Arrangement of the Score to a few chosen judicious & competent Individuals, leaving to their Election such Portions of the Work as they might feel most eligible & pleasant to work upon.

I could name (I think) at least *six* in the musical Profession, whom I consider competent to the Undertaking, but we will only suppose that *three* are needful, & then we shall have the three Acts of the Oratorio prepared for Publication in the same (nay in less) Time than had the whole Arrangement been consigned to a single Individual.

Hereby then, much Time is saved: but moreover, much Expence would be saved also: for several professional Persons could (compatible with their general Engagements) devote *one Week* to a Business of the Kind for a moderate Compensation, to whom the Sacrifice of *a Month* would be of such serious Importance as to render *that* Sum apparently exorbitant, which upon a fair Analysis is of the Fact, would be in reality, reasonable.

[1] Mary Ann Russell, née Morcott (1781–1854), widow of William Russell.   [2] Not preserved.

[3] Russell's oratorio *Job*, which was to be published by subscription.

[4] Probably William Drummer. For the links between him and the Russells, see SW to Glenn, 25 Nov. [1813], n. 4.

You will probably feel surprized that I have left myself entirely out of the Question in the above Statement: the Fact is, that I am at the present Time so closely confined to a similar Task of musical Arrangements,[5] that I could not with any decent Regard to previous Engagements break off suddenly on the present urgent Occasion: I am so well aware by sad Experience that 'Procrastination is the Thief of Time'[6]—that I should ill deserve any favourable Opinion with which you have honoured me either for Talent or Honesty, were I not to recommend your immediate Application to two or three Men of high musical Eminence, with a Proposal on the Plan I have ventured to recommend;[7] & I beg Leave to add that I shall be most willing & ready to render any possible Assistance in the Revision of the desired Arrangement, in the Correction of Proofs, or in any other Way I can become useful, in the sense of Friendship *only*, & totally excluding that of *Trade*.

Believe me,
My dear Madam,
With most cordial Wishes for your Success,
faithfully yours
   S. Wesley

To Vincent Novello   [Euston Street], 19 April [1825][1]

ALS, 1 p. (BL, Add. MS 11729, fo. 179)
Addressed To | Mr Novello | Shacklewell Green | near | Kingsland | Tuesday Morning
Pmk 19 AP 1825

Tuesday Morn^g
19 April

D^r N

You will see the Drift of the enclosed.—I believe you know Williams[2] (the Subject of this Application to you)—he is clever, & worthy, & you may safely give

---

[5] Doubtless his arrangements for the Royal Harmonic Institution.

[6] Young, *Night Thoughts*, i. 393.

[7] Nothing came of this suggestion, and SW eventually took on the whole of the task of arranging the score himself (see SW to Novello, 10 May [1825]). It was published over a year later; SW's preface is dated 8 May 1826.

[1] The year is given by the postmark.

[2] Robert Williams (b. 1794) of Hatfield Street, Blackfriars Road, a pupil of SW, and the organist of St Andrew-by-the-Wardrobe, Victoria Street, from 1816 to 1842. He was also a subscriber to SW's Service.

him a favourable Word without Dread of a Charge of Falsehood from the Editors of the Harmonicon or musical quarterly Review.—

He will write to you upon his Business, the Settlement of which (it seems) 'cries Haste.'

Yours (in Haste also)

SW

Tuesday

Is it not Ld Chesterfield who says that a sensible Man is often in Haste, but never in a Hurry?[3]—So you see I add this Postscript, (as long almost as the Letter) to shew you that I am a sensible Man.—If you doubt it, enquire of Mrs Barstable[4] & Dr Sutherland.

To Vincent Novello [Euston Street, 27 April 1825][1]

ALS, 1 p. (BL, Add. MS 11729, fo. 247)
Addressed To | Mr Novello | Shacklewell Green | near | Kingsland | Wednesday
    Morning
Pmks AP 27 1825, 27 AP 1825

Dear N

I am paying great Attention to my Judge or Judges in your Review:[2] I have little Doubt that Horsley[3] is the Lord Chief Justice in the Cause, & have written him an *inquisitorial* Line upon the Subject: in whatever Way he may give his

Novello had supported his application for membership of the Royal Society of Musicians in 1818. His request for a reference from Novello was no doubt in connection with his application for the post of organist at the newly consecrated St Matthew's, Brixton, for which SW was adviser or umpire, and which the Select Vestry was to discuss at their meeting on 25 Apr. (RSM; Dawe; St Matthew's Brixton Select Vestry minutes (London Metropolitan Archives, P85/MTW/82/1)).

[3] Philip Dormer Stanhope, *Letters written by the . . . Earl of Chesterfield to his Son Philip Stanhope*, 2 vols. (1774), letter 241, 28 Jan. 1751: 'A man of sense may be in haste, but can never be in a hurry, because he knows, that whatever he does in a hurry, he must necessarily do very ill.'

[4] i.e. Mrs Bastable, the keeper of Blacklands House.

[1] The date is given by the postmark.

[2] i.e. in Novello's copy of the current number of *QMMR*.

[3] Horsley was closely involved with *QMMR*, acting as Bacon's ears and eyes in London and contributing many articles and reviews. SW was correct in his supposition: Horsley's authorship of this review is indicated in his own copy of *QMMR*, now at the Sibley Library, Eastman School of Music, Rochester, NY.

Answer, I shall be quite sure of getting at the Truth by *telling him that I know he would disdain Evasion*; so that if he do evade I have him fast, & if he do not, the Point of Course is gained this Way.

He is certainly a Musician of abundant Merit, which however I have long known to be lamentably counterbalanced by an Exuberance of Envy.—He always personifies Pope's true Account of those worthy Criticks who

'Damn with faint Praise, commend, with civil Leer,
And, without sneering, teach the Rest to sneer.'[4]

Adieu—

SW

To Vincent Novello [Euston Street], 2 May 1825

ALS, 1 p. (BL, Add. MS 11729, fo. 249)
Addressed Monday Morning | To | Mr Novello | Shacklewell Green | near | Kingsland
Pmks MY 2 1825 2 MY 1825

Monday. May 2. 1825

Dear N

I expected you to have looked in here on Friday Evening,[1] when I should have talked over the Letter with you which I now enclose:[2]—I guess that our Opinions of the *quo Animo* will not be very widely dissentient, & that with all the Affectation of Mystery, it will be found an entirely *transparent* Document.

I shall return no Reply 'till I have seen you on Thursday[3] when you will give me your final Judgement of its Contents, upon which I shall then act without further Delay.

I hope you will be able to make some more commodious Arrangement in the Disposition of your Orchestra on Thursday: when I deputized for you on the last Evening,[4] about two Thirds of the Performers had no Sight of the Piano Forte,

---

[4] Pope, *Epistle to Dr Arbuthnot* (1735), ll. 201–2: 'Damn with faint praise, assent with civil leer, | And without sneering, teach the rest to sneer.

---

[1] 29 Apr.
[2] Not preserved: probably Horsley's reply to SW's 'inquisitorial line' mentioned in the previous letter. [3] At the concert of the Classical Harmonists on 5 May: see next letter.
[4] i.e. at the previous meeting of the Classical Harmonists on 7 Apr., when Novello was away in Cambridge.

consequently were assisted only by one Sense in a Matter where *two* are always requisite for Precision.—

Perhaps you can give me a Call To-morrow after your Mill-Horse Career.

Yours as usual

SW

To Vincent Novello [Euston Street, 3 May 1825][1]

ALS, 1 p. (BL, Add. MS 11729, fo. 251)
Addressed To | Mʳ Novello | Shacklewell Green | near | Kingsland | Tuesday Evening
Pmk 4 MY 1825

Dear N

Thank you for your Letter, but not much for the sickly Part of the Intelligence.—All is up or down in this whirligig World: I too have very strong Doubts of my attending your Society on Thursday.—My loving Wife has caused me to be arrested, & To-morrow (not being able to advance £25 tout d'un Coup) I am going to Prison:[2] any sudden Release is far from certain, & hardly probable, & I am rather puzzled how to be in Durance vile & at Church at one & the same Time on Sunday next.[3]—The Duty must be done *somehow*; but that *how* is the *Crux possibilitatis*, upon which I fear the Reputation of my general Punctuality at *that there Shop* may be in the sinking Line.—

You will hear from me shortly either from this House or my Prison-House, very shortly, but you see the Necessity of my warning you against my *certain* Appearance at the Crown & Anchor on Thursday.[4] Pray make no Secret *there* of the real Cause of my Absence.[5]

Yʳˢ as in general

SW

---

[1] The date is given by SW's 'Tuesday evening' and the following day's postmark.
[2] SW was imprisoned in a debtor's prison in Cursitor Street, off Chancery Lane.
[3] In fact, SW was released from prison on Saturday, 7 May (see SW to Novello, 10 May [1825], n. 2).
[4] i.e. at the concert of the Classical Harmonists. The Crown and Anchor tavern was a historic meeting place for various societies and concert-giving organizations, including the Academy of Ancient Music and the Madrigal Society (*Enyclopaedia of London*; Argent).
[5] This sentence has been erased.

To Charles Smart Evans[1]   [Euston Street], 9 May [1825][2]

ALS, 3 pp. (BL, Add. MS 11729, fo. 253)
Addressed To | C. Evans Esqr | 44 | King Street | Soho | Monday Morning
Pmk 9 MY 1825

Euston Street
Monday 9th May.

Dear Sir

In Reply to your Letter, allow me to state candidly Matter of Fact, & the Result I will leave to your Impartiality.

Having taken no Benefit during the last nor the present Season, I had (long before the Arrival of yours) fixed in my own Mind to play no where in public, except in the Way of a professional Engagement, & I have signified this Resolution very generally among my musical Acquaintance, and as a Proof of it I have lately declined (tho' most reluctantly) Acquiescence upon a similar Application to yours, in Conformity to the Purpose I have above specified.—Although the Party in Question has never rendered me such active Service as yourself, yet, as I am not one of the many who feel a Pleasure in *refusing* to oblige, it gave me much Pain to answer in the Negative.—

Should I live another Year, & my Brains & Fingers remain unimpaired, I shall feel a real Gratification in offering you my Services.—At the present Time you (as a Man of equitable Feeling) must readily perceive that without a manifest Inconsistency I cannot do what in other Circumstances I most readily would; but my Determination with Regard to *this Season* is very extensively known, & you would do me Injustice by imagining me for a Moment *reluctant* to come forward for *You*: I tolerably well know the Delight the World has in putting the most cruel Construction upon the most innocent Action: in the present Case I should be complimented with the Title of a *Weathercock*, which tho' a useful Implement upon a Steeple, becomes rather contemptible when it walks on two Legs & calls itself a rational Animal.

I can hardly believe that you will be offended at my Frankness, but should it be so, I shall still remember your past Exertions[3] gratefully, & continue

very sincerely yours

S Wesley

---

[1] For Evans, see SW to Novello, 8 Mar. 1824, n. 3.
[2] The year is given by the postmark.   [3] Presumably at SW's benefit concerts.

To Vincent Novello   Euston Street, 10 May [1825]¹

ALS, 1 p. (BL, Add. MS 11729, fo. 255)
Addressed To | Mʳ Novello | Shacklewell Green | Kingsland
Pmk 10 MY 1825

Euston Street.
Tuesday 10ᵗʰ of May.

Dear N

Here I am, *safe*, (which I was when locked up by my loving Wife last Week) but to add, *sound*, is hardly true, for I am not well recovered from the Effects of close Air, & what is still worse, the witnessing Scenes of Misery impossible for me to relieve.²

I have agreed to attempt serving Mʳˢ Russell by arranging the Oratorio: *if* her Patrons prove true to their Promise, she may be a Gainer: but not only 'much Virtue in **IF**,'³ but much Danger also, and this Consideration has held (*holden*) me back from acquiescing sooner.

Mʳ Palmer⁴ whom I mentioned to You, is desirous of your meeting me with him on some early convenient Day, at the Savoy Chapel, or where a great Organ is *manutractable*, hoping that you will afterwards dine with him at Home.—The Family are of the right Sort.—His Mother is a frank charming Woman, the Father a frank blunt *honest* Man, and a *Lawyer*: so that at last I shall force you to believe in Miracles.

Adieu

SW

To [Robert Williams]¹   Euston Street, 10 May [1825]²

ALS, 1 p. (Rylands, DDWF 15/26)

Euston Street
Tuesday 10. May

---

¹ The year is given by the postmark.

² SW had been released from prison on 7 May (see SW to Sarah Wesley, 8 May 1825 (Rylands, DDWes 6/36)).   ³ *As You Like It*, v. iv. 100.

⁴ Not certainly identified: either he or his father may have been the W. H. Palmer of Doughty Street who subscribed for two copies of SW's Service.

¹ For Williams, see SW to Novello, 19 Apr. [1825], n. 2. He is identified as the addressee of this and the next letter on the basis of the reference to the 'bouncing paragraph', concerning his recent non-appointment as organist at St Matthew's, Brixton (see n. 3).

² The year is given by 10 May falling on a Tuesday and SW's Euston Street address.

Dear Sir

I presume that you read the bouncing Paragraph in last Night's Courier,[3] & I am desirous of some Chat with you thereupon.—

The Trustees, Vestry or whatever they call themselves are no better than a Bundle of Swindlers, & were I you I would expose them to the uttermost.— There ought in fact to be an entirely new Election.

If you can call this Evening between 8 & 9 you will find me at Home.

Yours faithfully

S Wesley

To [Robert Williams]   Euston Street, 12 May 1825

ALS, 1 p. (Rylands, DDWF 15/27)

Euston Street
Thursday May 12. 1825

Dear Sir

On my Return from Hampstead I found the enclosed,[1] which I am anxious to forward to you: the Writer best knows whether he has produced a true State of the Case: for my own Part, bitter Experience has forced me to distrust the Professions of every Man, & when Lord Byron declared in the Epitaph upon his Dog[2] that he was the only true Friend he ever had, I can hardly believe he exaggerated the Fact.

---

[3] A brief paragraph in the *Courier* for 9 May discussing the recent election for the post of organist at St Matthew's, Brixton. According to the minutes of the Select Vestry, four candidates were short-listed for the post: William Thomas Ling, Henry Boys, John George Emett, and Williams. Each was required to play three pieces before a meeting of the Select Vestry on 2 May: an own-choice voluntary lasting not more than ten minutes, the 104th Psalm, and the Pastoral Symphony from *Messiah*. In the ensuing ballot Ling received twelve votes, Boys five, Emett two, and Williams one, and Ling was duly elected. The appointment evidently caused some upset: the *Courier* paragraph referred to the fact that SW (who was not present at the election) had recommended not Ling but Williams, that the Select Vestry had disregarded his recommendation, and that Williams and SW had subsequently published letters to this effect. According to the *Courier* account there were only three candidates for the post. Ling, who was simultaneously organist at St Dunstan-in-the-West, was dismissed in June 1829 for neglecting his duties; he was succeeded by Joseph Mundie.

[1] Not preserved: presumably concerning the Brixton election.

[2] The final couplet of Byron's *Inscription on the Monument of a Newfoundland Dog* (1808) at Newstead Abbey, near Nottingham, reads: 'To mark a friend's remains these stones arise | I never knew but one,—and here he lies.'

I am desirous to hear from your own Mouth how your Matters are going on: I have been giving your Rival's Friend[3] a Lesson, who is ready & clever, but a most unequivocal & thorough-paced Dandy as any rational Being would wish to laugh at.

You will find me at Home To-morrow between 3 & 5, if you feel inclined to call in upon

Your hoaxed & belied Umpire

S Wesley

To Vincent Novello

Euston Street, 15 May [1825][1]

ALS, 1 p. (BL, Add. MS 11729, fo. 257)
Addressed To | Mʳ Novello | Shacklewell Green | near | Kingsland | Monday Morning
Pmk MY 16 1825

Euston Street
Sunday 15ᵗʰ of May.

Dear N

You will perceive, by perusing the enclosed,[2] that your speedy Comment is necessary; I shall therefore rely on your indulging me with the earliest Line in the Power of Inclination seconded by the Adjutancy of Goose Quill, (which I look upon as a very eloquent, elegant, & novel Way of expressing what is so much more rationally conveyed by 'pray write soon.')

It is plain that Dʳ Wait[3] is desirous of combining Propriety with Benevolence, & you will find by his Letter that I am to expect (hourly) his Appearance at

---

[3] Not identified: presumably a friend of Ling's.

[1] The year is given by the postmark.

[2] A letter of 11 May from Daniel Guilford Wait to SW (BL, Add. MS 11729, fo. 258), detailing the results of enquiries that he had been making about the possibility of SW transcribing and publishing his own selection from the Fitzwilliam collection at the University of Cambridge. Wait conveyed the Vice Chancellor's opinion that the Senate would probably be prepared to grant permission to SW to publish, but would not be willing to do so before Novello had finished making his own selection. Wait further reported that he was about to come to London and would visit SW on his arrival, and suggested that SW should accompany him on return to Cambridge to make a preliminary inspection of the Fitzwilliam collection. For a summary of SW's protracted negotiations with the University, see Biographical Introduction.

[3] Daniel Guilford Wait (1789–1850), Hebrew scholar, matric. University College, Oxford (1809), St John's, Cambridge (1812), LL B (1819), LL D (1824), appointed to catalogue the oriental manuscripts in the University Library (1824), Curate of Pucklechurch, Glos., Rector of Blagdon, Avon (1819–50). In 1833 he was declared bankrupt and imprisoned in the Fleet Prison. Some hints of his speculative business ventures and financial problems run through SW's references to him in subsequent letters (*DNB*; Venn).

N. 16.—It will be gratifying to have obtained your Reply previous to his Call, for his Candour imperiously demands the most delicate Attention.

I have Thoughts of coming in for a slice of Boyce's immortal Anthem on Tuesday, at St. Paul's:[4] this I fear is a Day when you are generally 'delivered over to the Tormentors' until Eventide, & so that I shall miss all Chance of meeting you there.

Yours as usual

SW

To Vincent Novello   [Euston Street, 10 June 1825][1]

ALS, 1 p. (BL, Add. MS 11729, fo. 261)
Addressed To | Mr Novello | Shacklewell Gree<n> | near | Kingsland
Pmk 10 JU 1825

Dear N

I do not know whether you are aware that a certain *Canonist*[2] is also a prodigious Church & King-Man, (as indeed all canonical Folk ought to be): I have therefore guessed that the following might a little *metagrobolize* him, as your favourite Rabelais may say:

> Billy Horsley (Mus. Bac.) is the Man (of all others)
> To shorten our Clergy's exorbitant Length:
> For (by gen'ral Consent of his classical Brothers)
> He denounces *two Fifths*, & they just make *a Tenth*.[3]

---

[4] 'Lord thou hast been our refuge', composed by Boyce in 1755 for the annual Festival of the Sons of the Clergy at St Paul's Cathedral, and at this time still performed at each festival. Tuesday 17 May was the day of the public rehearsal; the festival itself was on 19 May (*Grove*[6]; *The Times*).

---

[1] The date is given by the postmark.

[2] William Horsley, thus described because of his *A Collection of Canons* (1817).

[3] A reference to Horsley's accusation in his review of SW's Service that SW had broken the rules of harmony by writing consecutive fifths. Another attack by SW on Horsley's pedantry is contained in the manuscript of a short Kyrie written at about this time (BL, Add. 31239, fo. 106), where SW deliberately writes a series of consecutives and comments: 'this chain of fifths I beg leave to present with all due respect to Wm. Horsley Esq. Mus. Bac. Oxon. Fifth and Eighth Catcher in ordinary and extraordinary to the Society of Musicians.'

Do what you like with this; I think your friend Hunt (being a loyal Man)[4] would laugh at it.

On Tuesday I mean to set out to Cambridge,[5] in Spite of my Horror of Stage Coaches.—

O for Mercury's winged Feet! but perhaps after all, Mercury's a bad *Thing*, & as to *a good GOD*, I know that is among your Doubts.

SW

To Vincent Novello [Euston Street], 11 June 1825

ALS, 1 p. (BL, Add. MS 11729, fo. 263)

Dear N

The following, I think is a better Reading of my Squib upon orthodox *Canonists*, & as whenever I mend (which alas! is but seldom) I like my Friends to know it, Vanity furthers unto you the 2[d] Edition.—

> Billy Horsley (Mus Bac) is the Lad of all others
> To shorten our Clergy's exorbitant Length:
> From a Duty most due to the Pedants (his Brothers)
> He denounces *two Fifths*, & they just make *a Tenth*.

D[r] Wait supped here with me last Night, & it seems that we are likely to take our topsy-turvy Chance together, he being detained in London probably till Wednesday,[1] when we may whirl towards Alma Mater, Cheek by Jowl.

Adieu!

SW

Saturday Evening | 11th of June. 1825

---

[4] Ironic: Leigh Hunt's far from loyal comments on the Prince Regent in an article in the *Examiner* in Mar. 1812 had resulted in his trial and imprisonment for libel (see SW to Novello, 17 Feb. [1813], n. 6).

[5] 14 June. SW's departure was in fact delayed, and he did not go to Cambridge until 18 June.

[1] 15 June. SW in fact did not depart for Cambridge until 18 June.

To an unidentified recipient[1]   Euston Street, [14 June 1825][2]

ALS, 2 pp. (Rylands, DDWF 15/30)

Euston Street
Tuesday Evening

My dear Sir

When I found Webb[3] at his Door this Morning, he told me that you had not left him above 5 Minutes before, & that you were proceeding towards my House. I was pressed for Time or would have returned in the Hope of finding you there.— I am sorry to learn that you feel as if a little too late in the Promulgation of your lithographic Apparatus: the Scheme of such a Thing I learned only a few Nights ago, from D[r] Wait who is to accompany me to Cambridge, but I do not conceive that because somebody else has hit upon an Invention, therefore a similar one must prove abortive, especially since every mechanical Invention is so capable of continual Improvement.[4]

The Reference given by D[r] Wait on this Subject was to the *Typolithographic Press*—White Lion Court, Wych Street, Drury Lane.[5]—Here I suppose you will know all about it.

I met To-Day M[r] Warren, the Father of a young Organist whom you probably have heard of:[6] he is anxious to have all the Rights & *Wrongs* of the Brixton

---

[1] Evidently the inventor of a lithographic printing process, and a friend of SW.

[2] The date of this letter is established by SW's 'Tuesday' and his references to his impending visit to Cambridge and to the Typolithographic Press (see n. 5).

[3] Probably the Revd Richard Webb (1770/1–1829), a male alto and minor canon of St Paul's Cathedral, Westminster Abbey, and St George's Chapel, Windsor. Earlier he had been successively a chorister, clerk, and chaplain at New College, Oxford; he had also been connected with the Foundling Hospital Chapel. In 1808 he published *A Collection of Madrigals for Three, Four, Five, and Six Voices, Selected from the Works of the Most Eminent Composers of the 15th and 16th Centuries*, which he had transcribed on behalf of the Madrigal Society (Foster; Doane). Another possibility is the John Webb of Tottenham Court Road who was a subscriber to SW's Service, and who may have been Richard Webb's son.

[4] SW's correspondent had evidently invented a method of lithographic printing, and was disappointed to learn that a similar process had already been developed by others.

[5] The Typolithographic Press were pioneers in lithographic printing. They were the printers of the *Parthenon: A Magazine of Art and Literature*, the first journal to be produced entirely by lithography, and intended as a showcase for the process. The first number had appeared on 11 June and was doubtless the immediate cause of SW's correspondent's disappointment. For the *Parthenon*, see Michael Twyman, *Early Lithographed Books* (1990) 54–7; *Early Lithographed Music* (1996), 389.

[6] Joseph Warren (1804–81), who later had a distinguished career as a church musician, composer, editor, and writer of instruction books on music. In 1834 he became organist of St Mary's Roman Catholic chapel, Chelsea, and in 1849 brought out a new edition of Boyce's *Cathedral Music*. He also composed church music, wrote many music instruction books, and was a noted collector of music (*DNB*; *Grove*[6]; King, 56–7).

Squabble, and I have promised him your Papers upon the Subject, which I recommend to you to send without Delay directed to Mr Warren sen^r, Upper Lark-Hall Place, Clapham.

Depend on it, that your spirited Stir in that rascally Business has done much good, and Musicians will thank you, *secretly*: honest & open Gratitude you must look for *somewhere* else, & I cannot conveniently specify the Corner *where*, at this present Writing.—

So God be with you till I see you next, & he only knows when, as I am to *sit* (not to run) my Chance of a broken Neck or Skull in a Cambridge Coach within a Day or two.

Che sarà sarà—the Italians say; and they are pretty right: Prudence has its occasional Advantages, but what a Fool is the *Calculator* for To-morrow's Event!

Adieu
Yours in Truth
S Wesley

*Long Words of little Sense are all the Fashion you know.

To Vincent Novello [Euston Street], 15 June 1825

ALS, 3 pp. (BL, Add. MS 11729, fo. 264)
Addressed To | Mr Novello | Shacklewell Green | near | Kingsland | Wednesday Evening
Pmks 16 JU 1825, JU 16 1825

Dear N

Our late Duke of Cumberland,[1] the Brother of George the III^d, as the present one[2] is of George the IVth, was a preferable Character to the Gentleman who has swindled England so cunningly t'other Day out of a few cool annual Thousands:[3]

---

[1] Henry Frederick (1745–90), fourth son of Frederick, Prince of Wales, grandson of George II, described by *DNB* as 'notorious for excesses'.

[2] The deeply unpopular Ernest Augustus (1771–1851), fifth son of George III. At this time he was living in Germany with his wife and family.

[3] On 10 June, amidst a great deal of public controversy, the House of Commons had passed the Duke of Cumberland's Annuity Bill, which increased the Duke's annual allowance from £18,000 to £24,000, ostensibly for the education of his son. *The Times* devoted three leading articles to this 'odious measure', commenting that it was 'calculated to injure the people's respect for royalty' (*DNB*; *The Times*, 8, 10, 11 June 1825, Fulford, 217–18).

I mean *preferable* in one Particular: he always conducted his Amours *at the right End,* 'tho' he once defended his Detection in one of them in a singular Manner, & in a Way that at Oxford or Cambridge would not have been considered elegantly logical.—When some rude Intruders insulted Royalty to so vulgar a Degree as to catch him in Bed with Lady Grosvenor[4] (a most beautiful Animal, but a cursed Fool like himself) he bounced out of Bed with his Breeches à la Main into the adjoining Apartment, vociferating,—'Gentlemen, you all have ocular Demonstration that I am not in the *next* Room: & I'll take my Bible Oath I am not.'[5]

Bible Oath became proverbial *then,* as it is nugatory *now.*

What's all this to any Purpose? (say you). Perhaps I don't well know, but I must try.

I do not date this Letter from Cambridge, the Reason whereof is similar to the Duke's Defence of his Chastity: *I am not in the next Room,* but in that identical two-pair of Stairs Closet whence I directed to you my last Edition of Horsley's aukward Reform of the Church. In plain English, I am yet in Euston Street, & not at Cambridge, & I'll take my Bible Oath I am not.

And why?—that's the Question.—Our good little Doctor Wait has been worried in lovely London by a Chap who has disappointed him in every promise of settling business with him here, & instead of accompanying me to Cambridge on Tuesday last, as mutually agreed upon, he has been obliged to run off into Hertfordshire in Quest of this lying Yahoo, who necessitates him to defer his Return home till Friday next, where he will expect me on *Saturday,* & I shall miss the Pleasure I anticipated of the Converse of a Scholar & a Gentleman for 6 hours, to beguile the Tedium & Ennui of that vile Article of Utility, a Stage Coach.

'It must do as well as it can' must always be treasured as worthy of Reminiscence among the Proverbs of the wise.

My humble Apology for all my Pêchès mortels in the Te Deum &c is to be found in last Saturday's Literary Chronicle—Price 6[d]—to be had at most News-Mongers, & published by Davidson, Surrey Street, Strand.[6]—

---

[4] Henrietta, née Vernon, wife of Richard, first Earl Grosvenor (1731–1802), described by Walpole as 'a young woman of quality, whom a good person, moderate beauty, no understanding, and excessive vanity had rendered too accessible' to the Duke of Cumberland (*DNB,* under 'Grosvenor, Richard'; Horace Walpole, *Memoirs of the Reign of George III,* 4 vols. (1845), iv. 164).

[5] This notorious incident took place on 21 Dec. 1769 at the White Hart Inn at St Albans. In the criminal conversation suit which followed, the jury found for Grosvenor and awarded £10,000 damages against the Duke of Cumberland.

[6] SW had eventually succeeded in having his reply to the criticisms of his Service printed in the *Literary Chronicle and Weekly Review* for 11 June 1825 (pp. 377–81). It is an elegant and entertaining

Every fresh Reader of Horsley's Letter[7] confirms the Belief that he is the 'faithfully yours' with his Stiletto in the Dark.

I wish any humble Efforts of mine could be effectual in checking this mean Species of paltry Villainy, & that I could invent a potent Machine for cracking literary Lice.

> Adieu
> Je suis toute à vous[8]
>   SW

Wednesday Evening 15th of June. 1825

To Vincent Novello   Cambridge,[1] 21 June 1825

ALS, 2 pp. (BL, Add. MS 11729, fo. 266)
Addressed To | Mr Novello | Shacklewell Green | near | Kingsland | Midd^x | June 21st
Pmk JU 22 1825

Regent Street Cambridge
June 21st 1825

Dear N

According to your Command I pester you with another Scroll.—I am endeavouring to make the most of my Time here, which really is most agreeably employed, for the Kindness & Attention of my Host Dr Wait, make me very reluctant to think of Saturday next,[2] on which I am solemnly pledged to 'render up myself

---

rejoinder, showing SW at pains to take issue with his critic on every possible point, from his knowledge of musical repertoire and grasp of the rules of harmony to his knowledge of Greek and his use of English. The article is characteristically erudite, heavy with quotations from and references to the works of Shakespeare, Pope, Swift, Johnson, Horace, and Cicero, and at one point invoking the authority of Scapula's Greek Lexicon to point out an incorrect usage. On the musical side, all the accusations of harmonic incorrectness in the *Harmonicon* review are countered, with music quotations, by reference to the practice of Tallis, Farrant, and Purcell, taken from Boyce's *Cathedral Music*. For the *Literary Chronicle*, see Sullivan, *TRA* 230–9.

[7] Not preserved: doubtless a reply to SW's accusation that he was the author of the *QMMR* review.
[8] 'I am entirely yours'.

---

[1] SW had travelled to Cambridge on Saturday, 18 June and was staying with Wait and his wife. He gives an amusing account of his journey in his letter of 19 June to Sarah Suter (BL, Add. MS 3102, fo. 53).
[2] 25 June.

to sulphurous & tormenting Flames' alias London Streets with their glorious Gas Lights.[3]

You will render me much Service by writing immediately on receiving this: I want you to state *all* the Names of the Authors of whom you mean to avail yourself, that we may not clash in our Endeavours to benefit the musical World:[4] —I do not learn that you have meddled either with Paradies or Scarlatti, & conclude that they are among the Authors you leave to another Hand: a list of your intended Materials for Operation will save both of us much needless Trouble, & as I *must* return on the above mentioned Day you will readily excuse my Importunity.

I am much pleased with the Organs here, but it is grievous to think how much Mischief has been done to the noble Instrument in Trinity Chapel by that Brace of Quacks Flight & Robson.[5]—The Organ at Peterhouse[6] is a sweet little Instrument, & that at St Mary's[7] utters the true ecclesiastical Sounds.—Of the Organ at King's I am not enabled to pass a fair Judgement, the Provost[8] having in his scholastic Politeness *refused* the Key upon Dr Wait's Application.

I would write to the Extent of my Paper, but I must be obedient to the Annunciation, not of the blessed Virgin, but of Dinner.

Adieu

Yours always

SW

P.S. The Post brings us our Letters, soon after 9 in the Morning.

---

[3] Gas lighting had first been introduced into London in 1807 and had quickly become widespread (Roy Porter, *London, a Social History* (1994), 126). The quotation is perhaps a misremembering of 'sulphurous and thought-executing fires' (*King Lear*, III. i. 4).

[4] On his first visit to Cambridge to explore the riches of the Fitzwilliam collection, SW was understandably anxious to know what Novello was intending to transcribe and publish in his own collection. The Fitzwilliam collection contained substantial amounts of music by Pietro Domenico Paradies (1707–91) and both Alessandro Scarlatti (1660–1725) and his son Domenico (1685–1757); this reference is probably to Alessandro. No music by any of these composers was included in Novello's *Fitzwilliam Music*.

[5] The organ at Trinity College, begun by 'Father' Smith and completed after his death by his son-in-law Christopher Schrider, had been extensively altered by Flight and Robson in 1819–20. By all accounts their work was unsatisfactory, and they were unsuccessfully taken to court over it by the Master and Fellows of Trinity (Boeringer, i. 224; Thistlethwaite, 106).

[6] A small two-manual instrument by John Snetzler (1765), with unison pedal pipes added by Avery in 1804 (Boeringer, i. 220; Thistlethwaite, 62).

[7] i.e. St Mary the Great, the University church: a three-manual instrument by 'Father' Smith (1698) (Boeringer, i. 214–15; Thistlethwaite, 90).

[8] George Thackeray (1777–1850), Provost of King's College 1814–50 (Venn; *DNB*).

To Vincent Novello   Euston Street, ?25 June [1825][1]

ALS, 1 p. (BL, Add. MS 11729, fo. 268)

Euston Street
Saturday Evening
26 of June

Dear N

I am just imported to the 'Seat of Confusion and Noise,'[2] from the terrestrial Paradise of the Cambridge Walks, & that Edifice which might dignify the New Jerusalem, King's College Chapel.

Pray name the Day or Night you will come to me in the next Week.—I say *Day*, because I will give you *one* Mutton Chop, & *one* Gallon of Porter (which I confess is for *you* rather short Allowance) on any Day from Monday 'till Saturday you may best like.

Y^{rs} as usual

SW

I have a Letter for you from Wait,[3] which I must give you *propriâ manu*.[4]

To Vincent Novello   Euston Street, 2 July [1825][1]

ALS, 1 p. (BL, Add. MS 11729, fo. 269)
Addressed To | Mr Novello | Shacklewell Green | near | Kingsland | Saturday Afternoon
Pmk 2 JY 1825

Euston Street
Saturday July 2.

Dear N

You know that Paradox, 'take one from one, & there remain *two*:' this arithmetical Fact having happened since you last called on me,[2] I am thereby (very

---

[1] It is clear from its contents that this letter dates from 1825, and that SW has mistaken either the day of the week or the date. The correct date is probably Saturday 25 June.

[2] This description of London is from the song from *Love in a Village* quoted by SW in SW to Novello, 12 [Apr. 1825].   [3] Not preserved.

[4] 'With my own hand'.

[1] The year is given by the postmark.

[2] SW's cumbersome circumlocution announces the birth of his son John during the previous week.

unwillingly) necessitated to postpone our Chop & Porter 'till after Tuesday next; & after which I hope the Street Door Knocker may be safely untied without distracting the Brain of the Party for whom that unfashionable Virtue called common Humanity required the Operation.

As all this cannot be long ænigmatical to you, I will not trespass on your Time by a more every-Day mode of Statement of Matters at present.—Do not pass N. 16 without looking in on

Y^{rs} truly
SW

To Samuel Sebastian Wesley[1]   [Cambridge], 1 August 1825

ALS, 3 pp. (BL Add. MS 35012, fo. 109)
Addressed Master Wesley | N. 16 | Euston Street | Euston Square | London | August 1st
Pmk AU 2 1825

Dear Boy[2]

I have written to Harding, (& I think your Mother will hear from him by Wednesday,) nothing doubting that he will come forward with the requisite £5.

Buy a Shilling or 18 Penny Penknife, & I will give you the Money again when I return.

You say nothing of the poor Girls,[3] or whether the Baby has caught the Meazles.—I hope you 'dwell together in Unity,'[4] & if I find it otherwise I shall not patiently overlook it.

Mrs Wait is not yet confined, but as the House is necessarily in some Agitation, I do not *dine* there except on a special Invitation.—I breakfast & take Tea with them generally but provide for myself as to Dinner & Supper.

Novello & I have played over the Confitebor at Trinity Chapel,[5] which has pleased so much, that they are all urging me to publish it by Subscription: there

[1] SW's eldest son by Sarah Suter, aged 14: see SW to Hawes, 28 Nov. 1817, n. 3.
[2] The 'dear Boy' salutation and the sententious tone of this letter recall Chesterfield's *Letters to his Son*.
[3] SW's daughters Rosalind (b. ?1814) and Eliza (1819–95).   [4] Ps. 133: 1.
[5] SW described this occasion in an unsigned paragraph in the *Examiner* on 14 Aug.: he and Novello had performed the *Confitebor* as an organ duet to 'an auditory of selected judges of musical composition' who subsequently urged SW to publish it by subscription. SW also took the opportunity to outline his plans to perform the *Confitebor* in London during the coming season.

is a Mrs Frere[6] in the University who is a great Patroness of all musical Schemes, and who is likely to procure me a long list of Names.—Dr Wait would not encourage me in any Risk, nor suffer me to venture on proceeding until I should be sure of a very liberal Subscription before beginning to print.

The Manuscripts which I am copying[7] are likely to turn to excellent Account, and if Hawes has any Guts in his Brains (tho' he has but few in his Carcase) he will make me a liberal Offer for a Slice of the Concern.

I do not grudge Postage for any News from Home: therefore I desire you to write, by Wednesday's Post, but you must really put a little more Intelligence in your Letter and not leave me in the Dark about several Things that you know I am anxious about.

If Horsley's Letter[8] be not too long to copy without leaving out News of more Consequence, I should wish you to transcribe it.—The Original you could not send but with double Postage which I cannot afford.—I wish my Money may hold out without being obliged to borrow of Novello:—I would by no means ask Dr Wait, because he would conclude that I had reckoned on making my House his Home *in all Respects*, & therefore that I had not calculated upon the Expence which must be incurred by dining frequently away at my own Cost.

My Lodging will be 18 Shillings for the Fortnight, which is pretty moderate for Cambridge, but the People are remarkably civil & obliging, & I am perfectly comfortable in their House.

Give me a *full true & particular* Account of all Things you can cram into three Pages, for you must not leave an Inch of Paper unoccupied, and as with a *good* Knife you *may* make a good Pen, with a good Pen you may write a good Hand, which I assure you Master Sammy (I beg your Pardon, *Doctor* I meant) I wish you would set about to do.—At all Events you ought now to be a forward *English* Scholar, and I do not despair even of your becoming a Latin one, if you make good Use of the most valuable Article in Life, which is Time.

---

[6] Mary Frere, née Dillingham, wife of William Frere (1775–1836), Master of Downing College; she was largely responsible for making the college an important social centre during her husband's mastership. She was the mother of the agriculturist Philip Howard Frere (1813–68) and the grandmother of the liturgiologist Walter Howard Frere (1863–1938) (*DNB*).

[7] Not identified: they may have included motets from William Byrd's *Gradualia* from an 18th-cent. copy in score in the Fitzwilliam collection which SW was hoping to edit and publish. SW's transcriptions are now at BL, Add. MS 35001, and are erroneously described in the printed catalogue as being by SW himself. For SW's later account of this unsuccessful project, see his letter to Street of 25 May 1830.

[8] Evidently a further letter from Horsley, which had arrived since SW's departure from London.

I trust that your Mother is getting on, and that Fish,[9] & your Sisters are in no bad Condition of any Kind. Once more, be careful to apprize me of every Thing you know I wish to be apprized of, & I am,

Dear Sam always
Your loving Father

S Wesley

PS Spell *Wantes* so—wants
& *Knive*—Knife
Make your O's round, not ϽϽϽ

To Vincent Novello [Euston Street], 9 August [1825][1]

ALS, 1 p. (BL, Add. MS 11729, fo. 271)
Addressed To | Mr Novello

Dear N

According to command I have sounded my own Trumpet,[2] a job I am very aukward at, & which does not much increase my universal self Complacency:— it is written all with Blots & Scratches as you will see, which must pass (if you like) for Beauty Spots, as I have neither Time nor Patience for a corrected Copy.

I miss my Pen Knife, & Bach's Exercises.[3] You must give me what Tidings you are able about them.—the latter Article is Sam's property, & if I don't indemnify him he will indict me for Larceny prepense.—Perhaps (as it was dark when you scrambled up my Battle Traps) they were left in the Museum.[4]

Pray write directly to
Yours as always

SW

Tuesday Morning | Aug. 9

P.S. I hope you found the Queen Bee safely imported from Boulogne.[5]

---

[9] The pet name for SW's son Matthias Erasmus (1821–1901).

[1] The year is given by 9 Aug. falling on a Tuesday and SW's allusion to his paragraph for the *Examiner* (see n. 2).

[2] A reference to SW's *Examiner* paragraph, the copy for which he evidently enclosed in this letter.

[3] Not certainly identified: perhaps the Hoffmeister edition of *Clavierübung I*, published as *Exercices pour le clavecin*, a copy of which SW is known to have owned.

[4] The Fitzwilliam Museum.

[5] Novello's wife Mary Sabilla. She had evidently been visiting their eldest daughter, Mary Victoria (later Mary Cowden Clarke), who was at this time at school in Boulogne (Averil Mckenzie-Grieve, *Clara Novello 1818–1908* (1955), 10; Clarke, *My Long Life*, 25–31).

To Vincent Novello   Euston Street, [12 August 1825]¹

ALS, 3 pp. (BL, Add. MS 11729, fo. 272)
Addressed To | Mʳ Novello | Shacklewell Green | near | Kingsland | Friday Evening
Pmk 13 AU 1825

Euston Sᵗ Friday Evᵍ

Dear N

Major has lent me the Quarterly, N° 26.—the four first Pages contain incipient Scraps of the Te Deum, Jubilate, & Nunc dimittis, to which the Numbers 1, 2, 3, 4 &c refer *par avance* in the preceding Magazine.²

I think the best Plan is to return the Antidote to the Ground whence the Poison has been emitted, & send my Retort courteous³ to gentle Mʳ Bacon, who (by the Way) is not unlikely to prove his Right & Title to that Name by a Refusal of Insertion, especially as he is a profest Crony of the Canonist; but even the Refusal will furnish me with a *Sam*sonian Argument against the illiberal tout ensemble.

Major is engaged for a Fortnight to come; & *you* do not forget that you also are engaged for a Sunday *to come* & that Sunday the 21ˢᵗ of the present Month, at 5 of the Clock (or 29 selon *vos* Italiens⁴ if their Day commence from Midnight, for if from Noon, then it would be *our* 5 o'Clock, only changing Afternoon into Morning, & as it has been long fashionable to turn Night into Day, I think the sooner we adopt this Calculation the more consistent we shall appear.)

Nothing so beautiful as a Parenthesis, so galloping away from the Subject of the Sentence, that the only Way to regain it is to begin the Sentence all over again.

Well then—on Sunday the 21ˢᵗ, that is to say, Sunday Week next, you & I as Men of Honour & Musicians (which are always synonimous) have pledged our Words to dine with friend Pug⁵ at his Willa in Kentish Town, at the Hour (or Hours) above & aforesaid.

Your Logic seems to me very defective, when you profess to consider my Letters really more valuable than those of a pettifogging Attorney.—Is not every

---

¹ The date is given by SW's 'Friday evening' and the following day's postmark.
² The latest number of *QMMR*, dated June 1825. As SW states, it included four pages of musical examples referring to the review of the Service which had appeared in the previous number.
³ *As You Like It*, v. iv. 90.   ⁴ 'According to you Italians'.
⁵ The nickname of an amateur musician friend of SW, not identified, frequently mentioned in SW's letters of this period. From SW's subsequent remarks it appears that he was an organist, lived in Kentish Town, and was perhaps a lawyer.

thing that is valuable dear to us? and are there any Letters so dear to us as those of a Lawyer?

There, there! you erring Sophister, you draw false Conclusions, & I must send you to study Logic under Horsley & Attwood.—Has not the one demonstrated that all Breaches of old Rules are mortal Sins, & the other that the most sublime of all Instruments is the Piano Forte?[6]

The Letter which arrived when you called, & the Postage of which you kindly offered to pay, to save the Time for getting Change, contained the most obliging Invitation possible from S[r] James Gardiner[7] to pass a Week with him in Hampshire, & which (if I can manage it) I should be a Foe to both my Health & Interest to refuse, maugre the quondam 9 Guinea Demur.—N.B. he adds that *none* of the travelling Expence is to be a Shadow of Obstacle, or of Thought.

I enclose J. W's Apology for answering Fools according to their Folly,[8] which you so well liked, & which indeed the simple but masterly Style of Argumentation induced me to copy in the first Instance.—Had you known him you would have been tempted to acknowledge with the Whore in the Beggar's Opera (concerning the Character of Jews) that 'he was a very good sort of Man 'bating his Religion.'[9]—

And so are you, altho' I am quite convinced that on the grand Points where the *vital Essence* of Religion is concerned, you & I are not much further apart than 7 Furlongs are from a Mile.[10]

Adieu—Write—
Will our *Puff* appear on Sunday?[11]

SW

P.S. Miss Ogle!!![12]

---

[6] Attwood had presumably expressed these views in a periodical article (not traced) or in some public forum.

[7] Sir James Whalley Smith Gardiner, Bart (1785–1851), matric. Brasenose College, Oxford (1804); of Roche Court, Fareham, Hampshire (Foster; *Complete Baronetage*); the letter containing the invitation (which SW accepted) is not preserved.

[8] Preserved with SW's letters to Novello at Add. MS 11729, fo. 302. Another copy, also in SW's hand, is at Rylands, DDWF 15/50.

[9] By John Gay (1685–1732). The allusion is to *The Beggar's Opera*, II. iv., where Mrs Slammekin tells Suky Tawdry that 'I, Madam, was once kept by a Jew; and bating their religion, to women they are a good sort of people'. [10] A mile consisted of eight furlongs.

[11] The *Examiner* paragraph. [12] For Miss Ogle, see SW to Novello, 12 Sept. [1825].

To Vincent Novello   Euston Street, 17 August [1825][1]

AL, 1 p. (BL, Add. MS 11729, fo. 274)
Addressed Wednesday Evening | To | Mr Novello | Shacklewell Green | near | Kingsland
Pmk 17 AU 1825, AU 17

Euston Street.
Wednesday 17th of August.

Dear N,

The enclosed[2] will increase your Respect for the Candour & *Logick* of Batchelor Horsley: I have just received it, & you have the best Right of any man to the first over hawling thereof.

I often think of that excellent Remark of my Godfather Madan—'what a lamentable Affair it is that so many People cannot be quietly contented to remain Fools, but they must let all the World know it.'

As you did not call Yesterday I conclude that I am unlikely to see you before Sunday.—Sarah[3] is desirous to know whether you mean to honour her Blankets & S<heets> with the Deposit of your Corporalities <on> Sunday Night next.[4]

A Line *in Answer* will confer a great Favour on

Sir Yours &c &c &c

P. S. I really could not have believed Horsley to be such an egregious Ass as you will find him in a Minute or two.—But it is as true as that 'a standing P—has no Forethought,'[5] that Malice has no Prudence.

[Enclosure]

A new Parody upon the favourite old Song Sweet Willie O.[6]

1.

He would be a Critick, the sweet Willie O,
He would be a Critick, the sweet Willie O,
He sometimes quotes Latin,
Which seldom comes pat in,
For why?—he ne'er studied it, sweet Willie O

---

[1] The year is given by the postmark.
[2] Presumably another letter from Horsley; not preserved.   [3] Sarah Suter.   [4] 21 Aug.
[5] Eric Partridge, *A Dictionary of Slang and Unconventional English*, 8th edn. (1984), 1145, records 'a standing prick has no conscience' as the more usual form of this proverbial saying.
[6] This piece of doggerel, a parody of the words of a popular song from Charles Dibdin's *The Jubilee* (1769), is preserved with SW's letters to Novello. Annotated by Novello 'a skit at William Horsley; Mus Bac and pedantic canonist', it is likely that it was enclosed with this letter.

2.

He would play extempore, sweet Willie O,
He would play extempore, sweet Willie O,
    But his Fingers refuse
To help out his Muse
And they say he'll relinquish it, sweet Willie O

3.

He would be a Genius, the sweet Willie O,
He would be a Genius, the sweet Willie O,
    But *Materiel* for this,
He for ever must miss,
So he'd better sing smaller, the sweet Willie O

To [William Hone]¹   Euston Street, 18 August 1825

ALS, 2 pp. (Rylands, DDWes 6/103)
Endorsed To William Hone

Dear Sir,

'Ingratum si dixeris omnia dicis:'²—and I should verily be this odious Miscreant were I to neglect the earliest Opportunity of rendering most cordial acknowledgements, for the singularly kind Remark with which you concluded the short Memoir of him who now addresses you.³

¹ William Hone (1780–1842), who was 'in the course of more than forty working years a clerk, bookseller, book auctioneer, printer, radical pamphleteer, satirist, journalist, innovative publisher, poet and bankrupt' (John Wardroper, *The World of William Hone* (1997)). In his youth he was a member of the London Corresponding Society and later was in business with its former secretary, John Bone. From 1815 to 1821 he collaborated with the caricaturist George Cruikshank in a series of political satires, many of them directed at the Prince Regent. Three pamphlets attacking ministerial corruption in the form of parodies of the catechism, the litany, and the creed led to his prosecution for blasphemy. In three successive trials he spoke in his own defence for over twenty hours and was acquitted on all counts. His most substantial publications were *The Everyday Book*, *The Table Book*, and *The Year Book*, described by Wardroper as 'three unfading treasuries of high and low learning, humour, poetry, art and warmhearted reporting' (Wardroper, *The World of William Hone*; for the *Every-Day Book*, see pp. 10–14).

² 'If you call someone ungrateful, you have said everything there is to say about him': a Latin proverb of unknown date.

³ Hone's memoir of SW had appeared in the entry for 28 July 1825 of his weekly miscellany the *Every-Day Book*. After praising SW's compositions and his extempore performances on the organ, Hone concluded: 'the intellectual endowments of Mr Samuel Wesley equal his musical talents and . . . the amiable and benevolent qualitities of his nature add lustre to his acquirements. He is a man of genius without pretension, and a good man without guile.'

In predicating me to be one 'without guile' I feel that you have not flattered me; nevertheless you have bestowed upon my Character the highest, and (to me) the most valuable possible Encomium.

I certainly should have made a wretched Lawyer, and a worse Courtier; for Observation and Experience have very long convinced my Reason that nothing on Earth is worth a Lie.

Having pronounced me 'a good Man' you must suffer me to explain the extent to which alone I can admit the Truth of the Proposition.

Concerning Goodness in what is usually called a moral Sense, I feel not the slightest Temptation to boast: I am only conscious of feeling always inexpressible Gratification in any Occasion offered of relieving Pain, mental or bodily, and an utter Abhorrence of inflicting either without the most imperious Necessity; and I daily wish myself *a good Man*, in the Sense of the Stock Exchange, when witnessing the Wretchedness that wrings the soul at the Corner of every Street.

But in the religious (or rather the scriptural) Sense of a good Man, I shrink into self-Annihilation, and can best express my Sensations in a consoling Verse of my late dear and inestimable Father;

> Might I in thy Sight appear
> As the Publican distrest;
> Stand—not daring to draw near;
> Smile on mine unworthy Breast;
> Groan the Sinner's only Plea,
> GOD be merciful to me![4]

Believe me
Dear Sir
With highest Esteem
Yours faithfully
S Wesley

Euston S[t] Euston Sq[r] 18th of Aug[t] 1825

P.S. My Brother is not only living, but I trust enjoying Health at present either at Bristol (our native City) or in Wales, whither he designed to make an Excursion, this Summer.[5]

---

[4] The fourth verse of Charles Wesley's hymn 'Saviour, Prince of Israel's race'. For SW's setting of this text in 1807 and his quotation of its opening in a letter to Jacob, see SW to Jacob, [?21 Nov. 1808] and n. 10.

[5] Probably the visit mentioned in SW to Charles Wesley jun., 16 June [1825] (Rylands, DDWF 15/29).

To Vincent Novello   Euston Street, [19 August 1825]¹

ALS, 2 pp. (BL, Add. MS 11729, fo. 277)
Addressed To | Mr Novello | Shacklewell Green | near | Kingsland | Friday Morning
Pmk 19 AU 1825

Euston St. Friday Morn^g

Dear N.

I am not worth the 30 Variations² at this present Writing: My only MS. Copy³
I willingly made over to you:—I had a French Copy⁴ of them which is strayed
or stolen, & after all, I suspect that the Musick is almost above the Pitch of the
Stock Exchange.—Bring any Thing that you may think palatable: I will bring the
Song I spoke to you about, & which I think rather a better than the one in A which
tickled your Fancy.⁵

I cannot quite agree with the regal Organist that the Piano Forte is the Emperor
of all keyed Instruments, & I wish that Mr Pug's Organ were half as good as his
Piano, for in that Case, we might strum more to our Taste.

I have written to the Editor of the Quarterly, asking whether he will insert my
Reply: he has yet sent no Answer, & I suspect that H. has put him up either to
Evasion or Refusal: in either Case, I shall give the Paper to your friend Clarke:⁶
it is incumbent on me to call public Attention to the extraordinary Conduct of
Orator Horsley, by which I hope to check (a little at least) the vile assassinating
System which is at present so fashionable.—

Sam will be with us on Sunday, but alas! his Voice betrays Symptoms of Anti-
Vellutism,⁷ & moreover he begins to shew Signs that a Razor must before very
long form one Article of his Toilette.

---

¹ The date is given by the postmark.   ² The *Goldberg Variations*.
³ BL, Add. MS 14334, which may have been made for the performance given by SW and Novello for
Burney on 20 July 1810: see SW to Burney, 17 July 1810.
⁴ Presumably a printed edition; probably the one by Nägeli, entitled *Trente Variations fuguées pour
Clavecin ou Pianoforte* [1803].   ⁵ Neither song has been identified.
⁶ Charles Cowden Clarke (1787–1877), author and lecturer, and member of the Novello circle. In 1828
he married Novello's eldest daughter Mary Victoria; he was later in partnership with Novello's son
J. Alfred Novello, and was the first editor of *MW* in 1836 (*DNB*; Altick).
⁷ A reference to the imminent breaking of Samuel Sebastian's voice. The soprano castrato Giovanni
Battista Velluti (1781–1861) had arrived in London earlier in the year and had made his London début at
the Duke of Devonshire's concert on 6 May; his stage début was at the King's Theatre on 3 June. As the
first castrato to appear in London for more than a quarter of a century, he naturally aroused a good deal
of curiosity (*QMMR* 7/27 (Sept. 1825), 268–76; *Grove*⁶).

I wish you would bring your Song 'If in that Breast so good & pure.'[8]—I think Sam could get through it if transposed, & it is a great Favourite of mine.

Harding is desperately fond of Vocality, so that we must cackle him out a Stave* or two, if we ever mean to get House Room on a future Holiday.

Adieu.—I did not pay Postage, because you scolded me for it before; but abstaining rather inflicts a Wound upon my Conscience.

SW

* You know there is no such English word as *a Stave*; & that *Staves* is the plural of Staff.

Horsley

To Vincent Novello [Euston Street, ?c.26 August 1825][1]

ALS, 3 pp. (BL, Add. MS 11729, fo. 281)

Dear N

As I mean to leave Town on Thursday[2] for my Trip to Sir James G's (he having written since I saw you a quite irresistible Invitation) I thought to fire off my signal Gun to you, & you only, for I do not much love to 'prate of my whereabout,' especially if mine Host happen (as in the present Instance) to be bedaubed with a Title.

I send you two more prime Proofs of 'the Pot calling the Kettle black Arse'.[3] —My worthy Correspondent has forgotten a few of the Liberties he himself takes in his Harmony, & (I cannot but think) those as reprehensible as what he quarrels with in my Text: *Sam* furnished me with them from the Canon 'Audivi Vocem' composed on the putrescent Exordium of Parson Rennell's Guts & Garbage, a proud Limb of the English Church, who ceased to tyrannize on Earth a few Months ago.[4]

---

[8] Not preserved.

[1] This letter appears to refer to SW's visit to Sir James Gardiner in early Sept. 1825. The dating of 26 Aug. (a Friday) suggested here is derived from SW's reference to his departure on 'Thursday' (?1 Sept.) and his intended return 'tomorrow fortnight' (?10 Sept.). These dates are consistent with what is known of the chronology of this visit.   [2] 1 Sept.

[3] Examples of Horsley's infringements of the rules of harmony from his canon 'Audivi vocem de caelo', possibly brought by Samuel Sebastian on his visit the previous Sunday; not preserved.

[4] Horsley had written 'Audivi vocem de caelo' on the death of the prominent churchman Thomas Rennell (1787–1824), vicar of Kensington. Horsley was one of Rennell's parishioners, and possibly a friend.

I have seen Phillips[5] the Bass Singer & initiated him in the Confitebor Air 'Confessio & Magnificentia'.—he is hugely delighted with it, & will drain the Marrow of his Bones to give it Effect.—We must get him at the Oratorio:[6] Robertson tells me he asked too much last Season: but the Managers made an excellent Market *of us all*, & if they will not squeeze out an extra 10 or 20 Guineas for the Credit of a national Concern, they deserve the Amusement of the Gentleman Sailor who chose to 'cut & run.'

Robertson thinks that that Song & Paton's[7] 'Fidelia'[8] would form a *Jachin & Boaz*[9] in the Job: it is however much to be lamented that Griffin says I cannot write, & Horsley pisses upon what I have written, otherwise I do think that even one of the Choruses might be heard with Patience, & that after the Hunting Chorus in Der Freichutz[10]—(I hope I have spelt it wrong, I love it so dearly).

Adieu.

I go on Thursday, purposing to return To-morrow Fortnight.[11]

---

[5] Henry Phillips (1801–76), the leading operatic and oratorio bass of his day. After an early career as a boy soprano and subsequently in the chorus at the English Opera House, he made his solo début as Artabanes in Arne's *Artaxerxes* in 1824, and later in the same year was Caspar in the first English production of *Der Freischütz* at the English Opera House. He was the bass soloist in the first complete performance of SW's *Confitebor* in May 1826. For a contemporary account of his early career, see *QMMR* 7 (1825), 463–7.

[6] In his *Examiner* paragraph on the *Confitebor* (see SW to Samuel Sebastian Wesley, 1 Aug. 1825, n. 3) SW had taken the opportunity to state that he hoped that 'at the ensuing Lent season, the musical public will have an opportunity of hearing this meritorious and elaborate production, with all the advantages which a work designedly magnificent justly claims'. This projected first performance of the complete work with orchestral accompaniment, which SW presumably hoped would form part of one of the Covent Garden Lenten oratorio concerts, did not materialize. The *Confitebor* was eventually first performed at SW's benefit concert on 4 May 1826.

[7] Mary Anne Paton, later Wood (1802–64), Scottish soprano. She had made her concert début as a 'juvenile performer of music and reciter from Scotland' in June 1812. Her stage début in Oct. 1822 was as Susanna in *Le nozze di Figaro* and she also appeared that season as Polly in *The Beggar's Opera* and Mandane in Arne's *Artaxerxes*. She sang Agathe in the English Opera House production of *Der Freischütz* and created the role of Reiza in *Oberon* in Apr. 1826. Weber wrote of her to his wife: 'Miss Paton is a singer of the very first rank, and will sing Reiza divinely', but he found her acting lacking and had trouble with her in rehearsal (*Grove*[6]; *DNB*). She was the soprano soloist in the first performance of SW's *Confitebor*.   [8] 'Fidelia omnia mandata eius', a florid soprano aria from SW's *Confitebor*.

[9] The names given to the two bronze columns at the entrance to Solomon's temple: see I Kings 7: 21.

[10] The Hunting Chorus and other extracts from *Der Freischütz* were particularly popular in London at this time, and were included in almost every concert.

[11] Around 10 Sept., if the suggested dating of this letter is correct. In his letter of 9 Sept. to Sarah Suter from Winchester (BL, Add. MS 35012, fo. 57), SW wrote that he had intended to return to London on that day, but had been unable to secure a place in the stage, and was therefore intending to return the next day.

I am afraid that you will not condescend to read what is written on such coarse Paper; but it may serve to absterge a very fashionable Aperture in these Biblical Days.

SW

To Vincent Novello   Euston Street, 31 August [1825][1]

ALS, 1 p. (BL, Add. MS 11729, fo. 279)
Addressed To | Mr Novello | Shacklewell Green | near | Kingsland | Wednesday Morning
Pmks 31 AU 1825, AU 31 825

Euston Street
Wednesday 31st of Aug^t

Dear N

You will find the enclosed[2] to be another damning Proof of the Mus Bac's contemptible Falsehood, when declaring that he had '*no Interest whatever* in the Quarterly Music Review.'—You will I am sure quickly conclude that I should be as great a Fool as the Editor is a Rogue were I to commit a Word of my Writing to *his* Consideration.

What a silly Plan it is to resolve on being a Rascal! Swift has archly observed that 'it costs half the World much more Pains to be damned than it would cost them to be saved.'[3]

Your friend Clarke I see is the only Man to give my Paper to the World & I shall certainly send it to him.—

I met an *agreeable* old Maid at Drummer's yesterday who boasts of your Acquaintance & Approbation: Miss Jennings,[4] who is no everyday sort of a Yahoo.—Your Cheeks must have burned a little last Night, I trow.

Adieu
SW

---

[1] The year is given by the postmark.
[2] Presumably another letter from Horsley; not preserved.
[3] The source of this quotation has not been traced.
[4] No doubt Sarah Jennings, teacher of piano and singing, of 7 Trafalgar Place, Hackney Road. She subscribed to Novello's *A Selection of Sacred Music* in 1811 and to Russell's *Job* in 1825. Mary Ann Russell, the daughter of William and Mary Ann Russell, was at this time apprenticed to her (RSM, under 'Russell').

To Vincent Novello Euston Street, 12 September [1825][1]

ALS, 3 pp. (BL, Add. MS 11729, fo. 289)

Euston Street
Monday 12th of Sept^r

Dear N

Send me the Norwich editor's foolish Letter[2] as soon as you can, as I must quote a Part of it.—I have had no Leisure for preparing my Retort courteous to the worthy Mus. Bac. for Sir James kept me either eating, drinking, sailing, or laughing in so continuous a Series that I could rarely find Time to write even a Letter of Enquiry whether the Folk here were alive or dead.

By the way I was not a little affected at hearing from one of my fellow Travellers when going to Winchester[3] that our excellent Friend Miss Ogle[4] is no more— however I will not give the Report *full* Credit until I have learned the exact Truth from some of her Relations: I hardly know where it will be best to apply for Intelligence.—Linley is out of Town or he might probably give me the Address of one of her Brothers:—I am sadly vexed at the Idea of her leaving this World with the Probability of her ranking me among the many ungrateful Wretches whom she had served essentially.

Sir James G. knows Horsley, & was all Surprize when he found him the Hypocrite he has proved himself.—He thinks me perfectly right in exposing him, & that he deserves no Quarter whatever.

I have passed very good Days in the Country: the Family is a delightful one, & my Host introduced me to several prime sensible Folk—among the Rest to Earl

---

[1] The year is given by 12 Sept. falling on a Monday and SW's Euston Street address.

[2] Bacon's letter has not been preserved: it was no doubt in response to SW's letter to him, asking him to insert SW's reply to the *QMMR* review of the Service, mentioned in SW to Novello, [19 Aug. 1825].

[3] i.e. while on his way to visit Sir James Gardiner.

[4] Susannah Ogle (*c.* 1761–1825), one of the daughters of the Revd Newton Ogle (1726–1804), Dean of Winchester 1769–1804. Her sister Esther Jane (*c.* 1775–1817) was the second wife of R. B. Sheridan, whose first wife Elizabeth was the sister of Linley. Tantalizingly little is known of her relationship with SW. She is known to have owned at least two autographs of his music. A manuscript music book dated 1808 in the hand of, and once owned by J. W. Windsor (RCM, MS 1151) contains one piece by SW noted by Windsor as being 'copied from the author's MS in the possession of Miss Ogle', while another piece from the same volume subsequently appeared in Book 6 of Novello's *Short Melodies, Original and Selected, for the Organ*, where it was noted as being 'from an unpublished MS by Samuel Wesley formerly in the possession of Miss Ogle' (Venn; Robin Langley (ed.), Samuel Wesley, *Fourteen Short Pieces for the Organ* (Oxford, 1981)).

Northesk,[5] the Rear Admiral of the Navy, an excellent unaffected Scot of the old School, where we passed two extremely pleasant Days in unceremonious Luxury: he has a beautiful Seat within five Miles of Winchester,[6] at which latter Place I strummed the Cathedral Service twice in the Absence of Chard[7] who was gone to the Hereford Meeting,[8] but whom I saw previously, & found to be much less disagreeable than Musicians in general.

I dine next Sunday[9] with our host M[r] *Pug* at Kentish Town, who enquired yesterday very kindly after you.—I know he would be delighted if you would look in on that Day sans Ceremonie, & I leave you to consider of it: I wish you would, & should not wish it were I not certain of his receiving you as welcomely as myself.—He dines at 5.

Give me an early Line. This is very coarse Paper, but I had no other, & you must remember that I am not a *fine* Gentleman.

Adieu

Yours as usual

SW

P.S. Joe Major tells me that your Wife has eloped with a Man to York.[10]—I did not think you were such a fashionable Husband.

---

[5] William Carnegie, 7th Earl of Northesk (1758–1831), Rear-Admiral of Great Britain from 1821, Commander-in-Chief at Plymouth 1827–1830 (*DNB*).

[6] Longwood House, Owslebury, Winchester.

[7] George William Chard (1765–1849), organist of Winchester Cathedral and tenor singer. He received his early musical training in London as a chorister at St Paul's Cathedral under Robert Hudson and subsequently returned to Winchester. He became a lay vicar and assistant organist of the cathedral in 1791, and in 1802 succeeded Peter Fussell as organist and master of the choristers of the cathedral and organist of Winchester College, both of which positions he held until his death. He was succeeded by SW's son Samuel Sebastian (*Grove*[6]; Shaw, 301, 400).

[8] The Three Choirs Festival, held in 1825 at Hereford, for which Chard had been engaged as one of the vocal soloists. He appeared as the tenor soloist in *Messiah* on 7 Sept., taking the place of Thomas Vaughan, who was indisposed; on the following day his own *Offertorio* was performed (*Harmonicon*, 3 (1825), 204).   [9] 18 Sept.

[10] Mary Sabilla Novello had presumably gone to York to visit their children: Alfred, aged 15, was serving an apprenticeship in the music trade, and Clara, aged only 7, had recently been sent there to study music and singing under John Robinson, organist of the Roman Catholic chapel (Averil Mckenzie-Grieve, *Clara Novello 1818–1908* (London, 1955), 11; Michael Hurd, *Vincent Novello and Company* (1981), 15–16). Her visit was no doubt timed to coincide with the Second Yorkshire Musical Festival, which took place between 13 and 16 Sept: for a long report, see *Harmonicon*, 3 (1825), 174–85. The identity of her companion is not known, but could plausibly have been Charles Cowden Clarke, who may have written the *Harmonicon* report.

To Vincent Novello Euston Street, 14 September [1825][1]

ALS, 2 pp. (BL, Add. MS 11729, fo. 285; address portion Edinburgh
Addressed Mʳ Novello | Shacklewell Green | near | Kingsland | Wednesday Sepᵗ 14
Pmk EVEN SP 14 1825.
Endorsed by Novello: The Autograph of Samuel Wesley, one of the greatest musical
  Geniuses that England has ever produced.

Euston Street
Wedʸ 14ᵗʰ of Septʳ

Dear N

As you jaw me for my Gentility I send you some more brown Paper which you may apply to the Bishop's favourite Orifice the next Time you have the Gripes or as soon as you have read this here Letter, but not till then.

Your classical Brethren[2] did me the Favour to order three of my Books[3] extra, which were accordingly sent: I am still in Arrears to my Engraver & therefore am gathering in as many of the Halfpence as I may ask for without Injustice or Impudence, therefore tell me what to do without affronting your worthy Wights.

I shall now set to regularly with my Train of Compliments to the Mus. Bac.[4] whose Cause is so very weak, that were it not for his extreme Arrogance & Insolence it would be almost cowardly to strike him: however he has very long assumed so much of the lordly Tyrant that it has become high Time to force him to lower his Top Sails, & I think I may thereby save some *others* (whom he thinks he may kick & cuff as he likes) from similar Depredations on their Property.

What is the Title of the Magazine in which your friend Clarke is concerned?[5]— I mean to preface my Reply to the Quarterly by a short Address to *your* Editor explaining the cause of inserting that Paper in his Publication which had been originally intended for another.

---

[1] The year is given by 14 Sept. falling on a Wednesday and SW's Euston Street address.

[2] i.e. Novello's fellow members of the Classical Harmonists.

[3] i.e. copies of the Service.   [4] Horsley.

[5] The *London Magazine*, a literary magazine published between 1820 and 1829 and edited at this by time by Henry Southern. In spring 1825 Clarke had taken the place of John Hunt in a publishing firm set up in 1824 by Hunt and his nephew Henry Leigh Hunt which was the publishing agent for the journal (Altick, 51–2). SW was hoping to exploit this connection. Clarke was unsuccessful in his attempt to place SW's article: see SW to Novello, 23 Nov. [1825].

I wish you had said *when* you thought of looking in here, because I would take care to be within.

En attendant, Adieu.

SW

P.S. I have had a rich Treat in chewing the Cud of old Byrde's Minims:[6] they are full of my own Errors & Heresies according to his Holiness Pope Horsley.

Do call in soon, & let me know at what Time.

To Vincent Novello   Euston Street, 19 September [1825][1]

ALS, 1 p. (BL, Add. MS 11729, fo. 286)
Addressed To | Mr Novello | Shacklewell Green | near | Kingsland | Monday Afternoon
                                                                                    Euston Street
                                                                                    Monday 19th of Sept^r

Dear N

I have just received the enclosed.[2]—You must instruct me how to act upon it, although on second Thoughts I think that yourself had best write to Cambridge on the Business, & by D^r W's Account 'The Affair cries Haste'.

I hope you & your Headake are parted.—A Divorce for Life were the desirable Acquisition. I wish you would give Fuller's Pills a fair Trial.

We wanted you Yesterday. Pug & Harding were in high Order, & we were all very *cozey* together.

Cozey is a West Country Word, signifying snug *and confidential*.

Yours always,

SW

---

[6] Perhaps the transcriptions that SW may have made on his recent visit to Cambridge.

[1] The year is given by 19 Sept. falling on a Monday and SW's Euston Street address.

[2] Evidently a letter from Cambridge concerning the negotiations for SW to be allowed to transcribe and publish music from the Fitzwilliam collection.

To Vincent Novello [Euston Street], 22 September [1825][1]

ALS, 1 p. (BL, Add. MS 11729, fo. 288)
Addressed To | Mr Novello | Shacklewell Green | near | Kingsland | Thursday Morning
Pmks 22 SP 1825, SP 22 1825

Thursday 22^d of Sept^r

Dear N

If either you or I had chosen to play 'Life's subtle Game'[2] in the under-handed (or what is *called* the politic) Way, I think that with our moderate Allowance of Brain we might possibly have been half as rich as our worthy friend Mr Hawes.

I am inclined to believe your Notion right, & am certain that Wait voted for the manoeuvring System merely to defeat *Clarke*[3] whom he has Reason to know sticks at nothing shabby to serve his own Turn.[4]—I *can* have no possible Objection to put the Question strait forward to the University, & will not hesitate a Moment so to do, after learning the Formula of such a Ceremony.

Robertson has invited me to meet you To-morrow to see the Organ intended for the Theatre:[5] I have promised to come, & I will bring the Confitebor with me, as it will not be amiss to prepare him for my Intention of bringing it forward.[6]

Yours in Haste—I am just going to Brentford, & shall take the Liberty of presenting your compliments to Peat, although he be both a Knight & a Priest, each of which is sufficient to damn a Gentleman's Character with you.

SW

---

[1] The year is given by the postmark.   [2] Young, *Night Thoughts*, iv. 128.

[3] John Clarke-Whitfeld (1770–1836), Professor of Music at Cambridge from 1821 until his death, although rarely in residence. From 1820 until 1832, when he was succeeded by Samuel Sebastian, he was also organist at Hereford Cathedral.

[4] The significance of this remark is not clear, but appears to relate to SW's attempts to secure permission to publish selections from the Fitzwilliam collection. Novello's Preface to *The Fitzwilliam Music*, dated Dec. 1825, noted that Clarke-Whitfeld had himself been offered the opportunity to publish selections, but had declined.

[5] i.e. Covent Garden, where Robertson was Treasurer. The organ was by Bishop: see *Musical Gazette* 1 (1856), 103, cited in Boeringer, iii. 208. It was a one-manual instrument with pedals, installed under the stage with swell shutters opening into the orchestra pit.

[6] i.e. in the 1826 Covent Garden oratorio season.

To Vincent Novello   Euston Street, 3 October [1825]¹

ALS, 1 p. (BL, Add. MS 11729, fo. 290)
Addressed Monday Evening | To | Mr Novello | Shacklewell Green | near | Kingsland
Pmk 4 OC 182

Euston Street
Monday 3^d of Oct^r

Dear N

A Perusal of the enclosed,² just now received, will I think put Matters in a new Light concerning the necessary Plan of Operations, & I shall be glad if it prove satisfactory to you, for otherwise I really think I shall stumble at the Threshold & never be able to enter the House.

That you will digest Wait's Arguments candidly & judiciously I will not affront you by doubting.

I hope to come to you by 7 on Thursday,³ but wish you to write immediately after sifting the Letter.

 Yours in Haste

  SW

P.S. Sr James Gardiner has just written, insisting on haling me down to Winchester next Week.—I hardly know how to say either Yes or No. What a fine Thing Ubiquity would be!

To Vincent Novello   [Euston Street, 9 October 1825]¹

ALS, 1 p. (BL, Add. MS 11729, fo. 303)

Dear N

I send what I promised, & what I hope you may approve.²—I should like to convey the *real* Letter in a Frank, for postpaying a Letter to the *King*³ of a Place

---

¹ The year is given by 3 Oct. falling on a Monday and SW's Euston Street address.
² Not preserved: evidently another letter from Wait concerning the negotiations to secure permission for SW to publish selections from the Fitzwilliam collection.   ³ 6 Oct.

---

¹ The date of this letter, discussing the continuing negotiations for the granting of permission for SW to transcribe and publish selections from the Fitzwilliam collection, is given by SW's 'Sunday' and its subject matter (see n. 6).
² Not preserved: evidently a draft of a letter from SW to the Vice Chancellor, proposing that SW be granted permission to publish music from the Fitzwilliam collection.
³ i.e. the Vice Chancellor (see n. 5).

looks somewhat arrogant, & making him pay for asking him a Favour is a sort of Solecism the other Way.—Perhaps all Letters to such a Personages go free—you & I are aukward at aristocratical Calculations.[4]

If you could get me a Frank without real Inconvenience I wish you would.—I shall try, too, but two Applications have (arithmetically) a double Chance to one.

At all events write.—If Wait should be displeased at my boarding the Vice[5] sans Ceremonie, I can't help it:[6] I think quite with you that it is the most honest Way, & if I read the Character of the Chancellor rightly, he will prefer Openness of Conduct. I never liked the contrary, tho' Rascals sometimes force one to it se defendendo.[7]

Adieu in Haste

SW

Sunday *9 o'clock*

Going to Church loik a coot Poy.

To Vincent Novello — Euston Street, [10 October 1825][1]

ALS, 1 p. (BL, Add. MS 11729, fo. 292)
Addressed To | Mr Novello | Shacklewell Green | near | Kingsland | Monday Night
Pmk 11 OC

Dear N

Wait accedes to my addressing the Vice Chancellor, but particularly wishes you to signify to your Friend Dampier[2] that you mean to relinquish some Part of the

---

[4] There was an elaborate etiquette, alluded to here, concerning the dispatch of letters, and in particular whether the sender should or should not prepay postage. SW's proposed solution of sending the letter under a frank (the privilege of free postage extended to members of Parliament and certain others in public office) would have neatly side-stepped the problem. SW also alludes to the practice whereby letters to and from the King went free. The franking privilege was much abused and parliamentary franking was abolished in 1840, with severe restrictions on official franking. It is not clear how SW or Novello could have obtained a frank (Howard Robinson, *The British Post Office: A History* (Princeton, 1948), 113–19).

[5] Thomas Le Blanc (1773/4–1843), Vice Chancellor 1824–5.

[6] SW had evidently written to Wait with his suggestion that he should approach the Vice Chancellor direct. He had not at this stage received Wait's reply, but had discussed the matter with Novello, and they had both agreed that this would be an appropriate course of action, with or without Wait's approval. Wait's reply, concurring with this view, arrived on 10 Oct., the following day, and is referred to in SW's letter to Novello of this date.   [7] 'In self-defence'.

[1] The date is given by SW's 'Monday night' and the postmark.

[2] John Lucius Dampier (1793–1853) of King's College, matric. 1812, BA (1816), Fellow (1815), MA (1819), called to the Bar 1819; later Recorder of Portsmouth (1837–8) (Venn). A letter of 18 Jan. 1825 from

Selections to me: or in other Words that you are perfectly willing for me to transcribe from such Authors as are not within the Sphere of your own Plan to edite.[3]

I trust that you will not object to this.—I start To-morrow Morning for Winchester, but have previously finished my Work with Horsley.—I have lent the MS. to my Friend De la Fite, who has promised to convey it to you at Miss Campbell's[4] on Friday[5] about 1 o'Clock, which I named as a likely Time for the Messenger to find you, & deliver it into your Hand.

> Adieu,
> Yours always truly
>> SW

P.S. I hope to return the latter End of next Week.[6]
Pray write to me directly at the Post Office, Winchester.—I shall receive the letter on Wed^y Morning.—Wait's Letter to me was very kind & encouraging, & expressive of a firm Belief that my Point at Cambridge will be carried without any material Opposition.

To Vincent Novello   Euston Street, 24 [October 1825][1]

AN, 1 p. (BL, Add. MS 11729, fo. 232)

> Euston Street
> Monday Night 24th

Dear N

I this day received the enclosed,[2] & you will find that much depends upon you whether I can or cannot be the better for my Visits to Cambridge: I have no doubt that Wait states accurately the real Fact, & your Mode of considering it must determine my Plan of Operations or necessitate me to give up the Thoughts of operating at all.

---

him to Novello concerning Novello's cataloguing of the Fitzwilliam collection is in the Novello–Cowden Clarke Collection, Brotherton Collection, University of Leeds.

[3] This paragraph summarizes part of the content of the letter from Wait (not preserved) which SW was impatiently awaiting at the time of writing to Novello the previous day.

[4] Not identified: presumably a pupil of Novello's, whom Novello was to teach at her house at the day and time mentioned.   [5] 14 Oct.

[6] SW left Winchester on Friday 21 Oct. He travelled via Bagshot, where he met his friend Pug and visited Windsor Castle with him. After an overnight stay in Windsor he completed his journey to London on the following day (SW to Sarah Suter, 20 Oct. [1825] (BL, Add. MS 35012, fo. 59)).

[1] The month and year are given by SW's 'Monday 24' and the contents.

[2] Presumably a letter from Wait (not preserved) detailing the progress of the negotiations, and stating that permission would be likely to be forthcoming if Novello were to state that he had no objections to SW's proposals.

To Joseph Payne Street   [Euston Street], 30 October [1825][1]

ALS, 1 p. (Rylands)
Addressed To | Mr J. Street | Mansion House Place | N 3.
Pmk 31 OC 1825

Euston Street
Sunday 30 Oct^r

My dear Sir

I know of Nothing at present likely to prevent my meeting yourself and Mr Lewis[2] on the Vigil of Lord Mayor's Day[3] which I *guess* & *calculate* will happen on Tuesday the 8th of November instant, and when I shall endeavour to be at George's Coffee House[4] punctually at 5, remaining

> Dear Sir
> most sincerely Yours
> S Wesley

To Vincent Novello   Euston Street, 23 November [1825][1]

ALS, 3 pp. (BL, Add. MS 11729, fo. 294)
Addressed To | Mr Novello | Shacklewell Green | near | Kingsland | Wednesday Evening
Pmk 24 NO 1825

Euston Street
Wednesday Nov. 23.

Dear N

I hope by this Time you are become *convalescent*: however I have always thought that your utter Aversion from *all* Medicine was an extreme; & all Extremes (except of good, which seldom happens) are **unphilosophical**, you know.

I am puzzled to account for the very long Silence of Dr Wait: there is certainly an Ambiguity in the Negotiation very repugnant to the Spirit of a Man who feels

---

[1] The year is given by the postmark.   [2] Not identified.

[3] As SW surmised Lord Magor's day was on 9 Nov. For an account of the day's celebrations, see *The Times*, 10 Nov. 1825; for the significance of this annual event, see *Encylopaedia of London*, under 'Lord Mayor'.

[4] In the Strand, between Devereux Court and Essex Street, and a favourite haunt of wits and men of letters (*Encyclopaedia of London*).

[1] The year is given by the postmark.

acting de bonne Foi, which I do not flatter myself in saying that I do, & always will, while I have any Sense of right & wrong remaining.

It were, I own, somewhat vexatious after copying 100 Pages of MS. & waived Engagements of Importance during the Time, to be denied all Advantage resulting from the Labour; & I certainly shall be much gratified, if through the Interposition & Influence of your friend Mr Dampier, the original Intention may be carried into Effect.

Any Thing in the shape of Incivility or Disrespect to Dr W. I would studiously avoid, but really when Bread & Cheese are necessary (the former especially) the Means of providing it are neither to be neglected nor trifled with, & had I not fully relied on making much Progress in my Transcript long before now, I never would have engaged in the Speculation, by which it appears that *hitherto* I have been only prostituting Time.

I therefore leave to yourself & Mr Dampier the Mode which may seem most advisable to prevent an utter (& necessary) Dereliction of a Plan which lately promised so fair a Prospect, but which, if ultimately defeated, will be only one among the many cross Accidents to which I am pretty much habituated, & can tolerate without much mental Perturbation.

I have been a little surprized (after what your Friend[2] said to me at one of your classical Concerts) that there should have appeared a Difficulty to obtain Insertion of my Commentary upon Mr Horsley's Panegyric: however, when expecting to see it in the Novr Number of the London Magazine,[3] my Friends were baulked of their Sport; & upon Application to Mr Clarke, it seems that he had remonstrated with the Editor on the Subject, without Success, or even Apology.—

This appears so totally different from the paramount Authority which I understood from you that Mr C. possessed in the Publication, <that> the Omission, & Silence of the Editor are, I confess, to me demonstrative that his Influence is by no means omnipotent in that Quarter; & when Mr C. informed me that he had written three Times to this same Editor, whoever he may be, (for Mr C. says he conceals his Name)[4] I am much inclined to suspect that he has no due Veneration for the Behests of your Friend.

Yours always truly

S Wesley

---

[2] No doubt Charles Cowden Clarke.

[3] For the *London Magazine* and Clarke's connections with it, see SW to Novello, 14 Sept. [1825], n. 5.

[4] He was in fact Henry Southern (1799–1853), editor from around Nov. 1824 to July 1828 (*DNB*; Sullivan, *TRA* 288–96).

To Vincent Novello   [Euston Street], 12 December [1825]¹

ALS, 2 pp. (BL, Add. MS 11729, fo. 298)
Addressed Monday Evening | To | Mr Novello | Shacklewell Green | near | Kingsland
Pmk 13 DE 1825

Euston Street
12th of Dec^r

Dear N

Do you feel any Objection to declare in writing that your Intention is to transcribe & publish from the Fitzwilliam Compositions of the Italian masters *only*, & that a Selection from those of any other School remains open to any other Individual who shall obtain a Grace for the Purpose?²

It seems that a few Words confirming such a Determination will remove all Obstacle to the Attainment of my Object, to which you have always hitherto professed to be cordially favourable.

I am preparing for your next Evening, parts for the Chorus 'Magna Opera Domini', which I will further to you in due Time.³—

Adieu sans adieu
Y^{rs} always truly

S Wesley

P.S. I guess that had you been at all aware that so simple & harmless a Document would have been my infallible Passport to the Library, you would have transmitted one, Months ago.

Why will People not be explicit & strait forward at first? How much Time might thereby have been saved!

---

¹ The year is given by a just legible postmark and is confirmed by SW's Euston Street address and the content.

² Novello made this declaration in his Preface to *The Fitzwilliam Music*, dated December 1825. The negotiations over the Fitzwilliam music appear to have occasioned a quarrel between SW and Novello, and a cessation of their correspondence from the end of 1825: see Biographical Introduction. SW and Novello appear to have resolved their differences and to have resumed contact in May 1830: see SW to Novello, 10 June 1830.

³ From the *Confitebor*, to be performed at the next concert of the Classical Harmonists on 5 Jan. 1826.

To Vincent Novello [Euston Street], 29 December 1825

ALS, 1 p. (BL, Add. MS 11729, fo. 300)
Addressed To | Mr Novello | Shacklewell Green | near | Kingsland

Thursday Decr 29. 1825

Dear N

This is the first Moment I could secure for noticing your last (& for which I thank you): I presume that you intend to muster on Thursday next[1] (selon la Regle)[2] & I have therefore provided Parts for the Chorus 'Magna Opera', which accompany this: I think you said that Duplicates of each would be sufficient for the present State of your Orchestra.

I am not sure whether I mentioned to you a Lad[3] who has a good soprano Voice, & whose Father has committed him to my musical Care for *3 years*!—(the Climacteric,[4] if I live to reach it). I think to bring him with me on Thursday: he sings as yet principally by Ear, but can get through 2 or 3 Songs (& among them 'Angels ever bright')[5] sufficiently well to evince a Capability of high Improvement.

Mr Burgh (with whom I dined on Xtmas Day) informed me that you pleaded Indisposition for waiving his Invitation altogether. This was no very welcome News to your old Playfellow.

S Wesley

To [?John Eames][1] Euston Street, 23 January 1826

ALS, 1 p. (Rylands, DDWF 15/31)

Euston Street
Euston Square
Monday Jany 23. 1826

Sir

I hasten to acquaint you that several of my Friends and those of my young Pupil[2] feel particularly desirous that he may be permitted to sing twice in the

---

[1] 5 Jan. 1826: the meeting of the Classical Harmonists.   [2] 'According to the rule'.
[3] Presumably Thomas Francis (1812–87): see SW to Sarah Wesley, 29 May 1826 (Rylands, DDWF 15/34) and 14 June [1826], below.
[4] i.e. his sixty-third year, thought to be a critical time in life. SW would reach this milestone in Feb. 1828.   [5] A popular aria from Handel's *Theodora* (1750).

[1] The most likely recipient of this letter, concerning a forthcoming concert of the Choral Fund, is John Eames, the organization's Secretary and Collector.
[2] Francis: see previous letter.

Course of the Concert on the 6ᵗʰ Inst.³ and I know that there are Parties forming in various Directions for the Purpose of hearing him, and in Expectation of *two* Songs.—You will therefore oblige me by stating this Circumstance to the Committee, with my Respects, adding that I shall feel no Objection whatever to give an extemporaneous Piece upon the Organ on the same Evening.⁴

I remain
Sir,
obediently yours
　S Wesley

To Charles Wesley Junior　　　　　[Euston Street, 2 February 1826]¹

ALS, 1 p. (Rylands, DDWes 6/46)
Addressed　To | Charles Wesley | New Street | Dorset Square | New Road | No 1 |
　Thursday Morning
Pmk　2 FE 1826

Dear Charles
Here are two Tickets—² the Committee have behaved as Committees always do, pitifully and shabbily, having only sent me *Four* in all.—Each of the Tickets will admit two Persons into the Pit.—I hope you will make up your Mind to go, and that *as soon as possible*, because if you resolve *not* to go, I must request you to send me the Tickets back.

Yours sincerely
(and in much Haste)
　S Wesley

---

³ The Choral Fund's Annual Concert at the English Opera House on 6 Feb., conducted by Greatorex and led by Francis Cramer.
⁴ The advertisement for the concert (*The Times*, 3 Feb. 1826) announced that 'a young gentleman, a pupil of Mr S. Wesley' would sing, and that SW would give an extempore performance between the acts.

---

¹ The date is given by the postmark.　　　² No doubt for the Choral Fund concert on 6 Feb.

To Robert Glenn   Euston Street, 4 April 1826

ALS, 1 p (BL, Add. MS 35013, fo. 84)
Addressed To | Robert Glenn Esqre | Kirby Street | Hatton Garden | Tuesday Morning
Tuesday
April 4. 1826

My dear Sir

I returned Yesterday from Cambridge[1] whereat I have been very busily, but very pleasantly employed, having met the most flattering Encouragement towards my intended Publication of Wm Byrde's excellent Antiphones.[2]

I am very anxious to know how Mr Lawrence[3] gets on with his Transcript of the choral Parts.[4]—Not a Moment can be thrown away in Preparation for the 4th Inst. & I hope that Mr L. will name an early Day for assembling such of his Friends as have favoured me with the Promise of their Aid.

In Haste
I remain, Dr Sir
always truly yours
S W

---

[1] SW's long negotiations with the University of Cambridge had finally borne fruit on 1 Mar., when the Senate granted him a Grace to publish selections from the Fitzwilliam collection. He had set off for Cambridge on 27 Mar.

[2] Either during this or on his visit to Cambridge the previous summer, SW had transcribed fifteen antiphons from William Byrd's *Gradualia* (2 vols., 1605–7) from an 18th-cent. manuscript copy in score in the Fitzwilliam collection, with the intention of publishing them by subscription. Proposals were issued, names of subscribers were collected, and nine sheets of plates were engraved, but the project came to nothing. Further details of this abortive project are given in SW to Street, 25 May 1830.

[3] Not identified, but evidently a choral singer and a music copyist. A 'Mr Lawrence' and 'Mr Lawrence junior' were subscribers to SW's Service.

[4] Of the *Confitebor*, for the forthcoming performance on 4 May.

To Sir George Smart[1]   Euston Street, 13 April [1826][2]

ALS, 1 p. (LC, Hales Autograph Collection, i. 29)
Addressed To Sir G. Smart | 91 | Gᵗ Portland Street
Docketed by Smart: ansᵈ April 13 Per Copy

Dear Sir

I find that as I should not require the Services of your Pupils till the second Act,[3] and at a Time when their Performance at the Theatre[4] will have concluded, I presume that there will remain no Objection to my announcing them: I shall be much obliged by an immediate Line upon the Subject, as I am scolded by my Friends in all Quarters that my Advertisements are not in greater Forwardness.

I am
Dʳ Sir
Yours obediently
S Wesley

Euston Street | Thursday. 13ᵗʰ of April

To Sarah Wesley   [Euston Street], 27 April [1826][1]

ALS, 3 pp. (Rylands, DDWF 15/33)

Thursday Evening
27ᵗʰ of April

Dear Sarah

Your Hint is very friendly, and I accept it as such, but you have been misinformed, for I have not the most remote Expectation of receiving one third of 300l.

---

[1] For Smart, see SW to Novello, 12 Jan. [1813], n. 4.

[2] The year is given by 13 Apr. falling on a Thursday, SW's Euston Street address, and the discussion of arrangements for the forthcoming performance of the *Confitebor*.

[3] i.e. the second part of SW's Argyll Rooms concert on 4 May, which was to consist of the first performance of the *Confitebor*. Smart's pupils were presumably boy trebles, who would have been engaged to sing in the chorus.

[4] Probably at Covent Garden, where Weber's *Oberon* was to be performed, and where Smart's pupils may have been employed in the chorus or as extras. Smart was a close friend and professional associate of Weber; during his final visit to London in 1826 Weber stayed at Smart's house in Great Portland Street, and died there on 5 June.

---

[1] The year is given by 27 Apr. falling on a Thursday and the content.

by my first intended Publication from the Fitzwilliam Library:[2] indeed I should consider even £*100*, a tolerable Sum, although I am convinced that Exertions will be made at the University (whereat I have made a very favourable Impression) to promote the Encouragement and Advancement of future Publications from those valuable MSS.

(You will of Course give up to me your Author of so vague & silly a Report.— an avowed Enemy is (9 times out of 10) less mischievous than an imprudent Friend.)

I will write to Lord Pomfret[3] as soon as I have concluded this.—I know not how far the Earl's Generosity may extend towards me in the present Business, but Sam tells me that once at Xtmas he threw down half a Crown among four Boys, with this appropriate observation—'Boys, you see I like to be liberal.'—

However, his Influence may be serviceable, & you may tell Charles that he need not fear my Deficiency in the Etiquette which I perfectly well know that titled Men expect & insist on, and *that*, generally in an augmented Ratio of their *Demerit*.

You know I preach Sermons on Fridays among great Lords and Ladies,[4] and therefore am serving my Time to the proprieties of Ps and Qs.

I am sorely besieged on all Sides, touching Preparations for next Thursday,[5] and as the appointed Period approaches nearer & nearer every Hour, the Pressure of Bustle increases in a perplexing Proportion.

Remember me kindly to Charles, & tell him I wish to have his Glee 'Arno's Vale'[6] copied out as soon as possible, and *it must be very legibly & neatly*.

Y[rs] in g[t] Haste

SW

[2] SW's projected edition of Byrd.

[3] Thomas George Fermor (1768–1830), 3rd Earl of Pomfret.

[4] A reference to the course of six lectures that SW was currently giving on Fridays at the Royal Institution. The first lecture had been on 14 Apr. (*Harmonicon*, 4 (1826), 94); Royal Institution records.

[5] 4 May: SW's concert.

[6] SW's request was doubtless connected with a projected performance at one of his Royal Institution lectures: in a letter of 4 July 1827 to Miss Spence (Gloucester), SW's brother Charles remarked that this glee had been performed there by SW.

To Domenico Dragonetti[1]   Euston Street, [4 May 1826][2]

ANS, 1 p. (BL, Add. MS 56411, fo. 18)
Addressed To | —Dragonetti | La Sabloniere Hotel | Leicester Square
Pmk 4 MY 1826

Dear Sir

I hope & trust that you will favour me with your invaluable Assistance this Evening, otherwise my *Confitebor*, the new piece, will lose a very material Part of good Effect.

   I am
   D[r] Sir
   Very truly yours
     S Wesley

To Sarah Wesley   Euston Street, 10 June [1826][1]

Source *WBRR* 3 (1851), 452 (incomplete?)

                             Euston Street
                            Saturday June 10th

Dear Sarah

Here is the song you signified your wish to have.[2] I think you said it is a piece of Sir John Suckling;[3] but not being sure that I did not dream this, instead of hearing it, I abstained from affixing it.

I have offered to play the 'Requiem' for poor Von Weber on Friday next, at Moorfields Chapel;[4] but I shall be neither surprised or disappointed, if, through the jealousy of S——[5] and A——,[6] my civility be refused. Nothing *now* is a matter of wonderment to me but when people do right.

---

[1] The double-bass virtuoso Domenico Dragonetti (1763–1846), who had settled in London in 1794. He was the leading double-bass player of his time, renowned for his performances with the cellist Robert Lindley. The Sablonière Hotel in Leicester Square was his home from 1821 to 1840 (Fiona Palmer, *Domenico Dragonetti in England (1794-1846): The Career of a Double Bass Virtuoso* (Oxford, 1997), 27-9.

[2] The date is given by the postmark.

[1] The year is given by the reference to Weber's funeral (see n. 3).   [2] Not identified.

[3] Sir John Suckling (1609-42), English poet.

[4] 16 June. Weber had died on 5 June 1826; the funeral eventually took place at St Mary, Moorfields, one of London's principal Roman Catholic chapels, on 21 June. For details of Weber's death and funeral, see Warrack, 361-3; David Reynolds (ed.), *Weber in London 1826* (1976), 43-5.   [5] Smart.

[6] Attwood; he played the organ at Weber's funeral.

To Sarah Wesley   Euston Street, 14 June [1826][1]

ALS, 4 pp. (Rylands, DDWF 6/38)

Euston Street
Wed[y] 14th of June

Dear Sarah

I have not the slightest Objection to appropriate whatever Subscription you may gain for my Publication[2] to the lessening M[rs] B's[3] Demand: I know not now how much they have made it among them but I nothing doubt that 25 per cent Interest at least has been clapped upon it very long ago.—

I pity the Claimant[4] very cordially, but there is not much excuse for those two *base Legitimates*,[5] who refused to assist when *they* could, and when they well knew their Father could not—and why:—because their beloved Mother had thought proper to ruin him!

Ask worthy M[rs] Ball[6] of Duke Street Grosvenor Square a little about the several Sums I was robbed of by M[rs] W's Tradesmen, which sank every Penny I had in the Bank, *to begin with*! Were I wantonly to neglect, (much less to oppress or defraud) either the Widow or the Fatherless, I think I should happen to be the first of my Family who ever did so.

Allen's[7] Robbery of Charles I take special Care to circulate: he will lose many a 50 Pound Note by his Prank: but he has an infamous Name for every Thing but voicing the Reed Stops of an Organ.—What an enviable Reputation!

I am already under pecuniary Obligation to my excellent Friends Drummer & Street; which are the only two Sources I could at present think of: were it otherwise, I would cheerfully apply to them & send you the Money.

---

[1] The year is given by SW's reference to Weber's funeral.   [2] Of the Byrd antiphons.

[3] The wife of SW's former wine merchant Charles Bond, to whom SW owed a large amount, and whose bankruptcy was announced in *The Times*, 13 Dec. 1824. For other mentions of Bond, see SW to Sarah Suter, 3 August [1824] (BL, Add. MS 35012, fo. 51); SW to Sarah Wesley, 26 May 1826 (Dorset Record Office); Sarah Wesley to William Marriott, 27 May 1826 (Rylands, DDWF 14/52).

[4] Bond.   [5] Charles and John William, SW's sons by Charlotte.

[6] Presumably the wife of James Ball.

[7] The organ builder William Allen (*fl.* 1794–*c*.1826), who had evidently refused to pay Charles a commission which Charles considered his due. This was no doubt for the organ at Lincoln Cathedral, built by Allen in 1826 to SW's specification (Boeringer, i. 87–8; ii. 124–5). Almost two years later, Charles complained that Allen had refused to pay him the £60 commission due to him for recommending Allen to the Dean and Chapter (Charles Wesley jun. to Thomas Allan, 19 Apr. 1828 (Rylands, DDWes 6/75)).

I am glad Francis[8] sang out well.—He did not expect Money, neither do I:—I know that neither he nor his Father have any mauvaise Honte[9] upon that Subject; & I guess that he would not make any wry Faces at an effigy of our Sovereign Lord the King.—Do just as you like—but I w[d] never think of being paid for his singing any Song for Charles.—I think the Affair ought to rest entirely with M[r] Edmonds,[10] because it was *his*, not *your* Party, if I am rightly informed.

Hawes used always to get 3 Guineas at every Place where he sent my Sam, and always gave him afterwards, what?—not even Thanks.

But he has (God be praised) a pretty good Prospect of being able to scramble for a decent Livelihood himself, tho' in a Profession that I hate & despise.

I find that the musical Honours intended the German[11] are all superceded by Poynter, the popish Bishop,[12] who will not suffer more than 20 Performers in his Chapel at one Time, which is a Number much too inconsiderable to execute the Requiem of Mozart with proper Effect[13].—Poor Von Weber's Soul will not suffer much *in Purgatory* for the Omission, in the Opinion of yours truly (tho' in Haste, notwithstanding a long Scroll)

SW

Why do you spell the Word *Trifle* with a Brace of Fs?

To an unidentified recipient   Euston Street, 27 October 1826

ALS, 1 p. (Rylands, DDWF 15/35)

London, Euston Street, Euston Square
Oct. 27 1826

Sir

I have taken the Liberty to enclose the Prospectus of a musical Work,[1] now preparing for Publication, and which I trust will be found to prove a useful

---

[8] On 29 May, SW had written to his sister Sarah about another performance by Francis: 'I am glad that young Francis has entertained you & Charles—he certainly has a prime toned Voice, of which the most must be made *while it lasts*, & which I fear will be but for a short Season: if I had had him 3 Years ago, he would have sung me out of Debt long before To-day' (Rylands, DDWF 15/34). He was possibly Thomas Francis (1812–87), later an alto vicar-choral at St Paul's Cathedral (Brown and Stratton), and probably the 'young pupil' who had sung at the New Musical Fund concert on 6 Feb. (see SW to [?Eames], 23 Jan. 1826).   [9] 'False modesty'.
[10] Not identified: presumably a friend of Charles and Sarah.   [11] Weber.
[12] William Poynter, DD (1762–1827), Vicar Apostolic of the London District (*DNB*; Anstruther, iv. 222–3).
[13] This problem appears to have been solved: Mozart's *Requiem* was performed at Weber's funeral with full choral and instrumental forces.

[1] No doubt SW's projected Byrd edition.

Volume to all those who value and who study sound Church Composition: as such I can safely venture to recommend it, since the Name of the Author alone, is likely to excite Respect and Attention to any *genuine* Production of so learned a Pen.

I remain,
Sir,
very respectfully Yours
   S Wesley

To Eliza Tooth[1]   Euston Street, 31 October 1826

AL, third person, 2 pp. (Rylands, DDWes 6/22)

> Euston Street
> Euston Square
> Oct[r] 31. 1826

M[r] Samuel Wesley presents best Compliments to Miss Tooth, to whom he believes that his Sister has already communicated an Intention of publishing three curious MSS. of Handel, consisting of Hymn Tunes set to the Poetry of his Father, the late Rev[d] Charles Wesley, & also that the Fact is connected with some curious & interesting Circumstances.[2]

The said Tunes are eminently appropriate to congregational Singing, and having been composed in a beautifully simple Style, must speedily attract Notice & encourage general Zeal to join in them.

It seems therefore, that to render them universally useful, sufficient Publicity alone will be wanted, & that when once permanently established in the widely extended Wesleyan Connexion, they will be soon adopted by the numerous dissenting Congregations.

---

[1] Eliza (Elizabeth Telitha) Tooth (bapt. 1793–*ante* 1872) was one of two daughters of the builder Samuel Tooth, Steward of the Methodist Chapel in City Road, and a close friend of SW's parents. She and her sister Lydia were in their turn close friends of Sarah and Charles Wesley jun. She had much to do with the sorting and ordering of the family papers after their deaths and amassed a substantial collection on her own account (see Textual Introduction).

[2] On his visit to Cambridge in early Sept., SW had discovered in the Fitzwilliam collection the autograph manuscript of three hymn tunes by Handel, composed in the 1740s to words by his father (see SW to Sarah Suter, 13 Sept. 1826 (BL, Add. MS 35012, fo. 61)). Quickly realizing the commercial potential of this discovery, he took steps to have the hymns published.

S.W. moreover trusts, that in having fortunately obtained these valuable Relicks of Piety, he may prove in some Degree instrumental in assisting & increasing the Energies of vocal Devotion.

To Thomas Jackson[1] Euston Street, [8] November 1826[2]

ALS, 4 pp. (Rylands, DDWes 6/26).[3]
Editor's note Subsequently published with minor alterations and corrections in *WMM*, Dec. 1826, pp. 817–18 (see n. 3).

Euston Street
Euston Square. Nov[r] 1826

Rev[d] Sir,

I take the Liberty of addressing you upon a Subject which appears likely to prove both of Interest & Utility to the Wesleyan Connexion especially.[4]

Having been honoured by the University of Cambridge, with a Grace, empowering and authorizing me to transcribe and publish any Portions of the very valuable musical MSS. in the Library of the Fitzwilliam Museum, of which Privilege I have lately assiduously availed myself, I was very agreeably surprised at meeting with three Hymn Tunes, (most noble Melodies) composed by our great Handel (in his own Hand Writing) and set to Words of my good Father.—The first Hymn is

'Sinners obey the Gospel Word:'—

the second

'O love divine, how sweet thou art:'—

the third,

'Rejoice! the Lord is King.'—

---

[1] Thomas Jackson (1783–1873) began his long career as a Methodist minister as an itinerant preacher in Lincolnshire in 1804. From 1824 to 1842 he was Methodist Connexional Editor and editor of the Wesleyan Methodist Magazine. Among his large literary output was a substantial life of Charles Wesley (2 vols., 1841), an edition of Charles Wesley's Journals with selections from his poetry and letters (2 vols., 1849), and an edition of the works of John Wesley (14 vols., 1829–31). He was President of the Methodist Conference in 1838 and 1849 (*DNB*; Gordon Rupp, *Thomas Jackson, Methodist Patriarch* (1954)).

[2] This letter is undoubtedly the one referred to in the first paragraph of SW's letter to Eliza Tooth of the same date (below).

[3] This letter, apparently addressed to Jackson privately and not originally intended for publication, appeared with slight alterations and corrections in *WMM*, Dec. 1826, pp. 817–18, where it was accompanied by a note by Sarah on the background to the hymns. Both are reproduced in Burrows, 11.

[4] As the next letter makes clear, SW's approach to Jackson had been suggested by Tooth. SW was much encouraged by Jackson's reply (not preserved), and remarked in his letter of 13 Nov. to his sister Sarah that it was 'a Proof that the Cause of the Hymns will not be languid among the Society'.

Stanzas well known for many long Years to veteran Members in the Society, and to be found in all the Editions of the Hymns.[5]

You well know, Sir, that the Order of Verse in the 1st Hymn is, four Lines of eight Syllables in each Strophe: that of the 2d Hymn, six Lines in each Strophe; (four of eight Syllables, and the latter two, of six) and that of the 3d, six Lines also in each Strophe; the former four consisting of six Syllables, the two latter, of eight.

Hence it follows that the said Melodies are correctly applicable to every hymn in any of the three Metres above described; and consequently will be a valuable Acquisition in all Congregations where similar Metres are in use.

The style of the music is alike simple, solemn, and easy of Execution to all who can sing or play a plain Psalm Tune: therefore it were a culpable Neglect, to withhold from Publicity, articles so appropriate to the Purpose of choral congregational Devotion.

With full Persuasion of this Truth, I have resolved to print forthwith these combined Relicks of a real Poet and a great Musician; hoping and trusting that what will probably appear to giddy Thinkers, a merely fortuitous Coincidence (but which I firmly believe to be the result of a much higher Causality) will be ultimately effective of much good, by the Unition of what delights the Ear with that which benefits the Soul.

The Plates are already engraven, and the three Hymns will be inscribed to the Wesleyan Society.

That the Son of Charles, and the Nephew of John Wesley happened to be the first Individual lighting upon this MS. (after a Lapse of 80 or 90 Years at least)[6] is certainly a Circumstance of no common Curiosity; and if the Statement I have made be considered of sufficient Consequence to engage your attention to a publication, slight, *only in price,*[7] I cannot reasonably doubt, that Abundance of good, to the best of Causes, will accrue.

*The Tunes are comprized in three Pages.

Permit me to subscribe myself, Reverend Sir,
Very respectfully yours,

S Wesley

---

[5] All three hymns were included in *A Collection of Hymns for the Use of the People called Methodists* (1780; frequently reprinted), the standard Methodist hymnbook of the time. They also appeared, set to tunes by J. F. Lampe, in Lampe's *Hymns on the Great Festivals* (1746), and it was undoubtedly from this source that they became known to Handel (Burrows, 5).

[6] In fact, rather less. The printed version in *WMM* has 'a lapse of seventy or eighty years', a correction made no doubt by Jackson. Handel composed the tunes in the late 1740s, almost certainly in 1746: see Burrows, who establishes that they post-date the publication of Lampe's collection, and are on paper of a type used regularly by Handel only in 1746–7. [7] The first edition cost 1*s*. 6*d*.

To [Eliza Tooth]¹ Euston Street, 8 November 1826

ALS, 3 pp. (Rylands, DDWes 6/64)

Euston Street
Euston Square
Wednesday Evening, Nov 8. 1826

Dear Madam,

It is only within two Hours that I received the Favour of your *former* Notice of my Note,² and I hasten to return my most cordial Acknowledgements of the very energetic Interest which you so kindly manifest in Regard of my Publication.— I wrote, according to your Wish, to the Rev^d Mr Jackson, who has probably received my Letter at least 6 Hours before the present Pleasure I feel in thanking you for yours.

Mr Jackson the Artist, of Newman Street,³ is very desirous to promote the Success of the Hymns: in the last Letter I wrote to him (in Consequence of the Identity of the Name) I hinted the Supposition that he and the Rev^d were Relatives, which I presume to be true, since he did not signify the contrary to me in his Reply.⁴

I wish that the whole Society may be convinced, that I never felt so truly gratified from my Knowledge of Music, as when I discovered this most unexpected (and I trust generally important) Coincidence: and I cannot anticipate a greater musical Gratification (No! not even at your York or Birmingham Festivals) than that of hearing chaunted by a thousand Voices, and in the strains of Handel, 'Rejoice, the Lord is King'!

I wait for a Line from Mr Jackson,⁵ which will fix my Decision respecting a Title Page: indeed this is all that is now necessary concerning *the actual Execution of the Work*, because the Plates are finished, and 500 Copies can be struck off even in a few Days: therefore Copies might begin to be circulated, before any public Annunciation in Print: nevertheless, this latter is certainly of the utmost Consequence, as we wish 'the Sound to go out into all Lands'⁶ where the Gospel shall find its Way.

---

¹ Although this letter does not bear the name of the addressee, it is evidently to Eliza Tooth.

² Tooth's reply (not preserved) to SW's letter of 31 Oct., which evidently contained a suggestion that SW should write to Jackson.

³ John Jackson, RA (1778–1831), a Wesleyan Methodist who executed the portraits in *WMM*. His portrait of SW, painted at around this time, is in the National Portrait Gallery and appears as the frontispiece to this volume. He lived at 7 Newman Street.

⁴ SW was mistaken in his conjecture: the two Jacksons were not related. Neither SW's letter nor Jackson's reply is preserved.

⁵ i.e. John Jackson, whom SW may have consulted over the design of the title page.

⁶ Romans 10: 18, a text well known to musicians from its inclusion in *Messiah*.

I have to apologise for not having sooner replied to yours of the 4th Instant,⁷ but the above true Statement of the Fact will I think exonerate me from the Charge of ungrateful Inattention; therefore believe me what I really am,

Dear Madam,
With much esteem,
Your truly obliged & devoted Servant
   S Wesley

To John George Emett[1]   Euston Street, 23 November [1826][2]

ALS, 2 pp. (BL, Add. MS 35013, fo. 90)
Addressed To | Mr Emett | Organist | Ebury Terrace | Pimlico | N. 8.
Watermark 1825

Euston Street
Thursday 23^d of Nov^r

Dear Sir

As you were so kind as to promise me the Procuration of a Frank[3] upon any special Occasion, I avail myself of the Privilege by requesting the Favour of one for Monday next, 27th Inst. with the following Direction

Sir James Gardiner Bart.
Roche Court
Fairham
Hants

I have perused Forkel's Life of Sebⁿ Bach with some Satisfaction.—Too much Panegyric can hardly be lavished upon a Genius of such Universality of Style as

---

⁷ Evidently a second letter from Tooth; not preserved.

¹ John George (or George John) Emett, blind organist, Bach enthusiast, and collector of music. He was organist of St Michael, Crooked Lane (1826–30) and of St Mary Magdalen, Bermondsey (1830–47). He owned the incomplete 'London' autograph of Book I of Bach's '48' (now BL, Add. MS 35021), which he purchased at the sale of Clementi's effects in 1832. It was later owned by Emett's daughter, a close friend of Eliza Wesley; she bequeathed it to Eliza, who in her turn bequeathed it to the British Museum (see Walter Emery, 'The London Autograph of "The Forty-Eight"', *ML* 34 (1953), 106–23.

² The year of this letter is given by 23 Nov. falling on a Thursday and the 1825 watermark. It has hitherto been dated 1820 (see Lightwood, 187–8; Walter Emery, 'The English Translator of Forkel', *ML* 28 (1947), 301–2).

³ For franks, see SW to Novello, [9 Oct. 1825], n. 4. SW may have wanted one to write to tell Gardiner about the impending publication of the Handel hymns, but it is not clear how Emett could have procured one for him.

his Compositions every where evince, but Mr Kollmann's English is a grievous Disparagement of his Subject.[4]—His Sentences are always clumsy, and full often nearly unintelligible, from his close Adherence to the tiresome Pleonasm and Pedantry of Style in which the German Prose always abounds: and Forkel himself is not a little dogmatic & pedantic; sometimes running point blank contrary to the real Matter of Fact: for Instance, where he asserts such a gross and impudent Falsity, as that 'Handel's Melodies will not remain in Remembrance like those of Bach'[5]—the contrary is the direct Truth, and I boldly maintain that when we affirm the Melodies of the latter to be *as good* as those of Handel we bestow high Praise upon Bach.—

The constantly fine Melody which pervades the Choruses of Handel are a self evident Confutation of Dr Forkel's audacious Ignorance, and old Kollman[6] (who is well acquainted with Handel's Music) ought to blush at inserting such libellous Nonsense in a Work containing so many interesting Memoirs of the Prince of Harmonists.

The first Time you happen to travel my Way and will take your Chance of finding me within I need not say that your Company will be thoroughly welcome to

Dear Sir
Yours faithfully
S Wesley

To John Jackson   Euston Street, 29 November [1826][1]

ALS, 1 p. (NYPL (Berg))
Addressed J. Jackson Esqre | Newman Street

Euston Street
Wednesday 29th Nov.

My dear Sir
At last I have obtained a few Copies of the Hymns, which would have reached you several Days ago, had the Engraver performed his Promise; I must however

---

[4] It has hitherto been assumed that SW's reference is to the translation of Forkel's *Life of Bach* published by Boosey in 1820, and has been taken to establish that the translator was A. F. C. Kollmann. The redating of this letter to 1826 and a comparison of the style of the Boosey translation with other writings known to be by Kollman call this assumption into question: see Michael Kassler, 'The English Translations of Forkel's Life of Bach', in Michael Kassler (ed.), *The English Bach Awakening: From its Beginnings to 1837* (Aldershot, forthcoming).

[5] As Kassler points out, this phrase does not appear in the 1820 translation.

[6] i.e. A. F. C. Kollmann, as opposed to his son George Augustus Kollman.

[1] The year is given by 29 Nov. falling on a Wednesday and SW's Euston Street address.

in Justice own that they are very well brought out, without a single wrong Note, which is a Circumstance of rare Occurrence even in so brief a Work as the present.

> I remain
> Dear Sir
> faithfully Yours
> > S Wesley

To Thomas Jackson [Euston Street], 19 December 1826

ALS, 1 p. (Rylands, DDWes 6/27)
Addressed Revd Thomas Jackson

Tuesday Decr 19. 1826

Dear Sir,

I trust that you will pardon a short Trespass on your Time, concerning the Circulation of the three Tunes, which begin already to be pretty generally mentioned among Persons of various Denominations, wholly disjunct from the Methodist Connexion. Mr Kershaw[1] informs me that their Publication is as yet scarcely known, and that as early Notice as may be, *ought* to be given of the Fact.— I therefore conceive that the Hymns should be announced in your Magazine of the approaching Month, and new Year;[2] at the same Time I wish that the Slip I enclose may be added, relative to the Work of which I take the Liberty to forward one of the Proposals.[3]—I remain

> Dear Sir
> Very respectfully & sincerely
> Yours
> > S Wesley

P.S. I feel justly ashamed of not sending you a Copy of the Hymns sooner.

---

[1] The Revd John Kershaw (1766–1855), steward of the Methodist Book-Room and manager of the Methodist Printing House from 1823 to 1827. His career as a Methodist itinerant minister lasted for sixty-seven years and included periods in the north of England, in Scotland, and in large cities in the north of England and the Midlands. After his period as book steward he completed four further circuits in the south of England before retiring to Boston, Linconshire, in 1837 (*DEB*).

[2] The advertisement for the hymns appeared on the wrapper of the Jan. 1827 number of *WMM* and is quoted in Lightwood, 198.

[3] No copies of either the 'slip' (presumably an advertising insert) or the proposal have been preserved; both were presumably for SW's projected Byrd edition.

To Thomas Roberts[1]   Euston Street, 6 January 1827

ALS, 1 p. (Cheshire Record Office, D 5424)
Addressed To | Thomas Roberts Esqre
Endorsed Mr Saml Wesley | Jany 6th 1827

London. Euston Street.
Euston Square.
Saturday Jan 6th 1827.

Dear Sir

I beg you to accept my very cordial Thanks for your most friendly Letter,[2] as also for the excellent Print of my revered Uncle, which has been punctually forwarded to me, and is at this Moment in its right Position;—properly framed & glazed.

You probably have read in the Newspapers[3] (if not in the Methodists' Magazine for the present Month)[4] that the three Hymns are now universally attainable, & I have taken the Liberty to hope for your Acceptance of one Copy as a very trifling Testimony of sincere Respect from the Editor.

It is not a little gratifying to me, that the Sentiments expressed in my Letter which was published[5] (totally without any Intention of mine) have gained your Approval.—

They were as sincere as those with which I subscribe myself,

Dear Sir,
Very gratefully & faithfully yours
  S Wesley

---

[1] Thomas Roberts (1765/6–1832) was a Bristol-based Methodist itinerant preacher, active from around 1786 to his death. His friendship with the Wesley family and his interest in Methodist hymnody was of long standing: in a letter of 20 Apr. 1808 (Drew) addressed to him in Bristol, SW's mother thanked him for the interest he had taken in 'the hymns in manuscript' and stated that if he considered that another volume might be made out of those in his possession and the Methodist conference was of the opinion that they might be of use, she would 'willingly acquiesce' in his selection.

[2] Not preserved.

[3] No newspaper announcement of the publication of the hymns has been found.

[4] i.e. in the Jan. 1827 number of *WMM*.

[5] SW's letter to Jackson of [8] Nov. 1826, published in the Dec. 1826 number of *WMM*.

To Thomas Jackson   Euston Street, 12 February 1827

ALS, 2 pp. (Rylands, DDWes 6/28)
Addressed To | The Revd Mr Jackson

Euston Street
Monday 12 Feb^y
1827

Dear Sir

Several Persons who are zealous in promoting the Success and Extension of the Psalmody throughout the Society, have suggested to me the Propriety and Advantage of publishing the three Tunes of Handel (which have already begun to circulate briskly) in Parts for 4 Voices, thereby rendering them perfectly commodious for Choirs, where they sing all in *Score*, instead of (as formerly) in *Unison*.—I have followed the Advice, and the Hymns are now in the Hands of the Engraver, who promises to produce the Plates with the utmost Expedition.[1]

It has also been rationally observed, that the little Work would be rendered more generally useful were *all* the Verses of each Hymn added under the Tunes;[2] and to this I have also assented, and with the more Readiness, inasmuch as I learn that the noble Hymn, 'Rejoice the Lord is King' has (by some unaccountable Negligence) been omitted in the latest Edition of the Hymns.[3]

I have only to add that I feel myself truly honoured in having proved the unexpected Medium of ushering into the religious World those sacred Strains so appropriate to the sublime Poesy of their Author, and remain

Dear Sir,
respectfully & faithfully yours,
    S Wesley

P.S. A large Assortment will be ready for Delivery on the first Day of March.

---

[1] The first edition of the Handel hymns included melody and bass parts only. The new four-part edition was published as *Three Hymns from the Fitzwilliam Library Arranged in Score for the Convenience of Choirs by Samuel Wesley.* SW's fair-copy MS of this arrangement is at RCM, MS 4025, fos. 42–5. Among those advising him to publish a four-part arrangement was evidently Thomas Roberts (see next letter).

[2] As SW notes, the first edition of the hymns gave the words of only the first verse of each hymn. The second edition also included the words of subsequent verses.

[3] i.e. the 1825 edition of *A Collection of Hymns for the Use of the People called Methodists.*

To Thomas Roberts · Euston Street, 8 March 1827

ALS, 1 p. (Cheshire Record Office, D 5424)
Addressed To | The Revd Thomas Roberts
Endorsed Mr Saml Wesley | March 8th 1827

London. Euston Street
March 8 1827.

Dear Sir

I embrace the earliest Opportunity afforded me of proving my ready Adoption of your prudent Advice, relative to a re-Publication of the three Handelian Hymns; a Copy of which I have now the Gratification to present you, ramified into a Score for 4 Voices, and which will therefore suit all Parties and silence all Objections which may have been started against the *general* Utility of the Tunes for choral Purposes.

I am in hourly Expectation to receive a Large Lot of new Copies, which I have urged my Printer to forward without a Moment's unnecessary Delay.

Believe me,
Dear Sir,
Your truly obliged,
and faithful Servant
S Wesley

To Robert Glenn · Euston Street, 15 June [1827]¹

ALS, 1 p. (BL, Add. MS 35013, fo. 78)
Addressed Friday Afternoon | To | Robt Glenn Esqre | Kirby Street | Hatton Garden

Euston Street
Friday 15 June

Dear Sir,

Sunday the 24th is fixed for the Debut of the new Organ at Somers Town Church,² therefore favour me with a Call *To-morrow Evening*, when we may

---

¹ The year is given by 15 June falling on a Friday and the reference to the opening of the new organ at Somers Town church (see n. 2).

² Somers Town Chapel, now known as St Mary the Virgin, Eversholt Street, was like Camden Chapel a new church built to accommodate the recent upsurge in population in the St Pancras parish following the large amount of new building there. Although consecrated on 11 May 1826, it was not fully

arrange all the vocal Preliminaries.—I expect my last Pupil to be with me at *6*, therefore *by 7* I shall be quite at your Service until Sunday Morning.

Yours always truly
    S Wesley

To [William Crotch]¹   Euston Street, 7 July 1827

ALS, 1 p. (NRO, MS 11244, T140A)

Euston Street
Euston Square
Saturday 7 July. 1827.

My dear Sir

I request your Acceptance of a few old-fashioned Bars,² framed expressly in the Style of those whom you term the 'Minority,' and with whom I am likely to continue to vote, maugre the fashionable Mania for operatical Adulteration of Church Descant.

I cannot help suspecting that some of the *later* Masses ascribed to Mozart & published by Novello, are Forgeries, being sorely unwilling to believe that such monotonous Puerilities could have emanated from such a Pen as his.³

I am,
Dear Sir,
always very faithfully yours
    S Wesley

completed until the following year. Its first organ, by John Gray, was a temporary instrument which was used for little more than a year until the permanent organ was completed. It is the inaugural recital for this second instrument that is under discussion here (*Survey of London*, xxiv. 122–3; Boeringer, ii. 329).

¹ Although lacking an address portion, there can be no doubt from the preservation of this letter among Crotch's papers that he was the recipient.

² Not certainly identified, but possibly SW's six-part setting of 'Tu es sacerdos', two autographs of which (RCM MSS 2141b, 4022) are dated 6 July 1827.

³ Novello published editions of seventeen Masses attributed to Mozart from 1819 on; their precise publication dates are not known. Of these, Nos. 7 (K. Anh. 233), 12 (K. Anh. 232), 13 (K. Anh. 235a), 16 (K. Anh. 185), and 17 (K. Anh. 237) are now thought to be doubtful or spurious (CPM; *Grove⁶*). SW may have been thinking in particular of the popular 'Twelfth Mass', K. Anh. 232.

To [William Hasledine Pepys][1]

Euston Street,
23 November 1827

ALS, 1 p. (Kassler)

Euston Street
Euston Square
Friday 23^d of Novr 1827.

Sir

In Reply to your Application upon the Subject of Lectures,[2] I request to state that I feel no Objection to repeat a Course of Lectures similar to that delivered at the Royal Institution last Season.[3]—It is to be observed that an Organ was employed, as well as a Piano Forte, and that vocal Assistance was also rendered in numerous Examples. Mori's[4] Violin was occasionally added. The Number of Lectures was *Eight*, and the Terms six Guineas per Lecture.

I am
Dear Sir,
respectfully yours
S Wesley

[1] There can be little doubt from the subject matter of this letter and the existence of other letters explicitly addressed to him that its addressee was William Hasledine Pepys (1776–1856), Secretary of the London Institution. He succeeded to his father's cutlery and surgical-instrument manufacturing business, which he appears to have extended to include the manufacture of scientific instruments. He was one of the original managers of the London Institution, FRS (1808) and Treasurer of the Geological Society (1812). He was a member of the Glee Club and a subscriber to SW's Service. For the London Institution, which was founded in 1805 and had premises at Finsbury Circus, see Bernard Becker, *Scientific London* (1874), 189–200.

[2] At a committee meeting on 8 Nov. Pepys had suggested that SW should lecture in the coming season. The proposal was referred to the Lecture Committee, where it was agreed, and Pepys requested to write to SW. SW's course was on vocal music and ran for six weeks at 1 p.m. on Tuesdays from 4 Mar. 1828 (London Institution papers (London, Guildhall Library, MS 3076), 3, 131; *A Descriptive Catalogue of the Lectures delivered at the London Institution . . . from 1819 . . . to . . . 1854*, 47; *GM* 1827[1], 161). The first lecture was attended by R. J. S. Stevens, who recorded that SW was 'a bad speaker, a bad accompanier too violent! He quoted Thomas *Aquinas*, and Hesiod; and introduced both Latin and Greek quotations occasionally' (R. J. S. Stevens, Diaries (Cambridge, Add. MS 9110)). The texts of some of these lectures are preserved at BL, Add. MSS 35014–15.

[3] SW had given a course of lectures at the Royal Institution earlier in 1827, starting on or before 2 Apr.; he had also lectured there in Apr.–May 1826 (Kassler, 'Lectures', 19).

[4] Nicolas Mori (1797–1839), English violinist, music publisher, and composer of Italian descent. A pupil of Barthélemon, he first appeared in public at a concert for his own benefit at the King's Theatre on 14 Mar. 1805, when he was billed as 'the Young Orpheus, Master Mori'. He later studied with Viotti for six years. He was one of the original associate members of the Philharmonic Society, and for many years from 1816 one of the principal leaders at its concerts. The *Harmonicon* in 1824 called him 'one of the finest violinists in Europe', and SW described him in his Reminiscences as 'unquestionably the first Leader of his Day'. In 1819 he married Elizabeth Lavenu, widow of the publisher Lewis Lavenu. (*Grove*[6]; Humphries and Smith; SW, Reminiscences).

To William Thomas Brande[1]   Euston Street, 10 December 1827

ALS, 1 p. (BL, Add. MS 56411, fo. 28)
Addressed To | W. J. Brande Esqre | Royal Institute | Albemarle Street | Tuesday
  Morning
Pmk 11 DE 1827

Euston Street
Monday Evening
Decr 10th 1827.

My dear Sir

I know not how to attempt any Excuse of my indefensible Delay of thanking you for your Letter dated Novr 17[2]—True it is however, that ever since I received it, a perplexing Pressure of multiform Engagements has precluded my due Attention to Correspondence in various Quarters—Concerning the Subject of yours, I have to State, that *at present*, I have no Design of parting with the Copy-Right of the Lectures in question[3] but should I form such a Resolution, be assured that I shall make a Point of conferring with you, previously to any Bargain elsewhere.

Believe me,
Dear Sir
most truly yours
  S Wesley

W. J. Brande Esqre

---

[1] William Thomas Brande (1788–1866), FRS (1809), chemist and editor of *A Dictionary of Science and Art* (1842). The son of an apothecary, he was Professor of Chemistry at the Royal Institution from 1813 to 1854, was closely associated with Davy and Faraday, and was one of the leading chemists of his day (*DNB*).   [2] Not preserved.
[3] SW's lectures remained unpublished. In 1831 Crotch published the texts of some of his own lectures as *Substance of Several Courses of Lectures on Music delivered in Oxford and the Metropolis*.

To William Hasledine Pepys

Euston Street,
19 December [1827]¹

ALS, 2 pp. (Fitzwilliam)

Euston Street.
Euston Square.
Wednesday 19ᵗʰ of Decʳ

Dear Sir

I think I can safely engage to provide Singers at *two* Guineas per Head; but certainly not for less.—Phillips (the Base) will not 'give Tongue' under *three*, I know; having lately negotiated with him upon a similar Business.—It does not seem at all necessary, that three or four Singers should be employed at every Lecture, especially if an Organ be hired, but nota benè, the Organ must remain stationary for the whole Season (I mean till the Termination of the Lectures) & I cannot yet send you the Amount of the Demand for the Hire, until I have *haggled* with some of the Builders *sur le Sujet.*—I pledge my Word to do the best, & proceed upon the most economical Plan possible.—You seem anxious for an exact Statement of the Sum total, but this you see to be impossible until I know the Charge for the Loan of an Organ, and at *how many* of the ten Lectures² vocal Music may be indispensable.

An early Line will much oblige

Dear Sir,
Yours respectfully
S Wesley

To W H Pepys Esqʳᵉ

---

¹ The year is given by 19 Dec. falling on a Wednesday and the continuing discussion of SW's forthcoming course of lectures at the London Institution.

² The course eventually consisted of only six lectures.

To [William Hasledine Pepys][1]   Euston Street, 1 January 1828

ALS, 2 pp. (Fitzwilliam)

Euston Street.
Tuesday. Jan 1. 1828.

My dear Sir

Herewith is an Estimate of the lowest Terms on which the Lectures can be given, if the Assistance of only *three* Singers be required for *five* Attendances.— Yourself & your Committee are to judge of what *is required*; you intimated that Crotch's Course[2] having been solely instrumental, Antithesis must be desirable, & therefore the more Vocality, the better.

	Estimate	
	£	s.
6 Lectures at 6 guineas each	37	16
3 Singers in 5 lectures, at		
2 Guineas each	31	10
Hire of Organ	10	10
—of Pianoforte	3	3
	£82	19

Wherever you feel that any Retrenchment can be made (although of this I cannot discover a Possibility, without Injury to the Vitality of the Cause) you will of Course speedily communicate with me upon the Subject.—To tell you the plain Truth, I do not see how we can become at all vocally *brilliant*, without a Treble Voice, which, if any *4 Part* Pieces are to be sung, will be absolutely a *sine quâ non*.

I am
Dear Sir
Very respectfully
& cordially,
Yours
    S Wesley

---

[1] Although lacking an address portion, it is clear from its contents that this letter is to Pepys.

[2] Crotch had given a course of eight lectures on modern musical composition at the London Institution between 7 Feb. and 18 Mar. 1827 (*A Descriptive Catalogue of the Lectures delivered at the London Institution*, 47).

To [Edward Wedlake Brayley][1]   Euston Street, 2 January 1828

ALS, 1 p. (Toronto, Royal Ontario Museum, 934.43.277)
Addressed To | The Secretary | of | The Russel Institution[2]

Euston Street
Euston Square
Wednesday Jany 2. 1828

Sir

The lowest Terms upon which I can read six Lectures are 30 Guineas; and you will oblige me by an early Line of Information, whether vocal Additions, (such as are expected both at the Royal & London Institutions, & at each of these I am engaged this Season) will be required? I mention this, because *this* is (of Course) quite an extra Expense; as also the Hire of Organ, & Piano Forte; both of which will be necessary for the general good Effect of the Course.[3]

I remain,
Sir,
respectfully yours
 S Wesley

P.S. You must excuse the Superscription without the proper *Name*, as well as *Title*; but the Truth is that I have unluckily mislaid your Address.

---

[1] Edward Wedlake Brayley the elder (1773–1854), archaeologist and topographer, FSA (1823), collaborator with John Britton on parts of *The Beauties of England and Wales*, Librarian and Secretary of the Russell Institution from 1825 until his death (*DNB*).

[2] The Russell Institution was in Great Coram Street, off Russell Square.

[3] One of the lectures delivered by SW as part of this course can be identified among SW's lecture texts. Entitled 'In what respects may we be truly said to have improved in the knowledge and practice of music in the present period?', it is annotated 'Russell 6th' (BL, Add. MS 35015, fo. 32).

To William Haseldine Pepys

Euston Street,
[?5 or 12 January 1828]¹

ALS, 1 p. (BL, Add. MS 56411, fo. 30)

Euston Street 16
Saturday Night

Dear Sir

If convenient to You I will attend you on *Thursday* at 2 o'Clock, wherever you Shall appoint, for the Purpose of surveying the Lecture Room, when we may finally Settle the Point relative to the Organ.²—It certainly is a Desideratum of no Slender Importance, & ought to be admitted, *if possible*.

> I remain,
> Dear Sir,
> truly & respectfully Yours
> S Wesley

W. H. Pepys Esqre

To William Hasledine Pepys   Euston Street, 1 February [1828]¹

ALS, 1 p. (Fitzwilliam)
Addressed To | —Pepys Esqre | Poultry | Cheapside

Euston Street 16.
Friday Night. Feby 1

Dear Sir

Be so kind as to favour me, as soon as possible, with mine *Ordo Recitandi*; the *when*, both as to Day & Hour, when I am expected to mount Guard at my new Station; by which you will gratify & instruct

> Yours very sincerely
> S Wesley

---

¹ This letter, relating to SW's course of lectures at the London Institution, appears to follow SW's letter to Pepys of 1 January, and is evidently in response to a letter from Pepys (not preserved) questioning whether an organ could be used (see n. 2). The matter had evidently been resolved by the time of SW's letter to Pepys of 1 Feb. SW's 'Saturday' suggests 5, 12, 19, or 26 Jan. as possible dates, of which 5 and 12 Jan. are perhaps the most probable.

² Pepys had perhaps queried whether there was enough space for an organ in the lecture room.

---

¹ The year is given by 1 Feb. falling on a Friday and the continuing discussion of SW's forthcoming course of lectures at the London Institution.

To Joseph Fincher[1] Euston Street, 17 March [1828][2]

ALS, 1 p. (BL, Add. MS 38071, fo. 32)
Addressed To | Joseph Fincher Esqre

Euston Street
Monday 17th of March

My dear Sir

Mr Scott[3] having expressed himself so zealous for the Introduction of the Jew's Harp Artist,[4] I am anxious to know immediately whether the Preliminaries are already settled concerning his Performance, and it is necessary that I should have an Interview with him *here* in the Course of Wednesday.

A speedy Line will oblige

Yours faithfully

S. Wesley

To [William Hawes][1] Euston Street, 29 March [1828][2]

ALS, 3 pp. (BL, Loan 79.10/3)

Euston Street
Saturday March 29

Dear Sir

I find that no Plates of my Madrigal[3] were ever sent home to me.—*Skarratt* engraved them, but what has become of them is a Question of no easy Solution.

---

[1] The Assistant Secretary of the Royal Institution.

[2] The year is given by 17 Mar. falling on a Monday and SW's discussion of Eulenstein (see n. 4).

[3] Possibly Sir Claude Scott, one of the managers of the Royal Institution at this time, although it is difficult to see why SW should deny him his title. The 'Mr Scott' mentioned here appears elsewhere in family letters, where he is described as being engaged 'in the coal trade', and as being the former employer of SW's son John William.

[4] Charles Eulenstein (1802–90), a German jew's harp player and guitarist who enjoyed a brief celebrity in London in 1827 and 1828. The performance under discussion was presumably to occur during one of SW's Royal Institution lectures, which began some time in March. Eulenstein is also known to have demonstrated the jew's harp at Michael Faraday's Royal Institution lecture on the nature of musical sound on 9 May 1828 (*Grove*[5]; *A Sketch of the Life of C. Eulenstein, the Celebrated Performer on the Jews' Harps* (1833), 47–8; Kassler, 'Lectures', 19–20).

[1] Although lacking an address portion, internal evidence and the preservation of this letter with other letters to Hawes suggests that he was the addressee.

[2] The year is given by 29 Mar. falling on a Saturday and the reference to Willis (see n. 6).

[3] 'O sing unto mie roundelaie', which SW had written in 1812 as his entry for the Madrigal Society prize cup (see SW to Novello, 17 Feb. [1813], n. 8).

—I well remember that Gwilt[4] was so disgusted at the Adjudgement of the Prize to any other than the Madrigal in Question, he determined to publish it at his own Charge, which was accordingly done, but I know that I received only a few Copies of it, & certainly *never the Plates*.[5]

As you know the Worth of the Thing, at least as well as I, it is my Purpose at all Events that the Sounds shall 'neither slumber nor sleep.'[6]—if I cannot recover the Plates (which I think you might help me to do, by Enquiry) I will republish the Tune, in that cheap & clever Way that Willis exhibited to us yesterday.[7]

I am much inclined to conclude, that the Plates were sent from Skarratt to Gwilt; but as I have had not Communication with the latter for several Years past, I can gain no Information from that Quarter.—I know not how you & he stand at present together—for he is rather ready to dine with you or to die for you to Day, & swearing to Morrow that he never saw you before.

    SW

To [Thomas Jackson][1]   Euston Street, 21 April 1828

ALS, 1 p. (Rylands, DDWes 6/31)

Euston Street
Monday April 21ˢᵗ 1828

Dear Sir

I have had in Contemplation for some Months past, to compose a few Tunes appropriate to the Hymns of my Father in your Collection,[2] each to suit a separate Metre; and several of my judicious musical Friends are of Opinion, that such a Publication must prove an *Acquisition to the Psalmody* of the Connexion, which has long been so generally & so justly approved.

---

[4] i.e. Joseph Gwilt.

[5] For details of this incident, see SW to Novello, 17 Feb. [1813].   [6] Ps. 121: 4.

[7] The Dublin music publisher and seller Isaac Willis established his business in London around 1824 and published a good deal of sheet music. The 'cheap and clever way' mentioned by SW was doubtless lithography, which Willis used for some of his publications (Humphries and Smith). No copies of this projected new edition of SW's madrigal have been located, and it is not known whether or not it was published.

---

[1] It is apparent from the content of this letter that it is to Thomas Jackson.

[2] i.e. *A Collection of Hymns for the Use of the People called Methodists*. As SW states, many of its hymns were by his father.

You will much oblige me by an early Communication of your Sentiments upon the Subject, & believe me remaining

Dear Sir
Respectfully Yours
S Wesley

To Thomas Jackson   Euston Street, 17 May 1828

ALS, 3 pp. (Rylands, DDWes 6/32)

Euston Street
Euston Square
Saturday May. 17. 1828

Dear Sir,

According to your Suggestion, I address a few Words to you upon the Subject of the Hymn Tunes which I have had the Gratification of composing, & adapting to the various Metres in your Collection edited in 1825.[1]—I have endeavoured to render them as appropriate to the excellent Poetry as my musical Ability admits, and shall feel much mental Comfort should they hereafter prove a Vehicle of impressing more strongly & effectively the grand Truths which pervade the whole Volume.

I have submitted my Pages to the Criticism of a few whom I have long known to possess the most solid Judgement in every Species of Church Musick, & who have honoured me by pronouncing that the Melodies I have invented for the several Measures, are (what I especially wished them to be) easy of Acquirement, and every where suitably solemn to the sundry Subjects of the Words; & that whether sung in separate Parts (as they will be printed) or by a whole Congregation *in Unison only*, their Effect will prove powerfully devotional.

Considering as my Duty to offer to the Committee the Option of the Copyright of the MS. previous to making any decisive Engagement upon it elsewhere, I thought it well to consult a few impartial Men (on whom I have had Reason to rely in similar Negotiations heretofore,) with regard to a fair & moderate Price; and they tell me that £150 ought to be considered an undeniably just Requisition: this, of Course must be left to the Determination of Yourself and the other Gentlemen appointed to arbitrate similar Questions.[2]

---

[1] i.e. the 1825 edition of the *Collection of Hymns for the Use of the People called Methodists*.

[2] The timing of this letter is curious, as the Book Room Commmittee had a week earlier turned down SW's proposal that they should purchase the copyright of the hymns and publish them themselves, while agreeing that if SW himself were to arrange publication they would be glad to help with marketing and

Should even a Moiety of the new Tunes become popular, that the Demand for the Book would soon become general there is little Cause to Doubt: of the *three Tunes* from the Fitzwilliam Library (by Handel) I disposed of full 1800 Copies, & afterwards sold the Plates for a liberal Sum.[3]

Permit me to subscribe myself
Dear Sir
Very respectfully yours,

S Wesley

P.S. I purpose to prefix a Preface to the Tunes, giving a minute Explanation of every Point which could be possibly misapprehended in any Part of the Work.

Revd Mr Jackson

To William Upcott[1]   London Institution,[2] 20 August [1828][3]

ALS, 1 p. (Bath Public Libraries, AL 1523)
Addressed To | William Upcott Esqre

London Institution
Wed^y 20th of Aug^t

Dear Sir

I feel it right to announce to you, that a Set of 30 Hymn Tunes, all original Melodies of my own, adapted to every Metre in the Wesleyan Hymn Book is just issued into the World,[4] & I guess that they may not be unacceptable among

distribution (Book Room Minutes, 9 May 1828 (Rylands)). SW's collection was published in Aug. as *Original Hymn Tunes, adapted to every Metre in the collection by the Rev. John Wesley* (see next letter).

³ The identity of the purchaser of these plates, and the amount SW received for them, are not known.

¹ William Upcott (1779–1845), natural son of the artist Ozias Humphry, antiquary, and noted collector of autograph letters. After an early career in the book trade he was in 1806 elected to an assistant librarian's position at the recently founded London Institution at the same time as Richard Porson was appointed librarian. During his long period at the London Institution he bought and sold large quantities of autograph letters, resigning his position in 1834 in circumstances which suggest some irregularity. One of his executors was Charles Britiffe Smith (see SW to Smith, 4 Sept. 1828). Some of his extensive collection of autograph letters is now at BL, Add. MSS 15841–15957 (*DNB*; Munby, 13–32).

² SW presumably had called on Upcott at the London Institution, and had written this note there on failing to find him.

³ The year is given by 20 Aug. falling on a Wednesday and the reference to the recent publication of SW's hymns (see n. 4).

⁴ The Preface to the *Original Hymn Tunes* is dated 10 July 1828. The BL copy has a manuscript inscription to Crotch, dated 4 Sept. 1828.

your extensive Circle of Friends & Acquaintance.—I flatter myself that they are tolerably good, & may be had in five Minutes of your Neighbour Mr Mason,[5] Conference Office, City Road.

Believe me,
Dear Sir
faithfully Yours
   S Wesley

To | Wm Upcott Esqre

To Thomas Jackson   Euston Street, 2 September 1828

ALS, 3 pp. (Rylands, DDWes 6/29)
Addressed To | The Revd Mr Jackson | Brunswick Place | City Road | Tuesday Evening
Pmk 3 SP 1828

Euston Street Euston Square
Tuesday Septr 2. 1828

My dear Sir

As the recent Publication[1] (concerning which you have already witnessed my Anxiety) has been a Work of heavy Expense, the Remuneration of which must necessarily be *only expected* at present, and as I feel very desirous that the Money advanced by you should be refunded with all convenient Speed, I could not resist the Impulse I felt in earnestly requesting the united Efforts of your most efficient Engines towards the Promotion of its Publicity & Encouragement.—I acknowledge that the good Success of the three Hymns of my excellent Father set by Handel was the primary Stimulus to the present Undertaking, and it having been suggested to me by several judicious Persons (zealously affected towards the Methodists) that Tunes *for every individual Metre in the Hymn Book* were wanting, I eagerly embraced so favourable an Occasion of rendering a cordial Tribute of profound Veneration to the Manes of such a Poet, and such a Father!

I fear that Mr Mason (& probably others with him) may have quite mistaken my Motive for wishing a further Advancement of Cash;[2] it was the same which

---

[5] John Mason (1781–1864), Wesleyan Methodist minister and Book Steward, 1827–64 (*DEB*). The London Institution was very close to the City Road Chapel and Book Room.

[1] The *Original Hymn Tunes*.

[2] SW had evidently approached the Book Room for a short-term advance to cover his engraving and printing costs, and was now requesting a further £30 to pay for the cost of printing further copies. No

influenced me in the first Instance; namely the earnest Desire of promoting that Circulation of Copies which would most speedily ensure the Return of such Money: but without ready Money my Printer cannot proceed. 100 copies are immediately wanted: the Shops to which I have sent Title Pages object to exhibit them (& this very justly) because, when asked for a Copy, they have none to produce.

If, when I first announced my Design of issuing such a Publication, any Objection had been stated, to this I should have immediately attended; and if I had found myself incompetent to remove it, I would have given up all Thoughts of any future Proceeding in the Business: but on the Contrary, the Scheme appeared to meet very general Approbation, and I accordingly proceeded with all Promptitude to prepare for the Press a Work (certain to be popular, when thoroughly known) which stagnates for the immediate Lack of *Thirty Pounds*!

Whenever the Tunes in Question shall have attained *any Thing like* a general Circulation among the dissenting Congregations—[the *Church* κατ' ἐζοχήν,[3] is out of the Question: their Members will harbour them only as Matters of musical Amusement—][4] The dissenting Congregations will I think give them great Encouragement.—They are fond of new Tunes, & these, I flatter myself are fairly entitled to become *old*, and yet never *obsolete*.

I see that the former Advertisement remains upon your Number[5] for the present Month: so far, so good; it appears that great Progress in the Cause might be made by every Preacher who was informed of the Fact at the Conference, disposed to aid it.

Dii bene vertant[6]—the Heathens would say, upon the present Occasion. My Conclusion is, τὸ θέλημα τοῦ κυρίου γένοιτο[7]

> I am
> My dear Sir,
> Very sincerely yours,
>   S Wesley

record of this transaction is recorded in the Book Room minutes. Little more than a week later, however, the question of the *Original Hymn Tunes* was once more discussed at a Book Room committee meeting, where it was agreed that 'the Book Steward [Mason], with the consent of Mr Wesley be at liberty to negotiate with his Printer either for his Plates, or a certain number of copies of his musical work'. It is apparent from SW's letter of 10 Oct. to Jackson and subsequent Book Room committee minutes that they did not purchase the plates, but may have bought some copies of the *Hymns* as a result of these negotiations (Book Room Minutes, 11 Sept., 11 Dec. 1828 (Rylands)).

[3] 'Par excellence': i.e. the Church of England.   [4] The square brackets are SW's.
[5] i.e. in the current number of *WMM*.   [6] 'May the gods grant a successful outcome'.
[7] 'The Lord's will be done'.

To Charles Britiffe Smith[1]   Euston Street, 4 September 1828

ALS, 1 p. (BL, Add. MS 31764, fo. 27)
Addressed To | Britiffe Smith Esqre | Featherstone Buildings | Bedford Row | N. 2 |
    Thursday Evening
Pmk 4 SP 1828

> Euston Street. Euston Square
> Thursday Septr 4. 1828

Sir,

It appears to me that the English Translation of the following Epigram is far superior to the Original:[2]

Εκηνὴ πᾶς ὁ βίος καὶ παιγνιον. ἢ μάθε παίζειν, την σπουδήν μεταθείς, ἢ
φέρε τὰς ὀδύνας.

> Life is a Jest—mere Childrens' Play:
>   Go, learn to model thine by theirs:
> Go, learn to trifle Life away,
>   Or learn to bear a Life of Cares.

I remain
Sir
obediently yours
    S Wesley

---

[1] Charles Britiffe Smith was 'the earliest known collector of autograph letters of musicians' (King, 38; see also Munby, 66–7). As this is the only letter to him from SW and there is no other evidence of a friendship between them, it is possible that he deliberately solicited this letter to add to his collection. It is not known whether he was related to George Smith of Faversham, three of whose letters to SW concerning his daughter are also contained in the same manuscript collection.

[2] From *Anthologia Palatina* 10. 72, attributed to Palladas (4th cent. AD): a literal translation is 'All life is a stage and a comedy; learn to play, discarding earnestness, or else endure its pains'. The translation given by SW is by his son Charles; he had earlier set it to music as a glee (autograph at BL, Add. MS 71107, fo. 113^v, dated 17 Jan. 1807).

To John George Emett   [Euston Street, ?21 September 1828]¹

ALS, 1 p. (BL, Add. MS 35013, fo. 92)
Addressed John Emett Esqre

Sunday Night

My dear Sir

I will prepare the Papers in the Way you require as soon as possible, but am engaged (by the Advice of Mr Wakefield, my Aesculapius)² to go To-morrow, down to Gravesend on Account of my yet unsettled State of Intestines, in which I am concerned to find that you resemble me: I must return on *Saturday*³ next, & on Sunday shall be very glad to see you.—Whether my Sister be then in this or a better World, the Society of a Friend cannot be unseasonable.

Believe me
Most truly yours
S Wesley

To Thomas Jackson   Euston Street, 10 October 1828

ALS, 3 pp. (Rylands, DDWes 6/30)
Addressed The Revd Mr Jackson | Brunswick Place | City Road | Friday Octr 9
Pmk C 10 828

Euston Street Euston Square.
Friday Octr 10 1828.

My dear Sir,

I cannot but again express to you the strong Reluctance I felt to any Application upon the Subject of Money, which I think I may safely declare that I value no more *for its own Sake* than did my wise & good Father & Uncle: but as, while

---

¹ The dating of this letter, written at a time when SW's sister Sarah's death was in imminent prospect, is problematical. Sarah died in Bristol on Friday, 19 Sept., but 14 Sept. (the previous Sunday) is ruled out as a possible date for this letter as SW was in Leeds at this time (see SW to Sarah Suter, 13 Sept. 1828 (BL, Add. MS 35012, fo. 73)), and did not return to London until the following Thursday. The most probable date is 21 Sept: i.e. two days after Sarah's death, but evidently before news of it had reached SW in London.

² i.e. SW's doctor: not certainly identified, as there was more than one Wakefield in general practice in London at this time. He was SW's doctor at the time of SW's death, and is listed in *The Times* as among those attending his funeral.   ³ 27 Sept.

on Earth, 'the Mammon of Unrighteousness'[1] is a Sine quâ non of our mortal Existence, wholly to slight its momentary Value were to counteract both Experience & common Sense, I plead guilty to an insuperable Aversion from every Semblance of importunate Solicitation, & therefore hasten to explain the only Causes of my unseasonable Visit yesterday.

I believe that I did not mention to you the Circumstance of my losing £60 within the last three Months, by the unworthy Conduct of an Organ Builder,[2] whose Name I forbear to add, but who refused to pay the above Sum, (& to which he well knew I was justly entitled,) merely because the Agreement was not drawn up formally & legally upon Paper. £60 would have enabled me to proceed very independently with my Printer, so that there would have been no Scarcity of *Copies* in my late Work;—but at present, a Stagnation is caused, inasmuch as each 100 amount to nearly £12, for which my poor Typographer can afford no Credit.

That the Tune Book will ultimately find its Level, (& I will be bold enough to say, *obtain its Elevation*) you & I are well agreed; but the Time requisite for its *general Circulation* must be considerable, & I submit to you whether (all Things weighed well) my wiser & least troublesome Plan may be to part with the Copyright altogether, at a fair Valuation, rather than be worried from Time to Time as above described?[3]

You will much oblige me, dear Sir, by your early Thoughts upon the Business. —It certainly would be desirable that a Publication which I will venture to denominate *unique* in its Kind, should liberally reward the Labourer in the Vineyard, who is conscious of having devoted some of the best Sounds he could collect to assist the Expression, although they could never *improve* the Sense & Energy of that divine Poesy which will not be soon surpassed, in our native Tongue.

I am,
My dear Sir,
With great Respect & Regard,
Your truly obliged
   S. Wesley

---

[1] Luke 16: 9.

[2] Perhaps William Allen; the payment would have been for drawing up the specification for the Lincoln Cathedral organ, built by Allen in 1826. For a similar complaint from SW's brother Charles, which may relate to the commission which CW felt was his due for recommending Allen to the Dean and Chapter, see SW to Sarah Wesley, 14 June [1826], and n. 7.

[3] This suggestion had already been considered and turned down by the Book Room Committee (see SW to Jackson, 17 May 1828). Perhaps as a consequence of SW's request in the present letter, it was considered again by them in Dec., and once more rejected, on the grounds that the Book Room held sufficient stock of the *Hymns* for their anticipated requirements.

To Robert Glenn Euston Street, 30 October 1828

ALS, 1 p. (Rylands, DDWes 9/21)
Addressed To | R. Glenn Esqre | Kirby Street | Hatton Garden | N. 6 | Thursday 30 Oct^r

> Euston Street
> Thursday 30th of Octr 1828

Dr Sir

My Brother has written to inform us that he expects & intends to be in London on Saturday next: I design to call on Sunday, & I should think that on Monday you ought to see him, as nothing but Evil can result from Delay, when Circumstances are considered with a grain of Prudence.[1]

Y^rs truly
  S. Wesley

To John George Emett Euston Street, 15 January [1829][1]

ANS, 1 p. (BL, Add. MS 35013, fo. 95)
Addressed Mr Emmett | N. 2 | Elizabeth Street | Chelsea | Thursday Night
Pmk 16 JA 1829

> Euston Street
> Thursday Ev^g 15 Jan^y

My dear Sir

Particular Business will detain me *from* Home the greatest Part of To-morrow: Master Sam must also be an Absentee; therefore if you can name some Day in next Week for the Pleasure of our receiving you here, you will much oblige

Dear Sir
Yours very faithfully
  S Wesley

---

[1] This letter may relate to a dispute over SW's sister Sarah's estate: in a will dated 16 Nov. 1827 (Drew) she appointed her brother Charles as her executor and left her entire estate to him. For an undated letter to Glenn which may relate to the same subject, see Appendix, Letter 14.

[1] The year is given by the postmark.

To William Hawes   Euston Street, 24 January 1829

AN, third person, 1 p. (BL, Loan 79.10/3)

Nearly a Month ago Mr S. Wesley addressed a Note to Mr Hawes enquiring whether he would be disposed to engage his Services at the ensuing Oratorios,[1] to which a *verbal* Answer was returned, that 'Mr H. would write to Mr W. on the Subject.'—This Day the latter read Mr Adams's Name, for the Organ.—Query—Shall we call this the attentive Punctuality of a Man of Business, or the polished Manners of a Courtier?

Euston Street Sat^y 24th of Jany 1829

To Robert Glenn   Euston Street, 31 January 1829

ALS, 2 pp. (Rylands, DDWF 15/39)
Addressed To | Robt Glenn Esqre | Kirby Street | Hatton Garden

Euston Street Euston Square
Saturday Jan. 31. 1829

My dear Sir

I fully purposed to have been with you this Day, but two unexpected Scholars dropped in whom I could not dismiss without their Lessons; added to which I am so closely pressed for Time in the preparation of a new Lecture for *Tuesday next*[1] (the very Day on which the lousy Lawyer's Bill is to be paid) that really I am in a true, proper & orthodox Dilemma.

Now to the most perplexing Part of it: if you will do me the friendly Office of procuring for me the Loan of either 30 or at all Events £20, you shall not only receive my Note, payable on March 25th but also Property besides to the Amount of the Sum advanced.

I earnestly request you to look in here this Evening if possible. I would not become thus troublesome to you, were not the Affair so urgent & the impending Danger so closely imminent over the Head of

My dear Sir
Your *sympathetic* old Friend
S Wesley

To | R. Glenn Esqre

---

[1] Hawes was at this time the manager of the Covent Garden oratorio concerts.

---

[1] 3 Feb. The venue and subject of SW's lecture are not known.

To an unidentified recipient[1]   Euston Street, 7 March 1829

ALS, 7 pp. (BL, Add. MS 31764, fo. 28)

Euston Street, Euston Square
Saturday, 7th of March 1829

Dear Sir

The ingenious & profligate Author of 'Lacon', (viz, the *Reverend* Colston[2]) has truly said in his Book, that an 'intelligent Man is generally an intelligible Man.'— Now I wish to prove at least that I am the latter; & therefore will express my Judgement more exactly than can be conveniently done amid Bacchanalian Potations, upon the Contents of the Paper which you gave me on our last Lodge Night.[3]

I remain steadfast in the Conviction, that no multitudinous Addition of Instruments can ever in the least degree augment the Solemnity of Tone which the Organ inherently possesses & which will perpetually unite with the human Voice, in a Similarity of Effect, vainly attempted by any other Instrument than the *Flute*. It is true that some *Voices* resemble the *Reed* Stops of an Organ; (Braham's for example) but *then*, the Tone of the *human* Voice is either naturally bad, or vitiated by a false Mode of exerting it, which latter is *unquestionably Braham's case.*

The nearer the Approach of Tone in the human Voice to that of a fine Diapason; (whether of stopt or open Pipes) in that Proportion will be its Approximation towards Perfection.

In your Paper is stated, that 'the Introduction of stringed Instruments may increase the Flow of Harmony.' This is not correct, altogether; they certainly strengthen the Force of the Tones; but not the Power of the *radical & constituent* Harmony.—That they much embellish & diversify the general Effect will not be disputed; but then, that general Effect is rather *theatrical* than *ecclesiastic.*— therefore I agree with your Critic, that 'Requiems,' sung to the Organ, without stringed or wind Instruments, are indisputably the most 'consistent with perfect Taste;' & will be universally found 'more impressive upon every devout Mind, as well as upon every competent Judge of $\tau o \ \pi \rho \epsilon \pi o v$[4]

---

[1] The addressee of this letter was evidently a fellow Mason, a man of letters, and an amateur musician.

[2] The Revd Charles Caleb Colton (?1780–1832), author of the popular collection of aphorisms *Lacon, or Many Things in Few Words: Addressed to Those who Think*, 2 vols. (1820, 1822). For his profligate life-style and his addiction to gambling, see *DNB*, which states that he was 'a man of real talent, though unfitted by character, and, it would seem, by his real opinions, for a clerical career'. SW's slip of the pen was probably because of a confusion with the Bristol philanthropist Edward Colston (1636–1721).

[3] Doubtless of the Somerset House and Inverness Lodge. The Somerset House Lodge, of which SW was an honorary member, had amalgamated with the Inverness Lodge in Nov. 1828. If the new lodge continued the pattern of meetings of the Somerset House Lodge agreed on 23 May 1814, the meeting was on 23 Feb (Oxford). SW's correspondent's paper is not preserved.   [4] 'The decorous'.

Whoever begins & continues to practice ever so strenuously on the Piano Forte, & shall even be able to execute the marvellous Difficulties of Messrs Hummel & Moscheles,[5] will, when attempting the right Way of performing *even a Psalm Tune* upon an Organ, soon discover his Incompetency:—for even admitting that these Pianists are Harmonists, that is, that they understand how to modulate aright, (which is very seldom the Case), yet they are sure to treat the noblest of all Instruments in the most aukward & barbarous Way: for Instance, in striking any Chord, they do not put down the Keys simultaneously, *which on the Organ should always be done*, but one after another, beginning at the lowest note in the Base: so that (to use a harsh military Metaphor) the Effect on the Ear is not that of a general instantaneous *Explosion* but rather of a *running Fire*: To make this conspicuous, take the following Diagram:

We will name the Chord of C, E, G, in the Base, & its Reduplication in the Treble (though beginning in a different Order):—

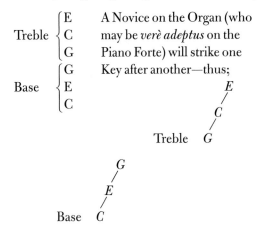

The Effect of which (in a Psalm Tune for Instance) is perfectly ludicrous. Added to this absurd mode of handling the Keys of an Organ, the Pianist constantly forgets that the sound of every Pipe is *continuous*, not fleeting, like that of the Piano Forte; & therefore although on the latter, the Finger may remain without Mischief upon a Key, for some Time after the temporal Value of the Note has been exhausted; the Fact is totally opposite as to the Organ, which necessarily preserves a Continuation of the Tone so long as ever the Finger may remain upon the Key: consequently, if the Execution of every Passage be not extremely nice, & accurate; if the Length of a Note, (either in Slow or brisk Measure), be protracted, even for Half a Second beyond its legitimate Duration, false Harmony will be the

---

[5] Johann Nepomuk Hummel (1778–1837) and Ignaz Moscheles (1794–1870), two leading composers of virtuoso piano music of the time.

instantaneous Consequence: so far are they miserably mistaken who imagine the Piano Forte an Instrument requiring *more* delicate Management than the other;—whereas the *direct Reverse* is the Truth.

He who wishes to be a good Player, *both on the Piano Forte & the Organ*, must learn the latter *first*: if he do otherwise he will never be an Organist deserving the Name of one.

And now for a little Masonic Confidence.—I shrewdly Suspect that you were the Suggestor of my Right & Title to all the Finery which I came down to the Banquet bedizened withal, the other Monday. If you were thus zealous to place me among the worthies,

'Stuck o'er with Titles, & hung round with Strings',[6]

let me express my Thanks for kind Intention at once to *you*: if someone other of the Brethren made the Motion, tell me his Name, that I may make a due Acknowledgement to *him*.

I fully believe that you give me Credit for a Fact, of which I am internally conscious, namely, that my Mind is not that of a *mere* Musician: I have (from a Boy) been a Lover of more of the Alphabet than the seven incipient English Letters, & had I not been an idle Dog, under the Instruction of my classical Father (whose Loss is by me daily felt, *more than 40 years since its Occurrence*) I might long ago have been well qualified to bandy Latin & Greek along with Parr & Porson.[7]

My *Trade* is Music, I confess; & would to Heaven it had only been destined for mine Amusement, which would certainly have been the Case, had I availed myself of the Advantages which were offered me in Juvenescence, of rendering myself eligible for any one of the learned Professions; but it was (it seems) otherwise ordained; & I was to attend only to the Cultivation of *one* Talent, which *unluckily cost me no Trouble to do*: had there been any up-Hill Work for me in Music, I should soon enough have sacrificed it altogether.

You will perhaps wonder at my pestering you with all this Egotism, but I will tell you my Motive: Although I am pretty closely occupied in drumming the intrinsic Value of Minims & Semibreves both into Paper Skulls & *impenetrable*; yet I contrive to *make* Time (somehow or other) for Attention to *the whole Alphabet*, & should feel no Objection to rendering myself useful among Persons engaged in literary Pursuits, as far as I should feel conscientiously warranted to take a Share in them.—In our boasted 'March of Intellect' are certainly Plenty of Opportunities to increase & strengthen the Battalions; & I think that I should not rashly volunteer any Promise which I might feel incapable of rightly performing.

---

[6] Pope, *Essay on Man*, iv. 195.

[7] The noted classical scholars Samuel Parr (1747–1825) and Richard Porson (1759–1808).

Perhaps I might lend a helping Hand in some critical Work, where I understand the Language, & the Subject, & if you will think a little upon this Proposal,
& hint some Information concerning it, you will thereby gratify

Dear Sir,
Your sincere Friend
& Brother,

S. Wesley

To [? Stephen Francis Rimbault]¹   Euston Street,
24 March [1829]²

ALS, 1 p. (Rylands, DDWF 15/37)

Euston Street
24 March 2 Tuesday

Sir

In reply to your Note I have to inform you that the three Hymns which I
transcribed in the Fitzwilliam Library are unquestionably *autographical*: I am
well acquainted with the Hand Writing, having seen Abundance of it; and it
exactly corresponds with all the other Specimens of Handel's Penmanship, which
cannot easily be mistaken.—Moreover I know the whole History of these Tunes,
& the Circumstance of Handel composing them at the Request of a particular
Friend of my Father,³ who wrote the Hymns as the Title Page announces.

I am, Sir,
obed^tly yours

S Wesley

P.S. Handel has written only the Melody, with a figured Base, which I have ramified for a
Choir.

---

¹ For Rimbault, see SW to Novello 20 Nov. [1820], n. 3. He is proposed as the addressee of this letter
on the basis of SW's note to him on the same subject less than a week later.

² The year is given by 24 Mar. falling on a Tuesday and the discussion of the Handel hymns.

³ i.e. Priscilla Rich, née Wilford (*c*.1713–83), the wife of John Rich (1691–1761), proprietor of Covent
Garden theatre. Before her marriage in 1744 she had (as Priscilla Stevens) been a well-known actress,
but had afterwards retired from the stage. She was a Methodist convert and a close family friend of the
Wesleys. SW's information probably came from his sister Sarah's account, printed in the Dec. 1826 number of *WMM* (see SW to Jackson, [8] Nov. 1826, n. 3) (*BD*; *Grove*⁶).

To Stephen Francis Rimbault   30 March 1829

Source Victor Schoelcher, *The Life of Handel* (1857), 51–2.
Editor's note Described by Schoelcher as a 'note', written for Rimbault by SW to explain
the 'somewhat singular origin' of the Handel hymns, and communicated to Schoelcher
by 'Dr Rimbault' (i.e. Edward Francis Rimbault).

The late comedian Rich, who was the most celebrated harlequin of his time, was
also the proprietor of Covent Garden Theatre, during the period when Handel
conducted his oratorios at that house. He married a person who became a serious
character, after having formerly been a very contrary one, and who requested
Handel to set to music the *three hymns* which I transcribed in the Fitzwilliam
Library, from the autography, and published them in consequence.

S. Wesley

March 30, 1829

To Robert Glenn   Euston Street, 10 April [1829]¹

ALS, 1 p. (Emory, Letter 79)
Addressed To | Mr Robert Glenn Esqre | Kirby Street | Hatton Garden

Euston Street
Friday Afternoon
10th of April

My dear Sir
Dr Wait delivers this to you, & is very anxious to converse with you forth-
with upon an Affair of the most vital Importance to him & every Individual in his
Family. It is of that Nature that you as a Man so deeply versed in Affairs of urgent
Business, will readily perceive the absolute Necessity of proceeding with the
utmost Promptitude.²

Yours most truly
in great Haste
S Wesley

¹ The year is given by 10 Apr. falling on a Friday, SW's Euston Street address, and by the reference to
Wait.
² The nature of Wait's financial crisis is unknown. It may possibly have been connected with his
editorship of the *Repertorium Theologicum*, which appeared for one number only in May 1829.

To an unidentified recipient   Euston Street, 23 May [1829]¹

ALS, 2 pp. (Rylands, DDWF 15/40)

Euston Street
Saturday May 23ᵈ

Sir

I must have appeared very remiss, & inattentive to your Letter of the 13ᵗʰ but really, were you to be acquainted with the various Obstacles to a *speedy* Answer of several Correspondents, which have occurred, ever since yours arrived, I am sure that you Candour would exonerate me from any *just* Charge of Neglect.

It is with Regret that I am obliged to confess my Inability of furnishing you with the Information your Friend wished for concerning the Annesley Family.²— If Messʳˢ Clarke³ & Moore⁴ can render no Assistance on the Subject (who have been sedulous in the Wesleyan Genealogy) I fear that any future Research of mine must be altogether ineffectual.—My late Sister might possibly have given some *Conjecture* concerning it, but I cannot believe she could have brought forward that correct Document which would have proved demonstrative upon the Point. Nevertheless, if any Clue can be found towards the Ascertainment of the real Truth, which you may be of Opinion that any subsequent Enquiry of mine might assist, I shall most willingly undertake the Negotiation in any Way you may guess to prove most successful.

Southey's Life of my Uncle⁵ you have probably seen; but I find therein no Mention of that collateral Relationship which is wanted in the present Instance.

I remain
Sir
Very truly Yours
    S. Wesley

---

¹ The year is given by 23 May falling on a Saturday, SW's Euston Street address, and his reference to his 'late sister'. For an undated letter of 1835–7, probably to Thomas Jackson, on a similar topic, see Appendix, Letter 16.

² i.e. the family of Susanna Wesley (1669–1742), wife of John Wesley of Epworth, SW's paternal grandmother. She was the twenty-fifth child of Dr Samuel Annesley (*c*.1620–1696) (*DNB*; see also Appendix Letter 13, n. 3).

³ Adam Clarke (?1762–1832), author of *Memoirs of the Wesley Family* (1823).

⁴ Henry Moore (1751–1844), Wesleyan minister and biographer, and one of John Wesley's literary executors. In 1792 he brought out a life of John Wesley in conjunction with Thomas Coke (1747–1814); it was written mostly by Moore, but without access to John Wesley's papers. He eventually gained access to Wesley's papers and wrote another life in 1824–5, described in *DNB* as 'a work of the first importance; though written with reverence, it displays intimate and discriminating knowledge' (*DNB*).

⁵ *The Life of John Wesley* (1820) by Robert Southey (1774–1843).

To John Thomas Smith[1]   Euston Street, 11 September [1829][2]

ANS, 1 p. (BL, Add. MS 45102, fo. 137)
Addressed J. Smith Esqre | British Museum

Euston Street
Friday Septr 11th

Dear Sir

I have encouraged young Mr Bennet[3] to enquire whether you are acquainted with any of the 24 Personages contained in the List he will present to you: he has been informed that any *one* of them is authorized to appoint whomsoever comes well recommended for Integrity & Steadiness, & that no pecuniary Security is requisite for the Election of the Candidate.[4]

Forgive this Trespass on your Time & believe me

Dear Sir
faithfully Yours
S Wesley

To Eliza Tooth   Euston Street [on or before
17 November 1829][1]

ALS, 3 pp. (Rylands, DDWF 15/41)
Addressed To | Miss Tooth | Hoxton Square

Dear Madam

It is not without much Reluctance that I am obliged to address you upon a Subject of immediate & serious Embarrassment.—A Tradesman with whom

---

[1] John Thomas Smith (1766–1833), topographical draughtsman and antiquary, keeper of prints and drawings at the British Museum from 1816 until his death, and author of *Nollekens and his Times* (1828) (*DNB*). Nothing is known of his acquaintance with SW.

[2] The year is given by 11 Sept. falling on a Friday, SW's Euston Street address, and the reference to 'young Bennet' (see n. 3), who is also mentioned in other letters of this period.

[3] Not identified: probably the 'young Bennet', presumably one of SW's pupils, who had accompanied him on his trip to Leeds the previous year (see SW to Sarah Suter, 18 Sept. 1828 (BL, Add. MS 35012, fo. 50)).

[4] The background to SW's request is not known. It clearly relates to an appointment, no doubt one for which either Bennet himself or Samuel Sebastian had applied.

[1] The date is established by SW's reference to his concert in Watford (see n. 2).

I have dealt for more than seven Years past, has, without any possible Cause that I can assign, (unless his Circumstances be in a desperate Condition, which I never had Reason to suspect) issued a Writ against me for £22, and proceeded so violently that I am at this Moment harboured in the House of a Friend, my own having been last Night besieged by several Officers, from whose search I very narrowly escaped.—Now, after the kind Proposal you made the other Day of an Application to my Brother on my Account, I am encouraged to believe that you would not feel averse from stating the Facts without Delay to my Brother, who if he will accommodate me with the said Sum *as a Loan*, I shall regard myself as responsible for the Return of the Money (at the first possible Opportunity) as though it were borrowed of an indifferent Person.— I can get out Town safely *To-Day*; & remain until Saturday Morning, so that if the Matter be adjusted *in the Course of To-morrow*, I may return without Danger; *but I must know before I leave Town*, otherwise my whole Business for several Days to come will be wholly disjointed, & confounded: Therefore indulge me by an immediate Line by the Bearer, which will be safely received directed to N. 16 Euston Street.—I am preparing a Concert at Watford in Herts, whither I am about to go To-Day, which cannot but prove abundantly profitable:[2] indeed my Prospects of pecuniary Advantages are by much brighter than they have been for several Years past.

With best Regards to your excellent Mother, believe me

My dear Madam
Your's ever faithfully

S Wesley

P.S. It will be best to apply for £25, inasmuch as there will be some legal Expense I fear.

---

[2] No details of SW's concert in Watford have been found; it was no doubt for the local organist William Bird (*fl. c.*1811–*c.*1840). In his letter of 17 Nov. to Sarah Suter (BL, Add. MS 35012, fo. 97), SW announced that he had arrived in Watford and had met Bird, and alluded further to his 'personal danger'. SW had assisted Bird with the revised edition of Bird's *Original Psalmody* and had contributed a letter of recommendation dated 27 Jan. 1829 as its preface (Brown and Stratton; *CPM*).

To an unidentified recipient   Euston Street, [?1 March 1830]¹

ALS, 3 pp. (Drew)
Docketed by SW in another ink: No 38
Watermark 1825
Editor's note The 'Monday' of the date has been scratched out but is just visible by
holding up the letter to a strong light. The appearance of an undecipherable squiggle
after the '1' is consistent with it being the superscript of '1ˢᵗ', but not with it being the
second digit of (e.g.) 15 March.

Euston Street 16
Monday March 1st

Dear Sir

I wish to remove from your Mind the Persuasion of my being disposed
to hypercriticize,² which I sincerely assure you that I am not: to indicate Faults
rather than to discover Beauties (which I believe is ever the Characteristic of a
thorough-paced Hypercritic) is an unamiable Employment in which I have no
Ambition to become sedulous:—the Individual,³ whose Blunder in Accentuation
I happened to notice with a little Asperity, is himself one of the most rancorous
musical Hypercriticks in Existence, and the Lex talionis can never be more
justly enforced than when he meets with par pro pari, which most of his Brother
Professors are afraid to give him, like cowardly Fools as they are.

I wish not to conceal that I have had a Quarrel with the Man, of which I
dare say you have long ago heard—He had assassinated my Church Service
anonymously, and when I cross examined him, hectored & prevaricated; & when
I got him between the *Horns* (of you know what) namely 'you *did* write this or
you did *not*;' his noble Retreat was—'I will not tell you which is true, but *this* I tell
you, that there is not a Word written in that Paper, to the Truth of which I would
not readily subscribe'.

---

¹ For difficulties in making out the date of this letter, see editor's note. The 1830 dating suggested
here is derived from 1 March falling on a Monday and the reference to criticisms of SW's Service. It is
not clear why the 'Monday' of the date should have been scratched out, and it is possible that the letter
dates from an earlier year. The 1825 watermark and the reference to the review of SW's Service make
the earliest possible year 1826, while SW's Euston Street address rules out any year after 1830 (see next
letter, n. 1).

² The addressee had perhaps heard SW's criticisms at one of the lectures SW gave in Bristol in
Jan. 1830.

³ No doubt Horsley, who SW believed to have written the review of his Service in *QMMR* in 1825.

—So much for l'Amende honorable!

I thought right to offer you some Apology for the Semblance of Irritation when insisting upon what you & I are alike conscious of being correct, that to lay a strong musical Stress upon grammatical *Particles* is a Demonstration of illiterate Education.

I am
Dear Sir
respectfully & sincerely yours
S Wesley

To John George Emett Mornington Place,[1] 23 April [1830][2]

ANS, 1 p. (BL, Add. MS 35013, fo. 97)
Addressed To | Mʳ Emett | 2 Elizabeth Street | Chelsea

Mornington Place
Friday 23ᵈ of April

My good Friend

Henry Gauntlett[3] has promised to be here this Evening, & is very desirous to meet you also: I am ashamed to trespass thus upon your Time & Patience, but your Acquiescence in this Instance will confer a fresh Favour on your greatly obliged

S Wesley

[1] SW moved to Mornington Place, at the northern end of the present Hampstead Road and immediately south of Mornington Crescent, on 22 Mar. 1830: this date is given on SW's prayer on moving to the new house, preserved among the family letters and papers bequeathed to the British Museum by his daughter Eliza (BL, Add. MS 35012, fo. 108). SW lived there until the late summer or early autumn of 1832, when he moved to 8 King's Row, Pentonville Road.

[2] The year is given by 23 Apr. falling on a Friday and SW's Mornington Place address.

[3] Henry John Gauntlett (1805–76), organist, composer, lecturer on music, critic, and collector of music, for a short time a pupil of SW. Despite his interest in music from an early age, in 1826 he was articled at his father's insistence to a solicitor, qualifying in 1831, and subsequently practising law for fifteen years. He became organist of St Olave's Southwark in 1827, and of Christ Church, Newgate Street, in 1836. He was active in the field of organ design, and active in campaigning for the introduction of the C compass organ into Britain. He was selected by Mendelssohn to play the organ part of *Elijah* at its first performance in Birmingham in 1846. From 1839 he was active in the compilation of hymn books and the composition of hymn tunes and chants: his best known tune is *Irby* ('Once in Royal David's City').

To William Henry Kearns[1]   Mornington Place, 1 May 1830

AL, third person, 1 p. (sold at Sotheby's, 21 Nov. 1978, Lot 392)[2]

SW asks Kearns to return the 'MS copy of Bach's Violin Solos . . . having particular Occasion for them in the Course of the next Week'.

To Joseph Payne Street   Mornington Place, 25 May 1830

ALS, 6 pp. (Osborn, file 179 58)
Addressed To | J. P. Street Esq[re] | Mansion House Place | City

> 1 Mornington Place
> Hampstead Road
> May 25th 1830

My Dear Sir

If I know aught aright of my own Heart & its sincere Desires, I can without any rational Fear of Self-Deception confidently declare that the two chief (if not the only) Wishes which I am anxious to accomplish before the close of my mortal & sorrowful Career, are, a just & punctual Discharge of my pecuniary Obligations in every Quarter where legal Demand may be equitably made, & the Claims of *kindly accommodating Friends* I feel even paramount to these; and my other Cause of intense Solicitude is the well-being of those young ones whom in all human Probability I must leave, nolens volens, long long before the Period at which they can be in a Condition to provide for themselves.

Among my Debts of Honour, which I am comforted in knowing not to be numerous, there is not one which more imperiously commands Attention or oftener recurs to Memory than mine to yourself: the Promptitude which you have so frequently evinced in rendering me kind Assistance, & your delicate

---

[1] William Henry Kearns (1794–1846), violinist, composer, and theatre musician. He came to London in 1817 and played in the Covent Garden orchestra; in the same year he wrote an operetta, *Bachelors' Wives, or the British at Brussels*. He was subsequently musical adviser to Samuel James Arnold and Hawes, and directed performances of *Der Freischütz*, Meyerbeer's *Robert le Diable*, and many other operas at the Lyceum Theatre. He wrote the additional wind accompaniments for *Messiah* and *Israel in Egypt* for the 1834 Handel festival, and collaborated with Gauntlett in editing his *Comprehensive Tune Book* (1845). He owned the autographs of SW's Trio for Three Pianos and his Organ Concents in C, both of which were sold at the same Sotheby's sale as this letter. (*DNB*; *Grove*[3]).

[2] The description and summary are from the catalogue entry.

Forbearance from any Application on the Subject must necessarily produce in a Mind of any Sensibility Impressions of indelible Gratitude.

Yourself, together with a few other friends are well aware that many Years of my Existence have been passed amid much domestic Turbulence & Persecution, that Some of my bitterest Foes have been 'of mine own Household,' & that there was a Period when I was rendered responsible for heavy Debts contracted without my Knowledge, & vilely exaggerated by Tradesmen who taking Advantage of Circumstances frequently presented Bills for 20 or £30, when I had no suspicion that a Demand for even £10 would have been a just one.

Having lived *on* Earth already 64 years, a very few more at most will require my Deposition *under* it: but as I am conscious that I never had any Propensity towards Idleness, so I yet remain desirous & prepared (as far as my Strength will yet permit) to work hard in whatever Department I may be in any Degree capable.

It has long been a Matter of Regret that hitherto the 15 fine Latin Anthems of Byrde, which I transcribed from the Fitzwilliam Collection have not (as announced) been ushered into the musical World: a numerous List of Subscribers' Names has long appeared, both in the Library and at several of the principal Music Shops, and *nine* of the Plates have been already engraven: as not a single Shilling has been advanced from any Quarter in Aid of the Work's Completion, and as I have always found musical Engravers not a little importunate for ready Money, without which they will hardly budge an Inch, also having omitted to mention in the printed Proposals that a Publication of that Extent required some auxiliary Encouragement in the necessary Expenses incurred by the Editor, it is not a little mortifying to reflect that a Work which must remain as a lasting Monument of the profound Skill & Learning of our Countryman has been withholden from the publick Eye & Ear by an Obstacle which in the Outset of the Business might have been obviated without Difficulty, but as the Time elapsed since its Commencement, has been very considerable (it having been announced in the year 1826)[1] it is now not easy to renew that lively Interest which seemed so general when the Design was first made known.

I have stated the Position of these Facts to several of the principal Music Sellers: they all acknowledge that the MS is a Treasure, not only in Regard to its intrinsic Worth, but also the Impossibility of obtaining a Copy by any other Mode than that in which I did, viz, by the Grant of a Grace from the University, *no easy Acquisition*: but they hesitate to undertake *on their own Account*, what they are pleased to term *so heavy* a Work (they mean as to Extent, not *Stile*,) but this seems no very solid Objection, inasmuch as it will not extend beyond 80 Pages. I offered to make over the Amount of the Subscriptions now to be received, & there are full 200 Names already on the List, in all, *even now*.

---

[1] See SW to Glenn, 4 Apr. 1826.

The 'Cantiones Sacræ' of Byrde are I believe among your Madrigal Collection,[2] & I presume occasionally performed at the Meetings: now I submit to you whether it were an improper Proposal to turn over the Work to the Management of the Society, upon a certain Consideration, rendering the whole of it their exclusive Property? It would certainly pay them well.

Having of late met several trying Disappointments, one of them the loss of £60 in a professional Concern,[3] I am of course anxious to beat about for the unum Necessarium[4] in every quarter where an honest Penny may be made, & I am well convinced by Experience, of your Promptitude to give me wholesome Advice on the Subject.

I trust to meet your Indulgence for so lengthy & verbose a Scroll, and that you will continue to believe me,

My dear Sir,
Your greatly indebted, but grateful Friend and Faithful Servant
S. Wesley

To Vincent Novello   Mornington Place, 10 June 1830

ALS, 4 pp. (BL, Add. MS 11731, fo. 17)[1]

Dear Novello

Two certain parties having been violently at Variance; one of them considering himself very deeply aggrieved appealed to my late Uncle John upon the subject; Concluding his Remonstrances with—'It was both impolitic and dangerous to quarrel with me, for he well knows that I never forgive.'—'Then' (replied my Uncle) 'I hope Sir, you never sin'[2]—

---

[2] i.e. in the collection of the Madrigal Society, of which Street was librarian.

[3] Probably from one of his Bristol engagements: either from his organ recitals in Sept. 1829 or his lectures at the Bristol Institution in Jan. 1830.   [4] 'The one necessary thing'.

[1] This letter is contained in a collection of letters to Novello on the subject of Purcell, all written at around this time, and relating to Novello's publications of Purcell's church music. Evidently written in response to a request from Novello for SW to send him any comments that he had made on Purcell in his lectures, it is the first surviving letter to Novello since the end of 1825, when SW and Novello appear to have quarrelled and to have broken off relations (see Biographical Introduction). Its formal salutation and close, SW's anecdote about the 'two certain parties' (see n. 2), and his comment about the delay in receiving the letter (see n. 7), all suggest that there had been no communication between him and Novello for some time, and that this letter signalled the end of their quarrel and the resumption of their friendship.

[2] No source for this anecdote has been found.

This pithy Reproof at once quenched all vindictive Feeling in the Complainant and there was an end of the Quarrel.

In rummaging my old Lectures,[3] I find only the two following Scraps Concerning Purcell: (We well Know that an elaborate Course might be given on the works of so transcendent a Genius.)

'Henry Purcell's immortal Church Service in B♭ is very rarely (if ever) sung at S[t] Paul's Cathedral, at Westminster Abbey or at the Chapel Royal; whereas all the harmless and hackneyed Chords of King[4] and Kent[5] are in Constant Request at the Cathedrals all over England.'

'Purcell bears a close Analogy with Shakespeare in his rare Faculty of exciting mental Emotions of every Kind, by his magical and marvellous modes of expression on all occasions. He is indeed a superb Acquisition to our Country and whose manifold & magnificent Powers very fairly excuse that hyperbolic Eulogy in his Epitaph:[6]—"He is gone to that Place where only his Harmony can exceed".—'

Should I meet with any matter relative to Purcell which may appear likely to be serviceable to you, I will most readily forward it, and am

Very truly yours

S Wesley

1 Mornington Place | Hampstead Road | Thursday June 10. 1830

NB Your letter is dated May 11.—I received it not before Friday last, June 4.[7]

P.S. I did not know before that the Tune called Burford[8] was attributed to Purcell, neither can I inform you whether there are any others among the English Psalmody of

---

[3] These quotations have not been found in SW's lectures at BL, Add. MS 35014–15.

[4] Charles King (1687–1748), who succeeded Jeremiah Clarke as Almoner and Master of the Choristers at St Paul's Cathedral in 1707. Among his output of church music were seven services, leading Greene to remark that he was 'a very serviceable man'. Five were included in Arnold's *Cathedral Music*; according to *Grove*[6] they are 'not so much bad as merely commonplace, and set a pattern of dullness in the writing of services hardly broken until the time of T. A. Walmisley and S. S. Wesley a century later.'

[5] James Kent (1700–76), successively organist of Finedon, Northamptonshire, Trinity College, Cambridge (1731) and Winchester College and Cathedral (1738). His church music publications included *Twelve Anthems* (1773) and *A Morning and Evening Service with Eight Anthems* (1777); his style is described in Grove[6] as being 'in a post-Croft style without the distinction of Greene, mildly florid or mellifluously charming'.   [6] In Westminster Abbey.

[7] The reason for the delay may have been that Novello had sent his letter to SW's former address in Euston Street, unaware that SW had moved to Mornington Place in March.

[8] This tune, usually sung to the words 'Behold, the Saviour of Mankind' by Samuel Wesley of Epworth, SW's grandfather, is very unlikely to be by Purcell. It first appeared in *Chethams's Psalmody* (1718), and was first attributed to Purcell in Edward Miller's *The Psalms of David* (1790). SW provides a harmonization of the tune and an interlude to it in BL, Add. MS 34999, fo. 136. It is included, attributed to Purcell and in a harmonization by Novello, in Novello's collection of hymn and psalm tunes *The Psalmist* (London, 1835–42). See also Franklin B. Zimmerman, *Henry Purcell 1659–1695: An Analytical Catalogue of his Music* (1963), 125.

which he may be ascertained to have been the Author.—The 104[th9] has been *Supposed* to be a Melody of Corelli, but on what Authority I know not:—The real Truth is that all the really good old Psalm Tunes are Gregorian Melodies in a metrical Form.[10]

Valeas![11]

To an unidentified recipient   Mornington Place, 26 April 1831

L, third person, amanuensis (S. S. Wesley) (RSCM)[1]
Endorsed M[r] Samuel Wesley | Musical Composer

No 1 Mornington Place
Hampstead Road

M[r] S Wesley informs the Advertiser in the 'Times['] of yesterday[2] respecting an Organ[3] that he has one for Sale that was built expressly for himself—the Price, 120 Guineas. It is nine feet high—has one octave and half of German Pedals and is of a powerful quality.

The Organ has been built but a short time—and may be heard by communicating with M[r] S Wesley at the above mentioned direction.

Tuesday April 26th 1831

---

[9] Probably the hymn tune now known as 'Hanover', sung at this time to 'Praise the Lord, O my soul', a metrical version of Ps. 104. The source of the attribution to Corelli is unknown, but the tune was often attributed to Handel. It is in fact most probably by William Croft.

[10] Part of this letter is quoted by Lightwood, 218–19, who adds at this point a passage neither in the original nor in the copy made from it by Eliza on 10 Aug. 1870 (BL, Add. MS 62928, fo. 46): '[Many of them] contain some portions of Gregorian descant, although their constant distribution into metrical lines prevents the immediate perception thereof. I cannot but think that the music in the old Gregorian masses is much more solemn and appropriate to the words than that of the modern composers, notwithstanding they boast the great names of Haydn, Mozart and Beethoven. Pope's distich is always pertinent:

Light quirks of music broken and uneven,
Make the soul dance upon a jig to heaven.'

[11] 'Farewell'.

---

[1] It has been suggested that this letter is in fact from Samuel Sebastian, writing *propria persona*. It seems unlikely, however, that he would have referred to himself as 'Mr S. Wesley' or that he owned an organ at this time.

[2] The advertisement, enquiring about an organ suitable for a church, had in fact appeared in that day's issue of *The Times*.   [3] Nothing is known about this organ.

To Lord Burghersh

ALS, 1 p. (BL, Add. MS 56411, fo. 32) Mounted
Docketed Received from Lord Burgersh March 21

My Lord

Understanding that there will be a grand Performance shortly, at the Abbey in Commemoration of Handel,[2] as an old member of the musical profession, and, I trust, not unknown by Reputation to your Lordship, I beg Leave to offer my Services to preside at the Organ on the Occasion, having been in that Department at the Oratorios for several Years, to the Satisfaction of the musical World and the Public in general.[3]

I have the Honour to be
My Lord,
Your Lordship's most
devoted Servant
S Wesley

8. King's Row | Pentonville | March 6. 1834

---

[1] SW moved from Mornington Place to 8 King's Row, Pentonville (later 138 Pentonville Road) some time in the late summer or early autumn of 1832: a letter of Oct. 1832 from Samuel Sebastian to SW (BL, Add. MS 35019, fo. 6) enquires if he has any people in his new house, implying that the move had been recent. SW lived at this address until his death, and Sarah Suter and the family continued there until at least 1848. They had moved elsewhere by the time of the 1851 census.

[2] The 1834 Handel Commemoration Festival, marking the fiftieth anniversary of the 1784 Commemoration and the supposed 150th anniversary of Handel's birth, was held at Westminster Abbey on 24, 26, and 28 June, and consisted of three large-scale choral concerts (for reviews, see *The Times*, 25, 27, 30 June 1834).

[3] The honour of 'presiding at the organ' was shared out among a number of musicians, including Novello, Adams, and Attwood. SW's offer was evidently declined: he took no part in the festival.

To Thomas Jackson [King's Row], 3 January 1835

ANS, 1 p. (Rylands, DDWF 15/45)
Addressed The Revd Thos Jackson

My dear Sir

You will much oblige me by a Pound to Day *instead* of next Friday, as I am pushed to make up a little Payment.[1]

Yours ever gratefully

S Wesley

3 Jany 1835

To John George Emett [King's Row], 27 February 1835

ANS, 1 p. (BL, Add. MS 35013, fo. 99)
Addressed Mr Emett

My dear Sir

I rec^d the enclosed[1] To Day,—from Sam.—I do not think with him about the Confitebor, but that I ought to have £200 for it.[2]—All the Parts are copied. Mrs W.[3] has been ill but is better. Mention to Novello what Sam says about the Performance, & see him tomorrow if you can.

Y^rs ever truly

S. Wesley

27 Feby 1835

---

[1] With the death of SW's brother Charles in May 1834, SW became the recipient of a small monthly allowance from the Methodist Book Room. The allowance, in lieu of copyright payments for Charles Wesley senior's hymns, had originally been paid to SW's mother, and after her death in 1822 successively to Sarah and to Charles. Collecting the allowance, which from the evidence of subsequent letters appears to have been paid at a rate of 10s. per week, brought SW once more into contact with Jackson and the City Road Methodist community. SW's letters to Jackson from this period indicate the financial hardship he and his family suffered at the end of his life.

[1] Not preserved.

[2] Following SW's performance of the *Confitebor* in May 1826 there had been a number of attempts to perform it again and to publish it, one projected performance being at the Three Choirs Festival at Hereford in 1834 under the direction of Samuel Sebastian. In an undated letter to SW from 1833 or 1834 (BL, Add. MS 35027, fo. 35), Novello discussed the possibility of a performance at Hereford and requested a copy of the soprano aria 'Fidelia omnia mandata eius' for his daughter Clara to study, at the same time stating his willingness to publish it in time for the festival. Neither the Hereford performance nor Novello's edition materialized.

[3] i.e. Sarah Suter.

To John George Emett King's Row, 3 March 1835

ALS, 2 pp. (BL, Add. MS 35013, fo. 101)
Addressed George Emett | N. 20 | Bermondsey New Road | Bermondsey | Free
Pmk MR 3 1835

My dear Sir

I really think the Confitebor with all the Parts worth £200—if Novello will not give more than £150 I must say that is the least I ought to take.—It may be advisable to try Birchall, Chappel & Cramer: but I think Novello knows the Value of it most, & the Parts are all ready, which cost a great Deal of Money to copy.—Perhaps you mentioned that Sam would have it performed, if that would be of any Advantage.—I would not be so urgent, but I have several little Bills pressing me.—I have got the Books from Hart's,[1] which are more valuable than you thought: they contain as follows:—the Songs in Semele,[2] Joseph,[3] 12 Songs by Chilcot,[4] those in Solomon, Susanna,[5] Lyra Britannica,[6] (Books) Sappho's Hymn to Venus,[7] Songs in Judas Macchabæus, Joshua,[8] 6 Cantatas by Stanley,[9] Songs in Alexander Balus, Deborah, Saul, Athaliah,[10] Felton's Concertos[11] & Dr Greene's Songs.[12]

If you can recommend me any one that will buy them, I will sell them for two Guineas & a half.—Erasmus[13] named that I was going to sell the Confitebor, & Glenn said he would give a little Money down for it, & then publish it after my Death, but he would probably offer only about £10 which would do no good.

We are glad to hear that Frederica[14] is getting better, & desire to be kindly remembered to all.—We hope to see you in a Day or two, & believe me

My dear Sir
Very sincerely yours
    S Wesley

8 King's Row | Pentonville | Tuesday March 3 | 1835

---

[1] Probably the engraver, printer, and music publisher Joseph Hart, at this time in business at 109 Hatton Garden. The books mentioned here may have belonged to SW's brother Charles, who had died on 23 May 1834. If so, SW would have acquired them from Elizabeth Tooth, to whom Charles had bequeathed them.   [2] By Handel.

[3] i.e. *Joseph and his Brethren* by Handel.

[4] Twelve English Songs (1744) by Thomas Chilcot (*c.*1700–1766).   [5] Both by Handel.

[6] A six-volume collection of songs, duets, and cantatas by William Boyce, first published 1749–59.

[7] A cantata (1749) by James Worgan (1715–53).   [8] By Handel.

[9] Either the Six Cantatas, Op. 3 (1742) or the Six Cantatas, Op. 6 (1748) by John Stanley (1712–86).

[10] All four by Handel.

[11] One or more of the five sets of concertos published by William Felton (1715–69) between 1744 and 1760.   [12] Probably *A Cantata and Four English Songs*, 2 vols. (1745–6) by Maurice Greene.

[13] Matthias Erasmus.   [14] Presumably Emett's wife or daughter.

To Thomas Jackson   [King's Row], 9 May [1835]¹

ANS, 1 p. (Duke)
Addressed Revd Thomas Jackson

My dear Sir

Ill Health obliges me to become again troublesome; I have been confined to the House all the Week, and must therefore request your kind Assistance *now*, *instead* of on Friday next, remaining gratefully yours

    S Wesley

9th of May. | Saturday

To [William Crotch]¹   King's Row, 5 August 1835

ALS, 1 p. (RCM)
Editor's note This letter is glued into Crotch's own copy of the Wesley–Horn edition of the '48' (shelfmark LXXVIII.D.19).

My dear Sir

Accept my cordial Thanks for your very kind & instructive Letter and valuable Present, in which I am gratefully joined by my Daughter.²—I am glad to find that you do not give up old Bach, nor think I have been *much* mistaken in my Opinion of him.

It gives me much Pleasure to hear of your good Health: of my own I cannot boast.³

    Believe me,
    My dear Sir
    faithfully yours
      S Wesley

8 King's Row | Pentonville. Wed^y 5. Augt 1835

---

¹ The year is given by 9 May falling on a Monday and by SW's request for money.

¹ Although this letter is not specifically addressed to Crotch, it is apparent from its contents and its present location that it is to him, and is a reply to Crotch's letter to SW of 3 Aug. 1835 (see n. 2).

² Crotch had sent a copy of his 'Elements' (presumably the second edition (1833) of his *Elements of Musical Composition*) as a present for SW's 'little daughter' (Thomasine, aged 7). His covering letter, dated 3 Aug. 1835, is in Eliza's scrapbook (BL, Add. MS 35027, fo. 9).

³ In his covering letter Crotch had reported on his continuing love of Bach and his good health.

To Thomas Jackson   King's Row, 12 November 1835

LS, 2 pp., amanuensis (Rylands, DDWes 7/45)

Pentonville. November 12. 1835.

Reverend Sir,

In the Edition of Cowper's Works published by the Revd T. S. Grimshawe,[1] there occurs in the 292^d page, an assertion said to have allusion to my late Father under the title of 'Occiduus' the falsehood of which I must trespass on your kindness, to afford me the means of publically declaring in the fullest and most unqualified manner.[2] The occasional performances by my Brother of some portions of sacred music on Sunday, (which, with the licence of amplification generally conceded to Poets, the author of 'The Task' has amplified into 'sabbatical concerts') were never desecrated by the admission of 'song tunes' or any other airs, but those dedicated exclusively to sacred subjects. The additional misrepresentation that my Father could for a moment so far forget his uniform objection to such places of fashionable resort as Vauxhall or Ranelagh, must lie to anyone who knew his consistent & unflinching enmity to vicious temptation so flagrantly untrue, that I should not condescend to deny it, had the slander originated from any source less respectable than Cowper, and I can

---

[1] *The Works of William Cowper*, ed. T. S. Grimshawe, 8 vols. (1835). This edition contained the *Life* of Cowper by William Hayley and some previously unpublished private correspondence of Cowper.

[2] In fact on p. 292 of vol. 1, in a previously unpublished letter from Cowper to the Revd. John Newton of 9 Sept. 1781, referring to some lines in Cowper's as yet unpublished *The Progress of Error*: 'I am sorry to find that the censure I have passed upon Occiduus is even better founded than I supposed. Lady Austen has been at his sabbatical concerts, which it seems are composed of song-tunes and psalm-tunes indiscriminately; music without words—and I suppose one may say, consequently, without devotion. On a certain occasion, when her niece was sitting at her side, she asked his opinion concerning the lawfulness of such amusements as are to be found at Vauxhall or Ranelagh; meaning only to draw from him a sentence of disapprobation, that Miss Green might be the better reconciled to the restraint under which she was held, when she found it warranted by the judgment of so famous a divine. But she was disappointed: he accounted them innocent, and recommended them as useful.' In *The Progress of Error* (ll. 124–7) Cowper had referred to Occiduus as 'a pastor of renown' who

> When he has pray'd and preach'd the sabbath down,
> With wire and catgut he concludes the day,
> Quav'ring and semiquav'ring care away.

The identification of Cowper's 'Occiduus' with Charles Wesley seems to have been general, but may have been erroneous. It is queried by Jackson in his *The Life of Charles Wesley, MA*, 371–6, who in a lengthy passage which includes a quotation from this letter argues strongly that Cowper's target was in fact Martin Madan. See also *The Poems of William Cowper*, ed. John D. Baird and Charles Ryskamp (Oxford, 1980), i. 265–6, 514–15.

only attribute his promulgation of such a slander to the facility of belief, which often accompanies a mind incapable of falsehood itself, and unsuspicious of it in others.

> I am
> Reverend Sir,
> Your obliged Servant
> S Wesley

> To the Revd Thomas Jackson | Editor of the Methodist Magazine

To [Joseph Payne Street][1]   [King's Row, early 1836][2]

ALS, 3 pp. (BL, Add. MS 56228)

My dear Sir

You will exceedingly oblige me, if you can possibly spare me one Pound, which nothing but very urgent Necessity could have induced me to request, and believe me always

> Most gratefully
> Yours
> S Wesley

P.S. I am preparing some Work for the Press,[3] with some Anecdotes of my own Life,[4] but can get no Money till the whole is finished.

My Son[5] who presents you this has been educated in the Blue Coat School,[6] which he is about to quit with a good Character.

---

[1] Although this letter does not bear the name of an addressee, there can be little doubt from its inclusion in the collection of letters to Joseph Payne Street that it is to him.

[2] The dating derives from SW's reference to the preparation of his *Musical World* article (see n. 3).

[3] SW's 'Sketch of the State of Music in England from the Year 1778 up to the Present', which appeared in the first number of *MW* on 18 Mar. Evidently intended as the first part of a two-part essay, it concluded with an account of the first English performances of Haydn's *Creation* in 1800. No second part appeared, but copy evidently intended to form part of it is included with the text of SW's Reminiscences (Olleson, 1111).

[4] SW's Reminiscences (BL, Add. MS 27593), a rambling collection of anecdotes and recollections written at various times on odd scraps of paper.   [5] Matthias Erasmus.

[6] In Caxton Street, Westminster. The building is currently a National Trust shop.

If you know of anyone who wants a Youth in an Office, you will confer on me a great Favour by recommending, be the Salary what it may.

To [William Crotch]¹ King's Row, 30 March 1836

ALS, 1 p. (BL, Add. MS 31764, fo. 32)

My dear Sir

My Son² requests me to forward to you a Copy of a few of his Compositions, & a Manuscript which he submits to you as an Exercise for the Degree of Bachelor in Music.³ He has some Fear that it is not precisely the Kind of Exercise which the Statutes require, but if it can be accepted, he would feel himself greatly indebted as the Distance at which he resides from London (being Organist & Sub-Chanter of Exeter Cathedral)⁴ makes every Communication between us, rather a lengthy & expensive Matter.

You have heard no Doubt that his Abilities (from a Child) were extraordinary, having been Organist at Camberwell, Waterloo, & Hereford Cathedral,⁵ and now at Exeter, and I rely on your great Kindness that if you can serve him in any Way, you will.

Trusting that you enjoy good Health, believe me, with the highest Esteem

My dear Sir
Yours very respectfully
and faithfully

S Wesley

8 King's Row | Pentonville | Wednesday March 30ᵗʰ 1836

¹ Although lacking an address portion and not addressed to him by name, there can be no doubt that this letter was written to Crotch in his capacity of Professor of Music at Oxford University.

² Samuel Sebastian.

³ It is not known what compositions were enclosed with this letter. Samuel Sebastian eventually received his B.Mus. and D.Mus. from Oxford together on 21 June 1839, his exercise being the anthem 'O Lord, thou art my God', written in that year.

⁴ Samuel Sebastian had been appointed organist at Exeter in Aug. 1835, moving there from Hereford Cathedral.

⁵ Samuel Sebastian was organist at St Giles, Camberwell from Jan. 1829 until Nov. 1832, resigning on taking up his appointment at Hereford. Between Nov. 1829 and Mar. 1831 he was also organist at St John's, Waterloo Road, where he succeeded Jacob (*Grove*⁶).

To Henry John Gauntlett [King's Row], 16 June [1836][1]

ANS, 1 p. (Rylands, Eng. MS 386 (3045))
Addressed Henry Gauntlett Esqre | Queen Street | Cheapside

Dear Sir

I conclude that by this Time you have examined the Music,[2] and if you will appoint any Hour tomorrow, will wait upon you to arrange what concerns it, as I really am at present sadly hampered for the Want of a little ready Cash.

Yours truly

S. Wesley

16 June | Thursday

To Domenico Dragonetti [King's Row, July–August 1836][1]

ANS, 1 p. (BL, Add. MS 56411, fo. 23)
Addressed Signor Dragonetti

Dear Sir

I have sent you my Daughter's[2] Album,[3] as she is making a Collection of the different talented Musicians a few Bars from your Pen she would most highly prize, if not troubling you[4]

Hoping you enjoy good Health, believe me
Dear Sir
Your sincere Admirer

S Wesley

---

[1] The year is given by 16 June falling on a Thursday, SW's shaky handwriting of this period, and the content (see n. 2).

[2] Not certainly identified: presumably some manuscript or printed music which SW was hoping to sell to Gauntlett, probably the 'motett' referred to in SW's letter to Gauntlett of 30 Sept. 1836.

[1] The date of this letter is given by SW's request for a contribution for Eliza's album (see nn. 3 and 4).

[2] Eliza Wesley (1819–95), SW's second daughter by Sarah Suter, was at this time 17 years old and at the beginning of her career as a church organist. For her role in promoting her father's music after his death, see Textual Introduction.

[3] Eliza's autograph album, begun on 28 June 1836, is at BL, Add. MS 35026. The first entry, dated 1 July 1836, was by SW himself: a setting for soprano and piano of the lines 'Orpheus could lead the savage race' from Dryden's *Ode on St Cecilia's Day*. Other early contributions came from Dragonetti, Crotch, Gauntlett, Attwood, Benedict, Ole Bull, Mori, and Mendelssohn.

[4] Dragonetti complied with SW's request. His contribution, a canzonetta 'Voi vorreste il nome amato', for high voice and piano, is the second item in the album, suggesting that it was inscribed shortly after SW's own.

To Thomas Jackson   [King's Row], 31 August 1836

ANS, 1 p. (Bristol)
Addressed Revd T. Jackson

My dear Sir

Will you be so kind as to spare me a Pound this Morning, as I am much embarrassed.

Yours gratefully

S Wesley

Aug. 31 | 1836

To Thomas Attwood   King's Row, 1 September [1836]¹

AN, 1 p. (BL, Add. MS 35013, fo. 103) Damaged
Addressed To | Thomas Attwood Esqre
Editor's note Part of the page, containing half of the first line of the postscript and no doubt also SW's signature, has been cut away.

My dear Sir

I send you my Daughter's Album, who is making a Selection of the various talented Musicians. A few Bars from your Pen she would consider most valuable if not troublesome to yourself.²

Trusting that you enjoy good Health, I remain with much Esteem

<S Wesley>

P.S. As our Resig <nation . . . > perhaps you would name to my Son³ the Bearer some Day convenient to yourself to the Return of the above, not that I wish you to hurry yourself, but it would prevent his having a long Walk to no Purpose.

8 King's Row | Pentonville | Thursday Sep^{tr} 1

---

¹ The year is given by 1 Sept. falling on a Thursday and the request for a contribution to Eliza's album.
² Attwood's contribution, an Amen canon, is at fo. 16.
³ No doubt Matthias Erasmus. Attwood must in fact have inscribed his contribution while Matthias Erasmus waited, for on the following day SW sent him on a similar errand to Crotch. Crotch's contribution to the album and a covering note to SW are both dated 2 Sept.

To Henry John Gauntlett [King's Row], 30 September [1836]¹

ALS, 1 p. (Rylands)
Addressed Henry John Gauntlett Esqre

My dear Sir

I suppose you will think I am always troubling you, could you oblige me with the other Pound for the Motett.² I am really most dreadfully embarrassed or I would not ask you. Have you seen Davison³ concerning the Psalms & Chants?⁴ or do you think he has done anything with them?—My Picture has been lying at Mr Huggins'⁵ in Leaden Hall Street for this last Month: there were several Gentleman he wished to shew it to, but Erasmus will bring it to you in his dining Hour if he can find Time.

Yours very truly

S. Wesley

P.S. I wish much to see you.

30 Sept^r | Friday

---

¹ The year is given by 30 Sept. falling on a Friday and the references to Davison and Matthias Erasmus.

² Not certainly identified, but probably SW's 1827 setting of 'Tu es sacerdos'. A copy in the hand of Novello of 'He is our God and Strong Salvation', Gauntlett's arrangement of this work to English words, is at RCM, MS 5253. In an annotation on the manuscript, Novello noted that the adaptation was by Gauntlett, that Gauntlett had purchased the copyright from SW, and that he later presented the MS to J. Alfred Novello for publication.

³ Frederick Davison (1814/15–89), an organ-builder, who in 1837 went into partnership with William Hill to form the firm of Davison and Hill.

⁴ Not identified: evidently other pieces which SW was attempting to sell.

⁵ William John Huggins (1781–1845), marine painter. After some years as a sailor in the service of the East India Company he set up in Leadenhall Street, where he specialized in nautical scenes, particularly drawings of ships in the service of the company. He is not known to have been a portrait painter, and the picture referred to here, presumably of SW, was probably by another artist; it may conceivably have been the one by John Jackson.

To Frederick Davison[1]   [King's Row], 12 October [1836][2]

ANS, 1 p. (BL, Add. MS 35013, fo. 107)
Addressed F Davison Esqre

Dear Sir

If I can be useful to you To-morrow I can be with you from half past 9 till *1*, when I must go forward to Morgan's.[3]

Yours truly

S Wesley

Wed^y 12 Oct^r

P.S. Could you call in this Evening?—Eliza has to do Duty To-morrow Ev^g at the West End of the Town[4] and her Mother will explain all to you.—She w^d be happy for you to go with her, for if she succeeds on Sunday, she will have the Place. Pray come.—She will not be nervous with you—if you can't come To-night, say you will go with her To-morrow.

The Service begins at 7, & she must go hence at 6. Y^rs truly again

SW

To Thomas Jackson   [King's Row], 28 January 1837

ANS, 1 p. (Bristol)
Annotated by Jackson: 'beggarly ending of a great line'.

My dear Sir

You would much oblige me by letting me have half a Sovereign this Morning instead of next Week my Son would have named it yesterday, but did not see you.

Yours gratefully

S Wesley

Sat^y 28. Jan^y | 1837

¹ See previous letter, n. 3.
² The year is given by 12 Oct. falling on a Wednesday, SW's handwriting, and the reference to Eliza (see n. 4).   ³ Not identified.
⁴ The church where Eliza was to play has not been identified, but was no doubt the one for which she had applied the previous month, and for which Thomas Adams had written her a testimonial (see Adams to SW, 18 and 20 Sept. 1836 (BL, Music Library Deposit 1995/19)). She was later organist at St Katherine Coleman (1837–44) and at St Margaret Pattens (1844–87), where she succeeded her brother-in-law Robert Glenn on his death.

To John Barnett[1]   King's Row, 15 March [1837][2]

AN, third person, 1 p. (BL, Add. MS 35013, fo. 108)
Addressed To | J. Barnett Esqre | Maddox Street | Hanover Square | N. 9

Mr Wesley presents his Compliments to Mr Barnett, and has sent him his Daughter's Album, who is making a Collection of the Hand Writing of the various talented Musicians.

If Mr B. will also contribute to it, Mr W. and Daughter will esteem it a Favour.[3]

8 King's Row | Pentonville. | 15 March | Wednesday

To [Thomas Jackson]   [King's Row], 17 March [1837]

ANS, 1 p. (Bristol)

My dear Sir

Can you oblige me To Day with a Sovereign instead of *half*, and I will not trouble you next Week.

Yours gratefully
    S Wesley

17 March Friday

---

[1] John Barnett (1802–90), English composer. He had begun his musical career as a boy singer, and made his first stage appearance under Samuel James Arnold at the Lyceum Theatre in 1813. His earliest compositions dated from before 1818. These were in a variety of genres, but from 1826 and 1833 he was mainly involved in composing for the theatre. In 1834 he wrote *The Mountain Sylph*, 'one of the first through-composed English operas since Arne's *Artaxerxes*' (*Grove*[6]) and a landmark in the history of English opera, for the reopened English Opera House at the Lyceum Theatre. Following quarrels with Arnold and other theatrical managers he abandoned the London stage in 1840 and in 1841 moved to Cheltenham, where he became a highly successful teacher of singing and wrote two books on the subject (*Grove*[6]).

[2] The year is given by 15 Mar. falling on a Wednesday and SW's request for a contribution to Eliza's album.   [3] Barnett's contribution, an extract from an Andante for string quartet, is at fo. 20.

To Thomas Jackson   [King's Row], 24 April [1837]¹

ANS, 1 p. (Bristol)
Addressed Revd T. Jackson

Dear Sir
Excuse my sending again on this Subject, but I think the Address had better be to XYZ at Mr Dean's Music Library 148 New Bond Street.²

Yours gratefully
S Wesley

Monday 24 April

To Frederick Davison   [King's Row], 24 May 1837

ANS, 1 p. (BL, Add. MS 35013, fo. 105)
Addressed Fred^k Davison Esqre

Dear Sir
Be so obliging as to send my Violin Pieces, as I have an Opportunity to dispose of them.
Mr Ole Bull¹ is coming in a Day or two to try some of them over.

Yours truly
S Wesley

24 May 1837

---

¹ The year is given by 24 Apr. falling on a Monday and the reference to Dean.

² John Dean, music and musical instrument seller, printer and publisher, at this address *c*.1831–1837. The context of SW's request is not known.

---

¹ Ole Bull (1810–80), Norwegian violinist, the foremost virtuoso of his generation. He arrived in London at the end of Apr. 1836 and gave four concerts at the King's Theatre in May and June (*Grove*⁶; Einar Haugen and Camilla Cai, *Ole Bull: Norway's Romantic Musician and Cosmopolitan Patriot* (Madison, Wisc., 1993), 41–7). Two letters from Bull to SW are contained in Eliza's scrapbook (BL, Add. MS 35027, fo. 83). One of them, dated 5 May 1837, evidently accompanied his contribution for Eliza's album (BL, Add. MS 35026. fo. 22), which bears the same date. In the same letter Bull also enclosed tickets for SW and Eliza for his farewell concert at the King's Theatre on 19 May.

To Thomas Jackson   [King's Row], ?27 June [1837]¹

ANS, 1 p. (Bristol)
Addressed Revd T. Jackson

My dear Sir

I hope you will forgive my applying to you *this* Day, but a pressing occasion has rendered it unavoidable.

Yours gratefully

S Wesley

Tuesday June 26

---

¹ This letter appears from its request for money to have been written after the death of SW's brother Charles in May 1834 (see SW to Jackson, 3 Jan. 1835, n. 1). SW's dating is faulty, however: 26 June did not fall on a Tuesday in any of the years between then and SW's own death in 1837. The proposed 1837 dating (when 26 June was a Monday) is on the grounds of the similarity of the content of this letter to others to Jackson from this time, and assumes that SW made a mistake in dating.

Appendix
Undatable Letters

1806–1837

1. To Mr Freebairn[1] [Camden Town, 1806–1808][2]

ALS, 1 p. (NYPL (Music))
Addressed —Freebairn Esqre
Watermark 1806

Sir

I take the Liberty of informing you that Mr Stokes has been prevailed upon by my very earnest Request to dine with me to-Day, which I had great Difficulty in effecting, by Reason of his expecting a Visit from You in the Evening: but I endeavoured to remove his Scruples by desiring You to do me the Favour of coming to my House, at N. 9 Arlington Street, Camden Town, near the Southampton Arms, & as I understand that you are partial to Musick, we may perhaps be able to afford you some little Amusement.

I must beg your Excuse for so abrupt an Invitation from an entire Stranger, & remain with Respect

Sir
Yours very obediently
S. Wesley

Sunday 5 o'Clock

2. To Robert Birchall Camden Town, [?1806][1]

ANS, 1 p. (BL, Add. MS 34007, fo. 45)
Addressed Mr Birchall

---

[1] Not certainly identified: possibly the engraver Robert Freebairn (1765–1808) (*DNB*).

[2] The watermark and SW's Camden Town address in the text of the letter give a dating range of between 1806 and June 1808, when SW moved from 9 to 27 Arlington Street. If the addressee is indeed Robert Freebairn, the dating range is further narrowed, as he died on 23 January 1808.

[1] The suggested year derives from the content: SW's *Variations on a Polish Air* was reviewed in *MM* for March 1806, and had presumably been published shortly earlier.

Sir

If convenient to you to settle for the Copy-right of the Polish Air by the Bearer (my Son)[2] I shall be obliged to you, and the Balance due to you, shall be adjusted in the Course of the midsummer Holidays.

I am
Sir
Your's very truly
S. Wesley

Camden Town | Monday Morn

3. To [Benjamin Jacob][1] [Camden Town, 1808–1809][2]

ALS fragment (Edinburgh)

< . . . > a Word to any of my Friends.—I however promise you that in the Course of a very few Days you shall have 'a full, true, & particular Account' of all the musical Hurly-Burly that is going on here from Morning till Night, & from Night till Morning. —With kindest Regards to Mrs Jacobs & all my your Friends, believe me as ever

My dear Sir
Your most cordially
S Wesley

4. To [George Cooper][1] 23 March [1810, 1821, or 1827][2]

AN, 1 p. (Edinburgh)

Friday 23^d of March

Dear Sir

No Friend of mine to me shall be a *Stooper*;
Therefore my Bellows-Blower shall not be
COOPER

S Wesley

---

[2] Charles or John William.

---

[1] Jacob is identified as the addressee of this letter by the reference to 'Mrs Jacobs' in the text.

[2] The content of the letter suggests that it was written during the period Aug. 1808–Dec. 1809, when SW was in frequent contact with Jacob.

[1] Probably George Cooper (*c*.1783–1843), or his son, also George (see SW to Novello, 25 Sept [1824]). [2] 23 March fell on a Friday in 1810, 1821, and 1827.

5. To Vincent Novello   Duke Street, [1811–25]¹

AN, 1 p. (BL, Add. MS 11729, fo. 108)
Addressed To | Mr Novello.

Sunday 24th
Duke Street
Grosvenor Square
N. 27

Dear N.

Mr Ball lives at the above directed Place, & SW will remain here till 9 o'Clock, with three Mottets of Sebastian, & *two Piano Fortes in Tune together*.

Sat Verbum sapienti²

6. To Vincent Novello   [1811–1825]¹

ALS, 1 p. (BL, Add. MS 11729, fo. 109)
Addressed To | Mr Novello.

Friday
Morning

Doctor

Pon Honour you are a funny Man.—I was detained at Paddington one Hour extra, therefore could not return Home at the Time I had intended.—Ball will tell you that I was in Duke Street *before 8*, with two prime Books full of Tunes under my *Oxter* (vide the Caledonian Vocabulary)—but you had taken your A—e in your Hand & were off.—St Paul² saith 'In Patientiâ vestrâ possidebitis Animas vestras.' 'In your Patience ye shall possess your Souls' is the Greek of it I believe.—Now where is your Patience, & where is your Soul, according to the Apostle's Doctrine?—O fie, fie! naughty Boy.

---

¹ The dating range is the period of SW's correspondence with Novello. The reference to a play-through with Novello of Bach motets suggests 24 January 1813 and 24 Sept. 1815 as two possible dates.   ² 'A word is sufficient to the wise.'

---

¹ The dating range is the period of SW's correspondence with Novello. This letter appears to refer to the engagement discussed in the previous letter and to date from the following Friday.

² In fact, Jesus: see Luke 21: 19.

471

Did I ever make you a Promise & did ever 'the Expectation cry out upon the Non-Performance?'—(NB Billy the Beau).—Stokes might have come, even if he *did* shit his Breeches which is a problematical Affair, referable to the Chancellor of the Exchequer or the Pope, I forget whether.

Sam Webbe w^d not give me up so, like *your* Honour & Glory.

SW

7. To Sir George Smart [*post* 1 January 1811]^1

AN, third person, 1 p. (Pierpont Morgan Library, New York)

S Wesley was at Sir G. Smart's Door exactly at 20 Minutes before 9 this Morning, & was informed that he had left Home about 10 Minutes before (consequently at $\frac{1}{2}$ past 8).—& also that there was no Probability of meeting with Sr G. before Sunday next.

11. Monday Morning

8. To Robert Glenn [?April–May 1813]^1

ALS, 1 p. (BL, Add. MS 35013, fo. 50)
Addressed Mr Glenn.
Watermark 1802

Saturday

My dear Sir

I never was laid under Contribution to any of the *stringed* Instrument Gentry before, but a principal 2^d Violin must be had, & if it cannot be had for Love, then

---

^{1} This letter must date from after 1 Jan. 1811, when Smart was knighted.

^{1} This letter refers to the necessity of engaging the violinist Arthur Betts for one of SW's benefit concerts. SW's first extant dated letter to Robert Glenn is 24 July 1812, and it seems unlikely that this letter was written earlier than this. It may relate to SW's concert on 4 May 1813, when SW experienced difficulties in engaging players (see SW to Novello, 30 Apr. [1813] and [?1 May 1813]). It may, however, relate to any other of SW's benefit concerts.

for money; therefore rather than be without this aid, we must have Mr Betts:[2] however my great Difficulty regards the Wind Instruments, & *Violoncellos*, which unless I can immediately procure, the Concert *must of Necessity* be postponed, to my great additional Expence, Disadvantage, & future Risk, as also to the Disappointment of the Public in general, & my Friends in Particular.—

Yours in much Discomfort
Very truly
   S Wesley

Saturday Night

9. To [?Robert Glenn][1]   Gower Place, [1813– *c*.1818][2]

ALS, 1 p. (Rylands, DDWF 15/24B)

Dear Sir

Pray come & breakfast with me on Sunday Morning next, *exactly at 9 o'Clock*; I have undertaken Novello's whole Duty for the Day at the popish Mass-House, & as the Morning Service is all in Score for the Organ, there is no getting on well without some skilful Man to turn the Leaves:—You know how good the Music is; indeed it is just as *good* as the Religion is *bad*, which is paying it the greatest of all possible Compliments.

Do not fail me, & believe me as always

Yours most sincerely
   S Wesley

Gower Place

---

[2] The violinist and teacher Arthur Betts (Doane; Sainsbury). From the list of his appointments given in Doane, it appears that he was probably an undistinguished player.

[1] The tone and content of this letter suggest Robert Glenn as a possible addressee.

[2] SW's Gower Place address establishes a dating range between 1813 and *c*.1818 for this letter, and its cheerful tone suggests that it is unlikely to have been written after early August 1816. A possible date is early August 1815, following SW's return from his visit to Norwich and Great Yarmouth, when he was asked by Novello to deputize for him on two Sundays (see SW to Pettet, 31 July 1815).

10. To Robert Glenn   Euston Street, [*c*.1818–1830][1]

ANS, 1 p. (BL, Add. MS 35013, fo. 76)
Addressed To | Robert Glenn Esq[re]

Euston S[t]
Sat[y] Morn[g]

My good Friend,
  If you can help me forth with the Accommodation of one small Portrait of our invalid Monarch, Pexy[2] will honestly refund the like to you on *Tuesday* next if you do me the Favour to look in.

  Yours truly
  (all in a Bustle)
    S Wesley

11. To William Nathaniel Dunn[1]   [Drury Lane Theatre, *c*.1818–30][2]

AN, 1 p. (NYPL (Music))
Addressed To—Dunn Esq[re]

D. L. T.[3]
2 o'Clock
Tuesday

  M[r] S. Wesley begs leave to acquaint M[r] Dunn, that he remained here for several Hours Yesterday & this Day in hope of meeting him, in vain.—He will therefore request a Line addressed to him, Euston St Euston Sq[re].

---

[1] SW's Euston Street address establishes the dating range for this letter.
[2] SW's pet name for Sarah Suter.

[1] William Nathaniel Dunn (1782–1855) deputy treasurer of Drury Lane Theatre (*BD*).
[2] SW's Euston Street address in the body of the letter establishes the dating range for this letter.
[3] i.e. Drury Lane Theatre.

12. To John George Emett [*c.*1826–1828][1]

ANS, 1 p. (BL, Add. MS 35013, fo. 94)
Addressed To | M[r] Emett | 25 | Ebury Terrace | Pimlico

D[r] Sir

I was obliged to send a Porter with this which I could not get at till late last Night

Y[rs] truly
in Haste
  S Wesley

Thursday Morning

13. To an unidentified recipient[1] Euston Street,
13 March [*c.*1818–1828][2]

ALS, 1 p. (Rylands, DDWF 15/38)
Addressed < . . . > Esqre | < . . . > Street | < . . . >side
Editor's note The left-hand side of the address panel is missing.

Euston Street
March 13th

Sir

That imperious Tyrant called *Necessity*, is the sole Cause of your not hitherto receiving the Balance of the Bill, which shall be handed over to you, within about *a Week* hence.—

---

[1] SW's first extant dated letter to Emett is dated 23 Nov. 1826, and is addressed to Ebury Terrace. By Apr. 1828, when Emett was a candidate for the organist's position at St Vedast, Foster Lane, Emett had moved to 2 Elizabeth Street, Pimlico (Dawe).

[1] The identity of the addressee has not been established; it may be the person who put a similar enquiry to SW in 1829 (see SW to unidentified recipient, 23 May [1829]).

[2] SW's Euston Street address and the reference to his sister Sarah, who died in September 1828, establish the dating range for this letter.

I cannot at this Moment solve your Question upon my great Grandmother's Maiden Name:[3] I expect to dine with my Brother & Sister To-morrow, when I will make Enquiry, & report to you the Result:

remaining,
Sir,
obed^{tly} Yours
   S Wesley

14. To Robert Glenn   Euston Street, [*c*.1818–1830][1]

ALS, 1 p. (BL, Add. 35038, fo. 1)
Addressed To | Robt Glenn Esqre | 6 Kirby Street | Hatton Garden | Friday Afternoon
                                                       Euston Street
                                                  Friday Afternoon

My dear Sir

Do pray contrive to call in here in the Course of the Evening: if the Business were not urgent, I would not be this importunate.—You will soon acknowledge that I do not ask Counsel without a Necessity of it.

Yours in Haste
very truly
   S Wesley

---

[3] The enquiry probably related to the mother of SW's paternal grandmother, Susanna Wesley, née Annesley, concerning whose family there was a good deal of interest. Her maiden name was White: she was the daughter of John White (1590–1645) (*DNB*, under 'Wesley, Samuel (1662–1735)'; Charles Evans, 'The Ancestry of the Wesleys', *Notes and Queries*, 193 (1948), 255–9).

[1] SW's Euston Street address gives the dating range for this letter. It may conceivably concern problems with SW's sister Sarah's will; if so, it can be dated to late 1828 (see SW to Glenn, 30 Oct. 1828).

15. To [John Capel][1]   King's Row, 27 April [1833–1837][2]

ANS, 1 p. (Rylands DDWF 15/46)

8 King's Row. Pentonville
27 April

Dear Sir

I have but this Moment received the enclosed, altho' my Address was left at the Tavern[3] before the Season commenced. Why the Letters were not sent to me rather than to Mr Cooper I cannot tell. It is plain that there was not Neglect on the Part of

Dear Sir
Your greatly obliged
& obedient Servant

S Wesley

16. To [?Thomas Jackson][1]   [King's Row, 1835–1837][2]

ALS, 6 pp. (Rylands, DDWes 6/57)
Watermark 1835

Revd & dear Sir

The following Answers are I know perfectly correct and I hope may suit your Purpose.

My Mother was the Daughter of the late Marmaduke Gwynne Esqre whose Family was one of the first and most ancient in Brecon, South Wales: the Name of the Family Estate was Garth which still remains, & which I am informed will at some time devolve to myself: the Gwynnes usually resided on the estate.—[3] At that Time were many highly respectable Families, with all of whom they were well

---

[1] John Capel (1767–1846), MP for Queenborough 1826–32, Governor (1818) and Vice-President (1832–7) of the Foundling Hospital. He was a subscriber to SW's Service and one of the signatories to a circular soliciting financial aid for SW following his breakdown in 1830.

[2] The dating range for this letter is determined by the fact that SW moved to Pentonville in the late summer or early autumn of 1832.

[3] Possibly the Crown and Anchor tavern, where the Glee Club and the Classical Harmonists met.

---

[1] Jackson is the most likely recipient in view of his closeness to SW and his interest in Wesley family history.   [2] The dating derives from the watermark.

[3] For Marmaduke Gwynne (?1694–1769) and his family, see J. E. Lloyd and R. T. Jenkinson (eds.), *The Dictionary of Welsh Biography: Down to 1940* (1959). Garth is between Builth Wells and Llanwrtyd Wells, Powys.

acquainted.—My Father had five Children, beside my Brother, Sister, and Self, all of whom died very young.[4]—two were named John, the elder of whom shewed an extraordinary Propensity to Music, for when he was but two years old, he was known to wave his Hands in just Time to the several Measures played or sung. He died at the Age of about two Years and a half.[5]

All the others died quite in their infancy, and were buried in the same Tomb in S[t] James's Church Yard Bristol.

My Father was educated at Westminster School, at the Time when my Unkle Samuel[6] was head Usher there, & was always considered an excellent Scholar[7]—Thence he went to Oxford to study at Christ's College[8] for Orders. He accompanied my Unkle John to America[9] as his Coadjutor, with Gen[l] Oglethorpe.[10]

In Latin Greek and Hebrew he was eminently well versed: he also read the German: I know not whether the Spanish.—

He was at Bristol when all the other Children were born, & came to London when I was about eight years old,[11] where he remained in Marybone with his Family until his Decease, which happened in 1787.[12]

My Brother Charles went early to a Grammar School at Bristol, M[r] Needham's,[13] where he was educated in Latin. On his leaving, he was devoted entirely to Music, but as early as two Years and three quarters old his strong Inclination to it was observable.

He then played a Tune on the harpsichord readily and in just Time.—Whatever his Mother sang or he heard in the Streets he could play.—M[r] Broderip,[14] Organist in Bristol heard him in Petticoats, & foretold that he would one Day make a great Player. His first Master was M[r] Rooke[15] at Bristol, & M[r] Kelway, Queen Charlotte's Master, in London, and D[r] Boyce, for Harmony & Composition.

My Sister Sarah was educated at Miss Temple's[16] School in Bristol for several Years, and my Father also gave her some Instruction in Latin: she had some Talent for Singing—but the musical Genius of our Family seems to originate in my

---

[4] John (1753–4), Martha Maria (b. and d. 1755), Susanna (1760–1), Selina (b. and d. 1764), and John James (b. and d. 1768) (Stevenson, *Memorials*).

[5] According to Stevenson, he lived for only sixteen months.

[6] Samuel Wesley (1691–1739): see SW to [Latrobe, *post* 22 Feb. 1799], n. 14. He entered Westminster School in 1704 and was appointed head usher in 1713. From 1733 he was headmaster of Blundell's School, Tiverton (Foster, *DNB*). [7] Charles Wesley attended Westminster School from 1716 to 1726.

[8] In fact at Christ Church, where he matriculated in 1726. [9] In Dec. 1735.

[10] James Edward Oglethorpe (1696–1785), general, philanthropist, and colonist of Georgia (*DNB*).

[11] According to SW's calculation, this would have been in 1774. He in fact came to London in 1771.

[12] In fact, in 1788. [13] Not identified.

[14] Edmund Broderip (1727–1779), a pupil of Geminiani and Kelway, or his brother Robert (*Grove*[6]).

[15] Described by SW's father in his account of his sons' musical progress as 'a man of no name, but very good-natured'. [16] Not identified.

Mother, who sang excellently.—My Unkle John's Wife[17] was heard invidiously to say of my Mother that she supposed 'the Methodist Cages' (Houses) 'were not fine enough for her Brother's singing Bird'. (My Mother, although frequently attending the Methodist Meetings, was not a regular Member of the Society)[18]

I am obliged to my Father principally for my Knowledge of Latin.—My Brother & Sister received the greater Part of their Education at School.

He[19] was for many years well acquainted with the Countess of Huntingdon,[20] the late Earl of Mornington,[21] Father of the present Duke of Wellington, the Hon[ble] Daines Barrington,[22] his Brother, the Earl,[23] General Paoli,[24] D[r] Samuel Johnson, and a Variety of other distinguished Personages.—The Countess of Huntingdon, my Father, and Unkle, were all intimate, on religious Subjects: they latterly differed on the Calvinistic Doctrines of Predestation & Elections.—Lord Mornington for several Years was accustomed to breakfast weekly at my Father's House, and play Quartettos for Hours together; he would bring his Tenor Violin under his Arm, & said that he should never be ashamed at being mistaken for a Musician.

D[r] Johnson was known not to be musical: he however said to D[r] Burney, 'I envy you your sixth-sense, your Relish of Music'.

My Father was not very *frequently* visited by the Methodist Preachers. Whenever his Brother John came to our House at Marybone, he always brought with him two or three of them.

When at Bristol my Father used to preach at the New Room in the Horse-Fair,[25] dedicated to divine Service, & when in London, had no constant Duty, but usually preached on Sundays at West Street Chapel,[26] where his Family also generally attended.

He was exceedingly fond of Music, and played a little on the Flute, but long before my Time.

---

[17] Molly Vazeille (1696–1781), who married John Wesley in 1751.

[18] This sentence appears as a footnote.   [19] i.e. Charles Wesley.

[20] Selina Hastings, Countess of Huntingdon (1707–91), founder of the branch of Methodism that bore her name.   [21] Garret Wesley, 1st Earl Mornington (1735–1781) (*DNB*; *Grove*[6]).

[22] Daines Barrington (1727–1800), lawyer, antiquary, naturalist, and writer, fourth son of John Shute (1678–1734), 1st Viscount Barrington. He examined the boy Mozart on Mozart's visit to London in 1764–5; for his account of Mozart's abilities, see *Philosophical Transactions of the Royal Society*, 9 (1770), 54–71, reprinted in his *Miscellanies* (1781). He subsequently examined Charles Wesley jun. and SW, and his account of their abilities, based on and substantially quoting material supplied to him by Charles Wesley, is also included in his *Miscellanies* (*DNB*; *Grove*[6]).

[23] William Wildman Barrington (1717–93), second Viscount Barrington (*DNB*).

[24] Pascal Paoli (1725–1807), Corsican general and patriot, ruler of Corsica 1755–69. Following his overthrow in 1769 he lived in London, where he was a member of the social circle of Samuel Johnson. He returned to Sicily in 1790.

[25] Now known as John Wesley's Chapel: still in use as a Methodist chapel.

[26] Off Charing Cross Road; at the time, the main Methodist chapel in the West End of London.

I do not know that my Father would have chosen the Profession of Music for his Sons.—he once asked Lord Chesterfield what he should make them? to which was answered 'whatever Nature seems to have designed them for.'

I do not remember the Year in which the Concerts commenced: I must have been about 14 or 15 Years old.[27]—they continued for several Seasons in Chesterfield Street: the Room admitted from 60 to 80 Persons, and was generally filled. L[ds] Barrington, Fortescue,[28] & Mornington attended them constantly: the last of these performed occasionally. Several others, & many Gentry were with us. My Unkle John came *once*, with some of the Preachers, & said 'I do this, to shew that I consider it no Sin.'—He loved Music much, but was no Performer.—His punctuality was extraordinary. When with D[r] Johnson, in an interesting conversation, one of his Preachers pulled out his Watch, & said, 'Sir, your have a Funeral to attend in half an Hour'—this caused him to start up & leave the Doctor quite abruptly.

On the 5th of November he made a Practice of giving to the boys with their Guy Fawkes, some Money, saying 'Now, mind & do not drink more than will do you good, my Boys.'

When he first preached in Ireland[29] he was much persecuted, but had the happy Art of gaining the Hearts of his Hearers.—He said it was 'always best to face a Mob,' and when he obtained a Hearing, he was sure to turn all in his Favour. At one of his first Sermons was an immense Mob, who were desperately outrageous, hooting & pelting him, when turning round to them, he so mollified them by his Gentleness of Speech, (begging them only to hear before they condemned), after which, they all unanimously espoused his Cause, applauding now as much as they had previously opposed.—

When legally required to render an Account of his Plate, he returned the following Answer:—I have two silver Tea Spoons, the one in London and the other at Bristol; and I do not intend to purchase any more, while I see so many Persons starving around me.'

D[r] Boyce was my Brother's Instructor in Composition who was a most amiable Man, as well as a profound Master and for whom he always entertained the greatest Respect and Regard.—M[r] Kelway, Queen Charlottes Master, was also his, for the Harpsichord, & my Brother was a very favourite Pupil.[30]

M[r] Ebenezer Blackwell[31] was for many years intimate with our Family, but I do not recollect any interesting particulars concerning him.

---

[27] The first season of family concerts started in January 1779, when SW was not quite 13.

[28] Matthew Fortescue, Baron Fortescue of Castle Hill (1719–85).   [29] In 1747.

[30] This paragraph has been deleted by SW.

[31] A banker and close friend of Charles and John Wesley; he died in 1782. He is also mentioned in two letters of 16 Apr. 1829 from Charles Wesley to Jackson, (DDWes 6/79 and 6/80) (Gill, 128–9, 134–6, 184; *GM* 1782, 207).

The above are the only Points I can at this Time call to Remembrance; but if you wish for further Information, & will take the Trouble to state any other Questions as in your former Letter, perhaps some Circumstances might occur, beside those already mentioned.

I remain
My dear Sir
Always gratefully
Yours

    S Wesley

17. To Christopher Lonsdale[1]   King's Row, [?1836][2]

AN (BL, Add. MS 34007, fo. 44)
Addressed To | Mr Lonsdale

Mr Wesley's Comp^{ts} to Mr Lonsdale & begs to return his best Thanks for the Fugues.[3]—He has the Organ Duet,[4] but the additional Fugues he has not seen therefore when Mr L. has a Copy to spare he will avail himself of his very kind Offer, but should feel happy at any Time to make some little Recompense should Mr L. ever require any Thing in his Line.

8 King's Row
Pentonville

---

[1] Christopher Lonsdale (?1795–1877), music publisher, successor to Robert Birchall, who was in business at 26 Old Bond Street from 1834 and published a number of works by SW (Humphries and Smith).

[2] SW's Pentonville address gives a dating range of 1832–37 for this letter. If the reference to the 'Organ Duet' is to SW's own composition (see n. 4), the letter dates from 1836.   [3] Not identified.

[4] Perhaps SW's organ duet of 1812, published by Lonsdale in 1836 according to the list of SW's work which accompanied his *MW* obituary.

Index

The names of recipients and the page numbers of letters to them are given in **bold**.